SEMANTICS

Primes and Universals

SEMANTICS
Primes and Universals

ANNA WIERZBICKA

Oxford   New York

OXFORD UNIVERSITY PRESS

1996

Oxford University Press, Walton Street, Oxford OX2 6DP
Oxford New York
Athens Auckland Bangkok Bombay
Calcutta Cape Town Dar es Salaam Delhi
Florence Hong Kong Istanbul Karachi
Kuala Lumpur Madras Madrid Melbourne
Mexico City Nairobi Paris Singapore
Taipei Tokyo Toronto
and associated companies in
Berlin Ibadan

Oxford is a trade mark of Oxford University Press

British Library Cataloguing in Publication Data
Data available

Library of Congress Cataloging in Publication Data
Semantics : primes and universals / Anna Wierzbicka.
Includes previously published material rev. and expanded
for this publication.
Includes bibliographical references and index.
1. Semantics.   2. Universals (Linguistics)   3. Grammar,
comparative and general.   4. Language and culture.   I. Title.
P325.5.U54W54   1996   401'.43—dc20   95–20740
ISBN 0–19–870002–4
ISBN 0–19–870003–2 (Pbk)

10 9 8 7 6 5 4 3 2 1

Typeset by Hope Services (Abingdon) Ltd.
Printed in Great Britain
on acid-free paper by
Bookcraft (Bath) Ltd.,
Midsomer Norton

Acknowledgements

□ □ _____

This book owes a great deal to my friend and colleague Cliff Goddard of the University of New England, who read and made very detailed comments on the first draft of it. I have revised all the chapters, some of them quite extensively, in response to Cliff's criticisms and suggestions. Over a number of years, Cliff has been my principal partner in the search for semantic primes and semantic universals, and interminable telephone discussions with him have been an unfailing source of insight and intellectual pleasure.

I am also very grateful to my old friend Andrzej Bogusławski of Warsaw University, who three decades ago initiated the search for semantic primes, who has continued this search throughout this period, and who, despite distance, has remained an invaluable interlocutor and colleague.

I would like to thank the colleagues who read and commented on an earlier draft of the Introduction to this book and thus enabled me to improve it, in particular Sasha Aikhenvald, Avery Andrews, Jerome Bruner, Bob Dixon, Mark Durie, Ian Green, Jean Harkins, Randy Allen Harris, Helen O'Loghlin, Andy Pawley, and Jane Simpson.

I am particularly grateful to my extremely able Research Assistant, Helen O'Loghlin, who went far beyond the call of duty in assisting me to prepare this book for publication, chasing references, tracking down inconsistencies and errors, discussing ideas, and suggesting possible ways of improvement. Her help was indispensable. I would like, too, to thank the Australian Research Council for a grant for research assistance, which made this possible. I would also like to thank Tim Curnow, who worked as my Research Assistant at an earlier stage of the preparation of the book (also under an ARC grant), and whose help was also invaluable.

It is also a pleasure to express my heartfelt gratitude and appreciation to Ellalene Seymour, for her expert, patient, and good-humoured typing and editing of the successive drafts of this book.

Finally, I would like to thank my students at the Australian National University, and in particular, the participants of my Seminar on Semantics, who have contributed both valuable data and ideas to the project.

Some portions of this book first appeared, in different form, as articles in journals or as chapters in collective volumes. I thank the publishers for permission to include revised and expanded versions of the following publications or parts thereof:

'Prototypes Save': On the Uses and Abuses of the Notion of 'Prototype' in Linguistics and Related Fields. In Savas L. Tsohatzidis (ed.). *Meanings and Prototypes: Studies in Linguistic Categorization.* London: Routledge & Kegan Paul. 1990. 347–367.

Semantic Primitives and Semantic Fields. In Adrienne Lehrer and Eva Feder Kittay (eds.). *Frames, Fields, and Contrasts: New Essays in Semantic and Lexical Organization.* Hillsdale, NJ: Lawrence Erlbaum. 1992. 209–27.

Semantic Complexity: Conceptual Primitives and the Principle of Substitutability. *Theoretical Linguistics.* 17. 1991. 75–97.

Semantic Universals and 'Primitive Thought': The Question of the Psychic Unity of Humankind. *Journal of Linguistic Anthropology.* 4/1. 1994. 1–27. 1667.

Ostensive Definitions and Verbal Definitions: Innate Conceptual Primitives and the Acquisition of Concepts. In Maciej Grochowski and Daniel Weiss (eds.). *Words are Physicians for an Ailing Mind.* Sagners Slavistische Sammlung, xvii. Munich: Otto Sagner. 1991. 467–80.

Back to Definitions: Cognition, Semantics, and Lexicography. *Lexicographica.* 8. 1992. 146–74. (Published in 1994.)

What are the Uses of Theoretical Lexicography? *Dictionaries.* 14. 1992–3. 44–78. Replies to Discussants. *Dictionaries.* 14. 1992–93. 139–59.

The Meaning of Colour Terms: Semantics, Culture, and Cognition. *Cognitive Linguistics.* 1/1. 1990. 99–150.

Dictionaries versus Encyclopaedias: How to Draw the Line. In Philip Davis (ed.). *Descriptive and Theoretical Modes in the Alternative Linguistics.* Philadelphia/ Amsterdam: John Benjamins. Forthcoming.

What is a Life Form? Conceptual Issues in Ethnobiology. *Journal of Linguistic Anthropology.* 2/1. 1992. 3–29.

Semantic Rules Know no Exceptions. *Studies in Language.* 15/2. 1991. 371–98.

The Semantics of Grammar: A Reply to Professor Palmer. *Journal of Linguistics.* 27/2. 1991. 495–8.

A Semantic Basis for Grammatical Typology. In Werner Abraham, Talmy Givon, and Sandra Thompson (eds.). *Discourse, Grammar and Typology.* Complementary Series of Studies in Language. Amsterdam: John Benjamins. 179–209.

Semantics and Epistemology: The Meaning of 'Evidentials' in a Cross-linguistic Perspective. *Language Sciences.* 16/1. 1994. 81–137.

Contents

◻ ◻ ──────────────────────────────

I General Issues

1 Introduction

◻️◻️ _____

1. Language and Meaning

Language is an instrument for conveying meaning. The structure of this instrument reflects its function, and it can only be properly understood in terms of its function. To study language without reference to meaning is like studying road signs from the point of view of their physical properties (how much they weigh, what kind of paint are they painted with, and so on), or like studying the structure of the eye without any reference to seeing.

Curiously, however, this is precisely how many linguists study language. A science of language in which meaning has at best a very marginal place is an anomaly and an aberration (which in itself will present an absorbing topic of study for the future historians of linguistics); and of course not all present-day linguists approach the study of language in that spirit. Yet in university curricula currently adopted in many linguistics departments throughout the world, "formal syntax" still occupies a far more central place than semantics (the study of meaning), and semantics is still often treated as marginal.

Two twentieth-century American linguists have been particularly influential in shaping a "linguistics without meaning": Leonard Bloomfield and Noam Chomsky.

Bloomfield (unlike his great contemporary and co-founder of American linguistics, Edward Sapir) was afraid of meaning, and was eager to relegate the study of meaning to other disciplines such as sociology or psychology. The reason he was afraid of it was that he wanted to establish linguistics as a science and that he thought that meaning couldn't be studied with the same rigour as linguistic sounds and forms. Bloomfield's behaviourism made him find all references to ideas, concepts, thoughts, or mind unscientific; "mentalism" was used by him, and by many other influential linguists of his generation, as a dirty word.[1] As Randy Allen Harris, the author of *The Linguistics Wars* (1993: 27–8), put it: "Bloomfield's ideas defined the temper of the linguistic times: that it [linguistics] was a descriptive and

_____

[1] As a close collaborator of Sapir, Morris Swadesh (1941: 59), pointed out, another confirmed behaviourist, Twaddell, "criticized Sapir as a mentalist dealing with an 'unknown and unknowable mind' ".

taxonomic science, like zoology, geology, and astronomy; that mental speculations were tantamount to mysticism, an abandonment of science; that
all the relevant psychological questions (learning, knowing, and using a language) would be answered by behaviorism; that meaning was outside the
scope of scientific inquiry."

It has often been said, in Bloomfield's defence, that it wasn't Bloomfield
himself but the "Bloomfieldians" or "post-Bloomfieldians" (and especially
Chomsky's mentor Zeillig Harris) who sought to banish meaning from linguistics. For example, Matthews (1943: 114) points out that even "in one
of his last general papers he [Bloomfield] continued to make clear that 'in
language, forms cannot be separated from meanings' " (1943; in Hockett
1970: 401). But it is not unreasonable to say that what the Post-
Bloomfieldians did was to take Bloomfield's largely (though not consistently) anti-semantic stand to its logical conclusion.

Matthews tries to explain why Bloomfield's successors "came to believe
that forms could and should be described without reference to meaning"
and "why, in adopting a theory in which the separation of form and meaning was axiomatic, they were so sure they were continuing his work". He
notes that the usual explanation given is "that however central meaning
may have been and however important its investigation, Bloomfield's
account of how it should be described effectively closed the door to scientific study" (1993: 115). Matthews seeks to distance himself from this conclusion but in my view it is inescapable.

Bloomfield didn't "reject" meaning in the sense of avoiding any mention
of it in linguistic description but he did want to exclude semantic considerations from linguistic analysis. For example, he ridiculed the idea that the
grammatical category of number (singular versus plural) has a semantic
basis and could be defined with reference to meaning: "school grammar
defines the class of plural nouns by its meaning 'more than one' (person,
place, or thing), but who could gather from this that *oats* is a plural while
wheat is a singular? Class-meanings, like all other meanings, elude the linguist's power of definition." (1933/1935: 266)[2]

Bloomfield himself denied that he had ever wanted to "undertake to
study language without meaning, simply as meaningless sound" (letter to
Fries; quoted in Hymes and Fought 1975: 1009); but the message of
Language was none the less loud and clear: there was no room for semantics within the "linguistic science", at least not for the foreseeable future.

We have defined the *meaning* of a linguistic form as the situation in which the
speaker utters it and the response which it calls forth from the hearer. . . . The sit-

---

[2] Curiously, Bloomfield didn't pay any attention to the fact that *oats* is not a "plural" contrasting with a singular (like, for example, *dogs* contrasts with *dog*) and that it doesn't really
belong to the same "form class" as *dogs* does. The "form class" to which *oats* belongs, and its
invariant meaning, is discussed in Chapter 13. (See also Wierzbicka 1988.)

uations which prompt people to utter speech include every object and happening in their universe. In order to give a scientifically accurate definition of meaning for every form of a language, we should have to have a scientifically accurate knowledge of everything in the speakers' world. The actual extent of human knowledge is very small, compared to this. We can define the meaning of a speech-form accurately when this meaning has to do with some matter of which we possess scientific knowledge. We can define the names of minerals, for example, in terms of chemistry and mineralogy, as when we say that the ordinary meaning of the English word *salt* is 'sodium chloride (NaCl)', and we can define the names of plants or animals by means of the technical terms of botany or zoology, but we have no precise way of defining words like *love* or *hate*, which concern situations that have not been accurately classified—and these latter are in the great majority. . . .

The statement of meaning is therefore the weak point in language study, and will remain so until human knowledge advances very far beyond its present state. In practice, we define the meaning of a linguistic form, wherever we can, in terms of some other science. Where this is impossible, we resort to makeshift devices.[3] (Bloomfield 1933/1935: 139–40)

Thus, for Bloomfield meaning could be referred to, but not studied, and given his "anti-mentalistic", behaviouristic conception of meaning, it could scarcely have been otherwise.

As Hymes and Fought (1975: 1010) put it, "Bloomfield included meaning in his conception of language structure but not in his short-term linguistic theory. . . . scepticism as to the practical possibility of incorporating meaning explicitly in linguistic analysis led to shifts . . . to reliance on distributional patterning . . . among the Bloomfieldians."

The "cognitive revolution" of the late fifties and the sixties banished (or so it seemed) the ghost of behaviourism, and made mind, and meaning, a central concern of human sciences in general, and of linguistics in particular. To quote one of the main actors of the "cognitive revolution", Jerome Bruner (1990: 1): "That revolution was intended to bring 'mind' back into the human sciences after a long cold winter of objectivism." For Bruner, "mind" is closely related to "meaning": "Now let me tell you first what I and my friends thought the revolution was about back there in the late 1950s. It was, we thought, an all-out effort to establish meaning as the central concept of psychology—not stimuli and responses, not overtly observable behavior, not biological drives and their transformation, but meaning" (p. 2). But, in his own words, Bruner's is not "the usual account of progress marching ever forward" (p. 1); for in his view, "that revolution has now been diverted into issues that are marginal to the impulse that brought it

---

[3] Bloomfield's reference to "NaCl" as "the ordinary meaning of the English word *salt*" highlights his failure to distinguish scientific knowledge from "ordinary meaning", as do also his remarks on the names of plants and animals. For detailed discussion of these matters see Chapters 11 and 12. As for the meaning of emotion terms (such as *love* and *hate*), see Chapter 5.

into being. Indeed, it has been technicalized in a manner that even undermines the original impulse" (p. 1). What has been lost sight of is meaning.

Very early on, for example, emphasis began shifting from "meaning" to "information," from the *construction* of meaning to the *processing* of information. These are profoundly different matters. The key factor in the shift was the introduction of computation as the ruling metaphor and of computability as a necessary criterion of a good theoretical model. Information is indifferent with respect to meaning. (p. 4)

Very soon, computing became the model of the mind, and in place of the concept of meaning there emerged the concept of computability.   (p. 6)

It was inevitable that with computation as the metaphor of the new cognitive science and with computability as the necessary if not sufficient criterion of a workable theory within the new science, the old malaise about mentalism would re-emerge.   (p. 8)

Bruner decries the "cognitive revolution" for abandoning meaning as its central concern and for "opting for 'information processing' and computation instead" (137); and he urges "that psychology stop trying to be 'meaning-free' in its system of explanation" (20).

But if psychology has been betrayed by the "cognitive revolution", with its escape from meaning, what is one to say of linguistics, in which the promising early references to "mind" (as in Chomsky's *Language and Mind*), have led to a preoccupation with formalisms, and in which "meaning-free" syntax has for decades usurped the place rightfully belonging to the study of meaning? Oliver Sacks (1993: 48) summarizes the "hijacking" of the "cognitive revolution" as follows: "Bruner describes how this original impetus was subverted, and replaced by notions of computation, information processing, etc., and by the computational (and Chomskyan) notion that the syntax of a language could be separated from its semantics." Sacks strongly endorses Bruner's position, and comments: "From Boole, with his 'Laws of Thought' in the 1850s, to the pioneers of Artificial Intelligence at the present day, there has been a persistent notion that one may have an intelligence or a language based on pure logic, without anything so messy as 'meaning' being involved."

Unfortunately, as noted by Sacks, this persistent notion was shared by the main *spiritus movens* of the "cognitive revolution" in linguistics, Noam Chomsky, whose influence on the field can hardly be overestimated.

Despite his mentalist, anti-Bloomfieldian stand, in his attitude to meaning Chomsky remained (and still remains) a Bloomfieldian. Like Bloomfield, "he . . . had a deep methodological aversion to meaning, and his work reinforced one of the key elements of the Bloomfieldian policy toward meaning: it had to be avoided in formal analysis" (R. A. Harris 1993: 99).

I agree with Harris (1993: 252) that while some "prefer to look at Chomsky's impact on linguistics as the last gasp of Bloomfieldianism", such a view is "far too narrow". But one also has to agree with Chomsky's critics that although he broke, in a way, Bloomfield's taboo on mind, Chomsky's professed mentalism proved to be as inimical to the study of meaning as was Bloomfield's behaviourism. To quote one critic (Edelman 1992: 243):

> One of the most pervasive and influential approaches to these critical questions [of how language and thought are connected] was pioneered by Chomsky. In his formal systems approach, the principal assumption is that the rules of syntax are independent of semantics. Language, in this view, is independent of the rest of cognition. I must take issue with this notion.
>
> The set of rules formulated under the idea that a grammar is a formal system are essentially algorithmic. In such a system, no use is made of meaning. Chomsky's so-called generative grammar . . . assumes that syntax is independent of semantics and that the language faculty is independent of external cognitive capabilities. This definition of grammar is impervious to any attempt to disconfirm it by referring to facts about cognition in general. A language defined as a set of strings of uninterpreted symbols generated by production rules is like a computer language.

This brings us back to Bruner's remarks quoted earlier. As he points out (1990: 1), "the new cognitive science, the child of the [cognitive] revolution, has gained in technical successes at the price of dehumanizing the very concept it had sought to reestablish in psychology, and . . . has thereby estranged much of psychology from the other human sciences and the humanities". The same can be said about linguistics.

In talking about a "linguistics without meaning" I do not wish to underestimate the work done in linguistic semantics over the last several decades. Nor would I question the significance of the other trends in linguistics that sought to transcend the limitations imposed upon the discipline by generative grammar. Harris (1993) and others are right to rejoice in the "greening of linguistics"of the last decade or two, with the dynamic development of functional linguistics, cognitive linguistics, pragmatics, and so on. At the same time, however, I think that the Bloomfieldian and Chomskyan anti-semantic bias is still hanging over linguistics like a dark shadow. The fact that "formal syntax" still occupies a prominent place in the curricula of many linguistic departments, at the expense of the study of language as an instrument for conveying meaning, gives sufficient substance to this claim.

In the latest version of Chomskyan linguistics references to meaning are apparently no longer disallowed. But this does not change its basically anti-semantic orientation. Chomsky no longer asserts that "if it can be shown that meaning and related notions do play a role in linguistic analysis, then . . . a serious blow is struck at the foundations of linguistic theory" (1955:

141). But he none the less remains what he has always been: "a deep and abiding syntactic fundamentalist" (R. A. Harris 1993: 139). Matthews (1993: 245) sums up his comments on the place of meaning in Chomsky's recent work as follows: "Where did that leave an account of meaning? Chomsky, as always, is primarily a student of syntax, or of 'grammar' in a traditional sense. Therefore we can expect, as always, little more than programmatic statements and passing remarks."

Nor has the semantic void created by the "syntactic fundamentalism" of Chomskyan grammar been filled by the so-called "formal semantics", which also features prominently in the teaching programmes of many linguistics departments.

Despite its name, "formal semantics" (or "model-theoretical semantics") doesn't seek to reveal and describe the meanings encoded in natural language, or to compare meanings across languages and cultures. Rather, it sees its goal as that of translating certain carefully selected types of sentences into a logical calculus. It is interested not in meaning (in the sense of conceptual structures encoded in language) but in the logical properties of sentences such as entailment, contradiction, or logical equivalence or, as Chierchia and McConnell-Ginet (1990: 11) put it, in "informational significance", not in "cognitive significance". (Cf. Bruner's (1990: 4) comments on the shift from "meaning" to "information", quoted earlier.)

To quote one noted formal semanticist (of the "Montague grammar" school), "the model theoretic intension of a word has in principle *nothing whatsoever* to do with what goes on in a person's head when he uses that word" (Dowty 1978: 379). Having explained that in model-theoretical semantics the meaning of a sentence is seen as "a set of possible worlds", Dowty acknowledges that "one may reasonably doubt whether sets of possible worlds have anything at all to do with the psychological process of sentence comprehension", and he admits that "there is no sense in which a person mentally has access to 'all the possible worlds that there are' " (376).

Thus, Chomskyans like to talk about "mind", but do not wish to study meaning, and "formal semanticists" like to talk about "meaning" but only in the sense of possible worlds or truth conditions, not in the sense of conceptual structures. One thing that both schools share is the great emphasis they place on being formal. This emphasis on formal models, at the expense of a search for meaning and understanding, brings to mind, again, Bruner's (1990: 65) remarks about psychology: "It simply will not do to reject the theoretical centrality of meaning for psychology on the grounds that it is 'vague'. Its vagueness was in the eye of yesterday's formalistic logician. We are beyond that now."

Despite all the promises of the "cognitive revolution" in human sciences in general and of the "Chomskyan revolution" in linguistics, now, at the close of the century, meaning (not the logician's "meaning" but the meaning which underlies human cognition, communication, and culture) is still regarded by many linguists as messy and as "the weak point of language study" (Bloomfield 1933/1935: 140). This book hopes to demonstrate that it doesn't have to be so.

2. Semantic Primitives (or Primes)

> To put it briefly, in human speech, different sounds have different meanings. To study this co-ordination of certain sounds with certain meanings, is to study language.
>
> Leonard Bloomfield (1933/1935: 27)

How is it possible to admit that to study language is to study the correlations between sound and meaning and, at the same time, to try to keep linguistics maximally "meaning-free"? Bloomfield's own reason for this contradictory position is quite clear: he wanted linguistics to be a serious and rigorous discipline—"a science"; and it was not clear at the time how, if at all, meaning could be studied in a rigorous and "scientific" manner. In fact, even today, many defenders of the central role of meaning in linguistics don't seem to mind if meaning is spoken of in a loose, vague, *ad hoc* way, without any coherent methodology. On this point, I must say that I agree with Bloomfield: if we really want to study, in a rigorous way, correlations between sounds and meanings (or between forms and meanings), our standards of rigour and coherence in talking about meaning should be just as high and exacting as in talking about sounds and forms.

As I have tried to demonstrate for a quarter of a century, the key to a rigorous and yet insightful talk about meaning lies in the notion of semantic primitives (or semantic primes).

To take an example. Two prominent researchers into child language and the authors of a very valuable study on the acquisition of meaning, Lucia French and Katherine Nelson (1985: 38), start their discussion of the concept 'if' by saying: "it is difficult to provide a precise definition of the word *if*". Then, after some discussion, they conclude: "The fundamental meaning of *if*, in both logic and ordinary language, is one of implication."

Two common assumptions are reflected in these statements. First, that it is possible to define all words—including *if*—and second, that if a word seems difficult to define, one had better reach for a scientific-sounding word of Latin origin (such as *implication*). In my view, these assumptions are not only false, but jointly constitute a stumbling-block for semantic analysis. One cannot define all words, because the very idea of 'defining' implies that there is not only something to be defined (a definiendum) but also something to define it with (a definiens, or rather, a set of "definienses").

The elements which can be used to define the meaning of words (or any other meanings) cannot be defined themselves; rather, they must be accepted as "indefinibilia", that is, as semantic primes, in terms of which all complex meanings can be coherently represented. A definition which attempts to explain the simple word *if* via the complex word *implication* flies in the face of the basic principle of sound semantic analysis put forward more than two millennia ago by Aristotle (1937: 141ª):

First of all, see if he [the analyst] has failed to make the definition through terms that are prior and more intelligible. For the reason why the definition is rendered is to make known the term stated, and we make things known by taking not any random terms, but such as are prior and more intelligible . . . accordingly, it is clear that a man who does not define through terms of this kind has not defined at all.

It could be argued that what is clear to one person may not be clear to another, and that therefore no absolute order of semantic simplicity can be established. To this, however, Aristotle had an answer: what matters is not what is more intelligible to particular individuals, but what is semantically more basic and thus inherently more intelligible:

For, as it happens, different things are more intelligible to different people, not the same things to all . . . Moreover, to the same people different things are more intelligible at different times . . . so that those who hold that a definition ought to be rendered through what is more intelligible to particular individuals would not have to render the same definition at all times even to the same person. It is clear, then, that the right way to define is not through terms of that kind, but through what is absolutely more intelligible: for only in this way could the definition come always to be one and the same.

The "absolute order of understanding" depends on semantic complexity. For example, one cannot understand the concepts of 'promise' or 'denounce' without first understanding the concept of 'say', for 'promise' and 'denounce' are built upon 'say'. Similarly, one cannot understand the concepts of 'deixis', 'demonstration', or 'ostension' without first understanding the concept of 'this', on which they are built; and one cannot understand the concept of 'implication' without first understanding the semantically more basic concept of 'if'.

When someone shows me a child who understands and can use the word *implication* but has not yet learned to understand and to use the word *if*, I will admit that everything is relative in semantics. Until such time, however, I will maintain that Aristotle was right, and that, despite all the interpersonal variation in the acquisition of meaning, there is also an "absolute order of understanding", based on inherent semantic relations among words.

This is, then, one of the main assumptions of the semantic theory, and semantic practice, presented in this book: meaning cannot be described without a set of semantic primitives; one can purport to describe meaning by translating unknowns into unknowns (as in Pascal's (1667/1954: 580) mock-definition "Light is the luminary movement of luminous bodies"), but nothing is really achieved thereby.

Without a set of primitives all descriptions of meaning are actually or potentially circular (as when, for example, *to demand* is defined as 'to request firmly', and *to request* as 'to demand gently'; see Wierzbicka 1987a: 4). Any set of primitives is better than none, because without some such set semantic description is inherently circular and, ultimately, untenable. This doesn't mean, however, that it is a matter of indifference what set of primitives one is operating with, as long as one has some such set. Far from it: the best semantic descriptions are worth only as much as the set of primitives on which they are based. For this reason, for a semanticist the pursuit of an optimal set of primitives must be a matter of first importance. " 'Optimal' from what point of view?" the sceptics ask. From the point of view of understanding. Semantics is a search for understanding, and to understand anything we must reduce the unknown to the known, the obscure to the clear, the abstruse to the self-explanatory.

As I pointed out in my *Semantic Primitives* (Wierzbicka 1972: 3), constructors and students of artificial languages often place great emphasis on the arbitrariness of "primitive terms". For example, Nelson Goodman (1951: 57) wrote: "It is not because a term is indefinable that it is chosen as primitive; rather, it is because a term has been chosen as primitive for a system that it is indefinable . . . In general, the terms adopted as primitives of a given system are readily definable in some other system. There is no absolute primitive, no one correct selection of primitives."

But the idea that the same applies to the semantics of natural language is a fallacy, and a recipe for stagnation in semantic research. There is of course no reason why linguists shouldn't invent arbitrary sets of primitives and "define" whatever they like in terms of such sets. But it will do little to advance our understanding of human communication and cognition. To quote Leibniz:

If nothing could be comprehended in itself nothing at all could ever be comprehended. Because what can only be comprehended via something else can be comprehended only to the extent to which that other thing can be comprehended, and so on; accordingly, we can say that we have understood something only when we have broken it down into parts which can be understood in themselves. (Leibniz 1903/1961: 430; my translation)

Semantics can have an explanatory value only if it manages to "define" (or explicate) complex and obscure meanings in terms of simple and self-explanatory ones. If a human being can understand any utterances at all (someone else's or their own) it is only because these utterances are built, so to speak, out of simple elements which can be understood by themselves.

This basic point, which modern linguistics has lost sight of, was made repeatedly in writings on language by the great thinkers of the seventeenth century such as Descartes, Pascal, Arnauld, and Leibniz. For example, Descartes wrote:

Further I declare that there are certain things which we render more obscure by try-ing to define them, because, since they are very simple and clear, we cannot know and perceive them better than by themselves. Nay, we must place in the number of those chief errors that can be committed in the sciences, the mistakes committed by those who would try to define what ought only to be conceived, and who cannot distinguish the clear from the obscure, nor discriminate between what, in order to be known, requires and deserves to be defined, from what can be best known by itself. (1701/1931: 324)

For Descartes, then, as for Leibniz, there was no question of "choosing" some arbitrary set of primitives. What mattered was to establish which con-cepts are so clear that they cannot be understood better than by themselves; and to explain everything else in terms of these.

This basic principle was applied first of all to lexical semantics, and was phrased in terms of the definability of words. For example, Pascal wrote:

It is clear that there are words which cannot be defined; and if nature hadn't pro-vided for this by giving all people the same idea all our expressions would be obscure; but in fact we can use those words with the same confidence and certainty as if they had been explained in the clearest possible way; because nature itself has given us, without additional words, an understanding of them better than what our art could give through our explanations. (1667/1954: 580)

Similarly, Arnauld:

Our first observation is that no attempt should be made to define all words; such an attempt would be useless, even impossible, to achieve. To define a word which already expresses a distinct idea unambiguously would be useless; for the goal of definition—to join to a word one clear and distinct idea—has already been attained. Words which express ideas of simple things are understood by all and require no definition . . .

Further, it is impossible to define all words. In defining we employ a definition to express the idea which we want to join to the defined word; and if we then wanted to define "the definition," still other words would be needed—and so on to infinity. Hence, it is necessary to stop at some *primitive words*, which are not defined. To define too much is just as great a failing as to define too little: Either way we would fall into the confusion that we claim to avoid. (1662/1964: 86–7; emphasis added)

Chomsky, despite his claims that generative grammar was a continuation of "Cartesian linguistics" (see Chomsky 1966), has always omitted any mention of this central thread in the Cartesian (as well as the Leibnizian) theory of language and mind. (See also the references to the "Cartesian conception" of language and cognition in Chomsky's more recent writings, e.g. in Chomsky 1991a).

My own interest in the pursuit of non-arbitrary semantic primitives was triggered by a lecture on this subject given at Warsaw University by the Polish linguist Andrzej Bogusławski in 1965. The "golden dream" of the seventeenth-century thinkers, which couldn't be realized within the framework of philosophy and which was therefore generally abandoned as a utopia, could be realized, Bogusławski maintained, if it was approached from a linguistic rather than from a purely philosophical point of view. The experience and achievements of modern linguistics (both empirical and theoretical) made it possible to approach the problem of conceptual primitives in a novel way; and to put it on the agenda of an empirical science.

Leibniz's theory of an "alphabet of human thoughts" (1903/1961: 435) could be dismissed as a utopia because he never proposed anything like a complete list of hypothetical primitives (although in his unpublished work he left several partial drafts, see Leibniz 1903). As one modern commentator wrote, having pointed out the difficulties involved in the proposed search: "In these circumstances it is understandable that Leibniz should consistently avoid the obvious question as to the number and type of fundamental concepts. The approach would be more convincing if one could at least gain some clue as to what the table of fundamental concepts might look like" (Martin 1964: 25).

The best clues as to what the table of fundamental concepts might look like come from the study of languages. In this sense linguistics has a chance of succeeding where philosophical speculation has failed. This book, which is based on linguistic research undertaken (by colleagues and myself) over three decades, does propose a complete (if hypothetical) table of fundamental human concepts capable of generating all other concepts (see Chapter 2). Crucially, this list purports also to be a table of lexical universals—a point which will be discussed in the next section.

3. Lexical Universals

In the theory presented in this book it was hypothesized, from the start, that conceptual primitives can be found through in-depth analysis of any natural language; but also, that the sets of primitives identified in this way would "match", and that in fact each such set is just one language-specific manifestation of a universal set of fundamental human concepts.

For example, it was expected that the concepts 'someone', 'something', and 'want', which are indefinable in English, would also prove to be indefinable in other languages; and that other languages, too, will have words (or bound morphemes) to express these concepts.

This expectation was based on the assumption that fundamental human concepts are innate, in other words that they are part of the human genetic endowment; and that if they are innate, then there is no reason to expect that they should differ from one human group to another.

It was also based on the experience of successful communication between native speakers of different languages. Since the indefinable concepts—the primitives—are the fundament on which the semantic system of a language is built, if this fundament were in each case different, speakers of different languages would be imprisoned in different and incommensurable conceptual systems, without any possibility of ever reaching anyone outside one's own prison. This is contrary to human experience, which points, rather, to the existence of both differences and similarities in the human conceptualization of the world; and which tells us that while cross-cultural communication is difficult, and has its limitations, it is not altogether impossible.

The assumption that all languages, however different, are based on isomorphic sets of semantic primitives is consistent with that experience.

Until recently, this assumption was based largely on theoretical considerations rather than on empirical studies of different languages of the world. This situation, however, has changed with the publication of *Semantic and Lexical Universals* (Goddard and Wierzbicka 1994*b*)—a collection in which conceptual primitives posited initially on the basis of a mere handful of languages were subjected to a systematic study across a wide range of languages from different families and different continents. The languages investigated in this volume included: Ewe (of the Niger–Congo family in West Africa), Mandarin Chinese, Thai, Japanese, the Australian languages Yankunytjatjara, Arrernte (Aranda), and Kayardild, three Misumalpan languages of Nicaragua, the Austronesian languages Acehnese (of Indonesia), Longgu (of the Solomon Islands), Samoan, and Mangap-Mbula (of New Guinea), the Papuan language Kalam, and—the only European language beside English—French.

This first large-scale attempt to test hypothetical conceptual primitives cross-linguistically did not answer all the questions, but except for one or two grey areas requiring further investigation, the studies included in the volume did strongly support the hypothesized set of primitives. In most cases, words (or bound morphemes) for the proposed primitives (e.g. 'I' and 'you', 'someone' and 'something', 'where' and 'when', 'big' and 'small', 'good' and 'bad', or 'do' and 'happen') could be readily identified.

In his discussion of "universalism" in semantics, John Lyons (1977: 331–2) stated that as far as he could see, no one advocates the most extreme form of "semantic universalism", that is, the position that "there is a fixed set of semantic components, which are universal in that they are lexicalized in all languages". But it is precisely this strongest universalist hypothesis which was tested in *Semantic and Lexical Universals*, and which also underlies the present book.

While the theory presented in this book is radically universalist, two provisos must be entered: first, that I fully accept the Humboldtian view that despite the presence of universals, on the whole the semantic systems embodied in different languages are unique and culture-specific; and second, that the presence of "embodied" (that is, lexicalized) universals does not mean perfect equivalence in language use. Both these points require some elaboration.

As all translators know to their cost, every language has words which have no semantic equivalents in other languages, and every language draws semantic distinctions which other languages do not. For example, translating the classic texts of the Hindu cultural tradition into European languages one must face the fact that these languages do not have words coming even near in meaning to key Sanskrit terms such as *nirvana, brahman, atman,* or *karma* (see Bolle 1979: 219–58). But even comparing languages which are genetically, geographically, and culturally very close, for example French and English, one constantly encounters examples of profound lexical differences. For example, the French word *malheur* has no counterpart in English, as pointed out by the English translator of Simone Weil's meditations on this concept, who finally in desperation decided to use, throughout his translation, the totally inadequate English word "affliction" (Weil 1972: 63).

In a sense, most words in all languages are like the French *malheur*, that is, unrenderable (without distortion) in some other languages. More than that, every language has words which are intimately bound up with one particular culture and which have no equivalents in any other languages. (See e.g. Wierzbicka 1991*b*, 1992*a*). At the same time, all languages also have words which—unlike *malheur*—do appear to have semantic counterparts in all other languages. The hypothesis explored in this book (and in the work which led to it) is that in every language the set of such readily "translatable" words coincides with the set of this language's indefinables.

Within a particular language, every element belongs to a unique network of elements, and occupies a particular place in a unique network of relationships. When we compare two, or more, languages we cannot expect to find identical networks of relationships. We can, none the less, expect to find corresponding sets of indefinables.

It is this (limited) isomorphism in the lexicon (and, as we shall see, also in grammar) that gives substance to the notion of universal semantic primitives.

For example, the English words *big* and *small* correspond in meaning to the Russian words *bol'šoj* and *malen'kij*, even though in English, *small* has also a special relationship with *little*, and even though in Russian, *malen'kij*—formally a diminutive—has a special relationship with diminutive adjectives such as *belen'kij* ('white' + DIM) or *kruglen'kij* ('round' + DIM). Whatever the differences in "resonance" (see Section 8.7) between *small* and *malen'kij* are, these differences cannot be shown through definitions; and so, from a definitional point of view, they constitute a "perfect" match (in the systems of English and Russian indefinables, they occupy the same slot). Similarly, regardless of any differences in "resonance" (and use), the Japanese words *ookii* and *tiisai* constitute a perfect semantic match for *big* and *small*, and the Japanese words *ii* and *warui*, for *good* and *bad*. (See Onishi 1994.)

Furthermore, it is only the postulated isomorphism of exponents of conceptual primitives which allows us to compare different semantic systems at all. For any comparison requires a *tertium comparationis*, a common measure. The hypothesized set of universal semantic primitives offers us such a common measure and thus makes it possible to study the extent of semantic differences between languages.

So the theory presented here combines, in a sense, radical universalism with thoroughgoing relativism. It accepts the uniqueness of all language-and-culture systems, but posits a set of shared concepts, in terms of which differences between these systems can be assessed and understood; and it allows us to interpret the most idiosyncratic semantic structures as culture-specific configurations of universal semantic primitives—that is, of innate human concepts.

4. Innate Concepts and Language Acquisition

Acquiring language consists in large part of learning how to map or translate from one representational system (the child's prelinguistic conceptual notions) into another (language).

(Bowerman 1976: 101)

As mentioned earlier, the idea that fundamental human concepts (semantic primes) are universal is closely linked with the notion that these concepts are innate. It is heartening to see, therefore, that over the last twenty years, child language acquisition studies have not only increasingly viewed language learning as, above all, a quest for meaning, but have also increasingly assumed that the child embarks on this quest not as a passive *tabula rasa* but as an actor equipped with some innate basic concepts.

To quote Bowerman (1976: 112–13), "the child is now commonly viewed as coming to the language-learning task well equipped with a stock of basic concepts that he has built up through his interactions with the world . . . Some early concepts undoubtedly develop autonomously (i.e. independently of language), particularly those which are universal (e.g. object permanence)." Bowerman quotes with approval Macnamara's (1972: 5) statement that "it is inconceivable that the hearing of a logical term (by which he means words such as 'and', 'or', 'more', 'all', and 'some') should generate for the first time the appropriate logical operator in a child's mind. Indeed the only possibility of his learning such a word would seem to be if he experienced the need for it in his own thinking and looked for it in the linguistic usage about him."

What is particularly interesting in Bowerman's (1976) discussion of the problem of innateness is her clear perception of the link between a child's first concepts, language universals, and semantic primitives.

The view that a central process in language acquisition is the child's search for links between cognitive and linguistic concepts and linguistic forms and operations has been strengthened and encouraged by recent developments in linguistics. Many linguists now argue, on grounds quite independent of child language, that the most basic elements of language are not abstract syntactic configurations like grammatical relations, but rather a universal set of prime semantic concepts that combine according to general and language-specific constraints to yield both words and sentences. (102)

The linguists to whom Bowerman refers at this point are generative semanticists, that is, representatives of a school which flourished briefly in the late sixties and early seventies but has now long ceased to exist (see e.g. R. A. Harris 1993). But the idea of a universal set of semantic primes was neither due to that school, nor linked in any way with its fate. On the contrary: as I argued at the time (e.g. Wierzbicka 1967*a,b*, 1972, 1976*b*), it was a lack of a strong commitment to that idea which made the position of the generative semantics school—suspended in mid-air between Chomskyan "meaning-free" syntax and genuine semantics—untenable.

The notion of innate and universal semantic primitives which underlies this book corresponds, in some ways, to Slobin's (1985) "semantic space" of "prelinguistic meanings", in which "core concepts and clusters of related notions can be identified" (1163). Slobin's central claim is that children construct "similar early grammars from all input languages. The surface forms generated by these grammars will, of course, vary, since the materials provided by the input languages vary. What is constant are *the basic notions* that first receive grammatical expression, along with early constraints on the positioning of grammatical elements and the ways in which they relate to syntactic expression" (emphasis added).

Slobin explicitly relates his innate "basic concepts" to Sapir's "absolutely essential concepts . . . the concepts that must be expressed if language is to be a satisfactory means of communication" (1949: 93).

Supporting, in principle, Slobin's "BCG" (Basic Child Grammar) hypothesis, Bowerman (1985: 1284) writes: I argue that the BCG hypothesis does contain a fundamental insight into early language development: that children's starting semantic space is not a *tabula rasa*, passively awaiting the imprint of the language being learned before taking on structure. Rather, children are conceptually prepared for language learning." At the same time, Bowerman (1985) argues that "the initial organization of semantic space is not fixed but flexible", that the child's "semantic space" does not "define a single, privileged set of semantic notions that strongly attracts the grammatical forms of the input", and that "one important factor that can influence the meanings children adopt is the *semantic structure of the input language*" (1284).

But there is no reason why the initial organization of the child's "semantic space" should not be flexible in the way Bowerman describes it and yet fixed in its minimum core of "absolutely essential concepts", as stipulated by Sapir. There is also no conflict between the tenet (which I will defend in further chapters of this book) that the universal innate concepts play a particularly important role in grammar and the perfectly plausible idea that from early on children pay a special attention to language-specific semantic distinctions, drawn by, and perhaps grammaticalized in, their native language. But to explore such issues in a meaningful way we need a coherent semantic theory, and a rigorous semantic methodology. (See Chapter 7.)

The converging perspectives of current theoretical reflection on language acquisition and the linguistically based search for innate and universal semantic primitives is perhaps best expressed by Bruner (1990: 72): "the case for how we 'enter language' must rest upon a selective set of prelinguistic 'readiness for meaning'. That is to say, there are certain classes of meaning to which human beings are innately tuned and for which they actively search. Prior to language, these exist in primitive form as protolinguistic representations of the world whose full realization depends upon the cultural tool of language."

Given the attention that Chomsky's writings on language continue to receive in the world market of ideas, it is perhaps worth mentioning here Chomsky's new theory on the acquisition of concepts, according to which most concepts (including, for example, 'chase', 'persuade', 'murder', or 'table', and perhaps even 'bureaucrat' and 'carburettor') are innate. Speaking of the semantic complexity of most concepts, Chomsky (1991*b*: 29) writes: "Barring miracles, this means that the concepts must be essentially available prior to experience, in something like their full intricacy. Children must be basically acquiring labels for concepts they already have, a view advanced most strongly by Jerry Fodor."

This theory, which Chomsky (1987: 33) himself acknowledges many find absurd, ignores the fact that the meanings of most words differ from language to language, that they are "cultural artefacts", reflecting aspects of the cultures that have created them.

In my view, what can be reasonably expected to be innate is not culture-specific concepts such as 'bureaucrat' or '*apparatchik*', 'table' or 'boomerang', 'persuade' or 'kow-tow', but only those which show up in all languages, such as 'person' and 'thing', 'do' and 'happen', 'where' and 'when', or 'good' and 'bad'. All the other concepts must be acquired via "the cultural tool of language".

Incidentally, the idea that the meanings of most words are innate rather than construed within a culture out of innate primitives, is used in Chomsky's writings (as well as in Fodor's; see Chapter 7), as an argument against lexical semantics: words are very difficult to define, but there is no need for linguists to try to define them, because they are simply labels for unanalysable innate concepts. "Ordinary dictionary definitions do not come close to characterizing the meaning of words" (Chomsky 1987: 21); none the less, they "can be sufficient for their purpose because the basic principles of word meaning (whatever they are) are known to the dictionary user, as they are to the language learner, independently of any instruction or experience" (ibid.).

This effectively absolves the linguist from the need to study the meaning of words or to take an interest in lexicography. Even the general principles of word meaning ("whatever they are") are clearly too hard to study. Here again, Chomsky's mentalism is as inimical to the study of meaning as was Bloomfield's behaviourism.

5. The Universal Syntax of Meaning

In what has been said so far, the emphasis was very much on the elements: the primitive concepts, the indefinable words. But to say anything meaningful we need more than words: we need sentences in which words are meaningfully put together. Similarly, to think something we need more than "concepts": we need meaningful combinations of concepts. Despite its obvious limitations, Leibniz's old metaphor of an "alphabet of human thoughts" is still quite useful here: conceptual primitives are components which have to be combined in certain ways to be able to express meaning.

For example, the indefinable word *want* makes sense only if it is put in a certain syntactic frame, such as "I want to do this". In positing the elements I, WANT, DO, and THIS as innate and universal conceptual primitives, I am also positing certain innate and universal rules of syntax—not in the sense of some intuitively unverifiable formal syntax *à la* Chomsky, but in the sense of intuitively verifiable patterns determining possible combinations of primitive concepts.

For example, the meaning of the sentence "I want to do this" is intuitively clear to any native speaker of English, and cannot be made any clearer by explanations, or by abstract elaborations. In particular, no explanations in terms of "agents", "actors", "volition", "action", "deixis", "self-reference", "subjects", "predicates", "objects", "clauses", "deletions", or any other technical terms and theoretical constructs can bring anyone a millimetre closer to understanding this sentence. On the contrary, it is our understanding of technical terms and theoretical constructs which has to rest, ultimately, on our intuitive understanding of simple sentences such as "I want to do this" or "I want you to do this".

If one wants to explain the meaning of a sentence such as "I want to do this" to a non-native speaker, the best one can do is to point to a semantically matching sentence in their own language. For example, to a Russian one could offer the following equation:

I want to do this = ja xoču èto sdelat'

where *ja* matches with *I*, *xoču* (1st Sg) with *want*, *èto* with *this*, and *sdelat'* with *do*, and where the combination *ja xoču* matches *I want*, the combination *èto sdelat'* matches *to do this*, and the whole combination *ja xoču èto sdelat'* matches the whole combination *I want to do this*.

This is, then, what the universal syntax of meaning is all about: it consists in universal combinations of universal conceptual primitives (see Chapter 3). From a formal point of view, the grammar of the Russian sentence differs a great deal from that of the English one. For example, the word *xoču* can be analysed into two parts, the verbal stem *xoč-* and the inflexional ending *-u* (first person singular, present tense), whereas the English word *want* (which in combination with "I" conveys the same meaning) is not similarly analysable; and the order of the elements *èto* and *sdelat'* is different from that of *do* and *this*. But formal differences of this kind don't detract in the least from the overall semantic equivalence of the two sentences, which is based on the equivalence of the primitives themselves and of the rules for their combination.

Thus, the theory posits the existence not only of an innate and universal "lexicon of human thoughts", but also of an innate and universal "syntax of human thoughts". Taken together, these two hypotheses amount to positing something that can be called "a language of thought", or *lingua mentalis,* as I called it in the title of my 1980 book.

Researchers into early child utterances have often noted how similar these utterances are, across languages and cultures (see e.g. Slobin 1985: 1189, 1243; Bowerman 1976: 139). The hypothesis of an innate and universal *lingua mentalis* as a basis of all future language development can, I think, go a long way towards explaining this. Of course, it will be said—and justly so—that it is, above all, the social needs of infants which explain the commonalities of infants' early speech and communication (see e.g. Halliday 1975; Donaldson 1978). But the semantic and the social point of view on language acquisition are fully compatible. What the child needs and wants to convey is messages such as 'I want something', 'I don't want to do this', 'I want more' (e.g. "more juice!"), 'I want you to do something', 'I don't want you to do this', 'there isn't (any)' (e.g. "allgone"), 'I want to know something', 'I see something bad' (e.g. "yukky"), and so on.

Messages of this kind, which rely not only on conceptual primitives such as WANT, DO, or NOT, but also on their "canonical" combinations, can indeed be called "social"; but being "social" doesn't make them any less meaningful. On the contrary, social interaction relies, to a considerable extent, on expressing and interchanging "social meanings" (such as, for example, 'I want you to do something' or 'I don't want you to do this').

Edelman (1992: 239) writes: "The syntax and semantics of natural language are not just special cases of formal syntax and semantics, the models of which have structure but no meaning. ... symbolic structures are meaningful *to begin with.*" Arguing against Chomsky's "language acquisition device", Edelman charges that it "ignores the fact that language serves to convey the thoughts and feelings of individuals who already think independently of language" (243), and he points out (with reference to Margaret Donaldson's (1978) critique of the Chomskyan position) that "a child first makes sense of situations and human intentions and *then* of what is said. This means that language is *not* independent of the rest of cognition" (245).

I, too, believe that language is not independent of the rest of cognition, and that meaning underlies language, not the other way around. Presumably, children "make sense" of what is said in much the same way as they "make sense" of non-verbal behaviours such as crying, smiling, frowning, beckoning, and so on. (See e.g. Wierzbicka 1993*a*, 1994*g*, 1995*b*.) Doesn't beckoning, for example, mean 'I want you to come here now'? And what could "making sense" mean if not interpreting people's observed behaviour in terms of meaningful "mental representations" such as 'I want you to come here' or 'I don't want you to do this'?

As Slobin (1985: 1243) put it, a child appears to be able "not only to scan linguistic input to *discover* meaning, but also to scan linguistic input for the means of expressing highly accessible, prelinguistic meanings". I believe that simple sentences formulated in lexical universals (such as "I want to do this" or "I feel something bad") allow us to give substance to such widely shared intuitions and claims about a child's "pre-linguistic meanings". More generally, my hypothesis is that in a latent state, the innate mini-language of universal semantic primitives constitutes the basis of a child's "readiness for meaning".

But while child language acquisition can undoubtedly be a fertile field of study for anyone interested in pre-linguistic semantic structures, at the moment the best avenue for studying the "universal syntax of meaning" is clearly cross-linguistic semantic investigation.[4] Preliminary evidence suggests, for example, that patterns such as "I want to do something", "I know this", "Where are you?", or "I can't move" are universal (that is, attestable in all languages). Facts of this kind are as important for the study of the innate conceptual system (or the "prelinguistic readiness for meaning"; Bruner 1990: 72) as the presence in all languages of words for 'I', 'you', 'where', 'want', 'think', or 'know'.

Just as attempts to separate syntax from meaning, and to absolutize syntax, have failed as a path to understanding how natural language works, how it is used, and how it is acquired, so too any attempts to separate meaning from syntax and to absolutize the lexicon would lead nowhere, for syntax and meaning are inextricably bound. To quote Oliver Sacks (1993: 48): "it is increasingly clear, from studying the natural acquisition of language in the child, and, equally, from the persistent failure of computers to 'understand' language . . . that syntax cannot be separated from semantics. It is precisely through the medium of 'meanings' that natural language and natural intelligence are built up."

6. The Natural Semantic Metalanguage (NSM)

I believe that the strongest support for the hypothesis of a language-like innate conceptual system comes from its proven merits as a working tool in the investigation of languages and cultures.

As pointed out earlier, any meaningful comparison requires a *tertium comparationis*, that is, a common measure. If by investigating as many diverse languages as possible we can establish a hypothetical shared core of all natural languages, we can then treat this shared core as a language-independent metalanguage for the description and comparison of all languages and cultures. Without such a language-independent metalanguage, we would be for ever condemned to ethnocentrism, for we could only describe other languages and cultures through the prism of our own language (whether colloquial or technical) (see e.g. Lutz 1985).

But if we can identify the shared core of all natural languages and build on this basis a "natural semantic metalanguage", we can then describe the meanings conveyed in any language, as if from inside, while at the same time using sentences from our own language, which—if at times unidiomatic—are none the less directly intelligible to us. To put it differently, the shared core of all languages can be seen as a set of isomorphic mini-

---

[4] In principle, data from language acquisition studies are very important to semantic theory. The difficulty is that to be directly relevant these studies should be conducted within the framework of a coherent semantic theory, and should be so devised as to test specific semantic hypotheses. In the past, this usually hasn't been the case.

languages, which can be used as language-specific versions of the same, universal Natural Semantic Metalanguage (NSM).

If we try to explain the meaning of Russian or Japanese sentences by simply providing them with *ad hoc* English glosses (using full-blown English), we inevitably distort their meaning and impose on them a semantic perspective inherent to the English language. On the other hand, if instead of full-blown English glosses we were to provide a gloss in the English NSM, that is, in the English version of the Natural Semantic Metalanguage, no such distortion would be necessary, for the English version of NSM can match exactly the Russian or the Japanese versions. For example, as pointed out earlier, the Russian NSM formula *ja xoču èto sdelat'* matches semantically the English NSM formula *I want to do this.*

The idea that all languages share an identifiable core is by no means new. Wilhelm Humboldt emphasized that in both lexicon and grammar, there is a "midpoint around which all languages revolve" (1903–36, v. 4: 21). Nor is it a novel idea that for semantic descriptions of different languages a special "intermediary language" is needed—and not just an artificial system of abstract features (like the Markerese of Katz and Fodor 1963) but a more language-like semantic metalanguage. The notion of "jazyk posrednik", 'language-intermediary', of the Moscow semantic school (see Žolkovskij 1964), is particularly relevant here.

What is new in the present theory is the assumption that an effective metalanguage for the description and comparison of meanings can be found in the common core of natural languages, and that it can be, so to speak, carved out of them. Incorporating this assumption, the NSM theory combines the philosophical and logical tradition in the study of meaning with a typological approach to the study of language, and with broadly based empirical cross-linguistic investigations.

Unlike various artificial languages used for the representation of meaning, the Natural Semantic Metalanguage, carved out of natural language, can be understood without further explanations (which would necessitate the use of some other metalanguage, and so on, *ad infinitum*), and thus offers a firm basis for a genuine elucidation of meaning.

As Ana Agud (1980: 457) put it in her *Historia y teoria de los casos*, "ninguna lengua formal puede ser, en última instancia, más precisa que el lenguaje natural que es su último metalenguaje", i.e. "no formal language can be, in the last instance, more precise than the natural language which is its ultimate metalanguage".[5]

---

[5] See also the following recent statement by Harré and Gillet (1994: 27–8): "Another important consequence of the second cognitive revolution is the priority that must be given to ordinary languages in defining what are the phenomena for a scientific psychology. We will endeavor as far as possible to present and understand cognition in terms of the ordinary languages through which we think, rather than looking for abstract representations of them. That

The need for a universally based metalanguage in human sciences has been well illustrated by the recent interdisciplinary debates on the nature of human emotions. (For detailed discussion, see e.g. Wierzbicka 1992*c*, 1994*h*). For example, it has been repeatedly pointed out that if we try to explain key emotion terms of other languages (such as the Ilongot *liget*, or the Ifaluk *fago* and *song*) by using English words and combinations of words such as "anger/passion/energy", "love/sadness/comparison", or "justified anger", we are imposing an Anglo cultural perspective on other cultures. For from an Ifaluk point of view, *fago* is a unified concept, not a mixture of the concepts encoded in the English words *anger, love, sadness* (for which Ifaluk has no equivalents).

The uncritical use of culturally shaped English words (such as *anger, shame, depression, emotion, mind*, or *self*) as "culture-free" analytical tools, and the reification of the concepts encoded in them, has been strongly criticized (in my view, with good reason) in recent anthropological literature (see e.g. Rosaldo 1980; Lutz 1988; Kondo 1990; see also Wierzbicka 1993*b*). But to move from "deconstruction" to constructive rebuilding of the metalanguage of human sciences, we need to go beyond conceptual relativism and reach for conceptual universals.

7. Semantic Invariants

In recent decades, semantics has suffered at the hands not only of its enemies but also of some of its friends. As I will argue in detail later (see in particular Chapter 4), especially harmful to its progress has been the doctrine of "family resemblances" and the associated attacks on the notion of semantic invariant—a corner-stone of effective semantic analysis.

One of the main tenets of this book is that words do have meanings, and that these meanings can be articulated. If they haven't been successfully articulated in the past, for example, by the proponents of semantic "features" and "markers", it is not because words do not have any constant meanings but because the methodology was inappropriate.

Of course, meanings can change, and they may vary from one dialect, sociolect, or "generatiolect" to another. But semantic change as such is not gradual; only the spread of semantic change is. (One meaning may gradually disappear, another may gradually spread, but both meanings are determinate, and the difference between them is discrete.) In any given speech community, meanings are shared. These shared meanings constitute the

is radical because it resists the idea that a new formal calculus must be devised to represent thought. Such calculi lie at the heart of the artificial intelligence project, the methodological principles of Chomsky and the transformational grammarians, and the assumption of formalists of all kinds."

basis of communication, and the mainstay of culture; to a large extent, they are also the vehicles by which culture is transmitted.

It should go without saying that to be able to fully understand cultures different from our own, we must be able to grasp the meaning of words encoding culture—specific concepts. For example, to understand Japanese culture, and to interpret it to cultural outsiders, we need to grasp the meaning of key Japanese words such as *amae*, *on*, or *wa* (see Wierzbicka 1991*b*; also Chapter 8); and to be able to understand Malay culture, we need to be able to grasp the meaning of key Malay words such as *malu*, *halus* or *lah* (see Goddard 1994*c*, forthcoming *c*). The use of the Natural Semantic Metalanguage allows us to state such meanings in a precise and illuminating way. It allows us to go beyond the vicissitudes of language use and to capture, and reveal, the semantic invariant of a word.

8. Methodological Issues

Summarizing the results of the cross-linguistic investigations reported in *Semantic and Lexical Universals* (Goddard and Wierzbicka 1994*b*), I wrote (Wierzbicka 1994*b*: 445): "Hunting for semantic and lexical universals is not like pearl-fishing. Primitives do not present themselves glittering and unmistakable. Identifying them is an empirical endeavour but one that calls for much interpretative effort." In this section, I will briefly survey the main methodological problems arising in the process of identifying universal semantic primitives and building a Natural Semantic Metalanguage. (For more detailed discussion, see Goddard 1994*a*; Goddard and Wierzbicka 1994*a*.)

8.1. Polysemy

Polysemy is extremely widespread in natural language, and common everyday words—including indefinables—are particularly likely to be involved in it. A semantic primitive cannot be identified, therefore, simply by pointing to an indefinable word. Rather, it must be identified with reference to some illustrative sentences. For example, the English word *want* has at least two meanings, as illustrated below:

(A) I want you to do something.
(B) This house wants painting.

Of these two meanings only A is proposed as a semantic primitive.

The NSM theory does not claim that for every semantic primitive there will be, in every language, a separate word—as long as the absence of a separate word for a given primitive can be convincingly explained (in a principled and coherent way) in terms of polysemy. The notion of different grammatical frames plays a particularly important role in this regard.

For example, if in the Australian language Yankunytjatjara (see Goddard 1994*b*) both the concepts THINK and HEAR, posited here as primitives, are expressed by means of the same verb, *kulini*, this is not seen as a counter-example, because (as Goddard shows) these two meanings of *kulini* are associated with different grammatical frames, and so this verb is demonstrably polysemous. Of course polysemy must never be postulated lightly, but neither should its presence be denied on dogmatically a priori grounds: each case has to be examined on its merits, with reference to some general methodological principles. (For detailed discussion, see Chapter 6; also Goddard 1994*a*, 1991*a*).

8.2. Allolexy

If one word (or morpheme) can be associated with two different meanings, one meaning can often have two or more different lexical exponents. By analogy with "allomorphs" and "allophones", such different exponents of the same primitive are called in NSM theory "allolexes".

To start with some relatively trivial examples, in English, *I* and *me* are allolexes of the same primitive concept (in Latin, EGO, in Russian, JA). Often, the allolexes of a primitive are in complementary distribution; for example, in Latin the three forms *hic, haec, hoc* are all exponents of the same primitive THIS, and the choice between them depends on the gender of the head noun.

Often, the combination with another primitive forces the choice of one of a set of allolexes. For example, in English, a combination of the primitives SOMEONE and ALL is realized as *everyone* or *everybody*, and a combination of ALL with SOMETHING is realized as *everything*. In these particular contexts, *-one* and *-body* can be seen as allolexes of SOMEONE, on a par with *someone*; and *-thing* can be seen as an allolex of SOMETHING, on a par with *something*.

The notion of allolexy plays a particularly important role in the NSM approach to inflexional categories (first articulated by Cliff Goddard at the 1992 Semantics Symposium held in Canberra). Consider, for example, the following sentences:

(A) I am doing it now.
(B) I did it before now (earlier).
(C) I will do it after now (later).

By themselves, the forms *am doing*, *did* and *will do* convey different meanings, but when combined with the temporal adjuncts *now*, *before now*, and *after now*, they are in complementary distribution and can be seen as allolexes of the same primitive, DO.

This is why NSM sentences can be said to match, semantically, across languages, even though the inflexional categories in these languages differ. For example, the Chinese NSM sentence adapted from Chappell (1994: 138)

> Chū-shǐ hòu, wǒ shúo-le xiē shénme
> happen after I say-PFV CL something
> 'After this happened, I said something.'

can be matched with the English NSM sentence:

> After this happened, I said something.

even though the English word for HAPPEN, in contrast to the Chinese one, is marked for past tense: when combined with *after*, the form *happened* can be seen as an allolex of HAPPEN, on a par with *happen*.

8.3. Obligatory or Semi-obligatory Portmanteaus

The notion of allolexy is closely linked with that of semantic portmanteaus, which I will illustrate with a simple example from Russian. The expression *like this*, common in both everyday English and in English NSM sentences, is normally rendered in Russian by means of the word *tak*, which expresses a combination of the two primitives LIKE and THIS.

> Ja sdelal èto tak
> I did this like-this

Since, however, Russian does have separate exponents for both LIKE and THIS (*kak* and *èto*), the use of an obligatory, or semi-obligatory, portmanteau for their combination does not present a problem for the NSM theory. It would present a problem if the postulated primitives did not have their own exponents usable in other contexts.

8.4. Valency Options

The notion of valency options (developed in Chapter 3) refers to different combinability patterns available to the same primitive. For example, the primitive DO can occur in the following combinations:

(A) *X* did something.
(B) *X* did something to person *Y*.
(C) *X* did something with thing *Z*.

Obviously, "doing something to someone", or "doing something with something" implies "doing something". None the less, sentences B and C cannot be analysed in terms of A and something else. It has to be recognized, therefore, that in each case the difference in meaning is due to the sentence as a whole, not to the predicate as such, and that the three sentences share in fact the same predicate (DO), albeit they realize different valency options of this predicate.

8.5. Non-compositional Relationships

Semantic primitives are, by definition, indefinable: they are Leibniz's ultimate "simples", Aristotle's "priora", in terms of which all the complex meanings can be articulated, but which cannot be decomposed themselves. They can, of course, be represented as bundles of some artificial features, such as "+ Speaker, – Hearer" for 'I', but this is not the kind of decomposition which leads from complex to simple and from obscure to clear. As pointed out earlier, the meaning of a sentence like "I know this" cannot be clarified by any further decomposition—not even by decomposition into some other meaningful sentences; and "features", which have no syntax and which are not part of natural language, have no meaning at all: they have to be assigned meaning by sentences in natural languages, rather than the other way around.

This means that, from a compositional point of view, elements such as 'I' and 'you' are semantically simple and have no identifiable part in common. At the same time, intuitively, these two elements are clearly related. Their relationship, however, is non-compositional.

A semantic system is not like a bag full of marbles, each of them perfectly round, self-contained, and independent of the others. Rather, it is a system "où tout se tient", to invoke (in a new context) Saussure's famous phrase. In this system, there are elements which "belong together" and which have the same combinatorial properties, such as 'I' and 'you', or 'good' and 'bad'. Elements of this kind are intuitively related, but this doesn't mean that one of them can be defined in terms of the other.

In the universal semantic system there are many different kinds of non-compositional relationships. For example, the elements I, YOU, THIS, HERE, and NOW, are all mutually related, although they do not all have the same combinatorial properties. We can acknowledge this relationship by putting on them all one label, "deictic", but doing this—while useful—has nothing to do with semantic decomposition.

The primitive THE SAME has a non-compositional relationship with the primitive LIKE, and also with the primitive ONE. The first is highlighted in sentences such as the following one:

This fish is like that other fish, but it is not the same fish.

The second relationship is reflected in the colloquial phrase "one and the same", and in the apparent paraphrase relation between sentences such as A and B below:

(A) These two shoes belong to one pair. ≈
(B) These two shoes belong to the same pair.

But close as the elements within each pair may be, neither THE SAME and LIKE nor THE SAME and ONE can be identified or defined in terms of each other. For example, in the sentence

I have one son and two daughters.

'one' has clearly nothing to do with 'the same'; and in the sentence:

They came at the same time.

'the same' has nothing to do with 'like'.

Non-compositional semantic relations of different kinds are real and important, and they offer an interesting field for research (see Goddard and Wierzbicka 1994*a*). But they must not be confused with compositional relations, which can be revealed by definitions (such as, for example, that between *asleep* and *awake*, or between *dead* and *alive*).

8.6. Recurrent Polysemies

Non-compositional semantic relations are often reflected in recurring polysemic patterns involving two, or more, different primitives. Of course, no natural language will ever be found in which the word for 'I' will be the same as the word for 'you', or the word for 'big', the same as the word for 'small': since the combinatorial possibilities of both elements within each pair are the same, polysemy of their exponents would lead to intolerable confusion. Other non-compositional relations, however, are often reflected in recurring polysemic patterns.

For example, in some languages the word for THE SAME is the same as the word for ONE, or the word for THIS is the same as the word for HERE; there are also languages in which the word for WANT is the same as the word for SAY, or where the word for DO is the same as the word for HAPPEN. This doesn't mean, however, that in those languages people do not distinguish the concept ONE from the concept THE SAME, or the concept WANT from the concept SAY; or that they have no words to express some of these concepts. They do have words for all of them, and if some of these words are polysemous (and mean, for example, (1) 'one', (2) 'the same', or (1) 'want', (2) 'say'), the different meanings of such polysemous words can be easily distinguished on the basis of distinct grammatical frames associated with each of them. (For examples and discussion, see Wierzbicka 1994*b*).

8.7. Resonance

Since every language embodies a unique semantic system and reflects a unique culture, the exponents of universal semantic primitives in different languages often "feel" different (to both native speakers and to linguistic experts on these languages). For example, it is easy to believe that in the Papuan language Kalam, where the words for KNOW, THINK, SEE, and HEAR all share the same verbal formative *nŋ* (Pawley 1994), these words "feel" somehow different in meaning from the corresponding English words (which are formally unrelated to each other). Or if the word for FEEL is polysemous between 'feel' and 'stomach' (as is the case with the word *tjuni* in the Australian language Yankunytjatjara, see Goddard 1994*b*), it is easy to believe that this word "feels" different from the English word *feel*, or from the Acehnese word *rasa* (a borrowing from Sanskrit; Durie *et al.* 1994).

Differences of this kind are real and important, and they are acknowledged in the NSM notion of "resonance" (first articulated by Goddard at the 1992 Semantics Symposium in Canberra). They must not be confused, however, with semantic differences *sensu stricto*.

8.8. Canonical Sentences

Most sentences uttered in any one language cannot be translated into other languages without some loss, and/or addition, of meaning. The NSM theory hypothesizes, however, that there are also some kinds of sentence which can be translated—without loss and/or addition of meaning—into any language whatsoever. These are sentences formulated in "local representatives" of universal semantic primitives, according to the universal syntactic rules (that is, rules for combining the primitives). Sentences of this kind include, for example, the following ones:

> You did something bad.
> I know when it happened.
> I want to see this.
> These people didn't say anything about this.
> If you do this, I will do the same.
> This person can't move.

Sentences of this kind are regarded in NSM research as "canonical sentences", which can be used to test the validity of the Natural Semantic Metalanguage (as developed until now), and to seek any weak points which may need revision.

For practical reasons (to make the testing more effective in working with native speakers) it is often useful to include in the set of canonical sentences some which are not composed exclusively of primitives. For example, if we want to check whether a language has words for the primitives ONE and TWO, it is practical to use sentences like the following:

I have two sons and one daughter.

even though the concepts of 'son' and 'daughter' are not universal, and the words glossed as 'son' and 'daughter' may not match semantically across language boundaries (for some languages may distinguish a man's son or daughter from a woman's son or daughter).

The notion of a canonical sentence both in the strict sense (primitives only) and in the broader sense (primitives with a controlled admixture of non-primitives) has proved to be a valuable tool in cross-linguistic semantic research (see Goddard and Wierzbicka 1994b). In the future, this notion may also prove useful in the cross-cultural study of language acquisition and cognitive development; and may answer, in some measure, the call frequently voiced by child language researchers "for a more powerful cross-linguistic methodology" (Johnston 1985: 996).

9. Past, Present, and Future of NSM Semantic Theory

Since its inception in the mid-sixties, the basic assumptions and goals of the NSM theory have remained unchanged: the search for universal semantic primitives, the avoidance of artificial "features" and "markers", the rejection of logical systems of representation, the reliance on natural language as the only self-explanatory system for the representation of meaning. At the same time, the theory has not stood still; on the contrary, it has been constantly developing. These developments could be said to have gone in six main directions:

1. the proposed set of primitives has considerably increased;
2. the search for primitives came to be identified with a search for lexical universals;
3. the search for lexical primitives came to be combined with a search for universal syntactic patterns (that is, for universally available combinations of primitives);
4. the pursuit of, first, primitives and then their combinations grew into a broader programme of building a full-scale "natural semantic metalanguage";
5. the theoretical underpinnings of the whole enterprise became gradually more and more clearly articulated (as discussed in Section 8); and
6. the range of domains, languages, and cultures to which NSM theory was applied, and against which it was tested, expanded substantially.

These developments cannot be discussed here comprehensively; a few brief comments on each of them, however, are in order.

1. NSM theory started as a search for lexically embodied indefinable concepts, or semantic primes, identified as such by trial and error, within one language (any language). The first tentative list of primitives identified in this search was published in my book *Semantic Primitives* in 1972. It included fourteen elements.

As the proposed primitives were tested against an increasing range of semantic domains, most of them (on present count, eleven of the fourteen) proved themselves effective tools in semantic analysis. But at the same time it became increasingly clear that the minimal set of fourteen was insufficient. (See Wierzbicka 1989*b*.)

A major impulse for their expansion was the Semantic Workshop held in Adelaide in 1986, and organized by Cliff Goddard and David Wilkins, where Goddard proposed a number of new primitives for further investigation. (See Goddard 1986*a*, 1989*a*.) As the consecutive expanded sets were tested in semantic analysis, the process repeated itself, and expansion continued. (For the current head count, see Chapter 2.)

The process of expansion greatly facilitated semantic analysis of numerous semantic domains and made it possible to formulate semantic explications that were much more readable and intuitively intelligible than those based on earlier, leaner sets. The theoretical "cost" of this expansion lay in the need to abandon the Leibnizian principle of mutual independence of primitives. In the early versions of the NSM theory, if the elements appeared to be semantically related (as, for example, 'good' and 'want', or 'the same' and 'other'), it was assumed that at least one of them must be semantically complex (on the grounds that if two elements share a common part they must have parts, and therefore cannot be semantically simple).

This assumption was never strictly adhered to, however. For example, I, YOU, and SOMEONE were regarded as primes from the outset, even though they are intuitively related (for every "I", and every "you", is a "someone"). In time, the assumption of mutual independence of primitives was rejected altogether, and it was recognized that primitives can be intuitively related (as "I" and "someone" are), without being compositionally related and without being decomposable (that is, definable).

2. The first proposed primitives were identified, by trial and error, on the basis of a handful of European languages. With time, through the work of experts on many diverse languages, the empirical basis grew considerably, including, among others, languages as diverse as Chinese (see e.g. Chappell 1983, 1986*a,b*), Ewe (Ameka 1986, 1987, 1990, 1991), Japanese (Travis 1992; Hasada 1994), Malay (Goddard 1994*c*), the Austronesian language Mangap-Mbula (Bugenhagen 1990), or the Australian languages Yankunytjatjara (Goddard 1990, 1992*a,b*) and Arrernte (Wilkins 1986;

Harkins 1992). This expansion culminated in *Semantic and Lexical Universals* (Goddard and Wierzbicka 1994*b*), mentioned earlier.

A priori, one might have expected that the process of testing a hypothetical set of primitives across a wider range of languages would lead to a reduction of the proposed set (as one proposed primitive after another would fail to show up in this or that language). On the whole, however, this has not happened. On the contrary, the list of primitives has shown a tendency towards gradual expansion.

3. For a long time, research into the syntax of the proposed primitives lagged behind that into the primitives themselves—a point commented on by several reviewers (e.g. McCawley 1983). This delay, though unfortunate, was dictated by the nature of things: one can hardly investigate the patterns of combination of primitives before one has some idea of what the primitives are. The first article devoted primarily to the syntax of the primitives was my "Lexical Universals and Universals of Grammar" (Wierzbicka 1991*c*). The Symposium on the Universal Syntax of Meaning held in Canberra in July 1994 (organized by Goddard and myself) launched a major programme of research in this area across a number of languages.

4. The building of the Natural Semantic Metalanguage was, and continues to be, a gradual process. In contrast to more speculative semantic theories, NSM constantly seeks confirmation—or disconfirmation—in large-scale descriptive projects. For example, in my *English Speech Act Verbs* (Wierzbicka 1987*a*) I attempted to analyse the meaning of more than 200 English verbs; and more recently, in a series of articles on another conceptual domain (see e.g. Wierzbicka 1990*c*, 1992*e*, 1994*c*) I have similarly sought to analyse at least 100 English emotion terms.

It is through descriptive projects of this kind that the inadequacies (as well as the strengths) of successive versions of NSM became apparent, and that future directions of development could be seen more clearly. Perhaps the most important direction had to do with the growing simplification and standardization of the syntax of explications, linked directly with the search for universal syntactic patterns.

5. The theoretical underpinnings of NSM research were gradually articulated more clearly, and its methodology formulated more explicitly, as important theoretical concepts like "polysemy", "allolexy", "valency option", "non-compositional relationship", and "resonance" were gradually clarified and more rigorously articulated (see Section 8; also Goddard 1994*a*; Goddard and Wierzbicka 1994*b*). The Symposium on Semantic and Lexical Universals held in Canberra in February 1992 and organized by Cliff Goddard and myself played an important role in this regard.

6. Over the years, the range of domains to which NSM research addressed itself has continued to expand, including not only lexical semantics (as in, for example, Goddard 1990, 1991*a*; Travis 1992; Hasada 1994;

Ameka 1990; Wierzbicka 1985, 1987*a*), but also the semantics of grammar (e.g. Ameka 1990; Chappell 1986*a,b*, 1991; Wierzbicka 1988) and pragmatics (e.g. Ameka 1987; Goddard 1986*b*; Harkins 1986; Wierzbicka 1991*a*; Wilkins 1986). Furthermore, this research has expanded into more direct comparison of cultures, via their lexicon, grammar, conversational routines, and discourse structure (e.g. Ameka 1987; Goddard 1992*b*, forthcoming *c*; Harkins 1994; Wierzbicka 1991*a*, 1992*a*; Wilkins 1992). Most recently, NSM research has moved into yet another direction, leading to the development of a "theory of cultural scripts", which offers a framework for comparing cultural norms operating in different cultures, a framework based on universal semantic primitives and universal syntactic patterns (e.g. Wierzbicka 1993*e*, 1994*a,d,e*, forthcoming *c*; Goddard forthcoming *b*; Goddard and Wierzbicka forthcoming).

But while all these developments are (as it seems to those involved) significant, NSM theory still has a long way to go. The pursuit of semantic primitives needs to be finalized, the study of the syntax of primitives needs to be more fully developed, the scope of cross-linguistic testing of both primitives and their syntax needs to be substantially widened, language-specific versions of the Natural Semantic Metalanguage need to be built, the NSM-based analysis of culture and cognition needs to be extended to new areas, the theory of cultural scripts needs to be further fleshed out, and so on. This book therefore constitutes an open invitation.

2 A Survey of Semantic Primitives

□ □ ⎯⎯⎯⎯⎯⎯⎯⎯⎯⎯⎯⎯⎯⎯⎯⎯⎯⎯⎯⎯⎯⎯⎯⎯⎯

A. OLD PRIMITIVES

1. Introduction

The set of primitives presented and discussed in this chapter has evolved in the course of nearly three decades of research by myself and colleagues—and it is still evolving. Some of the primitives proposed here are better established than others. Of the fourteen primitives posited in my *Semantic Primitives* (1972) ten have survived nearly a quarter of a century of critical assaults (by myself and others), and (with one exception: PART) the position of these original members of the set can be regarded as particularly strong. This old guard includes the "substantives" I, YOU, SOMEONE, and SOMETHING, the "mental predicates" THINK, WANT, FEEL, and SAY, and the demonstrative THIS.

But the main divide runs between those elements which were tested across a wide range of languages in the project reported in *Semantic and Lexical Universals* (Goddard and Wierzbicka 1994*b*), and those which were not included in that project, and which must, therefore, be regarded as less well established. Accordingly, the present chapter, surveying the primitives, is divided into two parts, called, for convenience' sake, "Old Primitives" and "New Primitives". The set of old primitives includes the following elements:

"substantives"	I, YOU, SOMEONE, SOMETHING, PEOPLE
"determiners"	THIS, THE SAME, OTHER
"quantifiers"	ONE, TWO, MANY (MUCH), ALL
"mental predicates"	THINK, KNOW, WANT, FEEL
"speech"	SAY
"actions and events"	DO, HAPPEN
"evaluators"	GOOD, BAD
"descriptors"	BIG, SMALL
"time"	WHEN, BEFORE, AFTER
"space"	WHERE, UNDER, ABOVE
"partonomy and taxonomy"	PART (OF), KIND (OF)

| "metapredicates" | NOT, CAN, VERY |
| "interclausal linkers" | IF, BECAUSE, LIKE. |

2. Substantives: I, YOU, SOMEONE, SOMETHING, PEOPLE

2.1. I and YOU

Joseph Brodsky's (1994) poignant recent poem entitled "Infinitive" starts as follows:

> Dear savages, though I've never mastered your tongue, free of
> pronouns and gerunds,
> I've learned to bake mackerel wrapped in palm leaves and favor raw
> turtle legs,
> with their flavor of slowness.

For the poet, the factual inaccuracy of the image does not matter, but the fact of the matter is that there are no tongues in the world (no matter how "savage") which would be "free of pronouns and gerunds". Of gerunds, yes, but of pronouns, no. In particular, there are no languages in the world which would be "free" of words for I or YOU (in the sense THOU). This is not to say that claims have never been made—not only in poetry, but also in scholarly literature—that languages "free of personal pronouns" do exist, but notions of this kind have never been substantiated and they must be regarded as fanciful. (See Wierzbicka 1994*b*.)[1]

It is true that many languages, especially South-east Asian languages, have developed a number of elaborate substitutes for "you" and "I", and that in many circumstances it is more appropriate to use some such substitute than the barest, the most basic, pronoun. For example, in a polite conversation in Thai, the use of the basic words for "you" and "I" would sound crude and inappropriate. Instead, various self-deprecating expressions would be used for "I" and various deferential expressions for "you". Many of the expressions which stand for "I" refer to the speaker's hair, crown of the head, top of the head, and the like, and many of the expressions which stand for "you" refer to the addressee's feet, soles of the feet, or even to the dust underneath his feet, the idea being that the speaker is putting the most valued and respected part of his own body, the head, at the same level as the lowest, the least honourable part of the addressee's body (see Cook 1968). But this does not mean that Thai has no personal pronouns, no basic words for "you" and "I".

---

[1] Harré (1993) claims to have shown that the concept 'I' has no lexical exponents in Wintu, Kawi, and Japanese; for detailed refutation of these claims see Goddard (1995).

A language may not make a distinction which would correspond to that between the words "he" and "she", and in fact many languages, for example Turkish, have just one word for "he" and "she", undifferentiated for sex. But no known language fails to make a distinction between the speaker and the addressee, i.e. between "you" and "I". This does not mean that the range of use of the words for "you" and "I" is the same, in all languages. For example, in Thai, the word *chăn*, which Thai–English dictionaries gloss as "I", has a range of use incomparably more narrow than its English equivalent. When used by women, it is restricted to intimates, and it signals a high degree of informality and closeness; when used by men, it signals superiority, rudeness, disrespect (Treerat 1986; Cook 1968). But since there are no invariant semantic components which could be always attributed to *chăn*, other than "I", the heavy restrictions on its use must be attributed to cultural rather than semantic factors. In a society where references to oneself are in many situations expected to be accompanied by expressions of humility or inferiority, a bare "I" becomes pragmatically marked, and it must be interpreted as either very intimate or very rude. But this pragmatic markedness should not be confused with demonstrable semantic complexity (see Diller 1994).

The universality of I and YOU (brilliantly guessed by Wilhelm Humboldt, in the early days of typological linguistic investigations, and reasserted by Boas (1911; see also Ingram 1978)) tallies well with the indefinable nature of these two concepts: while attempts to define them (e.g. in terms of "speaker" and "addressee"; see e.g. Reichenbach 1948: 811) have often been undertaken, these attempts have never been successful. Words such as "speaker" and "addressee" are neither universal nor semantically simple. Roughly speaking, "the speaker (of some words)" is "the person who says these words"; and "the addressee (of some words)" is "the person to whom these words are said".

Furthermore, if "I" doesn't mean "the speaker", "the speaker" doesn't mean "I". For example, if I whisper to the person next to me "I don't like the speaker", I mean neither that "The speaker doesn't like the speaker", nor that "I don't like myself". Similarly, if someone asks me "Who are you speaking to?" and I reply "I'm speaking to you", I can hardly mean that "I'm speaking to the person to whom I am speaking", or that "The speaker is speaking to the person to whom the speaker is speaking" (see Sørensen 1963: 96).

Finally, the idea of "I" is not necessarily tied to speech: we rely on the concept of "I" in our thoughts, as well as in our speech. For example, if I think to myself "I want to do something (X) today", I do not think of myself as "the speaker", but simply as "I".

From this point of view, Russell's attempted definitions of 'I' ('I—the person experiencing this' (1964: 85), and 'I'—the biography to which this belongs' 1965: 107)) are perhaps more plausible than Reichenbach's (since they do not refer to speech), but on the whole they are hardly convincing either: whether uttered aloud or thought silently, the sentence "I want to go now" can hardly mean 'the person experiencing this wants to go now', or 'the person to whose biography this belongs wants to go now'. As pointed out by Sørensen (1963: 96), " 'I' and 'you' are signs in the first and the second person respectively . . . Now, whatever the difference between first, second, and third person signs may be, *there is* a difference, a difference of meaning . . . Therefore, a sign in the third person cannot be semantically identical with a sign in the first or second person". (See also Castañeda 1988.)

Of course "I" can sometimes be intended as *referentially* identical to a "third person sign", such as, for example, "the author of these lines", or as the expression "this person" accompanied by a self-directed gesture; but clearly, neither "the author of these lines" nor "this person" mean the same as 'I', and even from a referential point of view, expressions such as "the author of these lines" or "this person" are not always equivalent to 'I'.

2.2. SOMEONE and SOMETHING

All languages have words for WHO and WHAT, and can distinguish lexically between the questions "What is this?" and "Who is this?" The distinction between 'who' and 'what', 'someone' and 'something', 'person' and 'thing' provides the most fundamental form of human categorization (for while YOU and I are also fundamental to human thinking, they do not categorize the contents of the world).

It is impossible to define 'someone' or 'something' in any simpler terms. In English, the apparent morphological complexity of the words *someone* and *something* may suggest the idea that these words are in fact decomposable (into 'some' + 'one', and 'some' + 'thing'). But of course *someone* doesn't mean the same as 'some one', and *something* doesn't mean the same as 'some thing'.

When the words *who* and *what* are used in questions, the concepts 'someone' and 'something' are combined with an interrogative meaning ('I want to know something', 'I want you to say something'), but this interrogative meaning is not an inherent part of the words *who* and *what* as such. For example, when used in so-called "embedded questions",

I know (don't know) who did it.
I know (don't know) what you see.

who and *what* do not express an interrogative meaning at all. Rather, sentences of this kind can be interpreted as follows:

I know this about someone: this someone (this person) did it.
I know this about something: you see this something (this thing).

(The expressions *this someone* and *this something*, which sound awkward in English, will be discussed in Chapter 3.)

In linguistic literature, the distinction between SOMEONE and SOMETHING, which plays an important role in the grammar of many languages, is often represented in terms of binary features, such as ± HUMAN, or ± ANIMATE, or ± PERSONAL. But accounts of this kind are a good example of pseudo-analysis, since the features which are invented to account for the difference between SOMEONE and SOMETHING themselves need to be defined (or explained) in terms of SOMEONE and SOMETHING. For example, the sentences

I met someone nice.
I saw something interesting.

can hardly be paraphrased (except in jest) along the following lines:

I met a nice human (animate, personal), thing (entity).
I saw an interesting non-human (inanimate, impersonal) entity.

As I argued in *Lingua Mentalis* fifteen years ago, to substitute "entity" for *someone* and *something* is to avoid the categorization embedded in all natural languages and to try to replace it with an artificial device alien to them. The distinction between "persons" and "non-persons" is quite fundamental to human conceptualization of the world. Natural languages differ in this respect sharply from artificial languages relying on the abstract notion of "referential indices". Linguists who have assumed that the language of symbolic logic is a suitable tool for analysing natural language have sometimes taken for granted that the notion of "semantic prime" can be identified with the notion of "atomic predicate", because what logicians describe as "arguments" can be simply thought of as indices. (This applies, in particular, to "generative semanticists"; see e.g. McCawley 1973: 334.) But natural languages don't work like that. The distinction between SOMEONE and SOMETHING is basic for them and cannot be reduced to any difference between predicates.

To put it differently, the concept of SOMEONE (a 'person') is essential to human conceptualization of the world, and despite all the differences in cultural context and cultural interpretation (see e.g. Shweder and Bourne 1984), it has a stable, irreducible core across all languages and cultures (see Spiro 1993; Wierzbicka 1993*b*); no language and no culture blurs the fundamental divide between SOMEONE and SOMETHING.

2.3. PEOPLE

As the evidence reported in *Semantic and Lexical Universals* (Goddard and Wierzbicka 1994*b*) illustrates, all languages appear to distinguish, in one way or another, between a more general notion of SOMEONE, or BEING (human or non-human), and a notion of PEOPLE (necessarily human). For example, *someone* (and *who*) can refer to God:

Who created the world?—God.
God is someone infinitely good and merciful.

But the word *people* (which is inherently "plural") cannot refer to any group of beings other than human beings (not even to the very human-like gods of the Greek Olympus).

The well-known fact that in many languages, the word for 'people' is also used as a tribal name is (as pointed out by Greenberg 1966*a*: 26) clearly a case of polysemy, comparable to the polysemy of the English word *man* (1) a male human being, (2) a human being, and not evidence that a word for 'people' may be missing.

It is a striking fact that in many languages the word for *people* has a different stem from the word for an individual human being, and doesn't look like an ordinary plural. The English word *people* is a good case in point. Similarly, in German, French, and Russian the words *Leute, gens,* and *ljudi,* 'people', are all different from the words for an individual human being (*Mensch, homme,* and *čelovek,* respectively). By itself, this formal difference doesn't prove anything about the semantic relationship, but it is certainly highly suggestive, and it tallies well with the semantic fact that it is impossible to define *people* in terms of *someone* and something else (or indeed in any other way).

On the other hand, if we accept that both *someone* and *people* are irreducible semantic primitives, numerous other concepts can be explicated via these two.

For example, every language has a large number of words referring to "cultural kinds" (see Lyons 1981), that is, to human artefacts, such as, for example, *cup, mug, bottle, boomerang, chair,* and so on. All these words make references (in their semantic structure) to people, because they designate objects "made by people", "used by people", and physically defined with reference to the human body. (For example, cups are made by people, for people to drink from; they are made in such a way that people can hold them in one hand, and so on. For discussion, see Wierzbicka 1985.)

In addition to names of material artefacts, there are also numerous words referring to social life (e.g. *society, tribe, family, committee,* and so on), to human emotions (e.g. *shame, embarrassment, pride*), to language (e.g. *language, dialect, slang*), and so on, which refer in their meaning to 'people'.

The status of PEOPLE as a fundamental element of human thought is reflected in various ways in the grammar of innumerable languages. For example, in Polish nominal declension, masculine nouns referring to people have an accusative plural identical in form with the genitive, whereas nouns referring to things and animals have an accusative plural identical in form with the nominative. (Cf. also the so-called "hierarchy of agentivity" discussed, for example, by Silverstein 1976, Dixon 1979, Comrie 1989, Mallinson and Blake 1981, and Wierzbicka 1981, in which the category "human" plays a prominent role.)

The hypothesis that the concept of PEOPLE is a conceptual primitive is consistent with the results of recent studies of language acquisition. For example, as pointed out by McShane (1991: 197), Carey (1985) "found that children initially organize biological knowledge around humans as a prototype. Inferences about biological properties of other species are based both on what children believe about humans and how similar the other species is to humans." Jackendoff (1992) talks in this connection about "a faculty of social cognition". Referring to Katz, Baker, and Macnamara's (1974) finding that children as young as 17 months know that proper names can be applied to people and people-like objects such as dolls but not to inanimate objects such as boxes, he comments: "That is, they seem predisposed to make a cognitive distinction between persons and everything else—the distinction I am claiming is pertinent to social cognition—and they are predisposed as well to find a linguistic distinction that encodes this difference." The evidence from cross-linguistic semantic investigations points in the same direction.

Finally, the hypothesis that the concept of PEOPLE is, in all probability, a semantic universal and a conceptual primitive offers a solution to the old and apparently insoluble problem of how the notion of 'human being' can be defined. Is a human being a 'featherless biped', as the cynics maintained in ancient Greece? Or is it a 'rational animal', as medieval philosophers used to claim? Or is it perhaps, as the French writer Vercors (1956) once maintained, 'a being endowed with a religious sense'? All these and other definitions are clearly deficient, and it is a relief to be able to go back to Pascal's (1667/1963: 579) view that the notion is basic and that all attempts to define it must fail.

Linguistic evidence suggests, however, that Pascal's view requires a correction. It is not the notion of an individual human being, *l'homme*, which appears to be universal and indefinable, but the notion of PEOPLE, a social, rather than biological, category. Given the universal presence of the concepts PEOPLE, SOMEONE, and ONE, the notion of an individual human being does not need to be regarded as primitive. But it is impossible to define both 'human being' and 'people'; and cross-linguistic evidence suggests that it is the latter, not the former, concept which is indeed universal (see Goddard and Wierzbicka 1994*b*).

If we think of universal semantic primitives as innate concepts, the idea that a social category of PEOPLE may be innate is unexpected, and it certainly gives food for thought. If we are 'rational animals' (with the notions of THINK and KNOW being part of our genetic endowment), we are also 'social animals', so much so that the idea of PEOPLE as a social category is also a part of this endowment. In fact, of course, according to the innate and universal folk model (see Bruner 1990), we are not 'animals' at all: we are PEOPLE, every single one of whom is also SOMEONE and 'I'—all irreducible and apparently universal human concepts.

3. Determiners: THIS, THE SAME, OTHER

3.1. THIS

The word *this* and its counterparts in other languages provide a basic means for identifying what we are talking about; and in any language, as in English, one can point to an object or a person and say something that means 'this', 'this thing', or 'this person'.

It is impossible to define the concept of THIS in terms of any simpler concepts; and while technical labels such as "deictic" or "demonstrative" are sometimes mistaken for a statement of meaning, presumably nobody would argue that, for example, *this dog* means 'deictic dog' or 'demonstrative dog'.

What linguists do sometimes argue is that *this* means 'near the speaker'. But this is an illusion, too—first of all, because *near* (in non-metaphorical use) always refers to spatial relations, whereas *this* is not restricted to space (compare e.g. *this day*, or *this song*), and second, because if I point to one of my own teeth and say "This tooth hurts", this can hardly be interpreted as "the tooth near the speaker" (see Fillmore 1975a).

Despite occasional claims to the contrary, careful examination of the available cross-linguistic evidence suggests that all languages have a clear and unproblematic exponent for THIS. The other demonstrative pronouns often do not match semantically across language boundaries (for example, of the three Japanese demonstrative pronouns *kono*, *sono*, and *ano*, neither *sono* nor *ano* corresponds exactly to English *that*, but *this* can be matched semantically with *kono*). In particular, it is not the case that (as has sometimes been claimed) some languages lexically distinguish 'this, which I can see' from 'this, which I cannot see', without having a basic, unmarked term for THIS.

For example, Cecil Brown's (1985: 287) suggestion that the Gidabal dialect of the Australian language Bandjalang doesn't have an exact semantic equivalent for the English word *this* because the nearest Gidabal equivalent implies 'visibility' as well as 'thisness' is refuted by Crowley's (1978: 72) authoritative study of Bandjalang, which makes it clear that the so-called "visible" demonstrative *gaya* is in fact unmarked, and that the closest Bandjalang equivalent of *this* doesn't mean 'this, which I can see', but simply 'this'.

What is controversial here is not the statement that the Gidabal word *gaya* has a range of use somewhat different from that of the English word *this*, but the claim that this difference in use is due to a specifiable semantic difference: 'this' (in English) versus 'this, which I can see' (in Gidabal). Differences in the range of use can sometimes be explained in terms of factors other than the semantic. But the presence of a *specifiable semantic* difference could not be reconciled with the claim that two lexical items have the same meaning. Experience shows, however, that reports concerning alleged semantic differences cannot be accepted at face value.

3.2. THE SAME and OTHER

The "determiners" THE SAME and OTHER appear to be used, universally, in sentences such as the following ones:

> It happened in the same place, not in another place.
> It happened at the same time, not at another time.
> She did (said/thought/wanted) the same.
> I saw it, and two other people saw it.
> It was not the same fish, but it was the same kind of fish.

(English sentences such as "Give me another beer!" illustrate a language-specific, not a universal, use of the word *other*.)

The element THE SAME corresponds to a fundamental logical relation of "identity", which occupies a prominent place in the philosophical and logical literature on thought, knowledge, and logical relations in general. OTHER may seem to be no more than a negated version of identity (as I argued myself in Wierzbicka 1989*c*), but in fact a phrase such as "I and two other people" cannot be reduced to 'the same' and negation.

Both concepts, THE SAME and OTHER, are lexical universals, and they both play a considerable role in the lexicon and in grammar. For example, they are needed to account for the meaning of many conjunctions and particles, such as *also*, *too*, or *otherwise* (see Goddard 1986*b*; Wierzbicka 1986*c*, 1991*a*), as well as for that of grammatical "reference-tracking" devices, such as, for example, "switch reference".

Exponents of both THE SAME and OTHER are often involved in common polysemic patterns, in particular, one linking THE SAME with ONE, and another, linking OTHER with SOMEONE (see Goddard and Wierzbicka 1994*b*); in each case, however, the polysemic knots can be disentangled and the distinctness of the two concepts in a given language can be upheld.

4. Quantifiers: ONE, TWO, MANY (MUCH), ALL

4.1. ONE, TWO, MANY (MUCH)

Fantasizing about his "UP" (Universal People), Donald Brown (1991: 139) writes: "UP language contains both proper nouns and pronouns. The latter include at least three persons and two categories of number. Their language contains numerals, though they may be as few as 'one, two, and many'." Empirical evidence surveyed in *Semantic and Lexical Universals* (Goddard and Wierzbicka 1994*b*) supports the view that all languages have words for at least these three quantifiers: ONE, TWO, and MANY (as well as for ALL, and, probably, SOME OF; see Part B of this chapter).[2]

The element ONE can appear, universally, in sentences such as the following ones:

> They have two sons and one daughter.
> They don't have two sons; they have one son.

In grammar, ONE plays an important role in the widespread (though of course not universal) category of "singular". In fact, the category of "plural", too, is based semantically on the concept ONE (since in its prototypical uses it means, usually, 'more than one').

The element 'TWO' is needed to account for the meaning of body part words such as *eyes*, *ears*, or *hands*, as well as for the meaning of numerals; and it plays a significant role in grammar in the widespread category of dualis (see Humboldt 1827/1973).

Turning now to the third quantifier listed by Donald Brown, that is, to MANY, I will note, first of all, that while all languages do appear to have a word to translate the English word *many*, this word doesn't have to make any overt distinction between 'many' and 'much'. Unlike the words for ONE and TWO, the counterparts of *many* do not necessarily imply discreteness.

---

[2] According to Popjes and Popjes (1986; as reported in Diana Green 1993: 1), "the Canela language, a member of the Jê language family [in Brazil], has no numerals at all; it is limited to general terms like "alone", "a couple", "few", and "many" to express quantities". I expect, however, that if the words in question are carefully tested for polysemy, it will transpire that the word glossed as "alone" can also mean 'one', and that glossed as "a couple" can also mean 'two'. The words for ONE and TWO can of course have many allolexes. For example, Diana Green (1993: 1) notes that the Palikúr language of Brazil has "twenty two words to express the concept of one", and that "nineteen of these words have eleven different forms, making at least 209 ways to say the number one, all spoken in everyday conversation".

For example, in Polish, the word for both 'many' and 'much' is *dużo*, in Russian, *mnogo*, in French, *beaucoup*, and in Japanese, *takusan*. It is true that in those languages which have an obligatory category of nominal number, the distinction between 'much' and 'many' will be reflected in the number of the head noun; for example, in Russian, in the phrase *mnogo vody*, 'much water' (a lot of water), the word for water is used in the genitive singular, whereas in the phrase *mnogo sobak*, 'many dogs', the word for dogs is used in the genitive plural. But in Japanese, which doesn't have an obligatory category of number, there is no corresponding formal distinction, and the word *takusan* covers both 'much' and 'many'.

From the point of view of a speaker of English, it may seem that a word like *takusan* must be polysemous and have two distinct meanings ('much' and 'many'). But from the point of view of a speaker of Japanese, such a conclusion would seem counter-intuitive, and it would seem more natural to say that the English words *much* and *many* are simply two allolexes (i.e. alternative exponents) of one primitive concept ('takusan'), and all things considered, this "Japanese" point of view appears to be more justified. It is true that to a speaker of English the words *much* and *many* appear to have different meanings, and that, for example, the phrase *many chickens* means something different from *much chicken*, but this difference (to do with discreteness) can be attributed to the head noun (with the assumption that, for example, *chicken* is polysemous in English), and so it can be argued that the two words (*much* and *many*) are in fact in complementary distribution.

Leaving aside, then, the issue of the distinction between *much* and *many*, let us turn to the question of the semantic simplicity (or otherwise) of the concept in question. Here, the only plausible approach to semantic decomposition would presumably be to try to reduce *much/many* to 'more', along the lines envisaged by Sapir (1949: 125):

It is very important to realize that psychologically all comparatives are primary in relation to their corresponding absolutes ("positives"). Just as *more men* precedes both *some men* and *many men*, so *better* precedes both *good* and *very good*. Linguistic usage tends to start from the graded concept, e.g. *good* (= *better than indifferent*), *bad* (= *worse than indifferent*), *large* (= *larger than of average size*), *much* (= *more than a fair amount*), *few* (= *less than a fair number*).

Quoting this passage a quarter of a century ago (Wierzbicka 1971), I argued that Sapir's thesis that all comparatives are primary (more basic) in relation to their corresponding absolutes is correct with respect to size, number, amount, and dimensions, though wrong with respect to *good* and *bad*, as well as to other "qualitative" kinds of adjectives.

However, in the course of a quarter of a century of research into this and other related matters, I have come to the conclusion that, attractive as

Sapir's thesis was, it was not partially wrong but altogether wrong. In particular, it no longer seems plausible that *much* and *many* are semantically based on 'more', whether this relationship is conceived of as 'more than a fair amount/number', 'more than one expects', 'more than the norm', or in any other way. Intuitively, the idea of 'many people' seems more basic than that of 'more people', and the fact that 'many(much)' is, apparently, a lexical universal (see Goddard and Wierzbicka 1994*b*) supports this intuition. The idea that 'amount' or 'number' may be more basic concepts than 'much/many' is entirely implausible: words such as *amount* and *number* are not universal, they are of course acquired by children much later than *much* or *a lot*, and they constitute abstractions built on the basis of simple ideas such as 'much', 'one', and 'two', rather than offering a foundation for them. (For discussion of this question, see Sections 6 and 7; see also Sections 16 and 23.)

Finally, is 'little/few' (as in "little butter" or "few people") also a conceptual primitive and a lexical universal, on a par with MANY/MUCH? Since 'few/little' appears to be an opposite of 'many/much', just as 'small' is an opposite of 'big', and since the latter two concepts have both been put forward as primitive and universal (see Section 9), it may seem quite clear that 'few/little' should also be proposed as such. But the matter is not so simple, and preliminary investigations suggest that the claim of 'little/few' to the status of a conceptual primitive and lexical universal is weaker than that of its apparent opposite 'much/many', as well as that of the two related opposites 'big' and 'small'. It is possible, in other words, that 'little/few' may prove to be reducible to a combination of 'much/many' and negation ('not much/not many'), whereas 'small' cannot be reduced to 'not big' (see Section 9 below).

Data from child language are certainly suggestive in this respect; while (in English) both the adjectives *big* and *little* appear very early and are used very frequently in child language (see e.g. Braine 1976; Section 8) and while the words *a lot* and *lots* also frequently occur in transcripts of child language (see e.g. French and Nelson 1985) the same does not seem to be true of the words *few* and *little* (as an opposite of *a lot*). But the matter requires further investigation.

4.2. ALL

ALL was proposed as a semantic primitive by Goddard (1989*a*). In *Lingua Mentalis* (Wierzbicka 1980) I had argued that this concept was not indefinable because it could be analysed along the following lines:

All dogs are faithful. =
    one can't say thinking of a dog:
    this (dog) is not faithful

As pointed out by Goddard, however, this kind of analysis may seem convincing from a purely logical point of view, but not from the point of view of psychological plausibility. The suggested analysis seems particularly unconvincing when applied to volitive or expressive utterances, such as "Regards to all!" or "To hell with it all!"; it seems hardly plausible to paraphrase them as follows:

> Regards to all. =
> one can't say thinking of someone:
> I don't (send) regards to this person

> To hell with it all. =
> one can't say thinking of something:
> I don't want this to go to hell

Similarly, the expression 'that's all', which frequently occurs in the transcripts of young children's speech (see e.g. French and Nelson 1985), can hardly be paraphrased along those lines.

The fact that the word *all* (and, apparently, the concept ALL) appears very early in children's speech (see e.g. Braine 1976) also supports the view that the analysis attempted in *Lingua Mentalis* was psychologically implausible.

ALL plays an important role in both lexicon and grammar. For example, English particles and conjunctions such as *at all, almost, altogether, although, all the same, also, already, all right* by their very form hint at the presence of the semantic component 'all' in their meaning, as do also adverbial and pronominal expressions such as *always, all over, overall, everywhere, everyone, whatever, whenever,* and so on; and similar examples could be quoted from other languages. (The evidence for ALL as a lexical universal will be discussed in Chapter 6; see also Goddard and Wierzbicka 1994*b*.)

Like negation and existence, ALL is accepted as one of the fundamental concepts in logic (as the so-called "universal quantifier"), and from a logical point of view the need for ALL as a universal semantic primitive will no doubt seem obvious and overdue rather than controversial. But semantics has its own point of view, and its own internal logic, which is different from the logic of logical systems. Above all, it requires an anchoring in language universals, which have to be confirmed empirically and not only on the basis of intellectual speculation. For this reason (among others) the concepts 'and' and 'or', indispensable to the logician, have not been proposed in the present system as semantic primitives. But ALL—like NOT—is one of the points where logic and semantics shake hands.

5. Mental Predicates: THINK, KNOW, WANT, FEEL

As argued elegantly by Bruner (1990: 35), "all cultures have as one of their most powerful constitutive instruments a folk psychology ... We learn our culture's folk psychology early", as we learn language early, and the two processes are inextricably linked. A good illustration of Bruner's thesis comes from the area of emotions: not only is the very concept of 'emotion' (and its counterparts in other languages) culturally shaped and determined, to some extent, by language, but every language includes its own taxonomy of emotions, which offers "a set of more or less connected, more or less normative descriptions about how human beings 'tick' " (Bruner 1990: 35).

But in addition to all those culture-specific systems of folk psychology there is, Bruner suggests, a universal, innate folk psychology which constitutes a basis and a starting-point of all further developments: "We come into the world already equipped with a primitive form of folk psychology" (1990: 73).

Cross-linguistic investigations reported in *Semantic and Lexical Universals* (Goddard and Wierzbicka 1994*b*) support and substantiate Bruner's claims; in particular, they allow us to state that the innate and universal "theory of mind" includes the following major constituents: THINK, KNOW, WANT, and FEEL—a finding which converges with recent data on language acquisition, as reported, for example, in Wellman (1990, and, especially, 1994).

The results of the research on lexical universals and on child language acquisition tally well with the results of purely philosophical reflection and conceptual analysis. The indefinability of THINK, of the basic 'cogito', was proclaimed three centuries ago by the Cartesians, and nobody has ever been able to refute their stand on this point. In fact, THINK was for the Cartesians a prime example of an indefinable word (Arnauld 1662/1964: 36): "Obviously, we conceive nothing more distinctly than we conceive our own thought. Nor is there a clearer proposition than 'I think; therefore, I am'. We can be certain of this proposition only if we can conceive distinctly what 'to be' and what 'to think' mean. We require no explanation of these words, since they are words so well understood that in explaining them we only obscure them." A look at dictionary "definitions" of *think* confirms the validity of this view. For example, *The American Heritage Dictionary of the English Language* (*AHDOTEL* 1973):

to think   — to have a thought
thought   — the act or process of thinking; cogitation
cogitation — 1. thoughtful consideration; 2. a serious thought

The circularity of these definitions hardly requires a comment. Generally speaking, "definitions" which try to analyse 'thinking' in terms of words and phrases such as "cogitation", "cognition", "cognitive processes", "conceptions", and the like are almost caricatural examples of the old and persistent practice of "defining" something that is clear via something that is obscure, and something that is simple via something that is complex. (For further discussion of THINK, see Wierzbicka forthcoming *f*.)

What holds for THINK holds also for KNOW, WANT, and FEEL. For example, *Longman's Dictionary of the English Language* (*LDOTEL* 1984) defines *know* via *cognition*, and *cognition* via *know*:

know — to have direct cognition
cognition — the act or process of knowing that involves the processing of sensory information and includes perception, awareness, and judgement

Not only are these definitions circular, but also they offer a good example of "progress" from simple to complex and from clear to obscure. The same applies to the definitions of *feel* and *want* (in the same dictionary):

feel — to have one's sensibilities markedly affected
want — to have a desire

(with *sensible* being defined as "capable of being felt or perceived", *desire* as "to wish for, want", and *wish* as "to have as a desire").

The universality of "mental predicates" has sometimes been disputed. For example, Hallpike (1979) has claimed that some languages lack exponents of THINK and KNOW, and that their speakers, like children at the "preoperational stage", have no clear concepts of 'thinking' or 'knowing'. As I argue in detail in Chapter 6, this claim is untenable (as is also the notion that pre-school children don't have concepts of 'think' and 'know'; see Wellman 1994).

It has also been sometimes suggested that some languages don't have a word for FEEL, or don't distinguish lexically between FEEL and THINK. On closer inspection, however, these reports, too, turn out to be unfounded. (See Wierzbicka 1994*b*, 1994*h*.)

The fundamental status of the concepts THINK, KNOW, WANT, and FEEL is manifested in the important role they play in grammar. For example, KNOW plays an essential role in the systems of mood—with the "declaratives" being based on the semantic component 'I know', and the "interrogative" on the components 'I don't know—I want to know'. Clearly, KNOW—as well as THINK—is also the basis of "evidentials" ('I know because I see', 'I know because I hear', 'I think, I don't say: I know', and so on; see Chapter 15, Section 8). FEEL underlies exclamatory constructions, diminutives, "experiencer constructions" of different kinds, and so on, whereas WANT forms the basis of the imperative.

6. Speech: SAY

The universal concept of SAY can be illustrated with the following canonical sentences:

I said something to you.
People say something bad about you.
I want to say something now.

Like the indefinability of mental predicates (e.g. THINK), the indefinability of SAY can best be appreciated by looking at contortions and vicious circles in the attempted dictionary definitions of this word.

The concept of SAY plays an important role in speech as a basis of different illocutionary forces (e.g. in questions which imply: 'I want you to say something'), in the thematic organization of utterances ('I want to say something about this'), and in the basic "subject–predicate" structure of sentences ('I'm thinking about *X*; I say: *Y*'). In the lexicon, its most important function lies in the categorization of discourse, since the distinctions between different "speech acts" and "speech genres" shape, to a considerable extent, our interpretation of human interaction. (See Wierzbicka 1987*a*.)

7. Actions and Events: DO and HAPPEN

The concepts of 'action' and 'event', that is, 'doing' and 'happening', play an extremely important role in human discourse. Essentially, that's what all stories are about: what happened, and what this or that person did. To quote Bruner (1990: 77): "one of the most ubiquitous and powerful discourse forms in human communication is *narrative* . . . Narrative requires . . . a means for emphasizing human action or 'agentivity'—action directed toward goals controlled by agents." The future, too, is mostly talked about in terms of future events and actions: what will happen to me (or to some other people)? What will I (or somebody else) do? Indeed, it is hard to imagine a language in which people couldn't ask questions of this kind, and to my knowledge no such language has ever been reported.

In human reflections about life the thought of "bad (or good) things happening to people" occupies a central place (see e.g. the characteristic title of a popular work *When Bad Things Happen to Good People*, Kushner 1982); and the notion of 'someone doing something bad' (or, to a lesser extent, 'something good') is at the heart of both ethics and the law.

In earlier work (Wierzbicka 1972, 1980) I tried to define 'happen' in terms of 'becoming', and 'doing' in terms of a combination of 'happening' and 'wanting', but these attempts were not successful, and I have come to recognize that (as argued by Bogusławski 1991), both DO and HAPPEN have to be accepted as irreducible semantic primitives. Paraphrases such as

> You did something bad. = something bad happened because you wanted it

are clearly incorrect, and even if it is true that 'doing' always implies some 'wanting' and some 'happening', these implications cannot be stated satisfactorily in terms of paraphrases. (It is also worth noting that in children's speech, *do* appears very early, and is used very widely; see e.g. Clark 1983: 822.)

Both the concepts DO and HAPPEN play an important role in the grammar of many languages. For example, in so-called "active" languages, such as Dakota, the case of the subject depends on whether the predicate refers to 'doing' or to 'happening'. In fact, the terms "agent" and "patient" (i.e. 'the person who does something' and 'the person to whom something happens') are widely used in the description of most languages, and fundamental grammatical phenomena such as transitivity, passives, or reflexives are defined if not in terms of 'doing' and 'happening' then at least with reference to these concepts (see Chapter 14).

8. Evaluators: GOOD and BAD

Over the centuries, there have been many attempts to define away the concepts 'good' and 'bad'. In most cases, in these attempts 'good' was linked with 'wanting', and 'bad', with 'not wanting': 'good' is what someone (I, people, God . . .) wants, 'bad', what someone doesn't want (see e.g. Schlick 1962: 10–11).

With time, however, it has become increasingly clear that attempts of this kind do not and cannot succeed, since it is always possible to present 'good' and 'wanting' (or 'bad' and 'not wanting') in opposition to one another. For example:

> I know it is bad to do it, but I still want to do it.
> I know it would be good to do it, but I don't want to do it.

It is also possible to juxtapose 'good' and 'want', as in St Paul's famous statement:

For I do not do the good I want, but the evil I do not want is what I do. (Romans 7: 19).

Both by contrasting and by juxtaposing 'good' and 'want' we show that we conceive of them as two separate concepts: if I can say that I can want to do what I think is good, and that I can also want to do what I think is bad, then it would make no sense to try to reduce 'good' to 'want', or 'bad' to 'not want'.

The (non-compositional) relationship between 'want' and 'good' can be compared to that between 'think' and 'know', in so far as both 'want' and 'think' imply a subjective, individual perspective, whereas 'good' and 'know' imply an objective and inherently valid one. What someone wants may be bad, and may be different from what somebody else wants; similarly, what someone thinks may be wrong, and may be different from what somebody else thinks. But what is "good" (or "bad") is good (or bad) regardless of individual differences in the point of view, and what is 'known' (to anybody) must be true.

Of course people argue about what is 'good' and what is 'bad', but this very fact indicates that by using these words they lay a claim to some objective validity. In other words, people regard different things (and different actions) as good or bad, but they all agree that some things or actions (no matter which ones) can be validly regarded as 'good' or 'bad' (although they may not agree which things or actions).

What applies to the speakers of English (i.e. to the users of the English words *good* and *bad*) applies also to all other languages and cultures: everywhere in the world, people may disagree whether something is 'good' or 'bad', but in doing so, they rely on the concepts 'good' and 'bad'. The fact that—as far as we know—all languages have words for GOOD and BAD (see Hill 1987; Goddard and Wierzbicka 1994b) strongly supports the hypothesis that these two concepts are innate and fundamental elements of human thought (experience can teach us to regard certain things as 'good' or 'bad', but it cannot teach us the very concepts of 'good' and 'bad').

But while the fundamental nature of the concepts GOOD and BAD appears to be well established and well supported by linguistic evidence, one puzzle remains: why is it that (as pointed out by Greenberg 1966a: 52) in many languages the word for BAD looks, from a morphological point of view, like a combination of negation and the word for GOOD, whereas the word for GOOD never looks like a combination of negatives and the word for BAD?

Donald Brown (1991: 131) writes this about his imaginary "Universal People" (UP):

However much grammar varies from language to language, some things are always present. For example, UP language includes a series of contrasting terms that theoretically could be phrased in three different ways, but that are only phrased two ways. To illustrate, they could talk about the "good" and the "bad" (two contrasting terms, neither with a marker added to express negation); or they could talk about the "good" and the "not good" (i.e., not having the word "bad" at all but expressing its meaning with a marked version of its opposite, the marking in this case to negate), or they could talk about the "bad" and the "not bad" (i.e., not having the word "good," etc.). Logically, these alternatives are identical: each arrangement conveys the same information. But . . . the third possibility never occurs as the obligatory or common way of talking.

But although, apparently, in some sense GOOD is "unmarked", whereas BAD is (perhaps) perceived as an absence, distortion, or perversion of GOOD, it appears that all languages have a word for BAD, as well as a word for GOOD. The word for BAD may or may not look like a negated version of the word for GOOD, but if the only "opposite" of GOOD to be found in a language looks like a negated version of the word for GOOD then it seems that this word means 'bad' rather than 'not good'.

Where cultures differ is in their willingness to contrast GOOD with BAD: clearly, in some cultures people prefer, in many contexts, to contrast 'good' with 'not good' rather than with 'bad' (presumably, to avoid giving offence). If this is the case, then the word for BAD may seem to be somehow "stronger" in meaning than the English word <u>bad</u>. For example, Chappell (1994: 142) writes this about Mandarin Chinese:

GOOD and BAD are semantically asymmetrical in Mandarin, *huài* 'bad' being semantically narrower in its range of application. In this case, the use of simple negation of the morpheme *hǎo* GOOD which gives *bù hǎo* might, in fact, be preferable since *huài* is more semantically specialized at its end of the scale to mean 'immoral', 'nasty' or 'evil' than *hǎo* is on the 'saintly' end of the scale.

I would suspect, however, that differences of this kind (interesting as they are) are due to cultural rather than strictly semantic reasons, and that BAD, like GOOD, is indeed a universal semantic primitive. (For further discussion, see Wierzbicka 1994*b*: 496–7.) The idea of a 'bad deed', a 'bad person', or 'bad people' may play a greater role in some cultures than in others; for example, it is no doubt more prominent in the Judaeo-Christian culture than, say, in Japanese culture, but this doesn't mean that in Japanese culture one cannot speak at all about 'bad actions' or 'bad people' (see Onishi 1994).

To say that 'bad' means the same as 'not good' is a bit like saying that 'black' is the same as 'not white'. If *not good* may sometimes be used as a euphemism for *bad*, it is precisely because the two do not mean the same, and to say to a child "It is bad to lie" is not the same thing as to say "To lie is not good".

To see this irreducible difference between 'bad' and 'not good' it is useful to consider "stronger" words such as *evil*, *vicious* (as applied to actions or people) and words such as *terrible* or *horrific* (as applied to events). It seems hardly necessary to argue at length that an "evil deed" or a "terrible disaster" is not simply "something that is not good".

As for Sapir's idea that, psychologically, 'better' precedes 'good' (and that, by implication, 'worse' precedes 'bad'), it is inconsistent with both cross-linguistic evidence and evidence from child language: it is 'good', and 'bad', not 'better' and 'worse', which emerge as lexical universals and which commonly occur in transcripts in the data of conversations with young children. Thus, data from cross-linguistic investigations and from child language research converge on this point with in-depth semantic analysis of natural language, pointing to the fundamental, irreducible character of the twin concepts GOOD and BAD.

9. Descriptors: BIG and SMALL

The concepts 'big' and 'small' are particularly easy to identify cross-linguistically: words for 'big' and 'small' are frequently used, easily acquired, and easy to identify (see Goddard and Wierzbicka 1994*b*). As frequently noted in the literature, the lexical exponents of these concepts are normally not symmetrical, with the word for BIG being treated as, in some way, more basic. For example, the question "How big is it?" does not imply that the object in question is big, whereas "How small is it?" does imply that it is small. (See e.g. Greenberg 1966*a*: 52–3.)

It is quite tempting, therefore, to try to define SMALL via BIG as 'not big'. But 'not big' does not mean the same as 'small', and one can easily say of something (for example, a dog, or an apple) that 'it is neither big nor small'.

Both BIG and SMALL are of course "relative" terms, in the sense that a small elephant is still quite a big animal, whereas a big mouse is not. As argued by Aristotle in his *Categories*:

Things are not great or small absolutely, they are so called rather as the result of an act of comparison. For instance, a mountain is called small, a grain large, in virtue of the fact that the latter is greater than others of its kind, the former less. Thus there is a reference here to an external standard, for if the terms 'great' and 'small' were used absolutely, a mountain would never be called small or a grain large. (1937: 5[a])

Aristotle's argument is of course persuasive, and it was this kind of reasoning which led me to posit in earlier work (Wierzbicka 1971) an analysis of 'big' and 'small' based on the comparative:

This dog is big. = this dog is bigger than one would expect

(See also Žolkovskij 1964*b*.) I have now repudiated such analyses, however, and for a number of reasons. First, there is the question about the meaning of the comparative itself: if we define 'big' via 'bigger' we couldn't define 'bigger' via 'big', and we would probably have to accept 'bigger' as a conceptual primitive—a very dubious move, given the apparent universality of words for 'big' and 'small' and a well-known non-universality of comparatives (see e.g. Longacre 1985: 243). Second, it has become clear that the "relative" character of the concepts 'big' and 'small' can be accounted for without any comparatives, along the following lines:

> This is a big dog. =
> when I think of dogs, I think: this is a big dog

As mentioned earlier, the words *big* and *little* appear very early in children's speech, and are used very frequently. For example, Braine (1976: 32) draws attention to a productive pattern of two-word combinations with the words *big* and *little* in the speech of his son, Jonathan, before his second birthday. Interestingly, Braine points out that "Jonathan often contrasted two objects in consecutive utterances, for example, *big stick* followed immediately by *little stick*, indicating the relative sizes of the two sticks" and he comments: "This sort of behavior seems sufficient evidence for the productivity of these size-attribution formulae."

But while the kind of behaviour exemplified by Jonathan shows that the words *big* and *little* are felt to be semantically linked, and that their juxtaposition is indeed used for comparison, it does not mean that the concepts in question are semantically "relative" in the sense suggested by Sapir (as discussed in Section 4). The idea that *large* (or *big*) means 'larger than of average size' seems completely incompatible with the frequent and competent use of the words *big* and *little* by infants in the second year of life.[3] The pattern of use described by Braine supports the hypothesis that a comparison of size ("*X* is bigger than *Y*") is based on a juxtaposition of opposites (next to *Y*, *X* is big; next to *X*, *Y* is little). It is also consistent with the hypothesis that an "absolute" assessment of size (as in "This is a big dog") refers not only to "this" but also to "dogs" in general ("For a dog, this is a big dog").

It is particularly interesting in this connection to compare Braine's comments on little Jonathan's way of handling comparison and that described by Longacre with respect to the languages of Papua New Guinea:

Comparison in Papua New Guinea is not expressed within a single sentence, but by a pair of sentences within a paragraph. It is, furthermore, really not comparison, but contrast. In Safeyoka (a dialect of Wojokeso), for example, we find pairs of sentences such as 'The black man's boats are small. The white man's boats are huge'. There is no direct way of saying 'The black man's boats are smaller than the white man's boats' or 'The white man's boats are bigger than the black man's'.

---

[3] As Johnston (1985: 980) points out (from a child's point of view), "How can one small shoe be bigger than another small shoe, or a single object be both bigger and smaller?" What this observation shows is that the idea of a "small shoe" or a "big shoe" is (*pace* Sapir) psychologically simpler than that of a "smaller shoe" or a "bigger shoe".

The fundamental nature of the concepts 'big' and 'small' is reflected in the role that they play in the grammar of many languages, in particular in the categories of so-called "diminutives" and "augmentatives".

10. Time: WHEN, BEFORE, AFTER

As pointed out by Keesing (1994), time tends to be exoticized in Western accounts of non-Western languages in cultures. The best example of this exoticization is the account of the Hopi language given by Whorf, who claimed that the Hopi conception of time is radically different from that reflected in European languages. "After long and careful study and analysis, the Hopi language is seen to contain no words, grammatical forms, constructions or expressions that refer directly to what we call 'time', or to past, or future, or to enduring or lasting" (Whorf 1956: 57).

But Whorf's ideas about Hopi have now been refuted in a careful study of the Hopi language by Malotki (1983), whose overall conclusion is that "Whorf's claim about Hopi time conception being radically different from ours does . . . not hold" (530).

In a similar vein, Keesing argues that the Kwaio language of the Solomon Islands, which he has studied in detail, has the same basic temporal categories as Western languages do, and that "Kwaio talk about duration and temporality in everyday life much as we do" (1994: 5). In particular, Kwaio has a common word (*alata*) "referring either to points in time or periods in time. . . . *Alata* is used as well as equivalent to English 'when' or French 'quand', to introduce temporal clauses, as in: *alata miru nigi i 'Aoke*, 'When we get to Auku'." Keesing concludes (6): "All the evidence available on everyday talk in non-Western languages would indicate that other 'exotic' peoples, like the Kwaio, situate events precisely in time in complex ways, are concerned with duration, and have intricate linguistic devices for coordinating plans and activities."

The cross-linguistic investigations reported in *Semantic and Lexical Universals* (Goddard and Wierzbicka 1994*b*) point in the same direction: despite all the differences in the conceptualization of, and attitudes to, time, discussed, for example, by Geertz (1966) or Hall (1983), and despite the considerable differences in the linguistic encoding of temporal notions (see e.g. Hopper 1982; Bybee and Dahl 1989), the fundamental temporal concepts encoded in languages of the world appear to be the same. They include: WHEN, AFTER, and BEFORE. (For discussion of durational concepts, see Part B of this chapter.)

Cross-linguistic investigations suggest that, for example, questions such as the following ones are readily available and frequently used in all languages:

When did it (will it) happen?
When did you (will you) do it?

For example, Kwaio "abounds with terms . . . that mark times in the diurnal cycle. . . . Kwaio talk is sprinkled with these markers of the daily cycle, based on angles of solar deviations diurnally (and such phenomena as dusk and subsequent insect noises, such as *keeani* 'crickets cry'), which allow precise planning and coordination of work, rendezvous, and travel" (Keesing 1994: 6).

It would be quite futile to try to reduce such *when*-phrases to something simpler; and it would be equally futile to try to reduce phrases of temporal succession ('after' and 'before') to something simpler.

If it has often been claimed that a sense of 'whenness' is lacking in "primitive thought" (including, for example, medieval European mentality; see Le Pan 1989: 113), even stronger claims have been made about the alleged absence of the idea of 'temporal succession' in many languages and cultures, and a linear conception of time has often been contrasted with a cyclical one (see e.g. Le Pan 1989: 89). Cross-linguistic investigations suggest, however, that whatever the differences in cultural emphasis and elaboration might be, all languages have words for AFTER and BEFORE, and that in any language one can easily make statements such as "*A* was born after *B*" and "*B* was born before *A*", or "*A* died after *B*" and "*B* died before *A*".

What is particularly interesting about these findings is the apparent redundancy of the exponents of temporary succession; for why should all languages have words for both BEFORE and AFTER, rather than for just one of these concepts? Aren't they reducible to one another?

From a logical point of view, indeed, they might be reducible to one another. But the fact that natural languages have lexical resources for expressing both of them suggests that from the point of view of human conceptualization of reality, "*Y* happened after *X*" means something different from, and irreducible to, "*X* happened before *Y*". Clearly, what matters is a different perspective on the events in question, a different point of view, and, as pointed out by Slobin (1985a: 1181), "the ability to view scenes from different perspectives" is a salient feature of human cognition, clearly reflected in all languages.

It is particularly interesting to see in this connection the early emergence of both 'before' (sometimes realized as *first*) and 'after' in child language. For example (French and Nelson 1985: 110–11; see also Carni and French 1984):

After the birthday, they go home. [age: 3 years, 1 month]

Well, *first* I didn't know how to, but now, when I get dressed, I can put on my pants. [age: 4 years, 2 months]

And my daddy just wants to eat them. Like chocolate cookies. I had one *before* we came here. [age: 3 years, 10 months]

In a narrative, AFTER is realized as a simple portmanteau "then", or "and then" (i.e. 'after this'). As Bruner (1990: 79) notes, "Children early start mastering grammatical and lexical forms for 'binding' the sequences they recount—by the use of temporals like 'then' and 'later', and eventually by the use of causals."

11. Space: WHERE, UNDER, ABOVE

What applies to the temporal triad WHEN, AFTER, and BEFORE appears to apply also to the spatial triad WHERE, UNDER, and ABOVE. First of all, evidence suggests that all languages have a word for WHERE (SOMEWHERE, PLACE) distinct from the word for WHEN. (See Goddard and Wierzbicka, 1994*b*.) This word can apply to both entities and events; for example:

Where are you? (Where is this thing?)
Where did it happen?

Since for entities (in contrast to "happenings") 'where' is interpreted as 'being somewhere', in the system posited here 'being somewhere' is regarded as an allolex of 'somewhere'.

As the universality of the words for WHERE confirms, WHERE is a fundamental human concept, incapable of being defined. In earlier work (Wierzbicka 1972), I have tried to analyse WHERE via PART, but this attempt led to bizarre and intuitively unacceptable results; and to my knowledge no other, more successful attempts to analyse this concept have ever been proposed.

As for ABOVE and UNDER, they present the same apparent redundancy as AFTER and BEFORE do, for if *A* is above *B* then *B* must be under *A*. By itself, this redundancy would not be a reason for not positing them both as primitives: since human minds are not disembodied computers (see Johnson 1987; Edelman 1992), our conceptualization of the world reflects our "embodiment", and also our position on the ground: since we normally walk with the head up, the contrast between ABOVE and UNDER may not be conceived of as reversible.

None the less, it must be admitted that the case for positing both 'under' and 'above' as semantic primitives (as it was done in Goddard and Wierzbicka 1994*b*) is not nearly as strong as that for 'before' and 'after'. Intriguing data bearing on this question come from research into child language. In particular, this research shows that while both the concepts 'before' and 'after' emerge early (apparently before the end of the third year; see Carni and French 1984), the spatial pair ('under' and 'above') behaves in a curiously asymmetrical way, with 'under' apparently emerging much earlier than 'above'—and not only in English but also in a number of other languages (see Johnston and Slobin 1979).

Another relevant fact emerging from child language research is that the concepts linked in English with the words *up* and *down* appear very early in children's speech, and are used very frequently (so much so that, for example, in the speech of the 16-month-old Allison Bloom they were among the seven most frequent one-word utterances; see Bloom and Lahey 1978: 114; also Clark 1985: 746). At first, these words apply predominantly to the movements of the child's body, as he or she is being lifted or put back down by the parent (see Bowerman 1976: 167). By contrast, the earliest uses of *under* (and its equivalents in other languages) are no doubt stative, and presumably refer to manipulable objects located temporarily under large objects with more or less fixed location, such as a table or a bed. (The idea of looking for things under the table or under the bed is no doubt more relevant to a small child than that of looking for things "above" something—presumably, partly because of the child's own size and partly because things fall down, rather than rise.)

It is interesting to note in this connection Clark's (1985: 744) observation about the prepositions *sous,* 'under', and *sur,* 'on', being in contrast in French children's speech. It makes a lot of sense to assume that from a child's point of view the likely choice is between interesting objects being *under* the table or *on* the table, rather than *under* the table and *above* the table.

Considerations of this kind suggest that while 'under' can be seen as a well-established semantic primitive, 'above' cannot; and also that in future research the notion of 'on' (as in "the box is on the table") should be scrutinized as a possible conceptual primitive (presumably, along with the notions 'up' and 'down').

From a purely logical point of view, 'above' and 'under' may seem to be related in the same way as 'before' and 'after', that is, as converses (see e.g. Apresjan 1974, 1992; Cruse 1986). But since in human experience the spontaneous movement of things is unidirectional (because they fall to the ground, unless supported on some stable surface), the contrast between 'on' and 'under' may be psychologically more real (as far as location of things is concerned) than that between 'under' and 'above'. On the other hand, as far as human action is concerned, the movement 'up' may indeed seem to be directly related to the movement 'down', and at this stage it is difficult to see how one of these concepts could be defined in terms of the other. (For discussion of 'in' and 'inside', see Section B of this chapter.)

12. Partonomy and Taxonomy: PART (OF) and KIND (OF)

12.1. PART

PART is a controversial primitive, partly (no pun intended) because many languages don't have a word with a range of use similar to that of the English noun *part*, and partly because some languages don't seem to have a word for *part* at all.

In proposing PART as a universal semantic primitive, therefore, it is important, first of all, to clarify what uses of the English *part* are meant to illustrate the postulated primitive; and second, to examine how the meaning in question is expressed in a language which doesn't seem to have a word corresponding to the English *part* at all.

In English, *part* can be used in (at least) three different ways. First of all, it can refer to "things" identifiable, so to speak, within larger things, as in the following sentences:

> The foot is a part of the leg.
> A knife has two parts: a blade and a handle.
> A petal is a part of a flower.

Second, *part* can refer to a "piece" of something, that is, to something which cannot be thought of as an identifiable thing before it gets detached from a larger thing (see Cruse 1986: 157). For example:

> He ate part of the melon (not the whole melon).

Third, *part* can be used to refer to a subset of a group of discrete entities, including people:

> Part of them went to the right, and part went to the left.

In the system of primitives proposed here, the second and third uses illustrated above, which can both be linked with the traditional label "partitive", exemplify the newly proposed primitive SOME (OF) (see Part B of this chapter). It is only the first use, then, which is regarded as corresponding to the primitive element PART.

It is inconceivable how the word *part*, as used, for example, with reference to body parts, could be defined in simpler concepts. It is also inconceivable that a language would fail to provide its speakers with some means for referring to body parts and for saying that, for example, the head is a part of the body, or that the foot is a part of the leg. (See Andersen 1978; C. Brown 1976; Chappell and McGregor 1995).

How does one express such thoughts in a language which does not have a noun corresponding to the English noun *part*? Different languages provide different solutions. For example, in the Australian language

Yankunytjatjara, PART is expressed by means of the so-called 'having' suffix *-tjara* (Goddard 1994*b*: 254–6):

Yunpa mulya-tjara, tjaa-tjara, kuṟu kutjara-tjara.
face nose-HAVING mouth-HAVING eye two-HAVING
'A face has a nose, mouth and two eyes (as parts).'

Puntu kutju, palu kutjupa-kutjupa tjuṯa-tjara.
body one but something many-HAVING
'(It is) one body, but with many parts.' (Romans 12:4)

As noted by Goddard, the suffix *-tjara* is polysemous, but in certain contexts it can only mean 'part'. In particular, Goddard points out that a sentence whose "word-for-word calque rendition . . . could be read as 'This thing has two whats?' has a very clear meaning in Yankunytjatjara, and refers unambiguously to the number of 'parts' ":

Puṉu nyangatja nyaa kutjara-tjara?
thing this what two-HAVING
'What two parts does this thing have?'

It is undoubtedly true that cultures differ in the amount of interest they show in the concept of 'part'. As argued in Goddard 1989*a*, modern Western culture places a great emphasis on viewing various aspects of reality in terms of complexes analysable into 'parts', whereas, for example, Australian Aboriginal culture does not. But cultural differences of this kind should not obscure the fact that the concept of PART can also be expressed in those languages whose speakers are less inclined to talk about "parts" in the abstract (in contrast to heads, feet, handles, and other specific kinds of "parts") than are speakers of technologically complex modern societies. (For further discussion, see Wierzbicka 1994*b*: 488–92.)

The concept of PART plays an important role in the grammar of many languages, mainly because it underlies so-called "possessive constructions" of various kinds. The label "possessive", frequently used in grammatical descriptions, has no constant semantic content, but it is usually used with respect to constructions whose meaning involves the concept of PART.

For example, the so-called "inalienable possession" is usually based on the notion of 'a part of a person' or 'a part of a person's body' (often extended to things which are seen as 'like a part of a person'; see Chappell and McGregor 1995). On the other hand, "alienable possession" is based on a combination of PART and, so to speak, 'disponibility'. The conceptual links between 'parthood' and 'ownership' can be represented along the following lines (partial explications only):

my hand — a part of my body
        if I want, I can do many things with it

my car   — a car
> if I want, I can do many things with it
> like I can do many things with a part of my body
> other people can't do the same with it

It is not clear when the concept PART first appears in children's speech, although utterances such as "Mommy hand" or "cow tail" are attested at a very early stage (see Braine 1976: 15, 19). Interestingly, Braine (1976: 7) includes also the combination "other part" in his record of one child's earliest two-word combinations. Apparently, 3- or 3-and-a-half-year-olds can already be quite competent in talking about "parts". For example (French and Nelson 1985: 109):

> Eat the green part first. ["green part" refers to icing on the cake.]

12.2. KIND

The concept of 'kind' is at the heart of the human categorization of the "contents of the world". The lexicon of every language is full of taxonomic concepts which rely crucially on this concept. For example, in English, a *rose* is 'a kind of flower', an *oak*, 'a kind of tree', and a *parrot*, 'a kind of bird'.

The important role of taxonomic (i.e. 'kind'-based) classification in all languages and cultures has often been denied in the past. In particular, it has often been claimed that in traditional non-Western societies ethnobiological classification is predominantly non-taxonomic—unlike the Western scientific classification, which is based on a hierarchy of kinds. In a classic statement of this position Lévy-Bruhl (1926: 176) wrote:

In spite of appearances, then, these minds, which evidently have no idea of genera, have none of species, families, or varieties either, although they are able to delineate them in their language.

To illustrate this claim, Lévy-Bruhl (1926: 170) repeated with approval remarks made by a traveller about Australian Aboriginal languages:

He states that generic terms such as tree, fish, bird etc. were lacking, although specific terms were applied to every variety of tree, fish or bird. ... The Tasmanians had no words to represent abstract ideas, and though they could denote every variety of gum-tree or bush by name, they had no word for tree.

Similarly, of American Indians Lévy-Bruhl (1926: 171) says the following (again quoting, with approval, travellers' reports):

almost every species has its particular Indian name. But it would be in vain to seek among them words for the abstract ideas of plant, animal, and the abstract notions colour, tone, sex, species, etc. ... In California, "there are no genera, no species: every oak, pine, or grass has its separate name."

But while trustworthy recent investigations by anthropologists and linguists have shown that general terms such as 'tree', 'bird', or 'fish', not to mention 'animal' and 'plant', may indeed be scant in a language while more specific words for creatures and plants may be present in abundance (see e.g. C. Brown 1984; Berlin 1992), the idea that a hierarchy of kinds is either absent from, or marginal to, folk-biological classifications has not stood the test of time. (See in particular the evidence and discussion in Berlin 1992.)

First, the apparently universal presence of at least some hierarchical categorization reflected in the lexicon (e.g. 'tree'–'oak'; or 'bird'–'cuckoo') does support the view that taxonomies play an important role in the conceptualization of living kinds, despite Hallpike's (1979: 202) and others' unsupported assertion to the contrary. The semantic relation between terms such as 'tree' and 'oak' can be verified by a variety of linguistic tests, and wherever such tests have been applied they support the view that class inclusion is indeed involved. (See Chapters 11 and 12.)

Second, as pointed out by Berlin (1992: 52–3), in every known language there is a set of words regarded as the "real names" of certain classes of living things. When asked "What is this called?" informants might reply with a folk generic term, with a "horizontal extension" of such a term (e.g. "It is like lilac"), or might say "I don't know", but they will not say, for example, "It is called a bird", or "It is called a bush". The presence of such "real names" establishes beyond any reasonable doubt the psychological reality of the notion of biological species (or "folk genera").

Third, and most importantly (from the present point of view), linguistic evidence suggests that the concept of 'kind' (or 'kinds') is a lexical universal. Ellen (1986: 88) mocks the idea that informants may in the course of their ordinary lives use sentences such as "Is *X* a kind of *Y*?" or "How many kinds of *Y* are there?", but in fact sentences referring to "kinds" of living things are widely attested in traditional non-Western languages. (See Goddard and Wierzbicka, 1994*b*.) This applies, in particular, to the following types of sentence:

> There are three kinds of bat (yam, mango, etc.).
> This is not the same fish, but it is the same kind of fish.

It is particularly important that cross-linguistic evidence supports the universality of the distinction between KIND and LIKE (or between categorization and similarity), as illustrated in the following sentence:[4]

---

[4] It seems natural to think that things which are "of the same kind" (e.g. cats; or oaks; or daffodils) are also "like each other". Yet recent work in cognitive psychology as well as linguistics has led to the growing conviction that human categorization cannot be reduced to notions such as "likeness" or "similarity". (See e.g. Atran 1990; Carey 1985; Gelman and Coley 1991; Keil 1986; Medin and Ortony 1989; Rips 1989.)

This tree doesn't look like that other tree, but they are the same kind of tree.

But if the concept of KIND cannot be reduced to the concept of LIKE, it can hardly be reduced to any other concept or concepts, and, to my knowledge, no viable decomposition of KIND has ever been proposed. On present evidence, therefore, KIND must be regarded as a universal semantic primitive. (See Wierzbicka forthcoming *d*.)

Finally, it is worth noting that, in children's language, the question "What kind of?" is attested as appearing relatively early, though after 'what', 'where', or 'who' (see e.g. Clancy 1985 on Japanese; Savić 1975 on Serbo-Croatian).

13. Metapredicates: NOT, CAN, VERY

13.1. Negation: NOT

The *not*-relation is one of the simplest and most fundamental relations known to the human mind.

(Royce 1917: 265; quoted in Horn 1989: 1)

Negation is probably the least controversial of all the lexical universals which have ever been proposed. Nobody has ever reported coming across a language without negation, and exponents of negation—unlike those of most other conceptual primitives posited here—are routinely reported in all descriptive grammars.

But while the question of negation as a lexical universal is quite straight-forward, the same cannot be said about its status as a conceptual primitive. In fact, to many readers' surprise and even dismay, negation was missing from the list of primitives which I postulated in *Semantic Primitives* (Wierzbicka 1972) and in *Lingua Mentalis* (Wierzbicka 1980); instead, my 1972 and 1980 lists included the elements 'don't want' ('diswant') or 'I don't want' ("I diswant"). (See also Wierzbicka 1967.)

In postulating 'diswanting' rather than negation as a semantic primitive, I was trying to come to grips with the fact that the semantic relation between the phrases "I want" and "I don't want" seems to be different from that between, say, "I know" and "I don't know", or "I do" and "I don't do". "I don't know" (or "I don't do") means, roughly speaking, that 'It is not the case that I know (or do)'. "I don't want", however (on one reading at least), does not seem to mean that 'it is not the case that I want' (as in "I don't particularly want"); rather, it seems to mean that I positively 'dis-want' something. It is also true that the interjection *No!* can be used to express a strong 'diswant' ("rejection"), rather than merely a denial of wanting. By assuming that 'diswanting' was semantically simpler than negation, I seemed to be able to explain such facts. (What was more difficult to explain in that approach was the use of negation in declarative sentences—a point to which I will return below.)

But although my analysis of negation as "rejection" was consistent with a long philosophical tradition of thinking about negation (see e.g. Bergson 1911) and although there is considerable empirical evidence which appears to support it, I have now come to doubt whether it is tenable.

Undoubtedly, acts of "rejection" ('I don't want this!') play an important role in human life, and it is not surprising that "rejection" should have special lexical exponents in many languages (e.g. in Acehnese, Longgu, Samoan, and Kayardild; see Goddard and Wierzbicka 1994*b*). But although these exponents of "rejection" are often identical with the exponents of negation, this does not necessarily mean that "rejection" is a simple semantic notion, which can be said to underlie all negation. After all, many languages (e.g. Samoan) have also special negative imperatives ('don't!')—despite the fact that 'don't!' is not a simple concept but a semantic molecule analysable as 'I don't want you to do this'.

While accepting the old philosophical notion that all negation implies "rejection", I experimented with a whole series of analyses of declarative sentences, such as, for example, A, B, and C below (for "This is not black"):

(A) I don't want to say "this is black".
(B) I don't want someone to think: "this is black".
(C) I don't want to say: I can think: "this is black".

But none of these analyses seemed quite right, and the "details" seemed always impossible to work out. In particular, it has always seemed difficult to see how complex sentences (e.g. with negation embedded in an *if*-clause) could be plausibly analysed via 'not wanting'. What has finally convinced me that this whole approach to the semantics of negation was probably misguided was a closer examination of data from child language acquisition. Since negation appears very early in children's speech (in the second year of life; see e.g. Braine 1976), it is very hard to believe that spontaneous utterances such as "no wet" (meaning 'I'm not wet'; see Braine 1976: 7) can be somehow based on the idea of 'not wanting someone to think or say something'.

It is true that in early child utterances 'no' frequently means 'I don't want' (e.g. "no mama" is interpreted by Braine 1976: 7 as 'I don't want to go to mama'), but it seems more plausible to analyse "no mama" as 'I don't want . . . mama' than "no wet" as 'I don't want someone to say/think that I am wet'.

I have come to accept, then, that 'not' is simply 'not', and that it cannot be reduced to anything else—not even to the intuitively appealing notion of 'rejection'.

Having reached this conclusion, I would now interpret the three earliest uses of negation identified in child language as "non-existence", "rejection", and "denial" (see Bloom 1991) along the following lines: (1) 'there isn't an *X* (here)', (2) 'I don't want this', and (3) 'this is not an *X*', assuming that all these uses involve the use of the same semantic primitive NOT. For example (Bloom 1991: 163):

"non-existence"
(Kathryn not finding a pocket in Mommy's shirt, which had no pocket:)
KATHRYN. no pocket [i.e. 'there is no pocket here']
"rejection"
(Kathryn pushing away a sliver of worn soap in the bathtub, wanting to be washed with new pink soap:)
KATHRYN. no dirty soap [i.e. 'I don't want dirty soap']
"denial"
(Kathryn, Mommy, and Lois looking for the truck:) Where's the truck?
(Mommy picking up the car, giving it to Kathryn:) Here it is. There's the truck.
KATHRYN. no truck [i.e. 'this is not the truck']

Horn (1989: 163) comments on Bloom's "rejection" category of negation as follows:

Bloom's rejection category corresponds to what philosophers—at least since Peirce—have long identified as the SUBJECTIVE or PRELOGICAL negative. Heinemann (1944: 138) glosses this 'prelogical use of negation' as 'I do not wish (will, desire, etc.) that' or 'It is not in my interests that', alongside the 'logical' negation of 'It is not true that'. On this view, the rejection category should antedate both nonexistence and denial; that it does not (at least in Bloom's data) may reflect the difference between possessing a concept and expressing it syntactically.

From a "semantic primitives" point of view, the question boils down to choosing between two solutions (A and B) to the problem of negation: should the "rejection" use of negation be seen as based on a simple semantic element 'I don't want' (in Latin, *nolo*) and the "non-existence" or "denial" use be seen as based on a combination of 'I don't want' and 'say' (solution A); or should rather the 'non-existence' and 'denial' use be seen as based on a simple semantic element 'not', and the 'rejection' use, as based on a combination of three primitives: 'I + not + want' (solution B)?

In earlier work (Wierzbicka 1967, 1972, 1980) I opted for solution A (despite strong opposition from my colleague Andrzej Bogusławski, who for a long time has argued for negation as a semantic primitive against my attempts to reduce it to a simpler notion of 'rejection'); but the language acquisition data suggesting that 'rejection' doesn't antedate 'non-existence' and 'denial' have finally convinced me that solution B is more justified, after all.

What remains to be explained (on the assumption that NOT is always NOT) is why the semantic relation between the phrases "I don't want" and "I want" does not seem to be the same as that between "I don't know" and "I know", or "I don't do" and "I do", and why "I don't want to do *X*" often appears to imply that I positively want "not to do *X*". At present, I do not have a fully satisfactory answer to this question; but the possibility of an analysis in terms of invited inferences (perhaps along Gricean lines e.g. Grice 1975) is no doubt worth exploring.

13.2. CAN

CAN is a relatively recent addition to the list of primitives. From a cross-linguistic point of view, 'can' is particularly difficult to identify, partly because it is often involved in complex patterns of polysemy, and partly because its exponents often appear to be bound morphemes rather than distinct words. From the point of view of decomposition, there is also a temptation to try to treat 'can' as complex, because of its intuitively 'iffy' character (discussed, for example, by Austin 1961). Yet all attempts to define away 'can' (including my own) have proved unsatisfactory (for general discussion, references, and for my earlier analysis of 'can', see Wierzbicka 1987*b*). The conclusion that 'can' is semantically elementary, despite its apparent intuitive links with 'if', had a significant liberating effect on subsequent analyses across numerous semantic domains (as had the earlier conclusion that 'because' was semantically elementary, despite its intuitive links with 'if'; see Section 14). Because of the close links between CAN and the newly proposed primitive MAYBE, the two elements will be discussed jointly in Part B of this chapter.

13.3. VERY

The concept of VERY might be seen as dispensable in a universal system of semantic primitives, as it is inherently subjective and "imprecise". But evidence suggests that all natural languages have a word corresponding to the English word *very* and that despite (and perhaps because of) this subjectiveness and imprecision this concept is not dispensable at all.

The area where VERY seems most relevant is that of expressive evaluations. For example, expressions such as *wonderful, marvellous, terrific, awful,* and *horrible* seem to rely crucially on the combinations of the elements GOOD and BAD with VERY ('very good', 'very bad').

In earlier work (Wierzbicka 1972) I tried to define 'very' away via 'more', along the following lines:

This is very good (big). = this is more than good (big)

and later (Wierzbicka 1980) I tried to link this interpretation to a performative analysis, as follows:

This is very good (big). = I say: this is good (big)
I want to say more than this

This analysis was questioned at the time by Dwight Bolinger (personal letter), who argued that *very good* does not mean the same as *more than good*, and that the expanded version 'I want to say more than good' does not ensure the desired interpretation.

In children's speech (in English), VERY is often realized as *so*, for example (French and Nelson 1985: 119):

Yeah, sometimes if you're so hungry, go to a restaurant that gives ya a lot of stuff.
... and then we go to the next door parking lot and it is so cold there and everything.

Examples of this kind make it particularly clear that an analysis of 'very' via 'more' is intuitively untenable ("sometimes if you're more than hungry ..."). Since no other, more plausible, analyses of 'very' have been proposed, and since accumulated cross-linguistic evidence points strongly to the universality of this concept, it seems reasonable at this stage to accept it as a universal semantic primitive.

14. Interclausal Linkers: IF, BECAUSE, LIKE

14.1. IF

In logic, "conditionals" (*if*-sentences) are defined in terms of truth conditions: "if p then q" is taken to mean that either p and q are both true, or p and q are both false, or p is false and q is true. It has often been pointed out, however, that this definition does not correspond to the use of *if*-sentences in natural languages. As Comrie (1986: 80) notes, according to the logical definition "the only relation that need hold between protasis and apodosis is that expressed in the truth table, so that otherwise totally unrelated propositions may appear as protasis and apodosis, subject only to the condition that they have appropriate truth values, as in

If Paris is the capital of France, two is an even number."

According to Comrie, in natural language (in contrast to the artificial language of logic) sentences of this kind are anomalous because in natural language *if*-sentences require a causal connection between the two propositions in question. Comrie's own definition proposed for conditionals "combines material implication with the relevance of a causal relation from the protasis to the apodosis" (1986: 96).

This amounts to an attempt to define *if*-sentences via a combination of concepts such as 'or', 'and', 'true', 'false' ('not true'), and 'because', along the following lines:

> If it rains, I will stay at home. =
> Either it will rain and because of this I will stay at home
> or it will not rain and because of this I will not stay at home
> or it will not rain and I will stay at home (despite this?).

This analysis may seem like an improvement on a purely truth-functional definition, but in my view, it is not tenable either, if only because it is not the case that 'if' always implies 'because'. It is true that 'if' implies some sort of connection between two propositions, and also that a causal link is often involved, too; I claim, however, that the 'if' connection is *sui generis*, and cannot be reduced to anything else; and that a link with 'because' is not always present. For example, the sentence

> If he insults me, I will forgive him.

does not imply that I will forgive him *because* he has insulted me: it is true that I can forgive him only if he has done something bad to me (e.g. if he has insulted me), but it is not true that the insult will be the "cause" of my forgiveness. Similarly, the sentence

> If he invites me to dinner I will not go

does not mean that I will not go *because* he has invited me: if he doesn't invite me I will not go either.

It hardly needs to be pointed out that a truth-functional analysis of *if*-sentences is highly counter-intuitive, as well as inadequate from the point of view of natural language (because of the lack of the requirement that the two clauses should be somehow connected). Since attempts to make it less inadequate by adding to it a causal component do not work, the conclusion suggests itself that—from the point of view of natural language—this analysis is simply irrelevant and should be abandoned altogether. Instead, we must conclude that the IF-relation is fundamental, irreducible to anything else; in other words, that it is a conceptual primitive.

It is worth noting in this connection that—contrary to what one might expect—the concept of IF appears relatively early in child language, although apparently later than BECAUSE. Here are some examples of *if*-sentences from the speech of American 4-year-olds (French and Nelson 1985: 114–15):

What do you do if you wanna make oatmeal cookies?
. . . well, you see, after, if you eat your food up, ya eat dessert.

(What do you do at a birthday party?)
you do a movie, and then if you have time, you play, and then you go.

(For a discussion of the universality of IF, see Chapter 6.)

14.2. BECAUSE

According to Kant, causation—with time and space—constitutes one of the basic categories of human cognition; it is not a category that we learn from experience but one of the categories which underlie our interpretation of experience.

Data from language acquisition, as well as from cross-cultural semantics, are consistent with Kant's view. The finding that apparently all languages have a lexical exponent of causation (whether it is a conjunction like *because*, a noun like *cause*, or an "ablative" suffix) is particularly significant in this regard. (For discussion, see Chapter 6; see also Wierzbicka 1994*b*.)

From the point of view of language acquisition, too, it is significant that despite the highly abstract and "non-empirical" character of the concept of causality, *because*-sentences appear quite early in children's speech. Here are a few characteristic examples from the speech of American 2-year-olds (Bloom 1991):

I was crying because I didn't want to wake up, because it was dark, so dark. (375)

(tiny blue barrel is inside other barrels)
You can't see it cause it's way inside.   (384)

(going towards disks)
Get them cause I want it.   (270)

(telling and demonstrating how she sleeps on the sofa)
Cause I was tired but now I'm not tired.   (271)

(regarding TV, which is on)
I left it open because I wanna watch it.   (339)

Bloom (1991) comments on the results of the study of causality in young children's speech as follows:

The concept of causality attributable to these children's thinking, from the evidence of what they talked about, emphasized the actions, feelings, and perceptions of persons in everyday causal events, or intentional causality. They discovered causal connections through their own and others' actions or heard them in everyday discourse about everyday events. Causality for them was neither the 'cement of the universe' that provides the structure of reality nor an innate quality of the mind that determines reality [as per the theories of Hume and Kant, respectively]. Rather, the construction of a theory of causality begins in infancy with the emergence of an understanding of the regularities in the relation between change and the actions of oneself and others that bring about change.

But while the results of studies such as Bloom (1991) do indeed appear to support the view of Searle (1983) and others that "we discover causality by experiencing it through our actions and perceptions" (Bloom 1991: 378), this is fully consistent with Kant's view that causality is an innate form of human perception of the world. It is also consistent with the view that causality (or, more precisely, the notion of BECAUSE) is a simple concept, rooted in our subjective experience of 'wanting' and 'doing', and not in any theoretical speculations about "might-have-beens", along the lines proposed in my *Semantic Primitives* (Wierzbicka 1972: 17):

> X happened because Y happened. =
> if Y hadn't happened X wouldn't have happened

As I have pointed out elsewhere (Wierzbicka 1989*b*: 321), while it may be true that "If Mary hadn't met John, she wouldn't have married him", it doesn't follow from that that "Mary married John because she had met him".

All the evidence leads, then, to the conclusion that BECAUSE is indeed a universal semantic primitive, an irreducible category of human language and cognition. (For a discussion of the universality of BECAUSE see Chapter 6.)

14.3. LIKE

The concept of LIKE can be illustrated with the following sentences:

> I did it like this: . . .
> I am not like these people.
> I think of people like you.

The importance of the concept LIKE in the human conceptualization of the world was justly emphasized by J. L. Austin in his *Sense and Sensibilia* (1962*b*: 74), where he wrote:

Like is the great adjuster-word, or alternatively put, the main flexibility-device, by whose aid, in spite of the limited scope of our vocabulary, we can always avoid being left completely speechless.

Commenting on Austin's words, Tamar Sovran (1992: 342) writes:

The concepts of similarity and its operators seem to have the same function in language and in thought, in the process of acquiring new concepts, and in the process of scientific growth. They help us to leave the safe ground of known, labeled, categorized terms, and to expand our knowledge and language to newly discovered areas.

I agree entirely with the spirit of these remarks (both Austin's and Sovran's). As for the phrasing, however, I would insist that it is Austin's 'like' rather than Sovran's 'similarity' which is the great "adjuster-word" and the main "flexibility-device" in English, and which can be matched with other such words and devices in other languages. For example, a medieval Latin hymn ("Regina coeli laetare") includes the following line:

> Resurrexit sicut dixit.
> 'He has risen as he said.' ('He has risen like he said he would.')

I imagine that the word *sicut* represents here the universal semantic primitive LIKE, and yet it could hardly be said to indicate 'similarity', either in the logical or, for that matter, colloquial sense of the word.

Furthermore, I would claim that among "similarity operators" listed by Sovran (" 'like', 'the same', 'as', and others"), one—'the same'—is not an exponent of the same concept 'like' at all, but an irreducible conceptual primitive in its own right. LIKE does have a number of exponents (allolexes) in English, as it does in other languages, and *as* (in some of its uses) is indeed a good example, but *the same* is not. In natural language, it is essential for people to be able to make distinctions such as the following one:

> This fish is like that other fish, but it is not the same fish

and cross-linguistic evidence suggests that in all languages people have lexical resources for making such distinctions. (See Goddard and Wierzbicka 1994*b*.)

The addition of 'like' to the list of primitives (proposed in Goddard 1989*a*) has simplified semantic analysis of numerous aspects of language. In particular, it has allowed explications couched in semantic primitives to account, in a simple and natural way, for the role of prototypes in human language and cognition. In my work, I have tried to use the notion of prototype from the start, and, for example, my 1972 analyses of emotion concepts or 1980 analyses of kinship and colour concepts were based on this notion (see e.g. McCawley's (1983: 656) comment: "Wierzbicka makes extensive use of prototype analyses"). But my early lists of primitives were lacking an element which would allow me to phrase these analyses in a simple and natural way. The addition of 'like' to the list changed this. As pointed out by Goddard, 'like' was "a semantically primitive hedge, built into NSM [Natural Semantic Metalanguage], with obvious benefits in terms of reducing the length of *Lingua mentalis* style explications, which lean heavily on expressions such as 'can be thought of as' and 'in the same way as' " (1989*a*: 53). Thus, the addition of 'like' facilitated a radical simplification of the syntax of the explications, as well as making the semantic account of prototypes, hedges, metaphors, and vagueness more accurate and intuitively satisfying.

B. NEW PRIMITIVES

15. Introduction

In the last two years, the system of semantic primitives has been radically expanded, from 37 to as many as 55. Despite this rapid expansion, the new primitives offered here for the reader's consideration have not been proposed lightly. Indirectly, they are the product of many years' thinking, searching, and experimenting. More directly, they have been born out of careful reconsideration of the whole system and lengthy discussions, particularly those with my co-editor Cliff Goddard, following our collective work on the volume testing the earlier, more restricted set of primitives (Goddard and Wierzbicka 1994*b*).[5]

As mentioned earlier, the new primitives haven't yet been extensively tested, and cross-linguistic evidence is vital for deciding their future fate. Their present status must be regarded as quite different from that of the old primitives, which have already been subjected to extensive cross-linguistic testing.

The order of presentation of the "new primitives" will follow, roughly, that of the old primitives (except, of course, for the areas to which nothing has been added). Thus, I will start with determiners and quantifiers, following on with mental predicates and with a section on movement, existence, and life, which can be seen as roughly corresponding to Section 7, "Actions and Events", in Part A. This will be followed by sections on space and time (this time, first space, then time), and by a section entitled "Imagination and Possibility", which corresponds to the final section of Part A, "Interclausal Linkers". Finally, the most recent and the most tentative of all, the concept of WORD will be briefly discussed—the least solid (at this stage) of all the proposed primitives. The chapter will close with a general discussion and a brief conclusion.

The new primitives tentatively posited in this part include the following:

| "Determiner" | SOME |
| "Augmentor" | MORE |

[5] The whole new set has been extensively discussed with Cliff Goddard, and has undergone a number of revisions, following his suggestions. A large part of the new set has also been discussed with Jean Harkins, and my understanding of some aspects of the new system has greatly profited from these discussions. Apart from Jean, I am also indebted to a number of other colleagues in Canberra, in particular, Tim Curnow, Bob Dixon, Nick Enfield, David Nash, Helen O'Loghlin, and Tim Shopen. I am also deeply indebted to my colleague Andrzej Bogusławski in Warsaw, despite the distance, an unfailing critic, debater, and co-thinker. Last but not least I would like to acknowledge my indebtedness to my daughter Clare, who discussed most of the new primitives with me and who offered many helpful criticisms and suggestions.

"Mental predicates"	SEE, HEAR
"Non-mental predicates"	MOVE, THERE IS, (BE) ALIVE
"Space"	FAR, NEAR; SIDE; INSIDE; HERE
"Time"	A LONG TIME, A SHORT TIME; NOW
"Imagination and possibility"	IF . . . WOULD, MAYBE
"Words"	WORD

16. Determiners and Quantifiers: SOME and MORE

16.1. Determiner: SOME

The English word *some* is polysemous. The sense posited here as primitive is that of "indeterminate number", as illustrated in the following passage from a text in the Australian language Guugu-Yimidhirr (Haviland 1979: 163; Haviland's numbers):

(32) Dhana   gada-y   waguurr-nganh,
3sg + NOM come-PAST outside-ABL
They came from the outside [i.e. from inland];

(33) gurra buurraay-nganh dhalun-nganh galmba gada-y,
and   water-ABL   see-ABL   also   come-PAST
and they also came from the water, from the sea;

(34) mundal   bubu-wi   badi = badiimbarr gada-y,
some + ABS ground-LOC under = underneath come-PAST
some came underneath the [surface of] the earth;

(35) mundal   wanggaar = nggarr bubu-wi   gada-y,
some + ABS above = REDUP   ground-LOC come-PAST
others came above the ground;

(36) mundal   birri wanggaar gada-y.
some + ABS river- above   come-PAST
and others came up the rivers.

The primitive proposed here is realized in Guugu-Yimidhirr as *mundal*. As Haviland's glosses show, in English this sense can sometimes be rendered as *some*, and sometimes as *others*. It is important to stress, however, that it is a concept which functions as a quantifier, situated somewhere between ONE and ALL.

The quantifier SOME was proposed as a universal semantic primitive by Bogusławski (1965: 58), alongside two other quantifiers: ONE and ALL. I confess that it took me more than twenty years to come to believe in ONE and ALL (which were also independently posited by Goddard at the Adelaide Workshop in 1986); and it has taken me close to another decade to come to believe in SOME. But looking at sentences such as those in the Guugu-Yimidhirr passage (which, as Jean Harkins, personal communication, points out, are very common in Aboriginal stories), one has to recognize that they couldn't be fully explicated with a set of primitives which didn't include SOME.

In works on languages and logic, the English word *some* is frequently linked with the so-called "existential quantifier". For example, McCawley (1981: 101–2) writes:

The so-called universal quantifier corresponds to several different English words: *all*, *every*, *any*, *each*; the existential quantifier corresponds to certain uses of the words *some* and *a/an*. . . . The existential quantifier, henceforth represented by the symbol ∃, is also the common element in a number of things that natural languages often distinguish, for example, various uses of *a/an* and *some* in English.

McCawley goes on to point out that the English language distinguishes obligatorily between singular and plural, but that the logical concept of existential quantifier is indifferent to this distinction:

The formula (∃: man $x)_x$(admire x Hitler) is supposed to be true if at least one man admires Hitler and false if no man admires Hitler. It is non-committal on whether exactly one man or more than one admires Hitler. However, English sentences must draw the distinction between one and more than one:

(*a*) Some man admires Hitler.
(*b*) Some men admire Hitler.

But the concept SOME proposed here as a semantic primitive corresponds only to sentence (*b*) above, not to sentence (*a*). What is meant could perhaps be better expressed as SOME OF, as in the following sentences:

Some of them admire Hitler.
Some of them turned right, and some (of them) turned left.

In Polish, the word *część* 'part' can sometimes be used as an exponent of this notion, for example:

Część z nich poszła na prawo, a część na lewo.
Part of them turned right, and part turned left.

Similarly, in many other European languages the exponent of the primitive PART can be used as a quantifier, to express the primitive SOME. Curiously, as Cliff Goddard (personal communication) notes, the same is true of the Australian language Yankunytjatjara. But in many other languages there is no lexical overlap between SOME and PART. (Moreover, even in English sentences SOME cannot always be paraphrased in terms of the word *part*. For example, *sometimes* (*at some times*) cannot be defined as 'part of the time'.)

It is important to note that while in works on language and logic *some* may be regarded as an equivalent of the verb *exist* (or the expression *there is*), from a semantic point of view SOME and THERE IS are two different notions, which cannot be reduced to one (see Section 16.2 below). For example, it seems clear that the Guugu-Yimidhirr passage adduced at the outset cannot be paraphrased in terms of *exist* or *there is*. One could of course say (in English), "There were people among them who went under the ground; there were people among them who went above the ground"; but a paraphrase of this kind relies on a relative clause—a structure which is not universally available (as well as on the expression "among them", which looks suspiciously like another way of saying "some").

Similarly, it is true that a sentence such as "Some people admire Hitler" does seem to be paraphrasable (in English) as "There are people who admire Hitler". But if we try to define away the complex and language-specific relativizer "who", on which this paraphrase depends, we have to fall back on *some* ("Some people admire Hitler"):

> Some people admire Hitler. ≠
>   there are people
>   these people admire Hitler

Finally, it might be suggested that *some* (in the relevant sense) can be defined away as "not all", along the lines of "Some people admire Hitler = Not all people admire Hitler". But a paraphrase of this kind is not valid, since "not all"—in contrast to *some*—implies something like "most".

16.2. Augmentor: MORE

The element MORE, included in one of his tentative lists of indefinables by Leibniz, appears on the list of semantic primitives not for the first time. I tentatively included it in one of the 1989 lists (Wierzbicka 1989*b*: 105), only to replace it later with the element MUCH (MANY), proposed at the time and convincingly argued for by Goddard. To have both MUCH (MANY) and MORE on the list seemed intolerably uneconomical, given the close semantic links between the two concepts, and so it seemed imperative to try to define 'much' via 'more' or the other way round.

Given the intuitive closeness of the two concepts it is certainly worth trying to reduce them to one. In my judgement, however, none of the attempts undertaken in the past were really convincing.

If we want to try to define 'much' via 'more' the obvious way to go is to refer to some expectations, along the following lines:

> much (many) = more than one could/would expect

But this approach, reasonable as it may seem at first, is not always convincing. For example, in the sentence

> Many people came (e.g. to see the Pope), but not as many as expected.

the word *many* can hardly mean 'more than expected'.

In the Moscow semantic tradition, the key word used in this and many other similar contexts was "norm" (see e.g. Žolkovskij 1964*b*):

much (many) = more than the norm

But the word *norm* doesn't always make sense in sentences with *much* or *many*. For example, the sentence

Many people are afraid of lightning.

could hardly be paraphrased in terms of the phrase "more than the norm". Of course it could be argued that what was meant was not the ordinary Russian word *norma* ('norm') but an artificial word with a different meaning, but it is not clear what exactly such a statement would mean or how it could be verified.

On the other hand, if we try to define 'more' via 'much/many' we run into other difficulties. At first sight, the approach which appears to work with other comparatives seems to work here as well (see Section 9 above):[6]

A is bigger than *B*. =
if someone thinks of these two things at the same time
this person can think: "*A* is big, *B* is not big"

But there are many situations when a paraphrase of this kind would not work for "more". For example, if I say that I want more to eat, a paraphrase along the lines proposed above doesn't seem to make sense. Similarly, the sentences:

I want to say more.
I want to see more.
I want to know more about this.

can hardly be paraphrased in the "these two things" format.

It is not a comparative 'more', then (a converse of 'less'), which I am positing here as a universal semantic primitive, but, so to speak, an "augmentative" one, illustrated in canonical sentences such as

I want more.
Give me more.
I want to see/know/hear more.

---

[6] An analysis along these lines, which was proposed by Cliff Goddard (personal communication), is simpler, and, I think, better, than the following one, which I proposed in Wierzbicka (1971):

A is bigger than *B*. =
if people can say about *B* "it is big"
they can say the same about *A*
I can't say:
"if people can say this about *A*
they can say the same about *B*"

When the presence of lexical exponents of MORE is cross-linguistically tested, it is probably worth including questions about 'less' as well. At this stage, however, 'less' seems to be a much less likely candidate for a lexical universal than MORE. I would expect that many languages will be found which have a word for MORE (in an augmentative sense) but not for 'less'.

The study of language acquisition strengthens this expectation (based on internal semantic grounds), since first, children start using the word *more*, in contrast to *less*, very early (see e.g. Braine 1976), and second, those early uses of *more* are augmentative, not relative. As, for example, Johnston (1985: 974) put it: "although we think of *more* as expressing judgments of relative quantity/extent, the child's *more* is at first non-quantitative and non-comparative". As shown by Braine, a combination of *more* and a word designating an object of desire (e.g. "more juice!") is in fact among the most common early two-word utterances in child language (Braine 1976; McShane 1991), whereas *less* does not appear on the list of the early two-word patterns at all. Bowerman (1976: 128) notes that her daughters Christy and Eva initially used the word *more* "in connection with a restricted set of objects at first—food and drink" and that "Bloom's (1973) daughter Allison likewise first produced . . . 'more' as a request for an additional serving of food or drink, although within only a few days she began to use these words across a range of more varied contexts."

Reflecting on the apparent asymmetry between the concepts 'more' and 'less' one is tempted to think that perhaps there is indeed some special psychological link between the concepts MORE and WANT. As we know them, human beings are perhaps more inclined to think, and to say:

> I want (to have, to eat, to drink) more.
> I want to see more.
> I want to know more.
> I want to say more.

than to use the corresponding sentences with 'less'. It is also worth noting that VERY—another quasi-quantitative concept—has no universal opposite either.

Finally, I would like to suggest that the augmentative element MORE plays a crucial role in our understanding of numbers. For what is "three" if not "one more than two"?

17. Mental Predicates: SEE and HEAR

See baby/See pretty/See train.
(from a 2-year-old's first word-combination list; Braine 1976: 70)

The concepts 'see' and 'hear' play a fundamental role in human communication.

As pointed out by Bowerman (1976: 138), in transcriptions of two-word child utterances from diverse languages one frequently finds sentences such as "this (that) doggie", "here (there) ball", or "see man". Generally speaking, the word *see* (alongside *this, that, here,* and *there*) appears to be one of the basic communicative tools in early interaction between children and adults. At that stage, the word *hear* doesn't seem to be nearly as important as *see,* but apparently, before long, it too begins to play a special role, alongside *look, listen,* and *watch* (see e.g. Bloom *et al.* 1975).

The concepts 'look', 'listen', and 'watch' are complex, and involve 'wanting' as well as 'seeing' or 'hearing' ('wanting to see' and 'wanting to hear'); but 'see' and 'hear' themselves cannot be similarly decomposed into simpler concepts.[7]

Admittedly, in earlier work (see Wierzbicka 1980) I have argued that SEE and HEAR (as well as 'smell' and 'taste') can be defined via the corresponding body parts: eyes and ears, nose and mouth. To see and to hear, I claimed, means to know something about something because of one's eyes or one's ears.

But there are problems with this account. First of all, it presents the notions of 'see' and 'hear' as very complex, and this is hard to accept in view of the role these elements play in many areas of lexicon and grammar of many languages (such as, in particular, "evidentials"; see Chapter 15).

Second, if we define 'see' and 'hear' via 'eyes' and 'ears', we cannot define 'eyes' and 'ears' via 'see' and 'hear', and we have to adopt purely anatomical definitions, along the following lines:

eyes — two parts of the face in the upper part of the face
ears — two parts of the head, on both sides of the head

But although in the past I tried to justify such definitions myself (Wierzbicka 1980), my readers and listeners always found them unsatisfactory, because they felt that 'seeing' and 'hearing' was an integral part of their meaning. I would now propose, then, defining 'eyes' via SEE, and 'ears' via HEAR, as follows:

eyes — two parts of the face
      these parts are alike
      because of these two parts a person can see

---

[7] At a Linguistic Forum held at the ANU in 1989, Bob Dixon said that if he were to propose his own list of universal semantic primitives, he would include in it "see" and "hear". I have now reached the same conclusion.

ears — two parts of a person's head
    these parts are alike
    because of these two parts, a person can hear

Third, while 'see' and 'hear' may seem to be notions derived from sensory experience, and therefore unlikely to be either universal or innate (because experience is variable), in fact they do not have to be viewed in that way. A person born blind may still "see" something (images or colours) in his or her mind, and may therefore have an innate notion of 'seeing'. Similarly, people deaf from birth may still "hear" something in their heads. It is interesting to note, for example, frequent references to 'hearing' (sometimes with, and sometimes without inverted commas) in the autobiography of a man who describes himself as totally deaf (Wright 1993: 10–11):

I do not live in a world of complete silence. There is no such thing as absolute deafness. Coming from one whose aural nerve is extinct, this statement may be taken as authoritative. . . . If I stand on a wooden floor I can 'hear' footsteps behind me, but not when standing on a floor made of some less resonant substance—for example stone or concrete. I can even partially 'hear' my own voice. This is not surprising, for people hear themselves talk mainly by bone-conduction inside their heads . . . Likewise, I 'hear' a piano if I place a finger on it while it is being played. . . . I cannot hear wind-instruments (flute, bagpipes, oboe). . . . I have a passion for military bands, though hearing little except the drumtaps, a sad boom-thud from the big drum and a clattering exhilaration from the kettledrums.

Whether or not all languages have separate words for SEE and HEAR is not always self-evident, because in a number of languages both SEE and HEAR share their lexical exponents with other concepts, notably with KNOW and THINK. But (as argued in Chapter 6), lexical overlaps of this kind can be shown to be due to polysemy. Apart from such common patterns of polysemy, to my knowledge no language without words for SEE and HEAR has ever been reported.[8]

The common polysemic patterns involving SEE or HEAR on the one hand and KNOW on the other are of course not accidental. They point to conceptual links, but I would argue that these links are not compositional.

---

[8] A particularly interesting case of polysemy involving SEE and HEAR has been reported by Sasha Aikhenvald (personal communication). In the Tariana language (from the Arawak family, spoken in Brazil), the same verb is used for both SEE and HEAR, but in the HEAR sense it requires an object which implies an "auditory" object ('words', 'sounds', 'language', etc.) In this language, the sentence of the form 'I Verb(see/hear) a bird' can mean either 'I see a bird' or 'I hear a bird'. But it is also possible to say, using the same verb, the equivalent of 'I hear a bird but I don't see it' or 'I see a bird but I don't hear it'. To do this, one would use sentences of the following form: 'I Verb(see/hear) the voice of a bird, but I don't Verb(see/hear) it', or 'I Verb(see/hear) a bird but I don't Verb(see/hear) its voice'. In my view this fact shows that the verb in question is polysemous (unlike, for example, the English verb *perceive*).

Definitions linking seeing and hearing with knowledge, along the lines of:

to see — to know something about something because of one's eyes
to hear — to know something about something because of one's ears

may seem plausible because they are consistent with a wide range of contexts where these words occur, but they cannot be said to capture their semantic invariant.

For example, when one sees a mirage in the desert this could hardly be interpreted in terms of gaining knowledge about something. Of course all auditive and visual experiences (including ringing in one's ears and seeing colourful dreams) can lead, indirectly, to some knowledge (e.g. about one's health, or about one's unconscious desires), but this is not what sentences about such experiences mean. Furthermore, an analysis of a 2-year-old's utterance "see pretty" as 'I want you/someone to know because of your eyes that there is something pretty here' is hardly convincing: apart from its precocious complexity, the baby wants someone to 'see', not to 'know'.

It is important to add that the approach to SEE and HEAR proposed here does not extend to the other senses. The supposed symmetry between the human "five senses" is spurious, and from a universal perspective there is no such thing as the human "five senses". Beyond "seeing" and "hearing", different languages draw their distinctions in different ways. As Classen (1993: 1–2) points out, "In the West we are accustomed to thinking of perception as a physical rather than cultural act. The five senses simply gather data about the world. Yet even our time-honoured notion of there being five senses is itself a cultural construction. Some cultures recognize more senses, and other cultures fewer."

Admittedly, Classen goes on to say that "the Hausa of Nigeria divide the senses into two, with one term for sight and one for all the other senses". This doesn't mean, however, that the Hausa word which stands for 'hear' as well all the other senses except 'see' is not polysemous. Polysemic patterns of this kind are common. For example, in Russian the word *slyšat'* can stand both for 'hear' and 'smell' (see the Academy dictionary of Russian: Akademija Nauk SSSR 1961, iv. 204). What matters, however, is not the term as such, but the term combined with a particular grammatical frame.

The hypothesis that SEE is a universal semantic primitive is consistent with the view widespread across cultures that there is a special relationship between seeing and knowing, and that eyewitness evidence is more reliable than any other kind of evidence, and the hypothesized status of HEAR as a universal semantic primitive tallies well with the special role of vocal speech in human communication: while SAY applies to both vocal and other signs, audible messages play a more important role in human societies than other kinds of messages; and spoken languages are not on a par with other semiotic systems.

The fact that of all the senses only SEE and HEAR are grammaticalized in the category of "evidentials" (see Chapter 15) is another reflection of their special status in human cognition, as is also the fact that "visibility" is often encoded in the systems of demonstratives.

One way to characterize this difference between the concepts 'see' and 'hear' on the one hand, and 'smell', 'taste', and 'touch' on the other, is to say that 'see' and 'hear' are, essentially, mental predicates, referring to events and processes which do not rely crucially on the body, whereas 'smell', 'taste', and 'touch' are, essentially, "sensory" predicates, referring to experiences which do rely, crucially, on the body. This difference is reflected in the fact that it is perfectly natural to attribute 'seeing' and 'hearing'—but not smelling, tasting, or touching—to God. For example, it is perfectly natural to say that God hears our prayers, or that he sees our hearts and indeed our actions; but it would sound ludicrous to say that he "smells" something.

Thus, we can conceive of 'seeing' and 'hearing' in a more abstract, less physical way than we can conceive of 'smelling' (or 'tasting' or 'touching'). This is consistent with the hypothesis that 'see' and 'hear', in contrast to 'smell', 'taste', or 'touch', are conceptual primitives.

18. Movement, Existence, Life: MOVE, THERE IS, LIVE

18.1. MOVE

The idea of 'movement' or 'motion' was put forward as indefinable by John Locke, who mocked attempts to reduce it to other concepts:

Nor have the modern philosophers, who have endeavoured to throw off the jargon of the schools, and speak intelligibly, much better succeeded in defining simple ideas, whether by explaining their causes, or any otherwise. The atomists, who define motion to be 'a passage from one place to another,' what do they do more than put one synonymous word for another? For what is *passage* other than *motion*? And if they were asked what passage was, how would they better define it than by motion? For is it not at least as proper and significant to say, Passage is a motion from one place to another, as to say, Motion is a passage, &c.? This is to translate, and not to define, when we change two words of the same signification one for another; which, when one is better understood than the other, may serve to discover what idea the unknown stands for; but is very far from a definition, unless we will say every English word in the dictionary is the definition of the Latin word it answers, and that motion is a definition of *motus*. (Locke 1690/1959: 35)

In *Lingua Mentalis* (Wierzbicka 1980: 5), I rejected Locke's claim and argued (following Leibniz 1765/1981: 297) that 'movement' was semantically related to 'change of place', and therefore could not be regarded as elementary. If, however, we allow elementary concepts to be mutually related (in non-compositional ways), then my argument can no longer be regarded as valid: if both 'I' and 'someone' ('person') can be regarded as elementary, despite being intuitively related, so can 'movement' and 'place'.

Furthermore, the notion MOVE, which I am now positing as a semantic primitive, is not necessarily linked with a passage of some object or person from one place to another. The prototypical examples of MOVE in the intended sense can be found in sentences such as the following ones:

> I see something is moving (in this place).
> I can't move.
> Something moved inside me.

In sentences of this kind, the idea of 'change of place' is not necessarily relevant at all (even if it is true that whenever something moves, something changes place, if only momentarily). Similarly, if we wanted to say that someone shivered, or that someone's lips trembled, it would seem rather ludicrous to try to paraphrase such sentences in terms of a repeated change of place. On the other hand, concepts such as 'go' or 'walk' do imply a change of place, but they also imply movement, and their explications would have to include both PLACE (WHERE) and MOVE.

18.2. THERE IS

Cartesians regarded it as self-evident that 'existence' (in French *l'existence*) was among those ideas which are so clear that no definitions could make them any clearer. For many years, I have rejected this view, in the belief that 'existence' could be defined in terms of, so to speak, "possible reference", that is, along the following lines (see Wierzbicka 1972, 1980):

> There are no unicorns (ghosts, black swans). =
> one can't say about something: "this is a unicorn (ghost, black swan)"

Paraphrases of this kind never seemed to me quite right, but I believed that with time they could be amended in some minor way and thus be rendered quite credible.

But after more than two decades of trying, and failing, to find the necessary "minor amendments", I now believe that the time has come to give up any attempts to define 'existence' away and to recognize that the Cartesians were right on this point as well (see e.g. Arnauld 1662/1964: 66).

Perhaps the only qualification which I would make is that both the noun *existence* (French *existence*) and the verb *to exist* (French *exister*) belong to philosophical, not everyday, vocabulary, and that it is more justified to nominate the expression *there is/are* (in French *il y a*) as the basic lexical exponent of the primitive in question. The point is not trivial, because the difference is not merely stylistic. Apart from stylistic differences, in some contexts, *exist* and *there is/are* may seem to be interchangeable, but in others they are not:

(1) There are no unicorns. ≈
    Unicorns don't exist.

(2) There are no cockroaches here. ≠
    ?Cockroaches don't exist here.

As sentence 2 illustrates, the verb *exist* does not co-occur with a place phrase. It is a verb used to make absolute statements, statements about the world as a whole, or about whole classes of entities rather than about individuals or groups. By contrast, the concept THERE IS (ARE) can apply both to the world as a whole and to specific individuals in specific places:

(3) There are no ghosts (ghosts don't exist).

(4) There are no ghosts in this place
    (?ghosts don't exist in this place).

In accepting THERE IS/ARE as a semantic primitive, and in choosing the English expression *there is/are* (rather than *be* or *exist*) as its primary exponent in English, I am following an idea put forward by Cliff Goddard at the Adelaide Workshop in 1986 (Goddard 1986a). The primitive proposed here corresponds to what Goddard called a "presentative/existential construction".

If the proposed primitive ALL approximates logicians' "universal quantifier", the proposed primitive THERE IS/ARE approximates logicians' "existential quantifier". As we will discuss in detail in Chapter 6, doubts have sometimes been expressed as to the availability of these two concepts in all the languages of the world. While I will leave discussion of the concept ALL for Chapter 6, I would like to suggest here that all languages do in fact have a lexical counterpart of the English *there is/are*. This lexical counterpart may of course be homophonous with the exponents of some other meaning or meanings, but if so, then we can confidently expect some basis for establishing polysemy (such as different grammatical properties linked with the different meanings). For example, in Polish (as in many other languages; see Verhaar, 1966–73) the concept THERE IS/(ARE) is expressed by means of the same verb which (in a different grammatical construction) serves also as a copula.

The hypothesis that all languages have a lexical exponent of the concept THERE IS should not be misconstrued as a claim that every language has an existential verb, or a verb phrase comparable to the English phrase *there is*. For example, in the Austronesian language Tolai (Mosel 1984: 157) 'existence' is expressed by means of the definite article (in a verbless sentence), as in the following examples (C stands for connective particle):

A   kilala-na-mulmulum.
ART season-c-hunger
'There was famine.'

Pata taina, a   tava   parika.
no   salt ART water all
'There was no salt, only water.'

Ma amana   a   vaden parika.
and formerly ART women all
'In former times only women (existed).'

But the fact that in other types of sentence the element *a* means, roughly speaking, 'the' (that is, 'I think you know which one I am talking about') does not invalidate the observation that in verbless sentences of the kind cited above it means 'there is'. Nor does the grammatical status of the element *a* (as a constituent of the noun phrase) disqualify it as a lexical exponent of the primitive THERE IS: there is no reason to expect that this conceptual element should always be lexically encoded as a verb or a verb phrase.

Data from language acquisition are highly relevant in this regard. Far from being a late development, 'existence' (in the sense postulated here as primitive) is in fact one of the first concepts emerging in infants' speech. The clearest early realization of this concept comes in the form of one-word utterances combining 'existence' with negation, such as 'allgone', and, at a later stage, with two-word combinations such as "milk allgone" (Bowerman 1976: 139). From an adult point of view, it might seem that utterances such as "allgone" are even more complex, and that they express 'disappearance' or 'cessation' rather than simply 'there isn't' (Bowerman 1976: 128), but these ('disappearance' and 'cessation') could, arguably, be ideas implicit in the situation as interpreted by the adult. But the meaning of 'non-existence' (i.e. 'there isn't') is clearly there. In any case, whatever the meaning of *allgone* in infancy, contextualized sentences such as "no pocket" (said by Kathryn not finding a pocket in Mommy's shirt, which had no pocket; Bloom 1991: 163) leave little room for doubt.

This clear early emergence of 'non-existence' sentences in child language matches, in an interesting way, clear marking of 'negative existence' in those languages which don't have a verb, or a verbal phrase, for 'there is' as such (such as Tolai; cf. the "no salt" example cited earlier).

I am not suggesting that 'non-existence' ('there isn't') is expressed in child language earlier than 'existence' ('there is'), but only that it is expressed at a very early stage more clearly (because it is not open to

different interpretations). In the speech of 2-year-olds, 'existence' ('there is')
can also be expressed with perfect clarity, as in the sentence of the 26-
month-old Julie Bates (Bates *et al.* 1988: 252):

There's a cleaning lady there.

At an earlier stage, 'there is' is frequently expressed in infants' speech by
means of a two-word combination, with the words *there* or *here* in the initial position; for example: "there book", "there rhino", "there hammer",
"here boat" (Braine 1976: 38). Commenting on utterances of this kind
included in his corpus, Braine notes: "All cases are consistent with the
hypothesis that the pattern "here/there + *X*" was used to show or to draw
attention to things, indicating their presence or existence".

Thus, far from being the philosopher's brain-child, 'existence' (that is,
'there is') is in fact something that "comes out of the mouths of babes and
sucklings".

18.3. LIVE (ALIVE)

> ADULT. Do you think the fire would listen?
> CHILD. No. Fires aren't alive, silly.
>
> (Kuczaj and Daly 1979: 575)

After many attempts, undertaken over the years, to define the concepts of
'life' or 'live' in simpler terms, I have come to the conclusion that all such
attempts are probably futile, and that when medieval philosophers defined
an animal as "vivens sentiens" ('a living thing, a feeling thing') they knew
what they were doing: one cannot define (in simpler terms) the concept of
'living', as one cannot define the concept of 'feeling'.[9] On the other hand,
if we accept that 'life' is a simple, irreducible concept, many other concepts
can be defined in terms of it.

To begin with, there are concepts relating to human age, such as 'old',
'young', or 'child':

These people are old. = These people have lived for a long time.

In English, the word *live* takes also adjuncts which describe places and conditions of life; for example:

These people live in the desert.
When I was young, I lived alone.
For many years, I lived in poverty (in constant pain).

---

[9] Recall also McCawley's (1973: 157) definition "to kill = to cause to become not alive". In
Lingua Mentalis (1980: 168–9) I argued, contra McCawley, that 'dead' is semantically simpler
than 'alive', but I now think that he was closer to the truth, on this point, than I.

It appears, however, that this is not universal. On the other hand, the combination of 'live' with temporal modifiers, as in the sentence

Turtles live for a long time.

appears to be universal.

Second, there are concepts relating to death, such as 'die', 'kill', 'murder', 'agony', 'resurrection', 'immortality', 'reincarnation', 'corpse', 'stillborn', and so on, all referring in their meaning to 'living'. For example:

At this time he died. = at this time something happened to him
before this, he lived (was alive)
after this, he didn't live (wasn't alive)

Third, there are concepts related to the human categorization of the "contents of the world": if all languages distinguish (as far as we know) SOMEONE from SOMETHING, and if they all single out a special category of PEOPLE, most languages distinguish also, in one way or another, living things from non-living things. For example, for English, we could propose the following definitions:

creatures ("animals", in the all-inclusive sense) — living things
these things can feel something
these things can do something

plants — living things
these things can't feel anything
these things can't do anything

machines — things, not living things
people make these things[10]
these things have many parts
when people do something to these things, some of these parts can move

---

[10] In the present system of primitives, "make" is not regarded as a primitive, and so it is used here as a semantic molecule. The relationship between "make" and DO requires further investigation.

	because of this, people can do something with these things
robots	— things, not living things these things are like people these things can do many things these things can do things as if they could think these things can't feel anything

Fourth, there is the mystery of people who are in a coma, on respirators or other artificial life-support systems, and so on. These people don't move, don't do anything, and, as far as we know, don't think, don't feel, don't know, and don't want anything; and yet they are considered "alive". Clearly, from lay people's point of view there is a mystery here: they couldn't explain what they mean by "alive" in such cases, and yet they feel that they somehow know what they mean. In fact, from a scientific point of view, too, a mystery is involved here, a mystery which has exercised the minds of many scientists over centuries. The constantly changing medical criteria of life and death point in the same direction.

Last but not least, in many cultures people talk a great deal about life—the lives of individual people, and human life in general. Life—human life—is one of the main subjects of folk philosophy in a wide variety of cultures. It is difficult to see how this important area of human discourse could be understood if we didn't all have a basic concept of 'living'. To quote just one example of such discourse (from Ecclesiastes 9: 3–5):

3. This is an evil among all things that are done under the sun, that there is one event unto all: yea, also the heart of the sons of men is full of evil, and madness is in their heart while they live, and after that they go to the dead.

4. For to him that is joined to all the living there is hope: for a living dog is better than a dead lion.

5. For the living know that they shall die: but the dead know not any thing, neither have they any more a reward; for the memory of them is forgotten.

The whole range of the universal concept LIVE (ALIVE) as envisaged here can be illustrated with the examples adduced in the recent dictionary of the Australian language Arrernte (Henderson and Dobson 1994), where the word *itethe* is glossed as "1. alive, living" and "2. life". I will only quote the English glosses of the Arrernte sentences:

1. The march fly is a big fly that sucks blood from people and from some other living things.
2. The rainbow snake swallows men, women or children alive.
3. A green tree is one that is still alive.
4. The life of a butterfly (a book title).
5. This is the story of my life.
6. That old man's heart stopped. Those women are thumping (his chest) to bring him back to life.

19. Space: FAR and NEAR, SIDE, INSIDE, HERE

19.1. FAR and NEAR

How could one try to define away the concept of NEAR?

The first temptation would probably be to try to reduce NEAR to FAR, along the lines of "near (close) = not far". But this won't do—if only because NEAR can combine with VERY, whereas "not far" cannot: (very near, very close, *very not far). (One can say, of course, "not very far", but this doesn't mean the same as "very close".)[11]

Another temptation would be to try to represent both NEAR and FAR in terms of a hypothetical primitive "distance" (near = small distance, far = great distance). But "distance" (in an abstract sense, covering both FAR and NEAR) is not a universal concept. We cannot be sure, without serious investigation, whether or not all languages have words for FAR and NEAR; we can be quite sure, however, that we will not find in all languages a word corresponding to *distance*. In fact, even in English *distance* is a fairly technical, learned word, which is not found in the everyday speech of all speakers of English. From the point of view of everyday language, *distance* is an artificial creation, forged (so to speak) on purpose to cover two simple everyday concepts: FAR and NEAR.

Furthermore, the word *distance* is probably chiefly necessary for talking about numbers and measures. But the words *far* and *near* (or *close*) are not concerned, primarily, with numbers and measures. They are fairly vague words, conveying an impression, not an accurate assessment. Consider, for example, the following words from a Christmas carol (Horrobin and Leavers 1990: 47):

---

[11] In some languages, the word for NEAR may look like a combination of negation and the word for FAR (just as the word for BAD may look like a combination of negation and the word for GOOD). It is always possible, however, that combinability tests will show that such a hypothetical 'not-far' word will mean NEAR, rather than NOT + FAR (just as a 'not-good' word may mean BAD rather than NOT + GOOD).

> Be near me, Lord Jesus;
> I ask You to stay
> Close by me for ever
> And love me, I pray.

It seems unlikely that anyone would want to paraphrase phrases like "be near me" and "close by me" via "small distance".

A related point is that both FAR and NEAR appear to embody a certain point of view: normally, "it is far from this place to that other place" rather than "between two places"; by contrast, the word *distance* implies that the speaker is not mentally associated with one place more than with the other, and so one speaks, normally, about the distance "between" two places rather than "from" one place "to" another.

Furthermore, FAR and NEAR appear to suggest a different perspective: while both refer to two places (it is far from *A* to *B*, it is close from *A* to *B*), FAR seems to be more particularly "far from", and NEAR, "near to". Thus, while one can say both:

> Is it far from *A* to *B*?
> ?Is it close from *A* to *B*?

one can only say:

> She lives far from us
> She lives near (to) us,

not

> *She lives far to us.
> *She lives near from us.

It seems, then, that in English at least, FAR has an inherently "ablative" perspective (FAR FROM), and NEAR, an inherently "allative" one (NEAR/CLOSE TO). Furthermore, it seems likely that FAR is, first of all, "far from here" ("far from this place"), whereas NEAR is, first of all, "near to" (see "be near me, Lord Jesus"). This difference in perspective ("ablative" versus "allative") offers additional support for the view that FAR and NEAR cannot be reduced to some unitary concept of 'distance'.

A third possible approach would be to try to reduce both FAR and NEAR to their respective comparatives, along the following lines:

> far = further than one would expect
> near = nearer than one would expect

But how would one then define the comparatives "further" and "nearer"? Presumably, in terms of "greater or smaller distance". But this would bring us back to the solution which we have already considered, and rejected. On the other hand, if we accept FAR and NEAR as semantic primitives, the comparatives can be defined in the same way as all the other comparatives (see Section 16.2).

Finally, why can't FAR be defined via "long"—either as "a long way" or via "a long time"? Aren't the sentences A, B, and C below quite close in meaning?

(A) Is it far from here to Tipperary?
(B) Is it a long way from here to Tipperary?
(C) Would it take a long time to get from here to Tipperary?

But first, the expression "a long way" has, so to speak, an "allative" perspective, not an "ablative" one, as the phrase "a long way to" shows:

It is a long way to Tipperary.
?It is far to Tipperary.

The phrase "a long way to" reflects the point of view of someone who is thinking about the destination, not about the point of departure.

Second, a decomposition of *far* into 'long' and 'way' wouldn't take us very far because it only generates two further questions: what is "long" and what is "way"? Without independent definitions of "long" and "way", even if we managed to convince ourselves that *far* means the same as *a long way*, this could mean only that the expression *a long way* is an unanalysable lexeme (an allolex of *far*).

An analysis of 'far' via 'a long time' cannot be accepted either. Under certain conditions, journeying-time may provide a satisfactory answer to the question "how far?", but generally speaking, the two questions "how far is it?" and "how long would it take to get there?" do not mean the same. For example, the sentence

It would take a long time to get from *A* to *B*.

doesn't really imply that it is far from *A* to *B* (e.g. places *A* and *B* could be separated by mountains). Similarly, the sentence

How far is the sun from the earth?

doesn't mean the same as

How long would it take to get from the earth to the sun?

I conclude, then, that both NEAR and FAR are, in all probability, universal semantic primitives. The fact that in many languages the concept of NEAR appears to play an important role in demonstrative systems provides additional evidence for the importance and "basicness" of this concept.

I would add, however, that by tentatively positing both these elements as primitives I do not mean to suggest that they are fully symmetrical, and, in some sense, perfect "opposites".

In the literature on language acquisition it has often been mentioned that the spatial notion of 'proximity' (see e.g. Johnston 1985: 969) or 'contiguity' (Slobin 1985*a*: 1180) emerges very early in child language; and the terms "proximity" and "contiguity", as well as "beside" (e.g. ibid.), are used interchangeably in those discussions. The generalization that the basic development order of "locative notions" is "in/on" < 'under' < 'beside' (ibid.) is based on research in which the label "beside" represents (for English) a series of expressions including *beside, by, near, next to,* and *close to* (Johnston and Slobin 1979: 534). For Italian, the label 'beside' represents the expression *vicino a,* 'close to' (Clark 1985: 745). This means, however, that what has been described as "the notion 'beside' " may in fact correspond better to the proposed primitive NEAR. On the other hand, given the early emergence and the use of the concept 'near/beside' in child language, the proposed primitive NEAR should perhaps be seen as referring, primarily, to a relation between people and things (*X* is near to/next to *Y*) rather than to a distance between places (like FAR).

Slobin's (1985*a*: 1180) observation that "All crosslinguistic acquisition data point to an initial salience of topological notions of containment, support and contiguity" can perhaps be related to the semantic evidence supporting the notions INSIDE ("containment") and NEAR TO ("contiguity"); and, perhaps, also to a possible primitive 'on' or 'touch' ("support/ surface"), not included in the present system.

19.2. SIDE (ON WHAT SIDE)

The concept of SIDE (suggested as a possible primitive by Goddard, personal communication) is crucial for people's spatial "orientation". A fundamental frame of reference for spatial orientation is provided by the human body, with its basic four sides, organized, conceptually, in the form of two pairs:

(1) on the right-hand side ("on the right side")
   on the left-hand side ("on the left side")

(2) "in front"
   "behind"

For the concepts of 'in front' and 'behind' two alternative analyses (see A and B below) can be proposed, both supported by widespread patterns of polysemy: one based on the concepts of 'face' and 'back' or 'behind' (as names of body parts) and the other based on the concepts of 'before' and 'after':

(A) in front of me = on the same side as my face
   behind me = on the same side as my back/behind

(B) in front of me = on one side of me
> I can see things on this side

behind me = on one side of me
> I can't see things on this side

The idea that the concepts 'front' and 'behind' are based on the notion of 'seeing' is consistent with the finding (Johnston 1985) that "the first uses of *behind* in English refer only to a smaller object totally hidden from view by a larger object" (Slobin 1985*b*: 1180).

Of the two body-centric orientational pairs ("front" versus "back", "on the right" versus "on the left"), the first one, "front" versus "back",[12] appears to play an important role in all languages and cultures, whereas the second one, "on the right" versus "on the left", is more restricted as a frame of orientation (see Levinson and Brown 1992).[13] If it is true, however, that the "body-centric" ideas of 'front' and 'back' are universal, this fact by itself supports Kant's (and Vico's) tenet that the human body provides an important frame of reference for human interpretation of space.[14]

Another important frame of reference is provided by the natural environment, and, in particular, by the sun. On analogy with the four sides of the body, the natural environment, too, appears to be almost universally interpreted in terms of four sides. If in the human body the four sides are distinguished with reference to the right hand and the face, in the natural environment the basic reference-point is provided by the sun.[15] Here, too,

---

[12] To speak of a person's front as a "side" may seem counter-intuitive, even absurd, because with reference to a person's body we normally speak of only two sides: the right side and the left side. But this is due to the polysemy of the word *side* in English. For example, in Polish, the two "sides" of a person's body, that is, the right side and the left side, are called *boki*, whereas *side* as a semantic primitive is expressed by the word *strona* (more precisely: ON SIDE X = PO STRONIE X, where *strona* is used in the locative case, and *po* is a preposition). (For a definition of 'face', see Chapter 7.)

[13] Levinson and Brown (1991) question the importance of the concepts 'in front of' and 'behind' in the conceptualization of space, referring, in particular, to the Australian language Guugu-Yimidhirr: "Instead of notions like 'in front of', 'behind', 'to the left of', 'opposite', etc., which concepts are uncoded in the language, Guugu Yimidhirr speakers must specify locations as (in rough English gloss) 'to the North of', 'to the South of', 'to the East of', etc." However, Haviland's (1979: 179) basic vocabulary list of this language does include a word (in fact, two) glossed as 'in front'.

[14] For a different view, see Levinson and Brown (1992).

[15] The importance of the four sides of the body as a basis for spatial orientation was recently disputed by Levinson and Brown (1992), who write: "Kant was wrong to think that the structure of spatial regions founded on the human frame, and in particular the distinctions based on left and right, are in some sense essential human intuitions." A counter-example to Kant's theory is provided, according to Levinson and Brown, by the Mayan language Tzeltal, of which they say: "It is true that they [the Tenejapans, i.e. the speakers of Tzeltal] have names for the left hand and the right hand, and also a term for hand/arm in general. But they do not generalize the distinction to spatial regions—there is no linguistic expression glossing as 'to the left' or 'on the left-hand side' or the like" (1992: 5). If this statement was accurate then SIDE couldn't be a universal semantic primitive; for if Tzeltal has words for the right hand and the left hand (as Levinson and Brown tell us), and if it also had an expression meaning

the four sides are divided, conceptually, into two pairs. Thus, for "east" and "west" explications along the following lines can be proposed: [16]

the east side = every day people can see the sun on this side
        before they can see it above them
the west side = every day people see the sun on this side
        after they see it above them

Like the four sides of the body, the four sides of the world, too, are widely used as a frame of reference for "orientation". To illustrate (from the Australian language Yir-Yoront; Alpher 1991: 165–6):

An kawrr nhilin.
'she is sitting just to the east here' [just off to your left]

This can be explicated along the following lines (where A refers to the Yir-Yoront sentence, and B, to the English gloss):

(A) every day people can see the sun on one side before they can see it above them
she is sitting on the same side, very near [to here]

'on [this, one, etc.] side of . . .', then presumably there would be no difficulty in putting the two together and constructing expressions meaning 'on the side of the right hand' and 'on the side of the left hand'. I suspect that this indeed is the case, although, needless to say, the matter requires verification. I do not doubt the accuracy or the importance of Levinson and Brown's findings that the concepts of 'right' and 'left' play a relatively minor role in the Tzeltal system of spatial orientation. But perhaps they go too far when they say that in Tzeltal 'right' and 'left' don't have "regional extensions" at all, especially since they themselves produce two Tzeltal sentences glossed as "The man is standing at the woman's right hand" and "The man is standing at her left hand". The interpretation of such sentences suggested by Levinson and Brown along the lines of 'The man is standing NEAR the woman's right hand' (rather than 'ON THE SIDE of the woman's right hand') seems to me unconvincing. One could say that a butterfly was hovering near a woman's right hand but not that a man was standing near her right hand (unless he was a Lilliputian standing on a chair). The two Tzeltal sentences in question bring to mind a line from the Apostles' Creed: "et sedet ad dexteram Patris", 'and is seated at the right hand of the Father'. Surely, the idea is not that Christ is sitting near the right hand of the Father, but that he is sitting near the Father, on his right-hand side. One can imagine a language in which the word for 'nose' is polysemous and means also 'front'. (In fact, Mary Laughren, personal communication, informs me that Warlpiri is a case in point.) In a language like that, to say 'the man was standing in front of the woman' one would have to say something homophonous to 'the man was standing at the nose of the woman'. On this basis, someone might argue that the sentence in question really means 'the man was standing near the nose of the woman'. But would anybody ever want to say a thing like that (speaking of normal-size people, both standing on the ground)? The same, I think, applies to the right hand. I conclude, then, that interesting as the Tzeltal examples may be, there is no reason to regard it as a counter-example to the hypothesis that SIDE (ON SIDE X of Y) is a lexical and semantic universal.

[16] I am not assuming that the words for the "four sides of the world" mean exactly the same in different languages. On the contrary, I expect that the details of the conceptualization—especially for 'north' and 'south'—may well differ from one language, or one group of languages, to another.

(B) your left hand is on one side of you
     she is sitting on the same side, very near [to you]

As this example illustrates, in Australian languages (as in many other languages of the world; see e.g. Levinson and Brown 1991; Haviland 1991),
the natural environment (especially the sun) plays a more important role as
a frame of reference for spatial orientation than it does in English and other
European languages. At the same time, the universal or near-universal divi-
sion of the world into "four sides" (two pairs of two sides) is undoubtedly
modelled on the "four sides" (two plus two) of the human body.

19.3. INSIDE

> You can't see it cause it's way inside.
>
> (from a 2-year-old; Bloom 1991: 384)

The concept of INSIDE (like SIDE, put forward as a possible primitive by
Goddard, personal communication) is relevant to all natural and human-
made "containers". Among the natural "containers", the most salient is
perhaps the mouth, presumably conceptualized all over the world as a part
of the body meant for, roughly speaking, "putting something in" (as well
as speaking; see Chapter 7). But presumably the whole body can be seen,
across cultures, as something INSIDE which there are various interesting
and important "things" (or "parts"). In the natural environment, the concept of INSIDE is clearly relevant to caves and also to animal dwellings:
burrows, tree-holes, nests, and the like. Among the human-made "containers", the most important ones are no doubt human dwellings (houses, huts,
and so on), and also containers for food and drink (pots, cups, bowls, and
so on).

In English, the word *inside* often appears to be interchangeable with in:

    inside the house = in the house
    inside the cave = in the cave
    inside the jar   = in the jar

But this is not always the case, either because a substitution of *inside* for *in*
changes the sense (A) or because the resulting phrase is unacceptable:

(A) in the garden ≠ inside the garden
     in the walls ≠ inside the walls (of the city)
(B) in the milk   ≠ *inside the milk
     in the air   ≠ *inside the air

Clearly, the English preposition *in* (like its closest translation equivalents
in many other languages) is polysemous; and this is not the place to try to
sort out its different meanings. *Inside*, too, has more than one meaning:

(1) People don't know what happens inside a volcano.
(2) I was inside when it happened.
(3) I went inside.
(4) Outside China, people don't talk about it much, but inside the country, people don't seem to be talking about anything else.

Inside$_4$ (as in sentence 4) has a contrastive meaning, built upon the notion of 'outside' (inside$_4$ = not outside). *Inside$_2$* is adverbial and refers specifically to a 'dwelling' (human or animal). *Inside$_3$* is directional and refers to a sequence of times (roughly: before I moved, I was not inside$_1$ the dwelling; after I moved, I was inside$_1$ it). *Inside$_1$*, however, appears to be indefinable. ("Outside" is not a candidate for a primitive, as it is clearly composed of INSIDE and NOT: outside X = not inside$_1$ X.)

As mentioned earlier, the prepositions *in*, *on*, and *under* (and their closest equivalents in other languages) emerge particularly early in child language, and in a particular order (*in* $\rightarrow$ *on* $\rightarrow$ *under*; Johnston and Slobin 1979; Slobin 1985*a*); and cognitive development has often been linked with the order of acquisition of locative prepositions. For example, Mills (1985: 237) writes: "If prepositions are classified according to the complexity of the conceptual relationships encoded in them, the resulting order of complexity could predict the order of acquisition . . . this classification will predict, for example, that the preposition expressing the notion 'in' will be learned before that expressing 'between'." But it is not clear what exactly is meant here by "the notion 'in' ". As mentioned earlier, *in* is a polysemous word and if one simply counts the occurrence of *in* in child language, one cannot be sure what concept or concepts are being expressed. For example, in the phrase *in the cup*, *in* means 'inside', but in the phrase *in this place*, *in* is only a part of the phrase *in a place* (which as a whole means 'somewhere').

It is possible that the data on the early use of the preposition *in* in English conflate the use of two different semantic primitives in child language, both supported by independent evidence: the early emergence of *where*-questions (see e.g. Ervin-Tripp 1970; Tyack and Ingram 1977) and the early comprehension of the preposition *inside* (see Bates *et al.* 1988: 190). For example, in a sentence such as "I no make duty in the potty!" (Bloom 1991: 198), *in* presumably means 'inside'. On the other hand, if a child takes his guinea-pig home from school "cause they don't belong in school" (Bloom 1991: 385), it is likely that *in* means 'where' rather than 'inside'.

I presume that Slobin's (1985*a*: 1180) observation (quoted earlier) about the initial salience of "the notion of containment" refers to the notion INSIDE, not to the notion PLACE.

19.4. HERE

HERE is a spatial counterpart of NOW, more of which will be said later (Section 20.2). Both these elements were put forward as possible primitives by Cliff Goddard (personal communication). On the face of it, 'here' is not a semantic primitive, because it seems to be clearly decomposable into 'this' and 'place', along the following lines: "here = in this place". The fact that in many languages (e.g. in Samoan; see Mosel 1994: 339) the three concepts 'here', 'now', and 'this' share the same lexical exponent appears to support this analysis.

But if we identify 'here' with 'this place', then we cannot use the expression 'this place' in explications with reference to any other place that we may wish to talk about (for example, "this other place"). On the other hand, if we tried to link the concept of 'here' more tightly with the concept of 'I' as "the place where I am", this would solve some difficulties but it would create others. For example, if I refer to two small objects lying in my open hand, such as two rings, as "this one here" and "this one", the phrase "this one here" can hardly mean 'the one which is in the place where I am'.

The problems which arise in the attempts to decompose HERE are similar to those which arise in the case of NOW. In both cases, the conclusion suggests itself that in fact the attempts at decomposition are futile, and that HERE and NOW are semantically simple, as the "deictic substantives" I and YOU are simple. (For further discussion, see Section 20.2.)

20. Time: A LONG TIME, A SHORT TIME, NOW

20.1. A LONG TIME and A SHORT TIME

Having once tried to reduce all temporal concepts to non-temporal ones, (Wierzbicka 1972, 1980), to have three temporal primitives (WHEN, AFTER, and BEFORE) seems a lot, and yet over the years it has become increasingly clear that even this set is not sufficient to deal with all the aspects of time. In particular, it is not sufficient to deal with duration and, more generally, "passage of time". Simple sentences such as:

> I did it for a long time.
> It happened a long time ago.

could simply not be paraphrased in terms of the available temporal concepts; and yet sentences of this kind appear to be very common in everyday discourse, in all languages. As Keesing (1994: 6) notes about the Kwaio, "Talk about the passage of time (in reference to how long garden work will be done, or when the pork will be cooked, or how long someone will be gone) is, for the Kwaio as with us, a constant theme of quotidian experience and communication." So finally it became clear that, in addition to the three basic "temporal" primitives WHEN, AFTER, and BEFORE, something else was needed to account for the "passage of time"; and the answer came in the form of two "duration" primitives, A LONG TIME and A SHORT TIME, analogous to the two "distance" primitives FAR and NEAR.

By introducing these two primitives, I am following, once more, in the footsteps of the Cartesians, who regarded both "time" (*temps*, presumably, in the sense of 'when', although they never bothered to make it clear) and "duration" (*durée*) as irreducible, clear ideas, which cannot be further defined. (See e.g. Arnauld 1662/1964: 66, 86.)

Since we aim always at a minimal set of primitives, it would be preferable, of course, to introduce one "durational" primitive rather than two, and, at first sight, this does seem possible: why not posit a neutral primitive, "some time", and then generate the meanings 'a long time' and 'a short time' by combining this neutral primitive with the available elements MUCH and NOT MUCH?

But there are strong arguments against such a move. First of all, experience and preliminary inquiries suggest that languages are more likely to have words, or phrases, for the concepts A LONG TIME and A SHORT TIME than for the putative concept "some time".

Having two "extreme" durational primitives rather than a single one covering the whole range may seem to create unnecessary difficulties in the area of measures. For example, how could one analyse in these terms a question such as "How long was he there?"?

But the semantics of measures is notoriously complex. In everyday discourse across cultures people are no doubt more likely to ask: "was he there (for) a long time?" than "how long was he there?"; and it would be wrong to treat the latter question as semantically simpler than the former.

Can all "durational" concepts be explicated in terms of the primitives A LONG TIME and A SHORT TIME? I do not claim that. It seems likely that some concepts which might be called "durational" would call for a different approach. For example, very tentatively:

> He did it from sunrise to sunset. =
> (Cf. He did it all day.)
>   he didn't do it before the sunrise
>   he didn't do it after the sunset
>   he did it at all times
>   after the sunrise before the sunset

But I do not think that we can explicate all references to time without some explicitly durational primitives, such as the two primitives proposed here: A LONG TIME and A SHORT TIME.

It should, however, be pointed out that of the two primitives proposed here one (A LONG TIME) is a stronger candidate than the other (A SHORT TIME). Unlike in the case of NEAR and FAR, there are perhaps no compelling arguments against an analysis of one primitive via the negation of the other (a short time = not a long time).

If we consider, for example, references to 'a short time' in transcripts of children's speech, they commonly take the form of the expression "for a little while", or "a little bit", and these could perhaps be paraphrased, without a loss of meaning, via "not long". For example (French and Nelson 1985: 106–7):

First I wake up and wake my mom and dad up then sleep with them for a little while.

And we wait for a little while, but not too long, then we go back in the school and play.

... and we go and wait for a little while and then the waiter comes and gives us the little stuff with the dinners on it, and then we wait for a little bit ...

On the other hand, it is not clear how words such as *moment* or expressions such as *at once* could be defined via negation and 'a long time'.

In a cross-cultural perspective, too, the evidence is mixed. Preliminary investigations suggest that finding matching equivalents for "a short time" is not as unproblematic as it is for "a long time". But the matter requires further investigation.

20.2. NOW

Another temporal concept, NOW, first proposed as a semantic primitive by Cliff Goddard at the Adelaide Semantic Workshop (Goddard 1986*a*), belongs to the "deictic" subset of the primitives, which includes also the "substantive" elements I and YOU, the "determiner" THIS, and the spatial element HERE. For a long time, this element was not included in the proposed set of primitives because it seemed to be decomposable into other primitives. In fact, there seemed to be not one but two plausible ways of decomposing 'now', which for ease of reference I will designate as A and B:

  (A) now = at this time
  (B) now = at the time when I say this

The fact that, as mentioned earlier, in some languages (e.g. in Samoan; see Mosel 1994: 332) the same word is used not only for 'this' and 'here' but also for 'now' appears to support this analysis.

As pointed out by Goddard, however, neither of these two analyses is really satisfactory.

Analysis A makes it very difficult, if not impossible, to refer to more than one time as 'this time'. For example, if we say in a semantic formula:

this happened a long time ago
at this time . . .

it is not clear whether the expression "at this time" refers to the time of reference or to the time of speech, and it seems impossible to differentiate between the two. Given that *ago* means 'before now', if *now* meant 'at this time', *ago* would mean 'before this time', and one couldn't refer to a time 'before this time' as 'this time'.

This particular difficulty is resolved in analysis B, where "the time when I saw this" can be clearly distinguished from "a time before the time when I saw this". But as pointed out by Goddard, the word *now* can be used, and is normally used, with reference to a period much longer than the moment of speech (cf. e.g. the English expression *nowadays*). Furthermore, the three tenses distinguished in many languages of the world, present, past, and future, are normally used with reference to a period much more extensive, or extendible, than the very moment of speech. For example, if I say:

I now live in Canberra, but before, I lived in Ballarat in Victoria.

I do not mean to suggest that I have moved to Canberra immediately before the moment of speech.

The hypothesis that NOW is in fact a universal semantic primitive simplifies enormously semantic analysis of the various tense systems and allows us to operate with very simple distinctions such as "now", "before now", "after now", "a long time before now", "before now, not a long time before now", and so on. At the same time, this hypothesis frees the expression "this time" from its links with the present time and allows us to use it freely with reference to any time that we wish to speak about.

What may seem objectionable about the present analysis is that it would present the word *now* and the expression *this time* as semantically unrelated, and would not allow us to account explicitly for the "deictic" nature of the concept 'now'. But the same objection could be raised with respect to I and YOU, both primitives of long-standing and apparently unshakeable status; and it would fall on the same grounds: I and YOU, too, have often been called "deictic concepts" and they do have a semantic link with the expression "this person", but this link is not compositional. If neither I nor YOU can be equated with "this person", NOW cannot be equated with "this time"; and if I and YOU cannot be equated with "the person who says this" and "the person to whom I say this", respectively, NOW cannot be equated with "the time when I say this".

21. Imagination and Possibility: IF ... WOULD, CAN, MAYBE

21.1. IF ...WOULD

If you would have eated all that turkey, your tummy would have ker-sploded.

(a remark by a 4-year-old; Kuczaj and Daly 1979: 575)

The discontinuous expression *if . . . would* can be used in English in two different senses (and in two different grammatical frames): as a hypothetical referring to a real possibility or as a counterfactual, as in the motto to this section. It is this second, not the first, use which is posited here as a universal semantic primitive. The hypothetical *if . . . would* can be defined in terms of 'if', as follows:

If *X* happened, I would do *Y*. =
if *X* happens, I will do *Y*
I don't say: I think: it will happen

But the counterfactual *if . . . would* cannot be similarly defined; and preliminary evidence suggests that the counterfactual *if . . . would* (in contrast to the hypothetical *if . . . would*) may well be a linguistic universal. (See Wierzbicka, forthcoming *g*.)

In English, and in many other languages, the counterfactual (*if . . . would*) overlaps formally with the conditional (*if*). In many other languages, however, the two elements in question do have distinct lexical exponents. For example, in Samoan the word for IF (the IF of real possibility) is *afai*, whereas the word for the counterfactual IF ... WOULD is *'ana* (Mosel and Hovdhaugen 1992: 656; GENR stands for general tense-aspect mood particle, DIR for directional particle and ES for ergative suffix):

(1) *'Ana* 'e lē sau, semanū 'ou te alu atu.
    if(irr.) 2.SG not come, probably 1.SG GENR go DIR
    'Had you not come, I was probably going to go and see you.'

(2) *Afai* ua lapoa se   puaa, *o le a* fana = ina loa
    if   PERF large ART(NSP.SG.) pig FUT   shoot = ES then
    ma faatau atu l = o = na   tino. . .
    and sell   DIR ART = POSS = 3.SG body
    'If a pig gets fat, then it will be shot and its body will be sold . . .'

A lexical overlap analogous to the English one occurs also in the Australian language Yankunytjatjara (Goddard 1994*b*: 249), where the word *tjinguru* by itself (used in a biclausal sentence) means IF, whereas the same word combined with a "potential" inflexion on the main verb of the main clause means IF . . . WOULD (Goddard's numbers):

(65) *Tjinguṟu-la wiyampa   iluma.*
     if-we   NO:INTEREST   die:POT
     If we'd been without (a radio) we would've died.

(66) *Ka   nyuntu tjinguṟu tjukurpa titjatjara*
     and you   if   story   long.ago:ASSOC:HAVING
     nyakula   kulintjikitja   mukuringkula, nyiri
     see:SERIAL   think:INTENT   want:SERIAL   paper
     pala palunya nyawa.
     that DEF:ACC see:IMP
     'So if you want to read Old Testament stories, look at that book.'

Both the elements IF and IF. . .WOULD are, so to speak, descendants of the notion 'imagine', posited as a primitive in *Semantic Primitives* (Wierzbicka 1972). The main reason why the mental predicate 'imagine' was later removed from the list was that as a predicate, it proved not to be universal. On the other hand, the interclausal linker IF emerged as both indefinable and universal (see Chapter 6), and for a long time it seemed that the notion of IF would be sufficient to account for the meanings associated, loosely speaking, with the area of imagination and "irrealis". Despite continued efforts, however, it has proved impossible to reduce counterfactual sentences to conditional ones. For example, the sentence

     If I were you I wouldn't do it.

cannot be adequately paraphrased along the lines of

     If I am you I will not do it.

As Tim Curnow (personal communication) pointed out, by virtue of their meaning, IF sentences put forward a real possibility, whereas IF. . . WOULD sentences allow for the impossible, and so one type cannot be used to paraphrase the other (without a change of meaning).

This is why no additional components disclaiming the reality of the supposed condition can make a paraphrase of IF . . . WOULD in terms of IF work. For example:

     If I were you I wouldn't go. ≠
         I am not saying that I am you
         if I am you I will go

     If I were the sun I would shine only for you.[17] ≠
         I know that I am not the sun
         I know that I can't be the sun

---

[17] The words from a Chopin song.

if I am the sun, I will shine only for you

Clearly, paraphrases of this kind do not make sense. (For further discussion, see Wierzbicka forthcoming *g*.)

Julian Evans (1993: 243) writes this, sardonically, about the Marshallese people of Micronesia:

There is something missing, some path in the mental process, an awareness of the conditional, an ability to envisage consequences, the conditional intelligence that motivates imagination, speculation, the control of the future. If this is right, if the Marshallese don't possess the ability to say 'what if . . .' or 'if . . . then . . .', then they and the Americans who have succeeded in treating them as children for so long must be made for each other.

Cross-linguistic evidence suggests that "an awareness of the conditional", an ability to say 'what if . . .' or 'if . . . then. . .', is indeed a human universal. I submit that "an awareness of the counterfactual", an ability to say 'had this not happened, that wouldn't have happened', may also be a human universal, a vital path in the human mental process, an indispensable element of human language and cognition. (See Landman 1993: 37.)

21.2. CAN and MAYBE

Can't.

(2-year-old unable to get out of large pot; Fletcher 1979: 280)

CAN and MAYBE are awkward primitives to posit because they seem to be inextricably linked. In many languages they share the same lexical exponents; for example in Polish, the word *może* can mean either MAYBE or CAN.

(1) Może   on to zrobi.
    maybe he it will-do
    'maybe he will do it'

(2) On to może   zrobić.
    he it can (3rd sg) do
    'he can do it'

The particle *może* means MAYBE; but the verb *móc* (infinitive) can mean either MAYBE or CAN (and there is no other word meaning only CAN). Yet the two meanings are clearly distinct, and can even co-occur in the same sentence:

Ona nie może tego zrobić, może ktoś   inny może
she Neg can this do,   maybe someone else can
'she can't do this; maybe someone else can'

Similarly, in English:

ADULT. What would happen if people were fish?
CHILD. Then if a whale came, they would get eated. But if they hided, the whale maybe couldn't find 'em. And, then they wouldn't get eated.

(Kuczaj and Daly 1979: 573)

The fact that, despite lexical overlaps, the concept MAYBE is realized in both English and Polish as a particle, whereas the concept CAN is realized as an "auxiliary" verb, is not accidental: it appears that MAYBE tends to be realized, in most languages, as a sentence particle, whereas CAN tends to be realized either as a quasi-verb or as a verbal suffix. An interesting example is provided again by Yankunytjatjara (Goddard 1994*b*: 248), where MAYBE is realized as a sentence particle *tjinguru* whereas CAN is expressed by the verbal inflexion *-ku* (which, Goddard notes, is frequently found in sentences also containing *tjinguru*. Goddard's numbers):

(62) Ma-pitja-ku-<u>na</u>?
 away-come-FUT-I
 'Can I come in?'

(63) Punkal-ku-n.
 fall-FUT-you
 'You could fall.'

In the list of primitives tested in *Semantic and Lexical Universals* (Goddard and Wierzbicka 1994*b*), the elements distinguished here as CAN and MAYBE were in fact regarded as variants of one primitive referred to as CAN. Further work in this area has shown, however, that it is necessary to split this supposed primitive into two.

The main argument in favour of the two separate primitives MAYBE and CAN is that neither of them can be adequately decomposed in terms of the other, or in terms of anything else. If anybody doubts this, I would invite them to have a go at a reductive analysis of the following sentences:

(1) I can't do it now; maybe someone else can.
(2) I can't do it here; maybe I can do it somewhere else.
(3) You can't see it now; maybe you can see it later.
(4) I can't say it is far, I can't say it is near.

The ideas of 'cannot' and 'can' reflect the fundamental human experiences of constraint and freedom from constraint. Perhaps the prototypical use of these ideas is in the context of movement:

I can't move/I can move.

(perhaps an archetypal experience of a baby, tightly held, or wrapped up, and then given the freedom to move).

I can't do it/I can do it.

Social rules also rely on the notion of CAN:

> You can't do this.
> You can't say this.
> You can't do it like this.
> You can't do things like this.
> You can do it like this.

Perhaps this is the crucial difference between moral rules, which are based on the concept of GOOD and BAD, and social rules, which are based on the concept of CAN.

Complex ideas such as 'power', 'rules', 'freedom', 'opportunity', 'ability', and 'skill' could never be explained and understood if we didn't have the concept of CAN at our disposal.

It could be suggested that CAN is linked in a special way with 'wanting'—so much so that one may even be tempted to explicate one in terms of the other (as I did in Wierzbicka 1989c: 318–19). For example:

> God can do everything. =
> If God wants to do something, he does it.

or, alternatively:

> If God wants to do something, he will do it.

An analysis along these lines seems also to have the virtue of accounting for the intuitively felt link between CAN and IF (as J. L. Austin (1961: 153) put it, "cans are iffy"). But neither of the above two paraphrases is really satisfactory, as neither of them conveys the intended idea of "omnipotence".

Consider also sentences such as the following ones:

> Her stomach cannot digest fatty foods.
> After we built a dam here, the water couldn't flow in this direction any more.

which can hardly be paraphrased in terms of WANT:

> When her stomach wants to digest fatty foods it does not do it.
> When the water wants to flow in this direction it doesn't do it.

We are forced to conclude, therefore, that while CAN is a pre-condition of doing what one wants to do, it cannot be simply reduced to it.

Turning now to the notion of MAYBE, we will note that it has nothing to do with 'power', 'rules', 'freedom', or 'wanting'. If CAN is related in a special (non-compositional) way to WANTING, MAYBE is related in a special (non-compositional) way to KNOWING (or rather, not knowing). One can't say, for example:

*I know she will come, but maybe she will not come.
*I know she will not come, but maybe she will come.

Nevertheless, MAYBE cannot be reduced to KNOW (or NOT KNOW) any more than CAN can be reduced to WANT. The sentence "maybe he did it" implies that "I don't know whether he did it", but cannot be reduced to it.

In a sense, then, the notions CAN and MAYBE can be regarded as clear and indispensable. On the other hand, in many contexts the distinction between these two concepts appears to be blurred. For example:

This can break.
Something bad could happen to them.
Bad things can happen to everybody.
They can't know about this.

In terms of the traditional distinction between 'possibility' and 'ability' the sentences above would no doubt be linked with 'possibility'; but it is difficult to see how these sentences could be paraphrased (without a change of meaning) with MAYBE and without CAN.

In earlier work (Wierzbicka 1972), I tried to account for the semantic links between CAN sentences with personal subjects (such as "I can move/do/see/hear/say") and those with inanimate subjects (e.g. "this can break", "something bad can happen") in terms of a "hidden" personal predicate, along the following lines:

This can break = I can think: this will break.

(A similar analysis was also proposed by Antinucci and Parisi 1976.) But I no longer regard this analysis as valid. To begin with, one could equally well try to 'recover' a hidden 'think' in all other CAN sentences:

I can't do it. = I can't think: I will do it.
I can't move. = I can't think: I will move.

But this is counter-intuitive and unconvincing, and sometimes can lead to absurd results:

God can do everything. = I can think: God will do everything.

Undoubtedly, the distinction between CAN and MAYBE in sentences with inanimate subjects requires further investigation. But in sentences with human subjects the distinction between these two concepts seems well established, despite the facts that both CAN sentences and MAYBE sentences can be paraphrased (approximately) in terms of 'possibility':

Maybe she will do it.   ≈ It is possible that she will do it.
God can do everything. ≈ Everything is possible for God.

To account for the fact that, on the face of it, two concepts posited as distinct and irreducible semantic primitives can both be replaced with one concept of 'possibility', I would suggest that the notion of 'possibility' is more complex than either MAYBE or CAN, and, in a sense, spans over both of them, rather like the abstract notion of 'distance' spans over both FAR and NEAR, or the notion of 'size' spans over both BIG and SMALL. The analogy is not perfect because FAR and NEAR, or BIG and SMALL, are intuitively felt to be 'opposites', whereas CAN and MAYBE are related in some other way. But maybe even this imperfect analogy can help us to accept that, related as they are, MAYBE and CAN may none the less be two distinct and irreducible semantic primitives.

It should also be pointed out that while the concepts CAN and MAYBE often share their lexical exponents (in different grammatical forms), this is by no means universal. (See for example the contrast between the verb *können,* 'can', and the particle/adverb *vielleicht,* 'maybe', in German). Recurring lexical overlaps are a common feature of many primitives (e.g. SOMEONE and OTHER, or MAYBE and IF), and while they are clearly not accidental, there is no reason to assume that they must be due to compositional semantics. (For discussion, see Wierzbicka 1994*b*.)

22. WORD

The concept of WORD (or 'words') may seem redundant in the lexicon of semantic primitives because it is intuitively related to the concept of SAY: a deed is something that one does, a word is something that one says.

But the analogy between "word" and "deed" is only partially valid: while one can indeed "say" a word, or some words, one can also say something "in" some words—in these words or in some other words. (In fact, this is what semantic analysis is all about: ways of saying the same thing in other words.)

Generally speaking, we can talk about speech (about "saying" things) without a reference to "words"; in some cases, however, a reference to "words" appears to be essential to the intended meaning, as the following contrast illustrates:

(A) You said something bad about this person.
(B) You said some bad words to this person.

Sentence A can refer to a criticism, whereas sentence B is more likely to refer to some swear-words.

The notion of "swear-words" is a good example of the apparent indispensability of the concept 'words': one cannot "swear" without saying what is regarded in a given society as some "bad words" (for a fuller discussion of "swearing", see Wierzbicka 1987*a*).

Other categories of speech which appear to involve crucially the notion of 'word' include names, counting performative verbs (e.g. *promise*), speech formulae (e.g. *Goodbye*), and magical formulae (see Goddard forthcoming *a*) . For example, a "name" is a word (or words) generally used to identify someone or something; "counting" involves saying a word that means 'one', after that a word that means 'two', then a word that means 'three', and so on; magical speech involves saying certain words to cause certain things to happen, and so on. (These are of course not full definitions, but only partial characterizations of the phenomena in question.)

"In the beginning was the word" (John 1: 1). Distant as this sentence is from normal everyday life, Bible translators seem to find less difficulty in translating it into numerous languages of the world than many much more prosaic and down-to-earth sentences (see e.g. Nida 1947). If the concepts BEFORE, ALL, SOMETHING, OTHER, HAPPEN, THERE IS, NOW, SOMEONE, SAY, and WORD are all universal human concepts, the relatively easy cross-translatability of this sentence would be easy to understand:

> BEFORE NOW
> BEFORE ALL THINGS HAPPENED
> THERE WAS A WORD (or: SOMEONE SAID A WORD)

23. General Discussion: Opposites and Converses

The present system of semantic primitives may seem uneconomical in so far as it includes some pairs of "opposites". To begin with, there is the pair of evaluators GOOD and BAD, the oldest and the best-established one. Although these two elements have, intuitively, something in common, I have rejected the temptation to extract from them some semantic common core ("value"), and to distinguish the two as a "positive" and a "negative" member of the pair. Rather, I have assumed that concepts such as 'value', 'positive', and 'negative' are more complex than the basic elements GOOD and BAD, and that although these two elements do form a coherent mini-system apart from all the other elements, none the less none of them can be further decomposed.

In addition to GOOD and BAD, the present system of primitives includes now two (and possibly three) further pairs of "opposites": BIG and SMALL, and FAR and NEAR (and possibly also A LONG TIME and A SHORT TIME). Aiming at a minimal system of primitives one must be tempted, of course, to reduce such elements further, extracting for each pair a common core, and positing for all pairs two "poles": + POL and − POL (along the lines suggested by Bierwisch 1967). One could try, then, to reduce BIG and SMALL to "size", FAR and NEAR to "distance", and A

LONG TIME and A SHORT TIME to "duration", with the addition of the two recurring features "+ POL" and "– POL".

Following this line of analysis, we would be able to account, in compositional terms, for the fact that within each pair the "+ POL" can stand for both members of the pair:

> How big is it? — Very big/very small.
> How far is it? — Very far/very near.
> How long? — A very long time/a very short time.

But attractive as such an analysis may seem, it has to be rejected—if we require that the basic units of semantic analysis are linked with "real (intelligible) words" rather than with analytical fictions, which have no meaning unless and until they are defined in terms of intuitively intelligible real words. In real (natural) languages there are simply no such words as "+ POL" or "– POL". In real speech, therefore, we cannot paraphrase a sentence such as "This dog is big" with something like "The size of this dog is + POL".

It might be suggested, of course, that the artificial words "+ POL" and "– POL" could be replaced with the "real" words *big* and *small*, along the following lines:

far — big distance
near — small distance

But this would be analogous to saying that *big* really means 'big size', and *small*, 'small size'. In fact, 'size' is not a simpler concept than 'big' or 'small', but a more complex one, and so it is 'size' which has to be defined in terms of 'big' and 'small', not vice versa. Similarly, it is not 'far' which should be defined in terms of 'distance', or 'good', in terms of 'value', but the other way around.

In natural language we simply cannot go beyond words such as *far* and *near*, as we cannot go beyond *good* and *bad*. Replacing *good* and *bad* with "positive value" and "negative value" we would engage in pseudo-analysis, not in real semantic decomposition; and the same applies to attempts to replace *big* and *small* with "size", or *far* and *near* with "distance".

In saying this, I am not denying the reality of the structural relations within the area of "opposites". On the contrary, I would like to add one further observation highlighting the close affinity between the two members of each pair, namely that within each pair of "opposites" both members appear to have similar combinatorial possibilities. Since this is an observation concerning all the pairs of "opposites", it provides also a further argument for the reality of this group as a distinct subsystem within the whole system of primitives.

In arguing that the relations between the "opposites" within each pair are not compositional (that is, that they cannot be accounted for in terms of further definitions), I argue that these "opposites" are more deeply ingrained in human cognition than they would be if they were reducible to some other elements. It is well known that "opposites" play an important role in all known human languages (see e.g. Apresjan 1974, 1992; Cruse 1986; John Lyons 1977; Lehrer 1974). I am suggesting that this is not a surface phenomenon but something that is rooted in the underlying system of primitives.

What applies to "opposites" applies also to some extent to converses: BEFORE and AFTER, and possibly to ABOVE and UNDER. The system of primitives would be more economical if each pair of converses were replaced with just one element, because from a logical point of view "*A* happened before *B*" is equivalent to "*B* happened after *A*", and "*A* is above *B*" is equivalent to "*B* is under *A*".

But a natural language has its own ("natural") logic, and in this "natural logic" BEFORE and AFTER, or ABOVE and UNDER, are not mutually equivalent. In both pairs, each element is linked with one particular point of view, and in human communication a difference in point of view may be as important as a difference between two predicates. For example, while both past tenses and future tenses situate events in time with reference to the present moment, past tenses do so in terms of the concept BEFORE, whereas future tenses do so in terms of the concept AFTER:

(A) It happened before now.
(B) It will happen after now.

24. Conclusion

The set of proposed universal semantic primitives has expanded from 14 (in 1972) and 13 (in 1977) to 37 in 1993, and now—dramatically—to 55. The question imposes itself: how many more primitives (or hypothetical primitives) are likely to emerge from future work?

For once, I feel that humble agnosticism is in order. I would like to recall, however, that when Bogusławski launched the search for semantic primitives in 1965, he mentioned the figure 100 ("almost certainly less than a hundred", he said, as I recall). Although I still expect that the ultimate figure will be closer to 50 than to 100, I now acknowledge that (as argued by Goddard at the 1986 Adelaide Workshop), my original sets of 14 and 13 were quite unrealistically small.

As the set of primitives expands, and as their grammar takes shape, the Natural Semantic Metalanguage grows in flexibility and in expressive power. In principle, then, the expansion of the semantic system is a positive, not a negative, development.

Looking at the expanded list of primitives and comparing it with the older one, one is bound to notice that the new list is less austere not only in its size but also in its composition.

The new spatial elements, of which there are as many as five (ON [THIS] SIDE, INSIDE, HERE, FAR, and NEAR), bring the set of primitives down to earth (from its previous heights of abstraction). At the same time, the element THERE IS links the system more closely to reality, as do also the new "deictic" elements HERE and NOW.

The paired opposites FAR–NEAR, and A LONG TIME–A SHORT TIME, strengthen the element of subjectivity and add an anthropocentric, experiential perspective (as do the old primitives BIG and SMALL).

SEE and HEAR bring colour and sounds to the system, and, if I may venture to say so, MOVE brings movement, and ALIVE brings life. MAYBE brings an element of uncertainty, linked with a human, psychological perspective (quite different from the logical perspective of "possible"), and IF ... WOULD brings, or rather restores, the element of fantasy, which was once brought to the system by the ex-primitive "imagine".

All in all, then, the changes can be seen as being all for the better. It must be remembered, however, that—quite apart from the obvious requirements of Occam's razor—we are looking for the shared lexical and grammatical core of all languages; and that given the tremendous diversity of languages as we know them, this shared core is bound to be small. It is imperative, therefore, to continue to subject every proposed primitive, and every proposed grammatical frame, to relentless scrutiny, so that only those remain which are truly indispensable and truly universal.

3 Universal Grammar: The Syntax of Universal Semantic Primitives

1. Introduction

Most grammatical patterns in any language are language-specific, but there may also be some patterns which are universal. In fact, if cross-cultural understanding is possible at all, despite the colossal variation in language structures, there must be a common core of "human understanding" relying not only on some shared or matching lexical items but also on some shared or matching grammatical patterns in which shared lexical items can be used. Arguably, this common core defines a set of "basic sentences" which can be said in any language, and which can be matched across language boundaries, and the grammar of these basic sentences consists in the possible distribution patterns of the "atomic elements" (that is, the lexical indefinables). To discover those patterns we have to look at the lexical indefinables themselves, to see what their possibilities of co-occurrence are. Therefore, in searching for universal grammatical patterns, we should not be looking for universals of form, but rather for universals of combinability. This chapter is a tentative and preliminary attempt to do just that.

Trying to write a sketch grammar of the universal semantic primitives is a daunting task.

First of all, such a grammar must make a large number of predictions concerning all the languages of the world. These predictions can be empirically tested, and it is highly likely, not to say inevitable, that upon further testing some of them will turn out to be incorrect.

Second, this grammar amounts to a hypothesis about the innate grammar of human cognition. As a hypothesis about human cognition, the system developed here is not as readily testable as it is as a hypothesis about linguistic universals. Exploration of linguistic evidence may prove to be, at least for some time, the main avenue of access to the grammar of human cognition. But no matter how difficult it may be to verify—or to falsify—

This chapter owes a great deal to long discussions with Cliff Goddard, who has contributed to it many important ideas. Cliff's criticisms and suggestions led to a substantial revision of the earlier draft.

the hypothesis about human cognition advanced here, the questions raised are disconcertingly heavyweight.

Third, this grammar has to be seen as the "real" grammar of NSM, the language of semantic description. It is proposed, therefore, as a set of constraints on NSM explications and paraphrases. These constraints will not always be adhered to in practice, but they will always have to be kept in mind, so that any departures from the rules of combinatorial semantics outlined here will be allowed only as short-cuts and compromises justified by practical considerations such as increased brevity or readability.

It hardly needs to be added that the word "always" in the last paragraph is not meant to preclude future changes in the proposed system. Despite the present attempt at codification, many areas of NSM grammar are still in a state of flux. The grammar proposed here is neither complete nor "final". It is put forward as a starting-point for testing and discussion.[1]

2. Preliminary Discussion

Before turning to the survey of primitives and their combinatorial possibilities, a number of general points should be made.

First, the grammar outlined below assumes a radically expanded set of primitives (55 instead of 37 as in Goddard and Wierzbicka 1994*b*). Since the status of some of the new primitives is still somewhat uncertain, so is, of course, the status of their grammatical characteristics.

Second, the meta-terminology of NSM grammar is still evolving. Terms such as "valency", "linkers", "subject", "object", "complement", and "adjunct" are used in the present chapter on a somewhat provisional basis. Hopefully, however, for the present purposes their intended meaning will be clear enough.

Third, this chapter makes an extensive use of a new theoretical concept: "valency of semantic primitives". For example, it is assumed that the predicate GOOD has two different valency options: it may combine with one "substantive" (which may be called a "subject"), as in sentence A below, or with two "substantives" (a "subject" and a "complement"), as in sentence B:

(A) This is good.
(B) This is good for me/you/these people.

---

[1] Strict adherence to the rules of NSM syntax, as sketched in this chapter, is not always desirable, as long as all the departures from the NSM rules can be regarded as convenient abbreviations, that is, as long as we have a clear idea of how the "ungrammatical" or "semi-grammatical" segments of the explications could be replaced with fully "grammatical" ones.

Some predicates—for example DO and THINK—may even open three "slots" for "substantives" (a first slot for a "subject", a second, for a "complement", and a third, for an "object"):

> someone (1) did something (2) to someone (3)
> someone (1) thought something (2) about something (3)

But although both DO and THINK can be said to open three slots, their valency options are different: DO has two valency options (A and B) whereas THINK has three (A, B, and C):

DO
(A) someone did something
(B) someone did something to someone

THINK
(A) someone thought something
(B) someone thought something about something
(C) someone thought about something

Fourth, it should be pointed out that the grammar sketched in this chapter allows for several types of complex sentences, and thus goes far beyond simple clauses offered as examples of NSM sentences in earlier work (e.g. in my *Lingua Mentalis* (1980) or *Semantics of Grammar* (1988)). A key role belongs in this respect to the primitives which function, or can function, as "interclausal linkers": BECAUSE, IF, IF . . . WOULD, LIKE, WHEN, AFTER, and BEFORE. These linkers provide a mechanism for combining two or even three clauses into one complex sentence.

Finally, the theoretical concept of "allolexy" (analogous to "allomorphy") should be mentioned here, too, for although it is not a new concept in NSM theory, it is one which raises important questions for NSM grammar. For example, the account of the combinatorial possibilities of the primitives SOMEONE and SOMETHING proposed here depends on the assumptions that in English, *person* (in some of its uses) can be seen as an allolex of SOMEONE, and *thing* (in some of its uses), as an allolex of SOMETHING.

3. Substantives: YOU, I; SOMEONE, PEOPLE; SOMETHING

3.1. YOU and I

YOU and I have a wide range of universal syntactic roles. Perhaps the most important one among them is the role of "psychological subject". What I mean by this is that YOU and I can universally occur in combination with the mental predicates THINK, KNOW, WANT, FEEL, SEE, and HEAR:

> I think/know/want/feel/see/hear.
> You think/know/want/feel/see/hear.

This is not to say that there are no restrictions on these combinations. In particular, in some languages (e.g. in Japanese, see e.g. Inoue 1979; or in Hua, see Haiman 1995), only I can freely co-occur with mental predicates in declarative sentences, whereas YOU normally combines with them only in questions (and third person subjects require the presence of special "evidential" markers, highlighting the limited character of our knowledge of other people's internal states).

YOU and I can also universally occur in combination with the action predicate DO, in a role which may be conveniently labelled as that of an "agent", for example:

> You/I did something bad.

They can also occur in the role of a "mover", in combination with the predicate MOVE:

> You/I moved.

Next, YOU and I can combine with the predicates of description and evaluation, as in the following sentences:

> You are a good/bad person.
> I am a bad/good person.

YOU and I can be used in the role of either of the arguments of a "relation" in relational sentences such as the following ones:

> You are like this other person/me.
> I am like other people/you.

They can also co-occur with spatial (though not with temporal) predicate phrases:

> I am in this place; you are in another place.
> I am under this thing; you are above this other person.
> I am here; you are here.
> I am far from you.

Furthermore, YOU and I occur as "patients" in combination with the universal predicates HAPPEN and DO, for example:

> Something bad happened to me/you.
> This person did something bad to me.

In combination with SAY, they can also occur in the role of an "addressee":

This person said something to me/you.

Finally, YOU and I can be used in the role of a "psychological object" in sentences such as the following ones:

I think about you.
This person knows everything about you/me.

3.2. SOMEONE and PEOPLE

By and large, SOMEONE and PEOPLE have the same combinatorial possibilities as YOU and I:

This person/these people think(s)/know(s)/want(s)/feel(s), see(s)/hear(s) something.
Someone did something (bad) to this person/these people.
Something bad happened to this person/these people.
This person/these people moved.
I said something to this person/these people.
This person is a good/bad person.
These people are good/bad people.
This person is (not) like other people.
These people are (not) like other people.
This person is in another place.
These people are in this place.
I think about this person/these people.

None the less, there are some systematic differences between YOU and I on the one hand, and SOMEONE and PEOPLE on the other. Apart from the restrictions on combinability with mental predicates mentioned earlier, SOMEONE and PEOPLE, in contrast to YOU and I, can co-occur with a wide range of "determiners", for example:

this person/these people (*this I, *this you)
the same person, the same people (*the same I/you)
another person, other people (*another you/I)
one person (*one I, ?one you)
two persons, two people (*two I-s)
many persons, many people (*many I-s)
all (these) persons, all people (*all I-s)

The reason why YOU and I, on the whole, don't combine with "determiners" and "quantifiers" whereas SOMEONE and PEOPLE do is of course clear, given the uniqueness of every "I" and every "thou" (YOU-Sg), and the non-uniqueness of "persons" and "people".[2]

It should be noted that in many languages the basic word for SOME-ONE doesn't readily combine with "determiners" either. For example, in English one doesn't normally speak of *this someone*, *one someone*, or the *same someone*; and in Russian the phrase *ètot kto-to* ('this someone') is even less acceptable than its English counterpart. Usually, however, SOMEONE has allolexes which can readily combine with determiners (e.g. *person* in English); and of course words more complex than SOMEONE (but including SOMEONE in their meaning) are widely used in combination with determiners (e.g. *this man*).

Perhaps the main reason for the awkwardness of expressions such as "this someone" lies in the fact that their meaning is usually encoded in a special portmanteau, that is, in the third person pronouns such as *he* and *she* in English. The fact that most languages have such portmanteaus (sometimes with, and sometimes without, an added reference to gender) highlights the importance of the combination of THIS and SOMEONE in human discourse.

Do both SOMEONE and PEOPLE combine with all the elements included here in the list of "determiners" and "quantifiers"? I would suggest that while both these elements combine with THIS, THE SAME, OTHER, TWO, SOME, MANY, and ALL, perhaps only SOMEONE combines with ONE (as in *one person*). In fact (as mentioned earlier), English itself provides a good example of the asymmetry between PEOPLE (plural) and its non-existent singular equivalent (with the word *person* not being as strictly restricted to humans as the word *people* is). (See Chapter 2.)

What I am suggesting, then, is that perhaps the semantic element PEO-PLE doesn't really combine with the "determiner/quantifier" ONE, or rather, that it can only combine with ONE in the "partitive" (or "selective") valency option ONE OF:

*one people (in the relevant sense of *people*)
one of these people

Finally, while YOU and I, as well as SOMEONE and PEOPLE, can be described as "good" or "bad" (e.g. "you are good"), only the latter pair can combine with these evaluators as attributes:

someone good/someone bad (a good person/a bad person)
good people/bad people

---

[2] The range of quantifiers with which YOU (that is, THOU) combines, may be different from that of I. The matter requires further investigation.

3.3. SOMETHING

SOMETHING (with an allolex "thing") has a wide, and, one might add, remarkably heterogeneous, range of syntactic roles. There is a large overlap with the roles of SOMEONE, but not all the roles of SOMEONE are equally applicable to SOMETHING, and some roles of SOMETHING are not applicable to SOMEONE at all. Normally, SOMETHING doesn't occur in the roles of a psychological subject:

?This thing wants (*thinks) something.

an agent:

?This thing did something.

or an addressee:

?I said this to this thing.

but under certain circumstances it can appear (at least semi-felicitously) in all these roles. (This applies, in particular, to animals and human collectives.)

In addition, SOMETHING (thing) can occur in the role of a "patient" or a "mover":

You did this to this thing.
Something happened to this thing.
This thing moved.

It can also occur as a "subject" of evaluation, description, relation, or location:

This thing is good/bad.
This thing is big/small.
This thing is like this other thing.
This thing is under/above all these other things.
This thing is on the other side.
This thing is far (from this place).

Unlike YOU and I, but like SOMEONE, SOMETHING can also be combined with an attribute:

something good/bad (a good/bad thing)
something big/small (a big/small thing)

Furthermore, SOMETHING—like SOMEONE—can combine with a wide range of determiners (with the same allolexic restrictions as SOMEONE):

this thing; another thing (someone else); the same thing; one thing
two things; many things; few things; all things (everything)

But perhaps the most important, and unique, role of SOMETHING is that of a complement, covering the range of a "psychological complement", a "speech complement", an "action complement", and an "event complement":

I want/know/think/feel/see/hear/something.
I said something.
I did something.
Something happened to me.

4. Mental Predicates: THINK, KNOW, WANT, FEEL, SEE, HEAR

Mental predicates (THINK, KNOW, WANT, FEEL, SEE, and HEAR) combine, first of all, with "psychological subjects" (I, YOU, SOMEONE, PEOPLE):

I/you think/know/want/feel/see/hear (something).
Someone thinks/knows/wants/feels/sees/hears (something).
People think/know/want/feel/see/hear (something).

Furthermore, they all take a "psychological complement" (SOME-THING, THIS), for example:

You want something.
This person knows this.
These people feel something bad.
I see/hear something.

The range of possible "complements" is no doubt different in each case. For THINK and KNOW, the complement slot is likely to be filled by a whole proposition (e.g. "I think that. . . .", "I know that . . ."). For THINK, it can also be filled by direct discourse (e.g. "I thought: gee! how strange!"). For WANT, the most likely complement probably takes the form of an "equi-clause" (e.g. "I wanted to go"), and in any case, even if the "complement" slot is filled by a "substantive" (THIS or SOME-THING), this "substantive" has to stand for a proposition (since sentences such as "I want an apple" have to be interpreted as an abbreviated form of sentences about having or getting an object, "I want to have/get an apple").

SEE differs from the other mental predicates in its ability to take SOME-ONE and PEOPLE in its "complement" slot, and also to combine with a place adjunct:

I saw someone.
You saw many people.
I see someone in this place.

(In English the verb *hear*, too, has these combinatorial possibilities, but this is unlikely to be universal.)

Perhaps the least clear of all is the semantic syntax of FEEL. In many languages (including English), sentences with FEEL and "complements" such as *something* or *this* are not fully acceptable. In English, sentences such as "I feel good", "I feel bad", and "I feel like this" sound of course better than "I feel something like this". The syntax and semantics of FEEL sentences in other languages require careful investigation before any firm hypotheses concerning the combinatorial possibilities of FEEL can be confidently put forward.

In addition to the "complements", some mental predicates open a slot for what we might call a "psychological topic"; for example: "to think about something" and "to know about something". These "psychological topics" can co-occur with the "psychological complements" "to think something about something", "to know something about something". (It is by no means clear, however, that in all languages the exponents of THINK and KNOW have as many as three different slots; the picture presented here is at this stage only a matter of conjecture.)

In the explications of various emotion concepts, I have often used the phrase "to feel something (good or bad) towards someone", which seems very useful in modelling similarities and differences between different emotion terms (see e.g. Wierzbicka 1992*e*). One can doubt, however, whether FEEL really has such a valency. It is more probable that both FEEL and WANT have, universally, only two slots: "psychological subject" and "psychological complement" (e.g. 'I want something', "I don't feel anything").

Finally, it must be noted that all mental predicates have also a time slot ("at that time, I thought/knew/wanted/felt/saw/heard . . ."), although the exact range of possibilities may be in each case different.

5. Speech: SAY

The primitive SAY occupies, one might say, an intermediate place between mental predicates and the action predicate DO. In a sense, "saying something" can be seen as a form of "doing something", and so the "subject" of SAYING can be seen as an agent. Since, however, SAYING can also be done in one's head, the "subject" of SAYING can also be seen as a "psychological subject", analogous to the "subject" of THINK or WANT.

Like DO, SAY has also an obligatory slot for a "complement": one "says something", as one "does something". (Mental predicates, too, have a slot for a "complement", but not necessarily an obligatory one; see e.g. "I thought about you".) For example:

You said something.
I said this.
This person said the same.
If you say one word . . .

There is also an obligatory time slot (though not a place slot). In fact, SAY-ING, like DOING, requires a fairly specific location in time (whereas mental predicates can have a more indefinite time span).

Importantly, SAY opens a slot for an addressee. I have often argued (against, for example, Ross 1970 or McCawley 1973) that SAY doesn't necessarily presuppose an addressee (see e.g. Wierzbicka 1976*a*, 1980), and I stand by this. But while there is no obligatory addressee slot, there is certainly an optional one. Thus, while the sentence

And God said: let there be light! (Genesis 1: 3)

is not elliptical for "God said to someone: let there be light!", the sentence

The angel said to her: "Don't be afraid, Mary"

cannot be analysed into a "monotransitive SAY" and something else, along the lines:[3]

The angel said something; the angel wanted Mary to hear this.

While it may be true that "saying something TO someone" implies wanting that person to hear what we are saying, this doesn't differentiate the addressee from other people whom the speaker may also want to hear the message. For example, one can say:

He said it to Mary, not to me, but I know that he wanted me to hear it.

This means that just as DO has two irreducible valency options (DO and DO TO), so has SAY (SAY and SAY TO).

In fact, I would suggest that SAY has one extra valency option (a third one), realized in English in the frame of SAY ABOUT, as in the sentence

I want to say something about these people.

By analogy to the "psychological topic" of THINK and KNOW, realized in English in the ABOUT frame (THINK ABOUT, KNOW ABOUT), the slot opened by the SAY ABOUT frame could be called (for convenience) the "locutionary topic". Like the addressee slot, the "locutionary topic" slot is optional.

---

[3] As I have proposed in Wierzbicka (1976*a*).

6. Actions, Events, and Movement: DO, HAPPEN, MOVE

6.1. DO

Obviously, the action predicate (DO) opens, universally, an "agent" slot:

I/you/someone/people did (something).

As the illustrative sentence above suggests, it opens also a slot for an "action complement":

I did something (bad).
You did this.
I did the same.

Clearly, there is also an (obligatory) time slot:

At that time, I/you did this.

as well as an (optional) place slot:

I did it in the same place.

The difference between the time and place slots is that time is relevant to all DO sentences, whereas place is relevant only to some of them. (Sentences with mental predicates do have a time slot, but they don't have place slots at all.)

What is perhaps less clear about the semantic syntax of DO is the presence of a "patient" slot. In earlier publications (see e.g. Wierzbicka 1981) I attempted to analyse sentences such as "This person did something (bad) to me" via "do" and "happen to", along the following lines:

This person did something bad to me. =
this person did something (bad)
because of this, something bad happened to me (at the same time)

I have come to recognize, however, that (as argued in Bogusławski 1991) this kind of analysis is untenable, if only because "DO TO" sentences view the situation as a single event, whereas a "DO + HAPPEN TO" sentence views the situation as two causally linked events.[4]

I cannot accept, however, Bogusławski's further suggestion that DO and DO TO are two different semantic primitives. Since the alleged two elements DO and DO TO appear to be realized, universally, by means of the same lexical exponents, I think it is more justified to conclude that they represent two different valency options of the same primitive; and that

---

[4] This is a point that Nick Enfield rightly insisted upon during a seminar discussion at the ANU, thus helping to clarify the difference between DO TO and DO + HAPPEN TO.

"patient" is an additional (optional) syntactic slot in the structure of DO sentences.

Finally, I foreshadowed in Chapter 1 the possibility of yet another valency option for DO, namely, an "instrumental option" DO WITH ("someone did something with something"), as in the following sentences:

> This person did this with one hand.
> This person did this with something of this kind (a knife, a hammer, a boomerang, etc.).

At this stage, however, this valency option is proposed only very tentatively.

6.2. HAPPEN

Turning to the element HAPPEN, we find a similar valency structure except for the absence of an "agent" (and an "instrument") slot and for the central position of the "patient" role. The "patient slot" of HAPPEN TO sentences (e.g. "something bad happened to me") corresponds to the optional "patient" slot in DO sentences (e.g. "you did something bad to me"). An obligatory "event complement" (e.g. something/this/the same happened to me) corresponds to the "action complement" in DO sentences (e.g. "I did something/this/the same"). The time slot is inherent in both DO and HAPPEN sentences (e.g. "at that time, I did the same", "at that time, the same happened to me"). Both DO and HAPPEN sentences have also place slots (e.g. "I did it in this place", "something happened to me in this place").

But in HAPPEN sentences, a place slot can also be an alternative to the "patient" slot. In a "patientless" sentence such as

> Something bad happened in this place.

the phrase "in this place" is an alternative to a "patient phrase" (e.g. "to me"), rather than an adjunct (as in "something happened to me in this place"). This means that just as the element DO has two alternative patterns, A and B:

(A) X did something
(B) X did something to Y

the element HAPPEN, too, has two alternative patterns (C and D):

(C) something happened to X
(D) something happened in place P

6.3. MOVE

MOVE occurs as a predicate in combination with all the substantives:

> I/you/someone/something/this moved.
> These two people moved.

It is possible that MOVE can also occur, universally, in combination with place (WHERE):

> Something is moving over there.
> Something moved here.

Possibly, this additional slot (the WHERE slot) is available only in sentences with an "indefinite" substantive, above all, with SOMETHING.

In an earlier draft of this chapter (distributed to the participants of the 1994 Canberra Symposium on the Universal Syntax of Meaning) I have suggested that MOVE can combine with "direction" (TOWARDS), as in the following sentence:

> The dog was running towards me.
> They were going south.
> She turned right.
> She was walking away from me.

It is quite impossible to paraphrase such sentences in a way which would dissociate "direction" from "movement". In fact, the two notions ("movement" and "direction") appear to be linked so closely that I have even suggested that MOVE and MOVE TOWARDS should perhaps be considered as two valency options of the same concept (rather like DO and DO TO, or SAY and SAY TO).

But cross-linguistic evidence does not support this suggestion. In many languages (including Polish) the verb corresponding to the proposed primitive MOVE does not combine with directional elements like *towards*, although more complex verbs of movement (such as 'go' and 'come') do. Clearly, the matter requires further investigation—as does also one further possible valency option of MOVE, discussed at the Semantics Symposium in Canberra in 1994: "person X moved body-part Y".

7. Existence and Life: BE (THERE IS/ARE) and LIVE

7.1. BE

The predicate BE co-occurs with the "substantives" SOMETHING, SOMEONE, and PEOPLE, and with the "classifiers" KIND and PART, usually in combination with some further determiners and frequently with a locational phrase. It is doubtful whether, for example, the Cartesian "sum", 'I am', 'I exist' (in "Cogito ergo sum") could be satisfactorily rendered, and make sense, in all the languages of the world.

Existential sentences which can be expected in all cultures include probably the following kinds:

There are three kinds of bat.
There is no such thing (as this).
There are many people like that (of this kind).
There are no trees in this place.
There is a lot of water here.
There is no water here.
There is someone in the garden.

As mentioned in Chapter 2, sentences of this kind do not have to include any "existential verb" and they may convey their existential meaning in different ways, but it can be expected that some lexico-grammatical means for conveying that meaning will always be available.

Sometimes, existence may seem difficult to distinguish from location (to be SOMEWHERE), and often BE and WHERE share their lexical exponents (see e.g. J. Lyons 1977, ii. 723a; Clark 1970):

(A) There are two people in the garden.
(B) (Where is everyone?)
    Two people are in the garden (and three in the house next door).

But the very fact that existence and location can co-occur (as in the sentence: "there is a lot of water here") shows that they are not different aspects of the same notion, and I would hypothesize that, despite overlaps, in all languages the two concepts in question can be overtly distinguished.

It should be noted, however, that (despite the abundant literature on the subject) the relationship between existence and location requires a great deal of further study.

7.2. LIVE (ALIVE)

LIVE is a very recent addition to the set of primitives, and at this stage little is known about its grammar. One could venture to say, however, that it is a predicate, and that it opens a slot or slots for temporal adjuncts:

These people lived for a long time.
These two people lived at the same time.
This person was alive at that time.

It would appear that for the purposes of classification, LIVE can also be used without any adjuncts:

These things are living things (= live?).

On the other hand, co-occurrence of LIVE with spatial adjuncts is probably not universal, although two separate types of sentences need to be distinguished here: those referring to temporary residence (e.g. "I live in Canberra") and those referring to permanent living conditions (e.g. "Fish live in water"). The use of the exponents of LIVE in the first of these types is certainly not universal; their use in the second type requires further investigation.

8. Determiners and Quantifiers; THIS, THE SAME, OTHER; ONE, TWO, MANY (MUCH), SOME, ALL

8.1. THIS

THIS has a wide range of roles, because it has, so to speak, a double class membership: it can function as both a "determiner" and a "substantive". (Sometimes two different forms have to be used in these two different roles, e.g. *kore* (substantive) and *kono* (determiner) in Japanese, but as I have argued in Wierzbicka (1991*b*), these two forms can be regarded as two allolexes of the same semantic primitive.)

As a "substantive", THIS can occur in the role of a "subject" of evaluation, description, relation, or location (that is, as an "evaluatum", "descriptum", "relatum", or "locatum"):

This is good/bad.
This is big/small.
This is like this other thing.
This is above/under this other thing.
This is not in the same place.

Like all the other "substantives", THIS can also occur in the "patient" role:

Something bad happened to this.

Like one other "substantive", SOMETHING, it can also occur as a "complement": with DO, HAPPEN, and SAY, and with at least four mental predicates (KNOW, WANT, SEE, and HEAR):

I did this/this happened to me.
I said this/I know this/I want this/I see this/I hear this.

It can also occur in a "predicate nominal" role in relational sentences:

All these other things are under/above/inside this.
All these things are like this.

At the same time, THIS can occur in the role of a "determiner" in combination with other "substantives": this thing, this person, these people, (in) this place, (at) this time, this kind, this part.

Furthermore, THIS can combine with some of the other "determiners", notably with OTHER, ONE, TWO, and ALL: this other person, this one person, these two people, all these people. It can also combine with the element LIKE, forming with it a quasi-determiner "like this", e.g. someone like this, something like this. "Like this" is an important semantic molecule, often realized as a single portmanteau morpheme like *so* (or *such*) in English. This molecule can combine with all the "opposites" in the semantic system: so good, so bad; so big, so small; so far, so close; so long, such a short time.

8.2. THE SAME

The universal syntax of THE SAME is not clear at this stage. It appears, however, that it can, universally, function as a "determiner" and can combine with the "substantives" SOMETHING, SOMEONE, and PEOPLE (though not with YOU or I):

the same person; the same people; *the same you; *the same I

It can also combine with "place" and "time":

at the same time; in the same place

and with the classifiers:

the same part; the same kind

It is also likely that THE SAME can, universally, play the role of a "complement", and so function as a quasi-substantive, for example:

I did the same/I said the same.
I thought/wanted/felt/(?)knew the same.
The same happened to me.

Like THIS, it can also occur in the role of a "psychological topic":

I thought about the same.

Last but not least, it should be said that presumably in all languages THE SAME can be used not only anaphorically but also cataphorically, and that in the latter case it opens a syntactic slot for the second member of the equation: THE SAME AS. For example:

I did the same as you.
This thing is of the same kind as this other thing.

8.3. OTHER

OTHER, unlike THE SAME, occurs only in the role of a "determiner":

> another person (someone else); another thing (something else); other
> people
> (in) another place; (at) another time
> another part; another kind

Possibly, OTHER—like THE SAME—opens a syntactic slot for an intended reference-point:

> I want something of another kind than this.
> anybody other than me
> I don't want to do it in a place other than this.

At this stage, I know of no evidence suggesting that this is—or is not—universal.

8.4. Quantifiers: ONE, TWO, MANY (MUCH), SOME, ALL

This subgroup of "determiners", which could all be called "quantifiers", combines, first of all, with the substantives SOMEONE (person) and SOMETHING (thing):

> one person, two persons, many persons, some persons, all persons
> (everybody)
> one thing, two things, many things, some things, all things (everything)

All the quantifiers except ONE combine also readily with PEOPLE:

> two people, many people, some people, all people
> *one people

Less commonly, but also quite readily, the quantifiers combine also with the primitives KIND, TIME, PLACE, and PART:

> one kind, two kinds, many kinds, all kinds
> (at) one time, (at) two times, (at) many times (often), (at) all times
> (always)
> (in) one place, (in) two places, (in) many places, (in) all places (everywhere)
> one part, two parts, many parts, all parts

In some languages, for example in Samoan (see Mosel 1994), quantifiers behave syntactically as verbs, but apparently in these languages, too, they can also function as "determiners" and "modifiers", as postulated here.

One question which requires testing is whether some of the quantifiers have, universally, a valency option associated with subsets:[5]

one/two/many of these people

It should also be asked whether some elements in the group under consideration can perhaps occur in the role of an independent "complement" (without supporting "substantives" or "quasi-substantives"). This applies in particular to MUCH and ALL. For example:

I didn't say much.
This person knows all about it.

It could be argued that sentences of this kind are elliptical (and that, for example, *much* stands here for "many things", and so on), but I doubt that a claim of this kind could be justified.

A final question which I would like to raise here for consideration is how phrases such as "one of these people" or "two (some, many) of these people" should be interpreted. My present suggestion is that in phrases of this kind we should see another valency option of the quantifiers. Just as the predicate DO has an additional valency option DO TO, SAY an additional valency option SAY TO, and GOOD an additional valency option GOOD FOR, the quantifiers appear to have an additional valency option linking a fraction of a set with the set as a whole.

A closely related point concerns phrases such as "some of it" or "much of it", and the contrast between the acceptable "some of it", "much of it" and the unacceptable *one of it, *two of it. Presumably, what this contrast shows is the inherent "countability" of ONE and TWO: while the other quantifiers can be vague with respect to countability, ONE and TWO, naturally enough, cannot.

9. Augmentor: MORE

The element MORE can combine with the substantives *people, someone,* and *something*:

more people/more persons/more things

It can also occur in the position of a verbal complement, in combination with the predicates *know, see, hear* (and possibly with some others):

I want to know/see/hear more.

[5] This valency was proposed, some time ago, by Cliff Goddard (in an earlier draft of Goddard 1995). At the time, I argued against that idea (mainly because at that time the notion of "semantic valency" had no place in the NSM theory); but now this idea strikes me as plausible and worth testing.

Like the "determiners" OTHER and THE SAME, MORE may (perhaps) open a slot for a complement of its own, for example:

more than two things of the same kind

Apparently, MORE can also combine with several determiners:

much more, one more, two more

10.　Evaluators: GOOD and BAD

Perhaps the central role of the evaluators GOOD and BAD is that of "attributes":

someone good/bad (a good/bad person)
something good/bad (a good/bad thing)
good/bad people

(Whether or not, or to what extent, such an attributive use can be extended to times, places, parts, and kinds remains to be investigated.)

It is not entirely clear whether GOOD and BAD can be used (in non-elliptical sentences) as predicates, as in:

You are good.
This is good.

or whether such sentences should be regarded as non-elliptical versions of sentences with attributive phrases:[6]

You are a good person.
This is a good thing.

It appears, however, that at least in some contexts GOOD and BAD *can* be used predicatively; in particular, that they can be so used with respect to "clausal subjects":

If someone does something like this, this is bad/good.

Perhaps the most interesting question which arises in connection with the evaluators is that concerning the relation between GOOD and GOOD FOR or between BAD and BAD FOR. My suggestion is that GOOD and GOOD FOR represent two different valency options of the same primitive (just like DO and DO TO or SAY and SAY TO do). Admittedly, one could try to reduce GOOD FOR to GOOD along the following lines:

This was good for me. =
because of this, something good happened to me

---

[6] This matter was brought to my attention by Nick Enfield (personal communication).

But I don't think that this analysis is valid. From a moral point of view, it may be important to distinguish something that is "good for a person" from "something good that has happened to a person". For example, for many moral teachers it may be important to be able to say things such as:

When something bad happens to you, it may be good for you.
If good things always happen to a person it may be bad for that person.

A language which wouldn't be capable of expressing such ideas could be regarded as impoverished, and we can hypothesize that all languages are capable of expressing them.

11. Descriptors: BIG and SMALL

The descriptors BIG and SMALL have, primarily, an "attributive" role:

(a) big/small thing (see also: something big)
(a) big/small person (see also: someone big)
big/small people
(a) big/small place
(a) big/small part

On the face of it, they can also be used predicatively; for example:

These people are big/small.

As in the case of GOOD and BAD, however, it is not clear whether such a "predicative" use should not be regarded as a crypto-attributive use:

These people are big/small people.

Sentences such as:

This is big/small.

may or may not be universally available, but even if they were, a case could perhaps be made for regarding them as elliptical, since the very notions of BIG and SMALL imply a reference to some standard of comparison.

12. Time: WHEN, AFTER, BEFORE, A LONG TIME, A SHORT TIME, NOW

WHEN (or AT A TIME) can be used, above all, as a "clause adjunct". It is obligatory in DO, HAPPEN, and MOVE sentences, and possibly in SAY sentences:

At that time, you did something.
At the same time, something happened to me.
At some other time, this thing moved.
At that time, I said something to this person.

To some extent, temporal adjuncts can no doubt also combine with mental predicates:

At that time, I thought that he was a good person.
At that time, I wanted to do it.
At that time, I felt something bad.
At that time, I didn't know anything about it.
At that time, I saw/heard something.

But the exact nature, and extent, of these co-occurrences requires further investigation.

In many languages, the exponent of WHEN can also be used in a biclausal construction, in which it functions as an interclausal linker (cf. Chapter 2):

When I did these things, I felt something bad.

It can be argued, however (as suggested by Goddard, personal communication), that when used as an interclausal linker, the English word *when*, and its counterparts in other languages, stand not just for the primitive WHEN (i.e. AT A TIME) but for a semantic molecule combining WHEN and THIS:

At some time before now, I did these things.
At this time, I felt something bad.

The element NOW cannot serve as an interclausal linker, and it cannot take "determiners" (compare, for example, *at this time* versus **this now*, and *at the same time* versus **the same now*), but otherwise the syntax of NOW appears to be similar to the syntax of WHEN: NOW can combine with the mental predicates, with DO, HAPPEN, MOVE, and LIVE, with spatial predicates, and so on. For example:

I now think/know/want/feel/see/hear/say . . .
This person is moving now.
These people live now.

The elements BEFORE and AFTER can perhaps be regarded as special modifiers (determiners) of time adjuncts, comparable to the universal determiner THE SAME:

at the same time; before this time; after this time

In past and future tenses, the elements BEFORE and AFTER are combined semantically with the element NOW ('before now', 'after now'). But if the basic temporal element WHEN (AT A TIME) operates, primarily, as a clause adjunct, the two time "modifiers" BEFORE and AFTER, which serve to establish the temporal sequence of two events, are often used as clause linkers (because the two events in question may well be referred to in different clauses). For example:

> You were born before I was born.
> I was born after you were born.
> Something bad happened after you did this.
> This happened before I saw you.

Cross-linguistically, however, the most common use of the element AFTER is probably in a narrative, where phrases meaning 'after this' ("and then") are used to introduce a new event. It is likely that BEFORE, too, is used primarily in combination with THIS ("before this"). It is important to note, however, that in phrases such as "after this" and "before this", "this" has to refer to the content of an entire clause.

Turning now to the two durational concepts A LONG TIME and A SHORT TIME, we will note that they combine, first of all, with the predicates DO, HAPPEN, MOVE, and LIVE, and also with all the mental predicates:

> I was doing it for a long time.
> It happened a long time ago.
> I felt something bad for a short time.
> He lived for a long time.

13. Space: WHERE; FAR, NEAR; UNDER, ABOVE; SIDE; INSIDE; HERE

13.1. WHERE and HERE

Like WHEN, WHERE (IN A PLACE), too, can be a clause adjunct, but the range of predicates with which it co-occurs is of course different: essentially, it co-occurs only with HAPPEN and DO (and possibly MOVE and SEE):

> It happened in this place.
> I did it in another place.
> Something moved in this place.

Sentences with mental predicates do not have a place slot, except perhaps for SEE. Sentences such as:

?I thought/knew/wanted it in another place.

if acceptable at all, must be regarded as elliptical. As far as FEEL is concerned, the situation is unclear.

The relation between SEE and WHERE (IN A PLACE), too, is at this stage far from clear. Can sentences such as

I see something over there.

be reduced to a combination of sentences about seeing and sentences about existence and location, along the lines of

I see something
this something is over there
(there is something over there)?

It could be argued that they cannot. For example, an oasis that I can see in the distance may be simply a mirage (and so may not be there at all, in the place where I see it), and an apparition which someone can see in a place may not be really there. (Recall Berkeley's (1713) point that the sentence "I see a silver speck in the sky" doesn't imply that "there is" a silver speck in the sky.)

Unlike WHEN phrases, however, WHERE phrases can also be predicates in their own right (as BE IN A PLACE or BE SOMEWHERE). For example:

This thing is in this place.
I know where it is.
I was somewhere else.

As predicates, WHERE phrases can be combined with all the "substantives" (YOU, I, SOMEONE, SOMETHING, PEOPLE, and THIS).

Finally, the syntax of HERE appears to be similar to that of WHERE, as the syntax of NOW is similar to the syntax of WHEN. Naturally, HERE (like NOW) does not combine with "determiners" (*in another place* versus *another here*). In contrast to the relationship between NOW and WHEN, however, the two spatial primitives can sometimes co-occur, as in the phrase "somewhere here". Like WHERE, HERE can also be used predicatively, as BE HERE. For example:

I am here.

13.2. FAR and NEAR

At first sight, the concept of "distance" ('how far?') appears to be parallel to the temporal concept of "duration" ('for how long?'). In fact, it could even be argued that the two represent two different faces of the same concept: "distance in space" and "distance in time". I would reject such an argument, however, because the notion of "distance" is, in my view, inherently spatial, and phrases such as "distance in time" are metaphorical.

Furthermore, while it could be argued that the idea of "boundaries" manifested in syntactic frames such as "from–to" is relevant to both "distance" and "duration",

(A) I did it for a long time (from 9 to 5).
(B) It is very far (from this place to this other place).

it should be pointed out that the "from–to" frame plays a different role in each case. In fact, the notion of FAR is inseparable from that of "from–to"; but the notion of A LONG TIME does make sense even without any explicit or implicit reference to "boundaries":

I did it for a long time (never mind from when to when).
It is far away (?never mind from where to where).

I submit, then, that the idea of "distance" (FAR and NEAR) makes sense only with reference to two specific places, whereas the idea of "duration" (A LONG/SHORT TIME) does not have to refer to two specific times. Consequently, the "from–to" syntactic frame (or an alternative frame discussed below) is obligatory in (non-elliptical) sentences about distance, but only optional in (non-elliptical) sentences about duration.

The alternative frame mentioned above takes in English the form of the preposition *from*, without an accompanying *to*; for example:

This thing is too far from me—I can't reach it.
You are too far from me—come closer.

What I am suggesting, in effect, is that while the predicate FAR always requires two reference-points, these reference-points don't have to be places, but can also be people or things:

(A) (It) is far from place *A* to place *B*.
(B) Thing/person *A* is far from thing/person *B*.

For example, I suggest that when we say of an object that it is long, what we mean is that (what is conceptualized as) the first part of this object is far from (what is conceptualized as) its last part. In other words, I suggest that perhaps we conceptualize length in terms of a distance between things (parts) rather than between places.

13.3. UNDER and ABOVE

Turning now to UNDER and ABOVE phrases we will note that at first sight they may seem to be similar in their functioning to the temporal modifiers BEFORE and AFTER. If the latter are to be interpreted as modifiers of the temporal notion AT A TIME (WHEN), the former can be seen as modifiers of the spatial notion IN A PLACE (WHERE):

This thing is under/above this other thing. =
this thing is in the place under/above this other thing

This interpretation, however, is not without some problems. To begin with, if we want to say that, for example,

The sky is above everything.

do we mean that the sky is in a place above everything? Or if we want to say that

The head is above all the other parts of a person's body.

do we mean that the head is in a place [which is] above the places where all the other parts of a person's body are? An interpretation along these lines seems counter-intuitive. It may be more justified, therefore, to regard UNDER and ABOVE as relational, rather than strictly locational, notions.

This approach would also solve another problem, namely that of the metaphorical application of the concept ABOVE (if not UNDER) to people (with reference to their status, position, power, and so on). It is quite likely that the metaphorical use of the notion ABOVE with reference to people is universal, and that, for example, the idea that God is "above all people" can be rendered, and be understood, in all languages (see Wierzbicka forthcoming *b*). But this metaphor would make little sense if it were to be interpreted in terms of places. It is true that "heaven" (God's place) is, metaphorically speaking, a place which is "above" the earth (people's place). But the metaphor of "heaven" is distinct from the metaphor of "father"; and the latter has clearly to do with the relation between God and people, and not between two places.

13.4. SIDE (ON WHAT SIDE)

The concept of SIDE is used to indicate location (WHERE) of people, things, and even places:

This person (thing) is on this side now; before, it was on the other side.

In addition to the person, thing, or place whose location is being described, SIDE requires also a point of reference. Often, this point of reference need not be mentioned explicitly, being provided by the person of the speaker, or the person spoken of.

The most important point about the grammar of SIDE is that it is not a "substantive", and that its full frame is "on side X of Y" (where X stands for some "determiner", for example, "this"; whereas *Y* stands for some "substantive"—prototypically, a person).

13.5. INSIDE

The concept of INSIDE may seem to be related to that of SIDE (ON WHAT SIDE), but I believe that the links between the two are not compositional: a sentence such as "*A* is inside *B*" does not mean that "*A* is on the inner side of *B*", because SIDE (ON (THIS) SIDE) implies an adjacent location, and the notions of 'inside' and 'adjacency' are not mutually compatible.

The syntax of the two concepts (ON WHAT SIDE and INSIDE) is not identical either, since one of them opens three slots, and the other, two:

> *A* is on side *X* of *B*.
> *A* is inside *B*.

It is not clear at this stage how many predicates can combine with INSIDE. Obviously, WHERE (be SOMEWHERE) can—so much so that we might be tempted to view INSIDE as a special case of "being somewhere". But things can also "happen" inside something (a house, a cave, a womb), and so we should allow, perhaps, that INSIDE can combine directly with HAPPEN.

14. Interclausal Linkers: BECAUSE, IF, IF . . . WOULD

Interclausal linkers constitute a powerful device for building complex semantic structures out of simple propositions. One such linker, WHEN, has already been introduced in Section 12, on time. But the primary function of WHEN is, arguably, that of a temporal adjunct. By contrast, the three elements discussed in the present section are primarily, or even exclusively, interclausal linkers.

14.1. BECAUSE

BECAUSE can function either as an interclausal linker or as a clause adjunct. Arguably, its primary role is that of a linker, as in the following sentence:

> The dog died because the man hit it on the head (not because of something else).

As a clause adjunct, BECAUSE commonly occurs in phrases such as "because of this", in clauses which present an event or a state of affairs as resulting from that described in the preceding sentence; for example:

The man hit the dog on the head; because of this, the dog died.

From a logical point of view, one would expect that BECAUSE always links events, and therefore that it has to connect a clause with another clause or with a clause substitute (a "substantive"—THIS or perhaps SOMETHING—referring to the content of another clause). In natural language, however, the role of BECAUSE does not seem to be similarly restricted, and phrases such as "because of me" or "because of you" may in fact be universally available. If they are, then there is perhaps no need to regard them as elliptical or polysemous. (See Jackendoff 1983: 176–8).

14.2. IF

IF is another interclausal linker. In contrast to BECAUSE, however, it can only combine with a clause (as a part of a complex sentence); it cannot combine with a substantive THIS or SOMETHING substituting for a clause:

> If you do this, people will say something bad about you.
> *If something, people will say something bad about you.

The phrase "if not" may seem to provide a counter-example to this claim, but it is probably not universal. (It cannot be universal if it is true that in some languages negation is realized only as a verbal suffix; and R. M. W Dixon (personal communication) informs me that this is the case in the Amazonian language Jarawara.)

In English (and in many other languages) the IF-clause can follow the other ("main") clause of an IF-sentence, but this option doesn't seem to be universally available. (For example, according to Tien (1994) it is not available in Chinese.)

14.3. IF . . . WOULD

The primitive IF . . . WOULD, too, is primarily an interclausal linker:

If you had been here, sir, my brother would not have died. (*The New English Bible*, John 11: 21)

> If I were you I wouldn't do it.

In many languages it can also introduce a wish clause (e.g. "if only I were there . . ."), but these can probably be regarded as elliptical, and, in any case, they are not universal (for example, they are not available in the Austronesian language Mangaaba-Mbula; see Bugenhagen forthcoming). Unlike IF, IF . . . WOULD can also be used as part of a complex interclausal linker "as if" (that is, IF . . . WOULD plus LIKE). For example:

He said it as if he didn't know anything.

We can hypothesize that in the unmarked order of clauses connected by IF, the IF-clause comes first; but the IF . . . WOULD-clauses can come second, notably when they occur in conjunction with LIKE/AS. (See Section 21 in Chapter 2.) Why is it that a sentence combining the elements WANT and NOT can be interpreted in two different ways? For example, why can the sentence "I don't want to go" be interpreted not only as denying that "I want to go" but also as affirming that "I want not to go"? And is this phenomenon universal? The matter requires further investigation. Other than raising this question, however, I will not discuss the semantic syntax of negation any further in the present context. (For a wealth of relevant observations and ideas, see in particular Jespersen 1917 and Horn 1989.)

15. Clause Operators: NOT and MAYBE

15.1. Negation: NOT

Negation is, universally, a "clause operator". Remarkably, it seems to be totally unrestricted: apparently any clause, of any kind, in any language, can be negated. As mentioned earlier, one difficult problem which arises in connection with negation is its relationship with "wanting". The matter requires further investigation.

15.2. Possibility: MAYBE

Possibility is commonly realized by means of a particle or sentence adverb, which can also be regarded as a "clause operator":

Maybe it will rain tomorrow.
Maybe this person did something bad.

In some languages, the same meaning can be realized by means of an auxiliary verb, or by means of a bound grammatical morpheme, but its semantic syntax seems to be always the same (a "clause operator").

There don't seem to be any restrictions on the combinability of MAYBE with different types of predicates. It combines with action, event, and speech predicates:

Maybe you will do it.
Maybe it happened.
Maybe someone else said it.

with mental predicates:

Maybe this person thinks/knows/wants/feels/sees/hears the same.

and also with predicates of description, evaluation, relation, and location:

> Maybe this is good/bad.
> Maybe this thing was a big/small thing.
> Maybe this thing was like these other things.
> Maybe all these people were in the same place at this time.

In this respect—its unconstrained combinability—MAYBE is like negation; for this reason, it may indeed be better to view it as a "clause operator" rather than a "clause adjunct".

None the less, MAYBE is not quite as unconstrained as negation. In "surface syntax" it doesn't combine with the imperative:

> *Maybe don't do it!

and in the "semantic syntax" it doesn't combine with "mental predicates" in first person (present tense) sentences, except in jocular or playful usage:

> ?Maybe I don't want to do it.
> ?Maybe I think about something else.
> ?Maybe I feel something bad.

The reason is that MAYBE implies that I don't know something, and normally one is expected to know one's own current mental states.

16. Metapredicate CAN

The metapredicate CAN combines, first of all, with the action predicate DO, and perhaps, prototypically, with "I" as an agent. Sentences such as:

> I can't do it/I can do it.
> I can't do it now/I could do it before.

reflect our experience of our own limitations, and also, of our freedom (within certain limits). Next to action, movement is perhaps another prototypical area within which CAN, and CANNOT, is most salient:

> I can't move.

But—perhaps by extension from these experiential prototypes—other predicates, and other "substantives", too, can combine with CAN:

> You/someone/people can do it.
> I/you/this person can say the same.
> I can't think about it for a long time.

But CAN can also occur in sentences with non-personal "subjects"; for example:

This thing can move.
When something bad happens to a person, it can be good for this person.
I know: something bad can happen to me.

It is not clear at this stage whether there are predicates which cannot combine with CAN at all.

17. Intensifier: VERY

The intensifier VERY combines, first of all, with the evaluators GOOD and BAD and the descriptor BIG:

very good/very bad/very big

Presumably, it also combines, universally, with the "determiners" MUCH/MANY, and also with the "distance primitive" FAR, and with the durational primitive A LONG TIME:

very much/very many/very far/a very long time

Curiously, preliminary cross-linguistic testing suggests that VERY does not always combine as readily and as freely with the, so to speak, "small" primitives SMALL, NEAR, and A SHORT TIME as it does with their opposites. Both the scope and the nature of these restrictions need to be investigated.

In many languages, VERY (or some allolex such as *very much* in English) combines also with the mental predicate WANT:

I want it very much ·

It is doubtful, however, whether this is universal, if only because in some languages (e.g. in Kayardild, see N. Evans 1994; also Harkins 1994) WANT is realized as a suffix, not as a full verb or adjective.

In most languages there are of course other "intensifiers", such as *at all*, *really*, *real*, *proper*, and *true* in English, and their combinatorial possibilities may go far beyond those listed here for VERY, but the meaning of these "intensifiers" may be different from the meaning of VERY.

18. Taxonomy, Partonomy: KIND OF, PART OF

The notion KIND co-occurs, as a rule, with a "determiner":

this kind; another kind; the same kind
one kind; two kinds; many kinds; all kinds

In English, and in many other languages, one can also use KIND in sentences without a determiner, for example:

An oak is a kind of tree.

but this usage doesn't seem to be universal (see e.g. Durie *et al.* 1994; or N. Evans 1994). On the other hand, evidence suggests (see Goddard and Wierzbicka 1994*b*) that in all languages one can say things such as the following:

There are two kinds of bat.
This is not the same fish, but it is the same kind of fish.

Presumably, it is also possible to say, in any language, the structural equivalent of the sentence

This fish (bird, tree, etc.) is of the same kind as this other fish (bird, tree, etc.).

(Of course the concepts of 'fish', 'bird', or 'tree' as such are far from universal. See e.g. C. Brown 1977, 1979.)

The notion of PART is at present more problematic than most of the other ones, and little is known at this stage about its syntax. On the basis of the data available, one would expect to find PART, universally, in metalinguistic sentences such as the following ones:

A blade is a part of a knife.
A stump is a part of a tree.
A foot is a part of someone's leg.

I would also expect that the concept of PART can be found, universally, in sentences of the following kind:

An axe has a handle and a blade.
A knife has two parts: a handle and a blade.
A flower has many parts which look alike.

Needless to say, I am not suggesting that all languages have a verb corresponding to the English verb *have*. Rather, I am suggesting that the English word *have*, when combined with a noun including in its meaning the concept of PART (such as *blade*, *handle*, *stump*, or *foot*), can perhaps be viewed as an allolex of the "existential" predicate THERE IS/ARE. The fact that in many languages this is precisely how the "part–whole" relation is expressed seems to support this idea:

A knife has two parts. =
"a knife, there are two parts (in it/to it)"

I am suggesting, then, that the concept of PART can combine, universally, with the concept of THERE IS/ARE; and also with "determiners" (e.g. TWO, MANY, SOME):

> The elephant has a long nose. =
> when people want to say something about things of this kind [ELEPHANTS]
> they can say something like this: this part [NOSE] is long

19. Similarity: LIKE

The combinatorial possibilities of LIKE are probably quite varied. To begin with, it can act as a predicative "linker", linking two "substantives":

> You are like me.
> I am not like other people.

It can also act as an "attributive linker" of substantives:

> someone like me; something like this; people like you

But there are restrictions here:

> *me like you; *you like someone else
> *someone like someone else; *people like someone else

In some languages, combinations of this kind are realized in the form of obligatory or almost obligatory portmanteaus. For example, in Polish they would normally be rendered as follows:

> ktoś   taki   jak ja
> someone such   as I
>
> coś   takiego
> something such-GEN.
>
> ludzie tacy jak ty
> people such as you

But differences of this kind can be regarded as superficial.

As an "attributive linker" LIKE can also apply to time and place:

> at a time like this; in a place like this

In attributive phrases, then, the "head" (the compared member) can be one of the following ("indefinite") set: SOMEONE, SOMETHING, PEOPLE, TIME, PLACE; whereas the point of reference appears to be restricted to the following ("definite") set: THIS, ME, YOU, THIS PERSON, THESE PEOPLE.

But LIKE phrases can also function as "clause adjuncts", at least in combination with the predicates DO, HAPPEN, and SAY:

It happened like this: . . .
I did it like this: . . .
He said it like this: . . .

It appears that as a clause adjunct, and also as a time and place linker, LIKE is restricted to a combination with THIS.

It seems likely that LIKE can also function, universally, as an interclausal linker, as in the following sentences:

Forgive us as (like) we forgive other people.
You want to do good things for me, as (like) we want to do good things for our children.

20. General Discussion

As can be seen from the above survey, the syntax of the natural semantic metalanguage can be characterized as analogous in some respects to, but much simpler than, the syntax of natural languages.

The basic unit of the NSM syntax is a "clause", which is constituted by a "substantive" and "a predicate", and some additional elements determined by the nature of the predicate.

In addition to this major type of clause (to be discussed below) there is also one minor type, which can be regarded as an analogue of "subjectless sentences" of the traditional grammar, and which includes "existential sentences", centred on the predicate THERE IS/ARE (e.g. "there are many kinds of birds"; "there is plenty of water here").

The set of "substantives" includes the elements I, YOU, THIS, SOMEONE, SOMETHING, and PEOPLE. Some of these (the last three) can be combined into a unit with "determiners" (THIS, THE SAME, OTHER, ONE, TWO, SOME, MUCH/MANY, LITTLE/FEW, and ALL) and "attributes" (GOOD, BAD, BIG, and SMALL).

The list of possible predicates includes the following elements:

[mental predicates]: THINK, WANT, KNOW, FEEL, SEE, HEAR
[speech] SAY
[action and events] DO, HAPPEN, MOVE
[existence and life] BE, LIVE
[relation] [be] LIKE; [be] a PART of
[space] [be] in a PLACE; [be] UNDER; [be] ABOVE; [be] ON [this]
    SIDE; [be] INSIDE; [be] FAR; [be] NEAR; [be] HERE
[evaluation] [be] GOOD, BAD

[description] [be] BIG, SMALL

Some of these predicates can combine into a unit with the "metapredicate" CAN.

Different predicates take different types of "complements" and "objects" (as discussed under individual predicates). In addition to predicate complements, some types of clauses (depending on the nature of the predicate) take also clause adjuncts: temporal, spatial, and causal (e.g. at this time/in this place/because of this).

All types of clauses can combine with the two universal "clause operators": negation and possibility (MAYBE). These two operators can co-occur, with NOT being within the scope of MAYBE (but not the other way round):

> Maybe they didn't do it.
> *They didn't maybe do it.

Clauses can be combined into complex sentences by means of "linkers": IF, IF . . . WOULD, BECAUSE, AFTER, BEFORE, WHEN, and LIKE.

A clause can be turned into an adjunct to another clause and thus "incorporated" into it if it is replaced (in discourse) with the "substantive" THIS (accompanied by the clause linker): after this/before this/because of this/like this. The only clause linkers which don't allow "clause incorporation" and which are, universally, strictly interclausal, are IF and IF . . . WOULD.

In addition to the use of linkers (IF, IF . . . WOULD, BECAUSE, AFTER, BEFORE, LIKE) clauses can also be combined by "nesting" (to use Weinreich's (1963) term), in the sense that they can be used as complements of certain predicates. Thus, the predicates SAY and THINK can take, universally, "quotative" complements; for example:

> You said: I didn't do it.
> I thought: this will never happen to me.

The predicates KNOW and WANT, too, can take "propositional complements"; for example:

> I know: people say something bad about me.
> People know: you didn't do it.
> I want you to do it (= I want: you do it).
> I want to know it (= I want: I know it).

One element (THIS) has, universally, a double status and can function either as a "substantive" or as a "determiner".

The evaluators and descriptors (GOOD and BAD, BIG and SMALL) can function, universally, as "attributes" (to the "substantives" SOMETHING, SOMEONE, and PEOPLE) as well as predicates.

As can be gleaned from the above discussion, NSM has a rudimentary parts-of-speech system. Elements which can occur only as predicates (THINK, KNOW, SAY, WANT; SEE, HEAR, DO, HAPPEN, MOVE) can be regarded as analogues of verbs; and those which can be used either as predicates or as attributes (GOOD, BAD; BIG, SMALL) can be regarded as analogues of adjectives. Elements which can function as "subjects" and which can take attributes (SOMEONE, PEOPLE, SOMETHING) can be seen as analogues of nouns, and those which can function as "subjects" without being able to take attributes (I, YOU, THIS) can be seen as analogues of pronouns.

The elements which can combine with "substantives" but which cannot occur predicatively (THIS, OTHER, ONE, TWO, SOME; THE SAME) can be regarded as an analogue of determiners, and those which can only occur in conjunction with substantives (PART and KIND) can be seen as an analogue of classifiers.

Elements which can link clauses (BECAUSE, IF, IF . . . WOULD, LIKE, AFTER, BEFORE) can be regarded as analogues of conjunctions, and those which can turn a substantive into a predicative phrase (UNDER, ABOVE, ON (ONE) SIDE OF) can be seen as an analogue of prepositions.

The universal intensifier VERY, which combines with the attributes GOOD, BAD, BIG, and SMALL, with the "determiner" MUCH/MANY and with the spatial and temporal predicates FAR and NEAR, A LONG TIME and A SHORT TIME, can be seen as an analogue of one type of adverb, whereas temporal and spatial clause adjuncts (WHEN, WHERE, A LONG/SHORT TIME) can be regarded as an analogue of another type of adverb.

Finally, the "clause operators" negation (NOT) and possibility (MAYBE) can be regarded as an analogue of sentence particles.

In addition, NSM has powerful iconic and indexical mechanisms, extending its grammar far beyond the boundaries determined by the combinability rules sketched above. Consider, for example, a typical NSM explication such as the following one (see Chapter 5):

I feel sad. =
(*a*) sometimes a person thinks something like this:
(*b*)   something bad happened
(*c*)   if I didn't know that it happened I would say: I don't want it to happen
(*d*)   I don't say this now
(*e*)   because I know: I can't do anything
(*f*) because of this, this person feels something bad
(*g*) I feel something like this

In a sense, the whole formula could be seen as one complex unit (an analogue of a "sentence"). This "sentence" includes as many as seven clauses, which jointly form an integrated whole. But the grammar of this whole goes beyond the links established by the linkers BECAUSE and IF, and by the complement structure of the verbs THINK and WANT.

One important linker binding the clauses of this sentence into a whole is the element THIS, referring either anaphorically (lines (*c*), (*e*), (*f*)) or cataphorically (line (*a*)) to whole clauses.

In the written form of NSM, there are also other devices which play an important auxiliary role. These include special spacing and indentation. The fact that a part of an explication is placed in a separate line indicates that this part forms a distinct semantic component, and a group of such components identically indented under a component including the element THIS (e.g. (*b*), (*c*), (*d*), and (*e*) in the explication above) form a larger unit.

In oral speech, NSM formulae would no doubt be often difficult to follow, but in principle a system of pauses and some rudimentary intonational contrasts could perhaps achieve the same effect.

As mentioned earlier, since NSM is intended to be a model of the innate and universal *lingua mentalis*, the NSM grammar sketched here can be seen as a hypothesis about the "grammar of human cognition". But there is no reason why one could not remain sceptical about the status of NSM (both in its lexicon and in its grammar) as a model of the language of human cognition and yet recognize its value as an effective universal system of semantic—and cultural—notation.

And, to repeat: the sketch grammar of NSM proposed here is highly tentative and is offered only as a necessary starting-point for testing and discussion.

4 Prototypes and Invariants

□ □ _____

1. Introduction

The role that the concept of prototype has played in contemporary semantics is analogous to that which the concept of Gricean maxims has played in generative grammar. A well-placed witness, James McCawley (1981: 215), identified this role with the excellent slogan "Grice saves". In grammar, if there was a conflict between postulated rules and the actual usage, it was assumed that "Grice" could rescue the grammarian: the usage could be accounted for in terms of Gricean maxims. (See Bach and Harnish 1982; for a critical discussion, see G. Green 1983; Wierzbicka 1991a.)

Similarly in semantics. Just as the failure of grammatical rules to work has often been presented as evidence of progress in linguistics (because it only illustrates the importance of Gricean maxims), the failure of semantic formulae to work has often been presented as evidence of progress in semantics. Semantic formulae *should not* "work"; to expect them to work means not to understand the role of "prototypes" in language and cognition.

Frequently, appeals to prototypes have been combined with a claim that there are two approaches to human categorization: the "classical" approach (linked with Aristotle) and the "prototype" approach (linked, in particular, with Rosch and Wittgenstein). When these two approaches were contrasted, it was usually argued that the "classical approach" was wrong and the "prototype approach" was right.

In this chapter I argue that the idea of contrasting these two approaches in this way has proved unhelpful in semantic investigations, and that what is needed is a synthesis of the two traditions, not a choice of one over the other. There is a place for prototypes in semantic analysis, but there is also a place for invariants: one does not exclude the other. Accordingly, in what follows, I will discuss two sets of examples. The first set will illustrate the tendency to abuse the concept of prototype (the "prototypes save" attitude); the second set of examples will illustrate the usefulness of this concept when it is used as a specific analytical tool and not as a universal thought-saving device.

2. Abuses of "Prototypes" in Semantics: Some Illustrations

2.1. The Meaning of *Boat*

Discussing the meaning of the English word *boat*, Verschueren (1985: 48) says:

> In trying to determine the meaning of the word BOAT, one could come up with a definition such as a 'man-made object that can be used for travelling on water'. A defender of the checklist approach, coming across a boat with a hole in it and deciding that he/she still wants to call it a BOAT (though it cannot be used for travelling on water anymore), would have to revise his/her definition: 'a man-made object that can normally be used for travelling on water, but in which there can also be a hole'. Further, he/she would have to determine how big the hole can be before the object in question is not a BOAT anymore, but simply a WRECK. The impracticality of the checklist approach is such that not even its proponents would want to be guilty of the absurdities mentioned. A defender of the alternative theory could simply stick to his/her definition and describe a boat with a hole in terms of deviations from the prototypical boat.

But instead of appealing to prototypes, couldn't we simply rephrase the formula just a little? Couldn't we say, in the first place, that boats are a kind of thing *made for* 'travelling on water' rather than *able to* "travel on water"? It is quite true that a boat with a very big hole can't "travel on water", but why phrase the definition in terms of *ability* rather than *intended function* anyway?

2.2. The Meaning of *Bachelor*

Extolling "fuzziness" and "prototypes" in language, Lakoff (1986: 43–4) writes:

> Fuzziness may also arise from non-graded concepts—concepts defined by models that have no scales built into them. Fillmore (1982) gives as an example the time-honoured case of *bachelor*. He observes that *bachelor* is defined relative to an idealized model of the world, one in which there is a social institution of marriage, marriage is monogamous, and between people of opposite sexes . . .
>
> This idealized model fits the classical theory of categories. Within the model, *bachelor* is a very clearly defined Aristotelian category. But this idealized cognitive model, or ICM, does not fit the world as we know it very well. When this model is placed within the context of the rest of our knowledge, fuzziness arises—not because of what is in the model but because of discrepancies between the background assumptions of the model and the rest of our knowledge. Here are some cases where the background conditions fail, and as a result it is difficult to give clear, unequivocal answers:
>
> > Is Tarzan a bachelor?
> > Is the Pope a bachelor? . . .

The answers to such questions are not clear-cut, and the reason is that the idealized model with respect to which *bachelor* is defined may not fit well with the rest of our knowledge. The source of fuzziness here is not within the model, but in the interaction of the model with other models characterizing other aspects of our knowledge. Fuzziness of the above sort leads to prototype effects—cases of better and worse examples of bachelors.

Thus the perennial *bachelor* turns up again in a new role. Thirty years ago, the most fashionable semantic theory of the time—Katz and Fodor's (1963) "new semantic theory"—made its triumphant entry into linguistics perched precariously on this same example; today, the theory of prototypes finds the *bachelor* example equally serviceable. But if the formula "bachelor—an unmarried (adult) male person" doesn't work, couldn't we perhaps revise it slightly, to make it work—couldn't we, to wit, replace it with the following definition: "bachelor—a man who has never married thought of as a man who can marry if he wants to"? (More precisely: "people think of this man like this: this man can marry someone if he wants to".)

What cases such as this make clear is that discussions of 'necessary and sufficient features' typically focus on physical features and ignore mental ones. Yet natural language concepts often constitute amalgams of both kinds of component. For 'bachelor', being thought of as someone who can marry is as necessary as being male and having never married.

2.3. The Meaning of *Congratulate*

According to Verschueren (1985: 47), "a typical congratulation is an expression of the speaker's being pleased about the hearer's success in doing or obtaining something important. The first aspect [i.e. the speaker's pleasure] of this prototypical meaning is completely absent from many formal acts of congratulating. The second aspect [i.e. the hearer's success] is being tampered with in the following headline from the *International Herald Tribune*: 'Begin congratulates Sadat on *their* Nobel [Prize].' "

But in fact, it is not true that the expression of pleasure 'is completely absent from many formal acts of congratulating'. Apparently, the *expression* of pleasure (i.e. *saying* that one is pleased) is being confused here with the *experience* of pleasure (i.e. with *being* pleased). Of course in many acts of congratulating, the experience of pleasure is absent; but if one doesn't say (or otherwise convey) that one is pleased, there is no act of congratulating. Surely, an expression of pleasure is part of the invariant of the concept 'congratulate', not just part of its prototype?

2.4. The Meaning of *Bird*

In a number of publications, George Lakoff has accused other linguists of dealing in various 'convenient fictions', and castigated them for failing to recognize that semantic categories are 'fuzzy'—a point which in his view has been established in Eleanor Rosch's work. For example, he wrote (Lakoff 1973: 458–9):

Eleanor Rosch Heider [1973] took up the question of whether people perceive category membership as a clear-cut issue or a matter of degree. For example, do people think of members of a given species as being simply birds or non-birds, or do people consider them birds to a certain degree? Heider's results consistently showed the latter. She asked subjects to rank birds as to the degree of their birdiness, that is, the degree to which they matched the ideal of a bird. If category membership were simply a yes-or-no matter, one would have expected the subjects either to balk at the task or to produce random results. Instead, a fairly well-defined hierarchy of 'birdiness' emerged.

(1) Birdiness hierarchy
    robins
    eagles
    chickens, ducks, geese
    penguins, pelicans
    bats

Robins are typical of birds. Eagles, being predators, are less typical. Chickens, ducks, and geese somewhat less still. Bats hardly at all. And cows not at all.

It is hard to see, however, how this reasoning can he reconciled with native speakers' firm intuition that whereas a bat is definitely *not* a bird at all, an ostrich *is* a bird—a "funny" bird, an atypical bird, but a bird. This would seem to support a conclusion opposite to Lakoff's: bats, which have no feathers and no beaks and don't lay eggs, are disqualified, because feathers, beaks, and eggs are thought of as *necessary* (rather than merely prototypical) components of the concept 'bird'[1] (see Wierzbicka 1985: 180); for further discussion of 'bird' see Section 3.5.

Of course, if informants are specifically instructed to rank a set of given species terms on a "scale of birdiness", and if the set they are given includes both bats and cows, one can understand why they might decide to place bats above cows, but does this really establish that bats are thought of as having any degree of "birdiness", and that it is impossible to draw a line between words for birds and words for things other than birds?

---

[1] When I speak of the concept 'bird' I mean the concept encoded in the English word *bird*. Other languages may of course have no word for 'bird', having lexically encoded slightly different concepts. For example, the closest counterpart of *bird* in the Australian language Nunggubuyu does include bats, as well as grasshoppers (Heath 1978a: 41). The closest equivalent of *bird* in the Australian language Warlpiri excludes bats, but it also excludes emus (Hale *et al.* forthcoming). The prototype may well be the same in all these languages, but the boundaries are drawn differently. An adequate semantic analysis should reflect this.

2.5. The Meaning of *Lie*

According to Coleman and Kay (1981), whether or not an utterance is a lie is a matter of degree, and there is no set of necessary and sufficient components characterizing the concept 'lie'. This conclusion, which has since been accepted and endorsed in countless linguistic articles and books, is based partly on so-called social lies and white lies and partly on cases of deception by evasion. For example, insincere utterances such as "What a lovely dress!" or "How nice to see you!" or "Drop in any time!" are claimed to be partial lies, rather than either lies or non-lies. Similarly, false reassurances given to terminally ill patients are regarded as partial lies, rather than either lies or non-lies. Finally, answers which are literally true but which are intended to mislead or deceive the addressee (e.g. "Where are you going?" "We're out of paprika") are also categorized as partial lies.

It is very interesting to see that many informants are prepared to classify "social lies", "charitable lies", and evasions as "partial lies" or the like. However, semanticists are not obliged to take informants' judgements at face value. Coleman and Kay's methodology—like Rosch's—tends to produce results expected and desired by the researchers. Since the informants were given a seven-point scale from 1 ("very sure not-lie") to 7 ("very sure lie"), they acted as expected and arranged all the instances offered them somewhere along the scale. In any case, Coleman and Kay's aim ("we intend to challenge the very notion of the discrete semantic feature") can hardly be said to have been achieved. The word *lie* can be given a perfectly valid definition in terms of "discrete semantic features" (see Wierzbicka 1985: 341–2):

> X lied to Y. =
> X said something to Y
> X knew it was not true[2]
> X said it because X wanted Y to think it was true
> [people would say: if someone does this, it is bad]

Of course there are similarities between lies and insincere or evasive utterances, as there are similarities between birds and bats, and informants are aware of that. But this does not demonstrate that the notion of the discrete semantic feature is not valid (see Tsohatzidis 1990; Jeffcott 1992).

The fact that informants' responses are often graded is interesting, but as Armstrong, Gleitman, and Gleitman (1983: 284) put it, it is probably "a fact about something other than the structure of concepts"—particularly in view of the fact that graded responses are also triggered by evidently

---

[2] The concept of 'true' is neither simple nor universal, but it is simpler than 'lie' and, for the present purposes, it doesn't need to be decomposed further.

discrete concepts such as 'odd numbers' (some odd numbers being rated by informants as odder than others, e.g. 3 being rated as odder than 501; Armstrong *et al.* 1983).

It might be added that Sweetser (1987: 62) goes even further than Coleman and Kay in the direction of "prototypical reduction", and claims that "a lie is simply a false statement". She realizes, of course, that the use of *lie* cannot be fully predicted from this simple definition, but, she claims "we all know from bitter experience how readily the complexities of meaning elude the reductionist formal analysis" (1987: 63)—that is, how difficult it is to define anything in a way which would make the right predictions. Fortunately, she thinks, the prototype theory can save us from the trouble and frustration involved in trying to do so. In the case of *lie*, it is enough to define it as a "false statement"; the lack of fit between the definition and the use can then be explained in terms of our cultural models of relevant areas of experience.

This explanation clearly collapses, however, when one realizes that a language may have two, or more, words designating "false statements", and that they may be used differently. For example, Russian has two words corresponding to lying: *vrat'* and *lgat'*, whose uses overlap rather than coincide. If students of Russian are told that both these words mean "false statement" and that any further guide-lines concerning their use should be deduced from the Russian "cultural model", how will they know how to differentiate the uses of *vrat'* and *lgat'*? On the other hand, carefully phrased definitions *can* guide the students in their use, and in their interpretation, of these words.

Cultural models are important indeed, but they are not "another important factor", in addition to meaning. Cultural models are reflected in the meanings of words. The model encoded in the meaning of *vrat'* is somewhat different from that encoded in the meaning of *lgat'*; and both of these models are somewhat different from that encoded in the meaning of *lie*.[3] It may be difficult to articulate these meanings adequately (that is, in a way which would ensure full predictive power), but it is not impossible to do so. (For a large body of predictive definitions of speech act verbs see Wierzbicka 1987*a*.)

---

[3] De Jonge (1982: 155) defines *vran'e* (a noun corresponding to *vrat'*) as "creative lying designed to make the liar appear interesting and important", and he calls it "a particular Russian habit" (*vrat'* being indeed the most basic Russian word corresponding to *lie*). Bogusławski (1983: 110) notes, however, that one can also say *termometr vret* 'the thermometer is "lying" ' or *časy vrut* 'the watch is "lying" ', meaning that the instruments in question are unreliable or inaccurate. The concept of *vrat'* embodies an important cultural model, and it is a challenging task to construct an adequate definition of this concept; it certainly won't do to say that *vrat'* means simply 'to make a false statement', as it won't do for the English concept of 'lying' (see Mondry and Taylor 1992; Shopen forthcoming; Kronhaus 1993).

2.6. The Meaning of *Mother*

According to George Lakoff (1986: 37), the concept of 'mother' cannot be given an invariant definition, because it is an "experiential cluster" and because no definition "will cover the full range of cases". The range of cases coming under this concept is, according to Lakoff, very wide, and cannot be reduced to any common core (such as, for instance, "a woman who has given birth to a child"), because the word *mother* refers not only to "biological mothers" but also to adoptive mothers, "donor mothers" (who provide eggs but not wombs), "surrogate mothers" (who provide wombs but not eggs), and so on. Lakoff's argument is so idiosyncratic that if one is not to be suspected of misrepresenting it, it is best to quote it verbatim:

> This phenomenon is beyond the scope of the classical theory. The concept *mother* is not clearly defined, once and for all, in terms of common necessary and sufficient conditions. There need be no necessary and sufficient conditions for motherhood shared by normal biological mothers, donor mothers (who donate an egg), surrogate mothers (who bear the child, but may not have donated the egg), adoptive mothers, unwed mothers who give their children up for adoption, and stepmothers. They are all mothers by virtue of their relation to the ideal case, where the base models converge. That ideal case is one of the many kinds of cases that give rise to prototype effects.   (Lakoff 1986: 39; see also Lakoff 1987: 83)

From a semantic point of view, however, Lakoff's claims carry little conviction. The crucial point which Lakoff overlooks is that foster mothers, adoptive mothers, "genetic mothers", "surrogate mothers", and so on are not "mothers" on a par with 'biological mothers' (see Bogusławski 1970). Without a modifier, the word *mother* ('*X* is *Y*'s mother') refers clearly to birth-givers, not to the donors of eggs, providers of wombs, caretakers, or fathers' spouses.

Lakoff points out that the expression *real mother* may refer to a caretaker as well as to a birth-giver ("She raised me and I called her mother, but she is not my real mother"; "She gave birth to me, but she was never a real mother to me"), but he overlooks the syntactic—and hence the semantic—difference between my *real* mother (either birth-giver or caretaker) and a *real mother to me* (caretaker only). Furthermore, he overlooks the fact that the test with *real* is not semantically reliable. For example, sentences such as "he is a real man" or "she is a real woman" may refer to the speaker's views or prejudices about men and women which have no basis in the semantics of the words *man* and *woman*. He doesn't appreciate the implications of the fact that the expression *biological mother* would be used only in a contrastive context, and that normally (without a contrastive context) one would not say "she is his biological mother", whereas expressions such as *foster mother*, *adoptive mother*, or *surrogate mother* are not restricted to contrastive contexts.

To treat "biological mothers" as being on a par with "surrogate mothers" or "foster mothers" is a little like saying that there are two kinds of horses: biological horses and rocking-horses (or that there are two diverging "models of horsehood": a biological model and an artefact model); and that we cannot define *horse* as 'a kind of animal . . .' because a rocking-horse is not a kind of animal at all.

I am not saying that the meaning of the word *mother* can be wholly reduced to that of 'birth-giver'; arguably, a social and psychological component is also present:

X is Y's mother. =
(*a*) at one time, before now, X was very small
(*b*) at that time, Y was inside X
(*c*) at that time, Y was like a part of X
(*d*) because of this, people can think something like this about X:
"X wants to do good things for Y
X doesn't want bad things to happen to Y"

But the social and psychological component (*d*) has to be formulated in terms of expectations (thoughts), not in terms of actual events; by contrast, the biological components (*a*), (*b*), and (*c*) have to be formulated as actual (see Wierzbicka 1980: 46–9).

2.7. The Meaning of *Furniture*

In a paper entitled "Cognitive Representations of Semantic Categories", Rosch (1975*a*: 193) wrote:

When we hear a category word in a natural language such as *furniture* or *bird* and understand its meaning, what sort of cognitive representation do we generate? A list of features necessary and sufficient for an item to belong to the category? A concrete image which represents the category? A list of category members? An ability to use the category term with no attendant mental representation at all? Or some other, less easily specified, form of representation?

This passage contains an implicit assumption that *bird* and *furniture* are the same sort of "category words". Following Rosch, many psychologists and, more surprisingly, linguists, adopted this assumption as self-evidently correct. There are, however, clear grammatical indications (as well as semantic evidence) to show that the two words embody completely different kinds of concept. *Bird* is a taxonomic concept, standing for a particular 'kind of creature'. But *furniture* is not a taxonomic concept at all: it is a collective concept (see Wierzbicka 1984, 1985, 1988; Zubin and Köpcke 1986), which stands for a heterogeneous collection of things of different kinds. One can't talk of "three furnitures" as one can of "three birds", and one can't imagine or draw an unspecified piece of furniture, as one can draw an unspecified bird. For *birds*, one *can* draw a line between birds and not-birds (bats being clearly in the latter category). For *furniture*, one cannot draw a line between kinds of things which are included in this supercategory and things which are not—because by virtue of its meaning, the word *furniture* doesn't aim at identifying any particular kind of thing. People may argue whether or not a radio is "furniture" (see Abelson 1981: 725), but not whether or not a pelican is a bird (see Armstrong *et al.* 1983: 268). The concept 'furniture' may indeed be said to be "fuzzy"—like those encoded in all the other collective nouns designating heterogeneous collections of things (*kitchenware, crockery, clothing*, and so on). But it is hard to see how the study of such collective nouns (mistaken for words of the same kind as countables such as *bird*) may constitute anything like "a refutation of the psychological reality of an Aristotelian view of categories" in general (Rosch 1975*a*: 225).

Bolinger (1992) has argued that both *furniture* and *bird* require "feature analysis" as well as "prototypes", and I agree with this. None the less, evidence suggests that they *are* fundamentally different in some respects, because a bird is, semantically, "a kind of creature", whereas furniture is conceptualized as "things of different kinds", not as "a kind of thing". The fact that bird is a "count noun" (e.g. *three birds*) whereas furniture is a "mass noun" (e.g. **three furnitures*) is not accidental, but reflects and provides evidence for this difference in the conceptualization. (For further discussion, see Wierzbicka 1992*b*).[4]

2.8. The Meaning of *Toy*

According to George Lakoff (1973) (who bases his claims on Rosch's investigations), *ball* and *doll* are among the "central members" of thc category

[4] Bolinger says that *furniture* is, in some respects, like *squash*, and that one can say, for example, "a crookneck is a kind of squash". He also points out that *bird* should be compared not with *furniture* but with *a piece of furniture*. But note the following contrasts:

> a sparrow is a kind of bird
> a crookneck is a kind of squash
> * a chair is a kind of furniture
> * a chair is a kind of piece of furniture

Contrasts of this kind suggest that the conceptual structures involved are different. These differences are quite systematic:

> a rose is a kind of flower
> an oak is a kind of tree
> * a shirt is a kind of clothing
> * a fork is a kind of cutlery
> * a shirt is a kind of piece of clothing
> * a fork is a kind of piece of cutlery

What applies to *furniture*, then, applies to all nouns which stand for heterogeneous collections of things (*clothing, cutlery, kitchenware*, and so on). What applies to *bird* applies to all nouns which stand for particular kinds of things, or creatures (*tree, flower, fish*, and so on).

'toy', just as *robin* and *sparrow* are among the "central members" of the category *bird*. *Swing* and *skates* are among the "peripheral members" of the category 'toy', just as *chicken* and *duck* are among the "peripheral members" of the category *bird*. Consequently, just as one cannot say whether chickens and ducks (and bats) are birds or not-birds, one cannot say whether swings and skates are toys or not-toys. All one can say is that they are toys to a certain degree (less than balls or dolls).

But the analogy between *bird* and *toy* is just as spurious as that between *bird* and *furniture*. While *bird* is a taxonomic concept which stands for a particular *kind* of thing, *toy* is no more a taxonomic concept than *furniture* is. It is a purely functional concept, which stands for things of *any kind* made for children to play with. One cannot draw an unspecified toy, just as one cannot draw an unspecified piece of furniture. The category 'toy' is "fuzzy"—because, by virtue of its semantic structure (entirely different from the semantic structure of 'bird') it does not aim at identifying any particular kind of thing. Words such as *sparrow, chicken,* and *ostrich* can be shown to contain in their meaning the component 'bird' (see Wierzbicka 1985), and it is quite legitimate to start their definitions with the phrase *a kind of bird*. But words such as *ball* or *doll* do not contain in their meaning the component 'toy'. They may be seen as "central members" of the category 'toy', but this is quite irrelevant from the point of view of their semantic structure. It would be completely unjustified to open the definitions of the words *ball* and *doll* with the phrase *a kind of toy*. There are many balls used in various sports (rugby, soccer, cricket, etc.) which are not thought of as 'toys' at all; and there are dolls (e.g. china dolls kept on the mantelpiece) which are not thought of as toys. Whatever we discover about the structure of purely functional concepts such as 'toy' (or 'vehicle', or 'weapon', or 'tool'), it cannot be transferred to taxonomic supercategories such as 'bird', 'flower', or 'tree'. The semantic relation between *sparrow* and *bird* is entirely different from that between *ball* and *toy*. (See Wierzbicka 1984, 1985.)

2.9. The Meaning of *Game*

The concept of 'game' has no doubt been the most influential example of the alleged "fuzziness" of human concepts which has been offered in the literature. It was brought up by Ludwig Wittgenstein, in a famous passage of his *Philosophical Investigations*. Wittgenstein didn't appeal to the concept of prototype, but he appealed to—and indeed introduced—the related notion of "family resemblance" between concepts. The underlying assumption was the same: concepts cannot be given clear definitions in terms of discrete semantic components; it is impossible to capture the semantic invariant of a concept such as, for example, 'game'—because all that different instances share is a vague "family resemblance", not a specifiable set of features.

Wittgenstein's idea of "family resemblance" has played a colossal role in the development of "prototype semantics", and the popularity of this school of thought is no doubt due substantially to his intellectual charisma.

In my view, Wittgenstein's writings contain some of the deepest and the most insightful observations on semantic matters to be found anywhere. But despite my gratitude to Wittgenstein I think the time has come to re-examine his doctrine of "family resemblances", which has acquired the status of unchallengeable dogma in much of the current literature on meaning (see e.g. Jackendoff 1983; Baker and Hacker 1980; Lakoff 1987). Wittgenstein (1953: 31–2) wrote:

Consider for example the proceedings that we call 'games'. I mean board-games, card-games, Olympic games, and so on. What is common to them all? Don't say: 'There must be something common, or they would not be called "games" '—but *look and see* whether there is anything common to all. For if you look at them you will not see something that is common to *all,* but similarities, relationships, and a whole series of them at that. To repeat: don't think, but look! Look for example at board-games, with their multifarious relationships. Now pass to card-games; here you find many correspondences with the first group, but many common features drop out, and others appear. When we pass next to ball-games, much that is common is retained, but much is lost. Are they all 'amusing'? Compare chess with noughts and crosses. Or is there always winning and losing, or competition between players? Think of patience. In ball games there is winning and losing; but when a child throws his ball at the wall and catches it again, this feature has disappeared. Look at the parts played by skill and luck; and at the difference between skill in chess and skill in tennis. Think now of games like ring-a-ring-a-roses; here is the element of amusement, but how many other characteristic features have disappeared! And we can go through the many, many other groups of games in the same way; can see how similarities crop up and disappear.

And the result of this examination is: we see a complicated network of similarities overlapping and criss-crossing: sometimes overall similarities, sometimes similarities of detail.

I can think of no better expression to characterize these similarities than 'family resemblances'; for the various resemblances between members of a family: build, features, colour of eyes, gait, temperament, etc. etc. overlap and criss-cross in the same way. And I shall say: 'games' form a family.

Passages like these have a hypnotic force, and it is not surprising that they have exercised a great influence on countless philosophers, psychologists, and linguists. But are Wittgenstein's claims really true? Is it indeed impossible to say what all games have in common, i.e. impossible to capture the invariant of the concept 'game'?

The only valid form of challenge in a case like this is to try to do the "impossible", to try to define the concept of 'game'. I would suggest that the following components are essential to this concept: (1) human action (animals can play, but they don't play games); (2) duration (a game can't be momentary); (3) aim: pleasure; (4) "suspension of reality" (the participants imagine that they are in a world apart from the real world); (5) well-defined goals (the participants know what they are trying to achieve); (6) well-defined rules (the participants know what they can do and what they cannot do); (7) the course of events is unpredictable (nobody can know what exactly is going to happen). Accordingly, I propose the following definition:

games

(*a*) many kinds of things that people do
(*b*) for some time
(*c*) "for pleasure" (i.e. because they want to feel something good)
(*d*) when people do these things, one can say these things about these people:
(*e*)   they want some things to happen
(*f*)   if they were not doing these things, they wouldn't want these things to happen
(*g*)   they don't know what will happen
(*h*)   they know what they can do
(*i*)   they know what they cannot do

Component (*a*) indicates that "games" are human activities and that there are many kinds of them, (*b*) that "games" are not instantaneous but have duration, (*c*) that "games" are undertaken for pleasure, (*d*) that "games" have certain constant characteristics: (*e*) games have some goals, (*f*) these goals have no meaning or value outside the game, (*g*) the course of a game is unpredictable, (*h*) and (*i*) games require certain rules, and the participants know what these rules are.

I believe that this definition[5] applies satisfactorily to board-games, card-games, ball-games, and countless other kinds of activity called "games". It does not apply to a situation when a child idly throws his ball at the wall and catches it again, but in English this activity would not be called a game. In German the word *Spiel* has a wider range of use, corresponding roughly to the English *playing*. But this very fact contradicts Wittgenstein's (1953: 33) claim that "we do not know the boundaries because none have been drawn". Boundaries do exist, and they have been drawn differently in dif-

---

[5] The definition of *games* proposed here is not meant to cover cases of metaphorical extension, ironic or humorous use, and the like, as, for example, in the case of the phrase "the games people play", or in the case of "games" played by mathematicians, generative grammarians, or other scholars who enjoy solving difficult problems for their own sake. Here as elsewhere in semantics, playful extensions have to be distinguished from the basic meaning (which explains both the "normal" use of the word and any extensions from that use).

ferent languages, and native speakers subconsciously know them and respect them. One feature which separates the concept of 'game' lexically encoded in English from the concept of 'Spiel' lexically encoded in German is the idea of rules: of knowing beforehand what one can do and what one cannot do. Another difference has to do with the idea of a well-defined goal, which may or may not be attained. If features like these are not identified and clearly stated, cross-linguistic lexical research cannot succeed. It is not surprising, therefore, that advocates of the theory of "family resemblances" usually do not engage in such research.

3. Uses of "Prototypes" in Semantics: Some Illustrations

So far, the discussion has been focused primarily on what I see as the abuses and misuses of the notion of "prototype". It is time to turn to the more positive aspects of the idea of "prototype". "Prototypes" can't save us, but they can help if they are treated with caution and with care, and, above all, if they are combined with verbal definitions, instead of being treated as an excuse for not ever defining anything.

Lexicographic practice suggests that the notion of "prototype" can be utilized in a number of different ways. Below, I will illustrate this with a bird's-eye survey of a number of different examples.

3.1. The Meaning of Colour Terms

As I have argued in Wierzbicka (1980, 1985), the meaning of words such as *green* or *blue* can be defined along the following lines:

green — colour thought of as the colour of grass
blue — colour thought of as the colour of the sky

Since this analysis was first proposed, a number of critics have questioned the use of the phrase *thought of as* in these definitions, and one critic (Goddard 1989a) has proposed the addition of the concept 'like' to my proposed list of universal semantic primitives. Taking this into account, one could rephrase the explications of colour terms roughly speaking along the following lines:

X is green — the colour of X is like the colour of grass
X is blue — the colour of X is like the colour of the sky

While simple formulae of this kind do not seem fully satisfactory either (see Chapter 10), there is a wide range of evidence to suggest that, in principle, the use of "prototypes" such as grass or sky in the explications of colour terms is well justified.

Jackendoff (1983: 113), among others, has tried to use colour terms as evidence that natural language concepts cannot be exhaustively defined into primitives. He wrote: "once the marker *color* is removed from the reading of 'red', what is left to decompose further? How can one make sense of redness minus coloration?" I hope that the formulae adduced above provide an answer to these questions (for fuller discussion, see also Chapter 10).

3.2. The Meaning of Words for Emotions

In a sense, one cannot convey to a blind person what the word *red* stands for (see Locke 1981: 38); or to someone who has never experienced envy what the word *envy* stands for. None the less, it is possible to define envy in terms of a prototypical situation, along the following lines (see Wierzbicka 1972, 1980, 1986*b*):

> X feels envy. =
> > sometimes a person thinks something like this:
> > > something good happened to this other person
> > > it didn't happen to me
> > > I want things like this to happen to me
> > because of this, this person feels something bad
> > X feels something like this

Definitions of this kind demonstrate, I think, the spuriousness of the dilemma of whether emotions are better thought of as prototypes or as 'classically definable' (see Ortony, Clore, and Foss 1987: 344). It has often been argued that emotion concepts cannot be defined because nobody has managed to define them. But, as pointed out by Ortony *et al.*, "the observation that philosophers and psychologists have so far failed to specify adequate definitions of emotion(s) does not establish that the goal is impossible". Whether or not definitions of the kind proposed above for *envy* constitute a "classical" account is a matter for discussion. They do establish, however, that emotions are definable; and that they are definable in terms of a prototypical situation, and a prototypical reaction to it. Without definitions of this kind, it would be impossible to account for the relationships between concepts such as 'envy', 'jealousy', 'hatred', 'contempt', 'pity', 'admiration', and so on. It would also be impossible to compare, and to interpret, emotion concepts cross-linguistically (see Wierzbicka 1986*a*). If the study of emotion concepts encoded in different languages is ever to get off the ground, it is crucial to understand that there is no conflict between prototypes and definitions. (For further discussion, see Chapter 5, section 4.)

3.3. The Meaning of *Cup*

According to Hersch and Caramazza (1976: 274), "Labov (1973) has shown that attempts to give well-defined characterizations in terms of traditional componential analysis of the semantic structure of a common concept such as 'cup' are inadequate." Strictly speaking, however, Labov has only shown that definitions of *cup* offered by conventional dictionaries, such as *Webster's Third*, are inadequate. This is hardly surprising, but does it really establish that no "well-defined characterizations . . . of a common concept such as 'cup' " are possible? Questions of this kind are best answered by simply doing what allegedly cannot be done. For 'cup', and for a host of related concepts, I believe I have done it in Wierzbicka (1985). The definitions provided in that work distinguish between characteristic components which are not part of the invariant and components which are absolutely necessary.

For example, a Chinese cup, small, thin, dainty, handleless and saucerless, can still be recognized as a cup—as long as it is clearly adequate for drinking hot tea from, in a formal setting (at a table), being able to raise it to the mouth with one hand. This means that while a saucer and a handle are definitely included in the proto-type of a cup (an 'ideal' cup *must* have a handle, and a saucer) they are not included in what might be called the essential part of the concept. On the other hand, the components 'made to drink hot liquids from' and 'small enough for people to be able to raise them easily to the mouth with one hand' have to be included in it. (Wierzbicka 1985: 59)

In that sense, these definitions cannot be criticized "for treating all components as contributing equally to the definition of a term" (Hersch and Caramazza 1976: 274). At the same time, they do contradict the assertion that "no subset of these components can conclusively be said to be necessary and sufficient to define a term" (ibid.); and they demonstrate that the opposite is true.

3.4. The Meaning of *Uncle*

According to Chomsky (1972: 85), it is obvious that expressions such as the following (Chomsky's numbers) "must have the same semantic representation".

(33) John's uncle
(34) the person who is the brother of John's mother or father or the husband of the sister of John's mother or father
(35) the person who is the son of one of John's grandparents or the husband of a daughter of one of John's grandparents, but is not his father

In my view, the meaning (and the "semantic representation") of expression 35 is vastly different from that of 34. What is more relevant in the present context is that 34 is not semantically equivalent to 33 either, and that it would be wrong to regard 34 as an explication of 33. Expression 34 treats the mother's or father's brother in the same way as a mother's or father's sister's husband, and therefore it distorts the meaning of 33. If a mother's (or a mother's mother's) sister's husband is categorized as 'uncle' at all it is done by analogy with the focal, prototypical uncle. A definition which would exclude marginal uncles completely (such as "*X*'s uncle = a brother of X's mother or father") would be empirically inadequate, but a disjunction which makes no difference between focal and marginal members is also inadequate. In my view, a satisfactory definition should account for both the invariant and the prototype. For *uncle*, the invariant consists in a certain type of human relationship; and the quality of this relationship is conveyed by the reference to the prototype. I propose (roughly) the following:

> *X* is *Y*'s uncle. =
> if someone were a brother of my mother or father
> I could say about this person: "this is my uncle"
> *Y* can think about *X* like I could think about this person

This definition leaves the denotational range of *uncle* vague, as I think it should, pointing at the same time clearly to the prototype, as I also think it should. (See Wierzbicka 1992a: 348–9.)

3.5. The Meaning of *Bird*

As I have argued earlier, bats, *pace* Rosch and Lakoff, are no more birds than cows are, but ostriches and emus—which do not fly—*are* birds. Does this mean that flying is not an essential part of the concept 'bird'? In my view, flying *is* an essential part of this concept, and the full definition of *bird*, which I have proposed in Wierzbicka (1985: 180), does mention flying (or the ability to move in the air), alongside components referring to feathers, beaks, eggs, and nests. But the definition of *bird* (like all the other definitions of 'natural kinds') is phrased in such a way that it doesn't imply that all the essential features of the concept 'bird' are realized in all creatures categorized as birds. The definition opens with the following frame:

> imagining creatures of this kind people would say these things about them
> . . .

Since the concept 'imagine' is no longer included in the set of primitives, and since in the present version of the NSM grammar 'would' requires a complex sentence ('if . . . would'), I would now rephrase this opening frame as follows:

> people think things like this about creatures of this kind

Accordingly, properties such as flying, feathers, and so on are presented as essential parts of the prototype, not as necessary features of every bird. In addition, however, the full explication of *bird* includes the following proviso: 'some creatures of this kind cannot move in the air, but when people want to say something about creatures of this kind they say something like this: "they can move in the air".'

What applies to *birds* applies also, *mutatis mutandis*, to *fruit* (and of course to countless other concepts). Thus, Geeraerts (1993) questions some components of my (Wierzbicka 1985) definition of *fruit* on the grounds that they don't apply to all fruit, even though the definition itself presents these features as part of the prototype, not a necessary feature of all denotata. This applies, in particular, to the component 'wanting to imagine such things, people would imagine them as growing on trees'. Geeraerts points out, quite rightly, that raspberries are fruit and yet they don't grow on trees. In my view, however, this indisputable fact does not disprove the existence of a conceptual link between 'fruit' and 'trees' (just as the fact that ostriches don't fly does not disprove the existence of a conceptual link between 'birds' and 'flying').

Geeraerts (1993: 266) observes that "we probably would not claim that other people tend to think of raspberries as growing on trees". But neither would we claim that other people think of ostriches as flying. From the fact that people think of ostriches as birds, and of birds as flying, it doesn't follow that they think of ostriches as flying.

It has to be stressed, however, that the two cases (*birds* and *fruit*) are not exactly parallel, because *bird* is a taxonomic category ('a kind of creature'), whereas *fruit*, like *furniture*, is a collective heterogeneous one ('different kinds of things'). The heterogeneity of the conceptual category *fruit* makes typical (but not necessary) features of *fruit* such as 'growing on trees' much less salient than typical (but not necessary) features of *birds* such as 'flying'.

3.6. The Meaning of *Tomato*, *Cabbage*, and *Apples*

It has often been claimed that the names of biological species and other "natural kinds" cannot be fully defined. (See Putnam 1975; Kripke 1972. For an excellent discussion, see Dupré 1981.) In Wierzbicka (1972, 1980) I advocated this theory myself. Since then, however, I have found—through extensive lexicographic research—that this is a fallacy, and that *tigers* or *lemons* are no more indefinable than other concrete concepts (such as *cups* or *mugs*) or than abstract concepts (such as *freedom*, *love*, or *promise*)[6] (see Chapter 5).

---

[6] For a definition of *love*, see Wierzbicka (1986b); of *freedom* (forthcoming *i*); of *promise* (1987a). For definitions of *cup*, *mug*, and many other similar concepts, see Wierzbicka (1985).

But to define either natural kinds or cultural kinds, we do need the concept of prototype. For example, for *cups* we have to predict both the fact that a prototypical cup has a handle and the fact that some cups (e.g. Chinese teacups and Turkish coffee-cups) don't have handles. Similarly, in the case of *tomatoes* we have to account both for the fact that prototypical tomatoes are red and for the fact that there are also yellow tomatoes, which are also called *tomatoes*, or at least *yellow tomatoes*. For *cabbage*, we have to predict both the fact that *cabbage* without modifier is greenish (except in elliptical sentences) and the fact that there is also the so-called *red cabbage*. For *apples*, we have to predict the fact that they can be red, green, or yellow; but also the fact that wanting to imagine (or paint) 'good apples', people are more likely to imagine them red than either yellow or green.

To account for facts of this kind, it is justified, I think, to have recourse to analytical devices similar to that which has been used to account for flightless birds. For example, in the definition of *cabbage* I have included the following components:

> the leaflike parts are greenish or whitish-greenish
> in some things of this kind the leaflike parts are reddish
> wanting to imagine things of this kind people would imagine them as greenish

In the present version of NSM, I would rephrase the last component as follows:

> when people want to say what things of this kind look like
> they say they are greenish

3.7. The Meaning of *Climb*

Alongside *bachelor*, the verb *climb* has played an important role in semantic theory as a key example of a word which—allegedly—cannot be defined in terms of any necessary and sufficient components and which can only be analysed in terms of a prototype. For example, Verschueren (1985: 46) wrote:

To show that a similar analysis is feasible for verbs, I adopt an example given by Fillmore (1978); the verb TO CLIMB typically describes an *ascending* motion in a *clambering* fashion. I quote: 'A monkey climbing up a flagpole satisfies both of these conditions. The monkey climbing down the flagpole satisfies the clambering component only, but is nevertheless engaged in an action that can be properly called climbing. A snail climbing up the flagpole satisfies the ascending condition and can still be said to be climbing. But the snail is not privileged to *climb down* the flagpole, since that activity would involve neither clambering nor ascending.'

However, this analysis fails to explain why a sentence such as "the monkey climbed the flagpole" cannot be interpreted as meaning that the monkey climbed *down* the flagpole. If the direction upward was part of the prototype but not part of the invariant, how could we be so sure that the monkey who "climbed the flagpole" was climbing upwards?

Difficulties of this kind have prompted Jackendoff (1985) to devote to the verb *climb* a whole study, and to use it as evidence for his own version of prototype semantics, developed in Jackendoff (1983). In essence, however, Jackendoff's analysis is not very different from Fillmore's: he, too, posits for *climb* components such as 'upward' and 'clambering fashion', and he, too, claims that either of these components can be 'suppressed', though they cannot both be suppressed at the same time. For example, in the sentence "the train climbed the mountain" the 'clambering manner' component is suppressed, and the component 'upwards' is present, whereas in the sentence "Bill climbed down the ladder" it is the other way round. The semantic formulae proposed for these sentences are as follows (Jackendoff 1985: 288–9):

The train climbed the mountain. =

$$\underset{\text{Event}}{\text{GO (TRAIN,}} \quad \underset{\text{Path}}{\overset{\text{TO TOP OF [}_{\text{Thing}}\text{ MOUNTAIN]}}{\text{VIA [}_{\text{Place}}\text{ ON [}_{\text{Thing}}\text{ MOUNTAIN])}}}$$
$$\text{UPWARD}$$

Bill climbed down the ladder. =

$$\underset{\text{Event}}{\text{GO (BILL, [}_{\text{Path}}\text{ DOWN THE LADDER])}} \quad \text{[}_{\text{Manner}}\text{ CLAMBERING]}$$

But this analysis is unsatisfactory, too, because it fails to predict, for example, that if a train went quickly up a hill it couldn't be described as 'climbing'. There is a difference in meaning between the two variants in the following pairs of sentences:

(1) The train climbed the mountain.
(2) The train shot up the mountain.
(3) The temperature climbed to 102 degrees.
(4) The temperature shot to 102 degrees.

Despite his rich arsenal of descriptive devices, including multiple brackets and "preferential features", Jackendoff's analysis cannot account for facts of this kind. In my view, what is really needed to account for such facts is a more careful, and more imaginative, phrasing of the necessary and sufficient components of the concept 'climb'. I would propose the following (cf. Taylor 1989: 108):

X climbed . . . =
X moved like people move in places where they have to use their arms and legs to move upwards

And a little more precisely:

> X climbed . . . =
> sometimes in some places
> if people want to move upwards
> they have to move both their legs and their arms
> X moved like people move at those times in such places

For temperature, the similarity in question can hardly be interpreted as referring to anything other than slowness. For trains, it can be interpreted as referring to slowness and apparent difficulty. For people, too, it can be interpreted as referring to slowness and apparent difficulty; but it can also refer to a quick and apparently effortless movement upwards in places where normally people would have to use their arms and legs to move upwards at all (see "Watching him climb the cliff quickly and effortlessly I was filled with pride and admiration").

Thus, a prototype is indeed relevant to the concept 'climb'. But this prototype is not "suppressed" in less typical uses of the verb. It is part of the semantic invariant itself.

4. Conclusion

There was a time when almost any problem in linguistic analysis could be "solved" by appealing to the distinction between "competence" and "performance". (For discussion, see e.g. R. A. Harris 1993.) These days, this particular solution to linguistic problems is usually viewed with suspicion. But the desire to find simple solutions to a range of linguistic problems has survived. "Grice saves" and a facile resort to prototypes are two characteristic examples.

Posner (1986: 58) wrote: "As impressed as I am with the insights obtained from Rosch's work, it is rather hard for me to get very excited about the great Aristotle versus Rosch debate." Rosch's work indeed contains interesting insights, but it would be difficult to maintain that they have contributed a great deal to semantic description. In too many cases, these new ideas have been treated as an excuse for intellectual laziness and sloppiness. In my view, the notion of prototype has to prove its usefulness through semantic description, not through semantic theorizing (see Wierzbicka 1985). But if it is treated as a magical key to open all doors without effort, the chances are that it will cause more harm than good.

Concepts encoded in natural language are, in a sense, vague (see Black 1937). The challenge consists in portraying the vagueness inherent in natural language with precision. I agree entirely with Hersch and Caramazza (1976: 273) when they say that "natural language concepts are inherently vague". But I cannot agree with them when they go on to say that "the meaning of a term could be specified as a *fuzzy set of meaning components*". Natural language concepts are characterized by referential indeterminacy in the sense that while "there are things of which the description 'tree' is clearly true and things of which the description 'tree' is clearly false . . . there are a host of borderline cases" (Putnam 1975: 133). This doesn't mean, however, that the meaning of the word *tree* can only be specified as a fuzzy set of meaning components. I have tried to demonstrate this point by providing precise, non-fuzzy definitions of *tree*, and numerous similar concepts in Wierzbicka (1985). I have also attempted to show that even the "fuzziest" concepts of all—"hedges" such as *approximately, around, almost, at least*, or *roughly*—can be given precise, non-fuzzy definitions, composed of fully specified discrete components (see Wierzbicka 1986*c,d*, 1991*a*).

If people argue whether or not a radio is "furniture", we don't have to account for this by saying that *radio* possesses the meaning component 'furniture' to a certain degree, less than *table* or *desk*. There are sufficient (linguistic) reasons for not including the feature 'furniture' in the meaning of either *radio* or *table* at all, as there are sufficient reasons for not including features such as 'kitchenware', 'tableware', or 'crockery' in the meaning of *cup*. It is not a matter of degree whether concepts such as *pelican, oak*, or *rose* contain in their meaning components such as 'bird', 'tree', and 'flower'; they simply do contain them. Nor is it a matter of degree whether concepts such as *table, radio, refrigerator*, or *cup* contain in their meaning components such as 'furniture', 'kitchenware', 'tool', 'device', or 'implement'; they simply don't. (For justification of this claim, and for detailed semantic analyses, see Wierzbicka 1985.)

Vagueness may reside in the semantic components themselves. Components such as 'like the colour of grass' (in 'green') are indeed vague, and this vagueness is mirrored in the referential indeterminacy of the corresponding words. Components such as (roughly speaking) 'thought of as a man who can marry' are perhaps not vague but are subjective, not objective; they refer not to the "reality out there", but to the speakers' ways of conceptualizing reality. But neither vagueness nor subjectivity of semantic components should be confused with any "presence to a degree". It is not the Aristotelian notion of necessary and sufficient features which causes trouble in semantic analysis; it is the tacit behaviourist assumption that the necessary and sufficient features should correspond to measurable, objectively ascertainable aspects of external reality.

Many psychologists and philosophers have embraced the prototype theory on the assumption that most concepts have resisted all attempts to define them and that "enormous efforts have gone into the attempt to identify a featural substrate" (Armstrong *et al.* 1983: 299). But this is an illusion. In fact, relatively little effort by professional semanticists has gone into that so far. Armstrong and her colleagues support their assertion with a reference to Katz and Fodor (1963) and Katz (1972). But, with all due respect to these writers, they are, essentially, semantic theorists, not practitioners of semantic description. It is a misunderstanding to credit theorists such as these with "enormous efforts to identify" the semantic components of any everyday concepts.

As Armstrong *et al.* (1983: 268) point out, "the only good answer [to the question 'why do so many doubt the validity of the definitional view?'] is that the definitional theory is difficult to work out in the required detail. No one has succeeded in finding the supposed simplest categories (the features)."

But how many bona fide semanticists have tried to do that? It is true that not only numerous philosophers and psychologists, but also "generations of lexicographers" (Armstrong *et al.* 1983: 301) have failed to produce successful componential definitions of everyday concepts. But lexicography has always lacked a theoretical basis. Theoretical semantics has flourished in an empirical vacuum, and lexicographers have grappled with their "practical" tasks without any theoretical framework (see Wierzbicka 1985). Given this lack of help from semantic theory, it is the lexicographers' achievements, not their failures, which are truly remarkable (see Chapters 8 and 9).

The era of systematic lexicographic research, based on rigorous theoretical foundations, has only recently begun (see e.g. Mel'čuk and Žolkovskij 1984; Mel'čuk *et al.* 1984, 1988, 1992; Apresjan 1991). The success of this research will depend partly on its ability to absorb and to develop insights from the psychological and philosophical inquiry into the role of prototypes in human thinking. In my view, however, it will also depend on the sustained efforts to establish, and verify, the basic stock of human concepts—universal semantic primitives—out of which thoughts and complex concepts are constructed (see Osherson and Smith 1981: 55; also Wierzbicka 1972, 1980, 1985).

The natural conviction that "the primitive conceptual repertoire *cannot* be as rich as the available repertoire of categories; hence that many concepts *must* be analysable" (Fodor *et al.* 1980: 52) is being validated in the ever-increasing body of careful definitions based on clear and rigorous theoretical foundations. Appeals to prototypes cannot relieve us from the labour of devising definitions which really work. Prototypes cannot "save us" from careful lexicographic research; on the other hand, they can certainly help us to construct the best, the most revealing, definitions, aimed at human conceptualization of reality reflected and embodied in language.

5 Semantic Primitives and Semantic Fields

□ □ _____

1. Introduction

It has often been said that the meaning of a word "depends" on the meaning of the other words in the lexicon (see e.g. Trier 1931). Strictly speaking, I do not believe that this is the case: since the meaning of a word is, as I have been arguing all along, a configuration of semantic primitives for each word, its meaning can (and must) be defined positively, regardless of the meanings of any "neighbouring" words in the lexicon. The meanings of different words can overlap (as *abc* overlaps with *bcd*), but both the similarities and the differences can be stated only after the meaning of each word has been identified.

Furthermore, what applies to semantic synchrony applies also to semantic diachrony: although the meaning of one of two semantically overlapping words can change without a concomitant change affecting the other (e.g. *abc* may change to *acd*, with *bcd* remaining what it was). In any case, a change in a word's meaning (e.g. from *abc* to *acd*) can only be established if we are able to describe both the original meaning (*abc*) and the subsequent meaning (*acd*). To do this, we must be able to analyse each meaning in terms of its components (that is, the relevant semantic primitives).

On the other hand, although the meaning of a word does not depend on the meanings of other words, to establish what the meaning of a word is one has to compare it with the meanings of other, intuitively related words. By comparing a word to other words that intuitively are felt to be related to it, we can establish what each of these words really means; having done this, we can compare them again, this time more precisely, being able to identify the elements that are different. Proceeding in this way, we can often discover remarkable symmetries and regularities in the semantic structure of many words—as well as unexpected asymmetries and irregularities. We can discover self-contained fields of semantically related words with analogous semantic patterning. We can also discover irregular and open-ended networks of interlacing networks.

The idea that words form more or less natural groupings, and that at least some of these groupings are non-arbitrary, is intuitively appealing, even irresistible. But if we couldn't decompose meanings into components, we couldn't really investigate this possibility in a systematic and methodical way. If we do, however, have a list of hypothetical indefinables, and if we learn how to discover configurations of indefinables encapsulated in individual words, we can reveal the hidden structure of these words and *ipso facto* we can reveal the structural relations linking different words together. For example, if we establish that the meaning of one word is *abc*, of another, *bcd*, and of a third, *bcf*, we will know that their common core is *bc*. Consequently, we can reveal non-arbitrary semantic fields, and we can investigate their nature. Thus, semantic primitives offer us a tool for investigating the structure of semantic groupings or fields. In particular, they can show us how to distinguish non-arbitrary semantic groupings from arbitrary ones; and how to distinguish discrete, self-contained groupings from open-ended ones.

In what follows, I illustrate the preceding tenets with a number of examples pertaining to different areas of the lexicon. Before doing so, however, I must clarify the notion of "configuration", which was just illustrated (perhaps somewhat misleadingly) with combinations of letters such as *abc* or *bcd*. In fact, meanings are very complex structures, built not directly from simple elements such as 'someone', 'want', or 'this', but from structured components such as 'I want something', 'this is good' or 'you did something bad'. Components of this kind are ordered, and because they often contain the temporal element 'after', or the causal component 'because', sequences of such components can often be regarded as "scripts" or "scenarios" (see Abelson 1981; Schank and Abelson 1977). This applies, for example, to words designating emotions or to words designating speech acts. (I return to this point later.) "Concrete" nouns (i.e. names of natural or cultural kinds) will usually exhibit a more static semantic structure, but, here too, many different components are usually involved, and these components refer not only to certain inherent features of the referents, but also to the "external frames"—such as habitat, behaviour or typical interaction with people in the case of animals, or the typical situation of use in the case of artefacts (see Fillmore 1975*b*, 1977). Here too, the components have to be seen as ordered (see Wierzbicka 1985). The general assumptions stated in this section are now illustrated with three sections devoted to specific semantic domains: (1) the names of "natural kinds" and "cultural kinds", (2) speech act verbs, and (3) emotion concepts. Since the first two domains have both been explored in considerable detail elsewhere (see Wierzbicka 1985, 1987*a*, 1992*e*), the present discussion of these domains will be brief, sketchy, and selective, and the section on emotions will be disproportionately longer.

2. Natural Kinds and Cultural Kinds

Names of animals (in the everyday sense of the word, not in the scientific
sense), of birds, fishes, flowers, or trees embody, I believe, taxonomic concepts, that is, concepts based on the idea of "kind". It is reasonable, therefore, that they are usually referred to as "natural kind" words. For
example, *dog* or *lion* can be defined as "a kind of animal"—plus, in each
case, a long sequence of components, specifying the habitat, appearance,
behaviour, relation to people, and so on (for illustrations, see Wierzbicka
1985; see also Chapters 11 and 12).

Words such as *dog, lion, tiger, squirrel,* and so on can be said to form a
well-defined, discrete semantic field because they all have definitions
headed, so to speak, by the same component, 'a kind of animal'. Similarly,
words such as *swallow, eagle, penguin,* or *emu* can be said to form a well-
defined, discrete semantic field because they all have definitions headed by
the same component, 'a kind of bird'; and words such as *oak, willow, birch,*
or *palm* can also be said to form a well-defined, discrete semantic field
because they all have definitions headed by the same component, 'a kind of
tree'.

Furthermore, the conceptual supercategories on which the names of
"natural kinds" are based have also a taxonomic character. For example,
animal, bird, or *fish* can all be justifiably defined as "a kind of creature"
(plus of course a number of additional components), whereas *tree* or *flower*
can be justifiably defined as, roughly, "a kind of thing growing out of the
ground" (plus, again, a number of additional components).

On the other hand, it is an illusion to think that words such as *doll, ball,
tricycle, rattle, swing,* and *teddy bear* can be similarly defined in terms of
one non-arbitrary supercategory such as toy. As I have tried to show in my
Lexicography and Conceptual Analysis (Wierzbicka 1985), words such as
toy, vehicle, container, or *weapon* embody functional concepts, not taxonomic concepts; and they are not related to "cultural kind" words (such as
tricycle, bottle, cup, or *knife*) in the same way in which taxonomic supercategories (*animal, bird, fish, flower,* or *tree*) are related to their subordi-
nates (such as *dog, canary, fruit, rose,* or *oak*). For example, *toy* doesn't
stand for any particular, describable, and recognizable *kind* of thing; rather,
it stands for things of *any kind* made by people for children to play with.
Therefore "toys", "weapons", and so on are not taxonomic supercategories,
in the sense that "animals", "birds", or "trees" are. Consequently, one cannot speak of "semantic fields" of "toys", "vehicles", or "weapons" in the
same sense in which one can speak of semantic fields of "animals", "birds",
"trees", and so on.

If one wishes to, one can of course group words such as *doll, ball, tri-*

cycle, and *rattle* together, and for certain purposes this may be useful (for example, as a list of various kinds of objects that can be bought in a toy department of a department store). But a grouping of this kind would not have a semantic basis.

This is not to imply that words such as *doll, ball, tricycle*, and so on are not all "headed" (in their semantic structure) by the same semantic component. They are. But the component in question is not "a kind of toy"; rather, it is a much more general one, subsuming a vast number of names of human artefacts: roughly "a kind of thing made by people". There is no reason, of course, why one should not speak of all the words headed by this component as forming one discrete, non-arbitrary semantic field. But it is a huge field, which itself is not hierarchically structured: it is not divided, semantically speaking, into "toys", "vehicles", "weapons", and so on, because these are functional categories, not taxonomic ones. Of course if we want to, we can classify cultural kinds into toys, weapons, instruments, kitchenware, and so on, but this classification would be arbitrary from the point of view of semantic structure. From the point of view of folk categorization reflected in the semantic structure, *cups* are not "a kind of kitchenware", *bicycles* are not "a kind of vehicle", *balls* are not "a kind of toy", and *knives* are not "a kind of weapon".

I suggest, therefore, that names of cultural kinds do not form non-arbitrary, discrete fields, whereas names of natural kinds do. In my view, it could be misleading to speak, for example, of "the field of containers" (see Lehrer 1974) as if there were a non-arbitrary, self-contained field of "names of containers". Of course, words such as *cup, mug, bottle, jar, jug, bucket*, and *barrel* are mutually closely related, and in fact their full explications reveal a degree of symmetry even greater than one might have expected (see the explications of these words in Wierzbicka 1985). But *bucket* is also felt to be related to *bowl* or *tub, bottle* is related to *carafe, carafe* is related to *vase, pot* is related to *pan*, and so on; and tubs, vases, and pans would not be naturally described as "containers". As argued in Chapter 4, birds do not fade off similarly into bats, fishes into animals (in the everyday sense of the word), or flowers into trees (for example, magnolias are thought of as a kind of tree, whereas roses are thought of as a kind of flower; emus are thought of as a kind of bird, whereas bats are not; and so on). Thus, semantically, *pots* and *pans, buckets* or *bowls* are not "a kind of container", whereas *sparrows* are "a kind of bird", and *roses*, "a kind of flower".

"Category membership" of words and meanings cannot be established by asking informants simple questions, or giving them simple sorting tasks. It can only be established by methodical semantic analysis. In the absence of such an analysis, different schemes of "semantic" and "conceptual" categorization proposed in recent literature, particularly in psychological literature, often reflect the pre-theoretical ideas of the researchers rather than results of valid, well-conceived empirical investigations. (For further discussion, see Chapters 11 and 12.) To illustrate:

parrot
a kind of bird
if people wanted to say many things about them,
    they could say these things: . . .

sparrow
a kind of bird
if people wanted to say many things about them,
    they could say these things: . . .

bird
a kind of creature
if people wanted to say many things about them,
    they could say these things: . . .

bucket
a kind of thing
if people wanted to say many things about them,
    they could say these things: . . .

barrel
a kind of thing
if people wanted to say many things about them,
    they could say these things: . . .

3. Speech Act Verbs

In English, and in other European languages, there are hundreds of verbs that can be said to form, together, one coherent, self-contained field; these are verbs referring to "different things that one can do with words", that is, to different types of speech acts. I have investigated some 250 such words in my *English Speech Act Verbs: A Semantic Dictionary* (Wierzbicka 1987a), and I have found a very high degree of patterning. What gives coherence to the field of "speech act verbs" is the presence of some well-defined semantic components. These components underlie what is usually called the "illocutionary force" (see Austin 1962a; Searle 1976) of the speech act described by a given speech act verb. This illocutionary force comprises components that spell out the speaker's intentions, assumptions, or emotions, expressed in speech. For example, the verbs *ask* and *order* describe an attitude that includes the following component:

(I say:) I want you to do it

In addition, *order* includes the component:

(I think:) you have to do it because of this

whereas *ask* contains the opposite assumption:

(I think:) you don't have to do it because of this

Forbid is in some ways symmetrical with respect to *order*, and it includes the component:

(I say:) I don't want you to do it

as well as a similarly confident assumption:

(I think:) you can't do it because of this

Complain includes the components:

(I say:) something bad is happening to me
I feel something bad because of this

Reproach, rebuke, scold, and *reprimand* include the component:

(I say:) you did something bad

Thank and *apologize* include, respectively, the components:

(I say:) you did something good for me
(I say:) I did something bad to you

And so on. It is not my purpose to provide here exhaustive explications of any speech act verbs. (The interested reader can find such explications in Wierzbicka 1987*a*.) Rather, I am trying to show here how the "field" of speech act verbs can be delimited in a non-arbitrary way.

The class of verbs that I am talking about does not coincide with the class of "performative" verbs. For example, whereas *ask, order, forbid,* or *apologize* can all be used performatively, *reproach, threaten,* and *boast* cannot:

I ask/order/forbid you to do it.
I apologize for what I have done.
*I reproach you shouldn't have done it.
*I threaten you I will do something bad to you if you do it.
*I boast I am the best.

None the less, all these verbs exhibit the same kind of semantic structure. They attribute to the speaker a certain attitude that can be portrayed in terms of first-person illocutionary components such as

(I say:) you did something bad [*reprimand*]
(I say:) I will do something bad to you [*threat*]
(I say:) I am good (other people are not like me) [*boast*]

I believe that components of this kind, all framed, explicitly or implicitly, by "I say:" do allow us to identify a class of words in a non-arbitrary way; and that this class does constitute a "real", relatively self-contained part of the English lexicon.

It is particularly interesting to note that the phrasing of components of this kind can be supported not only with semantic but also with syntactic evidence, as different speech act verbs that share certain semantic components (or combinations of components) can be shown also to share certain syntactic frames or combinations of frames. (See Lehrer 1988; Pinker 1989.) Consider, for example, the component

> you did something bad/good

which is associated with the following frame:

> X V-ed Y for doing Z.

For example, the following verbs share this component and this frame: *reproach, rebuke, reprove, reprimand, admonish, scold.* Utterances such as

> X reproached/rebuked/reprimanded/scolded/thanked Y for Z

imply that X said to Y something that included the semantic component "you did something bad (good)" (cf. *X rebuked/reproached/scolded Y, Z).

The frame "X V-ed Y for Z" is also used with verbs such as *criticize* or *praise*, which describe acts that can be performed, so to speak, behind the back of the target person: one cannot *reprimand* or *rebuke* people behind their backs, but one can *criticize* or *praise* them to a third person. However, the two groups of verbs can be distinguished in terms of another syntactic frame: "X V-ed Y's Z":

> X criticized/praised Y for Z
> X criticized/praised Y's Z
> *X rebuked/reprimanded Y's Z

Thus, speech act verbs that imply the component

> person Y did something bad/good

allow both of the syntactic frames in question:

> (1) X V-ed Y for doing Z
> (2) X V-ed Y's Z

whereas speech act verbs that imply the component

> you did something bad

allow only the first of these two frames.

As a second example, compare the syntactic possibilities of verbs such as *order*, *command*, *instruct*, *urge*, *ask*, and *beg*, all of which can be said to imply the semantic component

I want you to do this

and all of which can occur in the syntactic frame

X V-ed *Y* to do *Z*

Some of these verbs, however, have an additional frame:

X V-ed *Y* for *Z*
(e.g. *X* asked/begged *Y* for *Z*)

which the others don't have

*X ordered/commanded/urged *Y* for *Z*

This additional syntactic frame links *ask* (for) and *beg* (for) with verbs such as *plead* (for), *apply* (for), or *wish* (for)—all verbs that imply that the speaker cannot expect to have control over the outcome, that is to say, verbs that attribute to the speaker the intention to convey (among others) the following combination of components:

I say: I want you to do *Z*
I don't think you will do it because of this

On the other hand, verbs such as *order*, *command*, or *urge*, which take the frame "*X V*-ed *Y* to do *Z*" but not "*X V*-ed *Y* for *Z*", imply, as mentioned earlier, a more confident attitude on the part of the speaker:

I say: I want you to do *Z*
I think you will do it because of this

The interested reader is likely to raise at this point some objections pointing to apparent asymmetries and idiosyncrasies. For example, why can't *demand*, which should be similar to *order* and *command*, occur in the frame "*X V*-ed *Y* to do *Z*"? Or why can *plead* and *apply* occur with FOR (like *ask* or *beg*) but (unlike *ask* or *beg*) cannot occur in the frame "*X V*-ed *Y* to do *Z*"?

*X demanded *Y* to do *Z*
X allowed/forbade *Y* to do *Z*
*X pleaded for *Z*
X applied for *Z*
*X pleaded *Y* to do *Z*
*X pleaded *Y* for *Z*
*X applied *Y* to do *Z*
*X applied *Y* for *Z*

At first sight, differences of this kind may seem idiosyncratic and semantically arbitrary. But if one studies them more closely, one discovers that far from being arbitrary, they, too, point to very real semantic differences and thus confirm the reliability of syntactic clues in semantic analysis. For example, one *pleads* WITH a person, as one *argues* or *reasons* WITH a person, because *plead*, like *argue* or *reason*, involves an exchange of arguments rather than a direct appeal to the addressee's will. One *demands* SOMETHING, not SOMEONE, because what the person who *demands* something wants is, above all, a certain outcome (which may be brought about by somebody's action), not a specific action by a particular addressee. For the same reason, one *applies* for SOMETHING, and one doesn't apply SOMEONE, because what the *applying* person wants is, above all, a particular outcome, not a specific action of a particular addressee. At the same time, the attitude of a person who *applies* for something is less confident than that of a person who *demands* something; and this is why one *applies* FOR something, as one *hopes* or *asks* FOR something, whereas one *demands* SOMETHING, not FOR SOMETHING (for evidence and justification, see Wierzbicka 1987*a*).

Certainly, this method of verification cannot be applied to all areas of the lexicon. (Generally speaking, it is more applicable to verbs than to nouns.) It can, however, be reliably applied to speech act verbs; and for this reason alone, speech act verbs constitute a particularly fruitful domain for semantic experimentation. In particular, they offer a golden opportunity to investigate the structure of a large and highly patterned "semantic field"; and to explore, on an empirical basis, the very notion of a "semantic field".

4. Emotion Concepts

Emotion concepts encoded in the English lexicon constitute a coherent and reasonably self-contained (though not sharply delimited) cognitive domain, with a characteristic and specifiable type of semantic structure. All the words belonging to this domain can be defined in terms of cognitive structures that are typically associated with the emotions in question. In this section, I will try to substantiate this claim by analysing a reasonably large group of emotion concepts, drawn from two separate areas: roughly speaking, emotions linked with "events contrary to expectations", and emotions linked with "misfortunes". (For a discussion of a third group of emotion concepts, including 'terrified', 'petrified', and 'horrified', see Chapter 7.) The first group includes *frustration, relief, disappointment, surprise,* and *amazement*:

> *Frustration* (e.g. *X* feels frustrated)
> *X* feels something

sometimes a person thinks something like this:
   I want to do something
   I can do it
after this, this person thinks something like this:
   I can't do it
this person feels something bad because of this
X feels like this

Relief (e.g. *X* feels relieved)
X feels something
sometimes a person thinks something like this:
   something bad will happen
   I don't want this
after this, this person thinks something like this:
   I know now: this bad thing will not happen
because of this, this person feels something good
X feels something like this

Disappointment
X feels something
sometimes a person thinks something like this:
   something good will happen
   I want this
after this, this person thinks something like this:
   I know now: this good thing will not happen
because of this, this person feels something bad
X feels something like this

Surprise
X feels something
sometimes a person thinks something like this:
   something is happening now
   I didn't think before now: this will happen
   I want to know more about it
because of this, this person feels something
X feels something like this

Amazement
X feels something
sometimes a person thinks something like this:
   something is happening now
   I didn't know before now: this can happen
   I want to know more about it
because of this, this person feels something
X feels something like this

As these examples show, the definition of an emotion concept takes the form of a prototypical scenario describing not so much an external situation as a highly abstract cognitive structure: roughly, to feel a certain emotion means to feel like a person does who has certain (specifiable) thoughts characteristic of that particular situation (and to undergo some internal process because of this). Typically, though not necessarily, these thoughts involve references to 'doing' or 'happening', to something 'good' or 'bad', and to 'wanting' or 'not wanting'. (See e.g. Wierzbicka 1990*c*, 1992*e*, 1994*c*.)

These examples show also how by analysing individual concepts we can *ipso facto* show how they are mutually related. Thus the definitions of *relief* and *disappointment* (differing only in the choice of 'good' or 'bad') are symmetrical and in a way support one another. Similarly, the definitions of *surprise* and *amazement* are almost identical, and differing only in one point ('will' versus 'can'); and these two, too, support one another. On the other hand, *frustration* does not have a symmetrical counterpart; and yet its meaning, too, can be established with precision and clarity. On the whole, the relations between emotion concepts can be quite diverse (as the examples given above and those which follow illustrate); at the same time, a large number of such concepts can be shown to follow the same overall semantic pattern.

Turning now to the second group, we will note that in English, as in many other languages, many emotion terms refer to 'bad things' happening to people. They include (among others) *sad, unhappy, distressed, upset,* and *depressed,* which I will now define one by one, using the format illustrated above.

> *Sad* (e.g. *X* feels sad)
> *X* feels something
> sometimes a person thinks something like this:
> > something bad happened
> > if I didn't know that it happened
> > > I would say: I don't want it to happen
> > I don't say this now
> > because I know: I can't do anything
> > because of this, this person feels something bad
> *X* feels something like this

In a prototypical scenario, the "bad event" is in the past ('something bad happened'; for example, somebody died).

> *Unhappy* (e.g. *X* feels unhappy)
> *X* feels something
> sometimes a person thinks something like this:

something bad happened to me
I don't want this
if I could, I would want to do something because of this
because of this, this person feels something bad
X feels something like this

The main difference between *unhappy* and *sad* consists in the personal character of the former: if my neighbour's close friend dies I may be sad but not unhappy, but if my own close friend dies I may well feel unhappy.

Furthermore, *unhappy* suggests a less resigned frame of mind than *sad*. For example, if one says "I am unhappy about it" one may well intend to try to "do something about it", but one doesn't say "I am sad about it". This difference is accounted for by the unaccepting component 'I don't want this', and by the absence of the resigned component 'I can't do anything' in the explication of *unhappy*.

The combination of a past event ('something bad HAPPENED') with a current rejection ('I don't want this') may seem illogical, but in natural language "illogicalities" of this kind are very common. (One characteristic example was provided by the sign "1940 Annexation NO!", displayed by Lithuanian demonstrators in Vilnius in January 1990.)

Distressed
X feels something
sometimes a person thinks something like this:
    something bad is happening to me now
    I don't want this
    because of this, I want to do something
    I don't know what I can do
    I want someone to do something
    because of this, this person feels something
X feels something like this

The common phrase *distress signals*, used with reference to ships, points in the same direction. The ship's crew may well wish to signal a message along the following lines: 'something bad is happening to us', 'we don't want this', 'because of this, we want to do something', 'we don't know what we can do', 'we want someone (else) to do something'. But there would be no point in any ship sending out "signals of sadness", or, for that matter, "signals of unhappiness".

The word *now* in the explication of *distressed* proposed above may seem redundant, given the present tense of the verb in 'something bad is happening to me'; none the less it may be justified, as it helps to account for the short span of *distress*. *Joy*, too, has a present orientation ('something good is happening'), and so does *worry* ('something is happening'), but they can both refer to the "present time" in a broad sense; by contrast, *distress* always refers to the "present time" in a more narrow, more specific sense. For example, if I know that somebody that I love "is coming" next month, this may fill me with *joy* for many days; and if I *worry* about my child's poor progress at school, I may be thinking about months rather than days or hours. But *distress* seems to involve an immediate reaction to what is happening *now* ("today" rather than "in the present period").

> *Upset*
> X feels something
> sometimes a person thinks something like this:
>> something bad happened to me now
>> if I could, I would want to do something because of this
>> I don't know if I can do anything
>> I can't think now
> because of this, this person feels something bad
> X feels something like this

A person is *upset* by something that has happened to him 'before now', not by something that is happening to him 'now'. But the event in question is very recent; so much so that the experiencer hasn't had the time to regain his balance (as he is expected to do shortly).

The combination of the past tense with the word *now* in the explication is meant to capture both the pastness of the event and its immediate character (see the same combination in the sentence "It happened to me just now"). At the moment, the experiencer is off balance and cannot think as usual. His attitude is not passive, or resigned, as in sadness ('I can't do anything'); rather, he is confused and temporarily cannot cope ('I don't know if I can do anything'). But unlike a person who is *distressed*, someone who is *upset* is not crying for help or otherwise drawing attention to himself.

The semantic structure of most emotion concepts, then, can be represented as follows:

> X feels something
> sometimes a person thinks something like this:
>> .   .   .   .
>> .   .   .   .
>> .   .   .
> because of this, this person feels something
> X feels something like this

This structure can be said to define a large and coherent semantic field. The size of this field differs from language to language, but most, if not all, languages do appear to have a reasonably self-contained "field" of this kind.

5. Conclusion

If we want to establish what the meaning of a word is, and if we want to demonstrate the validity of our analysis, comparisons with other words are usually necessary. But the *meanings* of individual words do not have to be dependent on "whatever other lexical items may be available in the inventory"; and, ultimately, a definition, too, has to stand on its own. A definition expresses a hypothesis about the meaning of a particular word, and it is valid if it accounts correctly for the range of use of this particular word. The boundaries of this range may be "fuzzy", but even this fuzziness can and should be predicted by a well-phrased and well-researched definition. Meanings can be rigorously described and compared if they are recognized for what they are: unique and culture-specific configurations of universal semantic primitives. When the configurations of primitives conceptualized in individual words are revealed, the relations between different words also reveal themselves. I think, therefore, that the semantic primitives approach to semantic analysis also offers a necessary firm ground for the study of semantic fields.

6 Semantics and "Primitive Thought"

□ □ ————————————————————————————

> The functions of the human mind are common to the whole of humanity.
>
> (Franz Boas 1938*c*: 135)

1. Introduction

The question of universal semantic primitives is closely linked with that of the "psychic unity of mankind" (Boas 1938*c*). Just over two decades ago a leading American psychologist, George Miller, wrote:

Every culture has its myths. One of our most persistent is that nonliterate people in less developed countries possess something we like to call a "primitive mentality" that is both different from and inferior to our own. . . . No one would care to deny that differences exist. Any denial would be tantamount to saying that differences in experience that result from living in widely different cultures and technologies have no important psychological consequences. Rather, the argument concerns the nature of those differences, and their sources. (1971*a*, p. vii)

In linguistics and anthropology such terms as "primitive thought" became discredited rather more than two decades ago (although occasionally they still creep into print—witness the title of Hallpike's (1979) book, *The Foundations of Primitive Thought*, described in a serious recent publication (Le Pan 1989: 3) as "monumental"). But the precise nature of cognitive differences between different societies—in particular, Western societies and non-Western tribal societies—remains an open question (see e.g. Bain 1992).

Discussions of this question have always relied to a considerable extent on language. Rightly so, since language is "the best mirror of human thought" (Leibniz 1765/1981: 334) and evidence from language is crucial in determining the fundamental thought patterns of different human groups; but evidence from language can be misinterpreted, and data reported by field-workers require serious semantic analysis before they can be treated as a source of information about conceptual systems.

Discussing the alleged absence of abstract thinking in some human societies, Hallpike writes: "It is . . . necessary to do some preliminary semantic ground-work before we can usefully discuss the extent to which primitive thought is or is not abstract" (1979: 171).

The term "primitive" (which Hallpike defends on the grounds of ety-mology!) is unfortunate because it implies a value judgement, like Lévy-Bruhl's (1926) term "inferior". But the real question addressed in Hallpike's work is important, and should not be banned on a priori ideological grounds: Are there essential qualitative differences in the cognition of dif-ferent peoples? The view that there are such differences is not fashionable these days, and Hallpike deserves some credit for the courage he shows in defending it, as do its other recent proponents (see e.g. Bain 1992; Bain and Sayers 1990; Le Pan 1989). Instead of being simply dismissed, their views deserve to be examined. But for this examination to be fruitful, a prelimi-nary semantic groundwork must indeed be laid.

In this chapter, I will try to lay such a groundwork. I will argue that the reasoning of believers in "primitive thought" is fallacious, and try to show where exactly it goes wrong. In particular, I am going to argue that the pro-ponents of the "primitive thought" doctrine usually do not understand the phenomenon of polysemy and have no methodology which would allow them to establish whether a word has one or more meanings. In my dis-cussion, I will focus on several crucial concepts which have been alleged to be lacking in this or that language (notably, 'if', 'because', 'someone', 'all', 'know', and 'think'); I will start, however, with an example from a language not usually identified with "primitive thought".

Suppose someone were to claim that French speakers have no concept of 'daughter' and as evidence were to adduce the fact that both the English words *daughter* and *girl* are translated into French as *fille*. Would such a claim be accepted? Presumably not. Rather, it would be pointed out that the word *fille* is polysemous, having two distinct meanings: 'girl' and 'daughter'. In support of this assertion one could point to a number of lin-guistic tests of different kinds.

For example, one could point to conjoined phrases such as *le garçon et la fille* 'the boy and the girl' (not *'the boy and the daughter'), and *le fils et la fille*, 'the son and the daughter' (not *'the son and the girl'). One could also show that *fille*, 'girl', and *fille*, 'daughter', have different grammatical properties (e.g. the diminutive *fillette* can only mean 'little girl', not 'little daughter'); that they can occur in different syntactic frames (e.g. *la fille de Marie* can only mean 'Mary's daughter', not 'Mary's girl'); that *c'est une fille* can only mean 'it's a girl', not 'it's a daughter'; and so on.

It is not always easy to establish whether a word is polysemous. This doesn't mean, however, that it cannot be done. The question of polysemy cannot be ignored in the investigation of conceptual systems reflected in the lexicons of different languages of the world. (For further discussion of poly-semy, see Chapters 8 and 9.)

2. The Universality of BECAUSE

In English, the idea of causality is expressed in an absolutely unambiguous way in the simple everyday word *because*. In many other languages, however, there is no word which means 'because' and nothing else. For example, in Italian the basic word for 'because' (as well as for 'why') is *perché*—a word which literally means 'for what'. In French, the word for 'why' is *pourquoi* (again, literally 'for what'), and the basic word for 'because' is *parce que* (literally 'through this that').

Presumably nobody would claim, however, that speakers of French or Italian don't have, or cannot express, the concept of 'because' as such— partly because these languages have other words which express this concept unambiguously (e.g. the nouns *la cause*, 'cause', in French and *cagione* in Italian), and partly because nobody has any doubts that words such as *parce que* or *perché* do mean 'because', despite their formal analysability into morphemes with other meanings.

When it comes to 'exotic' languages (such as Australian Aboriginal languages), however, doubts concerning the availability of words for 'because' have sometimes been expressed. As Goddard (1991*a*) points out, "It was a commonplace of an older generation of ethnographic commentary, still sometimes encountered, e.g. Sayers and Bain (1989), that Australian Aboriginal languages and cultures are less explicit than Indo-European languages about the expression of causality, or even that they are positively indifferent to it."

Along similar lines (though more cautiously than Sayers and Bain) Evans (1986) argued in his paper entitled "On the Unimportance of 'Cause' in Kayardild" that the Australian language Kayardild has no straightforward exponent of 'because'; and that expression of causality is conflated in this language with a purely temporal notion of sequence. And indeed, if both the concepts 'because' and 'after' are rendered in Kayardild by means of the same "consequential suffix" *ngarrba*, how can we know that the speakers of this language distinguish the two concepts in question? Is it possible to establish that *ngarrba* is polysemous ((1) after, (2) because), rather than having only one meaning, with different interpretations being due to different context?

The most important thing to do in a case like this is to formulate precise hypotheses and to test them. One hypothesis is that the word in question always means 'after', with any causal overtones being contributed by context. On this hypothesis, any sentence with the word in question should make sense on the 'after' interpretation. If we find, however, that in some contexts the 'after' interpretation doesn't make sense whereas a 'because' interpretation does, then we have to postulate polysemy.

For example, in English the word *and* is often linked with a causal interpretation, but we don't have to posit a separate, causal meaning for *and* to make sense of all *and* sentences. For instance, in the sentence

He fell down and cried.

a causal interpretation is implied but it is not absolutely necessary, and the sentence makes sense even if we assume that *and* means here co-occurrence rather than specifically causation. Similarly, in the English sentence

After her husband died, she fell ill.

a causal interpretation is (contextually) implied, but there is no need to posit a separate causal meaning for the word *after* (because a sequential interpretation still makes sense).

On the other hand, in the Australian language Yankunytjatjara the ablative suffix (*-nguru*), which can be interpreted in different contexts as 'from', 'after', or 'because', can be used in sentences in which a temporal (sequential) interpretation would make no sense (Goddard 1994*b*). For example:

—Why are you crying?
—I have a toothache. That-ABL I am crying.

A sequential ('after') interpretation would not allow us to make sense of such sentences, and, as Goddard argues, a separate 'because' meaning has to be postulated. (See Goddard 1991*a*.)

In order to demonstrate the polysemy of the suffix *-nguru* ((1) after, (2) because) quite conclusively, Goddard (1991*a*) devised a test in the form of the following question: How, if at all, can one say in that language things like "sure, *Y* happened after *X*, but not because of *X*"? For Yankunytjatjara, this test shows conclusively that *-nguru*, which is fully acceptable in the second clause, does indeed have a separate meaning 'because' (the meaning 'after' can also be expressed by the monosemous word *malangka*).

A very clear example of the polysemy of an ablative suffix in an Australian language is also provided by the following sentence (Wilkins 1989: 186):

You should go visit your mother [because] she is very sick.

In the Arrernte counterpart of this sentence the morpheme glossed here as 'because' can in other contexts mean 'from' or 'after', but in this context the only possible interpretation is causal. The speaker is clearly urging the son to visit his mother at the time of her illness, not after it or away from it. If we assume that to the speakers themselves sentences of this kind do make sense we have to conclude that the morpheme in question is polysemous between 'from', 'after', and 'because' (as argued in Harkins and Wilkins 1994).

It is important to add that different meanings of a polysemous word or morpheme are often associated with distinct syntactic frames, and that differences of this kind can provide crucial evidence for the polysemy of lexical items. For example, in the Australian language Ngaanyatjarra the suffix *-tjanu* can mean either 'because' or 'after' (Amee Glass, personal communication; see also Glass and Hackett 1970). When one asks, however,

> Nyaatjanu   kukurraarnu?
> what-TJANU run-PAST

the sentence can mean only 'Why did he run away?', not 'When did he run away?' On the other hand, *-tjanu* can mean 'after' when it is used in an answer to a question about time:

> Wanytjawara kukurrarnu?
> when   run-PAST
> 'When did he run away?'

> Turlkutjanu.
> corroboree-TJANU
> 'After the corroboree.'

What applies to Yankunytjatjara, Arrernte, and Ngaanyatjarra applies also to Kayardild; and it is interesting to note that in a more recent paper on Kayardild, Evans (1994) also reached the view that the so-called "consequential" suffix *-ngarrba* is polysemous between 'after' and 'because'.

A word (or morpheme) which can be glossed as either 'because' or 'after' cannot have some unitary meaning "more abstract than either 'because' or 'after' ": there is no identifiable meaning more abstract than 'because' and 'after' and contained in them both. If someone claimed that there was some such meaning but that we had no word for it and couldn't articulate it, then I would say with Wittgenstein that what one can't say one should be silent about. Semantic hypotheses based on "ghost meanings" which cannot be articulated are not falsifiable and therefore have no place in semantic analysis.

It would be wrong, therefore, to think that by allowing polysemy we are rendering our hypotheses immune to empirical disconfirmation. Polysemy has to be established; it can never be posited without justification. For example, as pointed out earlier, the hypothesis that the English word *after* is polysemous between a "sequential" sense and a "causal" sense is disconfirmed by the fact that, in any context, *after* can be shown to be compatible with a sequential interpretation.

3. The Universality of IF

According to Bain (1992: 87), "The hypothetical conditional sentence is not found in Pitjantjatjara. In Pitjantjatjara one cannot put forward a purely hypothetical condition, something that is merely possible, or a supposition. In practice, when Westerners attempt to do so, the Aboriginal person receives the idea as a fact."

The claim is disturbing. Is it true that in some Australian languages "one cannot put forward a purely hypothetical condition, a supposition"? To put forward a supposition one needs a word for 'if'. Bain says that in Pitjantjatjara the concept 'if' does have a lexical exponent, but that, none the less, when a Westerner wishes to advance a mere hypothesis "his/her listeners treat the statement as fact. Accordingly, what is intended as, for instance, 'if you were to get the money . . .' is received as either 'when you get the money . . .' or 'as/since you are getting the money . . .' " (1992: 90).

It is easy to believe that sentences such as "if you (I) were to . . ." may lead to miscommunication in encounters between white people and Aborigines in Australia, but it doesn't follow from this that a purely hypothetical supposition cannot be expressed in Pitjantjatjara or any other Aboriginal language; or that one cannot forestall misunderstandings in this area when addressing Aboriginal persons in English. All one needs to do is to state explicitly (whether in English or in Pitjantjatjara) that one is not asserting the condition:

I don't know whether *X* will happen
if it happens, then *Y*

But what if a language doesn't have a word (or morpheme) for 'if', as it has also been alleged to be the case in some Australian languages? What if a language does not distinguish between 'if' and 'when', or 'if' and 'maybe'?

I believe that here as elsewhere allegations of this kind often stem from a failure to recognize lexical polysemy. As McConvell notes:[1] "lack of a formal distinction between *if* and *when* in Aboriginal languages, in contrast to English, is supposedly linked to absence of hypothetical conditional statements in Aboriginal discourse" (1991: 15). Rejecting such claims McConvell argues that Aboriginal languages do have lexical and grammatical resources to mark conditionality, and he points out that even if the words for 'if' and 'when' are identical, they may appear in different frames.

---

[1] McConvell doesn't draw a distinction between conditional (IF) and counter-factual (IF . . . WOULD) sentences, and it is not always clear which type he has in mind when he talks of "hypothetical conditional statements".

For example, "In the Ngarinman language the concept of *if* is distinguished from *when* by the use of the doubt suffix *nga* following the subordinate clause marker *nyamu* and the pronoun clitic complex" (16). McConvell points out that devices of this kind are frequently utilized in certain genres of spontaneous discourse, and that older people without Western education frequently describe "imaginary and hypothetical scenarios, including multiple chainings and embeddings of hypothetical statements within other hypothetical statements" (15).

The polysemy of the primary exponent of the concept 'if' can be illustrated with data from the Australian language Arrernte (Harkins and Wilkins 1994: 298). In a simple clause, the word *peke* means 'perhaps', but if a dependent clause is present then it means 'if'.

> Ingwenthe peke   kwatye urnte-me.
> tomorrow maybe water   fall-NPP
> 'It could rain tomorrow.' ['Perhaps it will rain tomorrow.']

> Kwatye peke   urnte-me ayenge petye-tyekenhe.
> water   maybe fall-NPP   1SG:S   come-VERB NEG
> 'If it rains I won't come.'

(If the dependent clause is affirmative rather than negative as above then the verb carries a special "subsequent" marker—*tyenhenge*.)

In another Australian language, Yankunytjatjara (Goddard 1994*b*), the same word *tjinguru*, shows an even more complex pattern of polysemy: when it is used in a simple clause, or by itself (as an exclamation), it means 'maybe'; but in a subordinate sentence it has either a conditional or a counter-factual meaning, depending on the absence or presence of an "irrealis" inflexion on the verb of the main clause (see Chapter 2):

(1) Tjinguru.
    Maybe!

(2) Ka nyuntu tjinguru tjukurpa irititjatjara
    and you   if   story   long.ago:ASSOC:HAVING
    nyakula   kulintjikitja mukuringkula, nyiri
    see:SERIAL think:INTENT want:SERIAL   paper
    pala palunya nyawa.
    that DEF:ACC see:IMP
    'So if you want to read Old Testament stories, look at that book.'

(3) Tjinguru ngayulu waringka, pulka palyanma.
    if   I   cold:LOC big   make:POT
    'If I was in cold (weather), I'd make a bigger (amount).'
    ("The speaker was explaining that she had not made a very large amount of spinifex gum because the weather was too hot to do this easily" (Goddard 1994*b*: 248.)

Data of this kind provide strong evidence for the presence of a linguistically encoded concept of IF (even if this encoding involves a polysemous lexical item).

As a final illustration of this point, consider some data from German, about which it has also been sometimes asserted (incorrectly) that it doesn't distinguish the concepts of IF and WHEN.

First of all, German does have some quite unequivocal exponents of WHEN, *wann* (used in questions and in relative clauses) and *als* (used in past tense temporal clauses), which can never be used in the sense of IF; so clearly, German does distinguish WHEN from IF. For example:

Wann warst du dort?
When were you there?

Als du dort warst, war ich hier.
When you were there, I was here.

Second, German does have a word for IF, namely *wenn*, and although in subordinate sentences referring to future events *wenn* can stand for either IF or WHEN, this doesn't mean that it is somehow vague and always covers both senses at the same time.

It is more justified to conclude that in future tense sentences *wenn* is polysemous, and means either IF or WHEN. For example (from *Die Bibel in heutigem Deutsch*),

. . . der Menschensohn wird kommen, wenn ihr es nicht erwartet. (Matt. 24: 44).
'The Son of Man will come when [not "when/if"] you do not expect it'.

Wenn ihr nur Vertrauen habt, werdet ihr alles bekommen, worum ihr Gott bittet.
'if [not "if/when"] you have faith, you will receive all that you ask God for.'

The fact that in certain grammatical frames (e.g. in the frame *wenn nicht* "if not" or in combinations with the past tense) *wenn* can only mean "if", and not either "if" or "when", supports the view that it is polysemous, not vague.

This conclusion is also supported by the fact that if one wants to contrast the two concepts IF and WHEN (e.g. "when you come—if you come . . ."), this is possible, too:

Wenn du kommst—WENN du kommst—wirst du es sehen.
'When you come—if you come—you will see it'.

What all these facts show is that German does distinguish, lexically, between the concepts IF and WHEN, even though in one type of sentence (complex sentences referring to the future) the exponents of these concepts overlap.

4. The Universality of SOMEONE

In her recent book similar in its general orientation to Hallpike's, Bain (1992) develops the thesis that Australian Aborigines use only "first degree abstraction and concrete logic", whereas Westerners use "second degree abstraction and formal logic". In support of this thesis, Bain argues (94) that, for example, in Pitjantjatjara "there are no terms for the indefinite pronouns such as 'someone', 'anyone', 'whoever' " and that to refer to an unspecified person the speaker would have to use the word *kutjupa*, 'other'. According to Bain, "linguistic features of this kind are antithetical to the formulation of purely general statements" (ibid.).

Couldn't one argue, however, that in Pitjantjatjara the word *kutjupa* is in fact polysemous and has two distinct meanings, 'other' and 'someone'? Bain rejects this possibility. Commenting on the sentence

> Kutjupa ngurakutu anu.
> another camp to   went
> 'Another (person) went to camp.'/'Someone went to camp.'

she writes:

With the last of these translations there is a move from the adjective 'another' to the more abstract pronoun 'someone'. That shift is acceptable in English but its appropriateness must be questioned for Pitjantjatjara. While to some extent the translation used may be a matter of personal preference, if we are to stay as close as possible to the Aboriginal thought, then the link with the real should be retained. (1992: 94)

But semantic analysis is not a matter of personal preference, and the hypothesis that *kutjupa* is polysemous can be tested. The simplest thing to do would be to conjure up a situation where 'other' would not make sense but 'someone' would, and to check if the word *kutjupa* could still be used. The fact that one can use *kutjupa* in such situations (Cliff Goddard, personal communication) shows that this word cannot always mean 'other'. On the other hand, one can make sense of all uses of *kutjupa* in terms of two hypothetical meanings: 'other' and 'someone'. For example, if one can say, using *kutjupa*, "I saw someone (*kutjupa*) there, it was the same person", then it is clear that *kutjupa* cannot mean 'another' in this context (?'I saw another person there, it was the same person').

In addition to semantic tests of this kind, one can also examine the environments in which the two senses occur and see if there are any differences between them. For example, Harkins and Wilkins (1994) show that in a related Australian language, Arrernte, the word *arrpenhe* can also be used in the same two senses ('other' and 'someone'), depending on whether or not a specific antecedent is present. The same applies to *kutjupa* (Cliff

Goddard, personal communication): if a specific antecedent is present (e.g. this man went first; then another (*kutjupa*) went), then it clearly means 'other'; but in the absence of a specific antecedent it can only mean 'someone'.

5. The Universality of ALL

Hallpike (1979) argues that what he calls "primitive societies" have no concept of 'all', adducing linguistic evidence from several languages. The implications of this claim are so serious that they deserve to be examined in some detail. He writes:

'Some' and 'all' are thus fundamental notions of logic and basic to propositions of inclusion which relate parts to wholes. 'All' denotes the totality of a set A, while 'some' denotes '$A - x$' (where x is greater than 0). In primitive usage, however, it is possible that while words are used that ethnographers translate as 'some' and 'all', 'all' does not denote 'all possible members of set A', but 'all those in our experience' or simply 'a lot'. In so far as primitive thought is not usually concerned with working out the theoretically maximum number of items in a set, it will tend to use 'all' in the sense of 'very many'; while if all possible members of a set are physically present, the primitive may indeed say 'all', but in the sense of 'full' or 'complete', which is derived from a spatial conception, as of a container that has been filled up.

Dr Neil Warren, for example, tells me (private communication) that the Kamano of the New Guinea Highlands use their word for 'many' to do duty for what we would translate as 'all'. In the same way, among the Tauade I found that the word that I was initially inclined to translate as 'all', *kuparima*, was more accurately rendered as 'many'. *Kupariai* is the word for 'two' or 'pair', *-ai* being the dual suffix, and *-ma* is one of the plural suffixes; thus *kuparima* seems to have the literal meaning of 'pairs', i.e. 'many', and is certainly so used in conversation. It should also be noted that *kuparima* is not an adjective, but a noun, and refers to a state of affairs, 'multiplicity', rather than being a property of a class. (Hallpike 1979: 181–2)

I believe Hallpike's conclusions are fundamentally wrong. It is true that in many languages the word glossed by ethnographers as 'all' is in fact a nominal rather than a determiner (that is, grammatically more like the expression *the lot* in English than the determiner *every*), and that sentences including a word whose basic meaning is 'many' can sometimes better be translated with the English word *all* than *many*.

But does this mean that these languages make no clear distinction between the concepts 'all' and 'many'? I think not. To begin with, Hallpike's remarks on the Tauade data are far from convincing. If the stem *kupari* combined with the dual suffix is the word for 'two' or 'pair', then by itself it is much more likely to mean 'all' than 'many' (cf. French *tous les deux*, lit. "all the two", that is, 'both'). A stem meaning 'many' could hardly be combined with a dual suffix, since the language clearly has a contrast between a plural ('many') and a dual ('two'); the combination 'many' + 'two' would be incoherent, whereas the combination of 'all' and 'two' for a pair has parallels in many other languages.

Furthermore, though I haven't been able to check Hallpike's assertions about Tauade (or about Kamano), his remarks on the apparent conflation of the concepts 'all' and 'many' also apply, for example, to Australian languages, with respect to which they have been studied in reliable linguistic literature. (The index of Hallpike's book shows clearly that next to the peoples of New Guinea it is Australian Aborigines who epitomize for him the notion of a "primitive society".)[2]

For example, Bittner and Hale's (1995) analysis of the Australian language Warlpiri shows that in this language, too, there is a word, also a nominal (*panu*), which is sometimes best translated into English as 'many' and sometimes as 'all'; and Harkins (1991) shows that the same applies to another Australian language, Luritja. But this does not mean that Warlpiri and Luritja do not have a concept of 'all' distinct from the concept of 'many'.

First, while the Warlpiri word *panu* can be translated into English as either 'all' or 'many' (depending on context), there is another word, *jintakumarrarni*, which can never be translated as 'many', but only as 'all' (or 'all of them', see below). Second, as Bittner and Hale's analysis shows, *panu* can be translated as 'all' only in those contexts which imply definiteness, that is, where it can be interpreted as 'the many', 'the lot', 'the group (composed of many)', by implication 'the whole group'.

In a case like this, the word which means, essentially, 'many' may appear to mean 'all'. From this, it is only one step to the conclusion that the Warlpiri people do not distinguish 'many' from 'all'. But such a conclusion would be fallacious. Equally well one could argue that English speakers do not distinguish the two notions in question because *a lot* means 'many', whereas *the lot* means (roughly) 'all'. The fact that Warlpiri has a separate word for 'all', *jintakumarrarni*, just as English does (*all*), shows that in fact the two concepts in question are distinguished, despite differences in use linked with other differences between the two languages, such as the presence versus the absence of articles.

These points can be illustrated with the following data (Bittner and Hale 1995, their numbers, and their glosses):[3]

---

[2] Australian Aborigines (along with Papuans) have often been used in the literature as an example of "primitive mentality"—by Lévy-Bruhl, by Hallpike, and by many others. The title of Wake's (1872) paper, "The Mental Characteristics of Primitive Man as Exemplified by the Australian Aborigines", is very characteristic in this respect. For discussion, see Chase and von Sturmer (1973).

[3] Bittner and Hale use the following abbreviations in their interlinear glosses: ABS—Absolutive, Loc—Locative, 1,2,3,—1st, 2nd, 3rd person, p—plural, s—singular, INF—infinitive, PROX—proximate, PRF—perfective, PRS—present, PST—past, NPST—non-past. Word internal morpheme boundaries are indicated by '—', clitic boundaries by '='.

1. *Panu* means 'many':

(17) (Q.) Nyajangu-Ø-Ø-ngku   karli   yu-ngu nyuntu-ku?
        NYAJANGU-PRF-3s-2s boomerang give-PST you-Dat
        'HOW MANY boomerangs did he give you?'
    (A.) Panu   Ø-Ø-ju   yu-ngu karli.
        PANU PRF-3s-1s give-PST boomerang
        'He gave me MANY boomerangs.'

2. *Jintakumarrarni* means 'all':

(10) Yurnmi-jarri   ka-lu   jintakumarrarni=lki
     ripe-become-NPST PRS-3p all=then
     'Then they get ripe, all (parts) of them.'

(11) Jintakumarrarni-jiki-jala ka-lu wapa   kankarlu-mipa
     all-A=of course   PRS-3p move-NPST above-only
     paarrpardi-nja-rla pinkirrpa-kurlu-Ø
     fly-INF-PROX   feather-ones.with-A
     'All of them of course live only up in the air flying [the feathered ones].'

3. *Panu* can be used in the sense of 'the many', 'the lot', 'the group', and, by implication, 'all' (i.e. 'the whole group'):

(19) Panu ka-rna-jana nya-nyi.
     many PRS-1s-3p   see-NPST
       (i) 'I see a large group (of them).'
     (ii) 'I see the large group (of them).'
    (iii) 'I see them, who are a large group.'

(35) Yapa   ka-lu nyina   panu nyampu-rla ngurrju?
     person-ABS PRS-3p be-NPST many this-LOC   well
     'Are all the many people here well?'

This is not to say that the Warlpiri word *jintakumarrarni* has exactly the same range of use as the English word 'all' (a point to which I will return later), but it does mean that Warlpiri distinguishes between the concepts 'all' and 'many', and has separate lexical exponents for each of them.

Furthermore, although Bittner and Hale (1995) gloss *jintakumarrarni* as 'all of them' rather than 'all', I see no evidence that this word means anything other than simply 'all'. In actual speech, it will usually refer, no doubt, to some previously mentioned group, and thus will be consistent with an interpretation along the lines of 'all of them'. But this is not necessary: when needed, the same word can also be used to make open-ended generalizations, of the kind that Hallpike claims are impossible in "primitive languages". Bittner and Hale's sentence 11 ("all of them of course live only up in the air flying [the feathered ones]"), which comes from an "oral essay" about living kinds recorded by Hale, and which doesn't refer to any particular group of birds but to birds in general, provides a good illustration of this.

Two further examples of such open-ended generalizations from another Australian language, Kayardild, are quoted in Evans (1985) (DT stands for detransitivized):

(6–279) Maarra diya-a-n-kuru.
       all   eat-DT-FUT
(Speaking of yams:) '(They) are all edible.'

(6–281) Maarra maku-karran-d.
       all   woman-GEN-NOM
(On lice as food:) 'Only women eat lice.' (Lit. "all lice are women's")

No doubt everyday life in a tribal community doesn't generate much need for generalizations of this kind, but if they are not made frequently it is not for lack of conceptual or linguistic resources (cf. Section 7). I conclude that as far as we know there is no human language which doesn't have some lexical means for expressing the concept of 'all'—not something roughly comparable to 'all' but exactly the same concept.

I think Hallpike is right in assuming that without a word (or some other lexical component) for 'all' a language wouldn't be able to express certain thoughts—more than that, that in a language without 'all' one wouldn't be able to think certain thoughts—and that thoughts crucially dependent on the concept 'all' have fundamental importance in European culture. But I believe Hallpike's conviction that such languages exist is not supported by the evidence.

This is certainly not to say that the range of use of words or morphemes which embody the concept 'all' is the same in all languages. In some languages, the range of use of the word or morpheme meaning 'all' is restricted to a relatively narrow range of semantic and/or syntactic environments. This is true, in particular, of the Australian language Marrithiyel (Green 1992) and of the Papuan language Yimas (Foley 1991). But the range of use is one thing and the existence of a lexicalized concept is another.

To see this, consider briefly the Marrithiyel facts. According to Ian Green (1992) the only word in Marrithiyel which could possibly be regarded as an exponent of the concept 'all' is the adverb/interjection *wakay*. Leaving aside the use of this word as an interjection, it appears that *wakay* (as an adverb) can only combine with "semantic undergoers" (that is, it can only apply to someone to whom something happened, not to someone who did something); and that, moreover, it can convey the idea of "completeness" as well as "totality". For example (Green's numbers):[4]

(11) Fiyi winjsjeni gani   -ya (wakay).
     head bad   3sSR "go" PST finished
     'He went (completely) silly.'

[4] Green uses the following abbreviations in interlinear glosses: Pst—past, "RR"—hands auxiliary, s—singular; SR—Subject Realis.

(12) ma   -meri ma-Merranunggu   gurringgi   -wanggal
      human ns man human ns Merranunggu 3nsSR "RR" finish
      -Ø -a   wakay
      pl Pst   finished
      'The Merranunggu people all "finished up" (="died").'
      (?The Merranunggu people died completely.)

What would it mean for a group of people to die "completely"? Surely, in a sentence like 12 *wakay* means simply 'all' (just as Green's gloss says). The fact that *wakay* can be used with non-gradable predicates such as 'die' suggests that this word doesn't encode some hybrid notion of 'completely/totally/all' but has two distinct meanings: (1) completely, (2) all. Other examples cited by Green (personal communication) support this conclusion. For example, if *wakay* is added to a sentence which means 'He gave away his daughters in marriage', the sentence can only mean 'He gave away ALL his daughters', not 'He gave away his daughters COMPLETELY'.

Given facts of this kind, we have to conclude, I think, that Marrithiyel does have a lexical exponent for the primitive concept 'all', even though this exponent's range of use is more restricted than that of the English word *all*. (For an interesting discussion of the concept of 'all' in Australian languages from a different perspective, see also N. Evans (forthcoming); for a discussion of the concept 'some' see Chapter 2.)

6. The Universality of KNOW and THINK

According to Hallpike (1979) there are languages which cannot express the notions of 'know' and 'think'. People who speak such languages are, according to him, like children at the "pre-operatory" stage of development (in Piaget's terms).

At this stage, the child is cognitively incapable of distinguishing clearly between subjective and objective, of recognizing the operation of his own mental processes . . . While he may use a word like 'think', he does not grasp its *cognitive* implications, and for him it means 'concentrating', 'making a mental effort', e.g. when trying to remember something . . . At the first stage . . . (at about six) he supposes that we think with the mouth when we speak, and by association also identifies thoughts with breath, air, and smoke, or else equates thinking with hearing, and hence regards it as something we do with our ears. (Hallpike 1979: 385–6)

According to Hallpike, "primitive" peoples, too, confuse thinking with speaking and hearing, and they, too, have no concept of purely cognitive processes and states such as those linked in English with the words *think* and *know*. He writes (1979: 393–4):

This inability to analyse private experience, as opposed to social behaviour, the paradigm of the knowable, is well illustrated by ethnographic evidence from the

Ommura, of the Eastern Highlands Province of Papua New Guinea. Like many primitive peoples in New Guinea and elsewhere, the Ommura use the same verb (*iero*) for 'understanding' or 'comprehending', and the 'hearing' of a sound etc. *Dapi* corresponds fairly closely to 'clear', 'distinct', as opposed to 'obscure' or 'confused', and thus the expression *dapi iena* means 'that sound which we can hear clearly' and also, when used in the sense of understanding, the notion of 'hearing' implied in such contexts relates to the sound of the name, *nrutu*, of the object being spoken.

Similarly, Hallpike (1979: 406) quotes with approval Read's statement about the Papuan people Gahuku-Gama:

The Gahuku-Gama do not ascribe any importance to the brain, nor have they any conception of its function. Cognitive processes are associated with the organ of hearing. To 'know' or to 'think' is to 'hear' (*gelenove*); 'I don't know' or 'I don't understand' is 'I do not hear' or 'I have not heard' (*gelemuve*). (Read 1955: 265 n.)

In a similar vein, Bain states:

There is no way to differentiate the concepts of thinking, listening and heeding in Pitjantjatjara. The same verb *kulini* does duty for all. . . . This feature suggests that the psychical and physical, the self and the environment, are not fully distinguished from one another, a characteristic noted by Piaget in connection with pre-operatory thought.   (1992: 86)

It is true that many non-Western societies use the same word for 'think' and 'hear' or for 'know' and 'hear'. But what exactly does that prove? In English one can use the word *see* to mean 'understand' ("I see what you mean . . ."), but this does not prove that the speakers of English do not distinguish the concept of 'understanding' and the concept of 'seeing'. (Similarly, in French *entendre* can mean either 'hear' or 'understand'; but this does not prove that the speakers of French do not distinguish the concepts of 'hearing' and 'understanding'.)

Admittedly, in English there is also a separate word, *understand* (and in French, *comprendre*), which has only a cognitive meaning. This doesn't change the fact, however, that *see* is polysemous in English, and that in a sentence such as "I see what you mean" it has a purely cognitive meaning. But if *see* can be polysemous between 'see (with one's eyes)' and 'understand', why can't the Ommura word *iero* be polysemous between 'hear (with one's ears)' and 'understand' or 'know' (just as the French word *entendre* is)?

In Polish (and a number of other Slavic languages) the word for 'knowing', *wiedzieć*, is cognate with the word for 'seeing', *widzieć* (see Brückner 1970). Both derive from the same proto-Indo-European root *veid*— 'know/see' (see also *video*, 'I see', in Latin and *véda*, 'I know', in Sanskrit; Ernout and Meillet 1963: 734).

Hallpike overlooks the crucial distinction between polysemy and vagueness (and so does Bain). If, for example, in the Australian language Yankunytjatjara the same word *kulini* can mean either 'hear' or 'think' (see Goddard 1992*a*), it is (as Goddard argues) a case of polysemy, not of vagueness. For example, in the sentence (Goddard 1994*b*)

Ngayulu alatji kulini, "tjingu_rula . . ."
I think (about it) like this, "maybe we . . ."

it clearly means 'think', not some hybrid between 'think' and 'hear' (for only the 'think' sense can take a quasi-quotational complement). On the other hand, in a sentence such as

Ngayulu a_nangu-ngku wangkanytjala kulinu
I   person-ERG   talk NOML.LOC near PAST
'I heard people talking'

kulini can only mean 'hear', not 'think' (for only the 'hear' sense can take a non-finite complement).

The case of the 'think'/'hear' polysemy in Yankunytjatjara (or Pitjantjatjara) is exactly parallel to the 'see'/'understand' polysemy in English. In both cases, the semantic difference correlates with a difference in syntactic frames: for example, "I can see why . . ." can only mean 'I understand', not 'I can perceive with my eyes', and *alatji kulini* can only mean '(I) think like this', not '(I) hear like this'. But even if there were no syntactic differences between the two semantic interpretations, two meanings would still have to be posited on purely semantic grounds: for example, *I see what you mean* simply cannot mean 'I perceive with my eyes what you mean'.

It is interesting that polysemy involving basic concepts such as 'think' usually is in fact correlated with a possibility of different frames. In the case of the Australian Western Desert Language (of which Yankunytjatjara is a dialect) particularly telling evidence is provided by Glass (1983: 40). This evidence involves the use of a suffix (*-kukantja*) and an enclitic (=*lkanyu*) meaning "mistaken thought" (glossed below as "mt"). Clearly, both these elements can co-occur only with the 'think' sense of the polysemous verb *kulini*. For example (Glass's numbers):[5]

(60) Tjilku pirni-lu=ya   tjiinya   kuli-ra palya-palya=lkanyu
     child   many-ERG=they you know think-PR fun=mt
     pitul-pa   ngarri-rranytjakukantja-lu kapi-kukantja-lu
     petrol-ABS lie-IPF.MT-ERG   water-mt-ERG
     The children, you know, mistakenly think that petrol is lying about for
     fun, they mistakenly think it is (as harmless as) water.

---

[5] I have rephrased slightly the English gloss of this example. Glass uses the following abbreviations for interlinear glosses: abs—absolutive, erg—ergative, ipf—imperfective, mt—mistaken thought, p—past, pr—present, pt—participle.

(61) Kuli-rnu   tjarrpa-ngu=lkanyu kapi-ngka palunya-kukantja.
     think-P.PT enter-P.PF=mt   water-in   that-mt
     '(They) thought that they had gone into the water, that's what they
     mistakenly thought.'

Examples such as these make it crystal-clear that even if the concepts
'think' and 'hear' share the same lexical exponent, this doesn't mean that
the concept of 'thinking' in a purely cognitive sense is missing. It is no less
present in the Western Desert Language than in languages where 'thinking'
has a unique lexical exponent, for example the Australian language Ngandi
(Heath 1978*b*: 147).

What applies to 'think' applies also to 'know'. A word which is used for
both 'hear' and 'know', and which can be used in a sentence incompatible
with a 'hear' interpretation, must be interpreted as polysemous; and when
one looks for syntactic differences linked with the difference in meaning one
can usually find them.

For example, in the Papuan language Gahuku-Gama (now called
Alekano), which Hallpike uses as one of his prime examples, the word for
both 'think' and 'know' is indeed the same as the word for 'hear', yet
according to one of the best experts on this language, Chris Deibler (personal communication), the three senses of this word ('think', 'know', and
'hear') can always be distinguished by the frame in which this word is used,
so that ambiguity does not arise.

If the word in question is glossed as 'perceive', as is usually done, then
the sense 'hear' can be associated with phrases such as "talk perceive" or
"say perceive", the sense 'think', with the phrase "one's ear perceive", and
the sense 'know', with phrases such as "thing perceive". For example
(Deibler, personal letter):

(1) na-gata gulumó
    my-ear I-perceived
    'I thought/I think'

(2) Óasímo gakó mukí geleneive.
    God   talk all   he-has-perceived
    'God has heard everything.'

(3) láa   loko   limó nene Óasímo geleake . . .
    thus saving he-said God   having-perceived
    'God hearing that he said thus . . .'

(4) Óasímo netá   mukí geleneive.
    God   things all he-has-perceived
    'God knows everything.'

(5) Óasímo netá   mukí-kumu geleneive.
    God   things all-about he-has-perceived
    'God knows about everything.'

The traditional gloss 'perceive' has an obvious value for describing facts of this kind, but it cannot be regarded as an accurate representation of the word's meaning, since quite clearly three different meanings are involved, not one. For example, sentence 1 can mean only 'I think', not 'I hear', and sentence 5 can mean only 'God knows everything', not 'God hears everything'. The fact that "ear-perceive" means in this language 'think' and not 'hear' is particularly telling, since in many other languages (e.g. in Kalam, see below) "ear-perceive" means 'hear', not 'think'; this shows that in Gahuku-Gama "ear-perceive" is in fact lexicalized in the sense 'think'.

Words for body parts often provide a convenient idiom for talking about inner states. One language which illustrates this particularly well is Hua (another Papuan language, geographically very close to Gahuku-Gama, and described authoritatively by Haiman 1980*b*, 1991). In Hua one feels, so to speak, with one's guts, one thinks with one's ears, and one knows with one's eyes. What this really means, however, is that Hua exhibits a certain pattern of polysemy (Haiman 1991 and personal communication):

( )geta	1. ear, 2. opinion
havi-	1. hear, 2. understand
( )geta havi-	think (lit. hear one's ear)
( )aipa	1. guts, 2. feel

In English one can refer to one's thoughts as one's "view", and in Hua, as one's "ear"; but it would be absurd to conclude from this that the speakers of either English or Hua lack the concept of 'thought'.

Lexical evidence is vital for establishing a culture's concepts, but without in-depth semantic analysis lexical evidence can be easily misinterpreted. For example, when one hears that in the Papuan language Kalam the same word (*nŋ-*) can translate both *know* and *hear,* one might conclude that the language makes no distinction between the two. In fact, however, Andrew Pawley's data and comments (Pawley 1966, 1975, 1986, personal communication) show that Kalam does distinguish between 'know' and 'hear': *nŋ* means essentially 'know', whereas *tmwd nŋ* (lit. "ear know") means 'hear'. In sentences referring to sounds (such as thunder) *tmwd nŋ* can be abbreviated to *nŋ,* but in this context the bare form *nŋ* can be regarded as elliptical for *tmwd nŋ.*

This analysis is supported by the fact that Kalam has many other lexical units including the stem *nŋ,* and that several of those other lexical units, too, can be abbreviated to a bare *nŋ.* For example:

wdn	nŋ	'see'	(lit. "eye know")
d	nŋ	'feel (by touching)'	(lit. "touch know")
ñb	nŋ	'taste'	(lit. "eat know")
gos	nŋ	'think'	(lit. "thought/mind know")

pk	nŋ	'nudge'	(lit. "hit know")
bwk	nŋ	'read, study'	(lit. "book know")
mapn	nŋ	'feel affection for'	(lit. "liver know")
sb	nŋ	'feel sorry for'	(lit. "gut know")

In a sentence such as

b   byn   nŋa-k
man woman know-he-past (punctual)
'The man saw the woman'

the bare stem *nŋ* can be used in the sense 'see' (and in fact only in that sense), but this doesn't mean that in Kalam the same verb (*nŋ*) means something "fuzzy" or intermediate between 'know', 'hear', and 'see' (as well as 'think', 'taste', 'read', 'feel sorry', and so on). Rather, we have to conclude that Kalam distinguishes lexically between 'know', 'hear', 'see', and 'smell' as follows: *nŋ*, know; (*wdn*) *nŋ*, see; (*tmwd*) *nŋ*, hear; (*kwy*) *nŋ*, smell.

Although the bare stem *nŋ* can be associated with different senses (know, see, hear, taste), in actual speech these senses are clearly distinguished: if the object refers to a sound, *nŋ* has to be interpreted as 'hear'; if it refers to an odour, it has to be interpreted as 'smell', and so on; and if the object refers to a concrete entity (e.g. a person or even a bell), then the only possible interpretation of *nŋ* is 'see', and never 'hear' or 'smell'.

It is also important to emphasize that in certain frames the only possible reading is 'I know', not 'I perceive' (see, hear, or whatever). For example (Pawley, personal communication):

yad Ulrike ñn akay ow-a-k   nŋ-b-yn.
I   Ulrike day when come-3sɢ-Past know-Pres-1sɢ
'I know (*perceive) when Ulrike came.'

yad Ulrike md-p-   nŋ-b-yn
I   Ulrike stay-Pres-3sɢ know-Pres-1sɢ
'I know (*perceive) where Ulrike is.'[6]

The case for positing distinct senses for verbs such as 'know/hear' (or

---

[6] Pawley usually glosses the stem *nŋ* as 'perceive, be aware', but from a strictly semantic point of view 'perceive' cannot be seen as an invariant meaning of this stem (just as it cannot be regarded as the invariant meaning of the Gahuku-Gama word *gelenove*, 'hear/know/think'). First, in some frames *nŋ* clearly means 'know', not 'perceive', as discussed earlier. Second, *gos nŋ* means 'think', not 'perceive'. For example, the "Kalam" sentence "I *gos nŋ* that he lives in Moresby" means 'I think that he lives in Moresby', not 'I perceive that he lives in Moresby' (Pawley, personal communication). I realize that in consistently glossing *nŋ* as 'perceive' Pawley doesn't mean that *nŋ* means the same as the English word *perceive*; rather, he means that *nŋ* has a meaning for which there is no word in English, and that he chooses the English word *perceive* as a label for this inexpressible something. But, from my point of view, this is a bit like saying that *nŋ* means '*X*' (the hypothesis is unverifiable). On the other hand, the hypothesis that *nŋ* by itself means 'know', and *gos nŋ* , 'think', can be empirically tested.

'know/hear/see') is strengthened by data from related and surrounding languages and cultures. Thus, if among geographically close and genetically closely related languages of Australia some have separate words for 'think' and 'know' (e.g. Arrernte; see Wilkins 1993; Harkins and Wilkins 1994), whereas others (e.g. Yankunytjatjara) use the same word for both 'hear' and 'think', it would be bizarre to infer that the Arrernte people do have a concept of 'think' whereas the culturally and linguistically closely related Yankunytjatjara people don't. The evidence available to date suggests that all languages do in fact have words for 'know' and 'think'. These words may or may not be polysemous, but this is irrelevant from the point of view of a language's conceptual resources.

Hallpike (1979: 391) writes: "Even when we encounter among the primitives a word we are disposed to translate as 'think', it commonly has the basic meaning of 'obvious mental effort', as it does among Piaget's pre-operatory subjects (see Tangu word *ngek'ngeki*, 'to think, ponder, cogitate, rack one's brains' (Burridge 1969: 176))." Hallpike is probably right: it is indeed quite possible that a language will have a separate word for 'think' as an activity, without having a separate word for 'thinking' in the more basic sense of 'think that . . .'. The Australian language Kayardild studied in depth by Evans (1985) is a good case in point. In Kayardild the word *nalmarutha* (lit. "head-put") means 'think of, recall, come up with something through thinking', for example *kakuju nalmarutha nithi*, 'uncle will think of the name, will recall the name' (Evans 1994: 211); and there is no word which would mean specifically 'think that' and nothing else (although the word *marralmarutha*, lit. "ear-put", can be used in the sense 'think that', as well as in the sense 'recall').

But Hallpike's argument rests on his assumption that if a word means 'hear' it cannot also mean 'think'. In fact, if a language has two words, one of which means, roughly speaking, 'think with effort', and the other is polysemous between 'hear' and 'think (that)', the argument fails. Referring to his earlier discussion of concepts such as 'all', 'some', 'number', and 'time', Hallpike (1979: 390) writes:

In the same way, when we are considering words that relate to cognitive processes, such as 'think', it would be prudent to remember that this word, together with those for 'know', 'remember', 'clever', 'stupid', and 'understand', can bear simpler interpretations than the purely cognitive, and that it is possible for primitives and the uneducated generally to use them in relation to behaviour, facial expressions, bodily movements, and speech, while leaving out of account their distinctively cognitive aspects. We would not expect to find discussions in primitive society about the difference between knowing and believing, for example, or appearance and reality.

But what is at issue here is not the use that different societies make of concepts such as 'think' and 'know', but the availability of such concepts. The claim that words for 'think' and 'know' may be present but may "bear simpler interpretations than the purely cognitive" is misconceived, since as Descartes (1701/1931), among many others, has pointed out, nothing can be "simpler" than 'think' or 'know' (see Bogusławski 1979, 1989). The claim that in some languages words for 'think' and 'know' are not available is, I think, false, but it is a claim which makes sense; the claim that such words are available but "bear simpler interpretations" doesn't make sense.

Referring with approval to Gilbert Ryle's view that "at the commonsense level our assessments of mental processes are in fact assessments of behaviour" (1979: 389), Hallpike goes on to say:

But Needham also lists translations of some other Nuer words and expressions which seem to refer more unambiguously and explicitly to inner states of a cognitive type, e.g. think, know, remember, forget, think back, change his mind, believe, imagine, etc. One would certainly concede that primitives are aware of some manifestations of cognitive processes and may have words for 'know', 'think', 'remember', 'forget', 'clever', 'stupid', 'understand', and so on. But the point is that all these aspects of cognition have behavioural manifestations, too . . .

In short, it is the external manifestations of inner states in which primitives are interested, and in these external manifestations the body has a crucial role.

The statement that a given word means 'think', or 'know', or 'hear', can be tested by the usual semantic methods; if the application of semantic tests shows that a word means 'think', or is polysemous between 'think' and 'hear', then the fact that mental processes can be expected to be associated with behavioural manifestations is irrelevant; it cannot invalidate the results of semantic analysis.

The semantic relevance of behavioural manifestations can be tested. For example, in English the words *merry* and *gloomy* refer in their very meaning to both emotions and external manifestations, whereas *happy* and *sad* do not:

> *He was merry/gloomy, but he didn't show it.
> He was happy/sad, but he didn't show it.

To my knowledge, no similar evidence for the relevance of behavioural manifestations to the meaning of the words for 'think' or 'know' in Australian, Papuan, or any other languages has ever been produced (by Hallpike or by anyone else).

I conclude that while Hallpike's claim that in many non-Western cultures "the realm of purely private experience receives very little elaboration or analysis at the level of public discourse" is undoubtedly correct (see e.g. Howell 1981; Lutz 1988), his assertions concerning the alleged absence of words for 'think' and 'know' (and the concomitant absence of the corresponding concepts) are unfounded.

7. General Discussion

Lave's (1981) critical review of Hallpike's *Foundations of Primitive Thought* bears the ironic title: "How 'they' Think?" Lave's irony reflects a belief which at the end of the twentieth century will no doubt be widely shared: a belief in what Boas (1938c) called "the psychic unity of mankind". To those who share this belief, all distinctions between "them" and "us" in terms of capacity for thought are unacceptable.

But the belief in the "psychic unity of (hu)mankind" can degenerate into an empty rhetorical posture if it is not linked with an empirical search for a shared conceptual basis linking different cultures and societies. To quote a leading anthropologist and one of the founders of the new discipline of "cultural psychology", Richard Shweder (himself the author of a very critical review of Hallpike's *Foundations of Primitive Thought*; Shweder 1982), "many anthropologists continue to be quite pious about the 'principle of psychic unity'" (Shweder and Sullivan 1990: 400); and further: "The current lack of a rich corpus of relevant data on the topic suggests that the 'principle of psychic unity' has been assumed more than it has been scrutinized" (1990: 401).

If a shared basis of universal concepts did not exist, the different conceptual universes associated with different languages would be mutually impenetrable, as some (e.g. Grace 1987) claim they indeed are. And if one believes in the psychic unity of humankind and in the principle that whatever one can say in one language one can also say (more or less easily) in any other, one cannot at the same time reject the hypothesis of a set of shared concepts. Those who believe neither in shared concepts nor in the psychic unity of humankind are at least more consistent.

Speaking of traditional non-Western societies, Lévy-Bruhl (1926: 147) wrote: "It is a mentality which makes little use of abstraction, and even that in a different method from a mind under the sway of logical thought; *it has not the same concepts at command*" (emphasis added). The question of whether native speakers of different languages have the same basic concepts at their disposal is crucial. Until recently, this question was not empirically investigated; and a theoretical framework was lacking within which it could be seriously and rigorously investigated.

Cole, Gay, Glick, and Sharp (1971: 215) wrote: "The almost universal outcome of the psychological study of culture and cognition has been the demonstration of large differences among cultural groups on a large variety of psychological tests and experiments. This has led to the widespread belief that different cultures produce different psychological (in the present case, cognitive) processes." They opposed to this widespread belief their own conclusion that "cultural differences in cognition reside more in the situations to which particular cognitive processes are applied than in the existence of a process in one cultural group and in absence in another".

Mutatis mutandis, the same conclusions emerge from research into cross-cultural semantics. On the one hand, the almost universal outcome of the semantic study of culture and cognition has been the demonstration of large differences among cultural groups with respect to their patterns of lexicalization, in particular, their key words and key concepts (see Wierzbicka 1991*b*). On the other hand, it emerges that in addition to the vast mass of culture-specific concepts, there are certain fundamental concepts which appear to be lexicalized in all languages of the world; so that cultural differences between human groups reside in ways in which these basic concepts are utilized rather than in the existence of some concepts in one cultural group and their absence in another. It might be added that there are also considerable differences between cultures in the extent to which certain basic concepts are called upon. For example, the concepts of 'because', 'if', and 'all' may indeed be utilized much less in the culture of Australian Aborigines than in Western culture (see N. Evans 1994 on 'because'; Bittner and Hale 1995 and Harkins 1991 on 'all'; also Goddard 1989*a*). But this doesn't mean that these concepts are absent, or that they are not lexically embodied.

It should also be mentioned that (as argued by Goddard 1991*a*) the low frequency of some indefinable words in some languages may be compensated for by high frequency of more inclusive "semantic molecules". Goddard argues that this is the case with the notion of 'because' in Australian languages, which is often included in "semantic molecules" encoded in various purposive constructions. Goddard (1991*a*: 44) writes:

Prime facie, I submit, the meaning of these constructions involves the notion of *because*, in combination with the complex notion of *someone wanting something to happen* . . . The purposive constructions, in other words, provide a compact means for articulating causal connections within a particular broad domain—that having to do with people's motives or reasons for doing things. In P/Y society, I would argue, people tend to be more interested in each others' reasons for doing things than in other kinds of causal links. Most talk about reasons for actions takes place in the idiom of the purposive, which services the main needs in respect of the expression of causality.

Leibniz (1765/1981: 326), who firmly believed in the psychic unity of humankind, recommended comparative study of different languages of the world as a way to discover the "inner essence of man" and, in particular, the universal basis of human cognition. Needham (1972: 220) commented on Leibniz's "grand proposal" as follows:

This bold suggestion . . . was based on the tacit premise that the human mind was everywhere the same. . . . Methodologically, Leibniz was thus proposing a comparative analysis of the kind that Lévy-Bruhl was to put into effect almost exactly two centuries later, and even in terms that find ready agreement today; but it is not premises, not the type of research that he recommended, that have since been called into renewed question. Underlying his proposal was the conviction that human nature was uniform and fixed, and it is precisely this idea that more recent conceptual analyses have made difficult to accept.

Hallpike (1979), who quotes Needham extensively, drew logical conclusions from these relativist statements (although one may doubt whether Needham himself would have endorsed Hallpike's theories of "primitive thought").

In a sense, however, *tertium non datur* (there is no third possibility): either Leibniz was right, and there is, behind the variability of cultures, a universal, "fixed and uniform" set of underlying human concepts, or Needham was right, and there is no "fixed and uniform" conceptual basis of different language-and-culture systems.

Linguistic evidence suggests that the truth is on Leibniz's side, as do conceptual analyses more recent than those referred to by Needham. Language-and-culture systems differ enormously from one another, but there are also semantic and lexical universals, which point to a shared conceptual basis underlying all human language, cognition, and culture.

But in order to establish what is and what is not universal in human linguistic and conceptual resources we need a rigorous methodology. In particular, we need a methodology which would allow us to recognize polysemy where it is really present without positing it in cases where it is not.

This point must be emphasized, because many scholars have deep-seated fears of ever positing polysemy for another language and imagine that by doing so one will inevitably fall prey to ethnocentrism. For example, one of the anonymous reviewers of an earlier version of this chapter (Wierzbicka 1994*g*) cautioned against "the assumption that if a term in language *X* requires more than one distinct translation to cover a range of cases that the translator/analyst devises, then it must be polysemous . . . i.e., if *we* can imagine a distinction, as for example, between 'hear' and 'think', for which a single term is used in *X* (but for which multiple terms are available in our language), this (putatively universal) conceptual distinction must be polysemously labelled in *X*", and illustrated this point as follows:

This is as if to say that if a term, e.g. *atníwa* (Sahaptin) is used to refer to a "bee" at one time and a "wasp" at another, that it must have these two distinct senses. Why reject out of hand the possibility that the distinction is simply of no consequence to the speakers of *X*? Perhaps, if it is a distinction we find difficult to imagine doing without, as between "all" and "some", we would want to argue strenuously for a polysemous interpretation.

But the question is not whether it is easy or difficult to imagine doing without a particular distinction, but whether the necessity of a particular distinction can be established by reductive paraphrases with full predictive power. For example, "bee" and "wasp" can no doubt be reduced to something along the following lines: "a small flying creature (small enough for a person to be able to hold it between a finger and a thumb); it has a sharp thin long part; it can sting people with that part; when this happens to someone it hurts". If this common core fits all the contexts in which the Sahaptin word *atníwa* can be used (a point which can be tested), then positing polysemy for this word would be totally unjustified.

But the relationship between 'think' and 'hear' is quite different from that between 'bee' and 'wasp' (or from that between 'girl' and 'daughter'). If a common core (substitutable in context) can be articulated for the Sahaptin word *atníwa*, no common core (substitutable in context) can be articulated for, say, the Pitjantjatjara word *kulini* (or for the French word *fille*).

One could of course suggest that 'think' and 'hear' have a common core which simply cannot be articulated, but this hypothesis is untestable (because a hypothetical meaning which hasn't been articulated cannot be tested in context), and therefore there is little point in entertaining it. The status of such an untestable hypothesis must be seen as quite different from the status of the testable hypothesis that, for example, the Sahaptin word *atníwa* has a unitary meaning.

If one takes into account that *kulini* occurs in two different grammatical frames, each of them associated with a different sense ('think' in one frame and 'hear' in another), whereas *atníwa* occurs (presumably) in exactly the same grammatical frames whether it is used with reference to bees or to wasps, one can see that the analogy between the two cases is more apparent than real.

Similarly unjustified (though understandable) is the fear of ethnocentrism expressed in the following comments (by the same reviewer):

Perhaps it is better to attack the assumption that every distinction *we* judge relevant and necessary for coherent abstraction must be basic to "adult" ratiocination. For example, re. the alleged "failure" to distinguish "causal relations" from relations of simple spatio-temporal contiguity: *our* philosophers argue interminably about the validity of causal inferences from observations of spatio-temporal contiguity. Why should all cultures make the same logical errors we are prone to?

But concepts such as 'because', 'if', 'think', 'know', and 'all' are not just "ours": they are well attested in numerous languages of Asia, Africa, America, Australia, New Guinea, and Oceania, and their exponents are by no means always polysemous (for evidence on this point, see Goddard and Wierzbicka 1994*b*).

Certainly, some of the universal concepts discussed here may be used more frequently in some cultures than in others. For example, it may well be that in some Australian languages, in which the concepts 'think' and 'hear' share the same lexical exponent, this exponent is used much more frequently with the meaning 'hear' than with the meaning 'think'; and also, that references to 'thinking' are much more common in English discourse than in, say, Pitjantjatjara discourse. But the question of the extent of use of certain concepts must be distinguished from the question of their availability.

More generally, the availability of cognitive resources should not be confused with the habitual use of these resources in different societies. Differences in the latter are particularly clearly illustrated by Luria's (1976: 111) interviews with Uzbek and Kirghiz peasants. For example:

[Q.] In the Far North, where there is snow, all bears are white. Novaya Zemlya is in the Far North and there is always snow there. What color are the bears there?
[A.] I don't know what color the bears there are, I never saw them.
[Q.] But what do you think?
[A.] Once I saw a bear in a museum, but that's all.

Luria comments that "the most typical responses of the subjects . . . were a complete denial of the possibility of drawing conclusions from propositions about things they had no personal experience of, and suspicion about any logical operation of a purely theoretical nature" (1976: 108). At the same time, however, Luria's interviews clearly show that his interviewees did have concepts such as 'all' and 'if', and that when pressed they could draw the desired inferences. For example (111):

[Q.] But on the basis of what I said, what color do you think the bears there are?
[A.] Either one-colored or two-colored . . . [ponders for a long time]. To judge from the place, they should be white. You say that there is a lot of snow there, but we have never been there!

And another example (109):

[Q.] But what kind of bears are there in Novaya Zemlya?
[A.] We always speak only of what we see; we don't talk about what we haven't seen.
. . .
[Q.] But what do my words imply? . . .
[A.] Well, it's like this: our tsar isn't like yours, and yours isn't like ours. Your words can be answered only by someone who was there, and if a person wasn't there he can't say anything on the basis of your words . . .
[Q.] But on the basis of my words—in the North, where there is always snow, the bears are white, can you gather what kind of bears there are in Novaya Zemlya?
[A.] If a man was sixty or eighty and had seen a white bear and had told about it, he could be believed, but I've never seen one and hence I can't say. That's my last word. Those who saw can tell, and those who didn't see can't say anything!

(At this point a young Uzbek volunteered, "From your words it means that bears there are white.")

[Q.] Well, which of you is right?

[A.] What the cock knows how to do, he does. What I know, I say, and nothing beyond that!

The availability of concepts such as 'all' and 'if' is crucial to deductive reasoning; all the rest can be learnt (as Luria's data show, quickly learnt, given sufficient cultural exposure). Different modes of thought do not make human cultures mutually impenetrable if the basic conceptual resources are the same. As Franz Boas wrote (1938*a*: 141–2):

In primitive culture people speak only about actual experiences. They do not discuss what is virtue, good, evil, beauty; the demands of their daily life, like those of our uneducated classes, do not extend beyond the virtues shown on definite occasions by definite people, good or evil deeds of their fellow tribesmen, and the beauty of a man, a woman, or of an object. They do not talk about abstract ideas. The question is rather whether their language makes impossible the expression of abstract ideas . . . Devices to develop generalized ideas are probably always present and they are used as soon as the cultural needs compel the natives to form them.

Discussions of conceptual and lexical resources in non-Western languages such as those contained in Hallpike's book tend to be based on anecdotal information (see Lave 1981) and often lack linguistic sophistication. But if claims like Hallpike's are to be successfully refuted, they have to be refuted on the basis of solid evidence and sound analysis.

The task of determining the full set of universal concepts which underlie the "psychic unity of humankind" is vital and urgent. Empirical linguistic investigations reported in *Semantic and Lexical Universals* (Goddard and Wierzbicka 1994*b*) suggest that in all probability the metapredicates 'if', 'because', and 'all', the mental predicates 'think' and 'know', and the basic "substantives" 'someone' and 'something' are among their number.

7 Semantic Complexity and the Role of Ostension in the Acquisition of Concepts

□ □ ─────────────────────────────────

1. Introduction

In modern semantics, progress seems to have been impeded, more than anything else, by unrealistic expectations. Familiar analyses of meaning along the lines of *to kill* equals 'to cause to die' or *bachelor* equals 'unmarried man' have seldom been regarded as satisfactory, but they have helped to perpetuate the illusion that if the meaning of a word cannot be stated satisfactorily in a simple formula of three or four words, then what is needed is a longer and more complex one, of five or six words.

However, most scholars who tried to go beyond formulae like *to kill* = 'to cause to die' found that trying to go just a little further didn't seem to help. Longer and apparently more sophisticated semantic formulae were proving to be just as open to criticism as the cruder and simpler ones. In fact, the deeper one looked into the meaning of words the more elusive this meaning appeared to be. Trying to catch it in verbal formulae was like trying to catch water in a net.

Perhaps as a result of this experience, many scholars previously interested in meaning abandoned semantic research altogether and turned to other, less frustrating pursuits, trying to justify their abandonment of semantic description in terms of new ideas about the nature of meaning. Meaning, some of them now declared, cannot be defined—not because we haven't yet learnt how to define it but because it is, by its very nature, indefinable (see e.g. Fodor *et al.* 1980; Fodor 1981; Chomsky 1987; Lakoff and Johnson 1980; Givón 1989).

This radical conclusion was frequently accompanied by attacks on Plato and Aristotle (or on Descartes and Leibniz), by almost ritualistic references to the late Wittgenstein, and by assurances that meaning cannot be described because it is "fuzzy". Often, "fuzziness" came to be celebrated as almost the ultimate truth about human language and cognition. One could almost hear a collective sigh of relief: meaning is "fuzzy", so we don't need to try to describe it.

But in linguistics there is no escape from meaning. Meaning is what language is all about, and the study of meaning encoded in languages is what linguistics is, ultimately, all about. Obviously, not every linguist has to make the study of meaning his or her primary concern: there are other important tasks in linguistics. But linguistics as a whole cannot relinquish its responsibility for the study of meaning; and this means that it cannot avoid the problem of semantic complexity.

2. Complex Concepts as Configurations of Simple Ones

The complexity of a concept can be viewed as the distance separating it from the level of indefinables. Some meanings encoded in natural languages can be regarded as "simple" in the sense that they cannot be decomposed (without circularity) into any other meanings. For example, as argued earlier, one cannot decompose (or define) concepts such as 'this', 'someone', or 'know', and any attempt to do so must lead to circularity and obscurity (as when one tries to define *this* in terms of *deixis, ostension, definiteness, referentiality,* and so on; or *know* in terms of *information, factivity, verification,* and the like). One could of course say that concepts such as 'this', 'someone', or 'know' are "complex" in some other sense or senses of the term "complex"; I maintain, however, that they are not complex in the sense of being decomposable into any elements conceptually simpler than themselves. In this sense (and only in this sense), they must be regarded as the "ultimate simples" of any valid conceptual analysis of natural language.

By contrast, most concepts encoded in any human language are "complex" in the sense that they *can* be decomposed in terms of simpler concepts. To state the meaning of a word is to reveal the configuration of simple concepts encoded in it—just as Locke said nearly 300 years ago:

a definition is nothing else but the showing the meaning of one word by several other not synonymous terms. The meaning of words being only the ideas they are made to stand for by him that uses them, the meaning of any term is then showed, or the word is defined, when, by other words, the idea it is made the sign of, and annexed to, in the mind of the speaker, is as it were represented, or set before the view of another; and thus its signification ascertained. This is the only use and end of definitions; and therefore the only measure of what is, or is not a good definition. (Locke 1690/1959: 33–4)

But to be able to present complex meanings (or concepts) as configurations of simple ones we must know in advance what the simple concepts are, just as to analyse chemical compounds into their constituent elements we must know in advance what the chemical elements are. Semantic analysis requires a list of semantic elements, just as chemical analysis requires a list of chemical elements. This crucial fact (that for semantic analysis to proceed we need a list of semantic simples) was pointed out not by Locke but by Leibniz.

Leibniz also saw clearly the dilemma stemming from the mutual dependence between our knowledge of simple concepts and our understanding of complex ones: to understand complex concepts we have to decompose them into what we assume are simple concepts; but to discover which concepts can be reasonably regarded as the simple ones we have to experiment with many different candidates, checking their power to "generate" complex concepts. It is only by trial and error that we can discover the ultimate simples; and before we have discovered them, all our semantic analyses must be seen as provisional and to a greater or lesser degree incorrect.

In what follows, I shall look briefly at a few different types of concept, trying to assess their complexity (relative to the postulated set of "simples").

As mentioned earlier (Chapter 1), data from child language are relevant here, but they have to be handled with care, since to study conceptual development a coherent semantic theory is needed in the first place. Unfortunately, linguists sometimes argue about such matters in a somewhat cavalier manner. For example, Chierchia and McConnell-Ginet (1990: 363) write:

Acquisition phenomena also might bear on the issue of lexical decomposition. Children acquire words like *kill* and *die* long before they learn words like *cause* and *become*. . . . Of course, the IPC [intensional predicate calculus] CAUSE and BECOME predicates need not be equated with *cause* and *become*; nonetheless, it is striking that what we have analyzed as the relatively more complex items semantically are apparently more directly salient for children. It is often said that young children, while being attuned to causal relations, lack explicit knowledge of abstract notions, like causation, that serve to cross-clarify many diverse types of events. But then how can children represent notions like those associated with *kill*, in which causation figures?

But empirical findings on child language demonstrate that the concept of causation (not in the form of the verb *to cause* but in the form of clausal linkers such as *'cause* and *because*) is quite common in the speech of 2-year-olds (see e.g. Bloom 1991). Whether the words *kill* and *die* are learned earlier than that I do not know: the authors probably don't know either but are simply guessing. Furthermore, they take for granted that when children do start using the words *kill* and *die*, they link them with the same concepts as adults do, again without reference to the relevant literature. Finally, the assumption that the best decomposition of the adult concept 'kill' should rely on the verbs *to cause* and *to become* (as suggested twenty-five years ago by generative semanticists) also shows that the authors' view of semantic analysis is outdated. (See e.g. Wierzbicka 1980a.)

The same applies to Fodor's (1987: 161) comments on the meaning of *father*: "Children know about fathers long before they know about males and parents. So either they don't have the concept FATHER when they seem to, or you can have the concept MALE PARENT without having access to internal structure; viz., by having the concept FATHER. Of these alternatives, the last seems best." I would certainly agree that the analysis of *father* as "male parent" is misguided (see Wierzbicka 1972), and that the child's concept of 'father' is not that of 'male parent'. But what does it prove? For adults, the knowledge of, roughly speaking, 'begetting' is a part of their concept of 'father'; it is necessarily true, then, that when children acquire the adult concept of 'father', they must also acquire this knowledge. Obviously, when small children use the word *Daddy* they don't need to have that knowledge; so it is not true that small children necessarily "know about fathers" (just because they use the word *Daddy*).

Words such as *Mommy* and *Daddy* are among the very first words learned by children (see Anglin 1977), but they are first learned as names for particular people, and the road from there to the adult concept of 'mother' and 'father' is a subject for serious study. Fodor's comments on the subject suggest limited familiarity with the work done thus far. His conclusion that children have an unanalysable concept of FATHER, which is the same as that of adults, denies the whole idea of conceptual development and overlooks the vast body of empirical research on child language and on the acquisition of meaning. And yet Fodor's musings on "father" and other similar passages are often adduced in books on "formal semantics" as evidence that the whole "decompositional approach" to meaning is untenable (see e.g. Chierchia and McConnell-Ginet 1990: 363).

3. Abstract Concepts: Words for Emotions

Generally speaking, abstract concepts appear to be less complex than concrete ones; but even so, they are usually much more complex than simple dictionary definitions or illustrative semantic formulae offered in scholarly literature would lead us to believe. But very simple definitions of this kind (e.g. *to lie*—'to say something untrue') do not have any predictive power, and they cannot account for the differences in the range of use of related concepts. For example, as pointed out earlier (Chapter 4), a definition of 'lie' which says that 'to lie' is to say something untrue cannot account for the differences in use between *lie* and its closest Russian counterparts *vrat'* and *lgat'*, both of which also mean, roughly speaking, 'to say something untrue'.

To my mind, if we want to assess a concept's real complexity we must seek to reveal its structure in a formula whose validity could be verified against its actual range of use. Otherwise, the formulae we devise will reflect nothing but our own preconceptions.

Consider, for example, the English word *happy* and the Polish word given by dictionaries as its equivalent: *szczęśliwy*. As Barańczak (1990: 12–13) points out, the range of use of the two words is not the same.

Take the word "happy", perhaps one of the most frequently used words in Basic American. It's easy to open an English–Polish or English–Russian dictionary and find an equivalent adjective. In fact, however, it will not be equivalent. The Polish word for "happy" (and I believe this also holds for other Slavic languages) has a much more restricted meaning; it is generally reserved for rare states of profound bliss, or total satisfaction with serious things such as love, family, the meaning of life, and so on. Accordingly, it is not used as often as "happy" is in American common parlance.

It is not only the Polish word *szczęśliwy* or its counterparts in the other Slavic languages which differs from the English word *happy* in the ways described: the German word *glücklich* and the French word *heureux* differ from *happy* in much the same way (see Wierzbicka 1992c). To account for these differences, I have postulated for these words the following two explications:

(A) *X* feels happy. =
    X feels something
    sometimes a person thinks something like this:
        something good happened to me
        I wanted this
        I don't want anything more now
    because of this, this person feels something good
    X feels like this

(B) *X* feels *szczęśliwy* (*glücklich, heureux*, etc.). =
    X feels something
    sometimes a person thinks something like this:
        something very good happened to me
        I wanted this
        everything is good now
        I can't want anything more now
    because of this, this person feels something very good
    X feels like this

The two explications differ in three respects: First, B has one additional component, 'everything is good now' (by implication, 'everything that is happening to me'); second, 'good' in A contrasts with 'very good' in B; and third, 'I don't want anything more now' in A contrasts with 'I can't want anything more now' in B. These three differences account, I think, for the "absolute" connotations of *szczęśliwy* and the more limited, more pragmatic character of *happy*, discussed by Barańczak and confirmed by numerous linguistic facts such as, for example, that one can say *quite happy* but not **całkiem szczęśliwy* or *ganz glücklich, or that one can say *I am happy with this arrangement* but not **jestem szczęśliwy z tego układu* or **ich bin glücklich mit dieser Anordnung*.

A few further examples from the area of emotion concepts (see also Chapter 5):

> *Terrified*
> *X* feels something
> sometimes a person thinks something like this:
>> something very bad is happening
>> because of this, something very bad can happen to me now
>> I don't want this
>> because of this I would want to do something if I could
>> I can't do anything
> because of this, this person feels something very bad
> *X* feels something like this

If one is *terrified*, what one is *terrified* of is seen not simply as 'something bad' but as something 'very bad'. What one is *terrified* of is very real—something that is already there. And yet the target of terror is also partly in the future, because the present 'bad event' is seen here as a source of a future threat ('. . . can happen NOW'). This future threat is necessarily personal ('something very bad can happen TO ME now'). The experiencer's attitude is one of an intense non-acceptance ('I don't want it'); at the same time, it is one of total helplessness ('I can't do anything').

> *Petrified*
> *X* feels something
> sometimes a person thinks something like this:
>> something very bad is happening
>> something very bad will happen to me now
>> I don't want this
>> because of this, I would want to do something if I could
>> I can't do anything
> because of this, this person feels something very bad
> because of this, this person can't move
> *X* feels something like this

Petrified appears to be a more specific version of *terrified*: it is a *terror* which leads to a kind of paralysis: 'this person can't move'. (Note, however, the difference between 'can happen' in *terrified* and 'will happen' in *petrified*.)

> *Horrified*
> *X* feels something

sometimes a person thinks something like this:
   something very bad is happening to someone
   I didn't think that something like this could happen
   I don't want this
   because of this I would want to do something if I could
   I can't do anything
because of this, this person feels something very bad
X feels something like this

The main difference between *horror* and *terror* concerns the relationship between the experiencer and the victim: in the case of *terror*, the two are identical, whereas in the case of *horror* they have to be different. One is *horrified* to see what is happening to someone else, as one is *appalled* to see what has happened to someone else. A second difference between *horror* and *terror* (which is not unrelated to the first one) has to do with the present orientation of the former: since *horror* is, essentially, the feeling of a spectator, it concerns primarily what is happening 'now' (in a broad sense), rather than what can or will happen after now.

Needless to say, explications of this kind are very different from so-called classical definitions, based on a set of necessary and sufficient conditions, applying not to concepts but to denotata (so that one can say of any extralinguistic entity or state whether it does or does not meet them). Rather, they could be called "semantic definitions". But a semantic definition of the kind proposed here is a fairly precise and flexible tool of conceptual analysis, and it allows us to capture subtle and elusive aspects of meaning far beyond the level of detail and sophistication which was aimed at in earlier analyses of emotion concepts. Most importantly, definitions of the kind proposed here are intuitively intelligible and intuitively verifiable; they can, therefore, be discussed with native speakers, tested against native speakers' intuitions, and revised and amended on the basis of such discussions. Though not perfect, therefore, they are perfectible, and a continued dialogue with native speakers never fails to result in an increased level of consensus.

But although all concepts encoded in natural language are reducible to simple, indefinable, universal, and inherently "clear" concepts such as SOMEONE and SOMETHING, SAY and KNOW, or GOOD and BAD, they can't always be so reduced, so to speak, in one go, that is in a single paraphrase, however complex. Often, they can only be reduced to the level of conceptual simples step by step. In saying this, I am relaxing a principle of semantic analysis which I have defended for two decades, and which was postulated by Leibniz as a necessary empirical check on semantic analysis, at least with respect to some words (notably, particles):

For a proper explanation of the particles it is not sufficient to make an abstract explication . . . but we must proceed to a paraphrase which may be substituted in its place, as the definition may be put in the place of the thing defined. When we have striven to seek and to determine these suitable paraphrases in all the particles so far as they are susceptible of them, we shall have regulated their significations. (Leibniz 1765/1981: 333).

I still believe that this principle is vitally important, but I no longer think that it can be applied as broadly as I suggested in a number of earlier publications (see in particular Wierzbicka 1972, 1980). In many cases, I now recognize, it can only be applied step by step. I will illustrate this with a number of examples of concrete concepts, beginning with relatively simple ones, and then turning to more complex ones.

4. Relatively Simple Concrete Concepts: Body Parts and the Natural Environment

Among the simplest concrete concepts are some spatial concepts such as 'top' and 'bottom':

top
a part of something
this part is above all the other parts of this something

bottom
a part of something
this part is under all the other parts of this something

A somewhat larger category of (relatively speaking) simple concepts includes those referring to body parts.[1] For example:

head
a part of a person's body
this part is above all the other parts of the body
when a person thinks, something happens in this part

Despite their relatively simple semantics, many body part concepts appear to involve a hierarchical (transitive) structure, with, for example, the 'eyes', 'ears', 'nose', and 'mouth' being defined via 'face', and 'face', via 'head' (see Cruse 1986; Wilkins 1981; Apresjan 1974, 1992; Mel'čuk 1974):

face
a part of a person's head
it is on one side of the head
it has parts

---

[1] For an earlier attempt at analysing the meaning of body part terms, see Wierzbicka (1980: 77–97).

often, when a person feels something,
   something happens in this part
other people can see this
because of this, when a person feels something,
   other people can often know something about it

eyes
two parts of a person's face
these parts are alike
one is on one side of the face
the other is on the other side of the face
because of these two parts, a person can see

ears
two parts of a person's head
these parts are alike
one is on one side of the head
the other is on the other side of the head
they are not parts of a person's face
because of these two parts, a person can hear

nose
a part of a person's face
one can think of this part like this:
   there are two parts above this part
   one on one side of the face
   one on the other side of the face
   there is one part under this part
because of this part, when a person is in a place, this person can feel
   something
because of this, a person can think something like this about a place:
   there is something bad in this place
   there is something good in this place

mouth
a part of a person's face
this part has two parts, one above the other
these parts are alike
because of this part, a person can say things to other people
other people can hear these things
often, there are some things inside this part
because this person wants to do something to these things with this
   part
people can think like this about this part:
   if there is nothing inside this part for a very long time a person cannot live

What applies to body part concepts applies also to environmental concepts such as 'sky' or 'sun' or 'cloud', for which I would propose explications roughly along the following lines:

sky
something very big
people can see it
people can think like this about this something:
   it is a place
   it is above all other places
   it is far from people

sun
something
people can often see this something in the sky
when this something is in the sky
people can see other things because of this
when this something is in the sky
people often feel something because of this

cloud
something
people can often see many things of this kind in the sky
sometimes people cannot see the sun because of these things
these things can move

Explicated in this way, a set such as 'eyes–face–head' or 'cloud–sun–sky' reminds one of a set of Russian wooden dolls. All this may seem not only very complicated but unnecessarily so: wouldn't it be better to admit, quite simply, that eyes are eyes, a face is a face, and a head is a head, and that's the end of the story?

Of course it would be simpler to do this. But consider what words such as these (e.g. *eyes*) can mean to a blind person like Helen Keller (1956), who could use them in ways that make perfect sense to sighted people. It seems to me that seen from the point of view of someone like Helen Keller the explications proposed here sound psychologically quite plausible. The words *eyes*, *face*, and *head* could have to Helen Keller an ostensive interpretation, because she could know their designata by touching. But surely, she knew not only which parts of her own face or of other people's faces were called *eyes*, but also that these parts—which she could touch—could give people some special, otherwise inaccessible, knowledge about places. She also knew that people's faces can reveal something about their thoughts and feelings, and that their heads are not only above other parts of the body but also have something to do with thinking.

In the case of 'cloud', 'sun', or 'sky' an ostensive definition is even less plausible, because Helen Keller could neither see nor touch their designata; and yet she clearly did understand the concepts.

I do not think, therefore, that the explications proposed here are unnecessarily complex. At the same time I acknowledge that they *are* complex—too complex for global, all-embracing, one-level paraphrases couched exclusively in terms of semantic primitives to be fully intelligible. It is desirable, therefore, and perhaps necessary, that our definitions of concrete concepts such as names of body parts or names of different parts or aspects of the natural environment should include semantic "molecules" as well as semantic "atoms".

It should be emphasized, however, that a semantic analysis conducted in terms of semantic "molecules" rather than directly in terms of semantic "atoms" makes no claim about the order of acquisition. Thus, if we define 'eyes' in terms of 'face', or 'sun' in terms of 'sky', this does not mean that we expect children to learn the word *face* before the word *eyes*, or the word *sky* before the word *sun*, because the acquisition of concepts is one thing, and the acquisition of words, another.

Though we may know that a child has started to use the word *eyes*, or the word *sun*, this does not mean that we know what concepts the child is associating with these words. Since a young child's use of words does not correspond to that of an adult (see e.g. Anglin 1970; Clark and Clark 1977; Clark 1983; Carey 1985), we cannot assume that the child's meanings correspond to those of the adult; on the contrary, we must assume that they may be different.

It seems reasonable to conjecture that children absorb the semantic universe of their native language gradually, moving, on the whole, from simpler concepts to more complex ones. It goes without saying that the acquisition of concepts by children requires much further study (across a wide range of languages) before any firm conclusions about the nature of this process can be reached. It is important to remember, however, that the task is exceedingly difficult, precisely because the acquisition of concepts cannot be equated with the acquisition of words. It would seem obvious that systematic and methodologically informed analysis of adult concepts is a condition *sine qua non* for the study of the gradual acquisition of these concepts by children.

5. Temperature Terms and the Concept of 'Fire'

It seems very likely that "temperature terms" are first learnt ostensively—for example, *hot* in connection with an oven or a heater, and *cold* in connection with cold water or drinks, or ice, or cold weather. At that stage of language acquisition, *hot* and *cold* may not even be thought of as opposites.

But the full adult meanings of these words are definitely thought of as opposites (although *cold* is also thought of as an opposite of *warm*). We can account for this if we try to reveal the conceptual point of reference contained in these concepts. I believe that such a point of reference for all these three concepts (*hot, cold,* and *warm*) is provided by the concept of *fire,* and that slightly different concepts are embodied in the temperature words referring to the ambient air and in those referring to objects. (It is interesting to note in this connection that in Russian two different words are used for "hot" weather and for "hot" things, e.g. water.) As a first approximation, I would propose the following explications:

> It is hot now. =
> if someone is very near fire
> this person can feel something bad because of this
> people can feel something like this now

> It is cold now. =
> sometimes people want to be near fire
> because they feel something bad
> people can feel something bad like this now

> It is warm now. =
> sometimes people feel something good
> because they are near fire
> people can feel something good like this today

As these explications show, both *hot* and *cold* as descriptors of ambient temperature incorporate value judgements, and in both cases, these judgements are negative. This suggestion is supported by Lehrer's (1990) observation that one can talk of a "warm jumper" and perhaps even of a "cool dress", but not of a "hot jumper" or a "cold dress": "warm jumpers" and "cool dresses" can be seen as functional, but hot jumpers or cold dresses would not because normally people don't want to feel hot or cold. The contrast in acceptability between *keep (oneself) warm* or *keep cool* on the one hand and *?keep hot* or *?keep cold* on the other points in the same direction.

On the other hand, hot food, or a hot bath, are not seen as undesirable (and *keep (food) hot* is perfectly acceptable); nor is a cold drink, or a cold compress on one's forehead, undesirable. The idea of something warm coming into such contact with our bodies implies a pleasant sensation, and while the idea of something cold coming into such contact is more likely to imply something unpleasant this doesn't have to be the case; for example, the collocations *cold beer* or *cold meat* do not imply anything undesirable (cf. *cold stethoscope*), and don't sound odd, unlike *cold jumper* or *hot socks.*

These differences between temperature words as applied to ambient air

or clothes and as applied to objects can be accounted for by assigning to
the latter type explications along (roughly) the following lines:[2]

This thing (*X*) is hot. =
if something is very near fire
something can happen to this thing because of this
if someone touches this thing this person can feel something bad
    because of this
X is like this

This thing (*X*, e.g. some soup, milk, water) is warm. =
if something is near fire
something can happen to this thing because of this
if someone touches this thing this person can feel something
    because of this
X is like this

This thing (*X*, e.g. some soup, milk, water) is cold. =
if something is near fire
something can happen to this thing because of this
if someone touches this thing this person can feel something
    because of this
X is not like this

Though relatively simple, all the above explications rely, crucially, on the
concept of 'fire'—and 'fire' itself is quite complex, much more so than the
other environmental concepts discussed earlier ('sky', 'sun', or 'cloud').

In view of this complexity, we might be tempted to say that "fire" is a
purely ostensive term ("fire is what people call fire"). But this would not be
any more satisfactory than saying, for example, that "sky" is "what we call
sky", or "sun" is "what we call sun". For any native speaker of English *fire*
is more than just a proper name, and it implies knowledge which can be
spelled out. If we do spell it out, we can see, among other things, how *fire*
is semantically related to *sun*.

Speaking informally, *fire* is a phenomenon which can be seen (even at
night), which can be felt by people nearby, which causes a profound change
("burning") in some things or substances, and which can hurt people if they
get too close to it. A more precise explication is given below. For the
reader's convenience, some "props" (in square brackets) have been included
in a number of places. These props should be helpful, but not essential, for
the understanding of the explication.

---

[2] The concept 'touch' (or 'on', 'contact') has been proposed as a possible semantic primitive by Cliff Goddard (personal communication). It has not yet been tested cross-linguistically.

There is fire in that place. =
(a)   something is happening in that place
(b)   people can see it
(c)   if at a time [at night] people couldn't see anything else in this place,
      they could see this
(d)   if someone is near that place, this person can feel something [warm,
      hot] because this is happening
(e)   something is happening to some things in that place [e.g. wood,
      coals] because this is happening
(f)   after this, these things will not be the same [they will turn to ashes,
      etc.]
(g)   people can think about it like this:
(h)   this is something
(i)   if someone touches this something, this person will feel something
         very bad

Component (a) indicates that fire is an event, or a process, (b) and (c)
that it is highly visible, (d) that it generates warmth, (e) and (f) that in the
process some substances are "burnt". Component (g) indicates that people
think of this event or process in a special way, namely, (h) that it is a
"thing", a tangible thing (i) which, however, should not be touched
(because one would burn oneself).

What is particularly important about this explication is that it doesn't
include words such as *hot*, *heat*, or *burn* (not to mention *flames, inflamma-
tion, combustion, fuel*, etc.) as conventional dictionaries usually do, which
all, inevitably, lead to circularity.

Long as this explication is, I have indicated that it may not even be complete, because it can be argued that the full concept of 'fire' includes also
some references to its role in human life: cooking, warmth, light as well as
destructive unwanted fires. In simple terms, these further aspects of 'fire'
can be articulated along the following lines:

(f)   often people do something in a place
          because they want this to happen [making fire]
(k)   sometimes people do it because they want something to happen to
      something [to some food]
(l)   sometimes people do it because they don't want to feel something
      bad [cold]
(m) sometimes people do it at a time when they cannot see things [at
      night] because they want to see things [light]

It could be argued, of course, that the formula above articulates not the
meaning of the word *fire*, but something else—say, English speakers' folk
knowledge and folk ideas about fire. In my view, however, this would really

be an argument about terminology (what is "meaning"), not about the substance: equally well, one could argue that the position of the head in the body (above the other parts), or the location of the sky ("above everything"), belongs to "folk knowledge". Whether we call such things "meaning" or "folk knowledge/ideas", they are part of the speakers' communicative competence, and they are associated, invariably, with the explicated words. (For further discussion, see Chapter 11.) The complexity of such meanings—or such folk knowledge—is quite remarkable, and it is hard to escape the conclusion that the human mind has an in-built capacity to acquire such horrors—or wonders—of complexity and to organize them along certain paths, for which the mind is perhaps somehow prepared. This conclusion is strengthened by consideration of words for cultural and natural kinds, which will be discussed next. (See again Chapter 11.)

6. Cultural and Natural Kinds: 'Bread' and 'Water'

According to many theorists of language and cognition, there are two kinds of concept: one kind is acquired via direct experience of the world, that is, ostensively, whereas the other is acquired via language. For example, Russell (1948: 78) wrote:

'Ostensive definition' may be defined as 'any process by which a person is taught to understand a word otherwise than by the use of other words'. Suppose that, knowing no French, you are shipwrecked on the coast of Normandy: you make your way into a farmhouse, you see bread on the table, and, being famished, you point at it with an inquiring gesture. If the farmer thereupon says *pain*, you will conclude, at least provisionally, that this is the French for 'bread', and you will be confirmed in this view if the word is not repeated when you point at other kinds of eatables. You will then have learnt the meaning of the word by ostensive definition.

Having in this way introduced the concept of ostensive definition, Russell goes on to suggest that there are two different kinds of words in language: those which are normally learnt by ostensive definitions and those which are learnt via other words. He exemplifies:

Most children learn the word *dog* ostensively; some learn in this way the kinds of dogs, collies, St. Bernards, spaniels, poodles, etc., while others, who have little to do with dogs, may first meet with these words in books. No child learns the word *quadruped* ostensively, still less the word *animal* in the sense in which it includes oysters and limpets. He probably learns *ant*, *bee*, and *beetle* ostensively, and perhaps *insect*, but if so he will mistakenly include spiders until corrected. .

Names of substances not obviously collections of individuals, such as *milk*, *bread*, *wood*, are apt to be learnt ostensively when they denote things familiar in every-day life. (Russell 1948: 83)

In a similar vein, Burling (1970: 80) distinguishes between what he calls "referential definitions" and "verbal definitions":

The conclusion seems clear: any theory of meaning must provide for two essentially different ways by which we can learn and define the meaning of words. *Mother* must almost always be learned in context, while *second cousin once removed* could probably never be learned without some degree of verbal explanation. *Water* is learned in context, *hydrogen dioxide*, with an explanation, and so on.

I would also agree that some concepts are learnt (partly) on the basis of ostension, and *bread, milk, water, dog*, or *bee* may indeed be of this kind. Whether any concepts can be acquired purely by ostension is a problem which I will discuss shortly. First, however, it should be pointed out that the alternative set up by Russell or Burling omits the third—and perhaps the most important—source of our concepts, that is our innate conceptual apparatus, which is both "logically and ontogenetically" prior to either verbal explanations or ostension.

It seems obvious that "verbal explanations" must rely on words which can be learnt without such explanations. Consequently, if ostension were the only alternative to verbal explanations then all concepts would have to be acquired, ultimately, by ostension. But how can one acquire by ostension conceptual distinctions such as that between *someone* and *something*, or between *you* and *I*? Astonishingly, Russell (though not Burling) does mention *you* and *I*, as well as *after* and *before*, among those words which are learnt by ostension. But how could one possibly "show" to a child what *you* or *I* means? Or how could one show to anyone what *someone*, as opposed to *something*, means? Of course, one could give examples of persons, and examples of things; but how could one *show* the grounds for the respective generalizations?

Assuming that universal human concepts such as SOMEONE and SOMETHING, YOU and I, or BEFORE and AFTER are prior to all experience, and to all explanation, and provide—like Kant's space and time—a priori forms of experience, let us return to the question of how concepts which *are* rooted in people's experience (such as Russell's 'bread' or 'pain') may be actually acquired, and what these concepts may really stand for.

Russell's charming vignette notwithstanding, to acquire the adult meaning of either *pain* or *bread* (which, incidentally, do not mean exactly the same, and which do not have exactly the same range of use)[3] children (or

---

[3] For example, English distinguishes lexically between *rolls* (bread rolls) and *bread*, whereas in French "rolls" are called *les petits pains* ("little breads"). This fact (among many others) reflects different culinary traditions and different expectations with respect to *bread* and *pain*: *bread* is expected to be sliced (and, consequently, *rolls* are conceived as a different cultural kind), whereas *pain*, which plays a far greater role in French culture than *bread* does in Anglo culture, is expected to be crusty on the outside and light and puffy inside, and is therefore less

shipwrecked mariners from distant lands) must do more than simply observe how these words are used in one type of situation, with respect to one type of object: they must also figure out how to extend their initial use to new situations, and to new, unfamiliar, types of referents. To do that, they must go beyond a mere observation of material objects (various pieces or kinds of bread), and come up with some (unconscious) hypotheses about the way people think about those objects; they must make the leap from ostension to conceptualization, from objects to construals.

They must learn that 'bread' is something that people eat; they must also learn that it is something that people, generally speaking, eat every day—even if they, or their own families, happen not to eat it every day; that it is something people normally eat in order not to be hungry (unlike cakes, which people normally eat for pleasure); that it comes in the form of large objects which can be shared and which can last for some time (loaves) and that people normally eat it with something else (e.g. butter). They must also learn that—unlike noodles or rice—it is something that people eat with their hands, and not with forks or spoons. (Words and expressions such as *breadwinner*, *bread and butter*, or *sandwich* provide linguistic evidence for the psychological reality of these components.)

The fact that bread is made from flour or from something like flour, and that it is baked, is probably less essential than the facts mentioned above, but it probably is, none the less, part of the adult concept of 'bread': to understand this concept, one must know that the thing in question is made from 'something that comes from plants, that is, something that grows out of the ground' (and that people do something to the ground for that purpose); and also that, while one doesn't normally eat bread hot, to prepare it one does need 'heat'.

For Europeans, 'bread' is such a familiar everyday phenomenon that it is often hard for them to imagine that this concept may need any explanation. When one looks at it from a cross-cultural perspective, however, it becomes obvious that bread eating is a highly culture-specific phenomenon, and that the word *bread* stands for a complex cultural kind, whose essential characteristics are by no means easy to identify to cultural outsiders (see Nida 1947). The fact that in many languages (e.g. in many Australian and Oceanic languages) the word for 'bread' is a recent loan from English highlights the "foreign" character of this concept in many cultures. It is also likely that although loan words of this kind may have the same range of denotata as the English word *bread*, the concept is in fact somewhat different. In particular, in Australian languages, which tend to contrast "flesh food" and "plant food", 'bread' (or, rather, 'burridi') is thought of above

suitable for slicing. (For example, a French *baguette* counts as *pain*, but it is not expected to be sliced.) The fact that in English *bread* is a mass noun (e.g. **two breads*) whereas in French *pain* can be used as a count noun (e.g. *deux pains*) points in the same direction.

all as a kind of "plant food". For example, in Marrithiyel bread is commonly referred to not just as *burridi* but as *mi-burridi*, where *mi* is a general classifier for food coming from plants (Ian Green, personal communication). As mentioned earlier, however, from an English speaker's point of view the 'plant' origin of *bread* may well be a less salient part of the concept, acquired relatively late.

As a first approximation we can, then, explicate the concept of 'bread' along the following lines:

> *bread*
> a kind of thing that people eat
> many people eat it every day
> when people don't eat something for a long time
>   they can feel something bad
> people often eat this kind of thing because of this
>
> people eat it like this:
>   they eat it with their hands, not with anything else
>   when they eat it, they eat something else at the same time
>   they don't eat all of it at the same time
>
> people make things of this kind
> because they want people to be able to eat them
>
> in some places things grow out of the ground   ORIGIN
> because people did something in these places
> because they want people to be able to eat this kind of thing
> people do some things to these things
> something happens to some parts of these things because of this
> people do something with these parts near fire

This explication, incomplete and imperfect as it no doubt is, is, I believe, psychologically more real than a typical dictionary definition, such as, for example, that provided by the *Shorter Oxford English Dictionary* (*SOED* 1964): *bread*—"an article of food prepared by moistening, kneading, and baking meal or flour, usually with the addition of yeast or leaven"; or the one provided by the *Macquarie Dictionary of Australian English* (1981): *bread*—"a food made of flour or meal, milk or water, etc., made into a dough or batter, with or without yeast or the like, and baked'.

Contrary to what definitions of this kind imply, one can know what *bread* means without knowing the meaning of words such as *yeast*, *leaven*, or *batter*; but if one doesn't know that *bread* is thought of as something that many people eat every day ("our daily bread"), and as something that they eat, roughly speaking, in order not to be hungry (rather than for pleasure, like cake); or that it is made from something that, roughly speaking, "comes from plants" (so that, for example, a "meat loaf" is not a kind of bread), then they do not know what *bread* means. The knowledge encapsulated in this concept goes far beyond ostension, and in this sense 'bread' is far from a purely ostensive concept. It embodies generalizations which are usually not made explicitly, verbally, but which none the less can be made verbally, and which sometimes have to be made verbally. For example, if a small child refers to a cake or to a meat loaf as *bread*, he or she is likely to be corrected: this is not bread, this is cake; or: this is not bread, this is a meat loaf. Somehow or other the child must build the generalization that things with meat in them, or sweet things that one eats for pleasure and which one doesn't spread with anything, are not *bread*. I am not saying that generalizations of this kind are given to the child verbally, or that they are made by the child consciously, but that if they are not made at all, the concept has not been learnt.

Similarly, how can one learn the concept of 'water' (Burling's example) by mere ostension?

Water is something that one can drink, but so is milk or orange juice. Water is "colourless", "see-through"; but so is vodka, and various other liquids that a child is not allowed to drink. Water is also the stuff one can go into in some places, for example, in a place called "the sea"; and this stuff one is not allowed to drink either. Water is also the stuff one can wash oneself with; but the idea of 'wash' presupposes, it seems, the knowledge of the concept 'water'. (One can 'wash' oneself only with water or with 'something like water'.)

Contrary to what is usually assumed, 'water' is not a universal human concept for which every language has a word. For example, the closest Japanese word, *mizu*, does not mean the same as *water* and refers exclusively to cold water (see Suzuki 1978). One cannot say, for example, **atsui mizu*, 'hot mizu', whereas *atsui miruku*, 'hot milk', is fully acceptable (Masayuki Onishi, personal communication). For 'hot water' Japanese has a different word: *yu* (with an honorific prefix, *oyu*).

Unlike the Japanese *mizu*, then, the English *water* can be either cold or hot. Water can come from a tap, but if it comes from the sky, it is normally called *rain*, not *water* (unlike the Pitjantjatjara word *kapi*, which applies also to the stuff falling sometimes 'from the sky'; Goddard 1992a). None the less, drops of rain can be called *drops of water*.

What, then, is *water*? Clearly, there is much more to this concept than what one can learn by mere ostension; and the most important components of this concept are not necessarily those that one learns first.

Interestingly, to have fully acquired the concept of 'water' one doesn't have to be able to tell it apart from all other substances. If scientists tell us of some liquid, "this looks like water and tastes like water, but it is not water", we do not refuse to believe them. We think of water as a particular KIND of thing, a kind which we may not always be able to recognize but which one can 'put into one's body, through the mouth' (i.e. drink it), and which one can 'see in various places not because people did something in those places' (rivers, creeks, lakes, seas, and so on). These two are perhaps the most crucial components of the (adult) everyday concept of 'water'. They cannot be acquired by ostension alone. There is more to the acquisition of concepts like 'bread' and 'water' than Russell's little fantasy about an Englishman "shipwrecked on the coast of Normandy" allows for.

My conclusion is this: the meaning of a "concrete" word like *bread* or *water* is indeed learnt "in context", but it is built, in the child's mind, gradually, and contains certain tacit knowledge which may not be verbal but which is verbalizable. The Japanese child learns "in context" that *mizu* is cold, but when she tries to use it with respect to boiling water she will be corrected (presumably, verbally corrected); and even if such an error, and such a correction, never occurs, the child must somehow make a mental note that a hot liquid which otherwise is quite like *mizu* is called *yu* and is never called *mizu*, and therefore that *mizu* must be cold. I am not saying that children make this mental note consciously or verbally; but they must make it somehow if they are to learn the proper range of use of the word *mizu*.

The same applies to names of animals, such as Russell's *dog*. How could a child learn this concept by ostension alone? Surely, sooner or later a moment will come when the child learns to apply the word *dog* to an animal that looks different from all those that were called *dog* in her presence. The word *dog* doesn't mean simply 'an animal that looks like those that we have heard people refer to as *dogs*'. A small child may call a fox, or even a cat, *dog* (Clark and Clark 1977). To develop a full adult concept of 'dog' one has to make in one's mind certain generalizations, such as that they bark, that they growl, that they can bite, that they live with people or near people, that they can do different things that people want them to do, and so on (see Wierzbicka 1985: 169–70; see also Tyler 1978).

Again, the ability to recognize dogs is not a necessary consequence of knowing the concept 'dog'. An adult person may mistake a wolf, or a dingo, for a dog, and this doesn't show that they don't know what *dog* means. To know this one has to have access to a number of generalizations about dogs (such as those mentioned above), not to a mental image ensuring that one can always tell dogs apart from other animals. How exactly these generalizations are built, and how they are stored in the mind, we don't know; but they are certainly verbalizable. (Cf. Chapter 11.)

Russell was convinced that *quadruped* is learnt via a verbal explanation whereas *dog*, *beetle*, or *ant* is learnt via ostension. He was less confident, however, about *insect*, and seemed in fact to recognize, implicitly, that *insect* cannot be learnt without a verbal explanation or at least a verbal correction.

But is *beetle* really very different in this respect from *insect*? Or, for that matter, from *ant*? In many Australian Aboriginal languages there is no word for *ant*, because, for example, "edible ants" are conceptualized as something quite different from 'red ants' or from "poisonous ants". In fact, different kinds of what speakers of English would describe as 'ants' are not even assigned to the same supercategory. (See Hale *et al.* forthcoming.) This suggests that each "species word" of this kind is learnt in terms of some abstract generalizations—not unlike those involved in *quadruped, insect,* or *second cousin once removed.*

Having said this, I hasten to add: I am not saying that there is no difference between *quadruped* or *second cousin once removed* on the one hand and *dog, ant, bread,* or *water* on the other. But the difference is not what Russell or Burling say it is.

Concepts such as 'quadruped' or 'second cousin once removed' are probably learnt by verbal explanation alone, so that ostension plays no role in their acquisition, whereas ostension clearly does play a role in the acquisition of concepts such as 'dog', 'ant', 'bread', or 'water'. However, this doesn't mean that the latter kind of concept can be acquired by ostension alone. Nor does it mean that they can be given a purely ostensive definition, along the lines of "an ant is a kind of creature that people call ANT" or "*bread* is a kind of stuff that people call BREAD".

Not every language has a word for 'bread' or for 'ant', and one could never teach the speaker of a language which doesn't have such words what they mean simply by showing them some appropriate specimens. Specimens are of course useful, but the learners have also to grasp how far they can go in applying the words in question to things which look different—or to things which look similar but are differently handled, differently interacted with. Abstract generalizations have to be built, and although the learner doesn't necessarily build them, and store them, in the form of verbal definitions, this is the only way, I believe, that testable hypotheses about their content can be formulated. How else?

When Burling (1970: 80) says that words such as *water* are "learned in context" (rather than with the help of other words) he is no doubt right. But this is different from saying that the meaning of such words can be stated without a verbal definition. The quote adduced at the beginning of this section seems to suggest that, in Burling's view, words learned in context do not require verbal definitions—and this is the point which I dispute.

7. Plugging Concepts In

So far, I have focused on the semantic complexity of words of different kinds. But, obviously, people don't speak just in words: they speak in sentences; and the semantic complexity of sentences depends not only on the complexity of the words of which they are composed but also on the mechanics of the composition itself.

Let us consider, for example, a simple sentence such as *I ate an apple*. In broad outline, its semantic structure can be represented as follows:

> [at some time before now]
> I did something [EAT] to something [APPLE]
> something happened to this something [APPLE] because of this

To apply this formula to a sentence, we need to 'plug in', somehow, the semantic information encapsulated in the words *eat* and *apple*. For *eat*, we could propose (as a first approximation) the following scenario: [4]

Someone ate something. =
(*a*) someone did something to something
(*b*) after this, something was inside a part of this person [MOUTH]
(*c*) this person did something to this thing with this part
(*d*) something happened to this thing because of this
(*e*) after this, parts of this thing were inside another part of this person [STOMACH]
(*f*) if people don't do this they cannot live
(*g*) if someone doesn't do it for a long time this person feels something bad

The crucial components which distinguish 'eating' from 'drinking' are (*c*) and (*d*): even though food doesn't have to be necessarily chewed or bitten, when one 'eats' it (as opposed to 'drinking') something happens to it in the mouth, and it happens because one does something to it with one's mouth. (For a definition of *mouth*, see Section 4.)

As for *apple(s)*, this could be defined, in essence, as 'a kind of thing that people eat', and in simpler syntax, 'a kind of thing—people EAT this kind of thing', a formula whose interpretation depends again on the explication of *eat*. But a full meaning of *apple* contains of course more than a basic categorization in terms of edibility. Trying to spell out this meaning (that is, the folk concept) fully, I found that I had to posit numerous components, some of great semantic complexity (see Wierzbicka 1985: 302–3).

But even if we ignored the enormous semantic complexity of a concept like 'apple', and if we defined this word simply as 'a kind of thing that peo-

---

[4] For an earlier attempt to state the meaning of *eat*, see Wierzbicka (1980: 90).

ple eat', or even as 'a kind of thing that people call APPLES', we would still have to conclude that the meaning of the simple sentence *I ate an apple* cannot be represented in terms of one global paraphrase. It can be represented in terms of semantic primitives, but only on a step-by-step basis. I conjecture, therefore, that—to some extent at least—this is how the human mind operates when it confronts the stupendous task of semantic interpretation in general; or at least, that it is capable of doing so when it is needed.

8. Conclusion

The semantic structure of an ordinary human sentence is about as simple and as "shallow" as the structure of a galaxy or the structure of an atom. Looking into the meaning of a single word, let alone a single sentence, can give one the same feeling of dizziness that can come from thinking about the distances between galaxies or about the impenetrable empty spaces hidden in a single atom. The experience can be disconcerting, and perhaps it is not surprising that many theorists of language and cognition prefer to take the view that meanings can't be analysed—as W. Lyons (1981: 73–4) put it, "for theoretically interesting reasons".

But no reasons, not even "theoretically interesting" ones, can absolve us from the effort of trying to explore the meanings of words to find out what unconscious principles determine the boundaries of their use. We have to try to pin down the elusive and culture-specific configurations of elements encapsulated in everyday concepts, and to face the formidable complexity of meanings which ordinary people appear to juggle effortlessly in everyday discourse.

If we don't tackle this complexity we shall also fail to achieve some of our basic professional tasks, such as laying the groundwork for a more effective lexicography, developing tools to revitalize language teaching, or promoting cross-cultural understanding via a non-ethnocentric description of cultural variation. We shall also throw away our chance of exploring and contemplating the dazzling beauty of the universe of meaning.

II Lexical Semantics

8 Against "Against Definitions"

□ □ _____

1. Linguistic Meaning

In this chapter I will not try to review the enormous literature on definitions but rather present my own conclusions on the subject emerging from work on hundreds of definitions, pursued over nearly three decades.

A "definition"—in the sense which is relevant to linguistics—is an expression which "shows", so to speak, the meaning of a word by articulating it into its components. (Cf. the quote from Locke 1690/1959: 33–4 in Chapter 7.)

Since to define a word is to decompose its meaning into its constituent parts, only complex concepts are susceptible of definition. Although Locke's "simple ideas" do not correspond exactly to semantic primitives as conceived here (see Wierzbicka 1980), his argument applies equally to both:

> This being premised, I saw that the *names of simple ideas, and those only, are incapable of being defined*. The reason whereof is this, That the several terms of a definition, signifying several ideas, they can all together by no means represent an idea which has no composition at all: and therefore a definition, which is properly nothing but the showing the meaning of one word by several others not signifying each the same thing, can in the names of simple ideas have no place.   (1690/1959: 34)

By "defining" a word, then, I mean, essentially, what Locke meant: "showing" the meaning of a definable (i.e. semantically complex) word in terms of indefinable (i.e. semantically simple) ones.

2. Definitions as a Tool for Cross-cultural Research

Why do we need definitions at all? One of the possible answers to this question is that we need them as a tool for understanding other cultures (and for making ourselves understood). Words are a society's most basic cultural artefacts, and—properly understood—they provide the best key to a culture's values and assumptions. But to avoid misinterpretation, definitions are needed that are free of ethnocentric bias; that is, definitions couched in terms of universal, culture-free, primitive concepts.

The need for such definitions is still not widely recognized. To quote one anthropologist: "It is perhaps a matter for some wonder . . . that in so many regards . . . social anthropologists should still so commonly write as though in their own language, and in the technical terms of their profession, they already possessed an ideal language" (Needham 1972: 222–3). I do not claim that the Natural Semantic Metalanguage is an "ideal language" in the sense of being the final answer to the search for lexically embodied conceptual universals. It is an approximation, to be improved by further trial and error. But it is better to have a tentative and imperfect set of indefinables than none at all.

Using the proposed set we can clearly define even those concepts which are widely regarded as "unique", that is, absolutely culture-specific and thoroughly "untranslatable". I will illustrate this claim here with just one example: that of the Japanese concept of 'amae' (for other examples, and more detailed discussion, see Wierzbicka 1991*b*, 1992*a* and forthcoming *e*).

According to Doi, *amae* is "a peculiarly Japanese emotion", although it has "universal relevance" (1981: 169). It is "a thread that runs through all the various activities of Japanese society" (1981: 26), represents "the true essence of Japanese psychology", and is "an important key to understanding the psychological differences between Japan and Western countries" (1974: 310).

Doi explains that "*amae* is the noun form of *amaeru*, an intransitive verb which means 'to depend and presume upon another's benevolence' " (1974: 307). It indicates "helplessness and the desire to be loved" (1981: 22). The adjective *amai* means 'sweet', both with reference to taste and with reference to human relations: "if *A* is said to be *amai* to *B*, it means that he allows *B* to *amaeru*, i.e., to behave self-indulgently, presuming on some special relationship that exists between the two" (1981: 29).

Amaeru can also be defined "by a combination of words such as 'wish to be loved' and 'dependency needs' " (Doi 1974: 309). The Japanese dictionary *Daigenkai* defines *amae* as "to lean on a person's good will" (quoted in Doi 1981: 72) or "to depend on another's affection" (167). Other dictionary glosses include "to act lovingly towards (as a much fondled child towards its parents), "to presume upon", "to take advantage of" (*Brinkley's* 1963); "to behave like a spoilt child", "be coquettish", "trespass on", "behave in a caressing manner towards a man"; "to speak in a coquettish tone", "encroach on [one's kindness, good nature, etc.]" (*Takenobu* 1918); "presume on another's love", "be coquettish", "coax" (*Kenkyusha's* 1954); and so on.

Morsbach and Tyler (1986), who analysed fifteen passages from Japanese literature referring to *amae*, used in their translations of these passages the following English glosses: "take advantage of", "play baby", "make up to [someone] and get their sympathy", "coax", "act spoilt", and so on.

On the basis of these and other similar clues, we can explicate the concept of *amae* as follows:

amae
(a) *X* thinks something like this:
(b)   when *Y* thinks about me, *Y* feels something good
(c)   *Y* wants to do good things for me
(d)   *Y* can do good things for me
(e)   when I am near *Y* nothing bad can happen to me
(f)   I don't have to do anything because of this
(g)   I want to be near *Y*
(h) *X* feels something good because of this

Doi emphasizes that *amae* presupposes conscious awareness. The sub-component (a) '*X* thinks something like this . . .' reflects this. The presumption of a special relationship is reflected in the component (b) 'when *Y* thinks about me, *Y* feels something good'. The implication of self-indulgence is rooted in the emotional security of someone who knows that he or she is loved: "it is an emotion that takes the other person's love for granted" (Doi 1981: 168). This is accounted for by the combination of components (b) 'when *Y* thinks about me, *Y* feels something good', (c) '*Y* wants to do good things for me', (d) '*Y* can do good things for me', and (e) 'when I am near *Y* nothing bad can happen to me'. The component (f) 'I don't have to do anything because of this' reflects the passive attitude of an *amae*-junior, who does not have to earn the mother-figure's goodwill and protection by any special actions. The component (g) 'I want to be near *Y*' reflects Doi's (1981: 74) idea that the baby in an "amae" relationship to the mother "comes to feel the mother as something indispensable to itself" and that "it is the craving for close contact thus developed that constitutes . . . *amae*".

Thus even "unique", thoroughly "untranslatable" words such as *amae* can be accurately and intelligibly defined in terms of universal semantic primitives.

3. The Concept of a Semantic Invariant

A linguistic definition is a scientific hypothesis about the concept encoded in a given word (see Robinson 1950: 41). Like other scientific hypotheses, it cannot be proved to be right, but it can be tested and proved wrong—in which case it is discarded, or revised and tested again. While the concept is not accessible to direct observation, it is manifested in a word's use. Accordingly, a definition can be tested against a word's range of use; this range of use may be very broad, but it has its boundaries, which are determined by the different components of the concept.

The components of the concept determine which aspects of a word's use are variable and which are invariable. It is the purpose of a definition to capture the invariable aspects of a word's use, that is, its semantic invariant.

One might ask at this point: How do we know that a word really encodes a concept with some invariable components, that is, that it really does have a semantic invariant? The answer is that we don't know it, but that this has proved to be a fruitful working hypothesis. The alternative hypothesis (that the meaning of words is changeable and "fuzzy", and cannot be captured in rigorous definitions) is sterile and can hardly provide an effective tool for large-scale lexicographic research.

The goal of capturing a word's semantic invariant by investigating its range of use was set out more than 2,000 years ago, by Socrates, in Plato's dialogue *Laches*, devoted to a search for the definition of the Greek concept 'andreia' (usually rendered in English as *courage*):

> SOCRATES. I meant to ask you not only about the courage of the heavily-armed soldiers, but about the courage of cavalry and every other style of soldier; and not only who are courageous in war but who are courageous in perils by sea, and who in disease, or in poverty, or again in politics, are courageous; and not only who are courageous against pain or fear, but mighty to contend against desires and pleasures, either fixed in their rank or turning upon the enemy. There is this sort of courage—is there not, Laches?
>
> LACHES. Certainly, Socrates. . . .
>
> SOCRATES. What is that common quality, which is the same in all these cases, and which is called courage?   (Plato 1970: 116–17)

Dictionary descriptions usually do not succeed in capturing a word's semantic invariant. Often, they don't even try to provide a definition, but instead offer more or less random lists of quasi-synonyms, as in *Webster's New School and Office Dictionary* (1965) entry for the word *courageous*: "courageous—brave, bold". Entries of this kind inevitably lead to vicious circles. For example, to continue with the same dictionary:

courageous	— brave, bold
brave	— bold, courageous, intrepid
bold	— courageous, venturesome
intrepid	— bold, fearless
fearless	— intrepid

If a rare dictionary does manage to define *courage* or *courageous* without a vicious circle, it is likely to pay for it by not even attempting to capture the invariant. For example, the *Longman Dictionary of the English Language* (*LDOTEL* 1984) defines *courage* as follows:

courage	— mental or moral strength to confront and withstand danger, fear, or difficulty

This definition doesn't say what *danger, fear,* and *difficulty* have in common (nor what is common to *mental strength* and *moral strength*). Lexicographic devices such as "or", "often", "usually", or "etc." are unmistakable signs of the lexicographer's failure to find a semantic invariant, as is also a proliferation of different senses and subsenses in a dictionary entry.

Since words don't have any meaning in isolation, but only in sentences, in looking for the semantic invariant of a word we have to start (contrary to common lexicographic practice) with some syntactic frame, and try to paraphrase the sentence serving as our point of departure in terms of words chosen earlier as indefinables. For example:

X is courageous. =
    X can do very good things when other people can't
    because when other people think something like this:
        I don't want bad things to happen to me
    X thinks something like this:
        it is good if I do this
        it is bad if I don't do it
        I want to do it because of this
    this is good

(For justification and discussion, see Wierzbicka 1992*a*.)

4. Determinacy of Meaning

A search for a word's semantic invariant presupposes a belief in the determinacy of meaning. In recent decades, this belief has often been questioned, by linguists and philosophers alike. Anyone who has engaged in lexicographic research can readily sympathize with such scepticism: constructing a definition which matches a word's entire range of use is a huge task requiring much more work than most are prepared to put in; and the temptation to give up after the first two minutes or the first two hours may well be overwhelming. But the fact that one has tried, and failed, to come up with a fully satisfactory definition in two minutes, or even two hours, hardly justifies the conclusion that meaning is indeterminate. (See e.g. Fodor's ideas about the meaning of *paint,* discussed in Section 9 below.)

In addition to unrealistic expectations about the amount of time and effort necessary for success, several other factors have clearly contributed to the widespread scepticism about the feasibility of definitions, notably the following: (1) the lack of a set of indefinables; (2) the lack of a coherent theory of polysemy; (3) confusion of lexical meaning with illocutionary and rhetorical devices such as metaphor, irony, sarcasm, hyperbole, and so on; (4) the seductive power of the theory of "family resemblances". The first of these four points has already been discussed. Of the other three, only fac-tor(3) hasn't yet been discussed at all, but while the question of polysemy has already been discussed in Chapter 6, and that of "family resemblances" in Chapter 4, both these topics need some elaboration.

5. Problems of Polysemy

As Zgusta justly points out, "the lexicographer will do well to reckon always with polysemy: this will cause him to undertake very deep analyses of the words' meanings" (1971: 66).

Polysemy can be obvious and unmistakable. For example, the English noun *spring* has at least four different meanings, defined by the *Oxford Paperback Dictionary* (*OPD* 1979) as follows:

1. the act of springing, a jump
2. a device (usually of bent or coiled metal) that reverts to the original position after being compressed or tightened or stretched . . .
3. a place where water or oil comes up naturally from the ground . . .
4. the season in which vegetation begins to appear . . .

It is obvious that if we tried to cover these four senses with one definition we would get nowhere; the notion of "semantic invariant" makes sense only with respect to specific senses of a word, not with respect to a mechanical sum of all its different uses, and to be able to construct adequate defini-tions, we have to separate the different senses of a polysemous word.

Here again we must proceed by trial and error, assuming always, to begin with, that there is only one meaning, constructing a tentative definition, checking it against a word's possible range of use, then, if necessary, posit-ing a second meaning, and so on. A great deal of hard work may be required, but this fact by itself has no bearing on the issue of discreteness of meaning.

Often the meanings to sort out will be much closer to one another than the four senses of *spring*. In sorting out closely related senses it is impor-tant that the differences between what we posit as two separate meanings be linked with the word itself and not simply with different contexts in which this word is used.

For example, it would not be justified to posit polysemy for the noun *love* along the lines of (1) romantic love, (2) parental love, (3) brotherly love, and so on, because all these supposedly different kinds of "love" can be seen as sharing a semantic invariant, and as differing only in ways implied by the modifying adjective.

Generally speaking, dictionaries tend to posit polysemy on a truly mas-sive scale; but it is usually posited on an *ad hoc* basis, without any clear guide-lines or general principles, and this applies to ambitious and innovative dictionaries as well as to commercial hack jobs. (For rare exceptions, see Mel'čuk & Žolkovskij 1984; Mel'čuk *et al.* 1984, 1988, 1992; or Apresjan and Rozenman 1979; for a critique of one ambitious and innovative dictionary, the *Longman Dictionary of Contemporary English* (*LDOCE* 1978), see Wierzbicka 1987a: 4–7.)

For example, the *American Heritage Dictionary of the English Language* (*AHDOTEL* 1973) postulates the following three meanings for *if*:

1. in the event that: If I were to go, I would be late.
2. granting that: Even if that's true, what should we do?
3. on condition that: She will sing only if she is paid.

I agree that the meaning of *if* in sentence 1 is indeed different from the meaning of *if* in sentences 2 and 3 (see Chapter 2). But the difference between the supposed senses 2 and 3 can be attributed to different contexts, not to the word *if* itself (note, in particular, the contrast between "even if" in 2 and "only if" in 3). The following rephrasings of the same sentences (without "even" and "only") show better the similarity in their meanings:

(1) If [we suppose that] that's true [we have to decide:] What should we do?
(2) If she is paid she will sing. [If she is not paid she will not.]

In the case of *spring*, different contexts may help clarify which meaning the speaker had in mind but they are not the source of the four different interpretations, which are inherent in the word *spring* itself.

Or consider the three distinct meanings postulated by the same dictionary for the verb *advise*:

1. to offer advice to; to counsel
2. to recommend; suggest
3. to inform; notify

In fact, there is no evidence of any semantic difference between the alleged meanings 1 and 2 (while 3 is indeed different). It is true that *advise* can occur in two different syntactic frames, with either a person or an abstract noun as its object (e.g. *The doctor advised Bill to have complete rest, The doctor advised complete rest*), and different syntactic frames can be associated with differences in the semantic structure. But the verb itself does have an invariant meaning, evident in both these frames (associated with the alleged meanings 1 and 2). (For justification and detailed discussion, see Wierzbicka 1987a.)

Finally, consider the verb *feel*, for which the same dictionary, *AHDOTEL* (1973), posits several different meanings, including the following ones:

1*b*. to perceive as a localized physical sensation: feel a sharp pain.
1*c*. to perceive as a nonlocalized physical sensation: feel the cold.
3*a*. to experience (an emotion): I felt my interest rising.

However, the distinction between 1*b* and 1*c* implies that a sentence such as *She felt pain* is ambiguous, and that it means two different things, depending on whether the pain is localized or non-localized. Furthermore, the distinction between the *feel* of sensation and the *feel* of emotion implies that sentences such as *How are you feeling?*, *I feel good*, or *I feel better* are also all ambiguous. But in fact, the two supposedly different meanings can be easily conjoined, as genuinely different meanings cannot:

I felt cold and miserable.
*He ordered several books and an inquiry into the matter.

But while dictionaries often posit a great deal of unjustified polysemy, they also frequently fail to recognize polysemy which is really there. (For a striking illustration see, for example, the discussion of the word *ribbon* in Chapter 9.)

Zgusta is of course right when he states that "taken on the whole, polysemy will always prove a hard riddle for the lexicographer" (1971: 73). We do not have to assume, however, that this riddle cannot be solved. In a system of semantic analysis based on a finite set of indefinables and on the principle of reductive paraphrase, meanings re-emerge as discrete, determinate entities, and the "riddle of polysemy" ceases to seem insoluble.

6. Lexical Meaning and Illocutionary Rhetorical Devices

A word can be adequately defined only if its literal meaning is distinguished from its metaphorical use, ironic use, playful use, euphemistic use, and other similar uses. Dictionaries frequently fail in this respect, and, for example, treat a word's metaphorical use as a separate lexical meaning.

For example, *OPD* lists (among others) the following two meanings of the English word *friend*: (1) a person with whom one is on terms of mutual affection independently of sexual or family love; (2) a helpful thing or quality, e.g. darkness was our friend. In fact, this second use can be satisfactorily accounted for in terms of the first on the basis of a general principle which allows us to use words of different kinds in the sense 'like *x*' (where '*x*' stands for the word's literal meaning). Thus, in the example above, darkness was not a 'friend' in some separate lexical sense of the word *friend*, but it was 'like a friend'. Since the 'like *x*' device is productive in English (as it is in many other languages), there is of course no need to mention it in individual dictionary entries. One can also say, for example, that "darkness was our refuge", but *OPD* (rightly) refrains from mentioning this use as a separate sense of the word *refuge*.

If metaphorical uses and other similar rhetorical devices are not distinguished from lexical polysemy, then meanings may indeed appear to be indeterminate and not amenable to precise definitions. But this is not the "fault" of the meanings themselves.

7. Family Resemblances

A key factor militating against large-scale study of the lexicon until recently was not just the absence of a suitable methodology but also the widespread belief that such a methodology could not be devised. Particularly damaging in this respect was Wittgenstein's doctrine of "family resemblances", which has gained extraordinary popularity (see Wierzbicka 1990*b*; also Chapter 4).

If it is assumed that meanings have no clear boundaries and that they are mutually related by vague and elusive family resemblances, then it is natural to conclude that no precise definitions are possible. But without such definitions meanings can be neither stated nor compared. As a result, all serious investigation of the lexicon comes to a halt.

The doctrine of family resemblances never had any empirical basis. It was the speculative idea of a philosopher—to be sure, a philosopher of almost unparalleled genius and charisma, but none the less one who was not immune to error. I believe that lexicographic research of recent years has proved Wittgenstein wrong on this particular point.

As pointed out by van Brakel (1991: 6), in recent literature on the nature of meaning and categorization, the notion of family resemblances is usually linked with the notion of prototypes ("it is almost canonical to refer to Wittgenstein and Rosch in the same breath when prototype theory is introduced"). Van Brakel argues against the prevailing current use of the concept of prototype, and against the whole "prototype approach" to language and cognition, and tries to separate prototypes from family resemblances, of which he does approve.

But while I agree with much of what he says about the prototype approach to meaning (see Wierzbicka 1990*b* and Chapter 4), I believe that the doctrine of family resemblances is equally at fault. Van Brakel writes:

With the notion of "family resemblance" Wittgenstein wanted to illustrate that there is no uniform set of attributes which constitutes the meaning of a linguistic expression. There are only similarities between different uses of an expression. Whatever rules are proposed, they only conventionally define some aspects of the language use. It is not possible to grasp, or theoretically pin down, *the* meaning of expressions or *the* competence of a speaker-hearer. (1991: 6)

But the proposition that "It is not possible to grasp, or theoretically pin down, *the* meaning of expressions" is refuted by hundreds of definitions which have been worked out by semanticists in the last two decades (e.g. Apresjan 1974/1992; Mel′čuk and Žolkovskij 1984; Mel′čuk *et al.* 1984, 1988, 1992; Wierzbicka 1985, 1987*a*, 1992*a,e*; Goddard 1991*a*, 1992*a*, 1995; or papers included in Wierzbicka 1990*c*).[1] Once the different senses of a polysemous word (or expression) have been sorted out, every meaning can be pinned down, and the semantic formula representing it can be tested against a wide range of examples and hypothetical counter-examples.

Van Brakel's conviction that every analysis of the meaning of a word that one may come up with "gives no more than one way of looking at it" is not borne out by the experience of methodical lexicographic work based on a systematic semantic theory. Van Brakel states: "As I hope my examples have shown, the meanings of words have a vagueness and flexibility that resists ultimate rational reconstruction" (1991: 16). But there is no necessary conflict between precision and vagueness. As I have tried to show in my study of English "approximative expressions", even a vague meaning such as 'around' (e.g. *around twenty*), 'about' (e.g. *about fifteen*) or 'roughly' (e.g. *roughly half*) can be captured in a precise semantic formula (see Wierzbicka 1986*c*, 1991*a*).

Van Brakel's examples, intended to show that the meanings of words "resist rational reconstruction", are worth considering because they illustrate some of the fallacies (as I believe) on which the belief in the indeterminacy of meaning is based.

Thus, according to Karl Heider (1970) the Dani people of the New Guinea Highlands have more than seventy words referring to sweet potatoes, which is not surprising, given that "sweet potatoes are extremely important in the Dani culture" and that "more than half of all conversations are directly or indirectly about sweet potatoes" (van Brakel 1991: 8). None the less, "After having spent some time trying to find out which sweet potatoes were called by what name, Heider gave up, concluding that 'although there are more than seventy terms for sweet potatoes, they are

---

[1] Important work on the structure of the lexicon has of course been done by many other semanticists, e.g. by David Cruse (1986), R. M. W. Dixon (1982), Charles Fillmore (1971, 1977), Dirk Geeraerts (1993), Jeffrey Gruber (1965), Ray Jackendoff (1983, 1990), Adrienne Lehrer (1974, 1983), John Lyons (1977), Eugene Nida (1975), Leonard Talmy (1985), Jef Verschueren (1985), and Uriel Weinreich (1980). To my knowledge, however, none of these authors has attempted to test their ideas, original and fruitful as they may be, in large-scale lexicographic studies, involving hundreds of lexical items and hundreds of definitions. (One outstanding exception is the work of Russian semanticists, in particular Jurij Apresjan and Igor Mel′čuk; see Wierzbicka 1976*d*, 1986*b,c*.) This relative lack of interest in lexicography as a testing-ground for semantic theories is in marked contrast to the attitude of the two great semanticists of the seventeenth century, Leibniz and Wilkins (see Leibniz's 'Table de définitions' 1704/1903, and John Wilkins 1668; for discussion, see Wierzbicka 1975, 1994*f*; Dolezal 1992).

used with considerable imprecision'" (1970: 33). He also noted that the Dani explicitly denied that different types of sweet potatoes have different susceptibilities" (van Brakel 1991: 8).

Heider's reasoning goes like this: (1) there are many different names for sweet potatoes; (2) these names do not seem to be linked with different types of sweet potatoes; (3) therefore, these names are used "with considerable imprecision".

This reasoning is, I believe, fallacious, because the different names may be associated with semantic distinctions other than purely referential ones. For example, in Russian the words *osel* ('donkey') and *išak* ('donkey') are not linked with different types of donkey, and yet the semantic difference between these two words is stable, and can be captured with full precision in an adequate semantic description (see Apresjan 1974/1992). (Roughly speaking, *osel* presents the animal in question as a symbol of stupidity and stubbornness, and *išak* as a symbol of willingness to work hard without complaining.) The conclusion, therefore, that the Russian words *osel* and *išak* are used with considerable imprecision would be false; and in all probability what applies to these two words applies also to the Dani words for sweet potatoes. And yet it is on false conclusions of this kind that the doctrine of the indeterminacy of meaning rests.

Consider also van Brakel's second example, that is, the area of English words used for describing wine. He writes:

Another way to look at the inconsistency of the way many of the Dani words for sweet potatoes are used—not *the* way to look at it—is to contemplate that also in English such inconsistencies may occur. For example, vocabulary for the description of the taste and odour of wines does not seem to have any fixed meaning, even among experts, but seems to function primarily in constructing a vague tone of knowledgeableness and concern about wine among a group of speakers [Lehrer (1983)]. Such use of language is what Malinowski called *phatic communion*: "language does not function here as a means of transmission of thought . . . Each utterance is an act serving the direct aim of binding hearer to speaker by a tie of some social sentiment or other." Hence, in such a case it doesn't make sense to look for a particular cognitive model that underlies the speaker's specific thoughts and utterances. (1991: 9)

Van Brakel appears to assume that an expression whose function is mainly "phatic" cannot have a specific meaning at the same time. But in fact, although sentences such as

> Lovely day, isn't it?
> Nice day, isn't it?
> Beautiful day, isn't it?

can be said to have the same phatic function, this doesn't mean that in this context there are no semantic differences between the words *lovely*, *nice*, and *beautiful,* or that these words cannot be assigned constant meanings. The same applies to adjectives used to describe wine.

Consider, for example, the following dinner-party conversation about wine:

—This [wine] is soft and sensuous—quite an improvement over the 67s, which were unstylish and flabby.
—Yes, it's soft, but I would say that it's graceful rather than sensuous.

(Lehrer 1983: 3)

It may well be that the main purpose of remarks of this kind is "to amuse or impress other people, allowing the speaker to show off his knowledge, experience, and expertise" (ibid.), but from this it doesn't follow that the words themselves have "little or no meaning", as Lehrer says she "used to assume" (ibid.).

What is presupposed in such a view is that words have meaning only when they are used to inform, not when they are used, for example, to impress or amuse. But one can also try to impress people with lies, and lies wouldn't be lies if they didn't mean something.

Words such as *soft, sensuous,* or *graceful* may or may not be associated with some objective differences between various wines (as the words *nice, pleasant,* and *lovely* may or may not be associated with objective differences between the people or things to which they are applied), but this doesn't mean that in certain contexts these words have no meaning.

The meaning of the word *soft* as applied to wine can be explicated as follows:

> This wine is soft. =
> when this wine is in a person's mouth
> this person feels something good
> this person can say then something like this:
> if I was touching something soft
>   I could feel something like this

It is not difficult to see how this analysis could be applied to other "wine words" such as *smooth, velvety,* or *silky:*

> This wine is smooth (velvety, silky). =
> when this wine is in a person's mouth
> this person feels something good
> this person can say then something like this:
>   if I was touching something smooth (or: some velvet, some silk)
>   I could feel something like this

When applied to wine, words such as *soft, smooth, velvety,* or *silky* are a kind of simile, and they make sense in the way similes or metaphors make sense. The literal meaning of the word is essential to the overall meaning of the sentence in which it is used, but overall meaning of the sentence depends also on other elements and aspects of the sentence, including various rhetorical and illocutionary devices (such as similes, metaphors, irony, and so on).

The range of semantic stratagems used in talking about wine is quite wide (as shown by Lehrer 1983), and I am not suggesting that all adjectives used in this context work in the same way. The component of pleasurable experience ('I feel something good') is quite common, but equally common is the component of unpleasant experience ('I feel something bad', as when the words *hard, harsh, sharp, rough, bitter,* or *flabby* are used to describe wine). I will not discuss the semantics of wine conversation here any further, but explications of the other two adjectives mentioned earlier (*graceful* and *sensuous*) are in order.

> This wine is graceful. =
> when this wine is in a person's mouth
> a person feels something good
> a person can say then something like this:
> if I saw someone moving gracefully
>   I could feel something like this

> This wine is sensuous. =
> when this wine is in a person's mouth
> this person feels something good
> this person can say then something like this:
> if I felt something in my whole body
>   because of one sense (or: because of one part of the body)
>   I could feel something like this

Explications of this kind may be very different from traditional definitions put forward by either philosophers or lexicographers, but they do offer an accurate representation of meaning.

8. Dictionary Definitions

There is a widespread view that no matter what reservations a semanticist, or a philosopher, or a cognitive psychologist may have with respect to dictionary definitions, these definitions are basically all right—because dictionaries are sold in millions of copies and therefore they must be useful. For example, speaking of the ubiquitous circularity of dictionary definitions, Fetzer writes:

The dictionary for an ordinary language, such as English—*Webster's New World Dictionary* (1988), for example—appears to succeed in providing useful definitions for the terms that it contains in spite of resorting to definitional circularity. If there is a problem here, therefore, then it needs to be made apparent, because there seem to be no problems in practice with dictionary definitions.   (1991: 51)

This faith in dictionary definitions is based on an illusion. As pointed out by Sledd (1972), the users of a dictionary cannot know what is best for them, and how much information they could extract from a dictionary if dictionary definitions were as good as they can be (rather than as bad as they frequently are; see Wierzbicka 1992*d*). "The average man and the average reviewer cannot demand the best in a big dictionary, because they have no idea what the best might be: and even if they did demand the best, the businessmen who run commercial publishing houses would not give it to them unless they saw a direct relation between quality and profits" (Sledd 1972: 136; quoted in Landau 1984: 12). There are no reasons to think, therefore, that commercial success can provide an adequate measure of a dictionary's usefulness.

Among many people who have never practised lexicography themselves and who have (partly for that reason, no doubt) formed the strange view that it doesn't matter how good or bad dictionary definitions might be because their purpose is "merely practical", one finds, with some surprise, Noam Chomsky.

According to Chomsky, dictionary definitions don't offer anything like a faithful representation of a word's meaning, and yet they are all right as they are, because there is no need for dictionary definitions to be even approximately correct.

Anyone who has attempted to define a word precisely knows that this is an extremely difficult matter, involving intricate and complex properties. Ordinary dictionary definitions do not come close to characterizing the meaning of words. The speed and precision of vocabulary acquisition leaves no real alternative to the conclusion that the child somehow has the concepts available prior to experience with language, and is basically learning labels for concepts that are already part of his or her conceptual apparatus. This is why dictionary definitions can be sufficient for their purpose though they are so imprecise: the rough approximation suffices, because the basic principles of word meaning (whatever they are) are known to the dictionary user, as they are to the language learner, independently of any instruction or experience. The point is dramatically illustrated in the case of the blind, or even the deaf-blind, who can acquire knowledge of the visual vocabulary with remarkable precision though extremely limited evidence; the meanings of such words as *watch, gaze, glare, scrutinize*, etc.   (1987: 21)

What is most striking in Chomsky's remarks is the absence of any cross-cultural perspective, and the complete disregard for the fact that words differ in meaning across language and culture boundaries. For any language and culture learner, a good dictionary is a tool of prime importance, and it is an odd view for a linguist to take that there is no need to try to improve on existing dictionaries, however bad they may be, because one can always rely on one's innate conceptual apparatus.

To take Chomsky's own examples, how can students trying to learn English acquire the necessary knowledge of words such as *watch*, *gaze*, *glare*, or *scrutinize* (short of moving for many years to an English-speaking country) if dictionaries do not offer them any reliable guidance in this respect? In fact, dictionaries do offer some guidance, but their help is far from adequate and could easily be improved on (if practical lexicography and lexical semantics were to work hand in hand).

For example, *OPD* defines the relevant meaning of *watch* as follows: "to look at, to keep one's eyes fixed on, to keep under observation". This definition, which includes three different would-be paraphrases, does not show what the invariant meaning of *watch* is, or how it differs from the meaning of the closely related but more basic verb *look at*. In fact, the difference between the two lies partly in the temporal qualification (with *watch* implying the components 'for some time' and 'all the time') and partly in the nature of the object (to which I will return in a moment):

X was watching Y. $\Rightarrow$
for some time, X was looking at Y all the time

The validity of the component 'for some time' is supported by the fact that *look at*, but not *watch*, can be used with respect to a momentary event:[2]

At that moment, he looked at her.
*At that moment, he watched her.

The component 'all the time' is supported by the somewhat incongruous effect of the following sentence:

?While he was watching her, he was frequently looking at other girls.

As for the object of *watching*, it must be capable of change. For example, one can *watch* a film but not a painting in a museum (unless one thinks that something may happen in, or to, the painting, for example that it may get stolen). Hence:

X was watching Y. $=$
for some time, X was looking at Y all the time
because X thought something like this:
    something can happen in/to Y now
    I want to see it

---

[2] The expression *for some time* is not constructed out of semantic primitives and even the word *some* used in it is not used here in the sense of the primitive SOME (see Chapter 2). A more articulated version of the semantic component in question could read (perhaps): 'at all times after one time, before another time'.

Glare is defined by the same dictionary as "to stare angrily or fiercely", with *stare* being defined as "to gaze fixedly with the eyes wide open, especially in astonishment", and *gaze* as "to look long and steadily". These definitions, too, fail to show the exact relationship between *glare* and *look at*, the most basic of these words. In fact, the meaning added by *glare* to that included in *look at* consists in an intended message—roughly, 'I feel something bad towards you, I want you to know it'.

> *X* glared at *Y*. =
> *X* looked at *Y*
> if someone wanted to say something like this to someone else:
> > when I think about you I feel something bad
> > I want you to know this
> > this person could look at this other person like this
> > people can think: *X* wanted to say this to *Y*

The component 'long and steadily', attributed to *glare* by *OPD* (via *stare* and *gaze*) is incorrect, since one can *glare* at (though not *stare* at or *watch*) someone briefly or even momentarily.

As for *gaze*, it implies, in addition to 'looking', the following components: (1) 'for some time' (duration), (2) 'all the time' (steadily), (3) absence of a knowledge-seeking purpose, and (4) 'feelings' (wonder, delight, fondness, disbelief, etc.). The validity of these components is supported by the following negative material:

> *He gave her a gaze.
> *He gazed at her for a moment.
> *While he was gazing at her, he was throwing glances at the other girls.
> ?He was gazing at her intently, trying to read her thoughts.
> *He was gazing at her with hatred.

This leads us to the following definition:

> *X* was gazing at *Y*. =
> for some time *X* was looking at *Y* all the time
> if the person was looking at something for some time
> because this person felt something
> not because this person wanted to know something
> this person could look at this thing like this
> people could think this about *X*

Finally, *scrutinize* adds to *looking at* elements of, roughly speaking, thoroughness and search for knowledge. In this case, the *OPD* definition is basically right: "scrutinize—to look at or examine carefully". (See also the *Concise Oxford Dictionary* (*COD* 1964) definition: "look closely at, examine in detail".)

X scrutinized Y. =
for some time, X was looking at Y
during that time, X looked at all parts of Y
if someone wanted to know everything about all parts of something
this person could look at this thing like this

9. Fodor on Definitions

The idea that words are impossible to define has found its most spectacular expression in the writings of Jerry Fodor, according to whom most concepts are innate, "psychologically simple", and undefinable. Speaking of what he calls the "indices of membership" in the "primitive conceptual basis" of innate and indefinable concepts, Fodor writes:

ostensive definability, early acquisition in ontogeny and in intellectual history, lexicalization and universality and relative independence from prior concept attainment are among these indices . . . Current evidence suggests that there must be thousands of concepts which satisfy these criteria: . . . This population of *basic* concepts represents a very conservative estimate of the population of *primitive* concepts . . . Since all primitive concepts must ipso facto be unlearned, it looks as though the innate structure of the mind is going to be very rich indeed according to the present proposal.   (1981: 315)

Fodor's proposal is a challenge rather than a firm theory ("I don't expect you to be convinced. I am not convinced myself"; (ibid.). Since among his criteria he mentions "lexicalization and universality", his tentative conclusions are in fact disconfirmed by empirical research: research into lexical universals shows that universally lexicalized concepts can only be counted in tens, not in hundreds, let alone thousands. (See e.g. Wierzbicka 1989*a,b*, 1991*c*, 1992*d*; Goddard and Wierzbicka 1994*b*.)

But Fodor's real challenge lies in his claim that there is a "striking paucity of working examples [of definitions] in the standard literature" (1981: 284), that "there seem always to be counter-examples to the proposed definitions" (285), and that "most of the morphemically simple expressions of English are undefinable" (285).

I believe that, for example, the definitions of the verbs *watch*, *glare*, *gaze*, and *scrutinize* proposed here (and hundreds of others in, for example, my *English Speech Acts Verbs*) do provide satisfactory counter-examples to Fodor's claims. Since, however, Fodor has chosen as his crowning example the English verb *to paint*, I would like to at least sketch a definition of this verb, too (for a full definition a separate paper would be needed).[3]

---

[3] I am very grateful to Igor Mel'čuk, who discussed with me my definitions of the verbs *paint* and *krasit'*, and who offered a number of valuable insights.

Fodor writes (with reference to George Miller's 1978: 285 discussion of *paint*):

What we have here is a proposal for defining the transitive verb 'paint' in terms of the noun 'paint', together with some further conceptual apparatus (COVER, SUR- FACE, and WITH); and what I claim is that the definition doesn't work; *X covers Y with paint* may be a necessary condition for *X paints Y* but it is certainly not a sufficient condition.

He concludes his lengthy discussion of *paint* as follows:

I don't know where to go from there. For all I know—for all *anybody* knows— 'paint$_{tr}$' is undefinable; for all I know, you can't eliminate it even in terms of such a very closely related term as 'paint'. Or perhaps it *is* definable, but only in a reduc- tion base that includes 'dinosaur' and 'chlorodent'. Either way, the present point is that Miller's example doesn't work. That's not surprising; when it comes to defini- tions, the examples almost always don't work.   (1978: 288)

I agree with Fodor that the proposed definition (which, I notice, is the same as that given in *AHDOTEL* 1973) doesn't work (for reasons discussed by him, among others); but not that the verb *paint* is indefinable.

To begin with, the noun *paint* is semantically more complex than the verb (see Apresjan 1974/1992: 101–2), and *X covers Y with paint* is not a neces- sary condition for *X paints Y*. For example, when a woman is painting her finger-nails she is not putting paint on them, but nail polish. This does not mean that one can "paint" an object with just about anything; one would hesitate to use the verb *paint* unless the "stuff" used was habitually used for the activity in question.

A sentence such as *X painted Y with Z* (where the verb *paint* is used in the relevant sense *paint$_1$*) implies that a person (*X*) did something to some object (*Y*), putting some stuff (*Z*) on all the parts of *Y* that could be seen (that is, on the surface of *Y*); it further implies that the stuff *Z* was liquid or semi-liquid at the time when *X* was putting it on *Y*, and that *Z* had a definite colour (so that one could say what its colour was); and that *X* wanted that stuff *Z* to remain on the surface of *Y* and become, as it were, part of this surface. Finally, the verb *paint* implies a function: if one puts some liquid or semi-liquid stuff *Z* on the surface of object *Y* it is for a rea- son, and normally (though not always) this reason is to make this object look good (I will return to this point shortly). As a first approximation, then, the following definition can be proposed:

X painted *Y* with *Z*. =
(*a*) *X* did something to *Y*
(*b*)   like people do
(*c*)   when they want something to look good
(*d*) when *X* did it

(*e*) X put some stuff Z on all parts of Y that one could see
(*f*) if someone looked at Z at that time
(*g*) this person could say what colour Z was
(*h*) at the same time, this person could think that part of Z was water
(*i*) X wanted Z to be like part of Y
(*j*) after X did it, Z was like part of Y

Three brief comments on this definition are in order. First, while it is constructed mainly from primitive terms, it contains some intermediate concepts ('look', 'put', 'liquid'), which have to be defined separately (see Chapter 7), and also, some non-primitive syntactic constructions. Second, it is of course much longer and more complex than the familiar dictionary-style definitions consisting of one short sentence; in fact, it includes a fairly complex scenario, with a number of temporal and causal links between the components. Third, it includes a "prototypical component" 'like people do when they want something to look good', which states the "normal" (typical) function of the activity in question. With the "function" component being stated in this way, the definition accounts for the fact that paint can be extended to some activities with a different function (e.g. protection against rust), but only on condition that they can be perceived as similar to the activity with the prototypical function.

Concrete concepts such as *paint* are usually more complex and more difficult to define than abstract concepts (see Chapter 7). The definition proposed here is no more than an imperfect first approximation. I hope, however, that it is sufficient to show that Fodor's somewhat nihilist conclusions are unfounded.

In particular, it should be pointed out that the concept of 'paint' as explicated here is language-specific. For example, the closest Polish equivalent of *paint*, the verb *malować*, does not require a standard material (paint, nail polish, and the like), and can be applied, for example, to children daubing their cheeks with beetroot juice or to women putting on lipstick. And the closest Russian equivalent of *paint*, the verb *krasit'*, does not restrict the process to the surface of the target object, covering not only the range of the English verb *paint*, but also that of *dye* (for example, one can *krasit'* an object by dipping it in some solution); in addition, *krasit'*—like *dye*—places a special emphasis on colour. All these differences, as well as similarities, between *krasit'* and *paint* can be reflected in the following definition of *krasit'*:

X pokrasil Y Z-om (X krasit'-ed Y with Z). =
(*a*) X did something to Y
(*b*)   like people do
(*b₁*)   when they want something to be a certain colour
(*c*)   because they think that this thing will look good because of this

(*d*) when *X* did it
(*e*) *X* did something to some stuff *Z*
(*f*) if someone looked at *Z* at that time
(*g*) this person could say what colour *Z* was
(*h*) at the same time this person could think that part of *Z* was water
(*i*) *X* wanted *Z* to be like part of *Y*
(*j*) after *X* did it *Z* was like part of *Y*

The differences lie in the components (b_1), which has no counterpart in the explication of *paint*, and (*e*), which is less specific than the corresponding component of *paint*.

Thus, concepts such as those encoded in the words *paint, malować*, or *krasit'* are language-specific. Consequently, they cannot be innate and unlearnt; and since lexicological research shows that very few concepts are universal, the "primitive conceptual basis" of innate, "psychologically simple", indefinable concepts must be quite different from the picture painted (if I may say so) by Fodor and his associates.

10. Conclusion

To quote Chomsky again, "ordinary dictionary definitions do not come close to characterizing the meaning of words". For anyone seriously trying to learn another language and understand another culture, the proposition that words cannot be defined can hardly be anything but very bad news. Fortunately, this proposition is not true. As Armstrong, Gleitman, and Gleitman (1983: 268) say, "the only good answer [to the question "why do so many doubt the validity of the definitional view?"] is that the definitional theory is difficult to work out in the required detail". But "difficult" does not mean "impossible". As I wrote in my *Lexicography and Conceptual Analysis*:

Defining the meaning of words has been for at least twenty-five centuries a characteristic ingredient of European culture. With the advent of modern dictionaries this activity has become institutionalized and its place in Western civilization has become even more important. Yet the methodology of lexico-semantic analysis has not progressed very far, at least in the sense that no consensus has emerged among scholars as to what its basic principles should be. Certainly, the continuous lexicographic practice of the last two centuries has developed certain routines, certain habitual devices. But the theoretical assumptions implicit in these routines have seldom been the subject of serious analysis.   (Wierzbicka 1985: 11)

And in *English Speech Act Verbs*:

If modern linguistics were to be judged by the contribution it made to lexicography, it would be hard to understand why linguistics is said to have made dramatic advances in recent decades. It is not my intention to question these advances. It must be pointed out, however, that the extraordinary growth of nearly all aspects of linguistic science has been accompanied by a virtually complete lack of attention (at least on the part of the mainstream linguistics) to that aspect of language which is the most obvious, and in a sense the most important, to the ordinary language users—to the lexicon. This remarkable state of affairs reflects the wide gap which despite many linguists' declarations and actual efforts continues to separate academic linguistics from "real life" as manifested in the needs and concerns of ordinary language users. It reflects also the failure of linguistic science to develop adequate methodological tools for dealing with the lexicon—and a widespread lack of faith in the possibility of a purposeful, methodical and revealing scientific study of this aspect of language. (1987: 2)

There are signs that this attitude to the study of the lexicon is beginning to change: the twenty-first century may become in linguistics the era of the dictionary—and of an integrated approach to linguistic description[4] (see Malkiel 1980; Rey 1983).

Fodor, Garrett, Walker, and Parkes (1980) put forward the destructive slogan "Against definitions", which led to the conclusion that semantic analysis in general is impossible and should be abandoned. It is time to acknowledge the self-defeating nature of this slogan. Meanings can be rigorously described and compared if they are recognized for what they are: unique and culture-specific configurations of universal semantic primitives. If we recognize the role of these primitives as a foundation on which all complex meanings are based we can use them as an instrument for improving lexicography—a topic which will be developed in the following chapter.

---

[4] See Malkiel (1980: 45): "For reasons which perhaps have never been candidly stated, the tone-setting linguistic scientists of our 20th century have, with extremely rare exceptions, shown no inclination to meddle with lexicological and, even less, with lexicographic undertakings that could, by any stretch of the imagination, appeal to the taste of an educated layman."

9   Semantics and Lexicography

□ □ _____

1. Introduction

For years, I have argued that semantics as a scholarly discipline must prove itself in lexicography. "Lexicography needs linguistics, and linguistics needs lexicography. As Zgusta (1971: 111) points out, for the treatment of meaning in dictionaries to be radically improved, preparatory work has to be done by linguists" (Wierzbicka 1987a: 1–2). I believe that during the two decades which have elapsed since Zgusta made this comment, much of this preparatory work has in fact been done. In this chapter I will try to show that, as a result of this work, the treatment of meaning in dictionaries can indeed be radically improved.

2. Scope versus Adequacy and Truth

Dictionaries are books about words. Unlike, however, various more or less selective "studies in words" (e.g. Lewis 1960), dictionaries are meant to be relatively complete—at least with respect to one thematic domain, or one aspect of language. Since they are also meant to be practically useful and commercially viable, one of the first dilemmas for a dictionary-maker is how to combine completeness with a reasonable size.

It is at this point, I believe, that a practical lexicographer often becomes impatient with theoretical lexicography. Theoretical lexicographers tend to maintain that to describe one word adequately one needs a great deal of space (many pages, if not many dozens, scores, or even hundreds of pages). As one leading lexicographer and semanticist, Igor Mel'čuk (1981: 57), put it: "Not only every language, but every lexeme of a language, is an entire world in itself." In a sense this is true—but if so, then of course a practical lexicographer does not have the room to do justice to even a single word, let alone to the thousands of words with which he or she usually has to deal.

An earlier version of this chapter was published as one of two "lead papers" in a special issue of the journal *Dictionaries* (14. 1992–3: 44–78), devoted to the theory and practice of lexicography. In the same issue, a number of commentaries on the two lead papers were published, along with the authors' replies (*Dictionaries*. 14. 1992–3: 139–59). Several of these commentaries are referred to in this chapter.

One possible response to this situation on the part of practical lexicographers is to turn their back on theoretical lexicography and to continue doing what they have always done: to rely on experience and common sense. I believe that in doing that practical lexicographers have frequently produced valuable and useful works, and can still do so. But I also believe that if they try, instead, to look theoretical lexicography in the eye and to take from it what it has to offer, they can do a lot better.

Landau (1984: 5) writes: "A dictionary is a book that lists words in alphabetical order and describes their meaning." It is only as an afterthought that he adds: "Modern dictionaries often include information about spelling, syllabification, pronunciation, etymology (word derivation), usage, synonyms, and grammar, and sometimes illustrations as well."

I agree with Landau's emphasis: although a good dictionary has to include, as Apresjan (forthcoming) points out, morphological, syntactic, prosodic, pragmatic, and phraseological information, as well as information about meaning, it is the latter which normally constitutes the core of a dictionary. In what follows, I will not try to comment on all aspects of the relationship between theoretical and practical lexicography, but rather will focus, primarily, on the one feature which is truly essential: the description of the meaning of words.[1]

My main thesis with respect to this central problem is this: The description of a word's meaning may vary, legitimately, in completeness from one work to another, but it should not differ in its basic content. A "definition" is meant to represent the truth about a word's meaning, and there is only one such truth, whether it is to be presented in a research paper devoted to one particular word or in a dictionary intended for a general audience, including various dictionaries addressed specifically to "children", "learners", "students", and so on.

It is a curious but widespread illusion that by saying things which are untrue, meaningless, obscure, or theoretically untenable, the dictionary-maker can gain in either insight or space, and that the dictionary user is thus better served. If space is of paramount importance in a "commercially viable" dictionary, then all the space available, however limited, should be used for saying things which without being complete are none the less true, meaningful, illuminating, and clear.

It might be thought churlish to deny that reputable commercial dictionaries do say, by and large, things that are "true, meaningful, illuminating, and clear". But unfortunately they often don't.

---

[1] One particularly important area which has not been discussed at all in this chapter is that of relationships between the meanings of words and their syntactic properties. For both general discussion and ample exemplification, see Wierzbicka (1987a). See also Ch. 5.

3. Saying Something that is not True

Sometimes dictionary definitions say things which are simply false. For example, the *Oxford Australian Junior Dictionary* (*OAJD* 1980) offers the following definition of *sure*:

sure—knowing something is true or right

But of course "knowing" and "being sure" are two very different things, and even in a dictionary intended for children they should never be equated. An "adult" dictionary, the *Oxford Paperback Dictionary* (*OPD* 1979) offers a more complex and "sophisticated", but in fact equally false, definition:

sure—having or seeming to have sufficient reasons for one's beliefs, free from doubts

The apparent afterthought "free from doubts" is basically right, but *doubt* itself is defined by the *OPD* via *certainty*, and *certainty* via *doubt* (*doubt*—"feeling of uncertainty about something"; *certain*—"having no doubts"). Leaving aside this circular detour (see Section 10), we will note that for subjective certainty (being sure of something), having sufficient reasons for one's belief is neither necessary nor sufficient.

Similarly, *announce* is defined by the *OAJD* as "to say something in front of a lot of people". But in fact, one can also announce something (for example, an important decision) to one's parents, and the presence of a lot of people is not necessary at all.

Bold is defined by the *OAJD* as "brave and not afraid". But this is wrong, too: one can be bold without being brave, and be brave without being bold. In particular, boldness is shown in relation to other people, whereas one can be brave even in solitary confinement (see Wierzbicka 1992a: 208–9).

Standard is defined by the same dictionary as "how good something is". But in fact, it is rather "how good you think something has to be".

Threat is defined as "a promise that you will do something bad if what you want does not happen". However, a threat is not a kind of promise, although it can be called that ironically; and one can say, for example, *threats and promises*, whereas one cannot say **spaniels and dogs* (because a spaniel is indeed a kind of dog).

Ability is defined by the *OAJD* as "the power to do something". But although the notions of 'ability' and 'power' are related, the former cannot be reduced to the latter: 'power' implies that one can do things that someone doesn't want, and so it implies actual or potential conflict of wills; 'ability', however, does not imply this.

To show that errors of this kind occur also in ambitious, prestigious, and innovative modern dictionaries, I will conclude this section with two examples from the *Collins Cobuild English Language Dictionary* (*Cobuild* 1987).

Thus, *Cobuild* defines *empathy* as "the ability to share another person's feelings and emotions as if they were one's own". But in fact, as shown by Travis (1992), *empathy* does not imply that one *shares* another person's feelings (but rather, that one understands them, as if they were your own); and, for example, an empathetic counsellor cannot be expected to *share* his or her patient's feelings.

Similarly, *Cobuild*'s definition of *forgive* implies incorrectly that to be able to forgive someone one has to be first angry with them and want to punish them: "if you forgive someone who has done something wrong or forgive a bad deed that someone has done, you stop being angry with them, and no longer want to punish them". But stories of saints and martyrs abound in examples of sentences in which someone is said to have forgiven his or her persecutors without any implication that at first he or she was angry with them and wanted to punish them. Likewise, in the Gospel story of the prodigal son (which for many people epitomizes forgiveness) there is no implication that the father was at first angry with his son and wanted to punish him.

4. Saying Something that is Superfluous

Given space constraints under which practical dictionaries usually operate it is surprising to see how often they waste precious space by saying things which are entirely superfluous. For example, the *Longman Dictionary of Contemporary English* (*LDOTEL* 1984) defines the word *weapon* as follows:

weapon—an instrument of offensive or defensive combat; something to fight with

The simple phrase "something to fight with" is perhaps not a perfect definition of *weapon* but it is a pretty good approximation; the definition is spoilt, however, by the completely unnecessary addition of "an instrument of offensive or defensive combat". One can almost sense the nervousness of the lexicographer who, having produced an excellent short definition, realizes that he or she has nothing to add to it—and panics at what appears to be an unfamiliar, unconventional level of simplicity, and tries desperately to add something to make it longer, more complex, more "respectable". Theoretical lexicography can be very useful at this point if it can reassure the practical lexicographer: "There is no need to add anything; the simple short definition is okay; on the contrary, it is the longer one which is faulty, because, as Aristotle pointed out twenty five centuries ago, in a definition every superfluous word is a serious transgression."

5. Confusing Meaning with Knowledge

Another way to waste space in a dictionary is to include in it technical or scientific knowledge. For example, *LDOTEL* defines the word *dentist* as follows:

> dentist—a person who is skilled in and licensed to practise the prevention, diagnosis, and treatment of diseases, injuries, and malformations of the teeth, jaws, and mouth and who makes and inserts false teeth

It may be instructive for a reader to learn that a dentist does all the things enumerated in this definition, but information of this kind, however useful, is out of place in a dictionary. The short definition offered by *OAJD* (though not perfect) is much more satisfactory:

> dentist—someone whose job is to look after teeth

The line between knowledge and meaning is not always easy to draw, but in principle it can be drawn (see Wierzbicka 1985 and Chapter 11), and in any case dictionaries are often full of information which quite clearly belongs in an encyclopaedia, not in a dictionary. Consider, for example, the following definition of *sugar* (*LDOTEL*; my emphasis):

> sugar—a sweet substance that consists wholly of *sucrose*, is colourless or white when pure, tending to brown when less refined, is usually obtained commercially from sugarcane or sugar beet, and is nutritionally important as a source of *carbohydrate* as a sweetener and preservative of other foods

Clearly most of what the *LDOTEL* definition offers is not part of the everyday concept at all (not to mention the fact that *sugar* is defined here via *sugar-cane* and *sugar-beet*; see Section 10). As usual, the *OAJD* definition, though not perfect, is much more plausible: "a sweet food that is put in drinks and other foods to make them taste sweet". (It would probably be better still to say something like this: "something that people add to things they drink or eat when they want to make them taste sweet; it comes from some things growing out of the ground (i.e. plants); it is normally white".)

McCawley (1992–3: 123) suggests that, in one respect, the *OAJD*'s definition of *sugar* "is more accurate than Wierzbicka's, since *OAJD*'s initially puzzling use of 'food' in the definition neatly distinguishes sugar from such sugar substitutes as saccharine and Nutrasweet".

But while *sugar* should indeed be distinguished from saccharine, do we have to call *sugar* a "food" (something that McCawley himself finds counter-intuitive) to achieve this goal? If *food* stands, roughly, for things that people eat, then it is understandable why people would normally not call *sugar* "a food": one normally doesn't eat sugar (on its own). To distinguish between *sugar* and *saccharine* we could say that while both *sugar* and *saccharine* are "added" to some things that people eat or drink, only of sugar can it be said that people can "eat it as part of some things they eat".

Consider also the following definitions of *horse* from three different dictionaries:

a solid-hoofed perissodactyl quadruped (*Equus caballus*)   (*SOED* 1964)

a large solid-hoofed herbivorous mammal (*Equus caballus*) domesticated by man since a prehistoric period   (*Webster's* 1988)

a large solid-hoofed plant-eating 4-legged mammal (*Equus caballus*, family Equidae, the horse family), domesticated by humans since prehistoric times and used as beast of burden, a draught animal, or for riding; esp. one over 14.2 hands in height (*LDOTEL* 1984):

It hardly needs to be pointed out that definitions of this kind do not represent what ordinary speakers of English have in mind when they talk of horses. The information included in such "definitions" is, for the most part, entirely superfluous in a dictionary of English. It would be much better to say simply that a *horse* is "a kind of animal called *horse*". It would be better still to try to explicate, in an abbreviated form, the folk concept encoded in the English word *horse*; but if a dictionary cannot afford the space to do this, why waste space on information which is given in all encyclopaedias and which has nothing to do with ordinary speakers' knowledge of their language anyway? (For further discussion, see Chapter 11.)

6. Definitions which are too Broad

Definitions which are too broad do not contain any falsehood (because everything they include is true), but their implications are false (because they leave out certain necessary components).

For example, *talent* is defined by the *OAJD* as "the ability to do something very well". But this implies that an acquired skill could be called talent, which is not true. The definition misses the crucial component 'inborn' ("if someone can do things of a certain kind very well not because he/she did something to be able to do them well").

To succeed is defined as "to do or get what you wanted to do or get". By this definition if one gets a present that one wanted to get, this could be described as succeeding; once again this is not true. (To succeed one has to do something; the disjunction "do or get" is therefore wrong.)

To defy is defined as "to say or show that you will not obey". But if a child says to his or her brother or sister, "You are not my mother or father, I will not obey you", this would not be described as defying. (One can only defy orders given by someone who actually does have authority over one and can be expected to be obeyed.)

The definition of *steal* says "to take something that does not belong to you and keep it". But this could refer to robbery as well as to stealing. For stealing, it is essential that the actor does not want people to know what he or she is doing, and expects that they will not know it.

Secret is defined as "something that must be kept hidden from other people"; but this could refer to physical objects, whereas in fact *secret* stands only for something that one knows (and must not tell other people about).

Thirst is presented as "the need to drink"; but in fact it refers to a sensation, to what one feels ("when you feel you need to drink").

A *ribbon* is, according to the *OAJD*, "a strip of nylon, silk, or some other material". But if this were true, any strip of any material could be called a ribbon, which of course is not true. In fact, the word *ribbon* (in the relevant sense) refers only to a kind of thing made (by people) in order to make something look good. (See Section 9.)

To shed is defined as "to let something fall" (and it is illustrated with the sentences "trees shed leaves, people shed tears, and caterpillars shed their skins"). But this implies that if I let a book fall I am shedding it. The crucial concept missed by this definition is that of 'part': *A* can only shed *B* if before the event *B* can be thought of as part of *A* (and after the event, cannot).

Finally, *a woman* is according to the *OAJD* "a fully grown female", which turns a bitch or a mare into a woman.

Needless to say, definitions can also be too narrow, but this fault seldom occurs on its own, and I will discuss it in the context of other errors with which it is most commonly combined. Here, just one example will suffice.

The *OAJD* defines *appointment* as "a time when you have arranged to go and see someone". This is too restrictive, because the lawyer who receives clients or the professor who sees students can also have an appointment, without having to "go" anywhere outside their office.

7. Capturing the Invariant

Although this may sound too grand for (what tends to be seen as) the humble task of a lexicographer, the process of constructing a lexicographic definition is—or should be—a search for truth. To find the truth about the meaning of a word means to find the invariant concept which is part of the native speakers' tacit knowledge about their language and which guides them in their use of that word.

Yet lexicographers often lack the confidence, the resolve, the boldness to reach for the invariant, and thus become unfaithful to their task of searching for the lexicographic truth.

Consider, for example, the following definition of *complain*, offered by the *OPD*:

complain—1. to say that one is dissatisfied, to protest that something is wrong; 2. to state that one is suffering from a pain, etc.

Two meanings are postulated here, but for neither of them is an attempt made to capture the invariant: the alleged second meaning ends with an *etc.* which, as far as the reader knows, could stand for anything, whereas the alleged first meaning is stated in two different and non-equivalent ways. It hardly needs to be pointed out that one can complain without feeling (or even pretending that one feels) pain; that one can protest that something is wrong in a situation which could not possibly be described as complaining (e.g. Amnesty International protests, but does not complain, about human rights' violations in different countries); or that one can say that one is dissatisfied with oneself without complaining about anyone or anything.

But in addition to being wrong in almost everything it says, the whole entry exudes lexicographic despair and apathy: "It is impossible to capture the invariant, or even to decide how many different meanings are involved; or if it is, we do not know how to go about it."

If the lexicographers responsible for this entry had a reliable lexicographic theory at their disposal, they would have need of neither their half-hearted positing of (unjustified) polysemy nor their sad and defeatist *etc.*

In fact, the invariant of *complain* is not particularly difficult to capture. Roughly speaking (for a detailed and more precise discussion see Wierzbicka 1987*a*), the complaining person has to convey the following message: "something bad happened to me—I feel something bad because of this—I want someone to do something because of this". ("Doing something" does not necessarily refer to changing the situation and removing the grounds for complaining; it can also refer to expressing sympathy, commiserations, and so on.)

It may be pointed out, incidentally, that the definition of *complain* cited above illustrates the link between proposing definitions which are too narrow and the failure to even aim at capturing the semantic invariant. The lexicographer realizes that the phrase "to state that one is suffering from a pain" is too narrow as a definition of *complain*, but instead of looking for a less restrictive formula he or she simply adds an *etc.* (and, for good measure, posits polysemy as well).

The link between positing false polysemies and the failure to look for a semantic invariant is also manifested in the following definition (from the *OPD*) of *bold*: "1. confident and courageous; 2. without feelings of shame, impudent". There are concepts which are inherently positive (that is, which reflect a positive evaluation), for example 'brave' or 'courageous'; and there are others which are inherently negative (that is, which reflect a negative evaluation), for example 'reckless', 'foolhardy', or 'impudent'. 'Bold' belongs to neither of these two categories, being compatible with either a positive or a negative evaluation. By splitting it into two supposedly different meanings, one positive and one negative, the dictionary is misrepresenting the truth about this concept and blurring the difference between the neutral concept 'bold', the positive concept 'courageous', and the negative concept 'impudent'. (Needless to say, 'bold', 'courageous', and 'impudent' differ also in other respects; for detailed discussion see Wierzbicka 1992*a*: 203–11.)

Another characteristic example is the *OPD* definition of *boast*: "to speak with great pride and try to impress people, esp. about oneself". This time no polysemy is postulated, but the little *esp.* (especially) is no less of a sigh of resignation (or a moan of despair?) than the *etc.* of the previous definition. Clearly, the authors of the entry could not make up their collective mind as to what the essential features of *boast* are. If they had a reliable lexicographic theory to lean on, they would have known that an *esp.* is a sign of defeat and they would have felt obliged to think a little longer. If they had done this, they would have realized that the concept of 'boast' always involves oneself (whether directly or indirectly), and that it is not different in this respect from 'pride'. Again, for detailed discussion the reader is referred to Wierzbicka 1987*a*; here, it will suffice to say that boasting always involves the following attitude: saying something very good about someone or something, thinking something very good about myself, comparing myself with other people ('other people are not like me'), and wanting other people to think something very good about me. Thus, if a father says something very good about his children, evidently thinking something very good about himself, comparing himself with other people ('other people are not like me'), and wanting other people to think something good about him because of this, then this can indeed be described as boasting.

It may be noted in passing that the *OPD* definition of *impress*, via which the *OPD* defines *boast*, is equally inadequate: "to make (a person) form a strong (usually favourable) opinion of something". *Usually*, like *especially*, suggests that the component of "favourable opinion" is not necessary, whereas in fact it is absolutely necessary both for *boast* and for the relevant meaning of *impress* (as in "He wanted to impress her").

The failure to capture the invariant is manifested in a particularly spectacular manner in the use of the conjunction *or*, with which dictionary definitions are usually peppered.

For example, the *OPD* defines *tempt* as follows: "to persuade or try to persuade (especially into doing something wrong or unwise) by the prospect of pleasure or advantage". The first *or* can be dispensed with immediately:

tempting can of course be successful, but so can trying; it is enough, therefore, to say "try to persuade", there is no need for "to persuade or try to
persuade". The disjunction "something wrong or unwise" can be reduced
to "something bad" (not necessarily "evil" or "morally very bad", but
something that is thought of as a bad thing to do); and the "prospect of
pleasure or advantage" can be reduced to the prospect of "something good
(for the temptee)". The qualifier *especially* can be dispensed with altogether:
one simply cannot tempt somebody to do something good; it has to be
something that is seen as "something bad" (although the speaker can of
course be using the word *tempt* in jest).

In conclusion, devices such as *or, especially, usually,* the use of multiple
glosses (whether words or phrases) to portray the same meaning, or the
positing of arbitrary polysemies are all different manifestations of the same
basic failure of practical lexicography. This failure mars most entries in
most of the existing dictionaries, and makes them much less useful to the
reader than they otherwise could be (under the same limitations of space
and other practical constraints). A rigorous and consistent lexicographic
theory, with a firmly established principle of determinacy of meaning, can
easily remedy this weakness.

In particular, a sound lexicographic theory can prevent the common phenomenon of unfounded proliferation of meanings, as well as the (less common, but even more harmful) conflation of meanings which are related but
not the same. It can prevent the confusion of ironic, sarcastic, jocular, or
metaphorical usage with the literal meaning of words (as in the case of
threat, discussed earlier). It can offer lexicographic criteria on the basis of
which meanings can be firmly separated from one another, clearly identified, and intelligibly stated.

8. Standing Firmly on the Ground of Discreteness

One of the major reasons that most dictionary definitions are much less useful than they could be is the widespread lack of faith in the discreteness of
meaning. As Aristotle realized better than many contemporary linguists do,
there are few things harder than constructing a good definition. How can
a lexicographer be expected to undertake the necessary effort if he or she
does not believe that the task is feasible at all? Theoreticians who undermine the lexicographer's faith in the possibility of stating the meaning of
words truthfully and accurately are doing both the lexicographer and the
dictionary user grievous disservice. In fact, most of the problems which
plague practical lexicography are linked with the issue of discreteness.

For example, how can lexicographers search with all their might, and
patience, for an invariant if they do not know whether they can expect to

find a definite number of meanings? To recall the *OPD* definition of *complain*, cited earlier: "1. to say that one is dissatisfied, to protest that something is wrong; 2. to state that one is suffering from a pain etc.". On the face of it, two meanings are postulated here, but in fact the first alleged meaning is stated twice, in two different ways, and the relation between these two different attempts at a definition is left unclear. The use of the numbers 1 and 2 implies that this particular lexicographer does believe in the discreteness of meanings, but the constant practice of throwing together different formulations of what is counted as "one meaning" indicates the shakiness of this belief. If the lexicographer felt obliged to state just one definition for each (hypothetical) meaning, this would encourage him or her to look for the true invariant; as a result, the multiple meanings postulated in present-day dictionaries would often be reduced to a smaller number, invariants would be captured, superfluous phrases would be omitted, space would be gained, semantic relations between different meanings (and different lexical items) would be made much clearer, and, on top of all this, the language used would be much simpler and clearer, as well as more economical. For example, as pointed out earlier, for *complain* one could propose just one unitary formula, and there would be no need for positing polysemy, no need for an *etc.*, and no need for agonizing between two non-equivalent phrases "to say that one is dissatisfied" and "to protest that something is wrong" (not to mention other advantages linked with a standardization and reduction of the metalanguage used).

Or consider the way *LDOTEL* defines the English verb *to pray*:

1*a*. to entreat earnestly; esp. to call devoutly on (God or a god)
  b. to wish or hope fervently
2. *archaic or formal* to request courtesy—often used to introduce a question, request or plea
3. *archaic* to get or bring by praying: to address God or a god with adoration, confession, supplication, or thanksgiving; engage in prayer

Although three figures are used (1, 2, and 3), the actual number of meanings postulated is far from clear: Is (*a*) a separate meaning? Or (*b*)? and what about all those *especiallys*, *ors*, *oftens*, semicolons? The relationship between the different alleged meanings is even less clear than the number of meanings postulated. For example, why should the meaning "to address God or a god" be given under heading 3, and "to call devoutly on (God or a god)" under 1? Are these two alleged meanings more different from one another than those listed under 1(*a*) and 1(*b*) (only one of which mentions God)? Why is the alleged meaning "to engage in prayer" given under 3 and "to call devoutly on (God or a god)", under 1?

I am not saying that it is easy to define *pray* in a satisfactory way, and I sympathize with the lexicographer's painful efforts. But I believe this pain could have been alleviated, and the efforts rewarded with more satisfactory results, if theoretical lexicography had sent a clear and unequivocal message that meaning is determinate, that a definite (and minimal) number of meanings must be looked for, that there are no "shades" of meaning, no (*a*)s and (*b*)s, and that no hedges (no *especially*, *often*, *etc.*) are necessary or acceptable; and if, in addition to this message, clear criteria for establishing and distinguishing different meanings had been provided. I believe that if such a clear message had been sent, and if the necessary guide-lines had been provided, the entry for *pray* would have ended up with just two meanings, one archaic and one contemporary (without any submeanings), and that these two meanings would have been stated clearly and accurately (without any hedges, *ors*, *etcs.*, or other visible signs of indecision and analytical failure; see Wierzbicka 1993*d*).

Finally, consider the lists of quasi-equivalents offered in definitions such as the following ones from Webster's (1959):

reply (noun)   — an answer; response; counter-attack

resign (verb) — to yield to another; surrender formally; withdraw from; submit calmly

report (verb) — to give an account of; relate; tell from one to another; circulate publicly; take down (spoken words)

request (noun) — desire expressed; petition; prayer; demand; entreaty

order (noun)   — method of regular arrangement; settled mode of procedure; rule; regulation; command; class; rank; degree; a religious fraternity; an association of persons possessing a common honorary distinction . . .

What is most striking about such lists is the fact that the lexicographer is making no attempt to indicate how many different meanings are involved in each case. Should the first four entries above leave anybody in doubt about the lexicographer's motivation for this failure, the hotchpotch of quasi-equivalents thrown into the entry for *order* makes it quite clear that in fact the only possible motivation is despair. This despair is understandable, but it is not justified. As I have tried to show in my *Dictionary of English Speech Act Verbs* (which includes, in particular, the verbs *reply*, *resign*, *report*, and *request*), meanings *can* be sorted out from one another, and (*pace* Wittgenstein and followers) boundaries between meanings *can* be drawn. The doctrine of family resemblances must not be used as an excuse for lexicographic laziness or as justification for lexicographic despair. (For further discussion, see Chapter 4.)

As one final point related to the question of discreteness, let us consider Hank's (1982: 102) claim that there is no reason why "dictionary definitions are to be read as mutually exclusive", and that "in practice, the wording of definition 1 normally colors the interpretation of definition 2". I agree that, from a reader's point of view, the wording of one definition may colour the interpretation of the other definitions of a polysemous word. The main problem, however, is to establish whether the word in question is really polysemous, and to ensure that its meaning or meanings be correctly identified. If this is achieved, then I think there is no need for such a "cross-fertilization of definitions".

For example, Hanks quotes a sentence describing two girls as "simultaneously bold and innocent", asking: "Does *bold* here mean forward or impudent or daring?"; and he answers: "A bit of both, really". But why should we assume that *bold* really does have two meanings which can be stated as (1) forward or impudent and (2) daring? If none of these supposed "definitions" fits the sentence well, it is, I think, not because there are two meanings which colour one another, but because neither of the proposed "definitions" of *bold* is correct. (For an alternative definition, and justification, see Wierzbicka 1992*a*: 208–9.)

A definition should always be able to stand on its own. If a word is genuinely polysemous, then each of its meanings should be stated separately, and each definition should be able to defend itself. This is not incompatible with Hanks's statement that "secondary meanings have a tendency to contain traces of primary meanings". I, too, believe that different meanings of a word are usually interrelated, and that adequate definitions should reveal those links. (For many illustrations, see Wierzbicka 1987; also Mel'čuk's concept of "semantic bridges", Mel'čuk *et al.* 1984.) But this does not change the basic requirement that each definition should be able to stand on its own.

9. Distinguishing Polysemy from Vagueness

One of the main reasons why lexicographers often find it difficult, indeed impossible, to capture the semantic invariant is that they do not know how to distinguish polysemy from vagueness. It is not that lexicographers do not believe in polysemy: frequently, polysemy is posited in dictionaries on a truly massive scale; but it is posited on an *ad hoc* basis, without any clear guide-lines or general principles.

Consider, for example, the definition of *ribbon* mentioned earlier: "a strip of nylon, silk, or some other material" (*OAJD*). As pointed out, this definition implies that *any* strip of material could be called *ribbon*, whereas in fact many different "strips of material" (e.g. a piece of sewing-tape) would not be so called (because their function is clearly different from that of ribbon: sewing-tape is clearly not made for tying things and, equally clearly, it is not made for a decorative purpose).

But the generalization proposed here may seem to apply to *many* (even *most*) cases rather than to *all* cases. For example, what about *typewriter ribbon*? Is it meant for tying things? Or is it decorative? And yet it is called *ribbon*, too, isn't it?

Confronted with an apparent exception of this kind, lexicographers often tend to lose faith in the existence of a semantic invariant, take recourse to hedges, qualifiers, and various other *ad hoc* devices, and lose the generalization.

But in fact the counter-example is apparent rather than real: the so-called *typewriter ribbon* is not called *ribbon* but *typewriter ribbon* (even if it can sometimes be referred to, elliptically, as *ribbon*).

The common belief that a modifier-head construction must indicate a taxonomic ('kind of') relationship is based on a fallacy, which feeds on the fact that compounds with such a structure can often be abbreviated, in an appropriate context, to the head alone.

For example, it is often assumed that an artificial leg is a kind of leg, that a plastic flower is a kind of flower, that an electric chair is a kind of chair, or that a house of cards is a kind of house. Since people cannot live in a house of cards, and since "a house of cards is a kind of house", the generalization that houses are made for people to live in appears to be easily refuted. Similarly, since plastic flowers do not grow out of the ground, and since "a plastic flower is a kind of flower", the generalization that flowers grow out of the ground may also seem to be easily refuted.

Reasoning of this kind is fallacious because it confuses semantic relationships based on the notion of 'like' with those based on the notion of 'kind' (i.e. "horizontal" and "vertical" relationships; see Bright and Bright 1969; Berlin 1992). For example, a rose is a kind of flower, but a plastic flower is *like* a flower, not a *kind* of flower. Similarly, a deck-chair is a kind of chair, but an electric chair is not a kind of chair ("something for people to sit on . . ."); rather, it is an object which is like a chair, but whose function is quite different from that of a chair. Finally, typewriter ribbon is not a kind of ribbon; rather it is something which is like a ribbon, but whose function is quite different from that of a ribbon.

There is, however, one important difference between the case of *typewriter ribbon* and that of *plastic flowers*: the fact that one can call a plastic imitation of a flower a *flower* is language-independent, whereas the fact that the "typewriter strip" is called in English *ribbon* (*typewriter ribbon*) is language-specific (e.g. in Polish the corresponding compound is *taśma do maszyny*, lit. 'typewriter tape'). Consequently, *typewriter ribbon* has to be listed in a dictionary as a separate item, with its own definition, whereas *plastic flower* does not.

To prove that a *typewriter ribbon* is not 'a kind of ribbon' and that the definition of *ribbon* does not have to cover typewriter ribbon, we proceed as follows: we first assume, for the sake of argument, that *typewriter ribbon* does have to be covered in the definition of *ribbon* and we ask what the two categories have in common; when we establish the common denominator (roughly, "a strip of material") we ask whether any object which fits this common denominator can be called by the word in question (*ribbon*); we find that the answer has to be negative; from this we conclude that the supposed common denominator cannot account for the word's range of use; and from this we infer the existence of polysemy.

If we proceed in this way we can arrive at definitions with full predictive power, not in a diachronic sense, explaining why certain objects came to be called by certain names (e.g. why the "typewriter strip" came to be called in English by a compound including the word *ribbon*, whereas, for example, in Polish it came to be called by a compound including a noun which on its own means 'tape'), but in a synchronic sense, which means that the definition matches a word's actual range of use. This procedure will enable us to be precise and to dispense with hedges and qualifying expressions such as *usually*, *often*, *typically*, or *etc.*, which are meant to make up for the inaccuracy of the definition itself.

Another way of making basically the same point is this: a *hair ribbon* differs from other kinds of ribbons in only one respect, specified by the modifier (being used for tying hair with), so there are no grounds for positing polysemy in this case. But *typewriter ribbon* differs from other ribbons in more than one respect (it is used in typewriters, it is not suitable for tying things with, it is not decorative); in this case, therefore, polysemy has to be postulated (see Chapter 8).

Thus, although with respect to nouns polysemy often has to be established on purely semantic grounds, this does not mean that there are no guide-lines for establishing whether a word has one meaning or two (or more).

With respect to verbs, the task of establishing the number of meanings is often facilitated by differences in syntactic frames. This point can be illustrated with the English verb *to order*.

The *Concise Oxford Dictionary* (*COD* 1964) offers for this verb the following glosses: "put in order, array, regulate . . . ; . . . ordain . . . ; command, bid, prescribe . . . ; command or direct . . . ; direct tradesman, servant, etc., to supply (~ *dinner*, settle what it shall consist of)".

These glosses do not make it clear how many meanings are being posited (and perhaps the underlying assumption is that the different meanings of this verb cannot be sorted out from one another). But in fact, if the syntactic frames are sorted out in orderly fashion, clear semantic distinctions emerge, too.

Leaving aside (for reasons of space) the meaning illustrated with the sentences "He ordered his affairs" or "He ordered his troops", I will focus here on the distinction between what I will call *order*$_1$ and *order*$_2$, which can be illustrated with the sentences "She ordered him to leave" and "She ordered a steak", respectively. In fact, I will reproduce here with only minor changes the discussion of this distinction which appears in my *Dictionary of English Speech Act Verbs* (Wierzbicka 1987a: 86–7).

A person who *orders₂* a meal in a restaurant or a book in a bookshop wants the addressee to cause him to have that thing and expects him to do so; to that extent *order₂* is similar to *order₁*. But there are numerous assumptions which are present in *order₂* but absent from *order₁*. The person who *orders₂* something wants to have something; an action by the addressee is necessary for this desired state of affairs to eventuate, but it is only a means to the goal, not the goal itself; it does not matter who carries out the *order₂* (which waiter etc.), as long as it is carried out. This semantic difference is reflected in a syntactic difference: one *orders₁* a person (to do something), but one *orders₂* a thing (from a person). One cannot *order₂* a waiter, one can only *order₂* a steak, and one cannot *order₁* a steak (as one cannot *give orders* to a steak), even though concrete nouns can be reported as *orders₁* (" 'The door', he ordered").

The direct object represents the focus of the speaker's interest. For *order₁*, the direct object has to refer either to the addressee or to the action ("He *ordered₁* her to leave", "He *ordered₁* an inquiry"). For *order₂*, it has to refer to an object ("He *ordered₂* a steak"), with the addressee being conceptually and syntactically demoted to a prepositional phrase ('*X ordered₂ Y* from *Z*'). The speaker who *orders₂* something assumes that the addressee has things that many people may want to have, and that he is willing to provide people with some of these things, on certain conditions. The addressee's task concerns not only the product which the speaker wants to have, but also some services: the addressee has to do something to the object desired (i.e. get it, prepare it, wrap it, serve it, and so on). For his part, the speaker undertakes to do something, too: whatever is required (for example, to pay). He also has to wait, because his wish cannot be complied with immediately (as in the case of buying), but only after some delay, allowing the addressee to perform the necessary actions.

Finally, the person who *orders₂* something does not assume that the addressee has to do what he wants him to do; he does assume, however, that the addressee is willing to do so. A person who *orders₁* someone to do something is very confident about the outcome ('I think that you have to do it'). A person who *orders₂* something is a little less confident, because the addressee may be unable to carry out the *order₂*. But, in this case, too, the speaker is reasonably confident ('I think that if you can do it, you will do it').

One can hypothesize that *order₂* has developed out of *order₁* by a shift of emphasis from the addressee to the object provided by the addressee, and by a concomitant disappearance of certain assumptions concerning the relationship between the speaker and the addressee: *order*₁ implies that the addressee is subordinated to the speaker and has to do what the speaker wants him to do. In *order*₂, this assumption is absent; instead, there are new assumptions which emphasize the object ('something has to be done to it') and which de-individualize the addressee: he is not seen as an individual subordinated to the speaker but as a person or group of persons who willingly provide certain kinds of objects to unspecified customers.

Thus the last gloss in the *COD* entry for *order* ("direct tradesman, servant, etc., to supply") confuses two different meanings, associated with different types of social relationship and with different sets of assumptions: it is one thing to order someone (e.g. a servant) to do something, and another to order something from someone (e.g. from a tradesman). In an adequate lexicographic description, these two senses whould have to be clearly distinguished, and the readers would have to be informed of the different grammatical frames associated with the different meanings.

10. Avoiding Circularity

> There was one thing that Edith could not beat, and that was the dictionary. "The Larousse is a big cheat. You look for a word, you find it, they send you back to another word and you haven't got anywhere."
>
> (Berteaut 1973: 103)

Conventional dictionaries are, generally speaking, vitiated by all-pervasive circularity in their definitions. Some dictionaries are better in this respect than others (for example, the OAJD is much better than all the Oxford dictionaries addressed at adults), but while there are differences of degree, there are hardly any exceptions—circularity is a malady (in a more or less advanced form) to which virtually no conventional dictionary is immune.

Practical lexicographers are often well aware of the circularity of their definitions, but not knowing how to avoid it they try to make a virtue of "necessity", and attempt to justify this circularity as something that may bother theoretical semanticists but that is quite acceptable in a practical dictionary and which will never bother the ordinary user. In fact, however, they are deceiving themselves (and unwittingly insulting the intelligence of their intended audience). A few examples.

The verb *to jump* is defined by the *OPD* as "to move off the ground etc. by bending and then extending the legs or (of fish) by a movement of the tail" (first meaning) and "to move suddenly with a jump or bound, to rise suddenly from a seat etc." (second meaning). As for the first definition, one might query the unexpected attention it gives to fish (as well as its use of *etc.*), but it is the second definition which is relevant in the present context. For what is "a jump"? The *OPD* offers several definitions, but the relevant one appears to be the first : "a jumping movement". Thus *to jump* is defined via *a jump*, *a jump* via *jumping*, and *jumping* is not defined at all, being treated, naturally enough, as a form of the verb *to jump*. Substituting the definienses for their definienda, we obtain the following: *to jump*—"to move suddenly with a jumping movement"; that is, "to move suddenly with a movement characteristic of moving suddenly with a movement characteristic of moving suddenly with a movement". And so it goes on—like a record caught in a groove. It would take a real jump of faith to believe that that is the kind of definition which will serve the dictionary user best.

To take another example, the *OPD* defines *fate* as "a person's destiny", and *destiny* as "that which happens to a person or thing thought of as determined by fate". Replacing the word *fate* with its definition we get the following: *destiny* is "that which happens to a person or thing thought of as determined by that which happens to a person or thing thought of as that which happens to a person or thing" (and so on, *ad infinitum*). Quite apart from the fact that a definition of this kind is an insult to the readers' intelligence, what use could it possibly be to them? If somebody knows what *fate* means, what *destiny* means, and how they differ from one another, then they don't need any definitions at all; but if they do not know, or are not quite sure, the dictionary will not teach them anything. Both the producer's and the buyer's money is wasted on definitions of this kind.

It might be added that *fate* is also given another definition in the same dictionary, "a power thought to control all events and impossible to resist", and that *destiny* is also defined as "fate considered as power". This time, replacing *fate* with its definition we get: *destiny* is "a power . . . considered as power"—hardly a more illuminating result.

It might be objected that this last example is unfair because the concepts of 'fate' and 'destiny' are particularly difficult to define. But in fact circularity is so pervasive that the easiest concepts are often defined in the same way.

For example, *LDOTEL* defines *best* as "excelling all others". *Excel* is defined, in turn, via *superior* and *surpass*, *superior* via *surpass*, and *surpass* via *better*, as well as via *exceed*, with *exceed* being defined in turn via *superior*. What baffles the reader most is why *best* couldn't have been defined via *better* in the first place ("better than all the others"), instead of going round the circles involving *superior*, *surpass*, and *exceed*.

Similarly, *OPD* defines *question* as "a sentence requesting information or an answer", and *answer* as "something said or written or needed or done to deal with a question, accusation, or problem". Omitting, to save space, the numerous *ors*, we get something like this: an *answer* is "something said to deal with a sentence requesting something said to deal with a sentence requesting . . ."—and so on, *ad infinitum*. And yet the essence of a *question*, or an *answer*, is not difficult to state: the *question* refers to a situation when, roughly speaking, someone says "I want to know something, I want someone to tell me" and *answer* means, roughly, "telling someone something that they said they wanted to know" (for more precise definitions, see Wierzbicka 1987*a*).

The examples given above were relatively simple, with *A* being defined via *B*, and *B* via *A*. Typically, however, vicious circles are like huge webs enveloping whole extended families of words, or like gigantic tentacles extending throughout the pages of a dictionary. For example, *A* is defined via *B*, *B* via *C*, and *C* via *A*; or *A*, *B*, *C*, *D*, *E*, and *F* are defined via one another—in circles, criss-crosses, and all imaginable sorts of combinations and patterns (for example, *A* via *B* and *D*; *B* via *D*, *E*, and *F*; *D* via *A*, *B*, and *C*; *C* via *A* and *B*; and so on)—with repercussions throughout the entire dictionary, which becomes an entangled web of overlapping circles. For example, in the *OPD*, one can find a little circle (Fig. 9.1) and a larger one, with the little one within it (Fig. 9.2).

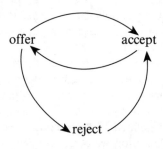

Fig. 9.1

In a system of this kind, every answer generates new questions, and these new questions either lead us to further questions or bring us back to the starting-point (or both). It is just as Descartes said in his "Search after Truth" (speaking through the mouth of Eudoxus and referring to the so-called metaphysical steps or the tree of Porphyry):

> EUDOXUS. You pay no attention to my question, and the reply that you make to me, simple as it may appear to you, will bring us into a labyrinth of difficulties, if I try ever so little to press you. Were I for example to ask Epistemon himself what a man is, and were he to reply, as is done in the Schools, that a man is a rational animal; and if, in addition, in order to explain these two terms which are not less obscure than the first, he were to conduct us by all the steps which are termed metaphysical, we should be dragged into a maze from which it would be impossible for us to emerge. As a matter of fact, from this question two others arise, the first is what is an animal? The second, what is reasonable? And further, if, to explain what an animal is he were to reply that it is a living thing possessed of sensations,

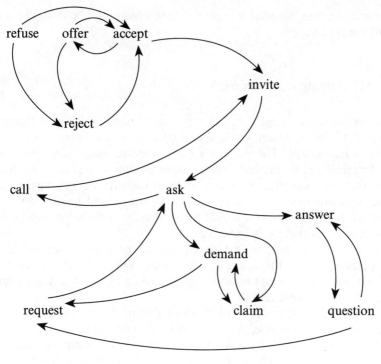

F<small>IG</small>. 9.2

that a living thing is an animate body, that a body is a corporeal substance, you see that the question, like the branches of a genealogical tree, would go on increasing and multiplying; and finally all these wonderful questions would finish in pure tautology, which would clear up nothing, and would leave us in our original ignorance.   (Descartes 1701/1931: 318)

Circularity involves the same kind of *regressus ad infinitum*.

Pascal denounced circularity with his mock-definition of *light*. He wrote:

There are people who go as far in absurdity as to explicate a word by itself. I know some who have defined *lumière* ('light') like this: "La lumière est un mouvement luminaire des corps lumineux" [Light is a luminary movement of luminous bodies]; as if one could understand the words *luminaire* and *lumineux* without understanding *lumière*.   (Pascal 1667/1954: 580)

Three centuries, and hundreds of dictionaries later, the problem of circularity has not only not been solved (in practical lexicography) but, on the contrary, has by and large ceased to be seen as a problem! The hydra of circularity is rearing its ugly heads with more and more self-assurance. There can be no doubt that—although dictionary makers are, naturally, reluctant to admit it—what is sacrificed to this hydra is, above all, the interest of the reader.

11. Relying on Indefinables

One cannot define everything. For any sound lexicographic undertaking it is crucial to decide which words are going to be defined and which can be taken as indefinable. The point has been made so many times, so clearly and forcefully, that one feels embarrassed having to repeat it again and again (see, for example, the quotes given in Chapter 1). Yet repeat it one must, until this basic point is generally understood and finally universally accepted. But how should a lexicographer decide on the set of indefinables on which the dictionary is to be based?

For obvious reasons, the set of indefinables must be reasonably small. For example, if half the words in a dictionary were defined and the other half not, the reader would have the right to complain, and perhaps even to demand a 50 per cent refund.

Second, the indefinables must be chosen from among words which are intuitively clear; otherwise, they are useless (or worse than useless) as building-blocks out of which the definitions of all the other (definable) words are constructed. For example, if the words *good* and *bad* are defined, directly or indirectly, via *moral* and *immoral* this is useless to the reader because the former pair is by far clearer and more intelligible to everybody (including small children) than the latter. Thus, explaining *good* via *moral* or *bad* via *immoral* is a parody of an explanation. And yet this is how dictionaries often proceed—not because their makers are foolish but because they do not have a firm and clear semantic theory at their disposal. To illustrate, the *OPD* offers the following:

bad   — wicked, evil
wicked   — morally bad, offending against what is right
evil   — morally bad, wicked

If one pursues the leads offered a little further, the web of vicious circles thickens:

to offend — to do wrong
wrong   — morally bad, contrary to justice or to what is right
moral   — of or concerned with the goodness or badness of human character or
            with the principles of what is right and wrong in conduct

This means *bad* → *wicked* → *bad*; *wicked* → *offend* → *wrong* → *bad* → *wicked*; *bad* → *wicked* → *moral* → *bad*; on and on.

The *OAJD* shows more wisdom, in that it does not attempt to define *bad* at all, and thus is free to define both *evil* and *wicked* via *bad*, imperfectly, no doubt, but at least without circularity:

evil   — very wicked
wicked — very bad

Unfortunately, the same wisdom was not shown in the case of *good*, which *is* defined, causing, predictably, a vicious circle (and, incidentally, committing the dictionary to a dubious and dangerous doctrine that 'good' is the same as 'socially acceptable'):

good   — of the kind that people like and praise
praise — to say that someone or something is very good

The solution to all this is very simple: to accept that both *good* and *bad* are among the most basic human concepts and that they neither can nor need to be defined—and then to define everything else clearly and accurately.

Critics are often sceptical of the defining power of simple and general terms such as *good* and *bad*. For example, Landau (1992–3: 115) asks how *bad* can be sufficient "to distinguish between, say, mistake, blunder, lapse, wrong, and sin"; but I believe that simple and general words such as *bad* can achieve this goal much better than the unrestricted set of words used in conventional dictionary definitions. Consider the set of circular definitions offered by *AHDOTEL* (1973) (abbreviated here for reasons of space):

mistake   — an error or fault
error   — . . . 4. a mistake
fault   — . . . 2. a mistake; error
sin   — 1. a transgression of religious or moral law, especially when delib-
                erate; 2. any offense, violation, fault, or error
violation   — 1. the act of violating . . . 2. an instance of violation; a transgres-
                sion
transgression — 1. the violation of a law, command, or duty

Pictorially this is represented in Fig. 9.3.

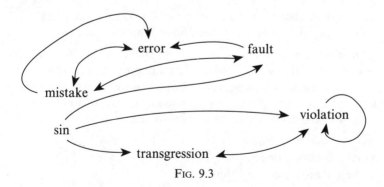

FIG. 9.3

Cobuild takes a different approach, but, in my view, it is also far from successful. For example:

mistake   1.1. an action or opinion that is incorrect or foolish, or that is not what you intended to do, or whose result is undesirable; 1.2. something or part of something which is incorrect or not right

The comment on the margin says, in addition, that "mistake = error". If the definitions offered by *AHDOTEL* are striking in their blatant circularity, those offered by *Cobuild* are striking in their failure to capture an invariant. In my view, however, *mistake* (noun) does have a unitary meaning, which can be stated as follows:

> *mistake* (*X* made a mistake)
> something bad happened
> because *X* did something
> *X* didn't want it to happen
> *X* wanted something else to happen
> *X* thought that something else would happen

By analysing the concept of 'mistake' into its components, we can not only avoid circularity and capture a unitary meaning, but also show the differences as well as similarities between related concepts such as 'mistake', 'blunder', and 'sin'.

For example, *Cobuild* defines *blunder* as "a big mistake, especially one which seems to be the result of carelessness or stupidity". But not every "big mistake", or even "terrible mistake", is a blunder, not even if it is due to carelessness. Something like "stupidity", on the other hand, is a necessary part of this concept (so it shouldn't be introduced in an "especially" frame). I would propose the following:

> *blunder* (*X* made a blunder)
> something bad happened
> because *X* did something
> *X* didn't want it to happen
> if *X* thought about it for a short time, *X* wouldn't have done it
> people can think something bad about *X* because of this

Landau doesn't believe that a general and simple word like *bad* could be used in defining both a word like *mistake* (with no moral or religious implications) and a moral and religious concept like *sin*. But if I am not mistaken, and if I am not sinfully over-confident, it can be done. Here is my *sin* (in the serious, non-jocular, use of the word):

> *sin* (*X* committed a sin)
> *X* did something bad
> *X* knew that it was bad to do it

X knew that God wants people not to do things like this
X did it because *X* wanted to do it
this is bad

The simplicity of all the elements used in this definition (except the concept of 'God', which is not very simple, but which underlies the concept of 'sin') allows us to avoid circularity, portray structural relations, and avoid blind alleys such as the one in which, for example, both *AHDOTEL* and *Cobuild* find themselves in their attempt to define *sin* via *law*. To illustrate from *Cobuild*:

sin or a sin — is an action a type of behaviour which is believed to break the laws of God

law — 1. is a system of rules that a society or government develops over time in order to deal with business agreements, social relationships, and crimes such as theft, murder, or violence.

Clearly, the definition of *law* quoted above does not allow for any "laws of God", so the attempted definition of *sin* via *law* does not allow for any coherent interpretation.

Finally, a few words about *wrong* (adjective), for which *AHDOTEL* finds itself obliged to posit no less than seven different meanings, and *Cobuild*, as many as eleven, without being able to show what all these supposed meanings have in common. Of course, one could write a whole study about the concepts of 'right' and 'wrong', but basically, the meanings of these two adjectives are quite simple. In essence, they could be stated as follows:

It is wrong to do this (like this). =
it is bad to do this (like this)
if one thinks about it one can know it

It is right to do this (like this). =
it is good to do this (like this)
if one thinks about it one can know it

Unlike the concepts of 'good' and 'bad', which are universal, the concepts of 'right' and 'wrong' are culture-specific, and in fact they are very revealing in the links which they postulate between values ('good' and 'bad') on the one hand and 'thinking' and 'knowing' on the other (see Wierzbicka 1989*a*; 1992*a*, ch. 1).

A list of indefinables that has proved itself valuable in lexical semantics should be of great potential benefit to practical lexicography. Since the same indefinables, and the same simple syntactic patterns, which appear to be most useful for analysing the English lexicon appear to be also very useful in analysing the lexical resources of other languages (including ones as diverse as Japanese, Pitjantjatjara, and Ewe), the conclusion does not seem premature that the same set of indefinables can be used as a core of a "natural lexicographic metalanguage" suitable for both monolingual and bilingual dictionaries in most, if not all, languages of the world. The practical advantages of such an outcome would seem to me to be huge, as any language learner would thus have relatively easy access to dictionaries of any language via their common core.[2]

12. Using Simple Language

The issue of indefinables is linked closely with that of simple language. The use of excessively complex and obscure language is one of the greatest obstacles to effective communication in any area of human endeavour; but in a dictionary, which seeks to *explain* the meaning of words, it is particularly out of place. Arnauld refers, in this connection, to the writings of the philosopher and mathematician Gassendi, and he writes: "Gassendi's exposition makes clear that there is scarcely a more reprehensible turn of mind than is exhibited by these enigmatical writers who believe that the most groundless thoughts—not to say the most false and impious ones—will pass for grand mysteries if reclothed in forms unintelligible to the common man" (Arnauld 1662/1964: 88).

Despite repeated pleas from thinkers like Gassendi, the use of complex and obscure language is a great plague of Western civilization, which mars, in particular, most encyclopaedias, textbooks, manuals, printed instructions for the use of machines and devices of different kinds, and so on. More often than not, it also mars, and diminishes the usefulness of, dictionaries of different kinds.

Consider, for example, the definitions of the words *obligatory* and *optional*, given by *AHDOTEL*:

obligatory — 1. legally or morally constraining; binding; 2. imposing or recording
        an obligation. 3. of the nature of an obligation; compulsory.

optional   — left to choice; not compulsory or automatic

Wouldn't it be better to explain what these words mean in very simple words, along the following lines:

---

[2] I am not suggesting that the Natural Semantic Metalanguage devised by the author and colleagues should be used, unaltered, as a lexicographic metalanguage, but only that it can be used as the core of a lexicographic metalanguage. Nor am I suggesting that all lexical items in a dictionary should be defined directly in terms of the indefinables. In particular, the names of natural kinds (e.g. *cat, mouse, butterfly*) or of cultural kinds (e.g. *bottle, bicycle, chair*) require a different approach, with a much larger defining lexicon than abstract vocabulary does (see Wierzbicka 1985; also Ch. 7).

obligatory — everyone has to do it

optional — one can do it if one wants to, one doesn't have to do it

(I'm not proposing these as fully accurate definitions, but only as an improvement on those offered by the dictionary.)

My respect for the work of practical lexicographers is so high that I would not wish to be seen as accusing them of passing (as Gassendi put it, according to Arnaud) "groundless and the most false thoughts" for "grand mysteries", but I think it is fair to demand of them that their definitions avoid being "clothed in forms unintelligible to the common man".

13. Exploring New Models of Definition

Lexicographic definitions can be improved immensely while maintaining a more or less traditional form. This can be done, above all, by simplifying and regularizing the language of definitions, by using a discrete model of definitions, by trying to capture invariants (and thus banishing all *ors* and *etceteras*), and by getting rid of circularity. It is possible, however, to improve definitions still further, if one is prepared to give up the traditional forms of definition and to explore new formats and new models (drawing on the discoveries of contemporary semantics).

Consider, for example, the *LDOTEL* entry for the verb *to punish*:

1*a*. to impose a penalty on for a fault, offence or violation
1*b*. to inflict a penalty for (an offence)
2. to treat roughly, harshly, or damagingly

Many weaknesses of this entry are quite apparent: the positing of a completely unjustified polysemy (1 versus 2) and semi-polysemy (1*a* versus 1*b*); the failure to capture the invariant (what do "fault, offence or violation" have in common?); the latent circularity.

The curious distinction between "impose" (1*a*) and "inflict" (1*b*) collapses in the entry for *inflict*, which is defined as "to force or impose (something damaging or painful) on someone". *Penalty* is defined, predictably, via *punishment*: "punishment imposed for, or incurred by, committing a crime or public offence". And if that much circularity was not enough, more is introduced via *crime*, which is defined as "an act or omission punishable by law" (*punish → penalty → punishment*; *punish → penalty → crime → punish*).

Here as in many other cases, the simple and unitary definition offered by *OAJD* is incomparably better:

to punish—to make someone who has done wrong suffer, so that he will not want to do wrong again

In fact, this simple short definition can be made even better by shortening it further: since one can speak of "capital punishment" (by death) or of "eternal punishment" (by hell), the corrective purpose cannot be a necessary part of the concept. We are left, therefore, with the short formula "to make someone who has done wrong suffer", and this is probably almost as good as one can get within the traditional model. The definition is no more, however, than an approximation: it does not capture correctly all the components of the concept, and in some respects it manages to be over-specific. In particular, it posits suffering as a necessary part of punishment, whereas in fact an intention to cause suffering is sufficient, even if no suffering actually occurs. What is missing from the definition is some indication of the relationship between the punisher and the punished, and of the punisher's view of the action as morally justified. For example, if a little boy (Johnny) hits his younger sister (Suzie) on the head, and Suzie retaliates by biting Johnny's finger, the *OAJD* definition would fit the situation (since Johnny did something wrong and Suzie made him suffer because of it), but the word *punish* would not. To portray the concept of 'punishment' accurately we need, I think, a scenario, not a definition of the traditional kind:

X punished *Y* [for *Z*]. =
(*a*) [*Y* did *Z*]
(*b*) *X* thought something like this:
(*c*)   *Y* did something bad [*Z*]
(*d*)   I want *Y* to feel something bad because of this
(*e*)   it will be good if *Y* feels something bad because of this
(*f*)   it will be good if I do something to *Y* because of this
(*g*) *X* did something to *Y* because of this

Component (*a*) refers to the culprit's action, (*b*) to (*f*) describe the punisher's attitude, and (*g*) refers to the punisher's action. The punisher's attitude includes, roughly speaking, a desire to inflict pain (*d*), and three assumptions: that the target person did something bad (*c*), that it will be right and just if he or she "suffers" (feels something bad) because of this (*e*), and that the punisher is called upon to inflict the necessary pain (presumably, as the person in charge).

Cruse (1992–3: 89) questions my analysis of the verb *punish* on the grounds that "the punisher may actually hate having to cause suffering". I entirely agree that the punisher may hate having to cause suffering; but this is not incompatible with an intention to cause suffering. For example, the father or mother imposing the punishment on the child may suffer intensely themselves; but if they didn't intend to cause some pain for the child they wouldn't be "punishing" him or her. On the other hand, if the child doesn't really feel any pain this doesn't stop the parents' action from being describable as *punishment*.

As a second example of the need for a scenario, consider the concept of 'revenge', which the *OPD* defines as follows:

revenge—punishment or injury inflicted in return for what one has suffered

The definition is unsuccessful for many reasons, two of which can be linked with the use of the words *punishment* and *return*. Contrary to what the definition implies, *revenge* is not a kind of punishment, because it does not imply the assumptions which as we have seen are part of the latter concept. The expression *in return* is not defined at all, and the definitions assigned to the noun *return* are useless and irrelevant from the point of view of defining *revenge* (e.g. "coming or going back").

Again, the definition offered by the *OAJD* is much more satisfactory ("a wish to hurt someone because he has hurt you or one of your friends"), but is not quite correct: *revenge* refers to an action, not merely to a wish, the mention of "friends" is superfluous, and the crucial idea of "doing the same" is missing. To portray the concept of 'revenge' accurately we need a scenario:

Y took revenge on *X* [for *Z*]. =
(*a*) someone (*X*) did something bad [*Z*] to someone (*Y*)
(*b*) because of this, *Y* felt something bad
(*c*) after this, *Y* thought something like this:
(*d*)   this person (*X*) did something bad [*Z*] to me
(*e*)   because of this, I want to do the same to this person (*X*)
(*f*) *Y* thought about it for a long time
(*g*) after this, *Y* did something bad to *X* because of this

Component (*a*) refers to the action of the offender, and (*g*) to that of the revenger; (*b*) shows what the revenger felt, and components (*d*) and (*e*) show his or her thoughts (with their focus on "paying in kind").

Finally, consider the concept of 'tempting', which *Webster's Dictionary* (1959) "defines" as follows: "*tempt*—to put to trial; test; persuade to evil; defy; allure; entice". It is hardly necessary to point out that this entry does not tell the reader whether the verb *tempt* is supposed to have one meaning or more, and if more, then how many; that no attempt is made to capture the semantic invariant or invariants; and that the entry offers no clues as to the differences in meaning between all the different verbs which it lists as supposed equivalents of *tempt*. It does not require much imagination to guess that the same dictionary will "define" *entice* and *allure* via *tempt*.

As pointed out earlier, a much more illuminating alternative is provided by the *OAJD*, which offers the simple, short definition "*to tempt*—to try to make someone do wrong". But of course this is only an approximation; for example, one can "try to make someone do wrong" by threats, and this could not be called *tempting*. To portray this concept adequately we need, I think, a scenario along the following lines:

X tempted Y to do Z. =
(a) X wanted Y to do Z
(b) Y thought something like this:
(c)   if I do Z it will be bad
(d)   because of this, I don't want to do it
(e) X knew this
(f) because of this, X said something like this to Y:
(g)   if you do it, something very good will happen to you
(h)   you will feel something very good because of this
(i) X thought something like this:
(j)   maybe Y will do it because of this
(k) X wanted this

I am not suggesting that new models of definition such as those illustrated here with *revenge, punishment,* and *tempt* should be necessarily accepted in all practical lexicography, although I think it would be useful to adopt—or to adapt—them for some types of dictionaries. But I believe it is useful for the practical lexicographers to know that new models of definition are available—and to let them draw on whatever is available in ways which they would judge most appropriate in any given case.

14. Conclusion

There is more to practical lexicography than getting the meanings right, but trying to get the meanings right is vitally important—more important, I think, than anything else. If theoretical lexicography could not help in this respect—by providing ideas, principles, criteria, models, and guide-lines—one could really doubt its *raison d'être*. I have tried to show, however, that theoretical lexicography indeed offers all these things.[3] Most importantly (from the present writer's point of view), it offers a tool which can by itself remedy a large proportion of the ills of traditional lexicography: a natural lexicographic metalanguage, derived from the Natural Semantic Metalanguage, and based on universal semantic primitives.

---

[3] For brilliant discussions of various aspects of theoretical lexicography and of the principles of lexicographic definition, see in particular Apresjan (1974, 1992, forthcoming); Mel'čuk (1974b); and Bogusławski (1988). For discussion of the lexicography of the concrete lexicon, see Wierzbicka (1985) and Ch. 8. For some recent dictionaries which overcome the indeterminacy and the circularity of traditional lexicography, and which aim at empirical adequacy without departing from traditional models, see e.g. Apresjan and Rozenman (1979); Bogusławski (1983); Goddard (1992a). For a new model of a monolingual dictionary, see Mel'čuk and Žolkovskij (1984); Mel'čuk *et al.* (1984, 1988, 1992); Rudzka *et al.* (1981).

10   The Meaning of Colour Terms and the Universals of Seeing

> Phenomenological analysis . . . is analysis of concepts and can neither agree with nor contradict physics.
>
> (Wittgenstein 1977: 16)

1. Introduction

'Colour' is not a universal human concept. It can of course be created in all human societies, just as the concepts 'television', 'computer', or 'money' can, but despite the rapidly increasing contact between human societies there are still many which have neither borrowed nor developed the concept of 'colour' (and of course there have been many more such societies in the past).

Nor are "colour terms" a universal phenomenon. It is certainly not true that, as has often been claimed, all languages have words for black and white. This point will be documented and discussed in detail later, but in a sense it is quite obvious: if a word is used to describe not only black, but also brown, grey, or dark-blue objects, then it cannot possibly mean 'black'.

In English, and in many other languages of the world, "colour" can be regarded as a reasonably self-contained semantic domain. But in the universe of human discourse it is not. To try to carve out, for all languages, a domain of "colour semantics" means to impose on the study of all cultures a perspective arising from only some of them (in particular, from modern, technologically complex, Western culture).

In all cultures, people are interested in "seeing" and in describing what they see, but they don't necessarily isolate "colour" as a separate aspect of their visual experience. All languages have a word for SEE (see Chapter 2), but not all languages have a word for "colour". From what we know about the vocabulary of 'seeing' in different languages, we can conclude that in most cultures the discourse of 'seeing' is contextualized, and the experience of seeing is described as a complex and integrated one, with colour, texture, shape, function, and many other attributes being treated as an indivisible

---

This chapter owes a great deal to many long discussions with Cliff Goddard.

whole. As van Brakel (1993: 113) writes, "In western languages, the domain of colour is clearly separated from other categories and there is a bias towards hue at the expense of brightness and saturation. In other cultures, the hue aspect of colour may, as it were, be subsumed under different categories, so that it isn't really present as a separate domain."

I do not doubt that there are some "universals of seeing", which can be discovered and validated through the study of the world's languages. But to establish what these universals are, the focus of research must shift from the search for "colour universals" to the search for "universals of seeing". There can't be any colour universals, if colour itself is not a human universal. But 'seeing' is indeed a universal human concept.

To say that the search for colour universals has been largely misguided is not to say that it has not been fruitful. The massive research into the description of colours initiated by Berlin and Kay's (1969) classic study has generated a great body of knowledge about the discourse of SEEing, and has contributed a great deal to any future theory of the universals of seeing.

In particular, this research has made it clear that the notion of colour is not only far from universal but that its role in human discourse is, relatively speaking, quite limited.

What does seem universal, or near-universal, in the domain of seeing is, first of all, the distinction between times when people can see ("day") and times when people cannot see ("night").

This universal or near-universal distinction between, roughly speaking, nights (dark times) and days (times of light), appears to be linked, universally or near-universally, with some distinction or distinctions in the description of what one sees. Roughly speaking, people tend to distinguish, universally, between seeing things which look "light" and "shiny" and seeing things which look "dark" and "dull" (that is, light-less, shine-less). Clearly, the first kind brings to mind the experience of "sun-time vision", and the second, that of "night-time vision". (It is worth recalling in this connection Birren's (1978: 3) observation: "All civilizations since the beginning of man's existence worshipped the sun, and from the sun came light and color.")

The distinction between "dark" colours and "light" colours appears to play an important role in most languages of the world. For example, Hargrave (1982: 208) makes the following comment about the Australian language Kuku: Yalanji (a "stage II language" in Berlin and Kay's colour-encoding sequence):

According to the investigators, *bingaji* and *ngumbu* mean 'light' and 'dark' as well as 'white' and 'black'. Several participants appeared to name chips light or dark in comparison with the frame around the chip or in comparison with the chip just shown them previously.

Hargrave adds:

Terms denoting light and dark have been recorded by other researchers in Australia. Jones and Meehan, carrying out an investigation of Anbarra (north-central Arnhem Land) colour concepts, concluded that there were only two real colour terms, those for light and dark. Four additional 'colour terms' were names for mineral pigments and could only be used to describe a limited range of objects (Jones and Meehan 1978: 26–30). Davis found that children at Milingimbi, also in Arnhem Land, first classified all colours as *watharr* 'light' or *mol* 'dark'. As they got older, they added further terms which classified colours by hue and saturation as well as brightness (Davis 1982).

Another universal or near-universal has to do with the importance of the environment as a fundamental frame of reference for any human description of 'seeing'. English words such as *view*, *scenery*, or *landscape* provide useful hints in this respect, since they link the idea of 'seeing' with the idea of 'place'. For what do human beings normally "see"? Presumably, objects, animals, or people positioned or moving against a background (cf. the "figure" and "ground" distinction in psychology). Of the two, backgrounds are no doubt more stable and more predictable than "figures": the sky (often blue), the ground (often brown), the grass (typically green), the sun (often yellow and brilliant), the sea (often dark blue), the broad expanse of snow (normally white).

Of course, the landscape doesn't look the same everywhere. Not all human beings are familiar with the sea or with snow, the ground is not everywhere brown (and in some places it may be seen as predominantly red, yellow, or black), and even the greenness of the grass depends on the availability of water and on the exposure to sun (e.g. in Australia the grassy landscape is, typically, yellowish or brownish rather than green). I am proposing, however, that the principle of using common features of landscape as a frame of reference for visual categories in general, and for 'colour' in particular, is an important human universal, and also that this principle is responsible for many recurring features of human discourse on 'seeing'.

Yet another universal or near-universal feature of human discourse on seeing is the important role of comparison, or, more precisely, of the universal concept LIKE, in the experience of visual experiences. The English adjectives *gold* and *golden* illustrate this mode of description very well, and so do numerous other "non-basic colour terms" such as *silver*, *navy blue*, *khaki*, *ash blond*, and so on. Another example is provided by some of the main colour terms in the Australian language Warlpiri: *yalyu-yalyu*, 'red' (lit. 'blood-blood'), *karntawara*, 'yellow' (lit. 'yellow ochre'), which, together with two "environmental" terms, *walya-walya*, 'brown' (lit. 'earth-earth') and *yukuri-yukuri*, 'green-blue' (lit. 'plants-plants'), and with something like 'dark/black' and 'light/white', form the core of the Warlpiri "colour" vocabulary (Hargrave 1982: 210).

But universals or near-universals such as those mentioned above could not be stated within the Berlin and Kay (1969) framework, with its emphasis on "basic" colour terms.

Shweder and Bourne (1984: 160) described Berlin and Kay's (1969) theory of "colour universals" as an example of the "data attenuation rule". They wrote:[1]

Not infrequently, the discovery of a universal is the product of a sophisticated process of data restriction and data attenuation. Berlin and Kay (1969), for example, discover universal prototypes for the definition of color categories, and a universal sequence for the emergence of a color lexicon. Their study begins with two applications of the data attenuation rule. First, "color" classification is equated with the task of partitioning a perceptual space, pre-defined in terms of hue, saturation, and intensity (thus, attenuating the referential range of the "color" concept as understood by, at least, some cultures (Conklin 1955)). Secondly, all color categories whose linguistic expression fails to meet certain formal criteria (e.g., superordination, monolexemic unity) are eliminated from consideration. The consequence of the application of these two data attenuation rules is that 95% of the world's expressions for color and most of the world's color categories are dropped from the investigation.

In the intervening time so much counter-evidence to Berlin and Kay's theory has been presented that one could no longer say that they discovered "universal prototypes for the definition of colour categories" or "a universal sequence for the emergence of a color lexicon" (see e.g. Kay *et al.* 1991; MacLaury 1987, 1992; Hewes 1992; Kinnear and Deregowski 1992; Saunders 1992; Toren 1992; van Brakel 1992, 1993).

I suggest that if we wish to discover, and to explain, the universals of human discourse on seeing, we must, so to speak, look in a direction different from that chosen in Berlin and Kay's (1969) classic and further explored in the huge body of research built on the foundations laid out in that work.

2. Meaning and Scientific Knowledge

The hardest things to observe are those which one sees every day. ("Il faut beaucoup de philosophie pour savoir observer une fois ce qu'on voit tous les jours"; Jean-Jacques Rousseau.[2]) The question "What do words like *red* and *blue* mean?" may sound, to many, offensively foolish. But in fact, it is

---

[1] Cf. also van Brakel's (1993: 112) comment: "all subsequent work in the Berlin and Kay tradition has been carried out with Munsell Colour Chips and standardized procedures to elicit BCTs [basic colour terms]. It has been estimated that in doing this 95% of the world's colour terms are eliminated."

[2] I borrow this quote from Moore and Carling (1982), who used it as one of the mottoes of their book.

very difficult to answer. Although the psychological, anthropological, and linguistic literature on colour terms is very extensive, it usually addresses itself to other questions. The simple, "naïve" question raised here tends to be largely overlooked—as simple and "naïve" questions concerning our everyday experience often are.

It is, of course, true that the meaning of colour terms has often been discussed by philosophers, and linguists and psychologists can profitably draw on the writings of thinkers such as Locke, Hume, Carnap, Russell, or Wittgenstein. But the philosopher's perspective is necessarily different from that of a psychologist and, even more, from that of a linguist. The crucial difference is that philosophers are interested in language, whereas linguists (*qua* linguists) are interested in languages. To a linguist, the problem is not only to discover what the (English) words *red* or *blue* mean, but also what the Hungarian words *vörös* and *piros* (roughly, types of red) mean, what the Russian words *goluboj* and *sinij* (roughly, types of blue) mean, what the Polish words *niebieski* and *granatowy* (roughly, also types of blue, but different from the Russian ones) mean, or what the Japanese word *aoi* (roughly, blue, but much broader in range than the English *blue*) means. Glosses such as *niebieski = blue* or *aoi = blue* or *sinij = blue* will clearly not do, since the range of each word is language-specific and cannot be correctly established on the basis of interlingual matching procedures of this kind.

But if *niebieski, sinij,* or *aoi* do not mean the same as *blue*, what do they mean? And what does *blue* mean, in the first place?

To some scholars, questions of this kind may seem foolish, because they believe that the meaning of every colour term can be identified in terms of physical properties of light such as wavelength or relative energy. For example: "When the wave lengths are between 400 and 470 nm [nanometres, 10^{-9} m], the field is reported to look violet for an average light level; around 475 nm it is seen as mostly blue" (Hurvich 1981: 39).

In fact, however, scientific knowledge of this kind is entirely beside the point, if we are interested in meaning, and if by meaning we understand, essentially, what people mean when they use the words in question. Clearly, when someone says *a blue dress, niebieska (FEM) sukienka* (Polish), or *sinee (NEUT) plat'e* (Russian), they may have no idea what wavelengths, or what relative energy, are associated with the words *blue, niebieski,* and *sinij*; and yet, surely, it would be foolish to conclude from this that they don't know what these words mean.

Scientific knowledge of wavelength associated with different colour terms is valuable in a textbook of physics, but when it is repeated in linguistic books and articles and presented as if it were an answer to questions about meaning, it only clouds the issue and stands in the way of our search for a real understanding of what people mean when they use these words. As pointed out by Russell (1948: 261), "names of colours were used for thousands of years before the undulatory theory of light was invented, and it was a genuine discovery that wave length grows shorter as we travel along the spectrum from red to violet". Should we conclude from this that for thousands of years people did not know what they meant when they used colour terms?

The same applies to the model representing colour sensations in terms of hue, brightness, and saturation generally accepted in chromatology, which, as the eminent Russian psycholinguist Frumkina points out, does not have any psychological reality:

A projection of the generally accepted scientific model of the description of colour sensations on to linguistic reality has given birth to an idea that the relations between colour terms (that is, between linguistic signs!) can be described via their denotata—entities from the realm of 'Reality' (that is, entities whose nature is entirely different from that of signs). It is important to stress here the word 'idea', because . . . we have found in the literature no actual description, carried out on this basis. This is hardly surprising: how could one, for example, describe by means of the three variables [hue, brightness, and saturation], the relations between *goluboj* ['light blue'] and *sinij* ['dark blue'], between *salatovyj* ['light green'] and *zelenyj* ['green'], or between *bežovyj* ['beige'] and *koričnevyj* ['brown']? Our knowledge of language tells us that *goluboj* is lighter than *sinij*, *salatovyj* lighter than *zelenyj*, and *bežovyj* lighter than *koričnevyj*. But 'lighter' cannot be translated, in any straightforward manner, as either 'brightness' or 'saturation'.   (Frumkina 1984: 24)

In my view, what applies to traditional chromatology applies also to more recent studies in the neurophysiology of colour perception, which, according to some scholars, can provide (or has already provided) a solution to the question of the meaning of colour terms. For example, Kay and McDaniel state that:

Research conducted in the past two decades has significantly increased our knowledge of the psychological processes which underlie the human perception of colour. This research is concerned, for the most part, with discovering how differences in the wavelength of light reaching the eye are transformed into response differences in the visual nervous system. . . . More recent studies of the visual processes have been concerned with the neural representation of colour at some remove from the retina, in the neural pathways between the eye and brain. These studies, which have used microelectrodes to monitor single neurons, indicate that, by the time wavelength-governed neural impulses reach lighter points in the visual pathway, the tripartite response of the retina's three-core system is transformed into a set of opponent neural responses.   (Kay and McDaniel 1978: 617)

This is all very interesting, but since the article in question is published in a linguistic journal, and since its title promises a paper devoted to the *meaning* of colour terms, one must ask the question: How are all those findings of neurophysiologists relevant to semantics? Kay and McDaniel appear to assume that progress in the understanding of the psychological processes which underlie human perception of colour must automatically lead to progress in our understanding of the meaning of colour terms. But why should this be so? They write:

Because hue, brightness, and saturation are all dimensions along which the neural responses that code colour vary, complete membership specifications for the fundamental neural response categories (*and hence the semantic categories defined in terms of them*), would require that membership in each of these categories be expressed as a function of all three dimensions. (1978: 629; emphasis added)

Thus, Kay and McDaniel simply assume that "semantic categories" should be defined in terms of "fundamental neural response categories", and that if something holds for the latter it automatically holds for the former.

The same leap from neurophysiology to semantics is evident in the following passage:

This and related observations developed below show that the meaning of basic colour terms cannot be accurately represented with discrete semantic features. We propose instead that colour categories, like the neurophysiological processes that underlie them, are continuous functions; and that a non-discrete formalism, in this instance fuzzy set theory, provides *the most concise* and *the most adequate* description of the semantics of basic colour terms. (1978: 612; emphasis added)

What the authors fail to take into account is that semantic categories differ from language to language. A description of colour categories which ignores this may indeed be "the most concise" one, but in what sense can it also be deemed "the most adequate" one?

To my mind, the question of the mechanics of colour *perception* has very little to do with the question of colour *conceptualization*. Colour perception is, by and large, the same for all human groupings (however, cf. Bornstein 1975). But colour conceptualization is different in different cultures, although there are also some striking similarities. Extreme universalism in the study of language and cognition is just as unfounded and just as dangerous as extreme cultural relativism. Whatever happens in the retina, and in the brain, it is not reflected directly in language. Language reflects what happens in the mind, not what happens in the brain; and our minds are shaped, partly, by our particular culture. Conceptual universals do exist, but they are found through conceptual analysis, based on data from many different languages of the world, not through research in neurophysiology. (See Bickerton 1981.)

To say this is not to deny that some aspects of our colour concepts may depend crucially on our common human biology, or that culture interacts with biology in the formation of colour concepts. I am only denying that we can elucidate our concepts in physiological terms. It is our brains, not our minds, which are shaped by our common human biology. The workings of our minds may, indirectly, reflect this; but the conceptualizations in our minds must be linked to something that can constitute the content of our thoughts.

The faith which some scholars have in the relevance of neurophysiology to the study of meaning can only be equalled by their faith in the relevance of formalisms. For example, Kay and McDaniel write:

We have found further that the facts of colour semantics are modelled felicitously in fuzzy set theory, and are not readily modelled in the traditional theory of discretely contrasting semantic features. This finding casts doubt on the general usefulness of the feature model, and suggests that more powerful formalisms, employing a range of structures much broader than the restricted Boolean algebra implicit in the discrete semantic-feature approach, are probably necessary to provide realistic accounts of the semantics of words.   (1978: 644)

The full title of their article reads: "The Linguistic Significance of the Meaning of Basic Colour Terms". This implies that the authors know what the meaning of basic colour terms is; and that they are going to build on that knowledge (which, one is to understand, has emerged from the neurophysiological research reported in the article). But all the reader is told, at the end, is that the authors believe that the facts of colour semantics can be modelled felicitously in fuzzy set theory, and perhaps in some other "powerful mathematical formalisms".

In my view, if some scholars are interested in translating linguistic facts into "powerful mathematical formalisms" (such as, for example, fuzzy set theory) they have every right to do so, but I do not think that by doing so they are bringing us any closer to discovering what words *mean*.

3. Meaning and Colour Charts

Another popular approach to the semantics of colour terms is based on the identification of meanings with denotata. One recalls in this connection the scholars from Swift's *Gulliver's Travels* (1728), who believed that verbal explanations could be replaced with the demonstration of denotata, and who carried everything they wanted to talk about on their backs. In the same vein, it is proposed that instead of defining colour terms in different languages we can simply produce samples of colours themselves. In particular, great faith is placed in commercially produced colour chips such as those which were used by Berlin and Kay (1969) in their investigation of universals of colour naming.

To some linguists it seems self-evident that the method which initially at least seemed to produce so much insight in Berlin and Kay's investigation of colour universals provides also an obvious solution to the problem of the meaning of colour terms. The attitude of these linguists can be portrayed as follows: What do words such as *blue, niebieski,* or *goluboj* mean? Simple: we can show this by circling appropriate areas in a universal colour chart. For words such as *blue, niebieski,* and *goluboj* these areas may overlap, but since they will not coincide with one another, the language-specific range of each word's use will be correctly accounted for.

But Berlin and Kay achieved the apparent success they did because they were investigating not the meaning of colour terms but the interlanguage stability of colour foci—and the method they chose seemed initially appropriate for the task which they had set themselves. They saw clearly, however, that their method was totally inappropriate for the investigation of colour boundaries. Thus, they wrote:

Repeated mapping trials with the same informant and also across informants showed that category foci placements are highly reliable. . . . Category boundaries, however, are not reliable, even for repeated trials with the same informant. (Berlin and Kay 1969: 13)

They concluded:

it is possible that the brain's primary storage procedure for the physical reference of colour categories is concerned with points (or very small volumes) of the colour solid rather than extended volumes. Secondary processes, of lower salience and intersubjective homogeneity, would then account for the extensions of reference to points of the colour solid not equivalent to (or included in) the focus. Current formal theories of lexical definitions are not able to deal naturally with such phenomena. (ibid.)

I believe that in 1969 this conclusion was correct; and that the concomitant decision not to pursue, at that time, speculations about the meaning of colour terms was prudent and justified. I think, however, that in the course of the intervening twenty years, enough progress has been made in the areas of both the theory and practice of lexical definition to enable us to tackle the problem which in 1969 may have—rightly—appeared intractable; Berlin and Kay had every right to limit their attention to colour foci, and to choose not to explore colour boundaries. But if we wish to reveal the concepts encoded in the colour lexicons of different languages of the world we have to take into account both the foci and the boundaries.

But to return for the moment to the possibility of "showing" the meaning of colour terms in colour charts, consider also Frumkina's observations:

any colour model is characterized by some degree of indeterminacy, as far as its possible naming is concerned. Often, people who are not professional colour experts . . . i.e. who have nothing to do with the science of colour or with other areas of knowledge where precision in the naming of colour perceptions is important, will not be able to find any intuitively satisfying colour terms to designate a given 'colour model'. In other cases, they will propose several terms for one colour model. Since in practice there are situations where denotative indeterminacy of colour designations and 'naming' indeterminacy of colour models may be very inconvenient, special normative charts are produced, which show what colour designations should be given to a given colour model. For example, the charts of the British Colour Council, 1939–1942, have such a normative character. Charts of this kind have purely pragmatic goals; for example, to achieve mutual understanding in the description of different genres and species of plants it is necessary to ensure, in an artificial manner, one-to-one correspondence between colour designation and colour models, despite the fact that in natural languages the correspondence is commonly of the many-to-many type. The charts of the British Colour Council, just like other normative charts, are a terminological guidebook, whose validity is strictly limited to that domain for which it was prepared, so that, for example, the nomenclature of colour designations for colour photo-reproduction (i.e. the system of pairs: colour designation–colour model) requires already a separate guidebook. (Frumkina 1984: 26)

Frumkina concludes:

The problem of colour naming, that is of assigning colour designations to specific colour models, deserves separate investigation as one aspect of the problem of naming in general. As for the possibility of describing colour designations by means of pictures, the fact that the relations between colour designations and colour models are of the many-to-many kind makes it rather unrealistic. (1984: 27)

This echoes Conklin's (1973: 940) remark: "There is obviously more to the study of colour categorisation than the matching of spectrographic readings with human verbal responses." I would add to this that the use of pictures and colour charts can be useful in the investigation of meaning if one makes proper use of them, without placing unreasonable demands on them. They cannot automatically show the meaning of a colour term, but they may help establish what the meaning of a colour term is. For example, Jones and Meehan (1978), who investigated the use of the two basic colour terms (-*gungaltja* and -*gungundja*) in the Australian Aboriginal language Gu-jingarliya with the help of the Munsell charts, obtained results which are indeed highly instructive from a semantic point of view. But they are instructive because they raise fascinating questions, not because they yield any ready-made answers.

Equally instructive is the fact (which the chart itself cannot show) of how the data were obtained:

At first, Gurmanamana (the informant) said there were no -*gungaltja* colours there at all and pointed from the chart to a piece of reflective foil used for coding, lying on a bench in the tent. 'That one here, properly number one *gun-gungaltja*, no more this mob.' . . . Having made his protest, Gurmanamana then proceeded to outline the approximate boundary of the -*gungaltja* colours as shown in Fig. 2 [not reproduced here]. It can be seen that only about 10% of colour chips are included in this category, the main bulk of the chart belonging to the -*gungundja* class. (Jones and Meehan 1978: 27)

The question of what the words *-gungaltja* and *-gungundja* mean is a fascinating one, and I believe it is the kind of question that is more pertinent to linguistic research than any questions concerning the neurophysiological bases of colour perception, important and interesting as the latter may be in their own right. I will return to this question later, after I have discussed the meaning of the English colour terms *white*, *black*, *blue*, *green*, *red*, and *yellow*, and their closest counterparts in a few other languages with complex colour lexicons. First, however, I should like to clarify what I mean by "meaning", and how "meaning" is related to "psychological reality".

4. Meaning and Psychological Reality

The meaning of a word can, roughly speaking, be defined as what people mean, or have in mind when they use it.[3] Since what they mean or have in mind may differ somewhat depending on context and situation, we should specify that "meaning" has to do with the constant, not with the variable, aspects of a word's use. These constant aspects can be ascertained in a variety of ways, including a methodical introspective study, a study of common phraseology, common metaphors, questioning of informants, psycholinguistic experiments of different kinds, and so on. All these methods reveal that, in the speakers' minds, words are mutually related in different ways, and they allow us to establish how they are related (see Wierzbicka 1985: 193–211).

For example, Frumkina (1984: 30) reports that she asked a number of informants to explain to her "what pink (*rozovyj*) is" and that she obtained from them the following kind of answer: "Pink is a very, very light red (*krasnyj*) colour, quite light, but sufficiently specific for people to be able to see that it is similar to red or has a shade like red." In Frumkina's view, answers of this kind help us to reveal "the organization of meanings in the speaker's linguistic consciousness". I believe this is correct, and I think that an adequate semantic description of the word *pink* (or *rozovyj*) should reflect its intuitive link with the concept encoded in the word *red* (or *krasnyj*) and with that encoded in the word *light* (or *svetlyj*).

It is important to keep in mind, however, that "linguistic consciousness" has many different levels and that while there are facts which lie on its very surface there are others which are buried deeply, even very deeply, under the surface. As was stressed forcefully by Boas (1911/1966: 63–4) and Sapir (1949: 46–7), and more recently by Halliday (1987), native speakers'

---

[3] Of course one could also define the term "meaning" in many other ways (see e.g. Ogden and Richards 1923), and I have no desire to argue about terminology. But the question of "what people mean" (when they use a particular word) is clearly a very important and worthwhile question to ask. Obviously, neurophysiology cannot answer questions like that.

knowledge of their language is, by and large, subconscious. It is important to distinguish tacit knowledge, which is hidden "in the depths" of a person's mind but which can be dragged to the surface (see Sapir 1949: 331), from scientific knowledge, which native speakers simply do not have and which no amount of searching could ever reveal. The latter, in contrast to the former, is not reflected in language and plays no role in the linguistic patterning. (See Chapters 11 and 12.)

Semantics is a search for meaning, not a search for scientific or encyclopaedic knowledge; but this does not mean that it is concerned only with facts which lie on the surface, or very near the surface, of speakers' consciousness. If we confuse "psychological reality" (see Burling 1969) with "consciousness" we shall never find out what goes on in people's minds and what conceptualizations are reflected in human languages.

Let us consider, for example, the following facts, reported by Frumkina (1984: 30): "While for Russian informants, *rozovyj* 'pink' and *krasnyj* 'red' are similar in colour . . ., *želtyj* 'yellow' and *koričnevyj* 'brown' are (for them) simply different colours, just as different as *krasnyj* 'red' and *fioletovyj* 'purple'." Should we then conclude from this that an adequate semantic description of Russian colour terms should present *krasnyj* and *fioletovyj* as totally unrelated—as unrelated as, say, *želtyj* and *fioletovyj*, or *zelenyj*, 'green', and *fioletovyj*?

I think that we should not. It is important, I believe, not to draw hasty conclusions from anything that informants may tell us. Rather, we should take their initial responses as one kind of evidence, to be used jointly with other kinds of evidence. Informants' responses should never be taken at face value; they should be interpreted and made sense of (see Wierzbicka 1985: 89–90; see also Chapter 12 Section 2).[4]

5. Colour Terms as Quotations

Once again, then: what do people mean when they say, for example, "I bought a blue dress" or "I saw a blue car"?

One "common-sense" answer to this question takes the following form. "Colour terms are learnt ostensively, and their meaning is also based on ostension. We have all heard the word *blue* applied to a variety of objects

---

[4] It should be emphasized, however, that "folk comments", as well as folk definitions, can provide precious insight into the meaning of colour terms. To see this, consider, for example, an informant's comments on the word *layi-layi*, 'grey', in the Australian language Warlpiri: "When a gum tree is first in good condition, in its foliage, it is first green. But if it should then (die and) dry up, its leaves would then become grey [i.e. *layi-layi*] . . . *Layi-layi* that is dry grass and dry foliage, old dry leaves. And *layi-layi* is white hair of people, that white . . . We also refer to old people as *layi-layi*" (Simpson 1989: 2). Clearly, the concept encoded in the Warlpiri word *layi-layi* is not the same as that encoded in the English word *grey*.

—and we have learnt, on this basis, what people mean by *blue*. *Blue* means 'what people call blue'."

I believe that an answer along these lines is probably correct, as far as it goes (although, as I shall argue shortly, it does not go very far). In particular, it is important to note that an answer along these lines is not circular, as it is not circular to say that, for example, the word *John* in the sentence referring to some particular person called John, means, roughly, "the person whom I call JOHN" (where JOHN, in capital letters, refers not to a person but a sound). Assuming, then, that colour terms are learnt, essentially, by ostension, and that their meaning reflects this, we could propose, as a starting-point for further discussion, the following explication:

X is blue. =
people say of things like *X*: "this is BLUE"

A formula of this kind represents the colour term as a kind of proper name: it implies that just as the word *John* means, essentially, "the person called JOHN", the word *blue* means, essentially, "the colour called BLUE".

Since to understand a word like *blue* one must know that this word has something to do with seeing (rather than, say, with hearing or tasting), we could expand our first formula as follows:

X is blue. =
when people see things like *X* they say of them: this is BLUE

It seems reasonable to suppose that a formula of this kind may reflect the child's first meaning of the word *blue*; and it is important to note that to sketch such a formula we do not even need the word *colour*, which, one must surmise, would be normally acquired much later than *blue* or *red*. (As pointed out by Leibniz (1966), the concept of colour is not indefinable: it can be defined via seeing, since colour is the only property which we can perceive only by seeing.[5])

Since, however, the formula sketched above refers to some specific models (such as a particular object "*X*", which would be different in each person's individual experience) without attempting to draw any boundaries, it cannot have full predictive power with respect to an adult's use of the word *blue*. After all, things that people call *green* or *purple* can also be seen as similar to those which they call *blue*—and yet mature speakers of English do not extend their use of the word *blue* to objects which they call *green*. As it stands, the formula sketched above does not account for this.

In learning a second language, we often acquire the boundaries with the help of negative feedback. For example, my daughters, who are bilingual

---

[5] The concept of 'colour' is actually quite complex, and I will not attempt a definition here. It is clear, however, that a definition of 'colour' would have to be based on the concept of SEEing.

but who live in an English-speaking environment and for whom English is their primary language, as children tended to extend the range of the Polish word *niebieski* ('blue', from *niebo* 'sky') to dark shades which in English are still called *blue*, but which in Polish would have to be described as *granatowy*, not as *niebieski*. When they did this, I corrected them: "not *niebieski*, *granatowy*". (See also Bartlett 1978.)

I don't know what role corrections of this kind may play in the acquisition of the first language; presumably, a more limited one. It is known, however, that in the first language, too, a child's lexicon of basic colour words is more limited than that of an adult, and that—from the adult's point of view—children "over-extend" even words such as *yellow* and *blue*, let alone *brown, pink, purple, orange,* or *grey*. (See Harkness 1973: 183; E. R. Heider 1972*b*.) This suggests that in the speakers' consciousness or subconsciousness, neighbouring terms may delimit one another's range, to some extent (although the boundaries are, of course, fuzzy).

In his discussion of the logic of colour terms, Bertrand Russell wrote:

We certainly know—though it is difficult to say how we know—that two different colours cannot coexist at the same place in one visual field. . . . More simply 'this is red' and 'this is blue' are incompatible. The incompatibility is not logical. Red and blue are no more *logically* incompatible than red and round. Nor is the incompatibility a generalisation from experience. I do not think I can *prove* that it is not a generalisation from experience, but I think this is so obvious that no one, nowadays, would deny it. Some people say the incompatibility is grammatical. I do not deny this, but I am not sure what it means.   (Russell 1965: 78)

Quoting this passage in my *Lexicography and Conceptual Analysis* (Wierzbicka 1985: 79–80; see also Wierzbicka 1990*a*) I suggested that the incompatibility between *red* and *blue* is in fact semantic, and I proposed semantic components to that effect, along the following lines:

X is blue. =
when people see some things they say of them: this is BLUE
X is like this
when people see other things they say some other things of them
they don't say these other things of *X*

I have come to doubt, however, whether "exclusionary" components of this kind are really necessary, for a number of reasons. First, not all pairs of "basic colour terms" are felt to be incompatible in the same way and to the same degree. For example, *white* and *black* are felt to be opposites, whereas *red* and *blue* are not. Furthermore, *red* and *pink*, though incompatible, are felt to be closely related, whereas, again, *red* and *blue* are not.

Even more importantly, some "basic colour terms" may not be mutually exclusive at all. For example, in Japanese both the terms *aoi* 'blue, blue-green, shining green' and *midori* 'green' appear to be "basic", and yet they are not mutually exclusive. (We could, of course, define the notion of a "basic colour term" in such a way as to make mutual exclusiveness mandatory, but this would be entirely arbitrary.)

Furthermore, exclusion follows, anyway, from identification (as argued in Goddard 1993). A person referred to as JOHN is normally not referred to as "Harry". This does mean that when I refer to someone as "John" I mean 'the person whom I call JOHN and whom I don't call anything else'; the shorter formula: 'the person whom I call JOHN' is sufficient. But if an explicit "exclusionary" component is not necessary for proper names, it is probably not necessary for colour terms either and a rudimentary formula such as 'X is blue = when people see things like X they say of them: this is BLUE' may be essentially correct (not for all colour terms but at least for the "abstract" ones, such as *red, blue, green, yellow, black,* and *white*).

Van Brakel (1993: 132) writes: "So perhaps . . . what all green objects have in common is that we've learnt to call them 'green' and what all *kwaalt* (roughly, 'yellow-green', a Shuswap term on the N.S. Pacific coast, which astonished MacLaury (1987)) objects have in common is that Shuswap speakers have learnt to call them *kwaalt* and can teach us which things are *kwaalt*, just as we can teach them which objects are green."

I think this is probably true; but, as I shall argue below, this is not the whole truth.

6. "Black" and "White", "Dark" and "Light"

If we say only that *white* means, essentially, "what people call WHITE", and *black* "what people call BLACK", we will fail to account for the fact that these words are felt to be opposites, and also for the fact that they are felt to be closely related to *dark* and *light*. For example, one can form in English compounds such as *light blue* or *dark blue*, but one cannot form compounds such as **light white* or **dark black*. Nor, for that matter, can one call something **dark white* or **light black*. The expressions *dark white* and *light black* sound self-contradictory, whereas *light white* and *dark black* sound foolishly tautologous.

To account for these facts we have to analyse both pairs of adjectives into components, and to see what they have in common.

I believe that (as hinted earlier) the clue to the semantics of *dark* and *light* lies in the concept of seeing, and that the prototypical use of these words has to do not with any objects but with the ambience. We say, above all:

It was (already) dark. It was (still) light.

Sentences including expressions such as "a dark ball" or "a light flower" seem neither as common or as natural as sentences with the words *dark* or *light* referring to the ambience.

One can also speculate that in children's speech the words *light* and *dark* refer, predominantly, if not exclusively, to the ambient, not to colours. Although I have no data to support these speculations, it is hard to imagine small children talking about a "dark dress" or a "light dress", whereas sentences such as the one quoted earlier (by a two-year-old, Bloom 1991), "I was crying because I didn't want to wake up, because it was dark, so dark" are of course well attested.

But what do we mean when we say that "it was (already) dark" or that "it was still light"? I would suggest that we mean something along the following lines:

> It was dark (at that time). =
> at some times people can't see much
> it was like this at that time

> It was light (at that time). =
> at some times people can see many things
> it was like this at that time

It could be argued, quite plausibly, that these definitions are too broad, and that they could be linked explicitly with, roughly speaking, daytime and night-time, along the following lines:

> It was dark (at that time). =
> at some times people can't see much
> because the sun is not in the sky
> it was like this at that time

> It was light (at that time). =
> at some times people can see many things
> because the sun is in the sky
> it was like this at that time

The matter requires further consideration.

For sentences referring to "dark" and "light" objects, we could then propose explications along the following lines:[6]

---

[6] The word *one* in the sense used here has no place in the Natural Semantic Metalanguage, and should, strictly speaking, be replaced with *someone*, along the following lines:

> when someone sees things like X, this someone
> (this person) can think of times of this kind

I have decided to use *one*, rather than *someone*, however, to make the explications easier to read.

X is dark. =
at some times people can't see much
when one sees things like *X* one can think of this

X is light (in colour).[7] =
at some times people can see many things
when one sees things like *X* one can think of this

I do not think that the words *dark* and *light* (as colour designations) are
learnt by ostension, with reference to some objects which provide models
of "a dark colour" or "a light colour". If there is a model of "darkness",
or a model of "lightness", it is to be found in the darkness of the night, or
in the light of the day. To put it differently, seeing dark objects reminds us
of the experience of seeing things at a time when it is dark; and seeing light
objects reminds us of the experience of seeing things at a time when it is
light. It is interesting to note in this connection that in some languages, for
example in the Australian Aboriginal language Luritja, one of the two basic
colour terms ("light" and "dark") is in fact identical with the word for
night-time (Ian Green, personal communication); and also that in Alice
Springs Aboriginal English, night is often called "dark time" (Jean Harkins,
personal communication).

Turning now to the English words *black* and *white*, I would suggest that
their semantic structure would reflect both their status of "basic colour
terms learnt by ostension" and their association with the concepts 'dark'
and 'light'. (Cf. Leonardo da Vinci's comment made in his "Treatise on
Painting": "We shall set down white for the representative of light, without
which no color can be seen; . . . and black for total darkness"; quoted in
Birren 1978: 4). As a first approximation (to be refined later) I would propose the following:

X is black. [partial explication]
when people see some things they say of them: this is BLACK
X is like this
at some times people can't see anything
because the sun is not in the sky
when one sees things like *X* one can think of this

For *white* (of which more will be said later) we could initially consider a
symmetrical explication:

X is white. [partial explication]
when people see some things they say of them: this is WHITE
X is like this

---

[7] One could also consider explicating 'light' via 'dark', so to speak (because even in broad
daylight, dark things still look dark, whereas when it is dark, even light things look dark).

at some times people can see very many things
because the sun is in the sky
when one sees things like *X* one can think of this

Explications of this kind account both for the intuitively felt antonymous relation between *black* and *white*, and for the intuitively felt links between *black* and *dark*, and between *white* and *light*. They do not imply that people think of the day as "something white" and of the night as "something black", as they might think of snow as something white and of charcoal as something black. Nor do they imply that white objects necessarily make us think of daylight, and black objects, of the darkness of the night. But they do imply a potential conceptual link: "when one sees things like this one can think of . . .".

There are good reasons to think, however, that the meanings of *black* and *white* should not be presented as fully symmetrical. The association between *black* and *night* is no doubt more straightforward and more transparent than that between *white* and *day*. The link between *white* and high visibility seems intuitively indubitable, but it is not white itself which is highly visible. Red and orange are no doubt more visible, or more obvious, than white. On the other hand, white provides the best background for all other colours: all other colours are better visible in "broad daylight" (in Polish, *w biały dzień*, 'in white day') than at dusk, and also they are better visible in places which provide a white visual background, such as, for example, a snowy landscape or the white paper on which we write or type. To account for this property of *white* as the best possible background for objects of all kinds (other than white) we could consider adding to its explication some further components along the following lines:

X is white. [partial explication]
in some places, people can see very many things
when one sees things like *X*, one can think of this

It should be added, however, that 'white' is a much more complex, and more problematic, concept than 'black', no doubt because 'black' has a universal prototype in a "pitch-black" (very dark) night, whereas 'white' doesn't have a similarly uniform universal prototype in a very bright day (because when it is very light people see lots of different colours), and may in fact embody in its meaning two very different points of reference: a temporal one (day versus night) and a spatial one (a white wintry landscape, covered with snow).

As mentioned earlier, snow (unlike day) cannot be a universal reference-point in the semantics of vision, but of course 'white' is not a universal concept either. For English, and for other languages which do have a semantic equivalent of the English word *white*, a snowy landscape seems a plausible reference-point, of course not as a necessary feature of every individual's personal experience but as a feature of the collective memory of speakers of English, reflected in their shared semantic universe (see expressions such as *snow-white*, *snowy white*, or *Snow White*, and *white Christmas*).

A number of observations about the concept 'white' made in the literature appear to support this suggestion. Thus 'white' is often described as a "surface colour", not a "volume colour" (see e.g. Westphal 1987: 14; Katz 1935: 7); a colour which "more than any other colour, offers resistance to the eye" (Westphal 1987: 14). It is also described as a quintessentially "opaque" colour, incompatible with transparency.

"White is an opaque colour", noted Wittgenstein (1977: 4), and he puzzled: "Why is it that something can be transparent green but not transparent white?" (1977: 5).

It seems to me that the prototype of the ground covered with snow explains, to some extent at least, intuitive observations of this kind. For if "white" is "the lightest of colours" (Wittgenstein 1977: 2), and is that "which does away with darkness" (1977: 15), this is explained by the fundamental contrast between day and night (roughly speaking, the night is "black", the day is the opposite of the night, and "white" is the opposite of "black"). But if "white" is also "opaque", a barrier to the eye, surely this is consistent with the image of snow covering and "hiding" the ground? The "blue" of the sky, or the "yellow" of the sun, can hardly be thought of as a "barrier" between the eye and something else; the green of the vegetation is also something that one can normally see through (except in the thickest jungle); and of course deep waters of the sea, or of a lake, are anything but opaque. But the white expanse of snow is indeed an exceedingly light and yet opaque "barrier" to the eye, a covering of the ground, which cannot be seen through, although it sets off, and lightens, the visibility of all "figures" visible against this light and opaque background.

Finally, it is worth noting that "black" and "white" are by no means symmetrical in the world's languages, and that "black" is a more common term than "white". For example, Hargrave (1982: 211) writes this of the Australian language Martu Wangka:

The primary question raised by the data in comparison with [Berlin and Kay's] colour-encoding sequence is the absence of a basic term for white—or even for 'macro-white'. According to the sequence, a language with two basic colour terms has the categories 'macro-black' and 'macro-white', and foci for the latter can be expected to vary between white and red, while the former may have foci in black, green or blue (Kay and McDaniel 1978: 639). The Martu Wangka data, however, show clear categories focused in black and red. Twenty-two participants *did* focus a colour term in the pure white area, but a variety of terms were used, and five participants used two or three terms. In all, twelve different terms were used which were focused in white.

Hargrave notes further that "This same lack of agreement on a term for white is found in the Warlpiri area" (1982: 212), and she concludes:

The above data suggest that Aboriginal groups who were traditionally desert nomads did not abstract the colour white as a separate property of a variety of natural phenomena, and therefore it cannot be considered a basic colour term in their language.

When Wittgenstein wrote that "white is an opaque colour" (1977: 4), that "transparent white is impossible" (1977: 19), and that "white water is inconceivable" (1977: 5), he was clearly thinking of the German word *weiss* ('white'). But the words from other languages glossed in English as *white* may have a different image. For example, Alexandra Aikhenvald (personal communication) reports that in the Tariana language of Brazil the word for "white" (*halite*) means also 'transparent' (as well as 'light'). Likewise, Birren (1978: 3) quotes (in English) the following (somewhat puzzling) line from the Upanishads: "The red color of burning fire is the color of fire, the white color of fire is the color of water, the black color of fire is the color of earth". Then, while the experience of snow is of course far from universal, so is the idea of an opaque, "surface colour", 'white'.

7. *Green*, *gwyrdd* (Welsh), *latuy* (Hanunóo)

In many languages of the world, the nearest equivalent of the English word *green* is either morphologically or etymologically related to words for grass, herbs, or vegetation in general. For example, in Polish the word *zielony* is etymologically derived from *zioło*, 'herb'. In Warlpiri (as mentioned earlier) the word for "green" or "green-blue" is a reduplication of the word for plants. In fact, even the English word *green* is believed to be etymologically related to *grow* (see Swadesh 1972; Klein 1966).

Native speakers of English, when asked to give some examples of green, usually mention grass, leaves, or fresh vegetation (most commonly, grass). This does not mean that their range of greens is restricted to the colour of grass, or even more generally, to the colours of vegetation; but it seems reasonably clear that they do associate the concept encapsulated in the word *green* with vegetation ("things growing out of the ground"). To account for this, I would propose the following (partial) explanation of this concept:

> *X* is green. =
> in some places many things grow out of the ground
> when one sees things like *X* one can think of this

I have deliberately refrained from using here the phrase "*X* is like this" because there are shades which native speakers of English would be prepared to call *green* although they would be reluctant to liken them to the colour of vegetation. None the less, a vaguer association of the kind implied by the explication sketched above seems to be valid.

But the association with "things growing out of the ground" is no doubt valid not only for the English word *green* and for its semantic equivalents in other languages (such as, for example, the Polish word *zielony*), but also for the nearest counterparts of *green* in languages in which this word does not have exact semantic equivalents.

For example, in Welsh the nearest counterpart of *green* is *gwyrdd*, whose range of application is narrower than that of *green*: and some English "greens" are lexically identified with "blues" in Welsh (see Hjelmslev 1953: 53). I do not have enough information on Welsh to interpret these facts in a very informed way, but it would appear that Welsh restricts *gwyrdd* to relatively livelier, brighter, fresher greens. Trying to account for this in terms of an intuitively plausible prototype, I would propose (as a starting-point for discussion) the following (partial) explication:

X is gwyrdd. =
in some places many things grow out of the ground
at some times there is water in these places (after rain)
when one sees things like *X* one can think of this

The reference to "wetness after rain" brings to mind, I think, fresh, glistening vegetation, more consistent with the range of *gwyrdd* than a mere reference to "things growing out of the ground". But it is not so much wet vegetation as such that is offered here is a point of reference; rather, it is a prototypical situation: "things are growing out of the ground, rain comes, everything gets wet, and then everything glistens with wetness". The whole script brings to mind a vivid, natural greenness evoked also by the images and phrases associated with Welsh culture lore ("How green was my valley . . ."). Of course, the referential boundaries of *gwyrdd* are as "fuzzy" as those of *green*; but the different phrasing of the conceptual reference-points suggests, in each case, a somewhat different range of reference.

The references to vegetation in the case of *green*, and to vegetation and wetness in the case of *gwyrdd*, may seem rather speculative, but they are both clearly evidenced in the case of the Hanunóo word *latuy*, described by Conklin (1964: 191) as "light green and mixtures of green, yellow, and light brown", the colour "which is most tangibly visible in their [the Hanunóos'] jungle surroundings", and whose focal point is "near light- or yellow-green".

Conklin shows that *latuy* is clearly associated both with plants and with wetness. Hanunóo has four basic colour terms, which can be loosely glossed as "dark/black", "light/white", "red", and "green/light green". "Green" is seen as opposed to "red" in terms of wetness versus dryness.

There is an opposition between dryness or desiccation and wetness or freshness (succulence) in visible components of the natural environment which are reflected in the terms *rara?* ['red'] and *latuy* respectively. This distinction is of particular significance in terms of plant life. Almost all living plant types possess some fresh, succulent, and often 'greenish' parts. To eat any kind of raw, uncooked food, particularly fresh fruits or vegetables, is known as *pag-laty-un* (*latuy*). A shiny, wet, brown-coloured section of newly-cut bamboo is *malatuy* (not *marara?*). Dried-out or matured plant material such as certain kinds of yellowed bamboo or hardened kernels of mature or parched corn are *marara?*. (Conklin 1964: 191)

On the basis of Conklin's comments I propose the following tentative explication:

X is latuy. =
in some places many things grow out of the ground
there is something like water in these things
when one sees things like *X* one can think of this

In this case, unlike the case of the Welsh *gwyrdd*, "juiciness" rather than external wetness appears to be part of the conceptual model. (I doubt if "a shiny, wet, brown-coloured section of newly-cut bamboo" could be called *gwyrdd*.) It is also interesting to note that although Hanunóo doesn't have a separate word for "blue", its word for "green" does not extend towards blue at all, dark blues being categorized with "black", and light blues with "white". The association between *latuy* and "juicy plants", which I propose as a part of the meaning of this word, is consistent with this fact.

Conklin's illuminating description of Hanunóo makes it particularly clear that the use of colour charts are not a suitable method for showing the meaning of colour terms. To understand words such as *latuy* and *rara?* we have to understand the conceptual prototypes to which these words refer. The prototype of *latuy* refers to fresh, juicy plants, whereas the association between redness and dryness can be explained if we assume that the word *rara?* refers, in its semantic structure, to fire and to burning. Munsell's colour chips cannot account for facts of this kind, but verbal explications can.

Of course one could say that the "wetness" implied by *latuy* is a separate semantic feature, which can be added to a description in terms of hue, brightness, and saturation. But the evidence presented by Conklin suggests that in the speakers' mind this "wetness" or "juiciness" is not an independent semantic feature: rather, it is an integral part of the same prototype which determines the kind of greenness associated with this word (vivid, warm, succulent, ripe, closer to yellows and to light brown than to blues).[8]

What applies to Hanunóo applies also, *mutatis mutandis*, to the Shuswap term *kwaalt*, 'yellow-green', which was mentioned earlier, and which,

---

[8] See in this connection Toren's (1992: 169) remark: "colour naming should not be abstracted from other domains of classification as if it formed a discrete system; for example, the Hanunóo *warm* and *cold* categories, with their connotations of desiccation and succulence . . . suggest a connection with plant classification, for which Hanunóo are renowned, rather than with colour as such".

"Much to the amazement of MacLaury (1987) reporting this fact . . . 'contradicts present physiological knowledge' " (van Brakel 1993: 118). To van Brakel's highly pertinent question "Would it really be possible that the meaning of a word in a far-away-culture contradicts our *physiological* knowledge?" I would add my own: Isn't it likely that in the natural surroundings of the Shuswap people there is something that is visually salient and that is 'yellow-green' (perhaps sun-burnt grasslands, like those which define the yellow-green Australian landscape)?

8. *Blue, niebieski* (Polish), *goluboj* and *sinij* (Russian), *aoi* (Japanese), and *fáa* (Thai)

In numerous languages of the world, the nearest equivalent of the English word *blue* is morphologically, or etymologically, related to the word for sky. For example, the Polish word *niebieski* is derived from *niebo*, 'sky', and the Latin *caeruleus* is derived from the word *caelum*, 'sky'. Words of this kind imply a clear association between the colour concept in question and the concept of "sky". The English word *blue* and the Japanese word *aoi* are not similarly related to the words for sky, but (judging by informants' responses) in these languages, too, there is a strong association between the colour terms and the concept of 'sky': when asked to give some examples of something *blue*, or of something *aoi*, informants invariably mention the sky. To account for these facts, I would propose not only for *niebieski* and *caeruleus*, but also for *blue* and *aoi*, the following semantic component:

> *X* is blue/aoi/niebieski/caeruleus. =
> at some times people can see the sun above them in the sky
> when one sees things like *X* one can think of the sky at these times

However, although words such as *blue, aoi* or *niebieski* are all semantically related to the concept 'sky', they are not identical in meaning, since the range of each of these words is unique. For example, as mentioned earlier, *niebieski* refers only to light and medium dark blues, not to very dark blues (which in English would still be called *blue*). To account for this, I would assign to *blue*, but not to *niebieski*, an additional reference-point: naturally occurring "big water places", such as the sea or lakes (especially seen from afar). This allows us to contrast the meaning of *niebieski* and *blue* as follows:

> *X* is niebieski. =
> (*a*) at some times people can see the sun above them in the sky
>   when one sees things like *X* one can think of the sky at these times
> *X* is blue. =

(a) at some times people can see the sun above them in the sky
  when one sees things like X one can think of the sky at these times
(b) in some places there is a lot of (very much) water
  when people are far from these places
  they can see this water
  when one sees things like X one can think of this

I have refrained from using in the explication of *blue* the phrase "X is like this" because people can distinguish the colour "blue" from the specific shade "sky-blue". None the less, I believe that a vaguer, more general association between *blue* and *sky* is valid, and my informal questioning of a number of informants confirms this.

I recognize that the "best", focal *blue* is darker than *sky-blue*, and more "vivid" than the "blue" of the sea. Its exact shade may indeed depend on some properties of the human perceptual apparatus rather than on the shades prevalent in the human environment, such as the sky or "big water places visible from afar". But the range of *blue* is language-specific and so it cannot be explained in purely biological terms. On the other hand, we can account for it if we assume that the concept *blue* does not have the kind of structure which is characteristic of the compound *sky-blue*, or of *apricot* or *pea* (as colour terms): it does not provide an exemplar, it only provides some points of reference.[9]

Polish has no phrase like "sky-blue", but it has a more specific adjective, *błękitny*, which is associated primarily with the sky. Accordingly, I have not used the phrase "*X* is like this" for the Polish word *niebieski* either, and I have used instead the vaguer formula: "one can think of".

Let us turn now to the two Russian counterparts of *blue*, that is, to *sinij*, 'dark blue', and *goluboj*, 'light blue'. Berlin and Kay (1969: 367) have raised some doubts about the "basic" character of *goluboj*, referring to some evidence showing that among Russian children *goluboj* is less salient than *sinij* (Istomina 1963). However, there is also some evidence showing that among Spanish children, the word for "blue" is less salient than the word for "yellow", which in turn is less salient than the word for "green" (see Harkness 1973); and yet all of these words are regarded as basic colour terms. Furthermore, Frumkina (1984: 31) reports that Russians are invariably surprised when they learn that English has only one word for both *goluboj* and *sinij* (i.e. *blue*). This suggests, it seems to me, that they perceive both *sinij* and *goluboj* as "basic". She also notes: "Some informants—educated native speakers of Russian—don't want to regard the words *koričnevyj*, 'brown', and *seryj*, 'grey', as basic 'because they are absent among the colours of the

---

[9] It is interesting to note, none the less, that according to van Brakel (1993: 114), "English speakers often volunteer two foci for 'blue' (one dark and one light)."

rainbow'." They are all convinced, however, that *goluboj* and *sinij* are there. (See also Corbett and Morgan 1988; Moss 1989.)

I believe that the semantic relationship between *goluboj* and *sinij* (and also between both these words and the English word *blue*) can be satisfactorily accounted for if we show, in the explications, that all three words refer to the sky, but that *goluboj* is directly likened to the sky, whereas *sinij* is said not to be "like the sky" although it can make people think of the sky, while *blue* is unspecified in this respect (so that it can include both the *sky-blue* and the *non-sky-blue* shades of the sky–sea range). In addition, the formulae proposed below link *goluboj* directly with broad daylight and *sinij* with absence of full daylight.

X is goluboj. =
(*a*) at some times people can see the sun above them in the sky
     when one sees things like X one can think of the sky at these times
(*b*) X is like this kind of sky
(*c*) at some times people can see many things
     when one sees things like X, one can think of this

X is sinij. =
(*a*) at some times people can see the sun above them in the sky
     when one sees things like X one can think of the sky at these times
(*b*) X is not like the sky at these times
(*c*) at some times people can't see very much
     when one sees things like X one can think of this

It should be pointed out that the explication assigned here to *sinij* does not present it as a "dark colour", although it does present it as darker than *goluboj*. To see this, compare the following two variants:

(1) at some times people can't see very much
(2) at some times people can't see much

It is variant (2), not (1), which I have assigned to the English word *dark*, and which I would assign to other words which stand for colours thought of as "dark". But *sinij* is not thought of as "a dark colour"; and it differs in this respect from the Polish word *granatowy*, also 'dark blue', which definitely is thought of as a dark colour. The fact that *sinij* has been assigned component (1), not (2), accounts for these differences.

Turning now to the Japanese word *aoi* (*ao*), we note that its range covers not only those shades which in English are called *blue*, but also some of those which in English are called *green*.[10] Thus, it is not only the sky which is called *aoi*, but also wet grass and the "Go!" traffic lights. In fact,

---

[10] My information on the use of *aoi* comes chiefly from discussions with Takako Toda, and from her reports of informants' responses. I am very grateful to her for her help in this matter.

Japanese has set phrases referring to both grass and traffic lights as *aoi* (Takako Toda, personal communication). For example, when teachers in Japan teach children traffic rules they say:

> Shingoo ga ao ni nattara, migi o mite, hidari o mite, watarimashoo.
> 'When the lights turn *aoi*, look to the right, look to the left, and then cross.'

When there is a need to contrast the colour of the sky with the colour of grass, a different colour adjective is used for grass: *midori*. But when there is no need for contrast, *aoi* is used to cover many "greens" (as well as all "blues"). Interestingly, however, the "best example" of *aoi* is not in the middle of the range, but clearly in its "blue" part; and in fact (according to my informants), it is unquestionably provided by the sky, *sora* (*aoi sora*).

Trying to account for these facts, it seems that we should propose for *aoi* two points of reference rather than one (roughly speaking, sky and grass, or, more generally, things growing out of the ground); and also that we should show that one of these models (sky) is more important than the other.

It should also be noted, however, that when applied to things described in English as *green* rather then *blue*, *aoi* appears to favour temporary states over permanent qualities. Thus, when speaking of grass or of trees as *aoi* (rather than *midori*) informants find it necessary to include a reference to a transitory state (after the rain). For example, they are happy to say that after the rain, the grass looks very *aoi*, but not that grass is *aoi*. There are also restrictions on the use of *aoi* as an attribute: one can say *aoi sora*, 'aoi sky', or *aoi umi*, 'aoi sea', but not **aoi kusa*, 'aoi grass', or **aoi ki*, 'aoi tree', though one can perfectly well use *aoi* as a predicate to describe a temporary state of trees or grass, for example:

> Ame no ato, ki ga ao ao to shite iru.
> After the rain, the trees are (look) very *aoi*.

The reduplication *ao ao* underscores the vivid, fresh look of the trees after the rain. Interestingly, *midori* would not be used like this:

> ?Ame no ato, ki ga midori midori to shite iru.

On the other hand, one can use *midori* as an attribute of *ki*, 'tree', or *kusa*, 'grass': *midori no ki*; cf. **aoi ki*. Clearly, the reason is that *midori* is seen as a permanent property of trees, whereas *aoi* refers to a temporary state, or to a temporary visual impression.

It is also interesting to note that while *aoi* is readily applied to changeable targets such as "green" traffic lights, a (permanently) green jumper or a book with a green cover would be described as *midori*, not as *aoi*. All these facts point to a link between *aoi*-ness and a possibility of change.

It is also relevant to note that the sea, *umi*, is normally described in Japanese as *aoi*; and, next to the sky, what could be visually more change-able than the ocean? In fact, according to my informants it is the ocean rather than grass or plants in general which provides the second best ex-ample of *aoi*: after the phrase *aoi sora*, 'blue sky', it is the phrase *aoi umi*, 'blue/green sea', which comes to mind most naturally in connection with the word *aoi*. Since the sea can be seen, at different times, as either blue or green, a triple model, based on the sky (primary point of reference), the sea (secondary point of reference), and vegetation after rain (a tertiary point of reference) might seem to accord better with the way *aoi* is used, and with informants' responses to it. Following this line of thought, one could pro-pose the following (partial) explication:

X is aoi. =
  (*a*) at some times people can see the sun in the sky
       when one sees things like *X* one can think of the sky at these times
  (*b*) in some places there is a lot of water
       when people are far from these places
       they can see this water
       when one sees things like *X* one can think of this
  (*c*) in some places things grow out of the ground
       at some times there is water in those places
       when one sees things like *X* one can think of this

Finally, let us consider briefly the situation in Thai, described authorita-tively by Diller and Juntanamalaga (forthcoming). In "lower", rural Thai, there are only four basic colour terms, with foci in the areas of white, black, red, and green. In the "higher", urban Thai, however, there are also two terms of the "blue" type: *fáa* (lit. 'sky') and *nam-ŋən* (lit. 'silver-tarnish'). The former refers only to very light blues ('sky-blue' or even lighter), whereas the latter designates, in particular, the dark blue of the Thai flag. What is considered in English the focal *blue* is too dark to be called *fáa* and too light to be called *nam-ŋən*, and informants regard it as a "difficult to classify" shade, although if pressed they may call it *fáa-kὲ* (lit. 'sky-dark' or 'dark-sky'). There is, therefore, a "no man's land" between the two "blues" and, remarkably, it is this no man's land which corresponds to the "focal blue" supposedly determined by universal human neurophysiology.

This fact highlights the irreducible gap between neurophysiology and meaning. Surely, what the Thais lack is not a perceptual category but a con-ceptual one. It is likely that sooner or later they will develop one—on the lines of the English *blue*, of the Polish *niebieski*, or of the Japanese *aoi*, or in some other way. (It seems most likely, in fact, that they will follow a path similar to the Russian one, with two "basic" words for "blue".) In any case, we cannot predict the exact shape of this future category on the basis of any past or future findings in either chromatology or neurophysiology.

Furthermore, the situation in Thai seems to be at variance with the general account of colour category formation proposed by Rosch (1975*b*: 184): "There are perceptually salient colours which more readily attract attention and are more easily remembered than other colours. When category names are learned, they tend to become attached first to the salient stimuli, only later generalizing to other, physically similar, instances. By this means these natural prototype colours become the foci of organisation for categories."

But in Thai (like many other languages) it is the sky which is treated as the "natural prototype" of a blue-like category; and this "natural prototype" is different from the kind of "blue" which is said to be perceptually most salient and which is (perhaps) most likely to become the focus of the not-yet-born basic "blue" category. For this category to be born, the focal, perceptually most salient "blue" must become conceptually linked with some noticeable reference-point in the speakers' experience—such as, for example, the idea of the sky on a sunny day.

9. "Red" and "Yellow"

The nearest equivalent of the English word *red* is in many languages etymologically related to the word for "blood" (recall, for example, the Warlpiri word for "red" mentioned in Section 1); it can, however, be related to many other putative models, such as, for example, various minerals (for example, red ochre) or other sources of pigments and dyes. The Polish word *czerwony* is synchronically no longer analysable, but it is believed to have come from the name of a red worm, *czerw* (Brückner 1970). The English word *red* is not synchronically analysable either. It is possible, none the less, that here, too, we can discover a common association which might unite the speakers of English in their conceptualization of the category in question.

In an earlier work (Wierzbicka 1980: 43) I proposed that *red* may be conceptualized via the concept of 'blood', and I proposed the following rough formula:

red—colour thought of as the colour of blood

Further work with informants, as well as an introspective exploration of my own concept of 'czerwony' (prompted by objections expressed by other linguists), have led me to question the adequacy of this kind of explication. The relevance of blood to the concept of 'red' can be compared to the relevance of milk to the concept of 'white', or to the relevance of charcoal to the concept of 'black'; while objects of this kind may provide good exemplars of certain commonly recognized colours, they are not things of extraordinary visual interest, things that dominate people's view (like the sky, the sun, the sea, or a white snowy landscape do). But if we do not define *red* via blood, or not just via blood, what else can we do to elucidate this concept?

Trying to approach the problem from a different angle, I shall take as my point of departure the suggestion made by Manning (1989) that *red* is "a rich, warm colour". The words "rich" and "warm" are used here metaphorically, but I think that these metaphors provide useful clues to the meaning of *red*. Of the four "basic colour categories" encoded in English as *red*, *yellow*, *green*, and *blue*, two, *red* and *yellow*, are thought of commonly as "warm colours". Why is that? What does the notion of "a warm colour" mean and why is it that people associate "warmth" with *red* and *yellow* rather than with *green* and *blue*?

The answer seems to me rather obvious: *yellow* is thought of as "warm" because it is associated with the sun, whereas *red* is thought of as "warm" because it is associated with fire. It seems plausible, therefore, that although people do not necessarily think of the colour of fire as red, they do associate red colour with fire. Similarly, they do not necessarily think of the colour of the sun as yellow, and yet they do think of yellow, on some level of consciousness or subconsciousness, as a "sunny colour". It seems likely that the association between *red* and fire, and between *yellow* and the sun, is a little further removed from the surface of speakers' consciousness than that between *blue* and the sky, or *green* and things growing out of the ground. None the less, it is not difficult to bring these links to the surface.

I have asked a number of informants what colour they think fire is, and several of them replied: orange. However, when I ask informants which colour fire makes them *think* of, many of them reply: red. I think the reason may be that when asked about the colour of fire people think of the flame; but when asked about "what fire makes them think of", they think of the whole situation involving fire, and this includes glowing red coals.

The association between fire and *red* is supported by the existence of set phrases such as *red-hot*, *red coals*, or *fiery red* (cf. also the name of the most popular Australian brand of matches: *Redheads*). Other European languages have similar phraseological reflexes of this association. For example, in Polish the expression *czerwony kur*, literally 'red rooster', is a synonym of fire. It is also worth noting that fire-engines and other paraphernalia used by fire brigades are often painted red; that fire extinguishers are also painted red; that red is generally used as a symbol of danger or warning (for example, in traffic-light systems). It seems reasonable to suppose that all of these facts reflect a common association between fire and red.

The common association of the colour red with fire is well attested from a wide variety of times and places. For example, Birren (1978) notes that "the Jewish historian Josephus in the first century AD associated . . . red with fire" (p. 3). He mentions the same association in Chinese culture; he adduces Leonardo da Vinci's statement "We shall set down . . . red for fire" (4); and he quotes from the Upanishads: "The red color of burning fire is the color of fire . . . The red color of the sun is the color of fire . . . The red color of the moon is the color of fire . . . The red color of the lightning is the color of fire . . .". (pp. 2–3).

It may also be worth recalling here Swadesh's (1972: 204) speculations on the possible etymological links between *red* and the Latin *ardere*, 'to burn' (as well as between *light* and the Latin *albus*, 'white').[11]

The fact that people tend to perceive the colour of fire as orange or yellow rather then red does not undermine the conceptual link between fire and redness. If it is true that "the four hue classes, red, yellow, green, and blue . . . are neurophysiologically 'wired' or 'programmed' in human beings" (Witkowski and Brown 1978: 442), for the purposes of conceptualization and communication these neurophysiological categories have to be projected on to analogues given in shared human experience. For "blue" and "green", the choice is obvious: the sky (and perhaps the sea) and vegetation. For "yellow", the sun offers—perhaps—one natural point of reference. (The fact that in children's drawings and paintings the sun is represented as yellow reflects this association).[12] For "red", however, there is no invariable environmental model. Although there is the invariable experiential model of blood, most human beings do not see blood nearly as often as they do the sky, the sun, or grass, and in any case, blood is not nearly as salient, visually, as is fire. It is natural, therefore, that in many, perhaps most, human cultures, in addition to "local" associations such as that with red ochre, a deeper association should have been established between "red" and its nearest analogue in human environment which is both visually salient and culturally, or existentially, overwhelmingly important: fire. The fact that we can find traces of such a conceptual association even in English provides, it seems to me, a striking confirmation of this fact.

These considerations lead us to propose the following (partial) explications:

X is red. =
when one sees things like X one can think of fire
when one sees things like X one can think of blood

X is yellow. =
when one sees things like X one can think of the sun

---

[11] Swadesh's speculations may seem to us rather fantastic in some of the details, but this does not invalidate his basic insight into the importance of light and fire to the human conceptualization of colour.

[12] As pointed out by Xu (1994), however, this is not universal. For example, in Chinese culture the sun is usually represented as red, not as yellow.

A further difference between *red* and *yellow* is that *yellow* is thought of as a light colour, whereas *red* is not thought of as either light or dark. Since we have already explicated the notion of a light colour, we can now use it in a fuller explication of the concept 'yellow':

> *X* is yellow. =
> when one sees things like *X* one can think of the sun
> at some times people can see many things
> when one sees things like *X* one can think of this

"Rich colours" are "deep" but not dark; they look as if "there was much colour in them", as if the dye, or the paint, was thick. They cannot be light, because light colours look as if "there was not much colour in them", as if the dye, or the paint, had been used thinly. On the other hand, red is certainly a "vivid" colour, that is, one that is very easy to see. If we think, then, that *red* is "a rich colour" as well as a "warm colour", and a "vivid colour", we might consider, initially, an explication along the following lines:

> *X* is red. =
> when one sees things like *X* one can think of fire
> when one sees things like *X* one can think of blood
> one can see things like *X* at times when one cannot see other things

On the other hand, additional components would presumably have to be postulated for the two Hungarian words for "red", *vörös* ('dark red') and *piros* ('light red'). As a starting-point for discussion, I would propose the following:

> *X* is piros. =
> when one sees things like *X* one can think of fire
> when one sees things like *X* one can think of blood
> at some times people can see many things
> when one sees things like *X* one can think of this

> *X* is vörös. =
> when one sees things like *X* one can think of fire
> when one sees things like *X* one can think of blood
> at some times people can see very little
> when one sees things like *X* one can think of this

These (tentative) explications present the two Hungarian words for "red" as analogous to the two Russian words for "blue".

10. Macro-white and Macro-black

Following the findings of Berlin and Kay (1969), it is widely believed that the concepts 'black' and 'white' are, in some sense, lexical universals. Berlin and Kay themselves (1969: 2) phrased the claims in question as follows: "(1) All languages contain terms for white and black. (2) If a language contains three terms, then it contains a term for red." As informal, abbreviatory ways of referring to generalizations precisely formulated elsewhere, statements of this kind can be seen as quite legitimate. It is unfortunate, however, that these informal abbreviations have led many scholars to conclude that if a language has only two basic colour words, we know what these words mean: "they must mean 'black' and 'white' ".

But, as mentioned earlier, this cannot be true. If a language has only two colour words, which divide between themselves all the colours perceived by the speakers, these words cannot possibly mean the same as what the words *black* and *white* mean. What do they mean, then? For example, what do the Gu-jingarliya (Burarra) words *-gungaltja* and *-gungundja*, discussed in Section 3, mean?

One suggestion which has sometimes been made is that words of this kind mean 'light' and 'dark', respectively. But this cannot be the whole truth either if the word supposedly meaning "light" includes red in its range. For example, the fact that the Gu-jingarliya counterpart of *white* includes also highly saturated, medium light red suggests that, in this case, the contrast between light and dark, that is, ultimately, between day and night, cannot constitute the only underlying model. Since the combining of light colours and red in one class proved to be a rule rather than an exception (see e.g. E. R. Heider 1972*a*; Turner 1966; Conklin 1973), the simplistic model opposing "light" to "dark" had to be abandoned and an alternative had to be sought.

At that point, a number of scholars suggested that the putative categories "light" and "dark" should be replaced with composite ones: "light warm" versus "dark cold" (e.g. E. R. Heider 1972*a*), and this is how "Stage I languages" are now often represented.

But this reinterpretation, which may seem quite reasonable, presents serious difficulties, too. For what evidence do we have that speakers of languages such as, for example, Dani or Gu-jingarliya possess a notion of a "warm colour"? In English, there is at least the expression "warm colours"; but in Gu-jingarliya and in Dani the only evidence we have is the very fact which we are trying to explain: that is, that the speakers of the languages in question include in one category colours which *we* (that is, speakers of English) think of as "warm colours". From the point of view of the Dani and the Gu-jingarliya, the idea of a "warm colour" or of a "cool colour" may be just as alien as the undulatory theory of light. Consequently, the expressions "warm colours" and "cool colours" may help *us* to identify the ranges distinguished by these speakers, but they tell us nothing about the meaning of the relevant terms—what the speakers mean when they use them.

To my mind, the fact that languages commonly (though not invariably) link red with light rather than with dark colours suggests that this type of categorization may have some explanation in common human experience. My hypothesis is that the explanation lies in the natural association between fire and sun, both of which are associated for human beings with warmth and light: even if the sun is seen as, primarily, a source of light, it must also be perceived as a source of warmth; and even if fire is seen as, primarily, a source of warmth, it must also be perceived as a source of light.

The natural association between fire and the sun (reflected, indirectly, in the notion of a "warm colour", applying to both yellow and red) may also account for the variation in the way different languages which have only two basic colour terms treat reds. If a language distinguishes light colours from dark and medium ones, one would expect red to go with the latter, and sometimes this indeed happens (for example, in the Papuan language Jale; see Berlin and Kay 1969: 23). In other languages, however, such as Gu-jingarliya, red "unaccountably" goes with very light colours. It seems to me that the association between sun and fire would explain this. The fact that reflective foil may be seen by Gu-jingarliya informants as the "best example" of the category in question ("properly number one *gun-gun-galtja*") suggests that in this particular language the idea of sunlight may be especially important for the conceptualization embodied in this category: shining, glistening, bright objects bring to mind things lying in the sun (and, possibly, reflecting sun).

The fact that some languages, for example the Papuan language Dani, put even deep dark reds with their light colours, and that they allow their speakers to think of dark red as the "best example" of the category in question, is also consistent with the idea that both the concept of sun and the concept of fire may play a role in the conceptualization of "macro-whites". Presumably, in Dani it is neither daylight nor sunlight which plays the central role in the conceptualization of "macro-white", but fire—and possibly not even fire but glowing embers. If we assume that universal human experience suggests a number of potential foci, interrelated but distinguishable (daylight–sunlight–fire–glowing embers), and that each of these potential foci can be given priority in conceptualization by a particular culture, then cross-linguistic variation in the behaviour of "macro-whites" begins to make sense.

In any case, it is quite clear that the differences between the different concepts of "macro-whites" call for carefully differentiated explications, and that the two colour terms of languages such as Jale, Gu-jingarliya, and Dani cannot be semantically identified with each other, as they cannot be semantically identified with the English words *black* and *white, dark* and *light,* or *warm* and *cool.* References to the neurophysiology of vision will not help, since this is, presumably, the same for all human beings.

Having said this, I will now try to construct some explications, hoping that they may become a starting-point for a constructive discussion.

To start with the two Dani colour terms investigated by Rosch (E. R. Heider 1972*a*), we note that "the focal points (best examples) of *mili* and *mola* were not 'black' and 'white'. . . . Examples of *mili* were reliably placed among the darkest greens and blues. *Mola,* however, appeared to have two focal points: the most common a dark red, the less common a pale pink" (1972*a*: 451). The point is important and one must be grateful to the author for stating it in quite unequivocal terms: "After each informant had pointed to an exemplar for *mili* and *mola,* I asked if he were sure that was a better example than the pure 'black' and pure 'white' chips which were available; informants reliably insisted that it was" (ibid.).

On the basis of Rosch's discussion, we can propose the following explication for *mola*:

X is mola. =
when one sees things like X one can think of fire
at some times people can see many things
when one sees things like X one can think of this
at some times one can see the sun
when one sees things like X one can think of this

This explication accounts for the fact that *mola* includes, as Rosch puts it, light and "warm" colours. Unlike the explication of *red,* it does not include a reference to blood; it does, however, include a reference to fire, and so it also accounts for, or at least is consistent with, the fact that most informants see red as the "best example" of *mola.* It does not account for the fact that some informants see pale pink, rather than red, as the "best example" of this category; this, however, can probably be explained in terms of a change in progress (those informants who chose pale pink appear to have moved to a system with three, rather than two, basic colour terms).

As for the opposite of *mola* (i.e. *mili*), we note that it includes both dark and "cold" colours; and that its focus is "among the darkest greens and blues". This description suggests that the concept in question has a largely negative character and centres around absence of light and absence of sun. This can be portrayed as follows:

X is mili. =
at some times people can't see very much

> when one sees things like X one can think of this
> at some times people can't see the sun
> when one sees things like X one can think of this
> when one sees some things one can think of fire
> X is not like this

Turning now to the Gu-jingarliya terms *-gungaltja* and *-gungundja*, we recall that they oppose light and brilliant shining colours to dark and dull ones, and that bright red is included in the former group. To account for these facts, I would propose the following explication for *-gungaltja*:

> X is -gungaltja. =
> (*a*) at some times people can see very much (many things)
>   when one sees things like X one can think of this
> (*b*) at some times in some places some things are in the sun
>   when one sees things like X one can think of this
> (*c*) when one sees things like X one can think of fire

The first component (*a*) of this explication is the same which has been posited for the English word *light*; component (*b*) accounts for the link between *-gungaltja* and "brilliance"; and (*c*) accounts for the link between *-gungaltja* and redness.

As for the "dark/dull" term *-gungundja*, we have even less basis for speculation about its possible meaning because we are not told what its "best examples" might be. It would appear, however, that at least the following components should be included:

> X is -gungundja. =
> (*a*) at some times people can't see very much
>   when one sees things like X one can think of this
> (*b*) at some times in some places things are not in the sun
>   when one sees things like X one can think of this

The existence of "macro-whites" and "macro-blacks" at the beginning of the alleged "evolutionary sequence" cannot in my view be explained in terms of either physics or neurophysiology of vision. "Black" and "white" are indeed opposites in terms of physical properties of light and "psychophysical" properties of vision, but the fundamental contrast between "light or warm" colours and "dark or cool" colours does not seem to be similarly explainable. It could, however, be explained if we gave credence to Swadesh's (1972: 205) speculations which place fire and light at the root of human conceptualization of colour. Given the importance of fire in human life, and given its perceptual salience, derived not only from its colours but also from its movement, and from its brilliance and luminosity, these speculations seem to me to be intuitively plausible.

This link of "macro-whites" with light, sun, and fire (in all their aspects, including brilliance and luminosity) highlights the fact that, contrary to what is commonly assumed, "colour" is not a universal human concept—not only because there are many languages which do not have a word for "colour" but also because in languages with only two "basic colour terms", like Gu-jingarliya, the alleged "colour terms" are not really "colour terms" but general descriptors of appearance, or of visual impression.

Witkowski and Brown (1978: 441) argue that if in primary macro-classes red is usually combined with yellow, and green with blue, this "provides evidence that a dimension based on wavelength order . . . is important in human colour categorization. Only conjunctive primary colours or, in other words, those adjacent to each other in wavelength order are combined in composite classes."

But this does not explain why yellow-green is a very rare (though not unattested) category. Nor does it explain why dark colours should be associated with green and blue, and light ones, with yellow and red. Witkowski and Brown try to explain this fact, too, in terms of "wiring" (1978: 442): "Wiring also underlies the pairings of warm hues with white and cool hues with black in the categories macro-white and macro-black respectively. (The converse associations, warm-dark and cool-light, are not attested.)" But this begs the question.

I believe that a hypothesis which links light, sun, and fire provides a better explanation of the recurring regularities than a mere reference to the supposed "wiring".

11. Macro-red and Grue

Those languages of the world which have only three basic colour terms appear to oppose the concept of a "coloured" (chromatic) visual experience to a "non-coloured" (achromatic) one. As a rule, the "coloured" colour is focused in "red", which is the most salient hue for human beings (Bornstein *et al.* 1976). At the same time, however, it is a "warm" colour, that is to say one which is opposed not simply to light and dark colours, but to light colours on the one hand, and to dark-cool or dull-cool ones on the other (see Kay and McDaniel 1978: 640). This means, in effect, that "macro-red", while focused in red, includes not only red, but also yellow and orange; and also, that it is associated with "brightness".

What could be the conceptual counterpart of a colour category which people intuitively call "warm" and which has the following properties: it is vivid ("colourful"), it is highly noticeable both during the day and during the night (and therefore is perceived as maximally distinct from both "light" colours and "dark" colours), it is bright (luminous), and it is focused in red but includes also yellows and oranges?

In my view the answer is clear: the concept in question must take fire as its point of reference. This leads us to the following type of explication:

> X is 'macro-red'. =
> things like X are "easy to see"
> (i.e. people can see things like X at times when they cannot see other things)
> when one sees things like X one can think of fire
> at some times when one sees things like X one can think of the sun

Moving now from "macro-reds" to the next stage of the alleged "evolutionary sequence", we note with Kay and McDaniel (1978: 630) that "many of the world's languages have a basic colour term that means grue". But what does "grue" mean?

For many writers on the subject, the first (and often, also, the last) answer which comes to mind is that "grue" means "cool". But vague metaphors like "cool" are not satisfactory explanations of meaning, although they may provide helpful hints. We must, therefore, ask further: and what does "cool" mean? Once this question has been asked, however, the answer is not difficult to find: "cool" (when applied to colours) means, essentially, "not-warm", and since "warm" makes sense only as an indirect reference to fire and/or sun, "cool" must mean a colour which—while vivid and highly visible ("coloured")—does not bring to mind fire or sun.

But this is not all. The most striking feature of "grue" is that, while it stretches over both blues and green, "focal grue selections have often proved to be bimodal, being chosen from both the focal blue and focal green regions. But grue has never been found to be focussed in the intermediate blue-green region" (Kay and McDaniel 1978: 630). This is an extremely intriguing finding, which requires an explanation. Kay and McDaniel imply that they have one: "The absence of focal choices from this intermediate region is strong evidence that these colours have lower grue membership values, and that grue has the membership structure stipulated by the fuzzy union analysis" (ibid.).

But how can "fuzzy union analysis" explain the fact that the "best" example of "grue" (that is, of a "cool" colour) is chosen either from focal blues or from focal greens, whereas the "best" example of a "macro-red" (that is, of a "warm" colour) is not similarly bifocal, and is always focused in "red"? Of course one can *model* the bifocal structure of "grue" in a "fuzzy union analysis", but I don't see how one could *explain* it this way.

It seems to me that both the bifocal character of "grue" and the "monofocal" character of "macro-reds" can be explained on the basis of the hypothesis that "grue" is, in a sense, defined negatively, as a "non-warm" colour, whereas "macro-red" is defined positively, as a "warm" colour. The notion of a "warm" colour refers us to a positive experiential model: fire. The concept of a "non-warm" colour is defined above all in opposition to that model. It is only in addition to this contrastive core that two positive models are involved; and these are, clearly, the sky and vegetation.[13] Admittedly, one could suggest that "grue" has its positive point of reference in natural "water places", that is, in lakes, rivers, or seas, which can be seen as blue, green, or blue-green. This, however, would not account for the bifocal character of "grues"; whereas the hypothesis that they are conceptualized primarily with reference to the sky and to vegetation would explain this.

These considerations lead us towards the following definition of "grue" (as it is understood by speakers for whom "blue" is more focal than "green"):

X is 'grue$_B$'. =
- (a) when one sees some things one can think of fire
  X is not like this
- (b) when one sees things like X one can think of the sky
- (c) in some places many things grow out of the ground
  sometimes when one sees things like X one can think of this

For speakers for whom "green" rather than "blue" represents the best example of "grue", we would place the components referring to the sky after, not before, those referring to vegetation, and we would include the word "sometimes" in the component referring to the sky:

X is 'grue$_G$'. =
- (a) when one sees some things one can think of fire
  X is not like this
- (b) in some places many things grow out of the ground
  when one sees things like X one can think of this
- (c) sometimes when one sees things like X one can think of the sky

It will be noticed that for "macro-red", too, two positive points of reference have been posited: fire and the sun; but the relationship between these two models is quite different than that between the sky and vegetation. First, one can presume that fire is visually much more salient than the sun, whereas the sky and vegetation are on the same level of salience. Second, fire itself can be seen as yellow, orange, and red, and therefore it is not

[13] Van Brakel (1993: 117) notes that Zulu speakers, who have one term for "blue" and "green", use at times expressions "grue like the sky" or "grue like grass" to differentiate between the two. It is also interesting to note that although the Tariana word for "red" is derived from the word for blood, its referential range (red, orange, dark yellow) points to fire, rather than blood, as a conceptual prototype (especially given that the language does have a separate word for "yellow").

opposed to the sun as something non-yellow to something yellow. Both in terms of colour and brilliance fire can be seen as a unitary model of all "macro-reds", although its focus is identified as red rather than orange or yellow. But neither the sky nor vegetation can be seen as a unitary model of all "grues". This is why grues are bifocal, whereas "macro-reds" are monofocal. But grues can also be bifocal because the category in question is united in a different way: by its "cool", "non-warm" character, that is, by its absence of, roughly speaking, "fire associations". On the other hand, "macro-reds" (which emerge as a category before "grues") are not defined in opposition to "grues", that is, they are not conceptualized as "non-cool" colours. Rather, they are defined with reference to a unitary positive model: fire. If there is a second positive model here (the sun), it plays a secondary role, and in any case it can be seen as similar to the first one in terms of two positive qualities: visibility and warmth. By contrast, the two models of "grueness" can only be united on a negative basis, as being different from "warm colours", that is from "fiery" and "sunny" "macro-reds".

12. Names of Mixed Colours

According to physicists, there are three primary colours in light: red, green, and blue. "White light can be made by mixing red, green and blue light" (*World of Science* n.d.: 163). But, of course, this is not how ordinary people think about colours.

According to psychologists, the smallest number of colour terms by means of which we can systematize our colour experience is not three but six. "If pressed to the greatest possible economy of colour terms we find that we can describe all the colours we discriminate by using only six terms and their various combinations. These are red, yellow, green, and blue, the four *unitary hues*, and black and white, the two extremes of the series of hueless colours. All other colour names . . . can be described by referring to these six terms and combinations of them" (Hurvich 1981: 3).

I believe that the meanings of colour terms in languages with an elaborated colour lexicon (such as English) accord reasonably well with the above statement: beyond the list of the first six colours in Berlin and Kay's sequence all the other ones (with the exception of brown, to which I will return later) are conceptualized, on some level, as "mixtures". Very roughly:

orange = yellow + red
pink   = red + white
purple = blue + red
grey   = black + white

This does not mean that we do not think of *orange, pink, purple*, and *grey* as "unitary" colours. We do, and I would postulate for all these words, too, a unitary ostensive ćomponent along the lines of: 'when people see things like *X* they call them ORANGE (PINK, PURPLE, GREY)'. But at some level of our linguistic consciousness we can also relate each of them to two other colour concepts, as indicated in the formulae above.

For *pink* and *grey*, their "mixed" nature lies relatively near the surface of our linguistic consciousness. For others, in particular for *purple*, it lies deeper and is harder to detect by introspection. But, as demonstrated by Hering (1920), it can be done. Being totally unaware of Hering's work, I proposed in an earlier book (Wierzbicka 1980: 43) definitions which closely corresponded to his analysis. Using the format of explication used in this chapter, I would now rephrase these explications along the following lines:

X is orange. =
one can think of things like *X*: this is like something yellow
at the same time one can think: this is like something red

X is pink. =
one can think of things like *X*: this is like something red
at the same time one can think: this is like something white

X is grey. =
one can think of things like *X*: this is like something black
at the same time one can think: this is like something white

X is purple. =
one can think of things like *X*: this is like something blue
at the same time one can think: this is like something red

Generally speaking, it would seem that "mixed colours" constitute one common way for extending the set of "basic" colour concepts. This is evidenced by the final bloc of four colour concepts ("grey", "pink", "orange", and "purple") in Berlin and Kay's sequence of eleven. It is also evidenced by concepts such as the Polish twelfth "basic" colour concept, *granatowy*, which is clearly decomposable into, roughly speaking, 'blue' and 'black'; or by the Polish semi-basic colour terms *beżowy* ('beige', that is 'brown' + 'white'), *kremowy* ('off-white', that is 'white' + 'yellow'), and *bordowy* ('maroon', that is, 'red' + 'black').

It is also worth noting that in the case of "mixed colour" concepts one component seems to be always more salient than the other. Thus, *pink* seems to be an offshoot of *red* rather than of *white*, *purple* of *blue* rather than of *red*, and *grey* of *black* rather than of *white*. Similarly, *granatowy* is an offshoot of *niebieski*, 'blue', *beżowy* of 'brown', and *kremowy* of 'white' (see the English term *off-white*). This is reflected in the explications, in which the first component refers to the more salient colour component.

13. "Brown"

Like pink, orange, grey, and purple, "brown", too, is often regarded as a "composite colour"—a kind of visual mixture of yellow and black, or yellow and black with an admixture of red—that is, in effect, a mixture of orange and black (see Wierzbicka 1990*a*).

But on the level of simple introspection, a composite formula for "brown" is problematic.

When we ask informants to "decompose" *pink, grey, orange,* and *purple* into two underlying colours their responses are uniform and predictable. With *brown,* however, they are not. It is easy enough to relate *brown* to *black,* because *brown* is generally thought of as a "dark" colour. But the other component or components of *brown* are harder to identify. Generally speaking, *brown* seems to be a more heterogeneous category than *pink, orange, purple,* or *grey.*

Hurvich (1981: 9) writes: "Browns are mainly dark-grayish orange and dark-grayish or blackish-yellow colours. But there are also red browns and olive browns. There are many browns in our environment. The earth, wood, leather, human hair, and human skin appear to contain different proportions of yellow and red as well as different proportions of black and white."

The remarkable fact is that despite the heterogeneity of the range of browns, and the speakers' frequent inability to agree on the "correct" decomposition of the concept 'brown', *brown* is, none the less, perceived as a more basic colour term than, for example, *purple*; and that the inter-informant agreement in the identification of "brown" colour chips is relatively high. For example, Harkness (1973: 183) writes with respect to the Spanish counterpart of *brown*: "The Spanish samples . . . did relatively well on naming the first five colours, but agreement on naming subsequent colours decreased markedly. . . . Adults, for the most part, correctly named all terms through Brown but did not agree on naming subsequent terms." It is also quite remarkable that in the "universal colour sequence" proposed by Berlin and Kay (1969) "brown" came before "purple", "pink", "orange", and "grey".

I think that in order to account for these facts we must recognize that the English word *brown,* and its closest counterparts in other languages, are not conceptualized in terms of a "mixture" of other colours, but rather have a positive model. I believe that if there is such a model it is to be found, like the models of *blue, green, red,* and *yellow,* in some universal or near-universal aspect of human environment. The choice seems obvious: *brown* can be thought of as the colour of the ground; or at least as that colour which is likely to make people think of the ground.

As mentioned earlier, in Warlpiri, where colour terms are formed by reduplication, the nearest counterpart of the English word *brown* means, literally, 'earth-earth'; just as the nearest counterpart of the English word *green* means, literally, 'grass-grass')[14]. This manifest association between something "brown" and the colour of the ground is instructive.

Of course, the colour of the ground can vary, and it varies more than the colour of the sky or the colour of the sun. This is consistent with the fact that "brown" was further down in Berlin and Kay's sequence than "red", "yellow", "green", and "blue". At the same time, the hypothesis that "brown" does have a positive model (albeit a notoriously heterogeneous one) would explain why it came in that sequence before "grey", "pink", "orange", and "purple".

These considerations lead us to the following (partial) explication of the English word *brown*:

> *X* is brown. =
> When one sees things like *X* one can think of the ground (earth)
> at some times people can't see much
> when one sees things like *X* one can think of this

In support of this "environmental prototype" approach to the concept of 'brown', I would add that "brown colour" is often regarded by scientists as a puzzle.

For example, Westphal (1987: 53) notes that if red, green, and blue are darkened, "the resulting maroons, navies and dark greens seem to retain their parent hue in a way in which brown does not" and he quotes Boynton's (1975: 315) view that "brown is certainly the most surprising [of the dark colours created by experiments of this kind] because it ceases almost entirely to resemble the original bright colour". (See also Gregory 1977: 127.)

Westphal (1987: 44) maintains, none the less, that "the colour brown is a kind of darkened yellow", but this is counter-intuitive and psychologically unconvincing. "What does it mean to say, 'Brown is akin to yellow'?" Wittgenstein (1977: 25) asked, incredulously, and he noted: "Brown is, above all, a surface colour, i.e. there is no such thing as a *clear* brown, but only a muddy one."

I would like to suggest that "brown" and "yellow" are seen as different colours, and not as different versions of the same colour, because they are associated, unconsciously, with different prototypes: if "yellow" is, primarily, the colour of the sun (light, "warm", and luminous), "brown" is,

---

[14] Similarly, Alexandra Aikhenvald (personal communication) reports that in her field notes on the Tariana language of Brazil (from the Arawa family), the nearest counterpart of *brown* is glossed as 'muddy, dirty, brownish', and that this word is clearly associated with the colour of the earth.

primarily, the colour of earth. Wittgenstein's observation that "brown" (like "white") is a "surface colour", tallies well with the idea that the concept 'brown' (like 'white') has its prototype in the surface of the earth.

From the point of view of chromatology, it might seem strange that human beings should treat "brown" as an important concept and honour it with a separate "basic colour term". But from the point of view of people's life on earth, "the naked earth" is an important visual (and existential) reference-point (like the sky above our head, or the vegetation all around us). It is this visual and existential salience of the earth which explains, I suggest, the scientist's "puzzle of brown". Hewes (1992: 163) writes: "Fixation on the spectrum colors and on physical and neurophysiological explanations for color perception obscures the fact that many colors of cultural interest to human beings, such as the variety of browns and tans, while now understandable as complicated mixtures of light of different wavelengths, etc., are not present as distinct components of the solar spectrum."

I agree with this, but I would add that the cultural interest of browns and tans (which, presumably, has to do with the value of soil and cattle in human life) must be seen in the context of the visual salience of big expanses such as the sky (often light blue), the sea (often dark blue), the grass-covered ground (typically green), the snow-covered ground (white), the naked earth (often brown).

It should be added that while I have explicated a number of colour concepts via "environmental" concepts such as those encapsulated in the English words *fire*, *sun*, *sky*, *grass*, *sea*, and *ground*, these "environmental" concepts are not postulated here as indefinable conceptual primitives in terms of which people conceptualize their experience. On the contrary, they, too, are regarded as constructs built by human beings on the basis of their experience of life on earth. (See Chapter 7.)

14. Names of Specific (Locally Salient) Referents

It seems to be a universal feature of language that colour perceptions are described, at some stage, not only with reference to visually salient features of the "macro-environment" (such as the night, the sky, the sea, or the sun), but also in terms of locally salient or particularly important referents, such as certain minerals, animals, or plants of characteristic appearance. This applies, for example, to the English words *gold* and *silver*, and presumably, it used to apply to the English word *orange*. Words of this kind provide evidence for the psychological reality of a comparative semantic component in colour semantics in general.

But words of this kind, like any words, are subject to semantic change. For example, the fact that the Russian word *goluboj*, 'light blue', is etymologically related to the word for pigeon, or that the Polish word *czer-wony*, 'red', is etymologically related to the name of a particular red worm, does not mean that the associations in questions are synchronically alive. They are definitely not: in present-day Russian, *goluboj* is clearly associated with the colour of the sky, not with the colour of pigeons.

Similarly, in the Dani language of New Guinea (E. R. Heider 1972*a*), three other colour terms are widely (though not universally) used in addition to the two basic words, *mili* ('dark-cool') and *mola* ('light-warm'), discussed earlier: *pimut*, the name of a kind of red clay, is also used for "red", *bodli*, the name of the root of the turmeric plant, is used for "yellow", and *itjuaiegen*, the name of the bud of a particular flower, is used for "blue" (whereas no special word is used for "green"). It seems to me that facts of this kind do not demonstrate that the Dani associate (what is called in English) the colour red with red clay and not with fire. For those Dani speakers who have moved, or are moving, towards a three-colour system, and who are beginning to differentiate the old concept of 'mola' (focused in fire but extending to sunlight and daylight) into two concepts, the name of red clay may constitute a useful point of reference, but it does not have to dominate one of the emerging new conceptualizations. At some stage the word *pimut* may be linked with both red clay and fire (and perhaps also with blood), and at some point it may dissociate itself from its etymon altogether and attach itself exclusively, in the speakers' linguistic consciousness, to a different, more salient perceptual model.

I conjecture that this is precisely what has happened in the case of the Russian word *goluboj* and the Polish word *czerwony*. It has also happened in the case of the English word *orange* and is probably happening in the case of the English word *silver* (if not yet *gold*).

15. Conclusion: Chromatology, Cognition, and Culture

The main conclusion which emerges from the analysis proposed here is that the language of 'seeing' is rooted in human experience, and that its basic frame of reference is provided by the universal rhythm of "light" days and "dark" nights and by the fundamental and visually salient features of human environment: the sky, the sun, vegetation, fire, the sea, the naked earth, the earth covered with snow. Since some of these fundamental and visually salient features of human experience are universal, it is only to be expected that they will be reflected, in some way, in recurring features of the vocabulary of seeing. Since, however, they are also variable, with different kinds of scenery prevailing in different parts of the globe, it is also to be expected that the vocabulary of seeing will be far from uniform—quite apart from such obvious and often discussed differences as the availability and the cultural importance of "durable coloring agents" (Hewes 1992: 163).

Consider, for example, the set of "colour words" in the Tariana language of Brazil, established by Alexandra Aikhenvald (forthcoming): *kadite*, 'black', *irite* (from *iri*, 'blood'), 'red, orange, dark yellow', *ewite*, 'yellow', *hipolite*, 'green, blue', *halite*, 'white, light, transparent', *kesolite*, 'muddy, dirty, brownish' (from *kesole*, 'mud').

In some respects, this set meets Berlin and Kay's expectations since among its six members it includes five which could be said to match with the first five in their "evolutionary sequence" (black, white, red, yellow, and green).[15]

In other respects, however, the Tariana set contradicts Berlin and Kay's predictions; in particular, it includes "brown", even though it doesn't have separate terms for "blue" and "green". If the word for "brown" is rejected from the set as non-basic (because it is derived from the word for "earth"), the word for "red" would have to be rejected too (because it is derived from the word for blood)—and this would contradict Berlin and Kay's expectations in a quite fundamental way.

Furthermore, the asymmetry between the terms for "black" and "white", and the curious overlap of the terms for "red" and "yellow", remain totally unexplained from this perspective.

On the other hand, the hypothesis that "colour terms" are oriented towards visually salient environmental prototypes makes perfect sense of all the Tariana data, and it allows us to interpret the set with reference to night (black), daylight (white, light, transparent—unlike a snow-covered ground, unknown to the inhabitants of the Amazonian tropics), fire (red, orange, dark yellow), sun (yellow), sky and vegetation (blue, green), and earth (muddy, dirty, brownish).

Our colour sensations occur in our brains, not in the world outside, and their nature is no doubt constrained by our human biology (which links us, in some measure, with other primates); but to be able to communicate about these sensations, we project them on to something in our shared environment.

As pointed out by Witkowski and Brown (1978: 42): "Several authors . . . have suggested that the four hue classes, red, yellow, green, and blue, and the additional categories, black and white, are neurophysiologically 'wired' or 'programmed' in human beings." In addition, however, it has

---

[15] As for the "evolutionary sequence" proposed by Berlin and Kay, it is no longer seen as tenable and it is not clear which, if any, parts or aspects of it will survive the current onslaught of criticisms. I believe, however, that an alternative interpretation of this "evolutionary sequence", which I proposed in Wierzbicka (1990a), is worth keeping on record as a different way of thinking about the issues involved, which can accommodate all the new insights emerging from the ongoing research into the history of human conceptualization of vision.

been claimed that these "neurophysiologically wired" categories are *directly* reflected in language. For example:

a particular structure is inherent in the human perception of colour, a structure which is not deducible from the physical properties of light alone. The opponent process analysis identifies and describes four specific categories of neural response: the R (red), G (green), Y (yellow), and B (blue) response states. . . . The semantics of basic colour terms in all languages *directly* reflects the existence of these pan-human neural response categories. (Kay and McDaniel 1978: 621; emphasis added)

But how can language be "directly" linked to neural responses? Language reflects conceptualizations, not the "neural representation of colour . . . in the pathways between the eye and brain" (Kay and McDaniel 1978: 617). The link between the neural representation of colour and the linguistic representation of colour can only be indirect. The way leads via concepts. Sense data are "private" (even if they are rooted in pan-human neural responses), whereas concepts can be shared. To be able to talk with others about one's private sense data one must be able to translate them first into communicable concepts.

Colour vision cannot be put into words. None the less, it can be talked about, because we can link our visual categories with certain easily accessible models. I suggest that these models include fire, the sun, vegetation, and the sky (as well as day and night); and that these models constitute basic points of reference in human "colour talk".

In presenting colour categories in terms of prototypes which relate colour perception to certain basic aspects of human existence we can lend meaning to what otherwise would be no more than a mysterious play of rods and cones in the human retina, and of the cells in the neural pathways between the retina and the brain, impenetrable to ordinary human beings and unrelated to anything in their experience or their culture.

Harkness (1973: 197) wrote: "It would seem that these colours [red, green, yellow, and blue] function as cognitive anchors for colour naming." I would argue, however, that colours as such cannot function as "cognitive anchors". It is the shared concepts of fire, sun, sky, vegetation, and so on, which function as cognitive anchors for colour naming. The visual categories themselves ("R", "Y", "G", and "B") may well be determined by what is neurophysiologically wired, but the "anchoring" is provided by concepts, because concepts, not perceptions, are potentially intelligible and communicable to others.

Since raw sense data can be conceptualized in different ways, different languages embody different colour concepts, and, for example, *blue* does not mean the same as *goluboj*, and *green* does not mean the same as *gwyrdd*. But the foci of these different semantic categories may be relatively stable, across languages and cultures, not simply because our neural responses are the same but because we share our fundamental conceptual models, which we base on our common human experience.

Rosch (E. R. Heider 1972*b*: 20) wrote:

Given the attributes of focal colours—their occurrence as exemplars of basic colour names, their linguistic codability across languages, and their superior retention in short- and long-term memory—it would seem most economical to suppose that these attributes are derived from the same underlying factors, most likely having to do with the physiology of primate colour vision. In short, far from being a domain well suited to the study of the effects of language on thought, the colour space would seem to be a prime example of the influence of underlying perceptual-cognitive factors on the formation and reference of linguistic categories.

But this is a false opposition. Granted, linguistic categories can be influenced—indirectly—by underlying perceptual-cognitive factors; but this is not inconsistent with saying that language can influence thought (see Lucy and Shweder 1979). Native speakers of English operate habitually with conceptual categories such as 'red', 'yellow', 'green', or 'blue', usually without realizing that these categories are not universal. 'Blue' is no more "pan-human" than 'sinij' or 'aoi'. The foci of these three categories may be similar, but the boundaries are different, because the concepts encoded in them are not exactly the same.

Despite their indirect links with human neurophysiology, the meanings of colour terms are cultural artefacts.

The huge variability of "colour talk" across languages and cultures, discovered in the last two decades, and especially in the last few years (see Berlin *et al.* 1991; Kay *et al.* 1991; MacLaury 1987, 1991, 1992) is compatible with a theory which links colour naming with common—but variable—features of human visible environment and human visual experience but not with theories trying to explain colour naming in terms of neurophysiology.

To quote a few characteristic recent comments, reflecting the changed perceptions of the validity of the Berlin and Kay paradigm, and of the explanatory value of neurophysiology in "colour semantics", Stanlaw (1992: 167) writes: "If color categorization is so strongly based on universal physiological and neurological constraints, we often seem hard pressed to explain the great diversity and inconsistency demonstrated by even one informant in a single interview."

Saunders (1992: 165) is even more emphatic:

A quote from MacLaury will show just how far it has been necessary to tailor the Berlin and Kay (1969) silhouette to explain the endless "colour-naming" anomalies: "Hue, brightness, similarity, and distinctiveness are not the only coordinates by which people compose color categories . . . There are also 'connotative coordinates'." "Colour categories" in other words, can be anything you like.

Similarly, Hewes (1992: 163) remarks on the harmful effects of the "fixation on the spectrum colors and on physical and neurophysiological explanation for colour perception"; and he comments that "The criteria employed by the color-name evolutionists for rejecting most commonly used color terms as 'not basic' are unrealistic" (ibid.).

Finally, van Brakel (1992: 169) comments as follows on MacLaury's (1992) attempt to "save" Berlin and Kay's theory:

I applaud MacLaury's recognition that if one "goes out into the field" with 320 Munsell colour chips, one doesn't always come back with pure hue words. He recognizes "the myriad complexities, subtleties, and differences" which may turn up in naming colour chips, and he allows many other "dimensions" to play a role. I am also very sympathetic to his suggestion that the first official "preliminary analysis of data" (Kay, Berlin, and Merrifield 1991) from the World Color Survey shows "the inevitable collapse" of the "empirical approach" to "color-category evolution".

The choice between linguistic arbitrariness and neurophysiological determinism in colour categorization is a false one. Human conceptualization of colour, which is reflected in language, may be constrained by the neurophysiology of vision, but it can be neither described nor explained in terms of neurophysiology. To describe it, we need to take recourse to human conceptual universals (such as SEE, TIME, PLACE, and LIKE). To explain it—in both its variable and its universal or near-universal features—we need to pay attention to the way people actually talk about what they see, without limiting our data in an artificial manner, and without, as Saunders (1992: 165) aptly put it, "reifying the neurophysiological into the phenomenal".

11 The Semantics of Natural Kinds

□ □ ────────────────────────

1. Introduction

How is knowledge stored and organized in the human mind? In particular, does the mind draw a distinction between "linguistic knowledge" and "non-linguistic knowledge", or between a "mental dictionary" and a "mental encyclopaedia"? For example, what do ordinary people know and how do they think about mice, crocodiles, or moths? Can the knowledge encapsulated in the everyday meaning of words such as *mouse, crocodile,* or *moth* be separated from the knowledge that people may have *about* mice, crocodiles, and moths?

There can hardly be a better way of approaching these questions than by analysing language. Language can allow us—better than anything else—to discover how knowledge is represented and organized in the human mind. If by analysing language we find evidence suggesting that "linguistic knowledge" differs somehow from "non-linguistic knowledge", and that a distinction between the two can be drawn in a non-arbitrary way, this would support the view that the mind itself draws a distinction between a "mental dictionary" and a "mental encyclopaedia". In this chapter I will argue that this is indeed the case, and that by examining linguistic evidence we can learn how to draw the line between "meaning" and "knowledge", or between "linguistic knowledge" and "encyclopaedic knowledge".

Surprisingly, until recently the structure of the lexicon was not subjected to intensive and methodical large-scale study of a kind which might throw light on the organization of knowledge in the human mind. The main reason for this was the absence of a suitable methodology and also the widespread lack of faith in the very possibility of developing such a methodology. Particularly harmful in this respect was the attractive but not very constructive doctrine of family resemblances, which was put forward by Wittgenstein in his *Philosophical Investigations* and which has gained extraordinary popularity in contemporary philosophy, psychology, anthropology, and also linguistics (see Chapters 4 and 8). As mentioned earlier, I believe that lexicographic research of recent years has proved Wittgenstein wrong on this particular point. Meanings do have boundaries, words can be rigorously defined, lexical fields with analogous semantic structures can be uncovered, and, on this basis, more or less reliable and accurate cognitive maps can be drawn.

Linguistic theories which deny the possibility of drawing the line between one meaning and another have the tendency to become self-fulfilling prophecies: they make the study of the lexicon an unpromising and unattractive enterprise, and so prevent the discovery of evidence which would test their validity.

The view that it is impossible to draw a line between "meaning" and "knowledge" or between "dictionaries" and "encyclopaedias" (see e.g. Haiman 1980*a*, 1982; Langacker 1987, 1990) has had, I believe, a similarly unfortunate effect on the study of the lexicon. For knowledge is open-ended. The belief that a dictionary definition represents nothing other than a selection from a (real or imaginary) encyclopaedia entry, with the choice being determined by practical considerations and having no theoretical justification, leads to stagnation in lexical semantics.

On the other hand, the hypothesis that the meaning of a word is determinate, that it can be established in a non-arbitrary way and clearly delineated, has the opposite effect. It encourages the semanticist to turn full attention to the lexicon, to examine carefully all available evidence, to come up with specific hypotheses, to look for possible counter-examples, and generally to engage in serious and thorough study of a language's lexical resources.

But to be able to discover the boundaries between meaning and knowledge we need to have a clear idea of what meaning is and how one can establish the meaning of a word or linguistic entity of any kind; in other words, we need a coherent semantic theory and a rigorous semantic methodology.

As was shown in Chapter 7, different types of words show different levels of semantic complexity. In particular, there are words whose meaning can be portrayed directly in terms of primitives (for example, emotion terms), and words whose meaning is so complex that it can only be reduced to the level of conceptual primitives step by step. The bulk of concrete vocabulary, and in particular the names of "living kinds" and "cultural kinds", is of the latter type.

None the less, although the tacit knowledge implicit in words such as *mouse* or *crocodile* is quite extensive, it can be separated, in a non-arbitrary way, from encyclopaedic knowledge about mice or crocodiles; and there are some types of information about denotata which can never become part of the folk concept (e.g. information about the average weight, in grams or kilograms, of a particular kind of animal).

2. Abstract Concepts and Concrete Concepts

As was shown in Chapter 7, both concrete concepts and abstract concepts are usually much more complex than one might expect before trying to analyse them. None the less, abstract concepts are usually sufficiently simple to be able to be defined directly in terms of the primitives, while an explication of a concrete concept written purely in terms of the primitives would be beyond comprehension (as a whole). I believe the correct conclusion to be drawn from this is that concepts associated with natural and cultural kinds are in fact immensely complex. One can, of course, try to deny this complexity, and claim that concepts of this kind are learnt largely by ostension, that they constitute "gestalts", not conceptual configurations, that explications of the kind proposed here belong in an encyclopaedia, not in a dictionary of any kind, and so on. But the fact remains that explications of this kind reflect a kind of knowledge which native speakers of a language have and which is part of their communicative competence. (For some psycholinguistic evidence of the reality of this knowledge, see e.g. Frumkina and Mirkin 1986; Frumkina and Mostovaja 1988.)

Given that it is one of the tasks of a (monolingual) dictionary to portray, as faithfully and accurately as possible, the knowledge encapsulated in words of a given language, it follows that explications of this kind belong, in principle, in a dictionary. Of course, practical considerations may impose more or less drastic abbreviations on the dictionary representations of knowledge associated with words, but this is an entirely different matter, independent of the theoretical line separating a "dictionary" from an "encyclopaedia". I am using the words "dictionary" and "encyclopaedia" in a metaphorical sense, referring to language-related "folk knowledge" (everyday knowledge) and to language-independent scientific knowledge (and certainly not to any concrete reference works such as the *Oxford English Dictionary* or the *Encyclopaedia Britannica*).

I will try to show that language-related folk knowledge is different, and can be distinguished in a principled way, from other kinds of knowledge and that it can be articulated in a coherent and rigorous manner, and I will try to do it with reference to a domain regarded as particularly difficult and controversial, namely the domain of "living kinds".[1]

---

[1] Whether or not "folk-knowledge" in general can always be distinguished, in a principled way, from "scientific knowledge", is another matter, which need not concern us here at the moment. (See Section 6.) I am talking here about the knowledge which has become entrenched in the words of a particular language.

3. Scientific Knowledge versus Everyday Knowledge

It is widely believed that the names of animals acquire their meaning from science. The Bloomfieldian claim that *all* words acquire their meaning from science has been generally rejected in contemporary linguistics as self-evidently unacceptable, and (as far as I know) no dictionary has ever sought to define words such as *hate, fear,* or *tenderness* on the basis of the latest findings of neurophysiology, as recommended by Bloomfield (1933/1935) (see Chapter 1). None the less, in the area of the names of animals and plants, the "scientific" approach has always been strongly represented, even in dictionaries, and is still widespread. For example, the *Shorter Oxford English Dictionary* (*SOED* 1964) defines *horse* as "a solid-hoofed perissodactyl quadruped (*Equus caballus*)", *Webster* (1976) informs us that *horse* is "a large solid-hoofed herbivorous mammal (*Equus caballus*) domesticated by man since a prehistoric period", and the *Longman Dictionary* (*LDOTEL* 1984) finds it necessary to mention that the animal designated by the word *horse* belongs to the family Equidae, and that the word is applied specifically to animals "over 14.2 hands in height".

It seems hardly necessary to argue that scientific definitions of this kind do not represent the native speaker's concept. Science is, or tries to be, universal and to reflect the knowledge accumulated by mankind as a whole (and, more specifically, by the professional experts in different fields of knowledge); languages are not universal, and each of them reflects the experience of a particular part of mankind, united by a common culture and a common existential framework (and not the experience of any local experts but that of the "people-in-the-street").

This point was argued by the Russian linguist Jurij Apresjan, in his masterly work *Lexical Semantics* (1992: 32–3, 35):

The folk picture of the world that developed in the course of centuries and includes folk geometry, physics, psychology, etc., reflects the material and spiritual experience of a people (native speakers of a certain language) and therefore is language-specific in the following two respects.

First, a folk picture of a certain portion of the world may be crucially different from a purely logical scientific picture of the same portion of the world that is shared by speakers of a variety of languages.

The task of a lexicographer (unless he wants to go beyond his discipline and turn into an encyclopedist) consists of discovering the naive picture of the world hidden in lexical meanings and presenting it in a system of definitions.

Second, folk pictures of the world, obtained through analysis of meanings of words in various languages, may differ in details, whereas a scientific picture of the world does not depend on the language used to describe it.

In the area of names for animals, the language-specific character of the concepts encapsulated in words manifests itself on a number of different levels. To begin with, the basic categorization of the "animal kingdom" may differ considerably from language to language. For example, in Warlpiri the basic categories lexicalized in language are these:

(1) kuyu — meat, creature with edible meat
(2) pama — edible, not meat, doesn't grow out of the ground
(3) jurlpu — flying creatures with feathers

(The data are from Hale *et al.* forthcoming; the phrasing of the glosses is mine.) *Kuyu* includes not only edible "meaty" animals such as kangaroo, hare, or mouse, but also edible birds, snakes, and fish, and it excludes animals which can't be eaten. *Pama* includes edible creatures such as larvae (e.g. witchetty grubs) and edible insects such as honey ants; it also includes edible substances due to such creatures, such as honey or nectar, but it doesn't include red ants, flies, or mosquitoes (the classification is not exhaustive). *Jurlpu* includes most birds, but, for example, doesn't include emu.

At the level of "folk genera", too, the categorization embodied in the lexicon may differ from language to language. For example, Japanese and Thai don't distinguish lexically between mice and rats, and for native speakers of these languages it is quite difficult to learn the difference in meaning between the ordinary English words *rat* and *mouse*. On the other hand, English doesn't distinguish lexically between the moths that eat clothes and the moths that fly around lamps at night, which native speakers of Polish perceive as two totally different kinds of insect (*mole* and *ćmy*).

The stereotypes and the "folk knowledge" embodied in the names of animals may also differ from language to language. For example (as mentioned earlier), in Russian *išak* ("donkey") epitomizes hard work, whereas in English one "works (and eats) like a horse" rather than "like a donkey". In Thai, hard work is epitomized by a buffalo, in Malay, by a bullock, and in Polish, by an ox. In English, cats are thought of as common pets (as well as catchers of mice), but in Warlpiri they are thought of as *kuyu*, "meat". In English, mice are thought of as small creatures which live "in or near places where people live because they want to eat things that people keep for people to eat, people don't want them to live there"; and rats are thought of as repulsive creatures spreading diseases among people. But in Warlpiri, the two words glossed as "hopping mouse, rat" (and regarded as synonymous) have quite different connotations for the native speakers: "*jungunypa* and *wijipardu* are what we call a small animal. It lives here in burrows. It digs a big burrow. . . . We kill them to eat. We eat them. The meat of that small animal is good. They dig down in the burrows to find that animal and they kill it in its burrow. They take it to cook it" (Hale *et al.* forthcoming).

4. An Illustration: Folk Mice versus Scientific Mice

To show more clearly the difference between scientific knowledge and the kind of knowledge which is encapsulated in a folk concept of a natural kind I will adduce here one detailed illustration. This will take the form of a reasonably full explication of the folk concept *mice* (a revised version of that proposed in my *Lexicography and Conceptual Analysis*, 1985), compared with the full entry for *mice* in the *Encyclopaedia Britannica* (1969).

To show that the folk concept of 'mouse' parallels in its basic structure folk concepts encoded in other animal names we would have to include here, and discuss, many other such explications. Since this is impossible for reasons of space, the reader is again referred to *Lexicography and Conceptual Analysis*.[2]

MICE—an explication of the folk concept

a kind of creature	CATEGORY
people call them MICE	NAME
people think that they are all of the same kind	"ESSENCE"
because they come from other creatures of the same	
kind	ORIGIN
people think these things about them:	
they live in or near places where people live	HABITAT

because they want to eat things that people keep for people to eat
people don't want them to live there
(some creatures of a similar kind live in fields)

a person could hold one easily in one hand	SIZE

(most people wouldn't want to hold them)

they are greyish or brownish	APPEARANCE

one cannot notice them easily

(some creatures of this kind are white
some people use them when they want to find out what happens to
    creatures when people do various things to them
some people keep them in or near their houses
because they like to watch them and to look after them)

they have short legs

---

[2] Both the lexicon and the syntax of this explication are quite complex. If we wanted to simplify the language, we could do so fairly readily, but at the cost of lengthening the explications considerably, and making them much harder to read. For example, instead of saying 'because they come from creatures of the same kind' we could say:

because before they were things of this kind
they were parts of other creatures of this kind

because of this when they move one can't see their legs moving
it seems as if their whole body touches the ground
because of this they can get quickly into small openings in the ground
they are soft
they can squeeze into very narrow openings

their head looks as if it was not a separate part of the body
the whole body looks like one small thing with a long thin hairless tail
the front part of the head is pointed
it has a few stiff hairs sticking out sideways
there are two round ears sticking up one on either side of the top of
the head
they have small sharp teeth that they bite things with

they don't want to be near people or other animals   BEHAVIOUR
when people or other animals are near they make no noise
they hide from people and animals in places where people and animals
can't reach them
animals of another kind living in places where people live (cats) want to
catch and kill creatures of this kind
people put special things in or near their houses to catch creatures of this
kind and to kill them

when they are caught they make little sounds
it sounds as if they wanted to say that something bad was happening to
them

they move in places where people live looking for something to eat
they can move very quickly
they can move without making noise
sometimes when they move one can hear little sounds
it sounds as if something light and rigid was moving quickly on
something hard

sometimes one can see very small, dark roundish bits of something
(dung) in places where they have been

people think of them like this: RELATION
they are small creatures   TO PEOPLE
they are quiet
they don't want people or other animals to come near them
one cannot notice them easily
they can do bad things in places where people live
they like to eat firm yellowish stuff of a certain kind (cheese)
that people eat

Before we proceed to an encyclopaedia entry for *mice*, a few brief comments are in order.

The explication of the folk concept proposed here starts with four components, labelled here (for the sake of convenience) as "category", "name", "essence", and "origin". Jointly, these components present *mice* as what Berlin (1992) calls a "folk genus": a category of living things which is thought of as having a biologically transmitted inherent nature linked with a name (see Chapter 12). What follows is a series of components spelling out what Putnam (1975) calls the stereotype: what people think about mice. As with most other stereotypes of animals, the stereotype is organized around the following signposts: habitat, size, appearance, behaviour, relation to people. The sequence in which the components are given is not arbitrary but seeks to elucidate the internal logic of the folk concept (see Wierzbicka 1985). All this is very different from a typical encyclopaedia entry, such as the one which follows.

MOUSE (an encyclopaedic description)
An imprecise term designating any small rodent but often meant to apply to the common house mouse (*Mus musculus*), the type of the genus *Mus* and the family Muridae. In North America most species of the widespread and varied family Cricetidae also are called mice. Specific kinds of mice are usually designated by a compound term such as harvest mouse (*Micromys* of Europe; *Reithrodontomys* of America), wood mouse (*Apodemus* of Eurasia), whitefooted mouse (*Peromyscus* of America) or pocket mouse (*Perognathus* of North America).

Mice are indigenous to almost every land area and in a given area are likely to be the commonest of mammals. Some species are of narrowly restricted occurrence and habitat; others are wide-spread and versatile. The genus *Mus*, for example, occurs naturally on all major land masses; the typical species has been distributed by man to all inhabited areas of the earth and has become naturalized. One species of *Peromyscus* occurs over most of North and Central America from the subarctic to the tropics, in swamps, deserts, forests, mountains and prairies. Mice eat a variety of foods, some consuming almost anything edible—seeds, vegetation, arthropods and flesh when available. They are in turn preyed upon by all manner of larger carnivorous mammals, rapacious birds and reptiles. Mice constitute the most important prey group of any of the mammals.

Mice mature relatively young; the house mouse typically is ready to mate two to three months after birth. Gestation periods, averaging about three weeks, is less than two in some species. From 1 to 18 young comprise a litter, the size of the litter depending upon the species, the number of litters already produced by the female (the second or third is usually the largest) and the season. Breeding may take place at any season in some species and be seasonally restricted in others; in a widespread species the climate of a given region is usually the determinant.

Some species are social and live in common burrows or in colonies. Others are solitary. Even in the social house mouse, however, excessive crowding produces metabolic disorders and abnormal behaviour patterns that may result in the decimation of the population, a phenomenon thought to be related to the well-known periodic "suicidal" migrations of lemmings to the sea (*see* LEMMING).

Many mice, notably the house mouse, seem to prefer dwelling in man-made structures and can become serious pests, not only for the destruction they cause but also for the disease-producing organisms they may harbour (e.g., murine typhus, plague). Serious infestations may require the services of trained exterminators because of the lethality of some of the poisons that are often used. A minor infestation can be handled adequately and most safely by trapping. Mice, especially the house mouse, together with their near relatives, the brown and house rats, are responsible for enormous economic damage annually. Even those living in natural conditions may be so numerous in limited areas as to become serious, although usually temporary, agricultural pests. Except in abnormal circumstances, however, mice are on the whole beneficial to man because they form the bulk of the diet of most fur-bearing animals and of predators that otherwise prey on more valuable species, including domestic livestock. The experimental decimation of populations of native mice in North America, for example, has produced a concomitant sharp increase in fox and coyote predation on poultry and of coyote predation on sheep.

The common white laboratory mouse is a domesticated variant of the house mouse and is widely used in medical experimentation. They also are commonly kept as pets. Many other variant strains of known genetic and/or nutritional history have been developed for experimental purposes. (*Encyclopaedia Britannica*, 1969, xv. 963)

According to the *Encyclopaedia Britannica* entry reproduced above, *mouse* is an "imprecise term" which doesn't correspond exactly to any biological taxon. In natural language, however (that is, in ordinary English), it is not felt to be any less precise than folk genera such as *horse, rabbit,* or *squirrel.*

The scientific category *Mus musculus* does not correspond to the folk categorization reflected in the concept 'mouse': in everyday English "the common house mouse" (*Mus musculus*) is not thought of as a specific variety of a wider category "*Mus*", and the expression "house mouse" is not used at all, because it is precisely the "house mouse" which is normally called "mouse", with "field mice" or "white mice" being seen as horizontal extensions of the basic category (see Bright and Bright 1969; Hunn 1976; Berlin 1977), not as other varieties, on a par with "house mice".

Thus, the folk concept 'mice' stands for what ordinary people see as a specific 'kind of creature', different from scientific categories and identifiable in terms of its name ('people call them MICE'), and of its presumed nature ('they are all of the same kind'); a nature which cannot be fully reduced to any verbal descriptions but which has something to do with their reproduction ('they come from creatures of the same kind').

Reading the encyclopaedia entry for *mouse*, one is struck by the mass of information which is clearly not part of the everyday concept, such as information on the geographical distribution of mice, on the length of the gestation period, on the maximum size of a litter, on metabolic disorders caused by overcrowding, and so on. On the other hand, a great deal of information which is essential to the everyday concept is missing. This includes, for example, information on what mice look like, on the way they move, on the sounds they make, on their special relationship with cats, on their "psychological" characteristics, and so on. This is the way it should be: the encyclopaedia is not aiming at capturing what is psychologically real and linguistically relevant (from the point of view of native speakers of English).[3] But there should also be another kind of compendium (a "cultural dictionary") which would explicate the everyday concept of 'mice'.

5. The Evidence for the Folk Concept

How do we know that the folk concept of 'mice' includes such information?

The methodology of establishing the content (and also the form) of a given folk concept is a complex topic which cannot be discussed here at length. (For more detailed discussion, see Wierzbicka (1985) and Chapter 11; see also Apresjan (1974/1992). I will, however, adduce here examples of different kinds of evidence that can be used).

To begin with, there is lexical evidence. In the case of mice, this includes words and phrases such as *mousy, mousetrap, mousehole, to mouse, mouser, mouse-ear*, or *mouse-tail*. The adjective *mousy* (as in *mousy hair* or *mousy appearance*) suggests that mice are indeed seen as particularly inconspicuous, hard to notice, greyish-brownish in colour. The noun *mousetrap* documents the fact that mice are seen as creatures that are unwelcome in human dwellings, that often people want to catch and kill them, and that there are special devices for doing that. Some dictionaries (e.g. *LDOTEL*) mention that in British English the word *mousetrap* or the expression *mousetrap cheese* is also used to refer to "inexpensive poor quality, usually Cheddar, cheese (from its being considered fit for use only as bait to trap mice)". This usage documents not only the psychological reality of the catching, killing, and getting rid of as parts of the folk concept of 'mice', but also that of the link (supposed or real) between *mice* and *cheese*.

The compound *mousehole*, defined by *OED* as "a hole used by a mouse for passage or abode; a hole only big enough to admit a mouse", supports the reality of the references to "small openings in the ground".

---

[3] On the other hand, the complexity of the language typically used in encyclopaedias is not justified either from a practical or from a theoretical point of view. For example, there is no reason why one should say that some species of mice are "versatile" rather than that they "can live in many different kinds of places"; that they eat "flesh" rather than "meat" or "arthropods" rather than "small creatures such as insects and spiders"; or that they are "indigenous to" rather than "native" (not to paraphrase it any further). By bringing the language of encyclopaedic explanations a little closer to the level of universal semantic primitives (such as 'do' and 'happen', 'know' and 'want', or 'kind' and 'part') one could make these explanations more accessible and more useful to potential users, without jeopardizing in any way their scientific validity and their distinct status (quite different from that of language-specific dictionaries).

The noun *mouser* (as in "she is a good mouser") documents the psychological reality of the link between mice and cats, which is further supported by expressions such as "a cat and a mouse" or sayings such as "when the cat is away the mice will play". This suggests that a reference to cats should be included in the explication of *mice*, just as a reference to mice should be included in the explication of *cats*. This can be done without circularity because we don't have to include the actual words *cat* and *mouse* in the explication; for *mice*, it is sufficient to include some component such as 'animals of another kind living in places where people live want to catch and kill creatures of this kind'.

According to many dictionaries, there is also a verb *to mouse*, which can be used not only with respect to mouse-hunting by cats (and perhaps owls), but also to describe human activities: "to go or move about softly in search of something, to prowl" (*OED*), "to search furtively for something, to prowl" (*AHDOTEL*). This use attests to the psychological reality of the components referring to noiseless, furtive movements in search of food.

The compound *mouse-ear*, noted in many dictionaries, stands for "any of several plants that have soft hairy leaves" (*LDOTEL*). Obviously, this is based on a perceived analogy with mouse ears, and thus it constitutes evidence for the psychological reality of ears in the folk concept of *mouse*. Similarly, the compound *mouse-tail* ("a plant of the genus *Myosurus*, esp. *M. minimus*, from the shape of its seed receptacle", *OED*) attests to the salience of the tail in the folk concept of mouse. (See also the reference to "tails" in the well-known rhyme about "the three blind mice").

It might be added that the recent use of the word *mouse* to refer to a piece of computer equipment also highlights the salience of certain aspects of size, shape, and type of movement perceived as characteristic of mice. In particular, this use appears to support the idea that "the whole body looks like one small thing with a long thin hairless tail". This is all the more interesting since from a physical, objective point of view the shape of a computer mouse is of course different from that of the animal. But one can see how the subjective impression of a compact, light little "body" with a long thin hairless "tail", capable of quick, light, noiseless movements, fits both mice and computer mice (or mouses).

In the case of many other names of animals, lexical evidence comes also in the form of words semantically (though not necessarily morphologically) derived from these names (in Cruse's (1986) terminology, "endonyms"). For example, in the case of *horse*, there is a whole family of "horse words" such as *neigh, gallop, trot, pony, saddle, reins, stirrups, star, stud, steed, groom, jockey, mustang, cavalry*, and so on (see Wierzbicka 1985: 201). In the case of *mice*, there are perhaps no such endonyms (other than those morphologically related to *mouse*, such as *mouser*), but there are words which are commonly associated with *mice*; these include *scurry, squeak*, *nibble*, and perhaps *scamper*. These words give evidence for various aspects of the folk concept, such as characteristic movements, sounds, and activities.

Common phrases such as *quiet as a mouse* or *poor as a church mouse* are also a source of evidence. The first of these two phrases underscores the perceived quietness of mice, and the second, their perceived connection with human houses as a place which (unlike a church) can be seen as a permanent source of food.

Another source of evidence is to be found in conventional metaphors. A person (normally a woman) who is called *a mouse* is perceived as quiet, shy, not very noticeable, not drawing attention to herself. As mentioned earlier, metaphors of this kind are partly language-specific and they often reveal important aspects of the folk concept.

Often, valuable evidence comes from proverbs and common sayings, such as the one about cats and mice cited earlier.

Literature, in particular poetry, is also a valuable source of evidence, although one which has to be used with caution, so that individual associations can be separated from shared ones. Children's rhymes, with their mixture of fantasy and stereotyped everyday experience, are particularly useful in this respect. For example, the well-known lines ". . . three blind mice, see how they run" highlight the importance of quick and apparently effortless movement in the folk concept of 'mouse', and so does the following rhyme:

> Hickory dickory dock,
> The mouse ran up the clock,
> The clock struck one,
> The mouse ran down,
> Hickory dickory dock.

Finally, we can mention ethnographic evidence of a non-linguistic type, such as the appearance of mice in common cartoons (e.g. Mickey Mouse's conspicuous round ears); the schematic drawings of mice emphasizing a long thin tail at the end of a compact, visually legless and undifferentiated little body; common children's games such as the one involving a farmer, a farmer's wife, a mouse, and cheese; and so on.

It is important to emphasize that the folk concept of 'mouse' cannot be established simply by putting direct questions to informants: the kind of knowledge which we are trying to establish is tacit knowledge, which is hidden below the surface of consciousness and which can only be brought to the surface through painstaking, methodical search. None the less, prolonged dialogue with a number of informants is very useful, too, though more as a method of verification than as a direct "discovery procedure". For example, one reviewer of the earlier explication of *mice* (in Wierzbicka

1985) has objected to "the statement that mice make no noise when moving around" and pointed out that "many people think mice make scratchy, rustling noises" (Malt 1987: 266). Other informants with whom I have since checked this point have agreed with the reviewer, and the explication has been amended in the relevant respect. I presume, however, that the reviewer hit upon the idea of the "scratchy, rustling noises" by exploring her own intuitions rather than by asking large numbers of informants. Obviously, we need both: methodical introspection and working with informants. But given the prevailing practice it is the former, not the latter, which needs to be stressed. It also needs to be stressed that methodical introspection can be supported with evidence other than the widely used procedures involving informants, in particular with linguistic evidence of various kinds. (For further discussion, see Chapter 12.)

6. General Discussion

Systematic, methodical exploration of folk concepts, using all available avenues of evidence, allows us to delineate their contours with a precision which, appearances to the contrary, is simply inaccessible to an encyclopaedia entry. The editor of an encyclopaedia has to decide, in an inevitably somewhat arbitrary manner, what to include from the mass of available information and what to ignore, how to arrange the information chosen, which aspects of it to highlight, and so on. In investigating folk concepts encoded in natural language, the position is quite different, because the linguist is not faced with the task of choosing what to include; here, the task consists in discovering the full concept as it really is, using all available evidence, and, at the same time, trying to use exclusively simpler (much simpler) concepts than the one which is being explicated. These two requirements—to articulate the concept fully, and to do it as far as possible in simple words—mean that far less room is left for individual choices than in an encyclopaedia entry.

To be able to delineate a folk concept accurately we need that attention to detail which was first postulated by Žolkovskij (1964b), who called for detailed lexicographic "portraits" of individual words. From the present point of view, however, the metaphor of a portrait is not fully apposite because it suggests a large measure of artistic freedom. By contrast, an explication of the kind envisaged here should leave no freedom of choice; the work of the analyst can perhaps be better compared to that of an archaeologist trying to uncover the outline of a statue or an artefact hidden in rubble or volcanic deposit.

Haiman (1982: 354) has argued against "the separation of dictionaries and encyclopaedias" on the grounds that "there are no hard facts, and all science is ethnoscience" (337), and that, for example, "our present knowledge of cats and elephants is as provisional, and specific to our culture, as the definitions of words like *care* and *taboo* in the languages where they occur" (337; see also the exchange between Frawley 1981 and Haiman 1982). But the conclusion doesn't follow from the premiss. The encyclopaedia entry for *mouse* quoted earlier may indeed be "provisional", "specific to our culture", and, I would add, based on a number of somewhat subjective and arbitrary choices. Yet the purpose of an encyclopaedia would not be served by replacing entries of this kind with the explication of the folk concept of the kind outlined in this chapter. Paradoxically, of the two, it is the dictionary entry, not the encyclopaedia entry, which can be said to be "objective" and non-arbitrary, and to represent a "hard fact". Psychocultural fact, of course, not biological fact. An encyclopaedia entry for *mouse* may be provisional, biased, and subjective in its choices and in its emphases, but it doesn't aim at establishing psychocultural facts; it does not aim at discovering conceptual structures. Encyclopaedic knowledge is cumulative and inexhaustible. By contrast, the meanings of words are discrete and finite. They embody a special kind of knowledge (and pseudo-knowledge, such as that about mice's fondness for cheese), and they constitute a vital point of reference for both communication and cognition.

It is true that the meanings of names of living kinds—unlike, for example, those of emotion terms—do have a measure of indeterminacy, since the amount of "folk knowledge" encapsulated in a naïve concept may vary somewhat from speaker to speaker (see Gal 1973; Gardner 1976; Hays 1976; and also Locke 1690/1959: 82). But there is a limit to this variation. For example, information such as that mice are ready to mate two or three months after birth, or that gestation period averages about three weeks, cannot be part of anybody's "naïve concept". It can, of course, be part of their individual knowledge, but not of that concept which they themselves see as a shared stereotype, on the basis of their life-experiences in the community (see Wierzbicka 1985: 212–18; Tyler 1978: 233–48).

This is not to say that living kind concepts such as 'mice' have, after all, the same kind of semantic structure as, for example, emotion concepts. The two domains are fundamentally different, and the greater variability of living kind concepts constitutes one of the important differences between them. But it doesn't follow from this that living kind concepts cannot be defined (or explicated); and from an explication the differences separating them from scientific concepts (and from scientific knowledge) can be clearly seen.

In rejecting the (theoretical) distinction between dictionaries and encyclopaedias Haiman (1982) was in fact defending the view that natural kind words such as *mice* or *horses* embody a great deal of "cultural knowledge" and that they could therefore be defined. In saying this, he was arguing against the earlier claims of Kripke (1972), Putnam (1975), and others, including myself, that natural kind words are like proper names and cannot be defined. I believe now that Haiman is partly right, and that natural kind words (such as *mice*) can indeed be defined, explicating the cultural knowledge encapsulated in them. (The reasons why I have abandoned my 1972 position in this regard are set out in Wierzbicka (1985).)

But a line can be drawn between cultural knowledge which has become deposited in language itself and other knowledge—whether scientific or non-scientific. Haiman argues that "the distinction between linguistic and cultural knowledge" is misconceived, and I would partly agree with this, in so far that, for example, the "linguistic" knowledge about mice, spelled out in the explication proposed in this chapter, represents cultural knowledge. But there is also knowledge about mice which is not part of the folk concept reflected in language—and a line can be drawn between that knowledge and the knowledge (and ideas) encapsulated in the word *mouse* itself.

The fact that different languages draw such boundaries in different ways demonstrates that these boundaries can indeed be drawn. For example, if Japanese doesn't distinguish lexically between mice and rats, or English between clothes moths (in Polish, *mole*) and other moths (in Polish, *ćmy*), this shows that semantic boundaries between different living kind concepts do exist, and that they are different from those drawn by biologists.

Haiman's claims that "all science is ethnoscience" (1982: 337) and that "the difference between everyday experience and scientific experience is a difference in degree of precision and generality" do not affect the present argument: the question is not how to draw the line between science and ethnoscience, or between cultural knowledge and linguistic knowledge, but how to draw the line between knowledge and ideas which are encoded in language and knowledge and ideas which are not.

7. Conclusion

Trying to discover how knowledge (or at least basic, "foundational" knowledge) is stored and organized in the human mind, we can rely in considerable measure on language. There may be concepts which are not lexicalized in natural language, but these are probably less common, less basic, less salient in a given speech community than those which have achieved lexicalization; they are also less accessible to study. Words provide evidence for the existence of concepts. Lexical sets, sharing a similar semantic structure, provide evidence for the existence of cohesive conceptual wholes (or fields). If it is hypothesized that knowledge is organized in the mind in the form of "cognitive domains", then conceptual fields detectable through semantic analysis of the lexicon can be regarded as a guide to those domains.

The organization of cognitive domains is reflected in language, and above all in the structure of the lexicon. The lexicon of a language is the speakers' fundamental cognitive resource; it is a treasury where the shared knowledge of the world, and the shared models of biological, mental, and social aspects of life, are held.

Exploring the lexicon in a systematic and methodical way we can discover how "ordinary people" (in contrast to experts and scientists) conceptualize the world; and we can learn to discern the line which separates language-related everyday knowledge from the specialist's knowledge, which is—or should be—largely language-independent.

12 Semantics and Ethnobiology

□ □ _____

1. Introduction

It is widely agreed today that "culture 'does not consist of things, people, behavior, or emotions', but the forms or organization of these things in the minds of people" (Frake 1962: 85, with reference to Goodenough 1957). The question which *might* cause disagreement is this: How can the organization of "these things" in the minds of people be discovered?

I believe that the best—and yet much neglected—path to discovery lies in the area of language, and that there is a whole battery of linguistic tests which can be put to use to reveal different aspects of the organization of the universe in the minds of people. In this chapter, I will try to show the usefulness of the linguistic approach with respect to some of the basic issues in ethnobiology.

The intensive and detailed study of botanical and zoological nomenclature in different languages of the world (especially that undertaken by Brent Berlin and his associates) has revealed that different societies differ considerably in their conceptualization of the biological universe; but it has also shown that "there are a number of strikingly regular structural principles of folk biological classification which are quite general" (Berlin *et al.* 1973: 214). Along different lines, universals have also been suggested by Cecil Brown (1977, 1979, 1987).

The apparent discovery of ethnobiological universals and the ensuing debate have further stimulated interest in the conceptualization of plants and animals, and they are largely responsible for the key position of this conceptual domain in current anthropology. In particular, the recent interest in "domain specificity", which is rapidly becoming one of the most topical issues in cognitive science, is focusing very much on this particular domain (see e.g. Gelman 1992; Keil 1989; Hirshfeld and Gelman 1994). In the current debate on the question of "whether there are domain-specific cognitive universals that account for the peculiar kinds of regularities apparent in folk systems of knowledge and belief . . . or whether those regularities are the product of general processing mechanisms that cross . . . domains" (Atran 1990: 47), the domain of "living kinds" is accorded a special place and is often treated as a natural testing-ground.

One issue which attracts particular attention in this context is that of the role of taxonomic structures in the human conceptualization of the world. Thirty years ago Frake stated that "the use of taxonomic systems . . . is a fundamental principle of human thinking" (1962: 81). More recently, however, it has been suggested that "hierarchical ranking of living kinds is apparently unique to that domain" (Atran 1990: 57; see also Wierzbicka 1984: 325). And while the importance of absolutely ranked taxonomies in human thinking and in human representation of knowledge has not been called into question (on the contrary, it has been reaffirmed), the universality of this principle (across domains, not across cultures) has been questioned. Indeed, the special link that this principle appears to have with the domain of "living things" has been used as a major argument in favour of domain specificity in human cognition in general.

Another topical issue involving folk biology in a special way is that of the nature of human categorization and of the role of prototypes in it. After a decade dominated by an obsession with prototypes and family resemblances and with the alleged fuzziness of human thinking (see Chapter 4; see also Atran 1990: 54–5), it is becoming increasingly clear that the notion of category (discrete category) plays a fundamental role in human thinking and cannot be reduced to the notion of resemblance. To put it in terms of the theory of universal semantic primitives, the notion of KIND (*"X* is a kind of *Y"*) cannot be reduced to the notion of LIKE (*"X* is like *Y"*). Similarity is not necessarily an adequate indicator of conceptual closeness (e.g. an Alsatian may be more "similar" to a wolf than to a Pekinese, but the folk category "dog" disregards this). In ethnobiology, horizontal extensions, based on the notion of LIKE (*mock orange, koala bear, jellyfish*), are universally distinguished from "vertical" subdivisions based on the notion of KIND (e.g. *polar bear, birch tree, king fish*). (See Berlin 1992.)

As Gelman and Coley put it, "similarity alone cannot explain why things belong to a given category" (1991; see also Rips 1989). The cross-linguistic validity of the concept of biological species (in the sense of folk genus) lends vital support to the emerging view that human thinking is not "fuzzy", as it was claimed to be by Rosch and her followers (Lakoff 1973; Rosch 1978; Rosch and Mervis 1975) and acccords a considerable place to discrete categorization.

A related theoretical issue, linked in a special way with folk biology, is that of the role of "essences" in human cognition (that is, the question of whether certain categories operating in human conceptualization of the world embody a presumption of an "essence" manifested in, but distinct from, "surface properties" (see Medin 1989; Medin and Ortony 1989). In particular, it has been suggested that the universal principles of folk-biological taxonomy include a presumption of "underlying natures" or "hidden essences" (corresponding, *mutatis mutandis*, to Locke's (1690/1959) "real essences"); and that—contrary to what Putnam (1975) and Kripke

(1972) asserted in this connection in their classic papers—this presumption is restricted to natural kind concepts (Atran 1990).

Thus, the study of folk biology, which has played a major role in the development of cognitive anthropology, promises to be a key factor in the development of cognitive science, and to throw light on such vital larger questions as the nature of human categorization, the existence of domain-specific cognitive abilities, the universality and perhaps innateness of certain concepts and certain principles of conceptualization, and so on.

To fulfil this role, however, ethnobiology needs a broad empirical basis involving the study of many different, and diverse, languages of the world, and it also requires an adequate conceptual framework; and an adequate framework cannot be developed without sufficient attention being paid to linguistic considerations.

2. Ethnobiological Analysis: Tools and Methods

To study the classification and naming of biological organisms in different languages of the world we need well-defined and language-independent conceptual tools. Among those proposed in recent ethnobiological literature the most important ones are undoubtedly the concepts "folk genus" and "life form" (Atran 1985; Berlin *et al.* 1973). So far, however, these terms have not been sufficiently well defined to be able to serve as precise tools in the cross-linguistic study of folk-biological systems and in the search for ethnobiological universals. In particular, the concept of "life form"—despite its widely recognized importance—is surrounded by a great deal of confusion.

Randall (1987: 146) is clearly sceptical about the concept "life form", and insists that it can only be valid if defined in purely perceptual terms. He assumes that what is needed is a detailed analysis of putative life forms for non-European languages (with the apparent implication that in European languages, and in particular in English, all is clear), and that the structure of conceptual categories can be revealed, above all, by interviewing (perhaps only by interviewing).

In my view, however, the situation in English with respect to the concept "life form" is far from clear. This lack of clarity, prevailing even with respect to a shared language to whose data all the writers on the subject have intuitive access, highlights the conceptual confusion which continues to surround the concept. In trying to clarify it we should begin, I believe, not with a range of non-European languages but with English, and not with large-scale interviewing of informants but with focused conceptual analysis. Furthermore, the experience of detailed semantic analysis of large bodies of data involving hundreds of lexical items (see e.g. Wierzbicka 1985,

1987*a*) shows that direct questioning of informants, and even experiments involving informants, can only be a subsidiary methodological tool. Information coming directly from informants is often superficial, unreliable, and misleading. Linguistic tests based on methodical examination of usage (such as, for example, those envisaged in the classic studies by Conklin (1962) and Frake (1962)) and on systematic examination of lexical and grammatical evidence (such as those applied in Apresjan (1974/1992), Berlin (1992), or Dixon (1982)) provide more reliable results.

To illustrate, in McCloskey and Glucksberg's (1978) sessions with college students it emerged that 3 per cent of their informants said "No" to the question "Are geese birds?", whereas as many as 17 per cent said "Yes" to the question "Are bats birds?" McCloskey and Glucksberg draw from such data the conclusion that the category "bird" in English is fuzzy. In fact, however, closer examination of linguistic evidence shows that this category is not fuzzy at all, and that while geese may be thought of as atypical birds, they are none the less conceptualized as "a kind of bird", whereas bats are not conceptualized as birds at all (see Chapter 4 and Wierzbicka 1985). The crucial point is that, in certain circumstances, an individual goose can be referred to as *bird* (as a turkey at a Christmas dinner may well be referred to as "the bird"), whereas a bat cannot.

Similarly, all the informants that McCloskey and Glucksberg worked with agreed that *butterflies* are *insects*, while 3 per cent stated that *bees* were not *insects*, and 7 per cent that *bats* were *insects*; for *fish*, 60 per cent of informants classified *jellyfish* as *fish*, 10 per cent classified *alligators* as *fish*, and 2 per cent stated that *tuna* and *salmon* are not *fish*. This, too, was interpreted as evidence for the alleged fuzziness of human thinking, and for the lack of clear boundaries between different categories.

But in fact such results are artefacts of the particular techniques of investigation. Generally speaking, directly classificatory questions ("Is an *X* a *Y*?" or "What is an *X*?") are unhelpful in the analysis of folk taxonomies. What is more illuminating and reliable is the acceptability of sentences referring to individual creatures, such as "Look at that fish over there!" said with respect to *jellyfish*, or "How many birds can you see?" with respect to groups including *geese*, *bats*, or *bees*; as well as other kinds of linguistic evidence (such as those discussed in Apresjan 1974/1992).

Similarly, Dougherty (1978: 78–9) reports that all students in one of her samples placed *butterflies* in the *insect* category (as does, incidentally, Cruse (1986: 136) in his discussion of English folk taxonomies). But presumably, the same informants would not say "See that insect over there?" or "What a beautiful insect!" with reference to a *butterfly*. This suggests that their responses were confusing scientific categorization with everyday language, and misrepresented the subconscious folk taxonomy reflected in their actual use of language.

As pointed out by Boas (1911) and Sapir (1927), the categorization reflected in language is unconscious, and it is for this very reason that language is such a revealing and valuable guide to culture and to social psychology. Direct questioning of informants appeals to their conscious knowledge, not to their tacit knowledge, and is unlikely to reveal much about their unconscious conceptualization of the world, which is revealed more clearly and reliably in linguistic structures and in linguistic usage (see Randall and Hunn 1984: 333).[1]

3. Types of Linguistic Evidence

There are many types of linguistic evidence which provide clues to the conceptualization of the biological universe. I will not try to undertake here a comprehensive survey or detailed discussion (see, however, Wierzbicka 1985), but the five types listed below (Sections 3.1–3.5) are particularly important. The last two of these have already been introduced, with respect to *mice*, in Chapter 11.

3.1. Ways of Referring

One can refer to a *rose* as "that flower" or to a *magpie* as "that bird"; but in ordinary (non-scientific) usage one cannot refer to a particular *tree* as "that plant" or to a particular *pumpkin*, as "that vine". This shows that, despite many claims to the contrary, a *tree* (singular) is not conceptualized in folk English as "a kind of plant", or a *pumpkin*, as "a kind of vine":

*Look at that plant over there! It's the oldest oak in this country.

Similar tests show, incidentally, that the recent wave of "anti-Roschian" thinking sometimes goes too far, as when, for example, it is claimed that in the English folk taxonomy dissimilar creatures such as caterpillars and butterflies, or frogs and tadpoles, are classified together (Atran 1990: 63;

---

[1] The difficulty in identifying life forms in different languages of the world is well illustrated by Randall and Hunn (1984: 334). I suggest that the operational criteria proposed in this chapter would lead to much more reliable results, although the resulting repertoires of life forms would not always coincide with those proposed by Berlin *et al.* (1973) or by C. Brown (1977, 1979). In particular, the difference between monolexemically and polylexemically labelled taxa, whose validity or importance Randall and Hunn (1984: 343) question, should continue to be regarded as important evidence pointing to differences in the underlying conceptualization. Furthermore, it should be kept in mind that "functional" and "utilitarian" concepts such as *vegetable* or *fruit* often behave differently (in linguistic usage) from "morphotypes" such as *tree* or *bird* (Wierzbicka 1984, 1985, 1988a). On the other hand, linguistic evidence shows that some categories, for example *flower*, which have been judged as "functional" and disqualified on this basis as a potential life form (Atran 1987a: 32; C. Brown 1977: 320), may in folk taxonomy play a role analogous to that of genuine, taxonomic life forms such as *bird*, *fish*, or *tree*.

Gelman and Coley 1991). For example, one cannot say in English while pointing to a *tadpole* or a *caterpillar*:

*Look at that frog!
*Look at that butterfly!

Linguistic tests of this kind show that while an *Alsatian* and a *dachshund*, despite their dissimilarity, are put into the same folk category (*dog*), a *tadpole* and a *frog*, or a *butterfly* and a *caterpillar*, are not.

3.2. Grammatical Congruity

Leach (1964: 41) has drawn a taxonomic tree of what he calls "the English language discriminations of living creatures", which implies that in English *pigs* are "a kind of farm animals", *farm animals* are "a kind of livestock", *livestock* is "a kind of tame beast", *tame beast* is "a kind of beast", and *beast* is a kind of "land creature".

Many different tests could be used to show that this is an arbitrary scheme invented by the researcher, not a faithful representation of the classification embodied in the English language. One of these tests is that of "grammatical congruity": *pig* is a countable noun, whereas *livestock* is a mass noun (cf. *three pigs* versus *three livestocks*); on these grounds alone we can establish that a *pig* is not conceptualized in English as "a kind of livestock", just as an *apple* (countable noun) is not conceptualized as "a kind of fruit" (mass noun), or a *chicken* (countable noun) as "a kind of poultry" (see Wierzbicka 1984, 1985, 1988a; see also Section 10 below).

3.3. Morphological Structure

The morphological structure of a linguistic expression provides an important clue to its meaning. For example, as pointed out by Mel'čuk *et al.* (1984: 41), the two Russian expressions *tešča* ('wife's mother', one word) and *mat' ženy* ('wife's mother', lit. 'mother of wife', two words) do not have quite the same meaning. Both *tešča* and *mat' ženy* specify a certain relationship, but *tešča* in addition identifies a certain (recognizable) *kind* of relationship and it is the latter, not the former, which is always used in the innumerable Russian jokes about mothers-in-law. Similarly, as pointed out by Langacker (1993), the two English expressions *venison* and *deer meat* suggest different conceptualizations. Likewise in Polish, *wołowina*, 'beef', is not used in quite the same way as *mięso wołowe,* literally 'ox meat' (referentially, the same thing as 'beef'). For example, in the context of meat exports, one would be more likely to use the phrase *mięso wołowe*, whereas in the context of a dinner menu one would be more likely to use the noun *wołowina*. *Mięso wołowe* differentiates this particular kind of meat from other possible kinds, whereas *wołowina* identifies a recognizable standard kind of food. Considerations of this kind support the significance of the distinction between "secondary lexemes" (such as *blue spruce* or *scrub oak*) and "primary lexemes" (whether analysable, such as *tulip-tree*, or unanalysable ones, such as *poplar* or *elm*), drawn by Berlin, Breedlove, and Raven (1973).

3.4. Phraseological Evidence

To elucidate the English concept of, say, 'butterfly', we can draw on the stock of common English phrases and secondary lexemes, such as, for example, "a social butterfly", "butterfly kiss", "butterfly clip", or "butterfly stroke"; for 'rabbit' we can, and should, draw on phrases such as "breed like rabbits", "a rabbit warren", "rabbit teeth", "rabbit mouth", "run away like a scared rabbit", and so on (see Jauncey 1990).

The fact that the common English collocations involving *mouse* differ considerably from the Japanese collocations involving *nezumi*, 'mouse/rat', suggests that the two folk concepts in question are very different. Analysis of the two sets of collocations shows in what respects these two folk concepts differ (see Miyokawa 1989).

3.5. Lexical Evidence

English has many different "endonyms" of the word *dog*, that is to say, words which are, so to speak, semantically derived from it (see Chapter 11)—first of all, names of kinds of dogs, such as *spaniel, poodle, fox-terrier, bulldog, boxer, dachshund*, and so on, but also other kinds of "dog-words", such as *bark, growl, muzzle, leash*, and *kennel*. All these words provide evidence for some aspects of the conceptualization linked with the English word *dog*. The existence of special nouns for kinds of dogs reflects aspects of the folk classification, and shows that the conceptual hierarchy is in this case more complex than it is for any other part of the English folk-biological system (see Wierzbicka 1985 and Section 7 below).

The fact that English has numerous nouns for kinds of dogs (e.g. *poodle, spaniel, boxer*, and so on) but no nouns for kinds of cats or kinds of mice suggests that the two domains are conceptualized differently. Moreover, it suggests that the domain of dogs, but not cats or mice, involves a special level of taxonomic categorization ("subgenus"; see Cecil Brown 1987; Wierzbicka 1985: 232–6). Roughly speaking, a word such as *poodle* or *spaniel* identifies a certain kind of dog, whereas an expression such as *blue whale, white mouse, silver fox*, or *bush turkey* identifies a kind of animal (namely, *whale, mouse, fox*, or *turkey*) and differentiates some subset or quasi-subset of the class of animals corresponding to that kind from other possible subsets. This distinction between positive identification and differentiation, whose importance was first pointed out by Berlin, Breedlove, and Raven (1973), is reflected in a number of ways in linguistic usage (see Wierzbicka 1985). It is also often reflected in diachrony, since a cultural change may lead to a change in conventional conceptualization, and hence to a linguistic change such as that from *Alsatian* (adj.) *dog* to *Alsatian* (noun).

I am not saying that linguistic evidence is the only reliable guide to human conceptualization in general and to human categorization in particular. There are, of course, many other types of ethnographic evidence that anthropologists have traditionally relied on. But linguistic evidence is particularly revealing.

4. "Life Forms" in English Folk Zoology

How many "life forms" can be found in the zoological folk taxonomy embedded in the English language? And by what criteria can we recognize them?

The first criterion proposed by Berlin, Breedlove, and Raven (1973) and Berlin (1981) is that of number: life form categories are few in number. This is useful, but it doesn't really help us to decide on individual cases (for example, on *slug*, *snake*, *spider*, or *butterfly*).

A second, and operationally much more useful, criterion is that of "polytypicity": a life form is a category which is thought of as comprising many different (named) kinds of entities. Applying this criterion to the folk zoology embedded in English, we could identify the following as life forms: *animal*, *bird*, *fish*, *snake*, and perhaps *insect*. All these words naturally invite the question "What kind of (animal, bird, fish, snake)?" and all are readily used in reply to questions of the form "What is a (platypus, emu, salmon, python)?" Interestingly, the words *bug* and *worm* are normally not used like that; rather, they suggest a lack of interest in the identity of the creatures in question:

> There are bugs on my windscreen.
> ?What kind of bugs?
> There is a worm in that apple!
> ?What kind of worm?

In most contexts, questions inquiring about the genus of *bugs* or *worms* sound either jocular or scientific, which is not the case with unfamiliar birds, fishes, or snakes, or with unfamiliar animals in a zoo:

> What kind of bird/fish/snake/animal/?worm/?bug is that?

Berlin, Breedlove, and Raven (1973) offer *mammal* as an example of a life form, and mention *animal* only as a "unique beginner", not as a life form. But *mammal*—like *quadruped, carnivore,* or *amphibian*—is a scientific concept, and doesn't belong to the English folk taxonomy at all. This can be proved by linguistic tests such as the following one:

> Look at that animal/bird/fish!
> *Look at that mammal/quadruped/amphibian!

Scientific concepts such as *mammal* stand for classes, not for individuals, and it is remarkable that although educated speakers of English are, so to speak, bilingual (in "scientific English" and in "folk English"), and can mix elements from both in their speech, none the less they unconsciously apply different rules to them and in particular do not use scientific concepts such as *mammal* with reference to individual creatures:

> What a beautiful animal/bird/fish!
> *What a beautiful mammal/quadruped/amphibian!

Using the same linguistic tests, we have to conclude that *animal* is not a "unique beginner" in folk English, as it cannot be used with reference to individual *spiders* or *ants*. For example, seeing an insect on somebody's collar one cannot say (except in jest):

> *There is an animal on your collar.

Similarly, one cannot (seriously) say of a spider or a butterfly:

> *What a beautiful animal!
> *Look at that animal over there!

If there is a zoological "unique beginner" in ordinary English it is *creature*, not *animal*, *animal* being rather a life form, on a par with *bird, fish, snake,* or *insect* (cf. phrases such as "animals and birds", or series of children's books such as "Animals of Australia", "Birds of Australia", and "Fish of Australia"). The word *creature* is perhaps not used very often in colloquial English, but it is certainly there (especially in the plural) as shown by phrases such as "all creatures great and small", or by sentences such as the following one:

> Diving in the Coral Sea, one can see all sorts of strange and fascinating creatures.

If the word *creature* did not exist in the English folk taxonomy reflected in ordinary English we could still speak of a covert category: 'something that can move and feel' (*movens sentiens*), opposed to the covert category of 'things that grow out of the ground'.

Returning to *animal*, in the non-scientific sense of the word, it is interesting to note that it is not just a colloquial equivalent of *mammal*, as has sometimes been suggested in the literature. For example, a crocodile can easily be referred to as an *animal*, whereas a spider or an ant cannot; and neither can a slug, a snail, or a butterfly. On the other hand, human beings are *mammals*, but they are not *animals* in the everyday sense of the word.

Atran (1987*a*: 55) writes: 'For the most part, vertebrate life forms correspond to modern [scientific] classes: mammals, birds, fish, etc. . . . Most often, folk views on the extensions of these life forms differ from scientifically construed extensions of the corresponding classes in regard to what, from the folk viewpoint, are rather marginal cases . . . bat, ostrich, whale, etc.'.

But in fact *mammal* is not a part of the folk-English taxonomy; and the folk English concept *animal*, whose extension is really quite different from that of *mammal*, does include *whale* and *bat* (as well as *crocodile* or *turtle*). Furthermore, in the present-day folk-zoological system, *ostrich* is a bird, though a highly atypical one. In some ways, then, English folk taxonomy is closer to the scientific one than is usually assumed. In other ways, however, it is much further from it—but to see this it must be recognized that words such as *mammal* or *quadruped* belong only to the language of science, and are not part of the English folk taxonomy at all.

It is worth recalling in this connection Russell's (1948: 83) remark that words such as *dog* or *ant* are probably learnt by ostension whereas words such as *quadruped* or *animal* ("in the sense in which it includes oysters and limpets") are definitely not. Russell doesn't spell out the intended generalization, and it might be conjectured that the distinction that he had in mind was similar to that between "folk genera" and higher-level categories. But presumably life form terms such as *bird* or *tree* are also learnt partly "by ostension"; on the other hand, scientific concepts such as *mammal, amphibian,* or *animal* (in the sense including *spiders*) are clearly never learnt that way. (Cf. Chapter 7.)

5. Are there Monogeneric "Life Forms"?

But if creatures such as spiders or snails are not thought of as *animals*, what (folk-English) life form do they come under? Clearly, they are not *insects, snakes, fishes,* or *birds*. Could we assume that they are life forms in their own right?

Among the many different criteria for life forms which have been suggested in the literature the taxonomic level (the first one underneath the "unique beginner") has often been mentioned (e.g. Atran 1985, 1987*a*). By this criterion, *spiders, ants,* or *snails* could count as life forms. Clearly, however, they are not (lexically) polytypic: ordinary English does not have names (primary lexemes) for different kinds of spiders, ants, or snails. There are, of course, expressions such as *redback spider*, or *funnel web spider*, and one could say, under certain circumstances, "I saw a redback today", but sentences of this kind are elliptical, and *redback* is used here as a modifier in the secondary lexeme *redback spider*, not as a primary lexeme in its own right. To see this, it is enough to compare the acceptability of the phrase *a redback spider* with that of **a swallow bird* or **a trout fish*.

But if we allowed *snails, spiders, ants*, or *bats* to count as "monogeneric life forms" (Atran 1987*b*), we would be undermining the main operational criterion we have for distinguishing folk genera from life forms: the linguistically recognized polytypicity (variety of kinds) of the latter. It seems much more justified to recognize (with Berlin *et al.* 1973) that categories of this kind are "unaffiliated generics" rather than "monogeneric life forms", and to accept the consequence that not all living kinds are thought of in terms of "transitive hierarchies, however shallow". Atran has argued explicitly that "life forms represent an exhaustive partitioning of the local flora" (1985: 308). If "unaffiliated generics" are, essentially, generics, not "monogeneric life forms", then this claim has to be rejected (see Berlin 1992: 211). But it has to be rejected anyway, given that (in English, at least) *bush, vine, grass*, and *herb* are not taxonomic life form terms (and that, semantically, *lilac* is not "a kind of bush" nor *pumpkin* "a kind of vine").

To do full justice to the special place of the categories under discussion in the English folk taxonomy (reflected in their semantics), it might be best to recognize terminologically their special status (for example, by calling them "isolates" or something like this). In any case, it is misleading and confusing to call them "monogeneric life forms", because the notion "life form" as an absolute rank is particularly useful and particularly revealing if it is construed as polytypic ("a kind including many kinds")—indeed perhaps only if it is so construed:

a kind of living thing
there are many kinds of things of this kind
all these kinds "have their names"
(i.e. there is a word for every one of these kinds)

6. "Life Forms" in English Folk Botany

Turning now more specifically to English folk botany, I will argue—in disagreement with most other writers on the subject—that only one of all the botanical life forms usually mentioned in the literature is really thought of by the speakers of English as something that comes in many different kinds and can therefore be recognized as a taxonomic life form, namely *tree*. Even urban dwellers in America who cannot tell an oak from a maple and for whom *tree* is psychologically more salient than *oak, maple,* or *birch* (see Dougherty 1978) are aware that there are many different named kinds of *trees,* as there are many different named kinds of *birds* or *fishes,* and the question "What kind of tree is this?" is perfectly natural to them, unlike the question "What kind of maple is this?"

This brings us to another putative criterion for distinguishing life forms from folk genera: that of psychological salience. Berlin, Breedlove, and Raven (1973: 216) described generic taxa as the basic, and psychologically most salient building-blocks of all folk taxonomies. On the other hand, Dougherty (1978) and others have shown that for urban dwellers *tree* and *bird* may be psychologically more salient than *oak* or *swallow*. However, as I have argued in detail elsewhere (Wierzbicka 1985), we do not have to conclude from this that for these speakers *tree* and *bird* are not life forms. Psychological salience may be a characteristic feature of folk genera in many speech communities (especially those living largely in a natural, not human-made, environment) but it need not be, and should not be, the basis for defining and distinguishing these categories (see Berlin 1992: 89). If it was, it would lose most of its value as a theoretical construct and as a tool for cross-linguistic comparisons. The criterion of polytypicity is incomparably more useful and more illuminating.

Assuming, then, that *tree* definitely is a life form in ordinary English, what of the other putative folk-botanical life forms—that is, what of *bush, shrub, vine, moss, grass, herb, fern,* or *mushroom*? In some sense, all these words can indeed be regarded as botanical "life forms"—not in the sense, however, in which *tree* or *bird* are life forms; that is not in the sense of being a taxonomic supercategory. Take, for example, the word *grass*. One can sometimes refer to "different grasses", in the plural; but if one asks a native speaker of English "What kinds of grasses are there?", they are usually unable to come up with different names. Some might mention *buffalo grass,* but this is a secondary lexeme, not a primary one. One could hardly say, for example, referring to grass, that someone "was sitting on the buffalo".

For most ordinary speakers, *grass* is simply *grass*. Not only do they not know of any named kinds of *grass,* they are unaware that there are such names, a situation quite different from that pertaining to *tree*. Similarly, when one asks native speakers of English "What kinds of mosses are there?" or "What kinds of ferns are there?", they look baffled and are generally unable to come up with any names.

With *bushes,* the situation is somewhat different. Admittedly, people know that bushes can be of different kinds (e.g. *lilac bushes, rose bushes, blackberry bushes, thorn bushes, gorse bushes, mulberry bushes,* and so on); but they do not think of *roses, lilac, blackberries,* or *mulberries* as "a kind of bush". Tyler (1978: 190) has actually defined *lilac* as "a kind of bush", but all my informants agree that this is counter-intuitive. An *oak* is "a kind of tree", but *lilac* is not "a kind of bush", and when asked "What is lilac?" or "What are blackberries?", people hardly ever reply "a kind of bush". *Mulberry* is actually thought of as a kind of *tree* (even though it can also grow in the form of bush, as in the children's rhyme, "Here we go round the mulberry bush"). *Rosebush* is a common compound, but *roses* are thought of, primarily, as a kind of *flower*, not as a kind of *bush*—and, according to my informants, so is *lilac*.

Vine is not an English folk taxonomic category at all. Tyler's (1978: 264) description of *pumpkin* as "a kind of vine" tends to produce a humorous effect. *Pumpkin* is, primarily, "a kind of thing that people eat", and, secondarily, "a kind of thing that people grow (for people to eat)"; it is certainly not thought of by ordinary people as "a kind of vine". One can say of an *oak* or a *birch* "Look at that tree!" (as mentioned earlier) but it is difficult to imagine anybody who would say "Look at that vine!", referring to a pumpkin plant.

The only clear taxonomic (polytypic) category available in the English folk botany, in addition to *tree*, appears to be *flower*[2] (Hunn 1982). When asked about different kinds of flowers, informants do not hesitate to name *roses, tulips, daisies, daffodils*, and so on. Conversely, when asked "What is a tulip (daisy, daffodil, and so on)?", they do not hesitate to reply "A kind of flower". Furthermore, informants do not hesitate to accept sentences in which the word *flower* refers to an individual tulip, daisy, or daffodil, as in the sentences "Look at that flower!"

Of course, the word *flower* can also be used in a different sense, as a PART, rather than a KIND, of a thing growing out of the ground, but in everyday use, the "kind" sense is as real as the "part" sense. Intuitively, a *flower* is, above all, a kind of thing which grows out of the ground, and which comes in many different kinds, just as a *tree* is a kind of thing which grows out of the ground and which comes in many different kinds.

Atran (1987*a*: 32) argues that "when living kinds enter the space of concern with human function and use, such as eating, gardening (weeds and flowers), farming (beasts of burden), entertainment (pets, circus and fair animals), they cease to be of taxonomic importance". I believe that,

---

[2] The fundamental nature of a folk-biological category can of course change, as in the case of the life form concept *flower* emerging out of a non-taxonomic (partonomic) concept (flower as a part of some things growing out of the ground → things growing out of the ground which have such parts). The mechanism of semantic change is in this case the same as in other areas of the lexicon: when a second meaning emerges it is first used side by side with the older one, and may gradually replace the older one altogether. In principle, a life form concept could change, in the same way, to a non-taxonomic concept, but whether such cases are attested remains to be established. For example, the fact that there was a period when many kinds of "vines" were known to everybody does not establish that *vine* was at an earlier time a life form (just as the fact that there are now many kinds of bushes known to everybody does not establish that *bush* is a life form in contemporary English folk biology).

generally speaking, this is quite true, and as I have argued in detail (Wierzbicka 1984, 1985, 1988*a*), linguistic tests show that, conceptually, *apples* are not "a kind of fruit", nor are *carrots* "a kind of vegetable". But the same linguistic tests show that just as *oaks*, *birches*, or *maples* are, conceptually, "a kind of tree", *tulips*, *daffodils*, or *roses* are, conceptually, "a kind of flower"; and that both *tree* and *flower* are, conceptually, comparable "kinds of things that grow out of the ground".

The circumlocution "thing which grows out of the ground" may seem clumsy and unnecessary: why not say, simply, *plant*? But the point is that *plant* does not really function as a botanical "unique beginner" in ordinary English. In particular, *trees* are not thought of as "a kind of plant", and neither are *mushrooms*. When asked whether a *tree*, or a *mushroom*, is a kind of *plant*, educated informants may of course reply in the affirmative, but they do not accept that *plant* could be used with reference to an individual oak or birch tree (cf. Section 3.1 above):

> Look at that plant over there!
> Which one?
> *That oak tree/that mushroom.

A *plant* (in the everyday sense of the word, and in the singular) has to be small (much smaller than a person), and it has to be green. A prototypical *plant* is a small green leafy plant such as a potted plant; but a *tree*, or a *mushroom*, is not just an atypical *plant*—it is not a *plant* at all (in the folk-English sense of the word *plant*).

In English folk taxonomy, then, *plant* is not a "unique beginner"; rather, it is a category comparable to *bush*, *shrub*, *grass*, or *moss*. As for the concepts *grass*, *moss*, *fern*, or *mushroom* it is quite obvious that they are not thought of as included in the concepts of some folk genera subordinated to them, because in ordinary English there are no such (known, named) folk genera subordinated to *grass*, *moss*, *fern*, or *mushroom*.

What are these categories, then? If they are not (taxonomic, polytypic) life forms, could they be unaffiliated folk genera, like *cactus*, *toadstool*, or *slug*? It seems clear that such a conclusion would be counter-intuitive (partly for reasons discussed below, in Section 7). It is intuitively much more satisfying to conclude that categories of this kind are in some sense more like life forms than like folk genera, but that they are not taxonomic (polytypic) life forms.[3] To sustain this point of view, however, we need a

---

[3] Hunn (1987: 146) appears to assume that to be a valid analytical category the life form has to be shown to be definable in purely perceptual terms, as Atran (1985, 1987*a*,*b*) expects it to be. But in fact, the life form may be an extremely useful analytical category even if it proves to be definable, in particular cases, in partly perceptual and partly functional terms. The actual term we use (e.g. "life form" or something else) is not very important, in comparison with the question of the existence of a "transitive hierarchy" of ranks in the domain of living things.

further construct: a "quasi-life form" as distinguished from a taxonomic, "polytypic life form". We also need some additional criterion distinguishing folk genera from both "life forms" and "quasi-life forms". I will try to suggest such a criterion in Section 9.

7. Polytypic Genera

I have claimed that life forms (such as *bird, fish, tree,* or *flower*) differ from folk genera in being thought of as polytypic and in including many named categories of a lower level. This characterization, however, needs to be supplemented by an additional criterion, referring to the position of a given category with respect to other named categories. To see the need for such an additional criterion, it is useful to consider the concept of *dog*.

The existence in English of nouns such as *spaniel* or *poodle* is a particularly telling (though not the only) piece of linguistic evidence showing that *dogs* are thought of in English as coming in many different kinds. But clearly, it would be absurd to conclude from this that *dog* is a life form in English, on a par with *animal, bird,* and *fish,* and that *spaniel* and *poodle* are folk genera, on a par with *cat* and *cow*.

First, *dog*, like *cat*, is thought of as "a kind of animal", and the phrase "animals and dogs" sounds absurd, whereas "animals and birds" is perfectly acceptable. (See also the following sentences: "It's not a bird, it's an animal" and "*It's not a dog, it's an animal".)

Second, linguistic tests involving co-ordination show that *dogs* are felt, intuitively, to be on the same level as *cats* or *sheep*, not on a higher level, whereas *spaniel* or *poodle* are felt to be on a level lower than that of *cat* or *sheep*: "John likes cats, but Mary prefers dogs", versus "*John likes cats, but Mary prefers spaniels".

Thus, linguistic evidence shows that primary lexemes such as *spaniel* or *poodle* belong to a special level lower than that of folk genera, though higher than that of specific taxa, normally represented by secondary lexemes, such as *Siamese cat* or *blue spruce*. I have suggested that this level, normally available only for taxa of particular cultural importance, can be called a subgeneric level (Wierzbicka 1985: 232–6); and a similar suggestion was put forward, independently, by Cecil Brown (1987). (Cf. Section 3.5 above.)

It turns out, then, that not only life forms but also some—rather exceptional—folk genera can be thought of as coming in many different kinds. We need, therefore, a proviso: not all biological categories thought of as coming in many named kinds are life forms. If a biological category comes in many named kinds but is treated linguistically (e.g. in conjoined phrases) as being on the same level as folk genera (that is, as categories which do not come in many named kinds) then it is not a life form but a (rather exceptional and culturally salient) folk genus subdivided into named subgenera.

8. "Gestalts" and "Distinctive Features"

It has sometimes been claimed in the literature that folk genera are conceptualized as holistic indefinable "gestalts", whereas life forms can be defined by means of a few abstract features. For example, *racoon* is conceptualized (it has been claimed) in terms of its unanalysed, global "racoonness", whereas *bird* can be represented in the speaker's mind in terms of a few abstract features such as feathers, beak, and eggs (see Berlin 1981: 96; Hunn 1976: 518).

But in fact, it is intuitively far from clear that we don't have a global gestalt of a *tree*, a *bird*, or a *fish*, just as we have a global gestalt of a *squirrel*. Indeed, elsewhere Hunn (1977: 47) himself mentions *bird*—alongside *raccoon, dog,* and *bumble-bee*—as an example of an "inductive" category, not a "deductive" one. And indeed, if we can have a global image of a *dog*, despite the wide variety of types of *dogs*, why shouldn't we have also a global image of a *bird?* In fact, Bruner, Goodnow, and Austin (1956: 47) offer *bird* as their prime example of a holistic concept: "A bird has wings and bill and feathers and characteristic legs. But . . . if it has wings and feathers, the bill and legs are highly predictable. In coding or categorizing environment, one builds up an expectancy of all of these features being present together. It is this unitary conception that has the configurational or Gestalt property of 'birdness'." What can be said of *bird* can also be said of *tree, fish,* or *snake,* as well as of *dog, squirrel,* or *spider.* The full definitions of life forms such as *bird, tree,* or *fish* arrived at in my *Lexicography and Conceptual Analysis* are at least as long as (in fact longer than) that of *squirrel* (see Wierzbicka 1985). It is doubtful, therefore, that life forms can be distinguished from folk genera along the lines of "a few abstract features" versus complex unitary gestalts.

Furthermore, as pointed out by Cecil Brown (1990: 38), we may well have unitary gestalts for "cultural kinds" too, whether relatively simple ones such as *bottle* or *jug* or relatively complex ones such as *bicycle* or *car.* The impression that artefactual concepts of this kind could be defined in terms of "a few abstract features" is just as illusory as the notion that life forms such as *tree* or *bird* could be so defined (for detailed analysis of these and other similar concepts, see Wierzbicka 1985).

9. "Hidden Natures" and "Proper Names"

One further possible difference between folk generic concepts and life form concepts is that the former—but perhaps not the latter—imply a "hidden nature" or an "underlying essence" which cannot be reduced to any observable attributes (see Atran 1987*a,b,c*; Keil 1989; Kripke 1972; Putnam 1975, 1977; Schwartz 1978). For example, we may think that some particular bird is a sparrow, but if other people, whose judgement we trust, assure us that this bird only looks like a sparrow but in fact is not a sparrow (but another kind of bird), we are quite likely to accept their judgement, assuming that the "underlying essence" or the "hidden nature" of this particular bird is not that of a sparrow. But could we similarly accept the judgement that a creature which looks and behaves like a bird in fact is not a bird?

Similarly, we could probably accept the judgement that a tree which looks to us like an oak in fact is not an *oak* (but another kind of tree), or that a flower which looks like a tulip in fact is not a tulip but another kind of flower. But would we similarly accept that what looks to us like a *tree* (not from a distance but from close by, in good visibility conditions) is in fact not a tree but some other kind of thing growing out of the ground (because it doesn't have the "hidden nature" of a *tree*)? Or that what looks to us like a flower in fact is not a flower (but, say, a mushroom), because it doesn't have the "hidden nature" of a *flower*? Similar questions can be raised with respect to non-taxonomic quasi-life forms such as *bushes* or *grass*, and in each case the answer appears to be in the negative: we assume that we know how to recognize a *tree*, or a *flower*, or how to recognize a *bush*, or *grass*, and we would not defer in such matters to experts; but with folk genera, we might well defer to an expert.

This suggests that the meaning of folk generic words like *sparrow* or *oak* may have some component absent from the meaning of life form words such as *bird* or *tree,* a component which would account for the assumption of "hidden nature". This component can be linked with the idea that a folk genus—in contrast to life forms and to various other groupings—provides a "real name" for living things which belong to it. For example, the explication of the word *tiger* could start as follows:

a kind of animal
there is a word for animals of this kind
this word is *tiger*

Atran, who assumes that the dividing line runs between living things and artefacts, has argued, in apparent support of a presumed "hidden nature" of *trees*, that "a given tree may not be as large as a person, but *bonsais* are still trees 'by nature' " (1985: 302).[4] But linguistic tests show that bonsais are not thought of in English as "trees". Just as a *crab-apple* would not be referred to, in ordinary English, as "an apple", a *bonsai tree* would not be referred to as "a tree" (as a sapling could not be so referred to):

> *Look at that apple!
> *Look at that tree!

It is interesting to note that "unaffiliated generics" appear to behave in this respect as the names of other generics, not like the names of life forms. For example, if we are told that a creature which looks like a *bat* (or a *snail*) in fact is not a *bat* (or a *snail*), we might well accept this claim—certainly more readily than the claim that what looks to us like a *bird*, or a *tree*, is in fact not a *bird*, or a *tree*.

In talking about a possible "hidden nature" of living kinds, I do not mean to abandon my earlier claim (Wierzbicka 1985) that folk genera are also definable in terms of specific features, such as stripes, claws, and teeth in the case of a tiger. On the contrary, I hope to have shown that folk genera can be fully defined, and that in this respect they do not differ from the names of cultural kinds (or any other words). The definitions which I have provided list the necessary and sufficient components of a *concept* such as 'tiger' or 'squirrel', not necessary and sufficient features of all the referents of the words in question.

I claimed in earlier work (1972) that biological kind terms, unlike the names of artefacts, cannot be defined and are a kind of generic proper name. In subsequent work (1985), on the basis of trial and error, I reached the conclusion that the names of natural kinds can be defined, and I showed that the resulting definitions (or explications), though complex, are no more complex than those of names of artefacts. My present suggestion is that these two earlier stands are in fact not incompatible; they can be reconciled if we supplement the definitions of natural kind words with an additional component hinting at their hidden underlying essence.

What I am suggesting now is that words such as *tiger* or *squirrel* may have one additional semantic component, referring to an "underlying essence" of a given genus, an essence which is felt to be something different from, though usually manifested in, typical perceptual features, such as stripes in the case of a tiger, or a bushy tail in the case of a squirrel. This means that in saying of something "This is a tiger (squirrel, etc.)" people mean not only that the animal in question can be expected to have all the features characteristic of tigers (squirrels, etc.) but also that it is an animal

---

[4] Cf. also the following statements: "Thus, 'tree' and 'sparrow' remain folk kinds, with presumed essences" (Atran 1990: 16); and "the definitions of lexical entries for living kinds at *all levels* pertain only to the essences of kinds, not the actual appearance of their denotata" (Atran 1985: 301; see also Atran 1990: 6).

of *the same kind* as animals that people call *tigers* (*squirrels*, etc.). This corresponds very closely to Putnam's (1975: 141–2) formula, summarized by Atran (1987*a*: 50) as follows: " 'natural kind' terms such as 'tiger' can be given an 'ostensive definition' with the following empirical presupposition: that the creature pointed to bears a certain sameness relation (say, *X is the same creature as Y*) to most of the things which speakers in the linguistic community have on other occasions labelled 'tiger'."

Fodor (1977: 148; quoted in Atran 1987*a*: 42) claims that *cows* differ from other animals in "familiar ways, but it is no part of the *meaning* of *cow* that cows say 'moo', and give milk, and look thus-and-so. These are not *necessary* truths—a cow that did not say 'moo' would still be a cow, and so would one that did not give milk or was purple."

But semantic theories equating "meaning" with necessary truths which have to hold for all the referents of a given term are so sterile that they have never borne any fruit in lexicological descriptions of any large bodies of data, either in English or in any other language of the world, and they have proved thoroughly useless as a basis for cross-linguistic and cross-cultural comparison of languages. By contrast, if we assume that stereotypes, expectations, value judgements, and so on can also be part and parcel of a word's meaning, then we have a firm foundation on which empirical study of lexicons can be based (see e.g. Apresjan 1974/1992; Goddard 1992*a*; Mel'čuk and Žolkovskij 1984; Mel'čuk *et al.* 1984; Wierzbicka 1985, 1987*a*, 1990*b*).

A purple cow which doesn't give milk or say "moo" can still be called a *cow* only if it is thought of as an animal of the same kind (that is, "having the same essence") as animals called *cows* which are not purple, do give milk, and do say "moo" (for a more serious and more complete explication of English folk concepts such as *cow*, see Wierzbicka 1985).

I suggest, however, that taxonomic supercategories such as *tree* or *flower* do not have a semantic component asserting "sameness" with respect to some "underlying essence". This means that when we refer to something as a *tree* we do not mean to imply that the entity in question has some "underlying essence" identical to that of all entities called *trees*. It seems particularly clear that we do not attribute "underlying essences" to non-taxonomic quasi-life forms, such as *bush* or *grass*. A *bush*, regardless of its observable properties, is not something which belongs to "the same kind" as things that people called *bushes*. But I think that what applies to *bush* or *grass* applies also to *tree*.

In the case of zoological life forms, it is perhaps less clear that they are not thought of in terms of "underlying essences", and the matter requires a further investigation. It appears, however, that they are not: if we see a creature that looks to us like a bird, or an animal, it is hard to imagine that we could be persuaded that in fact this creature is something else.

Atran (1987*a*: 48) writes: "living kind terms are conceived as 'phenomenal kinds' whose intrinsic nature, or (to use Locke's notion) 'real essence' is presumed, even if unknown". For folk genera (e.g. *squirrel* or *oak*) this is convincing, but it is inconceivable that *bushes* may have a "real essence" of a *bush*, or that *bugs* may have a "real essence" of a *bug*. It is less inconceivable, but still unlikely, that *trees* may have a "real essence" of a *tree*, and *birds*, of a *bird*. Presumably, the idea of a "real essence" has something to do with the notion of origin and of inherited hidden properties: a *cow* is a *cow* primarily because it "comes from" a *cow*. By contrast, artefacts don't come from other artefacts and to some extent the same applies even to life forms (e.g. a *tree* doesn't have to "come from" another *tree*, and a *bush* doesn't have to "come from" another *bush*).

It is interesting to mention in this connection a feature of Australian Aboriginal languages, which links folk genera with proper names and perhaps with an implied "hidden nature". In some of these languages one can ask about the "name" of a living thing in the same way as one can ask about the name of a person (e.g. "What name?" in Yankunytjatjara; see Goddard 1992*a*: 17), soliciting in this way an answer identifying a folk genus. Since questions of this kind can be asked neither with respect to life forms (*trees*, *birds*, etc.) nor with respect to artefacts (Goddard, personal communication) a distinction appears to be drawn between folk genera and everything else. This fact supports the psychological reality of folk generic concepts and the absolute character of the distinction between folk genera and life forms. It also supports the idea that folk genera are seen as a kind of "proper name" (in fact the "real name"; see Berlin 1992: 64) which cannot be reduced to a set of observable properties and which is linked with a presumed "underlying essence".

10. Living Things and Artefacts—Similar or Radically Different?

Atran (1987*a*: 28) argues that different cognitive domains may have different types of semantics, and that, in particular, the semantics of living things is different from the semantics of artefacts. Accordingly, "in work concerned with folk categorization researchers should clearly distinguish between the conceptual structure of living kinds and living kind terms as opposed to that of, say, artifacts and artifact terms". He criticizes the bulk of the literature on human categorization for taking it for granted that what holds for folk biology holds also for the domain of artefacts.

According to Atran, the differences between living things and artefacts have to do, first, with the question of "hidden nature" and, second, with the levels of categorization.

The notion that not only living things but also artefacts can be said to have a "hidden nature" is due to Putnam, who has argued that words such as *pencil, chair,* or *bottle* cannot be "defined by conjunctions, or possibly clusters, of properties" (1975: 160):

pencil is not *synonymous* with any description—not even loosely synonymous with a loose description. When we use the word *pencil,* we intend to refer to whatever has the same *nature* as the normal examples of the local pencils in the actual world. *Pencil* is just as *indexical* as *water* or *gold.*[5]   (1975: 162)

As pointed out by Schwartz (1978), however, the two cases—that of natural kinds and that of names of artefacts—are by no means parallel. It may make sense, intuitively, to attribute a presumed "hidden nature" to *lemons* or *tigers,* but certainly not to *chairs* or *pencils.* "What makes something a pencil are superficial characteristics such as a certain form and function. There is nothing underlying about these features" (Schwartz 1978: 571).

Similarly, Atran (1987*a*: 41) dismisses the idea of any "hidden nature" supposedly implied by names of artefacts ("Talk of artifact 'natures' is idle as well"), and he points out that "unlike living kind categories, labeled artifact concepts are not meant to classify particular items. Instead, they discriminate mental plans for serving functions" (1987*a*: 42).[6]

I hope to have demonstrated (Wierzbicka 1985) that the meaning of natural kind words such as *lemon* and *tiger* can be analysed as fully and precisely as that of names of artefacts such as *pencil, cup,* or *bottle.* In both cases, what is involved is not a "conjunction" of properties but a structured

[5] Putnam's idea that not only natural kind terms but also names of artefacts imply an "underlying essence" appears to be supported by Hunn (1987). But in fact, when Hunn (1987: 147) speaks of a "cultural essence" shared by artefacts of a given type, and when he points out that "having a flat surface" may be "of the essence of 'table' . . . as that is essential to a table functioning as such", he is talking of something quite different from the presumed "underlying essence" or "hidden nature" of folk genera. Hunn (1987: 147) argues (against Atran) that "the 'virtual nature' of a concept such as 'pine' is open to modification on the basis of additional experience. The possibility of encountering a truly coneless pine cannot be ruled out a priori. Thus 'cones' are an empirically contingent feature of 'pineness'." I think these arguments are valid, but they are not incompatible with the idea that the concept of *pine* includes a reference to cones, and that if a coneless tree was called a *pine* this would imply that it was seen as an atypical tree of the same kind as those trees which are called *pines* and which would normally be expected to have cones. I hope to have shown in my study of *cups, mugs,* and related concepts (Wierzbicka 1985) that names of artefacts do indeed include necessary (or essential) features, as well as prototypical ones; but these features should be distinguished from the assumed "hidden essence" contemplated by Putnam, Schwartz, and Atran.

[6] Actually, I don't think that Schwartz is quite right in referring to both form and function as "superficial characteristics". The function of a "cultural kind" such as, for example, *stool* (in contrast to *chair*) can be very complex and far from obvious. Usually, native speakers are not immediately aware why stools can be both much higher and much lower than chairs (e.g. *bar stools* versus *footstools*). Some aspects of the function of a cultural kind can be quite "hidden", too (e.g. the fact that stools are meant for "doing something", not just for sitting comfortably, with the upper legs supported on the seat and the feet on the ground). But this is different from the presumption of a hidden "real essence", which native speakers may not know at all, as in the case of living kinds.

network, with its own logic, involving both essential and prototypical features and comprising the causal relations between the individual features which explain their mutual presence (see also Keil 1989: 267). The fact that it may be justified to add one further component (accounting for the "hidden nature") to the explications of *lemons* or *tigers* but not to those of *pencils* or *bottles* does not change in any way the need for the full explication of the folk concept. Nor does it detract from the deep analogies between the natural kind concepts and cultural kind concepts demonstrated in the numerous explications given in Wierzbicka (1985).

As for the levels of categorization, Atran argues that "hierarchical ranking of living kinds is apparently unique to that domain" (1987a: 41). This corresponds also to Hunn's (1987: 147) position on this point: "I agree with Atran that the phenomenal reality beneath folk-biological classification does exhibit unique features . . . Most notably, a transitive hierarchy (however shallow) is to be expected in the classification of flora and fauna."

I believe this is correct. In fact, Atran's and Hunn's views on the uniqueness of hierarchical ranking to the domain of living things correspond closely to the claims put forward in Wierzbicka (1984). As I hope to have demonstrated in a number of works (e.g. Wierzbicka 1984, 1985, 1988a), linguistic tests show that in the area of artefacts there are no "supercategories" corresponding to the biological rank of life form. Semantically, *spoons* are not a kind of *cutlery* or a kind of *tableware*, *cups* are not a kind of *container*, *tables* are not a kind of *furniture*, *skirts* are not a kind of *clothing*, and *dolls* or *rattles* are not a kind of *toy*. Concepts such as *furniture*, *clothing* or *toy* are not taxonomic supercategories, in the way that *bird* is a taxonomic supercategory for *swallow* or *parrot*, *flower* for *tulip* or *rose*, or *tree* for *oak* or *maple*.

I have argued that there are other types of supercategories in the domain of artefacts, but that none of these types can be regarded as taxonomic, that is, based on the concept of KIND:

To summarize the discussion of nontaxonomic supercategories, purely functional concepts such as *toy* are defined in terms of what for; collectiva-singularia tantum such as *furniture* are defined in terms of what for and where; collectiva-pluralia tantum such as *leftovers* are defined in terms of where and why; and pseudocountables such as *medicines* are defined in terms of what for and where from. In addition, all four of these types of non-taxonomic supercategory are defined in terms of the mode of use: functional concepts stand for individual indivisible things; collectiva-singularia tantum stand for groups of indivisible things; collectiva-pluralia tantum stand for groups of things, divisible or not; and pseudo-countables stand for "stuffs" and divisible things.   (Wierzbicka 1984: 325)

I have also argued, as Atran (1987a: 42) does, that (at the level of supercategories) natural kind categories are not "fuzzy" in the way artefactual kinds are (see Wierzbicka 1984: 318).

Atran (1987*a*) links the greater "fuzziness" of artefactual concepts with a lack of presumption of "hidden natures" or "underlying essences". I have argued, however, that life forms don't carry such a presumption either. The presumption of "hidden natures" is a characteristic feature of folk generic concepts, not of all natural kind concepts. The "fuzziness" of artefactual supercategories is explained, I believe, by the fact that they are not taxonomic. Biological supercategories such as *tree* or *bird* are not "fuzzy" not because they imply some "hidden nature" but because they stand for "kinds of things" ("superkinds") rather than for heterogeneous collections, groups, and so on.

Furthermore, cultural kinds such as *chair*, *bottle*, or *bicycle* are not necessarily any more "fuzzy" than living kinds such as *dog* or *willow*. I do not accept the argument that "one and the same item can literally *be* an instance of 'waste paper basket' in one context and 'stool' in another if oriented differently" or that "it is the fact that artifacts are defined by the functions they serve, rather than by any inherent perceptual properties, that allows a given (morphologically selfsame) item to belong to different categories of artifacts in different circumstances. But, e.g., a dog is always a dog" (Atran 1990: 57). As J. Lyons's (1977) term "cultural kind" suggests, a *bottle* or a *bicycle* is not defined exclusively by the function it serves but also by its form (cf. the definitions in Wierzbicka 1985). It is only artefactual supercategories (such as *toy*, *weapon*, or *vehicle*) which are defined purely in terms of their functions—and these categories can indeed be "fuzzy" (in their range of reference). The same object, e.g. a *knife*, can be viewed as either a *weapon* or piece of *cutlery* (or a *kitchen utensil*), because artefactual supercategories such as *weapon*, *cutlery*, or *utensil* are indeed referentially "fuzzy". But a *bottle* is always a *bottle*, as much as a *dog* is always a *dog*. I agree, therefore, with Cecil Brown's (1990: 38) argument that *bottles* or *screwdrivers* imply as much "discontinuity" in the world as *squirrels* or *racoons* (and that they, too, evoke gestalts). It is not the presence or absence of gestalts or the degree of "fuzziness" which distinguishes living kinds from cultural kinds. It is probably true, as Schwartz (1978) and Atran (1990: 55) argue, that any "talk of artefact natures is idle", but cultural kind concepts can be discrete, and can imply clusters of perceptual properties, without implying any "hidden essence".[7]

Finally, living kind concepts are subject to inter-speaker variability and can expand with the speaker's experience with denotata (a process which

---

[7] Keil (1989: 53) suggests that "the dividing line between artifacts and natural kinds can be fuzzy in many cases", because complex machines, such as televisions, automobiles, and, above all, computers "take on many of the properties that supposedly distinguish natural kinds from artifacts". This is an interesting point, deserving further investigation. It seems to me, however, that the two cases are not truly parallel. Folk genera names such as *tiger* or *lemon* appear to attribute to the "kinds" in question an underlying essence which cannot be fully spelled out in words; but the names of complex artefacts do not seem to carry any such implications.

should not be confused with any increase in scientific knowledge); a similar variability does not seem to occur in the domain of artefacts (although names of technical inventions such as *television, radio,* or *computer* raise interesting problems in this connection, too, as they do with respect to "hidden natures"; see Keil 1989).

But as mentioned earlier, the most fundamental difference between the two domains (natural kinds versus names of artefacts) lies in the phenomenon of a transitive hierarchy of categories, which is unique to the realm of living things (although in that realm, too, there are many concepts which are not included in that transitive hierarchy, such as, for example, *bush*).

11. Conclusion

Despite the intensive and very fruitful work of the last two decades, the area of folk-biological categorization still suffers from a good deal of conceptual confusion. This confusion is due very largely to the fact that folk-biological taxonomies are frequently studied in the abstract, without the support of linguistic tests and linguistic evidence.

From lack of attention to linguistic evidence, scientific concepts such as *mammal* or *quadruped* continue to be confused with folk concepts such as *animal*; the scientific senses of the words *animal* and *plant* continue not to be distinguished from their everyday sense; and categories thought of as polytypic, such as *bird* or *tree*, continue not to be distinguished from categories which in everyday language are not treated as polytypic at all (such as *bush, grass,* or *moss*).

I have argued before (1984, 1985) and again here that the domain of living things is unique in presenting ranking taxonomies of primary lexemes, and that, as Atran (1987*b*: 306) put it, "science and common sense constitute logically independent approaches to knowledge, despite their subtle and pervasive interactions in Western society". I have also argued, in agreement with Berlin, Breedlove, and Raven (1973) and Berlin (1992), that the categories of life form and folk genus are non-arbitrary and can be identified on the basis of clear, absolute criteria. I have disputed, however, the claim that biological life forms "partition the everyday world of human experience" (Atran 1987*b*: 311), and I have questioned the correctness of the widely recognized repertoire of English life forms, including items such as *bush, vine, moss, grass, herb, mammal,* or *bug*.

I have supported Atran's claim that folk genera—unlike artefacts—imply a "hidden nature", and I have linked this implication with Putnam and Kripke's idea of terms for living things being a kind of proper name, while at the same time maintaining my earlier claim (1985) that all natural kind terms can, and should, be defined. I have also argued that the presumption of hidden nature cannot be extended to (taxonomic) life form concepts, such as *tree* or *bird*, or to quasi-life form concepts, such as *bush* or *grass*.

At the same time, I have supported Cecil Brown's (1990) claim that cultural kinds may imply a level of discreteness and discontinuity attributed by other scholars (e.g. Atran) only to living kinds. They may also imply gestalts as much as living kinds do.

Above all, I hope I have shown that linguistic tests can throw important light on the basic issues in the study of human categorization in general and ethnobiological categorization in particular; and that they can be used effectively as a source of verification, documentation, and insight.

III The Semantics of Grammar

13 Semantic Rules in Grammar

□ □ ──────────────────────────────────

1. Introduction

As I have tried to show (see in particular Chapter 5), a word's syntactic behaviour reflects, and depends on, its meaning. Thus, it is no accident that one can *ask*, *beg*, or *apply* FOR something, but not *order*, *demand*, or *command* FOR something; or that one can both *order* and *ask* someone TO DO something, but not *demand* or *apply* someone TO DO something.

So, the grammatical behaviour of words is governed by subtle semantic "rules"; and although at first sight these rules may appear open to exceptions, on further investigation even the apparent exceptions turn out to be semantically motivated. For example, as I have shown elsewhere, there are good semantic reasons why we say "the shirt IS old" but "the trousers ARE old", "rice IS warm" but "beans ARE warm", or "wheat IS good" but "oats ARE good" (Wierzbicka 1985, ch. 4).

Langacker (1987: 47–8) writes:

Linguistic theorists place much emphasis on the importance of making strong empirical claims. Several related factors determine whether a theory or description satisfies this requirement. For one thing, it should make clear predictions: the nature of supporting or disconfirming evidence should be readily apparent. A theory must also be restrictive, by limiting descriptive options to a narrowly specified range that rules out many conceivable alternatives. It should further provide a principled means of choosing among competing analyses.

Having said this, however, Langacker backs down (ibid.):

It is common for linguists to demand of a rule, principle, or definition what might be called *absolute predictability*. What this means, roughly, is that a statement pertaining to a certain class must be valid for all and only the members of that class if it is to be accepted as having any predictive value at all. Statements that achieve this level of predictability are obviously desirable, for they make the strongest and most precise empirical claims. Yet it cannot simply be assumed that language invariably or even typically lends itself to statements of this kind. In fact it does not. Expectations of absolute predictability are sometimes unreasonable for natural language and commonly lead to erroneous conclusions, dubious claims, or conceptual confusion. We must scale our expectations down to a level of predictability that is appropriate and realistic for the subject matter.

According to Langacker, then, the nature of language is such that it is "unrealistic" to expect "absolute predictability".

The expectation of absolute predictability has been prominent in diachronic and typological studies, and has not fared well. The most famous example is the neogrammarian doctrine that valid sound laws have no "true" exceptions: apparent exceptions can always be explained by analogy or by the operation of another sound law yet to be discovered, or in some other manner. Today it is generally agreed that this doctrine is wrong, whatever its heuristic merits; certain types of changes spread by lexical diffusion, typically leaving residues, so at no stage does a sound law necessarily hold true for all eligible forms (see Labov 1981 for a general review).

In Langacker's view, what applies to putative "sound laws" also applies to rules of grammar (1987: 49):

An expectation of absolute predictability is also apparent in the requirement that certain rules (syntactic rules in particular) be fully productive. The validity of a grammatical generalization is often denied unless one can predict exactly which forms it does and does not apply to.

The expectation of "absolute predictability" is linked, in Langacker's view, with the outdated "Aristotelian" model of categorization, to which he opposes—as more appropriate and more valid—the "Roschian" prototype model (ibid.):

The standard criterial-attribute model of categorization also exemplifies an expectation of absolute predictability. If the model is interpreted strictly, all and only the members of a class or category will possess the entire list of criterial properties, which thereby achieves absolute predictability with respect to class membership. We have already questioned the appropriateness of this model for linguistic categorization. . . . The prototype model offers a more realistic account in many instances, but adopting it implies that class membership is not predictable in absolute terms: it is a matter of degree, decreasing as an entity deviates from the prototype, with no specific cutoff point beyond which speakers abruptly become incapable of perceiving a similarity and thus assimilating an entity to the category.

But are expectations of absolute predictability *always* unrealistic? I do not wish to defend the old dogma that sound laws have no exceptions; but must we a priori assume that there is no absolute predictability anywhere in language? To my mind, statements such as the following take caution too far:

cognitive grammar emphasizes the importance of factors that make it unreasonable to expect rule applicability to be predictable in absolute terms.   (ibid.)

The question should rather be *what kind* of linguistic rules can be truly predictive.

Langacker himself acknowledges that "generality is a virtue" (1987: 45), and he elaborates:

Linguists properly seek general rules and universal principles. They merit our plaudits in stating obvious regularities, and our encouragement in finding others that are less readily apparent. And counting heavily in favour of a theory or description is its ability to capture nonobvious generalizations or to unify seemingly diverse phenomena.

I agree with Langacker that "we must recognize that language is a mixture of regularity and irregularity", and also that "Linguists have occasionally invoked suspicious devices to make things appear more regular than they really are" (ibid.). But being an empirical science, linguistics must—like any other empirical science—look for true generalizations.

2. Semantic Rules: The Past Practice

When arguing that grammatical categories do not have neat semantic correlates linguists have often invoked pairs such as *oats* and *wheat*. For example, Hudson (1976: 6) wrote:

A second reason for believing in the separation of syntax from semantics, as autonomous levels, is that the same phenomena can require different classifications on the two levels. The clearest instance of this that I know of is number in the noun-phrase. The argument runs as follows: there are some noun-phrases (or nouns—it makes no difference to the argument) which are syntactically plural but not semantically plural (such as *these bathroom scales*, which may be ambiguous semantically but in one of its readings must be as singular semantically as, say, *this bathroom weighing machine*; see also *these oats* versus *this wheat*); and there are others which are semantically plural but not syntactically plural, notably the following two cases. First, there are noun-phrases with collective heads, such as the *committee*, which can occur with verbs like *disperse*, which need to be marked as occurring only with subjects that refer to a group of individuals—i.e. semantically plural subjects; and second, there are noun-phrases with heads like *heap*, as in *a large heap of logs*, which can occur in a reciprocal construction ('A large heap of logs were piled on top of each other'), in contrast with *a large heap of sand*, which has to be semantically singular. I take it as axiomatic that this kind of situation requires two different levels, each with its own classification of the items concerned.

The argument goes as follows: there are two grammatical categories (singular and plural) and two semantic categories (singular and plural). The grammatical singular does not always correspond to the semantic singular, and the grammatical plural does not always correspond to the semantic plural, so syntax and semantics have to be separated from each other as two independent levels.

In my view, the examples discussed in this passage show something rather different; namely that the distinction between "singular" and "plural" is simplistic and does not fit the English language. Nouns such as *heap* or *committee* are not "semantically plural but syntactically not plural". Semantically, words of this kind stand for "multiple entities", or "entities composed of other entities"—and their grammatical behaviour reflects this. Far from being semantically arbitrary, the grammatical behaviour of words of this kind admirably reflects their distinct semantic nature. (See Jespersen 1924/1968: 196.)

Consider also the following passage of Gleason's (1969: 224) classic work:

> There is an old story of a man who was asked, presumably by a grammarian, whether *pants* was singular or plural. His reply was, "Well, mine are plural at the bottom, and singular at the top." Ultimately, the confusion, which many others have also felt, rests not so much in the shape of the garment as in the grammar of English. The object named is as clearly one entity as, say, a shirt or a coat. This does not matter; by a convention of English, *pants* is plural. Interestingly enough, this is not an isolated case; compare *trousers, breeches, shorts, slacks*, etc. This whole group of words are grammatically plural with no evident semantic justification . . . the distinction between these subclasses of nouns is purely arbitrary.

How can one fail to recognize that words such as *pants, trousers, breeches, shorts, slacks* (and also *scissors, goggles, glasses, tweezers, tongs, forceps*, and so on) do form a semantic class, as well as a grammatical one? Grammatically, these nouns have two shared features. They are all pluralia tantum, but—unlike *oats, chives*, or *coffee-grounds*—they are not uncountable; they can be counted, but they require a special classifier: *a pair of*. Semantically, all these nouns designate objects which are seen as having two identical parts, joined together, and performing the same function.

The word *pants* is neither singular nor plural. Rather, it belongs to a separate category (one among several categories of English nouns) which can be called "dual". The semantic unity of this group seems intuitively obvious—but we couldn't articulate this intuition if we were restricted to crude, a priori semantic categories like "semantically singular" and "semantically plural".

It is one thing, however, to acknowledge the semantic basis of a class such as the one including *trousers, scissors*, and so on, and another, to maintain that the semantic rule which assigns nouns to this class is "absolutely predictive". For example, Langacker (1987: 47) is willing to do the former but not, apparently, the latter.

> It is . . . fallacious to assume that a phenomenon is purely "syntactic" just because it is nonuniversal. For instance, it is a matter of convention (not cognitive necessity) that *scissors, pants, glasses, binoculars, etc.* are plural in form (and largely in behaviour), but contra Hudson (1976: 6), this does not imply that "syntactic number" is distinct from semantic number or that syntax constitutes an autonomous component of grammar. The plurality of these expressions reflects conventional imagery: they highlight the bipartite character of the objects named, so the assump-

tion that they are semantically singular is incorrect. Contrasting forms like *nostrils* vs. *nose, buns/buttocks* vs. *ass/bottom, stars* vs. *constellation,* etc. similarly construe the conceived entity by emphasizing either internal multiplicity or overall unity. The existence of an autonomous syntactic component hardly follows from the conventionality of such images.

Nouns such as *trousers* or *scissors* do indeed "highlight the bipartite character of the objects named" (Wierzbicka 1985: 322–4). But this generalization is not just an approximation open to counter-examples. In my experience, rules which are truly semantic in nature do not admit exceptions. If the grammatical class in question is governed by a semantic rule, then I would expect this rule to be "absolutely predictive". I will try to show that the various counter-examples which come to mind are in fact apparent rather than real. (See also Wierzbicka 1993*e*.)

3. "Dual Nouns" and Absolute Predictiveness

When we compare the "dual" noun *trousers* with the "singular" noun *shirt* the reason for their different grammatical behaviour seems to be—Gleason notwithstanding—crystal clear: trousers have a "bipartite" structure while shirts are essentially "unitary" objects. Of course, one could argue that shirts have sleeves, and that the role of sleeves in a shirt is analogous to that of trouser legs in trousers, but it seems intuitively obvious that the two cases are different: sleeves are not as essential to the function of a shirt as trouser legs are to the function of trousers (one can imagine a sleeveless shirt, but not legless trousers).

But what about *shorts*? And what about *"hotpants", panties, undies,* or *jocks*? Trousers, jeans, slacks, and so on have separate coverings for the legs, and these coverings constitute a large part of the object. Stretching the facts a little bit, one could make the same argument for shorts. But *underpants* and *briefs* don't have to have any separate coverings for the legs. So why do they, too, belong to the same grammatical class as *trousers* or *jeans*?

Of course, *underpants* still have two separate "holes", one for each leg; but why are these holes more important than the "holes" for arms in a shirt? Furthermore, why are they more important than the two "cups" in a bra, which would seem to be quite essential to the function of the garment in question?

Langacker would probably appeal at this point to "conventional imagery". People, that is, native speakers of English, think of *underpants* and *shorts* in terms of a "bipartite structure", but they don't think of *shirts* or even *bras* in these terms. I think this is correct but not sufficient. The question naturally arises: Do we have independent evidence for this alleged difference in "thinking"? Or do we have any other reasons to think that people think of garments in the dual noun class in a special way?

I think that we do have such reasons. Trousers, shorts, pants, and so on can all be thought of as "separate-leg garments", in contrast to "wrap-arounds" such as skirts or dresses. This distinction between "separate-leg garments" and "wrap-arounds" involves an important cultural principle. Traditionally (in the English-speaking world), "separate-leg garments" were associated with men, to whom they accorded a full freedom of movement, whereas "wrap-arounds" were associated with women, thus providing a symbolic protection (including visual protection) to the taboo area of the body. Of course, in special circumstances ladies could wear "non-feminine" leg-separating clothes such as *riding-breeches* and so on, but exceptions of this kind simply confirmed the rule. In the present (English-speaking) world, women too, wear trousers, and other outer garments separating the legs (jeans, shorts, and so on), thus discarding the traditional feminine image associated with "wrap-arounds" (normally not worn by men). But the choice is still there, and it is culturally important. Even if trousers are now thought of as gender-neutral rather than masculine, dresses and skirts are definitely associated with women, so the choice between "separate-leg garments" and "wrap-arounds" is still symbolically important. There is no similar culturally important choice in the case of garments worn on the upper half of the body, so there is, so to speak, no need to signal whether their structure is "bipartite" or otherwise.

But this is not the whole story. Turning now to *panties, undies, swimmers, bathers, trunks, scungies* (Australian), *jocks*, and so on, we will note that these, too, are all "separate-leg garments". Items of a similar nature which are not "separators"—for example, a *girdle* or a *petticoat*—are never pluralia tantum in English. It is true that—unlike outer garments such as trousers—*panties* or *swimmers* are not worn in preference to some type of "wrap-around". What matters, however, is that these garments, too, fall into the culturally salient category of "leg-dividers"—that is to say, garments which have two separate identical parts, one for each leg.

It hardly needs to be pointed out that this is culturally significant too: items of clothing which have two separate identical parts, one for each leg, are those whose function consists in tightly covering the parts of the body which have to be protected from being exposed to public view. The two separate holes for the two legs are relevant to this function: if instead of these two legs there was one big aperture, the parts of the body which are meant to be protected from view would not be so protected.

It is not, then, the bipartite structure as such which matters, but a *saliently* bipartite structure; and in the case of human artefacts (such as tools or items of clothing) functional salience may well be more important than perceptual salience.

This is, I think, why some garments with a visibly bipartite structure may have names which are not in the *trousers* class, whereas others, whose bipartite function is visually much less salient, may have names belonging to this class.

Consider, for example, the words *pyjamas* and *suit*. Physically, the structure of these garments may seem quite similar. Each is composed of two separate parts which can be called *trousers* and *jacket*, respectively (although a *suit* can also be composed of a skirt and a jacket). Why, then, is *pyjamas* a "dual" plurale tantum whereas *suit* is not?

My explanation is this: *pyjamas* is seen as an alternative to *nightshirt*, *nightgown*, or *nightie*, that is to say, it is seen as a leg-separating alternative to a unitary garment; but *suit* is not seen as a leg-separating alternative to a unitary dress. Rather, it is seen as a unitary substitute for two separate garments: a pair of trousers and a jacket (or a skirt and a top of some sort). Of course, from a physical point of view, a suit is not unitary, but from a cultural and psychological point of view, it is a unitary (though two-piece) alternative to a combination of two different garments.

I conclude, then, that in this area as in others, apparent exceptions are in fact no exceptions at all. On the contrary, even minor variation in grammatical behaviour corresponds to differences in the underlying conceptualizations. Although these underlying conceptualizations are not open to direct inspection in the way physical objects can be, we can have access to them through methodical introspection, and also through cultural analysis. The different grammatical behaviour of different nouns provides clues to different conceptualizations, and allows us to formulate semantic hypotheses. But these hypotheses can be verified in terms of knowledge derived from other sources.

For example, if we came across the name of a "wrap-around" belonging to the class of *trousers* it would not do to assert flatly that this particular "wrap-around" is conceptualized in terms of some sort of bipartite structure. We would have to defend such a claim with reference to some evidence other than the grammatical behaviour of the noun in question.

I do not claim, then, that any object with a bipartite structure will have a name analogous to *trousers*, because we do not know a priori just how important this bipartite structure is in the underlying conceptualization. Rather, I claim that for every word of the *trousers* class we can posit a conceptualization referring to a "bipartite structure" and justify such a hypothetical conceptualization in terms of some observations other than those that we have started from. This point will be elaborated and further illustrated in the following section.

4. Evidence for Different Conceptualizations

Consider, for example, the English word *mouth* and its nearest Polish equivalent *usta*. The first is a singular (countable), the second is a plurale tantum. Is this difference in the grammatical behaviour arbitrary or can it be linked with different conceptualizations? To maintain the latter we need independent evidence; and if we look for it such evidence is readily forthcoming: while both *mouth* and *usta* can refer either to the lips or to the oral cavity, differences in the collocations of these two words suggest that the lips are much more prominent in the conceptualization associated with the Polish word than in that associated with the English one. For example, in Polish not only *wargi* ('lips') but also *usta* ('mouth') can be described as *czerwone* ('red'), *różowe* (pink), *spękane* (cracked), *spierzchnięte* ('chapped'), and so on. By contrast, in English one would not speak of a ?*red mouth*, **pink mouth*, **cracked mouth*, or **chapped mouth*. These differences in collocations suggest a difference in meaning—and this difference in meaning is reflected in the different grammatical behaviour of the two words.

As a second example, let us consider the German words for "trousers": *die Hose* (singular, countable) and *die Hosen* (plurale tantum). Usually, informants are not aware of any difference in meaning between the two forms, so on the face of it the grammatical difference between them is, synchronically at least, perfectly arbitrary. But again, evidence for a difference in their conceptualization is not difficult to find.

For example, the same informants who claim to use both forms indiscriminately admit that in the case of shorts they would use the singular (*die kurze Hose*, 'short trousers') rather than the plural (*die Hosen*). Similarly, the same informants also admit that for underpants they would use the singular (*die Unterhose*) rather than the plural (*die Unterhosen*). Both these facts suggest that when the duality of the object is less salient (no trouser legs), the singular form is preferred.

On the other hand, in the proverb "die Frau hat die Hosen an", that is '(in that house,) the woman wears the trousers', only the plural form *Hosen* can be used. In this case, the word for trousers is used as a symbol of masculinity, and the leg-dividing nature of the referent is implicitly contrasted with the traditional feminine monowraps. In this case, therefore, it makes sense to emphasize the duality of the object—and this accounts for the use of the plural form.

As a third example, consider the words for "hair" in English, French, Italian, and German, which Palmer (1990) adduces as evidence for arbitrariness of grammatical patterns. Why, he asks, is *hair* singular in English whereas the corresponding words in French, Italian, and other languages are plural? He maintains that the correct answer to this question is that this is just the way it is. But this does not explain why, for example, in German, where there is a choice between two forms (*das Haar*, singular, and *die Haare*, plural), the speakers do not choose between these forms at random but appear to be sensitive to considerations of countability. For example, while both *lange Haare* (plural) and *langes Haar* (singular) can be used as a counterpart of the English phrase *long hair*, the singular *Haar* is highly preferable in the phrase *lockiges Haar*, 'curly hair'. On the other hand, only the plural *Haare* is acceptable in the sentence *mir stehen die Haare zu Berge* 'my hair is standing on end (out of fear)' (Ulrike Mosel, personal communication).

If we adopt Palmer's position, facts of this kind must be regarded as totally mysterious and inexplicable. But if we link grammatical number with semantic countability, an explanation is possible: a phrase such as *lockiges Haar*, 'curly hair', suggests a mass which is perceived as composed of interlocking curls, not of individual hairs. On the other hand, when a person's hair 'stands on end', it can well be imagined that it is the individual hairs which rise and straighten up (because of fear). The same point can, of course, be illustrated from English, where the plural *hairs* can also sometimes be used, but only with reference to conspicuously countable individual hairs, such as the first grey hairs on a person's temples. It is true that the two languages, German and English, draw the boundary in different ways, but the principle is the same in both cases: the contrast between a singular and a plural applies in situations of heightened countability; the *singulare tantum* is used in situations of lowered countability.

All these examples show that the differences in grammatical behaviour of apparent synonyms point in fact to differences in the underlying conceptualization, and that claims about differences in the conceptualization can be validated on the basis of independent evidence.

5. The Mystery of *Scales*

The view that nouns such as *heap* or *committee* "are semantically plural" and that the grammatical behaviour of such words is semantically arbitrary is quite surprising because it seems clear that far from being arbitrary, the "mixed" grammatical behaviour of such words reflects their "mixed" semantic nature, just as the "mixed" grammatical behaviour of *trousers*, *scissors*, or *forceps* reflects *their* "mixed" semantic nature.

When it is said, however, that the grammatical behaviour of *scales* is semantically arbitrary (recall the quote from Hudson 1976: 6), then I must admit that at first sight this looks reasonable: it seems clear that the grammatical plurality of *scales* has a historical rather than a synchronic explanation. *Scales* are a weighing instrument; and in the past, all, or most, instruments of this kind had a saliently bipartite structure. Thus, in the past, the grammatical plurality of *scales* was semantically motivated, but in the present it is semantically arbitrary. Or is it?

The first point to note is that at least in some dialects of present-day English (in particular, in American English) there has emerged an alternative to *scales* in the form of a countable noun *scale* (as a weighing instrument), noted, for example, by *LDOTEL*. This in itself points to a change in conceptualization, following the change in the material culture: the gradual disappearance of "bipartite" scales and the emergence of unitary scales (e.g. bathroom scales) has led to the emergence of a new grammatical form, matching the new meaning.

The second point to note is that in contemporary usage even the plurale tantum *scales* has changed imperceptibly in its grammatical behaviour. In the past, when scales were normally bipartite, the word *scales* took the classifier *a pair of*, just like *trousers*, *scissors*, or *glasses*. But in the present-day usage, this is no longer the case. For most of my Australian informants, bathroom scales can be described as *a set of scales* but not as *a pair of scales*.

When I questioned my teenage daughter about why she thought the name of the object in question was *scales* rather than *scale*, to my surprise she replied, without hesitation, that it was because of all the little numbers which one could see there. Thinking that this interpretation was fanciful and idiosyncratic, I asked a number of other children and teenagers—and to my even greater surprise, they all came up with the same answer. I conclude from this that these informants have, so to speak, reanalysed the word *scales*, endowing it with new characteristics, both formal and semantic. Formally, *scales* has lost (in these people's speech) its ability to take the classifier *a pair of*, and has become reanalysed as, roughly speaking, an object with a "multiple structure" rather than one with a "bipartite structure". (The usage of those people who can still say "a pair of scales" when speaking of bathroom scales will be discussed later.)

English has several classes of nouns which are "syntactically plural", that is, of pluralia tantum. One such class includes *trousers*, *scissors*, and so on. It also used to include *scales*, but (for most people) doesn't include it any longer. Nouns belonging to this class are countable, but to be able to combine with numerals they require the classifier *a pair of*.

Another class of pluralia tantum includes "plural mass nouns" such as *oats*, *chives*, or *coffee-grounds*. These nouns do not combine with numerals at all, and they do not co-occur with the classifier *a pair of*.

In most people's speech, the plurale tantum *scales* does not belong to either of these classes: unlike *oats* or *chives*, it does combine with numerals, but unlike *scissors* or *oats* it does not take the classifier *a pair of*. If these people want to count bathroom scales they can do so either using the classifier *a set of* ("we have three sets of bathroom scales") or without any classifier ("we have three bathroom scales").

But whenever we find an apparent freak in a language we should suspect that it is in fact a member of a class different from the one we are looking at—and that it obeys the rules of its own class.

As a first approximation the class which *scales* belongs to can be defined as follows: physical objects perceived as including a large number of identical parts or "bits" which are noticeable but difficult to count. The clearest examples of this class are provided by the nouns *beads* and *pearls*. When one says of a woman that she was wearing her *beads* or her *pearls* one doesn't mean a multitude of separate little beads or pearls (plurals of the countable nouns *bead* or *pearl*). One means an object composed of a multitude of such (countable) beads or pearls, threaded on a string; and the question: "how many beads (pearls) was she wearing?" would be totally inappropriate. Dictionaries of the English language usually miss this point and fail to include *beads* or *pearls* (as uncountable pluralia tantum) as separate entities. Similarly, the compound noun *rosary beads* does not designate a collection of individual *beads* (plural), but a single object, composed of many beads, though having a structure of its own.

Another good example of the class under discussion is the word *braces* (as it is used in Australia): a dental fitting used to correct irregular teeth, which seems to include separate metal bits for each tooth. A related example is *false teeth*—again a unitary fixture composed, or seemingly composed, of many individual parts which look the same. Yet another example is *blinds* (in particular, *venetian blinds*)—again, a unitary object visibly composed of a multitude of semi-separate identical parts. There are also games such as *checkers, draughts, skittles,* and so on.

This is, then, the category to which (for many speakers) the plural noun *scales* has become assimilated. The grammatical shift from *(a pair of) scales* to *(a set of) scales* has been accompanied by a semantic reinterpretation. For younger speakers, at least, *scales* no longer stands for an object with a salient bipartite structure but for an object with a salient multiple structure—like *draughts, checkers, braces, rosary beads,* or *blinds*.

Of course someone might assert that they personally do not regard bathroom scales as an object with a saliently "multiple structure". But this is beside the point. What matters is that younger speakers who had come across the plural form of the noun *scales* and who subconciously noted its plurale tantum behaviour have interpreted this behaviour by subconsciously assigning this noun to the class of nouns designating objects with a noticeable multitude of "things" all looking the same. This is evidenced by many informants' self-reports. Evidently, the object in question (bathroom scales) does lend itself to this interpretation. But if it does so only marginally, or not obviously, this only supports the argument developed here: speakers assume (tacitly) that semantic rules know no exceptions, and therefore they (subconciously) seek an interpretation which would be compatible with the rule. If they couldn't find it the grammatical behaviour of the noun would change.

What happened to *scales*, then, can be described as follows. At a certain point in time, changes in the material culture brought about an intolerable mismatch between this word's form (including grammatical behaviour) and its meaning. This mismatch could be rectified by a change either in the word's form (and/or grammatical behaviour) or in its meaning. American English opted for the first solution and moved from *scales* to *a scale*; on the other hand, British English, and Australian English, opted for the second solution, and (in many people's speech) moved from *scales* seen as an object with a salient bipartite structure to *scales* seen as an object with a salient multiple structure. As for those (rare) speakers who can speak of "a pair of bathroom scales" it can be hypothesized that they still think of the older bipartite scales as prototypical scales; so that they see a bathroom weighing device as an untypical instance of a category whose prototypical instances do have a bipartite structure. For these people, a bipartite structure is as crucial to the concept of scales as (for all of us) flying is crucial to the concept of 'birds', despite our common knowledge that not all birds can fly. If ostriches and emus can be seen as atypical examples of a category whose prototypes can definitely fly, so bathroom scales can be seen by some (older) speakers as atypical examples of a category whose prototype has a bipartite structure. But people who are not familiar with the older, bipartite scales would never speak of modern bathroom scales as "a pair of scales". Thus, all three words—*(a pair of) scales*, *a scale*, and *(a set of) scales*—obey absolutely general rules: the first one belongs to a class of words seen as designating discrete, countable objects with a salient bipartite structure, the second to a class of words seen as designating discrete, countable entities and thought of as unitary, and the third to a class of words seen as designating objects with a salient "multiple" structure (more precisely, objects which include many clearly noticeable distinct "things" of the same kind, which all look the same, and which in principle could be counted, but which would be difficult to count). I challenge anybody to find counter-examples to these rules.

6. Predictiveness and Different Languages

Some readers will no doubt raise the following objection: if semantic rules are fully predictive why is it that they are not universal? For example, why is it that the French word for "trousers" is singular (*le pantalon*), whereas German has two different forms: *die Hosen* (plurale tantum) and *die Hose* (singular)? Don't the trousers worn in France or in Germany have a salient bipartite structure, just as those worn in English-speaking countries?

To answer this question we have to consider how the notion of "predictiveness" can be applied to language. What exactly is expected to predict what?

If we start by examining physical objects (e.g. trousers, scissors, or scales) and if we expect to be able to predict the grammatical behaviour of their names on the basis of our physical examination, then undoubtedly we will be disappointed. One cannot predict the grammatical behaviour of a word on the basis of even the most careful examination of the denotata. It is the *meaning* which is predictive, not the *denotation*. One cannot discover the meaning of a noun by examining its denotation because meaning involves conceptualization, and the same physical objects may lend themselves to many different conceptualizations.

Meanings are not universal, because reality is, by and large, open to different conceptualizations, and different meanings embody those conceptualizations which have emerged within a particular speech community and are shared by its members (cf. Langacker's "conventional imagery"). The reasons behind those different conceptualizations may be explainable in terms of history, culture, living-conditions, religion, and so on. They are a legitimate field of study but they are outside the scope of semantics. (I will return to this point in the next section.) What semantics is concerned with is the discovery of language-specific meanings. The meanings which go beyond individual lexical items and which apply to whole classes of elements can be said to underlie certain "semantic rules", in the sense that they can determine the grammatical behaviour of the elements in question (not the grammatical *form* but the grammatical *behaviour*).

Gleason (1969: 226) observed: "The singular–plural contrast is common in languages. We must, however, expect that there will be considerable differences of detail or even of rather broad outlines between the assortments of concepts which various languages bring together into each of these categories." This is perfectly true: different languages draw their distinctions in different ways and, for example, we should not expect that the behaviour of the words for particular kinds of garments, or instruments, or whatever, will be the same in different languages.

But it is a mistake to conclude from this that within each language, the distinctions drawn by grammar are "arbitrary", as Gleason (ibid.) did:

What is important to note is that the category of plural in English gathers together a rather diverse assortment of concepts. All these have one thing in common: they contrast with another assortment of concepts which we call "singular". That is, the unity within the category is purely a feature of the linguistic system of the language which arbitrarily sets these two in contrast and imposes the requirement that every noun be assigned to one or the other.

As pointed out earlier English doesn't really draw a single distinction between "singular" and "plural", but a number of more subtle distinctions. Each resulting category gathers together not a "diverse assortment of concepts" but a class of concepts sharing a specifiable—and testable—semantic invariant. The unity within the category is a feature of this particular semantic system.

Semantic rules, then, are language-specific. They are "predictive" in the following sense: if we find, in a particular language, a group of words which share the same grammatical behaviour, and if we discover that this behaviour is governed by meaning (that is, that it obeys a "semantic rule"), then we can expect that any other word in that language which may come to our attention later and which shares the same grammatical behaviour will also be governed by the same semantic rule.

For example, if we notice that the English words *trousers, scissors, glasses,* and *forceps* have the same grammatical behaviour (pluralia tantum, countable, but only in combination with the classifier *a pair of*), and that this behaviour is governed by meaning (roughly, salient bipartite structure), then we can expect any other words exhibiting the same grammatical behaviour to be governed by the same rule. If we come across some words which do share the same grammatical behaviour but which do not appear to obey the semantic rule then we should suspect that we have formulated this rule incorrectly and seek an alternative formulation, which would be consistent with all the data. If we cannot find such a formulation then we should look again at the grammatical behaviour of the items which do not fit the semantic rule and see if they do not form a grammatical class of their own, different in some respects from the class governed by that semantic rule.

For example, as mentioned earlier, a grammatical distinction such as that between "singular" and "plural" is simply too crude to fit all the English nouns. English grammar has many categories based on something like "number", not just two. It has fully countable nouns such as *tree* or *knife*, it has "dual nouns" such as *scissors* or *trousers*, it has "plural mass nouns" such as *oats* or *chives*, it has various classes of nouns with a dual status, such as *hair/a hair, straw/a straw, thread/a thread,* and so on; it has pluralia tantum applying to unmoveable multiple structures such as *stairs, bleachers* (American), *gallows, library stacks, stalls,* and so on; it also has pluralia tantum which are countable but not in terms of the classifier *a pair of*, such as *scales, checkers, blinds,* or *braces*; and it has several other classes. These different grammatical classes are governed by different semantic rules, and in each case, the rule is fully predictive, in the sense that it applies to any item which shares the full set of the grammatical properties defining the class in question. Of course some of these classes are much larger than others, but this is beside the point; the point is that within its scope of application each rule is fully predictive. (For detailed discussion, see Wierzbicka 1985, 1988, ch. 10.)

When I say that semantic rules are truly predictive (i.e. have no exceptions) I do not mean that semantic rules can explain everything in grammar. For example, Moravcsik (1991) comments on my analysis of *oats* and *wheat* (in Wierzbicka 1988) as follows: "Strictly speaking, Wierzbicka cannot answer the unqualified question of 'why is the word for "oats" a plurale tantum in English while the word for "wheat" is not?' Her account provides an answer only to the following, more limited question: 'Given that one and only one of the two nouns, one to mean "oats" the other to mean "wheat", is to be plurale tantum in English, why is it the one for "oats", rather than the one for "wheat"?' "

I think this is essentially true—and perhaps as much as one can expect of semantic rules. Words such as *chives, coffee-grounds, hundreds-and-thousands, grits, groats, calf's feet*, and so on form a grammatical class governed by a semantic rule. Grammatically, these words are pluralia tantum (*these chives*, **this chive*), which do not co-occur with numerals (**three chives*) or with the classifier *a pair of* (**a pair of chives*). Semantically, words of this kind imply a conceptualization in terms of "multiplicity" and "limited countability" (referents occur in most speakers' experience in limited quantities and have visible particles which are neither totally uncountable nor fully countable, or worth counting (cf. the difference in this respect between a stretch of grass and a bunch of chives).

Since *oats* belongs to the same grammatical class, the rule predicts that its meaning is based on the same type of conceptualization, and since *oats* is primarily the name of a "foodstuff", occurring (in most speakers' experience) in limited quantities and in a visibly "multiple" form, it is consistent with the rule. (By contrast, *wheat* is thought of, primarily, as a crop; hence its different grammatical behaviour. For further discussion and justification, see Wierzbicka 1988, ch. 10.)

But would every English word referring to a foodstuff which occurs (in most speakers' experience) in limited quantities and in a visibly 'multiple' form be a plurale tantum? I do not claim this. There could be other factors affecting the underlying conceptualization. The conceptualization is not accessible to us directly and can only be speculated about. The grammatical form (and its behaviour) provides the best possible clues to the underlying conceptualizations, but to be able to verify such clues we must also look for other, independent evidence—and in my experience, when we look for it we always find it.

The reasoning involved here (Wierzbicka 1988) has often been misunderstood, so let me rehearse it once more: the perennial *oats*. First, we can establish a list of a number of English words which behave grammatically like *oats* and see if they have anything in common semantically. If a generalization emerges, we can treat it as a working hypothesis to be tested against all words of the same type. If we find a counter-example, the hypothesis is defeated; if we do not, it will not *ipso facto* be proved right, but it will be allowed to stand.

In the case of *oats* (my account of which was questioned recently by Palmer 1990) this procedure leads us to the following conclusion: the class to which *oats* belongs includes words which imply a conceptualization in terms of a combination of "multiplicity" and "limited countability". This is consistent with the common perception of *oats* as, primarily, a foodstuff.

Palmer (1990) asks why *rice* is not like *oats*, since it is essentially a food-stuff and not seen in fields in most English-speaking societies. I believe that the answer is that, first, whereas in English-speaking societies people do not eat rice raw, they often do eat oats raw (though processed in some way); and second, that oatflakes are bigger than grains of rice (just as beans are). Palmer quotes my statement: "Most commonly, rice is seen and handled as cooked, not raw", and adds: "Exactly the same could be said of oats!" What he overlooks is that when oats are cooked and therefore become less separate, their name changes, too: they are now called *porridge*, a singulare tantum just like *rice*. So the "counter-example" actually supports the hypothesis.

The same holds for Palmer's other counter-example: the fact that, unlike *noodles*, *spaghetti* or *macaroni* are singular 'in spite of their origin from Italian plurals'. According to my informants, however, when they think of *spaghetti*, they tend to think of a whole meal, involving a tangled mess of long "things" covered with meat sauce (as in spaghetti bolognese). The beginnings and ends of those "things" cannot be seen, and the 'things' themselves could hardly be counted. On the other hand, *noodles* are not thought of as a meal but rather as one component of a meal; they have no special association with a sauce; and they are shorter and more separate than spaghetti 'strings'. All these differences are consistent with the hypothesis that *spaghetti* is perceived, on an unconscious level, as less 'countable' than *noodles*—just as *porridge* is less 'countable' than *oatflakes*, or *rice* less countable than *beans*. The fact that there are commercial products called "spaghetti sauce" while there are no commercial "noodle sauces" provides independent evidence for this hypothesis.

Palmer accuses me of circularity: differences in grammar are explained, he charges, in terms of hypothetical differences in conceptualizations, while the conceptualizations themselves are posited on the basis of grammar. But this is not the case. First, a certain amount of independent evidence comes from our knowledge of denotata and of their countability. For example, beans on a plate would usually be easier to count than the grains of rice, chives (in a bunch, or in a little container) easier than the blades of grass on a lawn, oatflakes on a plate easier than porridge in a bowl, radishes easier than horseradish (as served at table), and Chinese noodles (as a side dish, or as an ingredient in what is known as "chicken noodle soup") easier than spaghetti bolognese "strings" (covered with meat-and-tomato sauce and sprinkled with Parmesan cheese). Second, there are many kinds of independent linguistic evidence which can be compared with the evidence from grammar. Among others, there is evidence from different collocations.

Returning now to bathroom scales, one couldn't predict whether speakers of English would name it with a countable noun (such as *a scale*) or with a plurale tantum (such as *scales*), and in fact both forms exist, one in American English, and the other in Australian and British English. What we can predict is that the plurale tantum *scales* will be associated with a conceptualization which attributes to this object some internal multiplicity; and this is consistent with what we otherwise know about the appearance of bathroom scales (and also with informants' responses).

One cannot predict the form (or behaviour) of the word from the physical structure of the referent; on the other hand, one can predict the conceptualization from the grammatical form—and having predicted it, one can verify it with independent evidence. (Cf. the discussion in Section 4 of *mouth* and *usta*, and of *die Hose* and *die Hosen*.)[1]

7. Different Cultures, Different Conceptualizations

Different languages embody different conceptualizations. The task of the linguist (*qua* linguist) consists in discovering the conceptualizations embedded in a language, not in explaining why this language embodies

---

[1] Disputing my claims concerning the semantic basis of grammatical patterns, Palmer (1990) refers also to the "anomalous contrast" of "the two verbs 'order' in Latin, *iubeo*, which takes the accusative and infinitive, and *impero*, which takes the dative and *ut* with the subjunctive" (1990: 225). He does not examine, however, the possibility that the two verbs glossed by conventional dictionaries as 'order' may in fact differ somewhat in meaning, and that this difference in meaning may account for their different syntax. In fact, *iubeo* implies greater control than *impero*—exactly as one would predict from the difference in syntax. One can say, for example, *iubere tributum*, 'to impose a tax', but never **imperare tributum*: one can only *imperare* a person, perhaps to no effect, but *iubere* implies an effect, and that is why it can take an abstract noun as its object (cf. in English: *to order/ask a person* versus *to order/*ask an inquiry*). Significantly, the law—*lex*—*iubet* rather than *imperat* (*lex iubet*, 'the law requires'), the assumption being that the law imposes a certain order. (Polish, too, has two 'order' verbs, *rozkazać* and *nakazać*; the first of them can take only a dative addressee phrase as its object, and the second can also take an accusative abstract noun, as in *nakazać dochodzenie*, 'to order an inquiry'; predictably, it is *nakazać*, not *rozkazać*, which is used in combination with *prawo*, 'the law'.) Similarly, Palmer asserts rather dogmatically ('Wierzbicka has her facts wrong') that 'the difference between *stop* and *cease* lies not in the suddenness of the end of the action but in the finality of it, *cease* being much more final' (1990: 231). This theory, however, collapses if one considers that one can say, for example, *The noise didn't cease for a minute* (cf. **The noise didn't end for a minute*, **John didn't finish his work for a minute*). Facts of this kind show that while *end* and *finish* do indeed imply "finality", *cease* does not.

these particular conceptualizations. The latter task belongs, as I have pointed out, to the cultural anthropologist.

Having said this, however, let me try on the hat of a cultural anthropologist and try to show how different conceptualizations of the kind discussed here can be explained in terms of cultural anthropology. Let us start by noting the following linguistic fact: English has more dual nouns for "separate-leg garments" such as trousers or shorts than other European languages do. For example, the French word for trousers, *le pantalon*, is syntactically singular, and so is *la culotte* (women's underpants), *le slip* (men's underpants), *le maillot* (swimmers), or *le pyjama* (pyjamas). In Russian the words for trousers and underpants (*štany, brjuki; trusy*) are pluralia tantum, but the words for pyjamas (*pižama*) and swimmers (*kupal'nik*) are not. In German, as pointed out earlier, the word for trousers can be either singular or plural (*die Hose/die Hosen*), and the word for swimmers is singular (*Badeanzug*); and so on.

The perceptual salience of the bipartite structure of many such garments, and the cultural importance of the distinction between "separate-leg garments" and "wrap-arounds", explain why most, if not all, European languages do place some nouns designating such garments in a category of dual nouns. But why should English put a greater emphasis on this distinction than French, Italian, Spanish, German, or Russian?

My suggestion is this: English treats the distinction between "separate-leg garments" and "wrap-arounds" more seriously than other European languages do because of the Puritanical heritage in Anglo-American culture. That the importance of this heritage explains a great deal about this culture is beyond doubt (see in particular Weber 1930/1968; also Morsbach and Tyler 1986). What matters here is that the importance of this heritage also explains a good many characteristic features of the English language, or rather, of Modern English (see Wierzbicka 1992*a*, ch. 2).

It is true that in the contemporary English-speaking world, sex is probably spoken of, or referred to, more freely and more matter-of-factly than in many other societies, including France, Italy, Spain, and Russia. This fact, too, has its linguistic reflexes. For example, French, Italian, Spanish, and Russian still don't have neutral, non-euphemistic counterparts of words such as *girlfriend* and *boyfriend* (as opposed to *fiancée, mistress, friend*, or *girl*); and they don't have neutral, non-technical and generally usable words such as *vagina* and *penis* (as opposed to medical terms or vulgarisms).

But grammar doesn't respond to cultural change as quickly as the lexicon. The conceptualization of garments in terms of "separate-leg garments" and "wrap-arounds" has become so entrenched in English grammar that it lives on and extends to new items and new words, such as, for example, *undies, scungies, G-strings* (in some varieties of English), and so on—even in the era of sexual permissiveness and unisex fashions.

This is, then, my tentative explanation for the grammatical difference between *trousers* and *le pantalon*, or between *underpants* and *la culotte*: native speakers of French are, of course, as capable of perceiving the leg-dividing nature of the objects in question as native speakers of English are; but the latter are, so to speak, conditioned to emphasize it more than the former are. In English there is a pressure from the language itself to conceptualize such items of clothing in terms of their leg-dividing character, and this pressure may be due, indirectly, to the Puritanical heritage. It should be noted, however, that if this tentative *cultural* explanation were to prove wrong, this would not detract in any way from the absolute predictiveness of the *semantic* rule stated here.

The question why different languages draw the boundaries in the way they do is not a semantic one. I believe these questions are also worth asking, and in some cases I have suggested answers. For example, in the case of names of fruit and vegetables, differences between, say, Russian and English may be due to different culinary traditions. (See Wierzbicka 1988.) But it is important not to confuse a quest for cultural explanations of this kind with the quest for a semantic invariant of a given linguistic category. Linguists do not have to engage in the former, however fascinating, but if they refuse to pursue the latter, they are neglecting a central issue. For what is linguistics if it is not a quest for meaning?

8. The Semantics of Gender

One "obvious counter-example" to the view of language advanced here is provided by the area of grammatical gender. This is a huge topic, which cannot be discussed here in detail (see e.g. Corbett 1994), but a few brief comments may be useful. I will draw my examples from Polish.

In Polish, the word for ceiling (*sufit*) is masculine, the word for floor (*podłoga*) feminine, and the word for window (*okno*) neuter. How can one explain facts of this kind?

The obvious answer to this question is that in Polish the "gender" (that is, the word class) of inanimate nouns is not governed by a semantic rule, and, in particular, that it is not governed by any rule based on "sex". Clearly, considerations of sex are inapplicable to such nouns. It would be absurd, then, to regard words such as *sufit*, *podłoga*, and *okno* as counterexamples to the claim that semantic rules know no exception. These words are simply not governed by any semantic rule whatsoever.

Let us turn, then, to animate nouns. The Polish word for elephant (*słoń*) is masculine, and the word for giraffe (*żyrafa*) is feminine; the word for rat (*szczur*) is masculine, and the word for mouse (*mysz*) is feminine; the word for fly (*mucha*) is feminine, whereas the word for mosquito (*komar*) is masculine. In the case of animals and other living creatures questions of sex may arise, so how can one explain such differences in gender? Here too, the answer seems quite clear: the assignment of elephants, rats, and mosquitoes to the so-called "masculine gender" and of giraffes, mice, and flies to the so-called "feminine gender" is not governed in Polish by a semantic rule.

Let us consider, then, human nouns. Here, the assignment of different nouns to different grammatical classes is, generally speaking, based on meaning. Let us see, then, if this assignment is governed by fully predictive rules.

Human categorization nouns such as *mężczyzna* ('man'), *chłopiec* ('boy'), or *staruszek* ('old man') all belong to one class "masculine gender". Human categorization nouns such as *kobieta* ('woman'), *dziewczyna* ('girl'), or *staruszka* ('old woman') belong to "feminine gender". Human categorization nouns such as *dziecko* ('child') or *niemowlę* ('baby') belong to another class ("neuter gender"). All this is clearly governed by meaning. But there are plenty of apparent "exceptions".

For example, there are expressive words such as *kobiecisko* ('woman'—neuter), *dziewczynisko* ('girl'—neuter), *chłopisko* ('man'—neuter), *chłopczysko* ('boy'—neuter), and so on. All such words may seem to be exceptions to the rule, but in fact they are not exceptions at all; rather, they form a grammatical category of their own, governed by its own semantic rule. Most words of this kind are derived from basic words which are either feminine or masculine, and the replacement of this basic "natural" gender by neuter gender signals the speaker's expressive attitude, an attitude which includes the component 'I don't want to think of this person etc. as a woman/girl/man/boy etc.'.

One or two nouns of human categorization are inherently expressive and are grammatically neuter even though they are not (or no longer) perceived as derivates of other, more basic nouns. The word *dziewczę*, 'girl'—neuter, for example, etymologically related to *dziewczyna*, 'girl'—feminine, evokes the image of an innocent young girl, nice to look at and generally endearing. The neuter gender of this word signals the speaker's attitude: the referent, while female, is not thought of as, primarily, a female, but as a young, innocent, and endearing creature.

In Polish there are also highly expressive masculine forms of feminine names such as *Marysik* (from *Marysia*, from *Maria*) or *Klarusik* from (*Klara*). In this case, the masculine gender signals an attitude of affectionate jocularity. (For detailed discussion, see Wierzbicka 1992a, ch. 7.)

There is also a group of expressive nouns such as *niedołęga*, *niedorajda*, *faitłapa*, or *ciapa*, which all designate incompetent people, without energy, initiative, and ability to get things done. Nouns of this kind take feminine agreement when they are applied to women, but when they are applied to men they can take either masculine or feminine agreement, the latter option being more pejorative and more insulting.

"Professional activity" nouns such as *żołnierz*, 'soldier', *stolarz*, 'carpenter', *doktor*, '(medical) doctor', or *pisarz*, 'writer', are marked by extremely complex gender behaviour and certainly cannot be reduced to any simple rule based on sex along the lines of male sex—masculine gender, female sex—feminine gender. (For discussion of similar complexities in Russian, see Rothstein 1973.) Even more complex is the gender-behaviour of titles such as *professor*, 'professor', *doktor*, 'Ph.D. holder', or *inżynier*, 'engineer' (in Polish also a title).

The semantics of gender in Polish or in other languages with similar systems of noun classes requires further study, despite the extensive literature on the subject which already exists. But it would be wrong to suggest that semantic rules governing the grammatical behaviour of Polish nouns are not predictive because this behaviour cannot be accounted for in terms of two biological features such as 'male' versus 'female'.

9. The Unconscious Character of Semantic Rules

Semantic rules operate below the threshold of consciousness. Linguists often miss this point, and declare that since there is no obvious reason why, for example, *oats* should behave differently from *wheat*, the difference between the two words is semantically arbitrary. But in fact, semantic rules are usually hidden, or at least partially hidden; and the fact that they are hidden is linked to the fact that they are unconscious.

Franz Boas's insight into the unconscious character of language is particularly apposite here. In his famous introduction to the *Handbook of American Indian Languages*, Boas (1911/1966: 63–4) wrote:

the very fact of the unconsciousness of linguistic processes helps us to gain a clearer understanding of the ethnological phenomena, a point the importance of which can not be underrated. . . . in all languages certain classifications of concepts occur . . . all these concepts, although they are in constant use, have never risen into consciousness, and . . . consequently their origin must be sought not in rational but in entirely unconscious, we may perhaps say instinctive, processes of the mind. . . . It would seem that the essential difference between linguistic phenomena and other ethnological phenomena is that the linguistic classifications never rise into consciousness, while in other ethnological phenomena, although the same unconscious origin prevails, these often rise into consciousness, and thus give rise to secondary reasoning and to re-interpretations. . . . if we adopt this point of view, language seems to be one of the most instructive fields of inquiry in an investigation of the formation of the fundamental ethnic ideas. . . . Judging the importance of linguistic studies from this point of view, it seems well worth while to subject the whole range of linguistic concepts to a searching analysis.

Linguistic rules can be unconscious while being open to exceptions and thus without being fully predictive. This applies, in particular, to phonological rules (see Sehuchardt 1895/1972; Venneman and Wilbur 1972). But paradoxically, perhaps, semantic rules are different. They appear to be truly absolute—obviously, not because they are "mechanical" or physiological, as neo-grammarians believed their *Lautgesetze* to be; but presumably because they are psychologically real (though unconcious): they are really "there", at the bottom of our minds (so to speak), and they apply across the board, to anything that falls within their domain.

The word *scales* illustrates in a striking way the difference between unconscious semantic rules, operating without exceptions, and conscious rationalizations, which are often open to "exceptions" and counter-examples. For example, some informants, when asked why they thought they called a bathroom "weighing machine" *scales* rather than *scale*, came up with a historical explanation: "because it derives from old two-bowl weighing scales, i.e. as in scales of justice, or because originally scales consisted of two scales, one for the weights and the other for the object to be weighed". And yet the same informants report, when questioned, that they are unable to apply to bathroom scales the classifier *a pair of*. This shows that while on a conscious level they link the plurality of *scales* with the previously bipartite structure of the referent, on a subconscious level they do not do that: if they still conceptualized *scales* in terms of a pair of identical parts they would be able to use the classifier *a pair of*. In fact, however, they report that they could only use the classifier *a set of* or no classifier at all. On the other hand, those informants who can still talk of "a pair of scales", even with reference to bathroom scales, show that a (prototypical) bipartite structure is still a part of their concept of 'scales', whether or not they are conscious of it and whether or not they could immediately articulate this aspect of their concept in reply to a question.

10. Conclusion

Stephen Hawking, the author of *A Brief History of Time* (1989: 10), has recently restated the criteria for a scientific theory as follows: "A theory is a good theory if it satisfies two requirements: It must accurately describe a large class of observations on the basis of a model that contains only a few arbitrary elements, and it must make definite predictions about the results of future observations." This may seem too hard a requirement for a theory of any human phenomena such as religion, customs, kinship systems, or language. In my view, however, this requirement does fit semantic rules operating in natural language. To retrace our steps: we started with a few arbitrary elements (*trousers, scissors, glasses,* and a few more), and on this basis we built a model: the combination of plural agreement and countability in terms of the classifier *a pair of* is correlated with a specific semantic structure (roughly, an object with a salient bipartite structure; for a more precise formula, see Wierzbicka 1988: 558). Furthermore, we made definite, testable predictions: any other English words we might come across that would have the two grammatical features in question would be correlated with the same semantic structure.

In the case of *scales* we started with just one arbitrary element, and again we built a tentative model on this basis: the combination of plural agreement with countability in terms of a classifier other than *a pair of* is correlated with another specific semantic structure (roughly, an object including a noticeable multitude of "things" all looking the same), and again, we made definite, testable predictions: any other English noun that we may discover which would have the same two grammatical features will also be correlated with the same semantic structure. In an earlier study, I followed this same procedure for *oats* and *wheat* (see Wierzbicka 1985, 1988).

I believe that so far our predictions concerning *trousers*, *scales*, and *oats*, and the classes to which these items belong, have held good. What matters more, however, is that these predictions don't *have* to hold good: they are formulated in such a way that they can, in principle, be disproved or falsified by further observation. To quote Hawking (1989: 10) again:

Any physical theory is always provisional, in the sense that it is only a hypothesis: you can never prove it. No matter how many times the results of experiments agree with some theory, you can never be sure that the next time the result will not contradict the theory. On the other hand, you can disprove a theory by finding even a single observation that disagrees with the predictions of the theory. As philosopher of science Karl Popper has emphasized, a good theory is characterized by the fact that it makes a number of predictions that could in principle be disproved or falsified by observation. Each time new experiments are observed to agree with the predictions the theory survives, and our confidence in it is increased; but if ever a new observation is found to disagree, we have to abandon or modify the theory.

As I have tried to show here and elsewhere (see in particular Wierzbicka 1988), a semantic theory of grammar can be predictive in the sense in which Popper, or Hawking, expect a good scientific theory to be predictive. Langacker stresses the empirical character of his version of cognitive grammar but, as a "realist", he fully expects to find counter-examples to his generalizations. The hypothesis advocated here, however, aims at the more demanding standards of Popper and Hawking: one could refute it by finding even a single observation that disagrees with its predictions.

14 A Semantic Basis for Grammatical Description and Typology: Transitivity and Reflexives

□ □ _____

1. Introduction

Grammar encodes meaning. Categories of grammar known, traditionally, as "plural", "dual", "past", or "imperative" encode semantic distinctions which in a given speech community are deemed (at a subconscious level) particularly important. The difference between a swallow and a lark can (at times) be ignored by the speakers of English because they can both be subsumed under a more general label "bird"; but the difference between a *bird* and two or three *birds* cannot be similarly ignored: for the speakers of English, the distinction between singular and plural is obligatory (for "count nouns").

But it is not just semantic distinctions (such as that between "one" and "more than one" or between "now" and "before now") which constitute the substance of a language's grammar. There are also notions which don't belong to any contrastive sets of this kind and which become grammaticalized—in one language, in several languages, or even in most languages of the world. (The so-called "imperative" construction, which will be discussed below, is an example of such a widely grammaticalized meaning.) One could say, then, that far from being an "autonomous" system, independent of meaning, grammar constitutes in fact concentrated semantics: it embodies a system of meanings which are treated in a given language as particularly important, indeed essential, in the interpretation and conceptualization of reality and of human life in that reality (see Boas 1938a; Jakobson 1962).

The semantic basis of grammatical categories is recognized in traditional labels such as "plural", "dual", "past", or "imperative". These labels embody insights which grammarians have gained from ancient times through their study of languages; and although the insights gained by earlier generations of grammarians are not fully adequate for the description and interpretation of the hundreds, even thousands, of often very different languages which have become accessible to study in the twentieth century, they are none the less valuable and can be built upon by modern linguistic science, with its broader empirical scope and more sophisticated theoretical frameworks.

Labels of this kind reflect the sound intuition that grammatical categories have a semantic basis, and also that they can be matched, to some extent, across languages—not by virtue of the grammatical form, or structure, because this differs from language to language, but precisely by virtue of some shared semantic core.

But valuable as labels of this kind often are, they carry with them a certain danger, because while they may hint at the meaning encoded in a certain grammatical category, they cannot represent this meaning accurately. Paradoxically, the realization that a traditional grammatical label does not give an accurate portrayal of the semantic range of a category often leads to claims that grammatical categories have no semantic basis whatsoever; or at least that they cannot be described in semantic terms.[1]

Such a conclusion amounts to throwing out the baby with the bath water, but scholars may find themselves in this absurd position if they have no coherent semantic theory to draw on, or can see no alternative to either taking semantic labels at face value or denying that the categories in question are based on meaning at all.

It is worth recalling in this connection John Lyons's comments on the status of linguistic labels, made specifically with respect to standard labels for moods, but applicable to other grammatical labels as well:

it is important to emphasize that, at the present stage of linguistic theory and descriptive practice, it is impossible to formulate any very clear notion of the distinctions that are grammaticalized, within the category of mood, throughout the languages of the world. The labels that are used in standard descriptions of particular languages are often misleading in that they imply that the functions of the moods are narrower or more specific than they really are. This is true, for example, of the term "conditional" as it is used with respect to French, or the "inferential" as it is applied to Turkish. In general, we cannot be sure that, because the same term is used in relation to two different languages, the moods that the term refers to have exactly the same function in the two languages. Nor can we be sure that, because two different terms are used, two different functions are involved. (Lyons 1977, ii. 847)

By linking grammatical labels with well-defined meanings we can standardize the use of these labels and thus help to overcome the confusion that Lyons is talking about. The range of meanings encoded in one construction which we want to call "imperative" (or "reflexive") may well not be the

---

[1] In private discussions, at least, many linguists express the view that grammatical labels don't matter, and that there is no point in trying to define terms such as "imperative", "reflexive", "passive", or "dative". But without some such terms grammatical descriptions of different languages cannot be compared. Linguistics as a discipline becomes a Tower of Babel, typological studies lose their necessary basis, and important generalizations about human languages cannot be made. (See Kibrik 1992: 43–4).

same as that encoded in another construction, in another language, to which we want to give the same label. But this doesn't mean that we cannot assign the label "imperative" (or "reflexive") a coherent definition. To show how this can be done, I will first discuss the notion of "imperative".

2. The Uniqueness of Grammatical and Semantic Systems

Every language has its own unique system of meanings encoded in grammar. Traditional grammatical labels do not make this point clear. Anyone who has had some experience with different languages knows that what is called "plural", or "past", or "imperative" in one language does not correspond exactly to what is called "plural", "past", or "imperative" in another. Is it justified, therefore, to apply the same labels to such different phenomena?

There is nothing wrong in using the same label for different phenomena as long as these phenomena have something in common, and as long as the label is defined in terms of a common core (and of course as long as the language-specific phenomena linked with such labels are rigorously described, from a language-specific point of view). In the past, definitions of this kind were usually not given; I believe, however, that since most widely accepted grammatical labels are based on sound linguistic insight, definitions of this kind *can*, in principle, be provided.

Consider, for example, the (so-called) English imperative construction, as in *Go away!*, *Give me that book*, *Keep the door closed*, or *Be quiet*. Formally, this construction can be described as a verb phrase with an uninflexed verb as its head. Semantically, it can be described as encoding, prototypically, the following core meaning: 'I want you to do something'. Since this core meaning carries with it a certain illocutionary force, a more precise formula would read as follows:

(1) I say: I want you to do something
    I think: you will do it because of this

In addition to this prototypical meaning, the same construction can also be used in a restricted number of set expressions such as *Sleep well!*, *Have a nice day!*, or *Have a good trip!*, that is, expressions which encode the following general meaning: "I want something good to happen to you".

Can the English "imperative construction" be equated with the "imperative constructions" in other languages—for example, in Polish? In a sense it can't, because the scope of the English construction is different from that of the Polish one; I will argue, however, that in another sense the two can indeed be identified with one another, and that traditional grammar was right in identifying them terminologically.

First, some facts.

Polish verbs have a special imperative form, or rather two such forms, singular and plural. What is normally regarded as the Polish imperative construction takes the form of a verb phrase with the imperative form of the verb as its head. For example:

(2) Chodź   tutaj!
     come: IMP:SG here
     'Come here!'

(3) Daj   mi   tę   książkę!
     Give: IMP:SG me:DAT this:ACC:SG:FEM book:ACC:SG:FEM
     'Give me this book!'

The basic (prototypical) meaning encoded in this construction is the same as in the English imperative construction 'I want you to do something'; but the extensions from this prototype are different.

First, one doesn't say in Polish things such as *Śpij dobrze, 'Sleep well', *Miej przyjemny dzień!, 'Have a pleasant day!' or *Miej dobrą podróż!, 'Have a good trip!'—that is to say, Polish doesn't have the 'I-want-some-thing-good-to-happen-to-you' extension. On the other hand, the same grammatical construction can be extended in Polish in ways in which the English construction cannot. For example, it can be used with stative adjectives or other expressions referring (explicitly or implicitly) to the addressee's thoughts:

(4) Bądź spokojny.
     'Be tranquil' (i.e. don't worry).

(5) Bądź pewny że . . .
     'Be certain that . . .'

(6) Bądź zadowolony, że tak sie skończyło.
     'Be pleased that it ended like this.'

(7) Bądź dobrej myśli.
     'Be hopeful' (lit. Be of good thought).

I suggest that the meaning encoded in this "psychological extension" can be formulated as follows:

(8) I want you to think something good

Adjectives such as *spokojny*, 'tranquil' or *pewny*, 'certain', are not inherently positive, but they are compatible with the positive meaning of the construction as such, and when they are used in this construction they are interpreted as referring to "good thoughts". On the other hand, terms for negative emotions such as *niezadowolony*, 'displeased', or *zły*, 'angry' (lit. 'bad'), cannot be used in this construction:

(9) *Bądź niezadowolona . . .
    'Be displeased that . . .'

(10) *Bądź na niego zła.
    'Be angry with him.'

—although one can use such terms in a negative construction (like in English):

(11) Nie bądź niezadowolona!
    'Don't be displeased!'

(12) Nie bądź na mnie zła!
    'Don't be angry with me!'

(13) Nie bądź smutna!
    'Don't be sad!'

Thus, the so-called imperative construction in English differs in scope from the so-called imperative construction in Polish. But they can reasonably be referred to by the same term, provided that we can define it in a way which would fit both languages. I suggest that this can be done in the following way: "An imperative construction is a special construction which is used in a given language to express the meaning 'I want you to do something', with possible extensions to some other related meanings." (The expression "related meanings" refers here to overlapping semantic formulae, such as 'I want you to do something' and 'I want something good to happen to you'.)

Of course a language may have no special construction encoding the core meaning 'I want you to do something' (in which case the speaker of that language wishing to express such a meaning may have to do so relying on purely lexical means). In a case like this, we would have to say that the language in question has no imperative construction. It is not clear at this stage whether there are in fact such languages, although there are, of course, languages without special imperative morphology, e.g. Vietnamese (see e.g. Bystrov and Stankevič 1988). According to Ogloblin (1988), there are no "active imperative constructions" in Javanese; there is only a passive irrealis construction, which, depending on the particle used, can be interpreted as either conditional or directive.

In those languages which do have a special construction for expressing the meaning under discussion, the construction in question has to be described, needless to say, in structural terms, so its description will be language-specific. None the less different imperative constructions found in different languages can be matched in terms of a unitary definition, referring to a language-independent semantic core.

I believe that if we didn't have such a unitary definition for the term "imperative construction", we would have no right to use the same term with respect to different languages. We have seen that at least for English and Polish a unitary definition is possible; it is possible, however, only if phrased in terms of meaning.

It should be pointed out that the proposed procedure for matching grammatical categories cross-linguistically is not based on the vague notion of "similarity", but on the rigorous notion of identity. For example, if the English and Polish imperative constructions can be matched, despite the differences between them mentioned here (and others, not mentioned for reasons of space), it is not because they are somehow "similar", but because they can be assigned exactly the same prototypical meaning (with different extensions in each language). "Similarity" would be too vague a notion for an effective matching procedure, because an English construction may be deemed similar, in different respects, to several Polish constructions, and vice versa. But a rigorously defined common core provides a sufficient basis for non-arbitrary matching of categories across language boundaries.

Common experience of linguists who have worked on different languages of the world suggests that an imperative construction defined as proposed here can be found in most (though not necessarily all) languages of the world. The notion of the imperative construction as defined here is therefore a useful part of grammatical theory. What is more important, however, is the fact that by defining the notion of an imperative construction in the way we have done here we can capture an important substantive generalization about human language and cognition; namely, that the meaning 'I want you to do something' plays such an important role in human cognition as to merit widespread grammaticalization across languages of the world.

If someone wished to define the notion of an imperative construction in a different way (for example, linking it with the formula 'I want something good to happen to you' as its core meaning), they would, of course, be free to do so, because a definition is no more than a tool. But I believe they would have provided themselves with a very inefficient tool. In particular, they would not be able to make the generalization that "most languages of the world have an imperative construction". Useful definitions are those which are based on insights emerging from prior linguistic investigation, and which can therefore lead to substantive generalizations. Of two alternative definitions we must judge as superior the one which allows us to make stronger generalizations.

3. Typology and Semantics

To compare languages (or anything else) we need a *tertium comparationis* (that is, a common measure). This common measure cannot be provided by linguistic form, or by linguistic structure, because these differ from language to language, but it can be provided by meaning. To quote a recent book on typology and language universals: "The characteristic feature of linguistic typology . . . is cross-linguistic comparison. The fundamental prerequisite for cross-linguistic comparison is cross-linguistic comparability, that is the ability to identify the 'same' grammatical phenomenon across languages. . . . This is a fundamental issue in all linguistic theory, in fact. Nevertheless, this problem has commanded remarkably little attention relative to its importance" (Croft 1990: 11). Croft quotes in this connection Greenberg's (1966b: 74) statement concerning cross-linguistic comparability of grammatical constructions: "I fully realize that in identifying such phenomena in languages of differing structure, one is basically employing semantic criteria"; and he comments: "These brief remarks summarize the essential problems and a general solution. The essential problem is that languages vary in their structure to a great extent; indeed, that is what typology (and, more generally, linguistics) aims to study and explain. But the variation in structure makes it difficult if not impossible to use structural criteria, or only structural criteria, to identify grammatical categories across languages." Croft concurs with Greenberg's conclusion that the ultimate solution to the problem is a semantic one; and he points out that the same conclusion was also reached by Keenan and Comrie in their cross-linguistic analysis of relative clauses (Keenan and Comrie 1977).

This conclusion would seem to imply that the reliability and validity of linguistic typology depends on the availability of an adequate semantic theory. Croft stops short, however, of spelling out this implication, and the other leading typologists tend to do the same. For example, Croft writes:

The problem of cross-linguistic identification should not be overstated. In most cases, it is not difficult to identify the basic grammatical categories on an intuitive basis. To a great extent this is accomplished by examining the translation of a sentence and its parts, which is of course based on semantics and pragmatics. On the other hand, the weaknesses of an intuitive cross-linguistic identification of categories become apparent when one focusses on an example which is not so intuitively clear after all . . . (1990: 13)

I would argue, however, that while the researcher's intuition is a valuable, indeed indispensable, starting-point, it cannot obviate the need for a coherent research methodology. As the remarks quoted earlier suggest, such a coherent methodology can only be provided by semantics. I suggest that the Natural Semantic Metalanguage, which is based on universal semantic primitives and which has been widely tested in lexical, grammatical, and pragmatic description of many languages of the world, can also provide a suitable semantic foundation for grammatical typology. In particular, relying on this metalanguage we can standardize the use of labels such as "reflexive", "causative", "imperative", or "subjunctive", and give a firm basis to the cross-linguistic study of grammatical categories. I have illustrated this claim with respect to causative constructions in my *Semantics of Grammar* (Wierzbicka 1988), and with respect to "evidentials" in Chapter 15. In this chapter, I will illustrate it mainly with respect to the grammatical category of "reflexives".

As Seiler (1986: 13) points out, "universal concepts are necessary prerequisites for all language activity. They are the *tertium comparationis* necessary for the comparison of languages, for translation; necessary also for assembling linguistic data."

The set of universal concepts arrived at on an empirical basis in the course of a quarter of a century of single-minded searching by myself and colleagues provides, I believe, a *tertium comparationis*, in terms of which grammatical constructions can be rigorously and insightfully compared. (See Chapters 2, 3, and 15; see also Wierzbicka 1988.)

4. Reflexive Constructions

Reflexive constructions are usually defined in terms of coreference of the subject and the object. For example, Givón (1990: 628) offers the following definition of what he calls "true reflexives": "The subject is coreferential with the object, and thus *acts upon itself* (reflexively)"; and Faltz (1985: 6) defines what he calls "primary reflexive strategies" as grammatical devices which "specifically indicate subject–object coreference".

According to this characterization, English sentences such as *Mary washed herself* or *Mary defended herself* are instances of a reflexive construction, since the object is marked in them as coreferential with the subject. But applying the same definitions to, for example, Polish, we might conclude (I believe incorrectly) that Polish has no "true" reflexive constructions at all. Consider, for example, the following pairs of sentences:

(14) (a) Ewa zabiła Adama.
     'Eve killed Adam.'
   (b) Ewa zabiła się.
     Eve killed REFL
     'Eve killed herself.'

(15) (a) Ewa skaleczyła Adama.
     'Eve injured   Adam.'
   (b) Ewa skaleczyła się.
     Eve injured   REFL

(16) (a) Ewa umyła Adama.
     Eve washed Adam.

(b) Ewa umyła się.
 Eve washed REFL

In each pair, sentence (*a*) is transitive, but sentence (*b*) is intransitive (see below), and so it cannot have an object, but only an intransitive subject; and so for (*b*) sentences the question of coreference between two arguments does not arise. English so-called reflexive sentences are also low in·transitivity by a number of criteria (for example, they can't be passivized); but at least their reflexive object can usually be conjoined with other objects.[2]

(17) Harry covered his wife and himself with a blanket.

In Polish, this is not possible:

(18) *Henryk przykrył się i żonę kocem.
 Harry covered REFL and wife:ACC blanket:INSTR

Thus if one can describe English reflexive sentences in terms of coreferentiality between the subject and the object, the same description would not apply to Polish sentences usually called by this name.

It might be objected that the Polish reflexive marker *się* cannot be conjoined with "other objects" because it is a clitic (see e.g. Rappaport, forthcoming). But the very fact that a would-be object is a clitic may point to the sentence's low transitivity. In many languages, "clitic objects" don't behave like "real objects" in a number of respects (e.g. they don't distinguish "direct objects" from "indirect objects", they don't respect the rules for the relative order of "direct objects" and "indirect objects", and so on). We should constantly remind ourselves that the number of syntactic core arguments depends not on the number of entities involved in the situation referred to, but on the manner in which the situation is conceptualized by the speaker, and that one cannot speak, for example, of a "transitive action" or an "intransitive action", because the same action may be viewed as "transitive" or "intransitive", depending on the point of view. (For further discussion, see Wierzbicka 1988.)

Furthermore, even if one wished to argue that in Polish sentences such as 19 and 20 below:

(19) Ewa zabiła Adama.
 'Eve killed Adam.'

(20) Ewa zabiła go.
 'Eve killed him.'

---

[2] The co-ordination test is, of course, only one test among many which can be used to judge the level of a sentence's transitivity. I think, however, that it is an important one, and that it provides a reliable key to the conceptualization, or at least to one aspect of the conceptualization. (For some other tests, see e.g. Wierzbicka 1988: 18–19; also Hopper and Thompson 1980.)

are equally transitive, despite the fact that *go* is a clitic, the fact remains
that the syntactic status of the "reflexive" clitic *się* is not the same as that
of the non-reflexive clitic *go*. Whether it is a full-blown direct object or not,
go behaves in some ways like a noun phrase, and in particular, it can combine with agreeing predicate nominals, whereas *się* cannot. For example:

(21) Zobaczył Adama   samego/pijanego.
     saw:3SG Adam:ACC alone:ACC/drunk:ACC
     'He saw Adam alone/drunk.'

(22) Zobaczył go   samego/pijanego.
     saw:3SG him:ACC alone:ACC/drunk:ACC
     'He$_i$ saw him$_j$ alone$_j$/drunk$_j$.'

(23) *Zobaczył się   samego/pijanego.
     saw:3SG   REFL alone:ACC/drunk:ACC

Facts of this kind suggest that in contemporary Polish the clitic *się*, traditionally called "reflexive pronoun" (*zaimek zwrotny*; see e.g. Szober 1966:
100), is better viewed not as a pronoun but as a "particle" (as it is indeed
viewed by Geniušienė 1987: 245). But if *się* is not a noun phrase in (contemporary) Polish, then it cannot be the direct object of any sentence where
it occurs, and consequently, a sentence where an otherwise transitive verb
combines with *się* cannot be regarded as transitive.[3]

It might be claimed, of course, that definitions couched in terms of coreference between subjects and objects refer in fact to "underlying objects",
not to "surface objects". A claim of this kind, however, presupposes the
now obsolete framework of transformational grammar, with its underlying
structures, surface structures, and transformations deriving the latter from
the former. Since the basic assumptions on which this framework was based
have been repeatedly refuted and since its inadequacy has been widely
acknowledged even by most of its former proponents, it seems hardly necessary to argue against the use of this framework any more. (Of course it
might be said that in the 1980s and 1990s syntactic "underlying structures"
are used only as convenient fictions. But if so, then they have no empirical
content and cannot be used as a basis for identifying and matching constructions across languages.)

Returning to Polish, it has to be recognized, I think, that most Polish
sentences usually described as reflexive (see e.g. Kwapisz 1978; Saloni 1976)
are intransitive and so can't have any coreferential subjects and objects. It
is true that Polish also has another "reflexive" construction, illustrated by
sentences such as the following:

---

[3] The element *się* has a number of different functions and different statuses in Polish grammar (see Bogusławski 1977). What is said about *się* in this chapter concerns only one of these
functions, and one of these statuses.

(24) Kochaj bliźniego   jak siebie   samego.
love:IMP neighbour:ACC like self:ACC EMPH:ACC
'Love your neighbour like yourself.'

(25) On nienawidzi samego   siebie.
he hates   EMPH:ACC self:ACC
'He hates himself.'

These sentences are transitive (as, for example, the test of conjoined objects shows), and their object, *siebie* (being a special "reflexive" pronoun), is inherently marked as coreferential with the subject. But sentences of this kind normally require the presence of an emphatic specifier, *samego* (*samej*, *samych*, etc; lit. 'the same'; homophonous with *samego*, 'alone') and they are highly marked. (Sentences without an emphatic specifier are not impossible, but they would have to be contrastive.)

Of the two patterns, the intransitive pattern is more basic and it is the only one which is normally used in physical action sentences (whether the action is voluntary or not):

(26) *Ewa okryła się kocem.*
'Eve covered herself with a blanket.'

(27) ?*Ewa okryła   siebie   samą   kocem.*
Eve covered self:ACC EMPH:ACC with a blanket

(28) ??*Ewa okryła   siebie   kocem.*
Eve   covered self:ACC with a blanket

(29) *Ewa skaleczyła się.*
'Eve injured herself (either accidentally or on purpose).'

(30) ?*Ewa skaleczyła samą   siebie.*
Eve injured   EMPH:ACC self:ACC
'Eve injured HERSELF.'

(31) ??*Ewa skaleczyła siebie.*
Eve   injured   self:ACC

In fact, even in a contrastive context, the intransitive pattern is usually much more natural in physical action sentences than the transitive one, with an emphatic marker (in the nominative) added to the subject:

(32) ?*Ewa okryła   samą   siebie, a   nie   okryła Adama.*
Eve covered EMPH:ACC self:ACC but didn't cover Adam:ACC
'Eve covered HERSELF, but didn't cover Adam.'

(33) *Ewa   sama   się   okryła, a   Adama   nie   okryła.*
Eve:NOM EMPH:NOM REFL covered but Adam:ACC didn't cover
'Eve covered HERSELF, but didn't cover Adam.'

(34) **Ewa okryła się samą, a nie okryła Adama.*
Eve covered REFL EMPH:ACC but didn't cover Adam.
'Eve covered HERSELF, but didn't cover Adam.'

(As sentence 34 above shows, the clitic *się* cannot combine with the emphatic pronoun *sam*; but the same is true of other clitics.)

In his study of the relationship between prosodic and syntactic properties of pronouns in Slavic languages, Rappaport (1988) presents the relationship between the Polish "reflexive pronoun" *siebie* and the "reflexive clitic" *się* as exactly parallel to that between tonic and atonic versions of personal pronouns such as *jego,* 'him' (tonic), and *go,* 'him' (atonic). I would argue, however, that in fact the relationship between the members of each pair is quite different, from both a syntactic and a semantic point of view. The clitic (which as we saw earlier has some properties of a noun phrase) points to a second participant in the speaker's conceptualization of the situation; but *się* (which as we have seen does not behave like a noun phrase) signals that there is only one participant in the speaker's field of vision (the one identified by the subject of the sentence). On the other hand, *siebie* is a noun phrase, and it does have a referring function, although by virtue of its lexical meaning it signals identity between its own referent and that of the sentence's subject.

Since sentences with *siebie* are transitive (by a number of criteria) and since *siebie* can be conjoined with other objects, it is understandable that acceptability of sentences with *siebie* depends on the extent to which one can treat oneself in the same way as one treats other people. For example:

(35) *Adam zastrzelił swoją żonę i samego siebie*
'Adam shot dead his wife and HIMSELF.'

is more natural and more acceptable than

(36) ?*Adam utopił swoją żonę i samego siebie.*
'Adam drowned his wife and HIMSELF.'

The reason is that the actions involved in shooting oneself and shooting someone else are fairly similar, in contrast to the actions of drowning oneself and drowning someone else: to drown someone else one would have to push a person into water, or hold their head under water, whereas to drown oneself one would have to simply jump into water; but in the case of shooting, the basic action is the same, regardless of who one is shooting at.

The fact that in Polish even "the best" transitive reflexive sentences sound more natural if they include an emphatic marker shows that from the point of view of Polish culture, reflected in the Polish language, one's relationship with oneself is normally expected to be different from one's relationship with another person. In this respect, Polish differs from English, since in English not only sentences such as

(37) Adam hates HIMSELF.

but also those without the emphasis on the pronoun:

(38) Adam hates himself.

are fully acceptable. (I will return to this feature of English in Section 5.)

To conclude our discussion of the differences between *się* and *siebie*, sentences with *się* and sentences with *siebie* suggest two different conceptualizations of a situation, and in fact very few verbs are semantically compatible with both *się* and *siebie*; this is not the case, however, with *go* and *jego* ('him'), which can combine with the same verbs.

Thus, when applied to Polish, the definition of "reflexives" couched in terms of coreference between subjects and objects makes the basic construction traditionally regarded as reflexive into a non-reflexive one, and allows only the more peripheral emphatic construction to be regarded as reflexive.[4]

Furthermore, under this definition many, indeed most, languages traditionally described as having a reflexive construction would have to be said to have no reflexive construction whatsoever. For example, Dixon (1980: 433) goes so far as to make the following general comment about Australian Aboriginal languages: "Reflexive and reciprocal verbs occur only in intransitive constructions—the single core NP is in s function and involves a noun in absolutive and/or a pronoun in nominative case."[5]

What do linguists normally mean, then, by a "reflexive construction"?

I believe that what they really have at the back of their minds is a certain meaning, and that they call different constructions in different languages "reflexive" if they sense that the central function of these constructions (though not necessarily the only one) is to express this unidentified but intuitively felt meaning. This unidentified meaning is often called "reflexive meaning". For example, Dixon (1972: 90) says that in Dyirbal "reflexive forms sometimes carry a reflexive meaning", whereas "in other cases, the reflexive affix appears just to derive an intransitive from a transitive stem, without carrying any reflexive meaning". (See also Marantz 1984: 152, quoted in footnote 5; or Geniušienė 1987: 355.)

I hypothesize that the prototypical meaning which, on a subconscious level, guides linguists in their actual use of the term "reflexive" can be represented as follows:

---

[4] Needless to say, for reasons of space, the account of Polish reflexives given in this chapter is very sketchy and does not aim at completeness. In particular, I am not going to survey here the existing literature on the topic.

[5] In fact, Marantz explicitly links "reflexivization" with intransitivity. He writes, for example: "Many languages include special intransitive verb forms with reflexive meaning" (1984: 152). (One wonders, however, what exactly he has in mind when he talks of "reflexive meaning".)

(39) (R) at some time, someone did something
  because of this,
  something happened to the same person at the same time

For example, a sentence such as

(40) Harry killed himself by cutting his wrists.

indicates that at some time Harry was doing something with some sharp object (bringing it into contact with some parts of his body), and that he died because of this (loosely speaking, "at the same time").

The condition "at the same time" has to be understood in a broad sense, as it is usually understood in ordinary language, not in the sense of strict simultaneity. For example, if a man kills himself by cutting his wrists, the action of his cutting his wrists precedes, strictly speaking, the event of his dying. Both events have to occur, however, at what is conceived of as the same time. Although one can say, for example,

(41) He killed himself: he cut his wrists on Thursday and he died on Friday.

one cannot say:

(42) *He killed himself on Friday by cutting his wrists on Thursday.
(43) *By cutting his wrists on Thursday, he eventually killed himself on Friday.

Reflexive sentences are similar in this respect to transitive clauses. (For discussion, see Wierzbicka 1975, 1980b.)

It must be stressed that formula R is proposed as a representation of the prototypical meaning of all so-called "reflexive" sentences, not as their semantic invariant: there are many types of so-called "reflexive" sentences in many languages which do not have the prototypical meaning in question. Nor am I proposing formula R as a full definition for the notion "reflexive construction"; rather, I am suggesting that a useful definition can be formulated with reference to this semantic formula.

I propose, then, the following definition of a reflexive construction:

A REFLEXIVE CONSTRUCTION IS A CONSTRUCTION WHICH ENCODES THE MEANING SPELLED OUT IN THE FORMULA R (AND POSSIBLY SOME OTHER MEANINGS).

A reflexive construction may have more than one meaning (''just as an imperative may have more than one meaning; cf. Section 2), but it must have the meaning spelled out in the formula R.

The formal characteristics of a given "reflexive" construction (in the sense defined here) will vary from language to language, and so will the additional meanings which it can serve, but the prototypical meaning stipulated by the definition (and spelled out in formula R) must be constant. (Otherwise, the definition would have no constant point of reference.)

Some readers may wonder at this point why I don't use instead conventional linguistic labels such as "agent" and "patient": can't the prototypical reflexive situation be defined in terms of coreference (or identity) between agent and patient? (For example, Dixon (1977: 280) writes, with respect to Yidiɲ: "If the agent and patient of an action described by a transitive verb are identical, then a reflexive construction must be used"; see also Mosel 1991.)

I believe that a definition based on the notions "agent" and "patient" would indeed be preferable to a syntactic definition along the lines of "subject = object".[6] But it would not be adequate either. What is missing from such a hypothetical definition is the causal and temporal link between the action and the resulting event or state. The formula proposed in this chapter, framed in terms of simple, non-technical verbs *do* and *happen*, allows us to present the prototypical reflexive situation in terms of a scenario including causal and temporal links. (Cf. Chapters 2 and 3.) The use of static (and highly technical) concepts such as agent and patient does not allow us to capture the dynamic character of the prototypical reflexive meaning. (For further discussion of the inadequacy of this definition see Section 5.)

It should be emphasized that the definition of the reflexive construction proposed in this chapter, while based on meaning, does take the structure into account, in a crucial way: a sentence which meets the semantic condition R will not be called "reflexive" if it doesn't meet the structural condition specified for the language in question. For example, the English sentence *Harry committed suicide* is not a reflexive sentence, because although the semantic condition is met, there is nothing in the structure of the sentence as such which would show this. On the other hand, the sentence *Harry saw himself in the mirror* does qualify as a reflexive sentence, even though it doesn't refer to any action (we can't say that Harry "did something") and thus does not correspond to the semantic prototype specified in the definition. The construction

(44)   NP $V_{transitive}$ Pronominal form + SELF

is identified in English on a structural basis, and of course a sentence such as *Harry saw himself in the mirror* has to be recognized as belonging to this construction. Similarly, in Polish the construction

---

[6] Compare the following comment by Kibrik (1991: 69), who also argues for a semantic basis for grammatical typology: "There is a widespread tendency to decribe the opposition of accusativity to ergativity in terms of subject and object . . . But the notions 'subject' and 'object', once they are studied more carefully, prove to be no less complicated than 'ergativity' and 'accusativity', and even less obviously universal." The same could be said, of course, about attempts to define "reflexivity" in terms of these highly problematic notions.

(45) NP_{transitive} SIĘ

is identified on a structural basis, and sentences such as

(46) Henryk zobaczył się w lustrze.
'Harry saw himself in the mirror.'

have to be recognized as belonging to this construction. But if these two constructions (44 and 45) are called "reflexive" at all it is because they both are also used to express the scenario stated in formula R.

From the requirement that a language-specific structural condition has to be met it follows that if two sentences, say one English and one Polish, mean the same, and if we call one of them "reflexive", we do not have to call the other one "reflexive", too. For example, of the following two sentences one (the Polish one) is reflexive (in terms of the definition proposed in this chapter), whereas the other one is not:

(47) Henryk położył się.
Harry   laid:TR REFL

(48) Harry lay down.

It also has to be recognized that the two constructions (the English and the Polish one) have a different scope; for example, as mentioned earlier, psychological attitudes towards oneself cannot be described in Polish, as they can in English, in the same construction as physical action:

(49) Harry hates himself.

(50) *Henryk nienawidzi się
Harry   hates   REFL

None the less, the two constructions (44) and (45) are matched under the same name "reflexive" because they can both be used to express the prototypical meaning R, as in the following examples (where (*a*) and (*b*) mean the same):

(51) (*a*) Henryk powiesił się.
(*b*) 'Harry hanged himself.'

(52) (*a*) Henryk ogolił się.
(*b*) 'Harry shaved himself.'

Alongside with the proposed definition, I put forward the following substantive hypothesis: Very many, perhaps the majority of, languages of the world do have a reflexive construction in the sense of this definition; in other words, the meaning spelled out in formula R is so important to human beings that it is grammaticalized in the majority of languages of the world.

It should be added that while the English and Polish reflexive constructions have been described here with reference to transitive verbs, the proposed semantic definition of a reflexive construction can also be met by intransitive verbs, and that it can account for the fact that, in many languages, reflexive markers are widely used with change of state verbs, regardless of their transitivity. For example, in Romance languages reflexive markers are often used with perfective verbs of physical position, in contrast to the corresponding imperfective verbs. For example, in Italian there is a contrast between the imperfective *sedere*, 'to sit, to be seated', and the perfective *sedersi* (with the reflexive marker -*si*), 'to sit down'; or between the imperfective *giacere*, 'to lie', and the perfective *sdraiarsi*, 'to lie down'. Facts of this kind can be explained with reference to the prototypical reflexive scenario: 'at some time, someone did something (e.g. made some movements); because of this something happened to the same person at the same time (roughly: this person came to be in a new position).'

Of course, one might declare that "reflexives" of this kind are purely lexical and have nothing in common with fully productive grammatical "reflexives"; but by doing so one would be losing a generalization which can be captured in terms of the semantic scenario.

The definition of reflexives proposed here corresponds, by and large, to the accepted usage (in the sense that it picks out, on the whole, those constructions which are usually called "reflexive"). But it doesn't necessarily correspond to the way the term "reflexive" has been used by every descriptive grammar—because the general usage of this term, not being controlled by any precise definition, is, predictably, shaky, inconsistent, and at times arbitrary.

Consider, for example, the possibility that a language may have two different constructions, one for describing a voluntary action, for example:

(53) Adam covered himself with a blanket.
(54) Adam cut himself (on purpose).

and another for describing actions with unintended results, for example:

(55) Adam burned himself (accidentally).

Should both these constructions be called "reflexive" or should the term "reflexive" be reserved for only one of them, namely, the voluntary one? Different authors have treated this problem in different ways (see e.g. the discussion in Dixon 1976*a*,*b*, 1977: 280).

In my view, however, whatever analysis may best fit this or that particular language, a universal definition of the notion "reflexive construction" should not take as its reference-point a semantic formula stipulating that the action must be voluntary (RV, as in formula 57 below), but rather should remain neutral on this point (as in formula R, repeated below as 56):

(56) (R) at some time, someone did something
            because of this
            something happened to the same person at the same time

(57) (RV) at some time, someone did something
            because of this
            something happened to the same person at the same time
            this person wanted this (to happen)

Formula R is clearly more fruitful as a basis for a universal definition because in most languages of the world so-called "reflexive constructions" (as described in the relevant literature) are not restricted to situations when the action is voluntary and the subject "acts upon itself", and in fact in many languages reflexive sentences can be ambiguous between a "voluntary action" reading and an "accidental event" reading. For example, in Spanish,

(58) Juan se   mató.
      Juan REFL killed

can mean either that Juan killed himself voluntarily, or that he died by accident, as a result of his own action. Similarly, in Polish,

(59) Jan zabił się.
      John killed REFL

can refer either to a suicide or to an accident. Even in English many reflexive sentences are similarly ambiguous; for example,

(60) John injured/burned/cut himself.

I suggest, therefore, that the meaning commonly (though not universally) grammaticalized in one way or another in different languages of the world in the form of some recognizable "reflexive" construction is the one proposed here, R, rather than a more specific one, requiring the presence of a voluntary action, RV. Reflexive constructions differ in this respect from "transitive constructions", whose semantic prototype refers indeed to a voluntary action. (See e.g. the data in Hopper and Thompson 1980, 1982; Plank 1984; Tsunoda 1981.) Although reflexive constructions in the sense defined in this chapter are very widespread, apparently they are not universal. For example, the Austronesian language Samoan appears to have no reflexive construction (Mosel forthcoming).

5. Transitive Constructions

The distinction between intransitive and transitive constructions, though by
no means sharp and clear-cut (see Hopper and Thompson 1980; Verhaar
1990), plays a fundamental role in most languages of the world. The current knowledge about the different ways in which this distinction can be
manifested in different languages suggests a certain prototypical scenario,
or what Givón (1990: 565) calls "the prototypical transitive event". (See
also Slobin 1982.) According to Givón, "Three semantic dimensions are
central to the semantic definition of transitivity. Each corresponds to one
central aspect of the prototypical transitive event, thus also to one central
feature of the prototypical transitive clause." Givón specifies these three
"dimensions" as follows:

(a) *Agent*: The prototypical transitive clause involves a volitional, controlling,
initiating, active agent, one that is responsible for the event, i.e. its *salient*
cause.

(b) *Patient*: The prototypical transitive event involves an inactive, non-volitional,
non-controlling patient, one that registers the changes-of-state associated
with the event, i.e. its *salient effect*.

(c) *Verb*: The prototypical transitive clause involves a compact (non-durative),
bounded (non-lingering), realis (non-hypothetical) verb and tense-aspect-
modality. It thus represents an event that is fast-moving, completed, and real,
i.e. *perceptually and cognitively salient*. (Givón 1990: 565)

In my terms, the prototypical transitive scenario can be represented as
follows (see Wierzbicka 1988):

(61) at some time, someone was doing (did) something to something
   .   because of this,
       something happened to this something at the same time
       this person wanted this (to happen)

Of course "transitive sentences" don't have to meet all the aspects of this
scenario, but a departure from any of them is likely to lead to a decrease
in syntactic transitivity (manifested in case assignment, passivizability, and
so on). The evidence for this assertion cannot be surveyed here for reasons
of space, but it can be easily found in the abundant literature on the subject (in particular Hopper and Thompson 1980; Moravcsik 1978; Tsunoda
1981; see also Wierzbicka 1988).

In an earlier work discussing the semantic basis of transitivity
(Wierzbicka 1981) I proposed a somewhat different semantic formula, with
a person or animal rather than an inanimate object as a prototypical
patient. I was in two minds about it, however, and left the question open,
adducing in fact a number of arguments in favour of my present position

(that the prototypical patient is inanimate). As I argued at the time (Wierzbicka 1981: 57–8), the fact that animate patients often receive differential case marking (ACC≠NOM) does not establish that clauses with animate objects are more highly transitive than those with inanimate ones.

The matter is complicated because a highly transitive clause requires two clearly individuated arguments, and human objects tend to be more highly individuated than inanimate ones. None the less the meaning encoded in a "cardinal transitive clause" (see Hopper and Thompson 1980) presupposes a maximum contrast between the two arguments, one active (a human agent) and one passive (an inanimate object purposefully acted upon).

Givón writes (1990: 630): "The prototypical transitive verb has an agent subject and patient direct-object. If reflexives and reciprocals were to apply to prototypical transitive verbs, they must be restricted to verbs that can take *human subjects.*" In reflexives, Givón points out,

the object must also be human, if it is to be coreferent with the subject. But the prototypical transitive object-patient is not human, but primarily a *dumb inanimate.* . . . Therefore, prototypical transitive verbs such as 'break', 'build', 'make', 'chop', 'destroy', 'bend', etc. cannot undergo the reflexives or reciprocals—unless their meaning is metaphorically extended *away from* the transitive prototype. (1990: 630)

I entirely agree that the prototypical transitive object is a "dumb inanimate" and that prototypical transitive verbs are physical action verbs such as *break, chop, build,* or *open.* A prototypical transitive scenario celebrates, so to speak, purposeful human action, in the course of which a human being controls and affects "dumb objects": chops a tree, breaks a branch, makes a fire, roasts an animal, builds a shelter, and so on. Actions of this kind are so vital to human survival that one can hardly be surprised to see the basic scenario enacted in them to be encoded, almost universally, in the grammar of human languages.

Purposeful actions directed at other people are also important in human life, but other people are potential agents themselves and they are less likely to be cast in the role of completely passive patients. They are likely either to co-operate with our action or to resist it rather to remain pure "undergoers" of it. This is why, I think, human undergoers are sometimes marked (for example, in Spanish) in the same way as recipients, beneficiaries, "maleficiaries", or addressees (for discussion, see Wierzbicka 1981).

As for purposeful actions directed at oneself (as a patient), they are hardly necessary for human survival. In fact, they often have self-destruction as their goal (as in killing, hanging, drowning, shooting, or poisoning oneself). The whole idea of "acting upon oneself" requires the ability, and the inclination, to look at oneself from outside, and to treat oneself as a person-in-the-world, on a par with other persons-in-the-world—as pointed out by Haiman (1995), hardly a universal human proclivity.[7] It is understandable, therefore, that human languages do not celebrate self-directed action on anything like the scale on which they celebrate purposeful action directed at the physical environment and "dumb matter". ("Self-directed" actions such as eating or getting dressed are, of course, vital for survival, but these are normally viewed as "doing something" rather than "doing something to oneself". Even in English, "eating" is distinguished from "feeding oneself".)

On the other hand, the idea that by doing something I can cause something to happen to me (whether something I want or something I don't want) is important, because it encourages people to take care, so that they don't cut themselves, burn themselves, injure themselves, and also that they can, when necessary, hide themselves, cover themselves, warm themselves, wash themselves, and so on.

The prototypical reflexive scenario differs, therefore, from a prototypical transitive scenario in several respects: it involves a person, rather than a person and an object (DO versus DO TO), it involves the idea of "sameness" ("something happened to the same person"), and it doesn't (necessarily) involve the idea of purposeful action.

The idea of "sameness" is missing, I believe, from sentences such as

(62) He washed/shaved/dressed.

Sentences of this kind are therefore not synonymous with their counterparts with a reflexive pronoun:

(63) He washed/shaved/dressed himself.

The situations described can, of course, be exactly the same, but the conceptualization is different, and in some situations one construction may be more appropriate than the other. In particular, if there is more emphasis on the details of the resulting state, the reflexive construction (64*a* and 65*a*) may be preferred to the non-reflexive one (64*b* and 65*b*):

(64) (*a*) She washed herself with special care.
    (*b*) She washed with special care.
(65) (*a*) She dressed herself slowly, paying attention to every detail.
    (*b*) She dressed slowly, paying attention to every detail.

---

[7] It is interesting to note, therefore, that the simple and therefore attractive formula "doing something to oneself", which might be suggested as an alternative to "agent = patient", is in fact culturally biased, as it implies the "self-alienation" discussed by Haiman. Not surprisingly, the number of languages into which this formula could be translated is rather limited. On the other hand, the semantic formula R proposed here is based on lexical and grammatical universals and can (I hypothesize) be translated into any human language.

Non-reflexive sentences such as *He washed* or *He dressed* suggest a routine action, and they indicate that this action is seen as a unitary event, not decomposed, in the speaker's mind, into different events involving "the same person". (For this reason, as pointed out by Faltz (1985: 7) one is also more likely to say *The cat washed himself* than *The cat washed.*)

Consider also the following contrasts:

(66) Mary hid.
(67) Mary hid herself.
(68) Mary was hiding in the shed.
(69) *Mary was hiding herself in the shed.

The reason why 67 and 68 are acceptable whereas 69 is not (in the appropriate sense) is essentially the same as the reason why in many languages (e.g. Romance languages) perfective verbs are often reflexive where their imperfective counterparts are not: the reflexive marker indicates a conceptual split between an action and a resulting change of state.

These examples highlight the danger involved in the common use of expressions such as "reflexive meaning" unaccompanied by precise definitions: grammar encodes different types of conceptualization, not different types of situation, and the same situation can be conceptualized in different ways. (See Langacker 1987.)

The prototypical reflexive scenario is not, then, a special case of the prototypical transitive scenario, with the additional condition that the "patient" is coreferential with the "agent". It is a different scenario, overlapping with, rather than subsumed under, the prototypical scenario of transitivity.

The idea that if I do something, something (wanted or unwanted) may happen to me does not require any "objectivization" of oneself, but it does encourage foresight and care; and—judging by the evidence of human languages—it does play an important role in human conceptualization of the world and of our life in the world.

It should be pointed out that in English, too, reflexive sentences are not always transitive to any extent. Using the co-ordination test again, we will note, for example, the following contrasts:

(70) He covered/defended/protected/shot himself and his child.
(71) *He hid himself and his child.
(72) *He warmed himself and his child.
(73) *He seated himself and his child.
(74) *He stretched himself and his child on the grass.
(75) *He threw himself and his child on to the grass.

Facts of this kind highlight the inadequacy of a semantic definition of reflexive constructions couched in terms of the notions "agent" and "patient": the so-called "patient" may stand for different semantic roles in sentences referring to oneself and those referring to another person. In the case of the sentence *He covered himself and his child with a blanket* English allows the speaker to treat the two "patients" in the same way, though many languages require here, too, conceptualization in terms of two distinct roles. But in cases such as bodily movements even English makes a distinction between oneself and other people. The cover-all term "patient" obscures such facts.

The scope of transitive reflexive sentences is wider in (modern) English than in other European languages, and, perhaps, wider than in any other language. This syntactic feature of (modern) English has an obvious semantic and cultural interpretation, of the kind suggested in Haiman (1985, 1995: 224). Speaking of sentences such as

(5*b*) I expect myself to win.
(6*b*) I got myself up.

(his numbers) Haiman writes:

My central claim in this essay is that the representation of reflexivity by a separate reflexive pronoun in sentences like (5*b*) and (6*b*) iconically signals the recognition of not one but two participants, and thus implies some kind of detachment from the self. . . . ordinary sentences like

(7) (*a*) I (don't) like myself
    (*b*) He restrained himself with difficulty

. . . reflect a degree of self-alienation which—unlike "reflexivization" in the middle voice . . .—is probably far from universal. The evidence for this comes not only from the large number of languages which have no reflexive pronoun at all . . . (1991*a*: 16)

I believe that Haiman is essentially right and that he is saying something important. I would point out, however, that in addition to the presence or absence of a "reflexive pronoun", we must also pay attention to the transitive or intransitive character of the reflexive sentence. For example, English sentences such as

(76) He hid himself.
(77) He stretched himself on the grass.

do contain a reflexive pronoun, but, as pointed out earlier, they are not transitive (at least judging by the co-ordination test), and, I would argue, they do not show any "self-alienation" (unlike, for example, *He restrained himself with difficulty* or *I don't like myself*).

I agree with Haiman that the emergence and current prevalence of the reflexive pronouns in English is itself a sign of semantic and cultural developments of the kind discussed in his paper. But on the level of individual sentences there may be no semantic differences between those with a reflexive pronoun (as in English), those with a reflexive clitic (as in French or Spanish), or those with a reflexive suffix (as in Russian or Dyirbal), provided that all the sentences in question are intransitive. For example, I don't think there is necessarily any semantic difference between the following three sentences, the first of which uses a reflexive pronoun (*himself*), the second, a reflexive clitic (*se*), and the third a reflexive suffix (*-sja*):

(78) He hid himself.
(79) Il s'est caché. (French)
(80) On sprjatalsja. (Russian)

On the other hand, a transitive reflexive sentence such as 81 may indeed differ in some aspects of its semantic structure from intransitive ones such as 82 and 83:

(81) He covered himself with a blanket.
(82) Il s'est enveloppé dans une couverture.
(83) On pokrylsja odejalom.

The fact that only 81 allows conjoined direct objects (*He covered himself and his child*) does indeed point to a different conceptualization.

Once again, what matters is not just the number of "participants" in a given situation (because this depends on the speaker's point of view), and not even the number of "core arguments" in a given sentence (because two core arguments can be associated with different degrees of transitivity): only a reconstruction of the full semantic scenario, in terms of which the speaker conceptualizes the situation, can explain all the aspects of a sentence's grammar. (For full discussion, see Wierzbicka 1988, chs. 5 and 6.)

6. Conclusion

Typologists have often recognized on a theoretical level that to compare languages (or anything else) we need a *tertium comparationis*. (See Kibrik 1992: 129–30.) For example, Faltz, in his cross-linguistic study of reflexives, writes: "Before settling in to an examination of a phenomenon in many different languages, it is necessary to have some language-independent idea of what that phenomenon is, so that we know what to begin to look for. The term *reflexive* must therefore be provided with some universal content" (Faltz 1985: 1). By using as its tools meaning-based categories such as "noun", "numeral", "plural", "past", "imperative", "conditional", or "reflexive", linguistic typology has also recognized that in the case of language the necessary *tertium comparationis* is provided by meaning. However, categories of this kind were usually not defined, or if they were defined, their definitions were not adhered to, and in fact, whatever the definitions, the actual analysis was carried out on the basis of intuition and common sense. The treatment of the category of "reflexives" illustrated in this chapter is a good case in point.

American structuralists such as Zellig Harris and Charles Fries, who refrained from using any traditional grammatical labels and from referring to any traditional grammatical categories (e.g. Harris 1946, 1951; or Fries 1952), were therefore more consistent and more rigorous in their approach to linguistic analysis than either traditional grammarians or present-day typologists. They did not, however, develop linguistic typology.

Languages differ in form and structure, but they all encode meaning. In their grammars (just as in their lexicons) different languages encode different configurations of the same semantic primitives. Some configurations, however, appear to be very widespread, and to play an important role in the grammar of countless and most diverse languages of the world. I believe that recurring configurations of this kind represent meanings which are particularly important in human conceptualization of the world. It is an important task of linguistics as a discipline to identify such meanings; by fulfilling this task, linguistics can contribute in a significant way to the study of humankind, transcending the boundaries of academic disciplines.

Among the meanings which linguistic investigations show to be grammaticalized most widely in the languages of the world, we can recognize certain scenarios such as the "transitive" scenario or the "reflexive" scenario; and we can see that large parts of grammars are organized around such scenarios, and can be described with reference to them. Other widely grammaticalized meanings are of a different nature. All types of meanings, however, can be rigorously described and insightfully compared in terms of the same set of universal semantic primitives and of the metalanguage based on them. I believe that without such a metalanguage, grammatical typology has no firm basis and no precise tools with which it could fully achieve its objectives.

15 Comparing Grammatical Categories across Languages: The Semantics of Evidentials

□ □ ————————————————————————————————

1. Introduction

In this chapter I am going to illustrate and document the claim that grammar encodes meaning by analysing one area of grammar in a number of different languages of the world: that area which is usually associated with the term "evidentiality". As the goal of this chapter is mainly theoretical, not empirical, my data will be drawn exclusively from one source: the volume entitled *Evidentiality*, edited by Wallace Chafe and Johanna Nichols (1986). I will re-examine the data presented in some of the chapters of this volume by experts on a number of languages, and I will try to show how these data can be reanalysed in terms of universal semantic primitives, and how in this way they can be made both more verifiable (that is, predictive) and more comparable across language boundaries.

As it is, the contributors to the volume operate with analytical categories such as "direct" (experience or evidence), "personal", "immediate", "first-hand", "witnessed", and of course "indirect", "non-immediate", "second-hand", "not-witnessed", "inferred", and so on. The trouble is that labels of this kind stand for different things in different languages; and that they have very little predictive value. For example, when we are told that a language distinguishes "direct evidence" from "non-direct evidence", or "immediate evidence (or experience)" from "non-immediate evidence", we may have no idea exactly what these labels mean with respect to this particular language, nor how the categories in question are used in this language; and if exactly the same labels are used with respect to another language, we can by no means expect that they will be used in the same sense, nor that the categories bearing these labels in the second language will correspond in use to those bearing the same labels in the first language. (See Kibrik 1992: 43, 129–30.)

By contrast, if we rely on universal semantic primitives such as I, KNOW, DO, THIS, and BECAUSE, SEE, or HEAR, we can posit intuitively clear categories such as 'I know because I see it' or 'I know because I did it', which will mean exactly the same with respect to any language for which they are postulated. Formulae of this kind are intuitively verifiable and they are empirically testable. They make clear predictions about the range of use of the categories which encode them, so that if we posit the same meaning for two categories in two different languages (e.g. 'I know it because I did it'), we can expect that these two categories will have the same range of use (except for possible differences due to some specifiable cultural factors). If our predictions are not fulfilled, the formulae are proved inadequate, or inaccurate, and have to be revised or adjusted. Proceeding in this way, we can obtain an optimal fit between semantic formulae and language use. Whether this fit can be perfect and absolute is an open question. But it can certainly be better than the fit between traditional labels such as "direct", "personal", "immediate", "first-hand" and language use.

The formulae proposed in the present chapter are meant, above all, to illustrate the proposed methodology. Since I have no knowledge of the languages for which these formulae are proposed, I have to rely entirely on the information provided by the experts. But in many cases this information is so rich and so clearly presented that it provides a sufficient basis for the formulation of semantic hypotheses. It would, of course, be ideal if, in the future, the experts themselves were to test these hypotheses against further data.

2. Kashaya

Kashaya (of the Pomo family of northern California) has a very rich system of verbal suffixes indicating evidentiality—as Oswalt (1986: 29) points out, one of the most elaborate and discriminating in the world. What is particularly interesting about this system is that although it is so elaborate it is also beautifully transparent in its semantics.

Doing

To begin with, Kashaya has two evidential suffixes (a perfective and an imperfective) which point to the speaker's personal experience as a self-explanatory source of information. Oswalt calls these suffixes "Performative", and defines them as follows: "The Performative suffixes signify that the speaker knows of what he speaks because he is performing the act himself or has just performed it" (1986: 34). In our terms the meaning of these suffixes can be represented very simply:

-ŵela   (Performative-Imperfective)
I know this
because I am doing it

-mela   (Performative-Perfective)
I know this
because I did it a short time before now

Oswalt's examples of the use of these suffixes include sentences 1, 2, and 6 (his numbers):

(1) qowá·qala. (Performative-Imperfective)
    (underlying form: qowaᵒq-ŵela)
    'I am packing (a suitcase).'

(2) qowáhmela. (Performative-Perfective)
    (underlying form: qowaᵒq-mela)
    'I just packed.'

(6) mi·-li   ʔa me-ʔe-l   pʰakúm-mela.
    there-VISIBLE I your-father-OBJ.   kill-PERFORM.
    'Right there I killed your father.'

Seeing

Another pair of complementary suffixes, one imperfective and the other perfective, is what Oswalt calls the "Factual–Visual" pair, -ŵă and yă. These suffixes "signify that the speaker knows of what he speaks because he sees, or saw, it." In addition, "the Factual (not the Visual) also applies to classes of actions or states which have been observed enough by the speaker for him to generalize them as true, and to classes which may simply be common knowledge" (1986: 36).

Clearly the meaning of the "Visual (Perfective)" suffix can be represented as follows:[1]

-yă   (Visual₁)
I know this
because I saw it

This can be illustrated with Oswalt's sentence 9:

(9) qowahy. (Visual₁)
    (underlying form: qowaᵒq-yă)
    '(I just saw) he packed, I just saw him pack.'

---

[1] The labels "Visual₁" and "Visual₂" used below are mine. Oswalt's labels are "Visual" and "Factual". Strictly speaking, the formula assigned to the "Specific (Imperfective)" sense of the "Factual" suffix should allow for both present and past events, extending over some time (cf. the gloss assigned to sentence 13). This could be achieved as follows:

    for some time I could say: I see this
    because of this, I can say: I know it

The "Factual" suffix appears to have two distinct senses, one manifested in sentences referring to specific events, and another, in generic sentences. The specific sense of this suffix parallels that of the "Visual$_1$":

-ŵă   (Visual$_2$)
I know this
because I see it

This is illustrated with Oswalt's sentence 8:

(8) qowá·q^h.   (Factual)
    (underlying form: qowa°q-ŵă)
    '(I see) he is packing.'

The generic sense of the 'Factual' suffix is quite different. It can be represented as follows:[2]

-ŵă   (Factual)
everyone knows it

This use of "Factual" can be illustrated with the generic interpretation of Oswalt's sentence 13:

(13) s̓ihta=yac^{h}ma cahno-w.
     bird=PL.SUBJ. sound-FACTUAL
     'Birds sing.'

The same sentence, however, can receive a different, specific interpretation, which (unlike the generic one) implies visual evidence:

(13) sihta=yac^{h}ma cahno-w.
     bird=PL.SUBJ. sound-FACTUAL
     '(I see/saw) birds are/were singing.'

It doesn't seem possible to reduce these two different uses of "Factual" to one; and it would perhaps be better to give the suffix in question two different labels: "Visual$_2$" for the specific use and 'Factual' for the generic use (at the same time renaming Oswalt's 'Visual' as 'Visual$_1$').

Hearing

In addition to its two "Visual" suffixes ("Visual$_1$" and "Visual$_2$") Kashaya also has an "Auditory" suffix, -*V̂nnă*, which "signifies that the speaker knows of what he speaks because he heard the sound of the action, but did

---

[2] Oswalt describes the use of the Factual suffix not only in terms of "common knowledge" but also of "classes of actions or states which have been observed enough by the speaker for him to generalize them as true" (1986: 36), but I think that both these uses can probably be subsumed under "common knowledge" and that the formula "everyone knows it" captures correctly the semantic invariant of this suffix.

not see it" (1986: 37). Unlike the "Performative" and the "Visual" suffix, it is indifferent to aspectual distinctions. Oswalt's examples include 14, 15, and 16:

(14) mo·dun. (Imperfective)
  (underlying form: mo-V̂°d-V̂nnă)
  'I hear/heard someone running along.'

(15) momá.cin. (Perfective)
  (underlying form: mo-ma°c-V̂nnă)
  'I just heard someone run in.'

(16) hayu cáhno-n. (Imperfective)
  'I hear a dog barking.'

The meaning of the suffix in question seems quite clear:

-V̂nnă (Auditory)
I know this
because I hear it

Hearsay and Personal Experience

Another suffix, which Oswalt classifies together with the "Performative", the "Visual", the "Factual" and the "Auditory" under the label "Direct Evidence", is -*yowă*, the suffix of "Personal Experience". In narratives, all the other evidentials described so far are replaced with this one suffix. This means that a radical simplification of the evidential system takes place, with all evidential distinctions replaced with just one: that between "Personal Experience" and "Quotative".

The meaning of the "Quotative" as such seems reasonably clear. It "is the one evidential for information learned from someone else, contrasted with the many for information learned through the speaker's own experience" (1986: 41). An example is provided by:

(27) mul =í-do-·   hayu cáhno-w.
  then =ASS-QUOT-NON-FINAL dog sound-ABS
  'Then, they say, the dog barked.'

Presumably, here as elsewhere, the meaning of the "Quotative" can be represented as follows:

-do (Quotative)
I say this because someone else said this
I don't say: I know it

What is much harder to establish is the meaning of the "Personal Experience" suffix -*yowă*, which in narratives constitutes the only "Direct Evidence" alternative to the "Quotative".

One possibility which comes to mind as a hypothetical meaning of -*yowă*
is this:

I know
because I was there

But this interpretation is undermined by the fact that -*yowă* can be used
with respect to "moving actions seen on television or in the movies" (1986:
42). It is also hard to reconcile with the fact that what is experienced in
dreams, visions, and revelations is also reported with -*yowă*. In the case of
television and movies, it could be argued that the speaker "was there" (in
front of the screen); but in the case of dreams, visions, and revelations
(which may or may not feature the speaker himself) such an interpretation
makes even less sense: if I know something because I have seen it in a dream
it is not my physical presence somewhere that matters but my psychological experience.

It seems to me, therefore, that we should look for a different, more plausible interpretation of the "Personal Experience" suffix. The fact that in
narratives all other devices are reduced to one—"Quotative" versus
"Personal Experience", suggests the following interpretation for the latter:

-*yowă*   (Personal Experience)
I don't say this because someone else said this
I know it

Compare this with the formula for the "Quotative" suggested earlier:

-do   (Quotative)
I say this because someone else said this
I don't say: I know it

Oswalt (1986: 40) comments: "The simplification in narratives of the
elaborateness of the evidential system is understandable—when one talks
of events that may have happened a considerable time previously, the precise type of evidence is less important and, indeed, is often not remembered
by the speaker." Thus, the only question which really arises with respect to
narratives is this: does the speaker say this or that on the basis of hearsay
or not? "Quotative" signals hearsay; the suffix of "Personal Experience"
signals no hearsay. Thus, the "hearsay" suffix does not signal (by virtue of
its meaning) an absence of "direct experience". Rather, it is the so-called
suffix of "Personal Experience" which signals (by virtue of its meaning) an
absence of hearsay. The fact that it is common for a story to have the -*do*
("Quotative") suffix "in almost every sentence" (1986: 44) lends, I think,
support to this analysis: if most, or nearly all, sentences in a story are
marked as based on hearsay, it makes good sense for the speaker to mark
those exceptional ones which are *not* based on hearsay.

Inference

The "Inferential I" suffix -*qǎ* "marks an inference based on circumstances or evidence found apart, in space or time, from an actual event or state . . . To a certain extent -*qǎ* is a default category for evidence through senses other than those that have specific sensory suffixes (Visual or Auditory) . . . The Kashaya Inferential suffix implies no lack of certainty, merely lack of higher ranking evidence" (Oswalt 1986: 38). These comments seem to suggest that the suffix in question means:

> I know this
> not because I see it
> not because I hear it

But this is a very implausible semantic formula. Consider, for example, sentence 20:

(20) cuhni· muʔṭa-qʰ,
  'Bread has been cooked.'

uttered by somebody coming into a house and detecting an odour. The formula 'I know it not because I see it' might seem to fit this situation, but why should anyone want to say, in addition, 'not because I hear it'?

Consider also sentence 24, when the same suffix is combined with a future tense:

(24) heʔén ya mihyáč-kʰe-tʰin =i-q-a·   mu·kito baq'o=·li.
  how we win-FUT -not   =ASS-INF-NON-FINAL him   what=in.
  'It appears we'll never be able to beat him in anything.'

Here, the formula sketched would make no sense:

> We'll never be able to beat him in anything
> I know this
> not because I see it
> not because I hear it

We have to agree with Oswalt, therefore, that the suffix in question is "inferential" rather than "sensory", even though it "implies no lack of certainty, merely lack of higher ranking evidence". I propose for this suffix the following semantic formula:[3]

---

[3] In his grammar of the Daghestani language, Archi, Kibrik (1977*a,b*) discusses similar phenomena under the heading "*zaglaznost'* " (lit. a noun meaning 'not in front of the eyes'). He remarks that "the meaning of '*zaglaznost'*' is composed of the meaning 'a participant in the speech event is present in the situation which is being described' and 'the binary meaning of negation'" (1977*b*: 143). The examples he offers, however (Kibrik 1977*a*: 228–31), include some where the speaker is actually present in the situation but for one reason or another fails to see some aspect of this situation. This suggests that Kibrik's heading ("*zaglaznost'* ") may actually be more accurate from a semantic point of view than the definition, and that the best

-qǎ   (Inferential I)
I know this
because I know something else

Kashaya also has another "inferential" suffix, *-bi*, which Oswalt labels "Inferential II", and another "experiential" suffix, *-miyǎ*, which Oswalt labels "Remote Past"; but not enough information is provided about these two suffixes to enable us to sketch more than very tentative semantic formulae. Virtually all that Oswalt says about these suffixes is that "Remote Past" is a remote past alternative to *-yowǎ* and that "Inferential II", in combination with another suffix *-w*, is close in meaning to the English "turn out" (e.g. 'it turned out to be my husband'). As a starting-point for further testing we could propose, therefore, the following formulae:

-miyǎ   (Remote Past)
I know this
not because someone else said something
it happened a long time before now

-bi-w   (Inferential II)
I know this now
because I know something else now
I didn't know it before now

3. Quechua

David Weber (1986) begins his discussion of the three evidential suffixes, *-mi*, *-shi*, and *-chi*, in Tarma Quechua (a language of central Peru), by referring to Adelaar's (1977: 79) statement that these suffixes "indicate the validity of the information supplied by the speaker". Adelaar assigns to these three suffixes the following meanings:

-mi   "indicates that the speaker is convinced about what he is saying",
-shi   "indicates that the speaker has obtained the information that he is supplying through hearsay",
-chi   "indicates that the speaker's statement is a conjecture".

These definitions suggest the following semantic representation:

---

semantic formula for the category in question (in Archi) may be 'I know this not because I saw something'. This formula seems to also fit examples such as 'he didn't come' or 'he had no intention to work', when there was actually nothing for the speaker to see: 'I know this not because I saw something'. It would be good if this formula could also be tested for categories such as the "inferential" in Kashaya and in the other languages described in Chafe and Nichols (1986).

-mi
I know this

-shi
someone else says this
I don't say: I know it

-chi
I think this
I don't know it

But Weber argues that while Adelaar's definitions may be appropriate for Tarma Quechua, they are not valid for the dialect that he has investigated himself, namely for Huanuco Quechua.

In Tarma Quechua, Weber says, -*mi* is used not only for personal experience, but also to indicate conviction, whereas in Huanuco -*mi* is used only for personal experience. Speaking of a number of Tarma texts that he had examined, Weber comments: "In all Ignacio Zarate Mayma's texts in Adelaar (1977: 308–407) and in Puente (1972), I have not found a single case of -*shi*. Even though much of the material is far beyond the realm of the teller's experience (including folktales about the fox and the condor), he uses -*mi* throughout. This is because he believes the stories he is telling . . . These facts justify Adelaar's claims for Tarma" (1986: 142).

But in Huanuco Quechua, Weber tells us, the situation is different. "To the Huanuco Quechua ear, Zarate's use of -*mi* seems exceedingly incautious with respect to the information he conveys" (142). Weber's informant also mentions a man, referred to by his neighbours as "loko", 'crazy', who constantly uses -*mi*. "No one believes what he says because he 'always speaks as though he had witnessed what he is telling about.' "

Apparently, then, there is a difference between the Tarma sense of -*mi* and the Huanuco sense of -*mi*: if in Tarma -*mi* means 'I know', or perhaps 'I can say: I know', in Huanuco it must mean something different. But what?

Weber glosses the Huanuco senses of -*mi*, -*shi*, and -*chi* as "direct" (DIR), "indirect" (IND), and "conjecture" (CNJ), respectively. He insists that in Huanuco, "-*mi* and -*shi* are basically evidential: -*mi* means 'learned by direct experience' and -*shi* means 'learned by indirect experience (hearsay)' " (139). In particular, -*mi* is not a "validational" ("indicating commitment to the truth of the proposition"; (139), but an "evidential" ("indicating the source of the information"). "A validational interpretation for -*mi* is often appropriate because of the axiom that direct experience is reliable (and thus one is convinced about it)" (140). The basic meaning of -*mi*, however, is not "validational" but "evidential", like that of -*shi*: -*shi* implies absence of direct experience, and -*mi*, its presence.

But what does it really mean that -*mi* signals "direct experience"? It could mean a number of things, such as the following:

(1) I know this
    because I saw it

(2) I know this
    because I heard it

(3) I know this
    because I perceived it

(4) I know this
    because I did it

(5) I know this
    because it happened to me

(6) I know this
    because I was there

(7) I know this
    not because someone said it

Would any one of these different possibilities cover the whole range of use of -*mi*? Let us examine Weber's examples, with these questions in mind.

Sentence 1*a* (Weber's numbers) refers to a diviner who has chewed coca and predicts death:

(1*a*) Wañu-nqa-paq-mi.
    die-3FUT-FUT
    'It will die.'

According to Weber, the "rhetorical force" of this utterance (in these particular circumstances) would be "I assert that it will die". Thus, the diviner doesn't mean 'I know because I saw it', or 'I know because I heard it', or 'I know because I was there', and, clearly, he doesn't mean 'I know because I did it', or 'I know because it happened to me', although he could conceivably mean 'I know because something happened to me'; and he might mean 'I know, not because someone said something'. The same two possibilities would also hold for sentence 3*a*:

(3*a*) Qam-pis maqa-ma-shka-nki-mi.
    you-also hit-1OBJ-PERF-2
    'You also hit me.'

Here, Weber provides the following additional gloss: "I saw/felt you hit me (and was conscious)". In this situation, some of the other possibilities listed earlier would also be applicable: 'I know this because it happened to me', 'I know this because I perceived it', or 'I know this because I saw it'. But none of these formulae would fit the case of the diviner. Let us consider, in turn, the (unnumbered) sentence glossed as:

'My mother's grandfather's name was John.'

According to Weber's informant, this sentence "is natural with -*shi* but not with -*mi*, even if the speaker is convinced that it is true" (1986: 140). Weber explains this fact as follows: "This is because with -*mi* it implies that the speaker has met his great grandfather. What is basic for -*mi* is the source of the information (direct experience), not commitment to the truth of what his name was" (140).

Weber also points out that "the same result obtains for a sentence that the speaker does not believe, e.g. 'The moon is made of cheese.' According to TCV [Weber's informant] this is natural with -*shi*, indicating that the speaker has been informed that the moon is made of cheese. With -*mi*, says TCV, it implies that the speaker has been to the moon" (140).

But these comments take us back to the question: What does -*mi* really mean? The last two examples appear to suggest the following interpretation: 'I know this because I was there'. But clearly, this cannot be the invariant of -*mi*, because this formula does not fit the case of the diviner, or, for that matter, the case of the person hit by someone. It would be odd to say 'I know that you hit me because I was there'.

Let us examine one further example provided by Weber—sentence 2*a*, uttered "in response to person(s) who have expressed doubt as to the speaker's ability to make it (e.g. to the top of a mountain)" (139).

(2*a*) Noqa -mi chaya-:-man aywar-qa.
    I   arrive-I-COND if:I:go-TOP
    'I would/could/might arrive, if I were to go.'

Clearly, the speaker does not mean here 'I know this because I was there'. Nor does he mean 'I know this because I saw it', or 'I know this because I did it', or 'I know this because it happened to me', or 'I know this because something happened to me'. It could be argued that in this case the speaker might mean 'I know this because I feel something' (i.e. 'I have a feeling that I could do it'). But this interpretation would not fit the case of the great-grandfather ('I know that my great-grandfather's name was John, because I feel something').

What, then, is the semantic invariant of -*mi*? It seems to me that we are left with only one possibility which would fit all of Weber's examples, namely, number 7: 'I know this, not because someone said something'. If this is right then -*mi* functions in Huanuco Quechua as a marked category, defined in opposition to the hearsay -*shi*:

-mi
I say this
not because someone else said it
I know it

-shi
I say this

because someone else said it
I don't say: I know it

It is not the case, then, that -shi indicates the absence of "direct evidence", and -*mi* its presence. Rather, -*shi* indicates the presence of hearsay (as the basis of the speaker's statement) and -*mi*, its absence.

Of course, a denial of hearsay could also be compatible with a conjecture and -*mi* is not compatible with conjectures. But this is accounted for by the component 'I know' assigned here to -*mi*: conjectures are not compatible with 'I know'. For the Huanuco Quechua element -*chi*, which Weber characterizes as "conjecture", we can propose the same semantic formula which we have assigned to the Tarma -*chi*:

-chi
I think this
I don't know it

The contrast between the component 'I don't know it' assigned to -*chi* and the component 'I don't say: I know it' assigned to -*shi* accounts, I think, for the different "validational" force of these two elements. Weber's examples suggest that -*shi* can be used in cases where the speaker is not at all certain of the information conveyed, or even when he is highly sceptical (as in the case of the sentence "the moon is made of cheese"), but also in cases when the speaker is convinced that the sentence is true (as in the case of the sentence "my mother's grandfather's name was John"). The component 'I don't say: I know it' is compatible with both these types of situation. On the other hand, the component 'I don't know it', assigned to -*chi*, suggests a lack of confidence, and would not be compatible with situations when the speaker reports second-hand information that he views as fairly reliable.

Of course, in Western culture, second-hand information regarded as reliable is usually not distinguished from first-hand knowledge. But as Weber points out, in Quechua culture "(only) one's own experience is reliable" (1986: 138), and the cultural norm is "Avoid unnecessary risk, as by assuming responsibility for information of which one is not absolutely certain" (138). This explains, for example, why in a booklet on Peruvian history (discussed by Weber), sentences such as "Their tools and things are found throughout Peru" has -*shi* rather than -*mi*: as Weber points out, it is so "because the author could not possibly have seen all those things found in all those places" (141). Clearly, the author of the booklet does not wish to imply 'I don't know'. But the cautious component 'I don't say: I know it' does not imply lack of knowledge; it implies only an unwillingness to assume personal responsibility for the information provided. Such a cautious attitude might seem unnecessary, and even odd, from a Western point of view, but it is understandable from the point of view of Quechua culture.

The analysis of Huanuco Quechua evidentials proposed here explains, it seems to me, the fact that *-mi*—though labelled by Weber "direct"—does not seem to be widely used in sentences based on the speaker's personal experience, and that many, perhaps most, such sentences occur without any evidentials. "For example, ATR [an informant], in telling of going to see a football game, did not use *-mi* in the parts describing his getting to and from the game (told in the first person), but he did use *-mi* in describing the events of other people (companions, players, referees)" (1986: 141).

If *-mi* meant something like 'I know this because I did it' or 'I know this because it happened to me', this absence of *-mi* in most personal narratives would be puzzling. But if *-mi* signals that the account is not based on hearsay, this absence of *-mi* in most personal narratives is understandable: normally, there is no need to say:

> I did it
> I know this not because someone else told me

If the speaker is not suffering from amnesia it would be assumed that he knows what he did without someone else telling him about it. But in the case of other people's actions, the report could well be based on hearsay, so if it isn't, it makes sense for the speaker to signal this non-hearsay basis of the sentence by means of *-mi*. Huanuco Quechua differs in this respect from some other languages (e.g. Wintu) described in the same volume, which have markers (also labelled as "direct") signalling "personal experience" of some sort in a positive way rather than "absence of hearsay". Understandably, in these languages the marker in question is used more widely than *-mi* is used in Huanuco.

4. Wintu

According to Schlichter (1986), Wintu, a language of northern California, has four evidential suffixes, which she labels as "nonvisual sensorial", "hearsay", "inferential", and "expectational". Here, as elsewhere, the labels at best provide hints, not explanations: they cannot tell the reader what each of the suffixes in question really means and in what range of situations it can be used.

Non-visual Sensorial

To begin with, the suffix *-nt^hEr* "is used if the speaker wishes to indicate that the statement he is making describes a fact known to him through one of his senses other than vision, i.e. his hearing, feeling, taste, smell, touch, or any kind of intellectual experience of 'sixth sense' " (1986: 47). As a first approximation, then, we could try to explicate the "evidential" in question as follows:

I know this
because I perceive(d) something
I didn't see it

Let us now test this explication against Schlichter's illustrative sentences:[4]

(1) Heket   wira wača·-bint^he·m.
    someone come cry   IM   DUB
    'Someone is coming crying (I hear).'

(2) Pi k'ilepma. daqčant^he·m.
    it awfully hot   DUB
    'It's awfully hot (I feel the heat).'

(3) Po·m yel-hurawint^he·m.
    earth destroy SE   DUB
    'The earth will be destroyed (I know, feel).'

(4) ʔUwebe·di war ʔunikint^he·m.
    don't   IMP QUOT.COM.DUB
    'He said 'don't do it!' (We heard him say not to do it.)'

(5) Q'otisa-bint^heresken.
    strong IM   you
    'You're strong (I feel).'   (Said while wrestling.)

(6) T'aqiqma·-bint^he·.
    hurt   IM
    'It hurts (I feel the pain).'

(7) Henuni mis yi·la-kint^heri·?
    how   you send COM-INTER
    'How did he instruct you (in your hearing)?'

(8) Č'epkal ne·l ba·-bint^hida.
    bad   we eat IM we
    'We've been eating bad things (I sense).'

(9) Hida naqalma·-bint^he·n.
    very pitiful   IM   you
    'You're so pitiful! (I am emotionally affected.)'

At first sight, all these examples seem to fit the proposed semantic description, but if one examines them more closely one is bound to develop some doubts. For example, could the person who says 6, "It hurts", or 2, "It's awfully hot", really mean 'I perceive it; I don't see it'? In other words, could the exclusion of visual evidence possibly be part of the speaker's

---

[4] Schlichter glosses her abbreviations as follows: "com"—"completive aspect", "imp"—"imperative", "dub"—"dubitative or third person subject", "se"—"sequential aspect", "quot"—"quotative", and "con"—"conditional aspect".

intended message? The supposition seems absurd: the very nature of pain, or heat, is such that one would feel it rather than see it, so there would be no need to specifically exclude visual evidence along the lines of: 'It hurts me; I know this not because I see something', or 'It's hot; I know this not because I see something'.

Clearly, it would seem to make more sense to explicate the meaning of the element in question more broadly, as:

> I know this
> because I perceive something

leaving the nature of the relevant perception to be specified by context.

If we do this, however, we will not be able to explain why a sentence such as 1, "Someone is coming crying -nt^hEr" will be interpreted as implying 'I hear', and never as 'I see'. There must be something in the meaning of -nt^hEr which excludes seeing. But what is it, if not an explicit component 'not because I see it', which would be inapplicable to sentences about pain or temperature?

A helpful clue is provided by Schlichter in the following statement: "We could say that evidentials are used to mark indirect evidence if we specify that the only evidence accepted as direct is visual evidence whose expression is unmarked. The speaker does not claim to be absolutely sure of anything unless he sees it right then and there together with the addressee" (1986: 54).

This statement suggests that our initial formula 'I know this not because I see it' may be simply ethnocentric. It would make sense for a Westerner—but perhaps not for a Wintu speaker—to say 'I know this not because I see it'; but for a Wintu speaker, if 'I don't see something', then I wouldn't want to say 'I know it'.

This is, then, what was wrong with our first tentative explication: the use of the phrase 'I know'. If the visual evidence is excluded, then it is not 'I know' that we should use in the explication but 'I think'. The phrase 'I think' will by itself exclude direct visual evidence because if I saw something I would say 'I know', not 'I think'. If, however, I say (in the semantic structure) 'I think' rather than 'I know', this exclusion of visual evidence is based on cultural assumptions and doesn't have to be articulated as part of the speaker's intended message.

So far so good. But 'I think' could also be based on inference or on reasonably reliable hearsay; how do we show, then, that this particular evidential (-nt^hEr) implies sensory evidence? I propose the following:

> -nt^hEr
> I think this
> because something happens (happened) to me

Pain, heat, a "gut feeling", a sound in my ears, a tension in my muscles (while wrestling), all these things can be seen as 'something that happens to me'. Even a sudden rush of pity (to which, I think, sentence 9 refers) can be interpreted in these terms. It might be argued that seeing, too, could be viewed as 'something that happens to me' but even if we accept this, we don't have to add anything to our formula (to exclude seeing explicitly), because from a Wintu perspective, seeing is already excluded by the phrase 'I think' (if one saw, then one would say 'I know' rather than 'I think').

The choice of 'I think' rather than 'I know' is supported by the fact that -nt^hEr is used in sentences such as 9, "You're so pitiful! (I am emotionally affected)". Clearly, what the speaker wishes to express here is what he/she thinks, not what he or she knows; and the implication that this thought is based on 'what is happening to me' makes perfect sense ('I am emotionally affected'). On the other hand, the component 'I think' might seem to be incompatible with sentences such as 2 and 6:

(2) It's awfully hot (I feel the heat).
(6) It hurts (I feel the pain).

Surely, experiencing heat, or hurt, is not a matter of opinion? But the phrase 'I think' does not have to be interpreted as an expression of (considered) opinion; it can also be interpreted as a record of a spontaneous thought passing through our mind:

I think: it's awfully hot.
I think: it hurts.

In this sense, sentences such as 2 and 6 are, it seems to me, compatible with the proposed semantic formula.

As for the second component of the proposed explication ('because something happens (happened) to me'), it might seem to have been chosen arbitrarily over possible competitors such as 'not because someone said this', which would also account for the "first-hand", "direct" and "personal" basis of the message expressed. But when tested against a whole range of examples, those competitors lose to the formula proposed here. For example, while the hypothetical component 'not because someone said this' could fit sentences such as 3 or 5:

(3) The earth will be destroyed (I know, feel)
    (I say this not because someone said it)

(5) You're strong   (Said while wrestling)
    (I say this not because someone said it)

it would not fit sentence 6:

(6) It hurts (I feel the pain)
    (? I say this not because someone else said it)

It would hardly make sense for anyone to wish to indicate that when they register their own pain they don't do so on the basis of what someone else has told them.

Hearsay

As Schlichter (1986: 49) defines it, "the second evidential [-*ke·*] indicates that the proposition expressed by the verb is known to the speaker through hearsay". This definition would seem to invite an explication along the following lines:

> I know this
> because someone said it

But this can't be right because, as we already know, in Wintu "evidentials" are used only when the speaker does NOT want to claim knowledge ("the speaker does not claim to be absolutely sure of anything unless he sees it right then and there . . ."). To account for the lack of certainty implied by the "hearsay" evidential we could try to represent its meaning as follows:

> I think [this]
> because someone said it

We can now test this formula against Schlichter's examples 10 to 14:

(10) Minel kir*ke·*m.
     die   COM.DUB
     'He has died (I'm told).'

(11) Le·ndada suke kila*ke·*.
     long ago   stand CON
     'Long ago they lived (I'm told).'   (Frequently used to begin a myth)

(12) Wi·ta čalit sukebi*ke·* m.
     man   good stand IM.DUB
     'It is said that he is a handsome man.'

(13) Čoyi·la*ke·* ni.
     drunk   I
     'I am drunk (I hear). They tell me I'm drunk.'

(14) K'ilepma. kuya·bi*ke·* mi.
     frightfully sick IM   you
     'Frightfully sick you are (I hear).'

Does the proposed formula fit these examples? In most cases, it does. It is not clear, however, that it fits example 11, and, in particular, whether it is consistent with the comment that 11 is frequently used to begin a myth. Presumably, what happened in a myth would be either accepted as true ('I know') or reported as something for which the speaker doesn't want to take personal responsibility ('I don't say: I know'). The phrase 'I think' doesn't really fit myths very well. On the other hand, the formula:

-ke.
someone says this
I don't say: I know it

fits both myths and all the other sentences with the "hearsay" evidential adduced by Schlichter. Furthermore, this last formula allows us to account for the difference between sentences with the "hearsay" evidential and those sentences with the "non-visual sensorial" evidential which report speech, such as 4 or 7:

(4) He said 'don't do it!' (We heard him say not to do it)
(7) How did he instruct you (in your hearing)?

Sentences such as 4 and 7 are consistent with the following interpretation: the speaker thinks 'that's what the other person said' because something happened to the speaker himself: the voice reaching his ears. I presume that the "non-visual sensorial" evidential would normally not be used in retelling a myth, because in this case it would make more sense for the speaker to wish to disclaim personal responsibility for the message ('I don't say: I know this') than to claim personal responsibility for it ('I think').

I conclude, therefore, that the most likely semantic structure of the "hearsay" evidential in Wintu is indeed this: 'someone says this; I don't say: I know it'.

Inferential

The third Wintu evidential, -re·, "indicates that the speaker believes his statement to be true because of circumstantial sensory evidence. This evidence turns out to be most often visual" (Schlichter 1986: 51). Illustrative sentences are:

(20) Heke   ma·n hara·kire· m.
     somewhere EX   go COM.DUB.
     'He must have gone somewhere (I don't see him).'

(21) Piya mayto·n dekna·sto·n piya ma·n biyakire·m.
     those feet   steps   that EX   be COM.DUB.
     'Those tracks of steps! That must have been him.'

(22) Hadi wintʰu·h minelbire·m.
     why! person   die IM.DUB.
     'Why, a person must have died (I see or hear someone cry)!'

Interestingly, in sentences of this kind "the action referred to by the verb stem always has a third person subject" (1986: 51).

I propose that the "sensory evidence", which is normally visual, can be represented as follows:[5]

-re. (partial explication)
I know something now
'because I see something'

whereas the "inference", which apparently has to concern a third person, can be represented as:

I think I can say something about someone because of this

It seems to me that these two components jointly fit all the examples adduced earlier, as well as Schlichter's two additional examples, 23 and 24:

(23) Hida k'aysa*re·* yo·!
    very hurry   EX
    'He must be in a great hurry (I see him run, I can't catch up with him)!'
(24) Ničay ʔewin suke*re·*.
    nephew here   stand
    'My nephew must have been here (I see tracks).'

For example, in 23, what 'I know now' is that 'he is running', and what 'I think I can say about someone because of this' is that 'he is in a great hurry'. Similarly, in 24, what 'I know now' is that 'there are tracks here' and what 'I think I can say about someone because of this' is that 'my nephew was here'.

Expectational

According to Schlichter (1986: 52), the fourth Wintu evidential, *-ʔel*, "denotes that the speaker believes his proposition to be true because of his experience with similar situations, regular patterns, or repeated circumstances common in human life". Schlichter's prime examples are (25) and (26):

(25) Tima minel*ʔel*, pira·*ʔel*.
    cold die   starve
    'He might freeze to death, he might starve (it's cold and he's alone, helpless, sick).'
(26) ʔImto·n nuqa·*ʔel*.
    berries ripe
    'The berries must be ripe (it's that time of year).'

But Schlichter's data also include several examples where the same evidential is used to indicate hearsay, as in 27 and 28, and she suspects that "this

---

[5] The question of whether the component 'because I see something' can be regarded as part of the semantic invariant is a matter for further investigation.

may represent a semantic change toward a single evidential for indirect evidence which includes both hearsay and expectation" (1986, 53):

(27) Ho·nʔukin bo·laheres wintʰu·h biya-kilaʔel ʔebasp'urit ko·t.
   long ago myth   people be CON   they   all
   'In the myths from long ago they (the animals) were all people.'

(28) ʔUni   ma·n pip'urit ʔuna· suke-kilaʔel ho·nto·n wintʰu·hto·t pip'urit.
   that way EX they   so   stand CON   long ago people   they
   'That's the way it was among the people long ago.'

It seems to me, however, that both the "expectational" and the "hearsay" use of the element in question can be accounted for in terms of a unitary semantic formula:

   -ʔel
   I think this
   I can't say: I know it

This would apply to the "expectational" examples as follows:

(25) I think: he will freeze to death, he will starve
   I can't say: I know it

(26) I think: the berries are ripe
   I can't say: I know it

But the same formula would apply to the "hearsay" sentences with the same suffix:

(27) I think: in the myths from long ago they (the animals) were all people
   I can't say: I know it

(28) I think: that's the way it was among the people long ago
   I can't say: I know it

If this is correct, then there is a subtle difference in meaning between "hearsay" sentences such as 10 to 14, with the suffix -ke·, and "hearsay" sentences such as 27 and 28, with the suffix -ʔel. This conclusion seems to me quite consistent with the illustrative sentences offered by Schlichter, but of course it needs to be checked against a more extensive range of data.

5. Maricopa

According to Gordon (1986), Maricopa has a number of suffixes which indicate the source of the information. Two of these suffixes, -(k)'yuu, "sight evidential" and -(k)'a, "hearing and other nonvisual sensory evidential", indicate "first-hand knowledge" of the speaker. Thus, "-(k)'yuu is

found on the final main verb of a sentence in which the speaker is asserting something which he or she knows about on the basis of having directly
seen the event expressed in the sentence" (1986: 77). Gordon illustrates the
use of the "sight evidential" with the following sentences (Gordon's num-
bering):

(4) M-iima-'yuu.
2-dance-SEE=EV
'You danced (I know because I saw it).'

(5) Iima-'yuu.
dance-SEE=EV
'He danced (I know because I saw it).'

(6) '-iima-k'yuu.
1-dance-*k*=SEE=EV
'I danced (for sure, in the past).'

But the third of these examples presents a problem. Clearly, in this case the
nice simple gloss 'I know because I saw it' does not fit, and has to be
replaced with something else ("for sure, in the past"). But if so, then what
is the real invariant of the suffix in question?

A similar problem arises in the case of the other sensory evidential,
-*(k)'a*, which is used "to mark that the information in the sentence is from
the speaker's first-hand knowledge, though in this case the knowledge is
gained not by having seen the event, but by having otherwise sensed (usually heard) the event or state" (Gordon 1986: 77). This is illustrated with
sentences 7, 8, and 9:

(7) M-ashvar-'a.
2-sing-HR=EV
'You sang (I know because I heard it).'

(8) Ashvar-'a.
sing-HR=EV
'He sang (I know because I heard it).'

(9) '-ashvar-k'a.
1-sing-*k*=HR=EV
'I sang (for sure, in the past; I heard/felt myself).'

But again, in sentence 9 the nice simple gloss 'I know because I heard it'
does not fit, and has to be replaced with something else. Gordon (1986: 78)
comments on this difficulty as follows: "When these suffixes are used on
verbs which have a first person subject, the evidential sense is less prominent and instead they convey a strong assertiveness about the actual occurrence of the event expressed by the sentence."

But what does it mean that "the evidential sense is less prominent"? To
say this is to dodge the crucial issue of the semantic invariant: is the sense

'I know this happened because I saw it' postulated as the invariant of the suffix *-(k)'yuu* or isn't it? Similarly, is the semantic component 'I know this because I heard it' postulated as the semantic invariant of the suffix *-(k)'a* or isn't it? Since these hypothetical components clearly do not fit sentences with first person subjects, they cannot constitute the invariants of the suffixes in question.

The reason why those hypothetical components do not fit sentences with first person subjects is quite clear. Normally, when we report our own activities we are certain that these activities have actually taken place because we know we have performed them, not because we have seen or heard ourselves performing them. It would make sense, therefore, to say:

> I danced (I sang)
> I know this happened because I did it

but hardly:

> I danced (I sang)
> I know this happened because I saw it (heard it)

But if we attribute these semantically plausible formulae to sentences with first person subjects we are left with no invariant. Can we find semantic components which could fit all the uses of the "sight evidential" (that is, both first person and non-first person uses)? And can we find such invariant semantic components for the "hearing evidential"? If we can't do that, could we at least find, for each suffix, two different but related formulae? It seems to me that we can. As a first approximation, I propose the following:

> -(k)'yuu
> I know this happened
> people could see it
>
> -(k)'a
> I know this happened
> people could hear it

I am not suggesting that these components will always, in all grammatical contexts, be interpreted in exactly the same way. It is possible, even likely, that in first person volitional sentences the 'I know' component will be interpreted as based on "internal evidence" rather than on visual evidence ('I know it happened because I did it'); but this is not incompatible with the presence of a component appealing to other people's visual evidence ('people could see it'). Thus, for first person volitional sentences I would propose the following analysis:

> I danced -(k)'yuu
> I danced

I know this happened because I did it
people could see it

A similar analysis can be proposed for sentences with the "hearing evidential", with two core components assigned to all the occurrences of this evidential, and with one additional component provided by the grammatical context.

I sang -(k)'a
I sang
I know this happened because I did it
people could hear it

Third person sentences can be analysed as follows:

He danced -(k)'yuu
he danced
I know this happened
people could see it

One further minimal pair, 23 and 24, may be helpful here (ss stands for same subject):

(23) Nyaa 'ayuu '-rav-k-'yuu.
     I   s.t.   1-hurt-ss-SEE=EV
     'I was sick.'

(24) Pam-sh 'ayuu rav-'yuu.
     Pam-SJ s.t.   hurt-SEE=EV
     'Pam was sick.'

Clearly, it makes more sense to posit for sentence 23 the following formula:[6]

I was sick
I know this happened because it happened to me
people could see it

rather than the unnatural "eyewitness report":

I was sick
I know this happened because I saw it
people could see it

For 24, we could propose the following formulae:

---

[6] The glosses "I was sick" and "Pam was sick" may seem incompatible with the component 'It happened', but this impression may be due to the English glosses: in Maricopa, the word referring to 'being sick' is a verb, and it probably has a more dynamic meaning than the English adjective *sick*.

Pam was sick
I know this happened
people could see it

It is one thing to assert that one has seen somebody dancing, and another, to assert that one has "seen" that somebody was sick. The vaguer formula 'people could see it' sounds more appropriate in this case than the explicit and specific claim 'I saw it'.

I would propose then that the "sight evidential" -*(k)'yuu* in Maricopa has the invariant meaning 'I know this happened; people could see it', and that a specific grammatical context can add to this core meaning a further component 'because I did it' in the case of volitional first person sentences and 'because it happened to me' in the case of non-volitional first person sentences. Similarly, I would propose that the "hearing evidential" -*(k)'a* has the invariant meaning 'I know this happened; people could hear it'.

One question which should be clarified at this point concerns the possibility of the suffix -*(k)'a* applying to sensory evidence other than hearing. Gordon is not as clear on this point as one would wish. She mentions the possibility of evidence other than auditory ("in this case the knowledge is gained not by having seen the event, but by having otherwise sensed (usually heard) the event or state", 1986: 77), but all her examples refer to sounds (singing, crying, saying). She says explicitly that "possibly the most typical place for this affix is on verbs of 'saying' which report information addressed to the speaker" (78). The only example when a sensory word other than *hear* appears in the gloss is 9:

(9) I sang (for sure, in the past; I heard/felt myself)

But the event referred to in this sentence is auditive, and it is likely that Gordon mentioned "feeling" as well as "hearing" in her gloss only because she felt uncomfortable attributing to the speaker the idea that he knew of his own singing because he heard himself singing. It seems much more reasonable to suppose that the speaker knew of his singing because he did it (that is, on internal grounds), not because he could hear himself do it.

This is not to deny the possibility of a language having a "sensory non-visual evidential" with a broader range of use, and I do not exclude the possibility that Maricopa is such a language. But the evidence provided by Gordon seems to suggest that -*(k)'a* is an "auditive", rather than "sensory non-visual", evidential.

In addition to the two sensory evidentials, Maricopa also has a "hearsay evidential", consisting of a form of the verb *'ii-m*, 'say', -*'ish*, followed by the "hearing evidential". This third evidential "is used to indicate overtly that the speaker does not vouch for the truth of the utterance, but instead is merely repeating something he or she has heard spoken of" (1986: 86). Sentence 32 is an example of this:

(32) Bonnie-sh chuy-k-'ish-'a.
Bonnie-SJ marry-*k*-say+*sh*-HR=EV
'(They said, I hear tell) Bonnie got married.'

(37*b*) Pam-sh Bonnie tpuy-m-'ish-'a.
Pam-SJ Bonnie kill-*m*-say+*sh*-HR=EV
'Pam killed Bonnie (I hear tell).'

The examples offered by Gordon suggest that the meaning of this evidential can be represented as follows:

-'ish-'a
people say this
I don't say: I know it

It is possible, however, that this formula is too restrictive, and that the evidential in question can also be used for information repeated after one specific person ("someone", rather than "people").

6. Bulgarian and Macedonian

Bulgarian and Macedonian have two past tenses, the so-called "definite past" and the "indefinite past". As pointed out by Friedman (1986), in the past these two categories have often been interpreted as evidentials, with the "definite past" signalling "direct" information, and the "indefinite past", "indirect", "distanced", or "reported" information. But Friedman himself argues that these past accounts are "greatly oversimplified and not, strictly speaking, accurate" (1986: 168) and that in fact "the forms under consideration do not mark the source of information or evidence, but rather the speaker's attitude toward it" (184–5).

To show that the "definite past" cannot mean personal witnessing, Friedman mentions the following fact:

for example, a Bulgarian colleague of mine, discussing which of his colleagues had attended a conference in America which he had not been able to attend, said of one of them:

(1) Beše tamo.
'(She) was there.'

This despite the fact that his only source of information was a report. (171–2).

What could this "definite past" mean, then? Clearly, it cannot mean "I know because I saw", or 'I know because I was there'; and it can't even mean 'I know, not because someone else said it'. It would seem, then, that the only possible invariant which can be attributed to it (in addition to "pastness", that is, 'before now') is 'I know'. This is consistent with the other examples cited by Friedman, such as 2 and 3 (both Macedonian):

(2) No podočna se slučija raboti za   koi   ne znaev.
but later   happened things about which not (I) knew
'But later things happened [PAST DEF.] that I didn't know about.' (I know this)

(3) Od   najstarite vreminja luǵeto   veruvaa   deka mesčina
From oldest   times   the-people believed (PAST DEF) that moon
vlijae   vrz životot na zemjata.
influences on the-life on the-earth
'Since most ancient times people have believed [PAST DEF.] that the moon influences life on earth.' (I know this)

The hypothesis advanced here is also consistent with the fact that the "definite past" cannot be used "in subordination to clauses which directly contradict the meaning of personal confirmation" (1986: 172), for example:

(4) *Toj ne veruva deka taa go napravi toa.   (Macedonian)
*Toj ne vjarva če   tja   napravi tova.   (Bulgarian)
he   not believe that she it did   it
*'He doesn't believe that she did [PAST DEF.] it.'

If we explicate the "definite past" in terms of the suggested component 'I know' we obtain a contradiction between 'I know' and 'I don't believe', and this would account for the sentence's unacceptability. On the other hand, sentences such as:

I don't know who did [PAST DEF.] it

are acceptable—presumably, because there is no conflict between 'I don't know (who did it)' and 'I know that someone did it'. The subordinate sentence does not identify the person in question, so the component 'I know' carried by its definite past tense can only be linked with the presupposition 'someone did it'.

The analysis proposed here is fully consistent with Friedman's assertion that "the definite past is marked for the speaker's confirmation of the information" (1986: 174); or at least with the spirit of this assertion. (Friedman's examples repeated here make it clear that he doesn't really mean "confirmation" as opposed to "affirmation"; rather, he means a confident assertion, viewed by the speaker as knowledge.)

On the other hand, Friedman's analysis of the Bulgarian and Macedonian "indefinite past" as "unmarked past" is harder to accept, given the fact that this supposedly unmarked past "has also developed a chief contextual variant meaning of nonconfirmativity, reportedness, or evidentiality" (174). Friedman attributes this apparent meaning of "nonconfirmativity" to the contrast "with the markedly confirmative definite past" (174). But this explanation does not account for the implication of "non-confirmativity" in contexts when there is no contrast between "indefinite past" and "definite past".

To take an example of an unmarked lexical category, the unmarked English word *dog* can be interpreted as 'he dog' when it is used in contrast to the marked word *bitch* (e.g. "I have a bitch and a dog"); but when it is used on its own (e.g. "we have a dog") there are no implications of maleness. Similarly, if the "indefinite past" was really unmarked we could expect it to imply "non-confirmativity" in those contexts where it is used in contrast to, or in combination with, the "confirmatory" "definite past"; in other contexts, however, we would not expect it to carry such implications. Why is it, then, that the "indefinite past" tends to imply "non-confirmativity" even in those contexts where it is used on its own? Friedman himself states that "it will ordinarily be assumed that the speaker is using this form [i.e. the indefinite past] in order to avoid personal confirmation of the information, e.g. due to its being based on a report" (174).

But why should it be assumed to be so if the "indefinite past" was really unmarked? For example, why should it normally be assumed that in the sentence

(7a) His father was [PAST INDEF.] very fond of flowers.

"the speaker was basing the statement on indirect information" (174) if there was nothing in the sentence itself to suggest such an interpretation? Friedman calls the "non-confirmativity" of the "indefinite past" its "contextual meaning"; but in the case of 7a no context is provided, so the "non-confirmatory" reading of the "indefinite past" cannot be attributed to the influence of the context.

I conclude from this that the "indefinite past" is not an unmarked category but carries a meaning of its own—even though this meaning is hard to establish. Friedman's motivation for treating the "indefinite past" as unmarked, despite its usual implication of "non-confirmativity", is quite clear. For example, he says: "As it is impossible to assign a single meaning which is present in all uses of the indefinite past, i.e. as there is no specific type of restriction on its occurrence as there is for the definite past, it must be treated as unmarked with respect to the definite past" (173).

But is it really impossible to assign a single meaning to all the uses of the "indefinite past"? I don't think it is; although I quite agree that traditional labels such as "indirect narration", "distanced narration", or "reported information" do not capture the invariant of this category (if there is one).

Let us consider Friedman's sentences adduced to illustrate the unmarked, "non-evidential" use of the indefinite past (Macedonian examples):

(6) Dosta sme   rabotele.
    enough (we) are worked

'We've worked enough.'   (One retired man commenting to another on their right to a pension)

(7) Tatko mi   bil   mnogu meraklija za cveḱa.
   father to-me was very   fond   for flowers
   'My father was very fond of flowers.'

(8) Sum   stanal noḱeska   vo eden.
   (I) am got up last night at one
   'I got up at one this morning.'

I can see why Friedman is reluctant to regard sentences such as these as based on "indirect" or "reported" information. However, I submit that if we look in a different direction we *can* find an invariant—that is, a formula which fits both "non-evidential" uses such as those in 6, 7, and 8, and "evidential" ones such as 7*a*. Essentially, I propose that the contrast between the "definite past" and the "indefinite past" is not that between 'I know' and nothing, but that between 'I know' and 'I think'. Let us test this hypothesis against all of Friedman's Macedonian sentences with the "indefinite past".

(6)   We've worked enough →
      I think we've worked enough

(7)   My father was very fond of flowers →
      I think my father was very fond of flowers
      (I remember him always buying flowers for our house, even when we had very little money)

(8)   I got up at one this morning →
      I think I got up at one this morning
      (I didn't have a watch)

(7*a*) His father was very fond of flowers →
      I think his father was very fond of flowers
      (I remember him always buying flowers for their house, even when they had very little money)

I think that the proposed interpretation fits all these sentences. At first sight, it doesn't fare quite as well when tested against Friedman's Bulgarian examples such as 9:

(9) Sto na sto *bili*   pokaneni.
   100%   (they)were invited
   'Absolutely, they were invited.' (I think they were invited; I'm absolutely certain of it.)

But Friedman helpfully supplies a clarifying context for this sentence:

it was uttered by a colleague of mine in Sofia during the course of a discussion as to whether a certain delegation had been invited to a congress. My colleague was convinced that they had been invited, although his conviction was not based on any kind of direct or indirect evidence, i.e. the statement was not based on a report or even a deduction, but only on the speaker's assumptions and expectations regarding the normal conduct of such matters. (1986: 175).

It seems to me that this explanation confirms the analysis proposed as it shows clearly that the statement was based on an 'I think' rather than an 'I know'.

Let us consider, in turn, Friedman's data on the Macedonian and Bulgarian pluperfect. Here, "the equipollent sharpening of the confirmative/nonconfirmative opposition . . . results in a set of restrictions which are truly evidential in nature—witnessed/nonwitnessed in Macedonian and confirmative/nonwitnessed in Bulgarian" (177–8). The evidence for this "equipollent sharpening of the opposition" is found in the fact that "in Macedonian the definite pluperfect cannot be subordinated to verbs of reporting, while the indefinite pluperfect cannot be subordinated to verbs of witnessing and direct perception but can only be used for reports and, rarely, deductions and suppositions" (178). The illustrative sentences are 15 and 16 (Macedonian):

(15) *Toj reče deka tie   ja *imaa svršeno* rabotata.
     he   said that they it had   finished the-job
     *'He said that they had finished [DEF. PLUPERF.] the job.'

(16) *Jas vidov kako/deka toj go *imal napraveno* toa.
     I   saw   how/that he it had done   that
     *'I saw how/that he had done [INDEF. PLUPERF.] it.'

These facts can be easily accounted for on the basis of the following semantic formulae:

> *definite pluperfect* (Macedonian)
> I know this
> not because someone said something

> *indefinite pluperfect* (Macedonian)
> I think this
> because someone said something

Friedman's idea of the "equipollent sharpening of the confirmative/nonconfirmative opposition" in the pluperfect is reflected here in the two symmetrical components: 'not because someone said something' and 'because someone said something'; but the contrast between 'I know' and 'I think' is preserved, and this accounts for the intuitive link between the "definite past" and the "definite pluperfect", as well as for that between the "indefinite past" and the "indefinite pluperfect". (In Bulgarian, the situation is apparently more complex; and as Friedman mentions it only in passing, without any details, I will not attempt to capture it in semantic formulae.)

One final point which requires a comment is the reference to 'saying' in the formula assigned to the Macedonian "indefinite pluperfect". ('I think this because someone said something.') Is this formula compatible with suppositions and deductions? I believe it is, even though suppositions and deductions don't have to be (and usually are not) based on hearsay. The proposed formula does not read: 'I think this because someone else said something', but 'I think this because someone said something'. Suppositions and deductions may well start with our "saying something" (not necessarily *viva voce*) along the following lines: "if we say that such and such, then we can think that such and such".

It would seem, then, that perhaps there was some truth in Jakobson's (1957: 4) view that Macedonian and Bulgarian have "true" evidential categories. If the formulae assigned here to the Macedonian pluperfects are correct, then Macedonian does have categories encoding epistemological meanings such as 'I think . . . because' and 'I know . . . not because'. On the other hand, Friedman is probably right in implying that there are no 'because' components in the meaning of the Macedonian (or Bulgarian) "definite past" and "indefinite past".

What is particularly satisfying is that we can account for both the "evidential" nature of the pluperfects, and the "validational" nature of the pasts, while respecting in our analysis the intuitive links between the pluperfects and the pasts; and reflecting them in the invariant components 'I know' and 'I think'.

7. Conclusion

Meaning is encoded not only in words but also in grammatical categories. The meanings encoded in grammar—just like those encoded in the lexicon—are language-specific. If one attempts to identify the meanings encoded in different languages by means of the same, arbitrarily invented labels, such as, for example, "first-hand" and "second-hand", "immediate" and "inferred", or "direct" and "indirect", one can only conceal and obfuscate the language-specific character of the categories to which they are attached. To be able to compare grammatical categories across language boundaries we need some constant points of reference, which slippery labels with shifting meanings cannot possibly provide. Universal semantic primitives can provide such constant and language-independent points of reference. They offer, therefore, a secure basis for a semantic typology of both lexicons and grammars. At the same time, they offer us convenient and reliable tools for investigating the universal and the language-specific aspects of human cognition and human conceptualization of the world.

8. A Summary of the Formulae

Kashaya

-ŵela   (Performative-Imperfective)
I know this
because I am doing it

-mela   (Performative-Perfective)
I know this
because I did it a short time before
now

-yă   (Visual (Perfective)) "Visual₁"
I know this
because I saw it

-ŵă   (Factual (Imperfective))
"Visual₂"
I know this
because I see it

-ŵă   (Factual—generic sense)
"Factual"
everyone knows it

-V̂nnă   (Auditory)
I know this
because I hear it

-yowă   (Personal Experience)
I don't say this because someone
else said this
I know it

-do   (Quotative)
I say this because someone else
said this
I don't say: I know it

-qă   (Inferential I)
 I know this
because I know something else

-bi -w   (Inferential II *-w*)
I know this now
because I know something else now
I didn't know it before now

-miyă   (Remote Past)
I know this
not because someone else said
something
it happened a long time before now

Quechua

Huanuco Quechua

-mi
I say this
not because someone else said it
I know it

-shi
I say this
because someone else said it
I don't say: I know it

-chi
I think this
I don't know it

Tarma Quechua

-mi
I know this

-shi
someone else says this
I don't say: I know it

-chi
I think this
I don't know it

Wintu

-nt^hEr   (non-visual sensorial)
I think this
because something happens
(happened) to me
-ke·   (hearsay)
someone says this
I don't say: I know it

-re·   (inferential)
I know something now
(because I see something)
I think I can say something about
someone because of this

-ʔel   (expectational)
I think this
I can't say: I know it

Maricopa

-(k)'yuu   (sight)
I know this happened
people could see it

(first person volitional sentences)
I know it happened because I did it
people could see this

(first person non-volitional
sentences)
I know it happened because it
happened to me
people could see this

(non-first person subject)
I know this happened
people could see it

-(k)'a   (hearing)
I know this happened
people could hear it

(first person volitional sentences)
I know it happened because I did it
people could hear this

(non first-person subject)
I know this happened
people could hear it

-'ish-'a   (hearsay)
people say this
I don't say: I know it

Macedonian

(definite past)
I know this

(indefinite past)
I think this

(definite pluperfect)
I know this
not because someone said something

(indefinite pluperfect)
I think this
because someone said something

References

◻◻ ───

ABELSON, ROBERT (1981). Psychological Status of the Script Concept. *American Psychologist*. 36/7: 715–29.

ABRAHAM, WERNER, TALMY GIVÓN, and SANDRA THOMPSON (1995) (eds.) *Discourse, grammar and typology*. Amsterdam: John Benjamins.

Academy Dictionary of Russian (1961). See Akademija Nauk SSSR (1961).

ADELAAR, WILLEM F. H. (1977). *Tarma Quechua*. Lisse: Peter de Ridder.

AGUD, ANA (1980). *Historia y teoria de los casos*.

AHDOTEL (1973). *The American Heritage Dictionary of the English Language*. Ed. William Morris. Boston: American Heritage and Houghton Mifflin.

AIKHENVALD, ALEXANDRA (forthcoming). *A Grammar of Tariana*.

AKADEMIJA NAUK (1988). *Imperativ v raznostrukturnyx jazykax*. Leningrad: Nauka.

AKADEMIJA NAUK SSSR (1961). *Slovar' russkogo jazyka*. Moscow: Gosudarstvennoe Izdatel'stvo Inostrannyx i nacional'nyx slovarej.

ALPHER, BARRY (1991). *Yir–Yoront Lexicon: Sketch and Dictionary of an Australian Language*. Berlin: Mouton de Gruyter.

AMEKA, FELIX (1986). The Use and Meaning of Selected Particles in Ewe. MA thesis. Australian National University.

—— (1987). A Comparative Analysis of Linguistic Routines in Two Languages: English and Ewe. *Journal of Pragmatics*. 11: 299–326.

—— (1990). The Grammatical Packaging of Experiences in Ewe: A Study in the Semantics of Syntax. *Australian Journal of Linguistics* (Special issue on the Semantics of Emotions). 10/2: 139–82.

—— (1991). Ewe: Its Grammatical Constructions and Illocutionary Devices. Ph.D. thesis. Australian National University.

—— (1994). Ewe. In Goddard and Wierzbicka (1994*b*), 57–86.

ANDERSEN, ELAINE S. (1978). Lexical Universals of Body-Part Terminology. In Greenberg (1978), iii: *Word Structure*. 335–68. Stanford, Calif.: Stanford University Press.

ANGLIN, JEREMY (1970). *The Growth of Word Meaning*. Cambridge, Mass.: MIT Press.

—— (1977). *Word, Object and Conceptual Development*. New York: W. W. Norton.

ANTINUCCI, FRANCESCO, and DOMENICO PARISI (1976). *Elementi di grammatica*. Trans. Elizabeth Bates as *Essentials of Grammar*. New York: Academic Press.

APRESJAN, JURIJ D. (1974). *Leksičeskaja semantika*. Moscow: Nauka.

—— (1991). On an Integral Dictionary of the Russian Language. *Semiotika i Informatika*. 38: 3–15.

—— (1992). *Lexical Semantics: User's Guide to Contemporary Russian Vocabulary*. Ann Arbor: Karoma. English version of 1974.

APRESJAN, JURIJ D. (1992–3). Systematic Lexicography as a Basis of Dictionary Marking. *Dictionariês.* 14: 79–87.
—— (forthcoming). *Theoretical Linguistics and Systematic Lexicography.*
—— and A. I. ROZENMAN (1979). *Anglo-russkij sinonimičeskij slovar'.* (An English–Russian dictionary of synonyms.) Moscow: Russkij jazyk.
ARISTOTLE (1937). Topics. In *The Works of Aristotle.* Ed. W. D. Ross. i. Oxford: Clarendon Press.
ARMSTRONG, SHARON L., LILA GLEITMAN, and HENRY GLEITMAN (1983). What Some Concepts might not Be. *Cognition.* 13: 263–308.
ARNAULD, ANTOINE (1662/1964). *The Art of Thinking.* Trans. James Dickoff and Patricia James. Indianapolis: Bobbs-Merrill.
ATRAN, SCOTT (1985). The Nature of Folk-Botanical Life Forms. *American Anthropologist.* 87: 298–315.
—— (1987*a*). Ordinary Constraints on the Semantics of Living Kinds: A Commonsense Alternative to Recent Treatments of Natural-Object Terms. *Mind and Language.* 2/1: 27–63.
—— (1987*b*). The Essence of Folk Biology: A Reply to Randall and Hunn. *American Anthropologist.* 89: 149–51.
—— (1987*c*). Origin of the Species and Genus Concepts: An Anthropological Perspective. *Journal of the History of Biology.* 20/2: 195–279.
—— (1990). *Cognitive Foundations of Natural History.* Cambridge: Cambridge University Press.
AUSTIN, JOHN L. (1961). Ifs and Cans. In John L. Austin. *Philosophical Papers.* Oxford: Clarendon Press.
—— (1962*a*). *How to Do Things with Words.* Oxford: Oxford University Press.
—— and G. J. WARNOCK (1962*b*). *Sense and Sensibilia* (reconstructed from MS notes by G. J. Warnock). Oxford: Clarendon Press.
BACH, E., E. JELINEK, A. KRATZER, and B. PARTEE (1995) (eds.) *Quantification in Natural Language.* Dordrecht: Kluwer.
BACH, KENT, and ROBERT HARNISH (1982). *Linguistic Communication and Speech Acts.* Cambridge, Mass.: MIT Press.
BAIN, MARGARET (1992). *The Aboriginal–White Encounter in Australia: Towards Better Communication.* SIL–AAB Occasional Papers. No. 2. Darwin: Summer Institute of Linguistics, Australian Aborigines Branch.
—— and BARBARA SAYERS (1990). Degrees of abstraction and Cross-cultural Communication in Australia. Paper presented at Sixth International Conference on Hunting and Gathering Societies, University of Alaska, Fairbanks.
BAKER, GORDON, and PETER HACKER (1980). *Wittgenstein: Understanding and Meaning.* Oxford: Blackwell.
BARAŃCZAK, STANISŁAW (1990). *Breathing under Water and other East European Essays.* Cambridge, Mass.: Harvard University Press.
BARTLETT, E. J. (1978). The Acquisition of Colour Terms: A Study of Lexical Development. In Robert Campbell and Philip Smith (eds.). *Recent Advances in the Psychology of Language: Language Development and Mother–Child Interaction.* New York: Plenum Press. 89–108.
BATES, ELIZABETH, INGE BRETHERTON, and LYNN SNYDER (1988). *From First Words*

to Grammar: Individual Differences and Dissociable Mechanisms. Cambridge: Cambridge University Press.

BERGSON, HENRI (1911). *Creative Evolution.* Trans. by A. Mitchell. London: Macmillan.

BERKELEY, GEORGE (1713/1965). *Three Dialogues between Hylas and Philonous.* In *George Berkeley's Philosophical Writings*, ed. D. Armstrong. New York: Macmillan.

BERLIN, BRENT (1977). Speculations on the Growth of Ethnobiological Nomenclature. In B. Blount and M. Sanches (eds.). *Sociocultural Dimensions of Language Change.* New York: Academic Press. 63–101.

—— (1981). The Concept of Rank in Ethnobiological Classification: Some Evidence from Aguaruna Folk Botany. In Ronald Casson (ed.). *Language, Culture and Cognition.* New York: Macmillan. 92–113.

—— (1992). *Ethnobiological Classification: Principles of Categorization of Plants and Animals in Traditional Societies.* Princeton, NJ: Princeton University Press.

—— DENIS BREEDLOVE, and PETER RAVEN (1973). General Principles of Classification and Nomenclature in Folk Biology. *American Anthropologist.* 75: 214–42.

—— and PAUL KAY (1969). *Basic Colour Terms: Their Universality and Evolution.* Berkeley: University of California Press.

—— —— and WILLIAM R. MERRIFIELD (1991). *The World Colour Survey.* Dallas: Academic Publications of the Summer Institute of Linguistics.

BERTEAUT, SIMONE (1973). *Piaf.* Harmondsworth: Penguin Books.

BICKERTON, DEREK (1981). *The Roots of Language.* Ann Arbor: Karoma.

BIERWISCH, MANFRED (1967). Some Semantic Universals of German Adjectivals. *Foundations of Language.* 3. 1–36.

BIRREN, FABER (1978). *Color and Human Response.* New York: Van Nostrand Reinhold.

BITTNER, MARIA, and KEN HALE (1995). Remarks on Definiteness in Warlpiri. In E. Bach *et al.* (1995), 81–105.

BLACK, MAX (1937). Vagueness. *Philosophy of Science.* 4: 427–55.

BLOOM, LOIS (1973). *One Word at a Time: The Use of Single-Word Utterances before Syntax.* The Hague: Mouton.

—— (1991). *Language Development from Two to Three.* Cambridge: Cambridge University Press.

—— and MARGARET LAHEY (1978). *Language Development and Language Disorders.* New York: Wiley.

—— PATSY LIGHTBOWN, and L. HOOD (1975). *Structure and Variation in Child Language.* Monographs of the Society for Research in Child Development. Vol. 40, no. 2, serial no. 160.

BLOOMFIELD, LEONARD (1933/1935). *Language.* London: George Allen & Unwin.

BOAS, FRANZ (1911/1966). Introduction to Handbook of American Indian Languages. In Boas, Franz and J. W. Powell. *Introduction to Handbook of American Indian Languages/Indian Linguistic Families of America North of Mexico.* Ed. Preston Holder. Lincoln: University of Nebraska Press.

—— (1938a). Language. In Boas (1938b). 124–45.

BOAS, FRANZ (1938*b*) (ed.). *General Anthropology*. Boston: Heath.

—— (1938*c*). *The Mind of Primitive Man*. Rev. edn. New York: Macmillan.

BOGUSŁAWSKI, ANDRZEJ (1966). *Semantyczne pojęcie liczebnika*. Wrocław: Ossolineum.

—— (1970). On Semantic Primitives and Meaningfulness. In A. Greimas, R. Jakobson, M. R. Mayenowa, and S. Żołkiewski (eds.). *Sign, Language and Culture*. The Hague: Mouton. 143–52.

—— (1977). Polskie 'się': Słowo nie do końca poznane. *International Review of Slavic Linguistics*. 2/1: 99–124.

—— (1979). Wissen, Wahrheit, Glauben: Zur semantischen Beschaffenheit des kognitiven Vokabulars. In T. Bungarten (ed.). *Wissenschaftssprache: Beiträge zur Methodologie, theoretischen Fundierung und Deskription*. Munich: Fink. 54–84.

—— (1983). *Ilustrowany Słownik Rosyjsko-Polski i Polsko-Rosyjski*. Warsaw: Państwowe Wydawnictwo Naukowe.

—— (1988). *Język w słowniku: Desiderata semantyczne do wielkiego słownika polszczyzny*. Wrocław: Ossolineum.

—— (1989). Knowledge is the Lack of Lack of Knowledge, but what is this Lack Lack of? *Quaderni di semantica*. 10/1: 15–31.

—— (1991). Semantic Primes for Agentive Relations. *Lingua Posnaniensis*. 32–3: 339–64.

BOLINGER, DWIGHT (1992). About Furniture and Birds. *Cognitive Linguistics*. 3/1: 111–17.

BOLLE, KEES (1979). *The Bhagavadgita: A New Translation*. Berkeley: University of California Press.

BORNSTEIN, MARC H. (1975). The Influence of Visual Perception on Culture. *American Anthropologist*. 77/4: 798.

BORNSTEIN, WILLIAM KESSEN, and SALLY WEISKOPF (1976). The Categories of Hue in Infancy. *Science*. 191: 201–2.

BOWERMAN, MELISSA (1976). Semantic Factors in the Acquisition of Rules for Word Use and Sentence Construction. In Morehead and Morehead (1976), 99–179.

—— (1985). What Shapes Children's Grammars? In Slobin (1985), ii. 1257–320.

BOYNTON. R. M. (1975). Colour, Hue and Wave Length. In E. C. Carterette and M. P. Freidman (eds.). *Handbook of Perception*, ii. New York: Academic Press.

BRAINE, MARTIN D. S. (1976). *Children's First Word Combinations*. Monographs of the Society for Research in Child Development. Vol. 41, no. 1, serial no. 164, Chicago: University of Chicago Press.

BRIGHT, J. O., and WILLIAM BRIGHT (1969). Semantic Structures in Northwestern California and the Sapir Whorf Hypothesis. In Stephen A. Tyler (ed.). *Cognitive Anthropology*. New York: Holt, Rinehart & Winston. 66–78.

Brinkley's Japanese–English Dictionary (1963). Cambridge: Heffer.

BRODSKY, JOSEPH (1994). Infinitive (A Poem). *New York Review of Books*. 41/13. 14 July 1994. 13.

BROWN, CECIL (1976). General Principles of Human Anatomical Partonomy and Speculations on the Growth of Partonomic Nomenclature. *American Ethnologist*. 3: 400–24.

—— (1977). Folk Botanical Life Forms: Their Universality and Growth. *American Anthropologist*. 79: 317–42.

—— (1979). Folk Zoological Life Forms: Their Universality and Growth. *American Anthropologist*. 81: 791–817.

—— (1984). *Language and Living Things: Uniformities in Folk Classification and Naming*. New Brunswick, NJ: Rutgers University Press.

—— (1985). Polysemy, Overt Marking, and Function Words. *Language Sciences*. 7/2: 283–332.

—— (1987). The Folk Subgenus: A New Ethnobiological Rank. *Journal of Ethnobiology*. 7: 181–92.

—— (1990). A Survey of Category Types in Natural Language. In Savas Tsohatzidis (ed.). *Meanings and Prototypes: Studies in Linguistic Categorization*. London: Routledge. 17–74.

BROWN, DONALD E. (1991). *Human Universals*. Philadelphia: Temple University Press.

BRÜCKNER, ALEKSANDER (1970). *Słownik etymologiczny języka polskiego*. Warsaw: Wiedza Powszechna.

BRUNER, JEROME (1990). *Acts of Meaning*. Cambridge, Mass.: Harvard University Press.

—— JACQUELINE J. GOODNOW, and GEORGE A. AUSTIN (1956). *A Study of Thinking*. New York: Wiley.

BUGENHAGEN, ROBERT D. (1990). Experiential Constructions in Mangap-Mbula. *Australian Journal of Linguistics* (special issue on the semantics of emotions). 10/2: 183–215.

—— (1994). The Exponents of Semantic Primitives in Mangap-Mbula. In Goddard and Wierzbicka (1994*b*), 87–108.

—— (forthcoming). The Syntax of Semantic Primitives in Mangaaba-Mbula.

BURLING, ROBBINS (1969). Cognition and Componential Analysis: God's Truth or Hocus-Pocus? In Stephen A. Tyler (ed.). *Cognitive Anthropology*. New York: Holt, Rinehart & Winston. 419–28.

—— (1970). *Man's Many Voices*. New York: Holt, Rinehart & Winston.

BURRIDGE, K. O. L. (1969). *Tangu Traditions: A Study of the Way of Life, Mythology, and Developing Experience of a New Guinea People*. Oxford: Clarendon Press.

BYBEE, JOAN L., and ÖSTEN DAHL (1989). The Creation of Tense and Aspect Systems in the Languages of the World. *Studies in Language*. 13: 51–103.

BYSTROV, I. S., and Stankevič, N. V. (1988). Povelenie vo v'etnamskom jazyke. In Akademija Nauk (1988), 33–5.

CAREY, SUSAN (1985). *Conceptual Change in Childhood*. Cambridge, Mass.: MIT Press.

CARNI, ELLEN, and LUCIA A. FRENCH (1984). The Acquisition of 'Before' and 'After' Reconsidered: What Develops? *Journal of Experimental Child Psychology*. 37: 394–403.

CARROLL, JOHN B. (1956). Introduction. In Benjamin H. Whorf. *Language, Thought and Reality*. New York: Wiley. 1–34.

CASTAÑEDA, HECTOR NERI (1988). *Thinking, Language and Experience*. Minneapolis: University of Minnesota Press.

CHAFE, WALLACE, and JOHANNA NICHOLS (1986) (eds.). *Evidentiality: The Linguistic Coding of Epistemology*. Norwood, NJ: Ablex.

CHAPPELL, HILARY (1983). A Semantic Analysis of Passive, Causative and Dative Constructions in Standard Chinese. Ph.D. thesis. Australian National University.

—— (1986a). Formal and Colloquial Adversity Passives in Standard Chinese. *Linguistics.* 24/6: 1025–52.

—— (1986b). The Passive of Bodily Effect in Chinese. *Studies in Language.* 10/2: 271–83.

—— (1991). Causativity and the *Ba* Construction in Chinese. In *Partizipation: Das Sprachliche Erfassen von Sachverhalten.* Ed. Hansjakob Seiler and Walfried Premper. 563–84. Tübingen: Gunter Narr.

—— (1994). Mandarin Semantic Primitives. In Goddard and Wierzbicka (1994b), 109–47.

—— and WILLIAM McGREGOR (1995) (eds.). *The Grammar of Inalienability: A Typological Perspective on Body-Part Terms and the Part–Whole Relation.* Berlin: Mouton de Gruyter.

CHASE, ATHOL, and JOHN VON STURMER (1973). 'Mental Man' and Social Evolutionary Theory. In George Kearney, Philip de Lacey, and Graham Davidson (eds.). *The Psychology of Aboriginal Australians.* Sydney: Wiley. 3–15.

CHIERCHIA, GENNARO, and SALLY McCONNELL-GINET (1990). *Meaning and Grammar: An Introduction to Semantics.* Cambridge, Mass.: MIT Press.

CHOMSKY, NOAM (1955). *Semantic Considerations in Grammar.* Georgetown Monograph Series in Linguistics. No. 8. 140–58.

—— (1966). *Cartesian Linguistics.* New York: Harper & Row.

—— (1968). *Language and Mind.* New York: Harcourt, Brace & World.

—— (1972). *Studies on Semantics in Generative Grammar.* The Hague: Mouton.

—— (1987). Language in a Psychological Setting. *Sophia Linguistica.* 22: 1–73.

—— (1991a). Linguistics and Adjacent Fields: A Personal View. In *The Chomskyan Turn.* Ed. Asa Kasher. Cambridge, Mass.: Basil Blackwell, 3–25.

—— (1991b). Linguistics and Cognitive Science: Problems and Mysteries. In *The Chomskyan Turn.* Ed. Asa Kasher. Cambridge, Mass.: Basil Blackwell, 26–53.

CLANCY, PATRICIA (1985). The Acquisition of Japanese. In Slobin (1985), i. 373–524.

CLARK, EVE V. (1970). *Locationals: A Study of the Relations between 'Existential', 'Locative' and 'Possessive' Constructions.* Working Paper on Language Universals. No. 3, June. Stanford: University of California Press.

—— (1983). Meanings and Concepts. In *Carmichael's Manual of Child Psychology, iii: Cognitive Development.* Eds. J. H. Flavell and E. M. Markman. General ed. P. H. Mussne. New York: Wiley. 787–840.

—— (1985). The Acquisition of Romance with Special Reference to French. In Slobin (1985), i. 687–782.

CLARK, H. H., and E. V. CLARK (1977). *Psychology and Language: an Introduction to Psycholinguistics.* New York: Harcourt, Brace & Jovanovich.

CLASSEN, CONSTANCE (1993). *Worlds of Sense: Exploring the Senses in History and across Cultures.* London: Routledge.

Cobuild (1987). *Collins Cobuild English Language Dictionary.* Ed. John Sinclair and Patrick Hanks. London: Collins.

COD (1964). *The Concise Oxford Dictionary of Current English.* Ed. H. W. Fowler and F. G. Fowler. 5th edn. Oxford: Clarendon Press.

COLE, MICHAEL, JOHN GAY, JOSEPH A. GLICK, and DONALD W. SHARP (1971). *The Cultural Context of Learning and Thinking.* New York: Basic Books.

COLE, ROGER WILLIAM (1977). *Current Issues in Linguistic Theory.* Bloomington: Indiana University Press.

COLEMAN, LINDA, and PAUL KAY (1981). Prototype Semantics: The English Verb Lie. *Language.* 57/1: 26–45.

COMRIE, BERNARD (1986). Conditionals: A Typology. In Traugott *et al.* (1986), 77–99.

—— (1989). *Language Universals and Linguistic Typology.* Oxford: Blackwell.

CONKLIN, HAROLD (1955). Hanunóo Color Categories. *Southwestern Journal of Anthropology.* 1: 339–44.

—— (1962). Lexicographic Treatment of Folk Taxonomies. *International Journal of American Linguistics.* 28/2: 119–41.

—— (1964). Hanunóo Color Categories. In Dell H. Hymes (ed.). *Language in Culture and Society.* New York: Harper & Row. 189–92. First published as Conklin, Harold G. (1955).

—— (1973). Color Categorization. (Review of Berlin and Kay 1969.) *American Anthropologist,* 75: 931–42.

COOK, JAMES (1968). *Pronominal Reference in Thai, Burmese and Vietnamese.* Berkeley: University of California Press.

CORBETT, GREVILLE G. (1994). *Gender.* Cambridge: Cambridge University Press.

—— and G. MORGAN (1988). Colour Terms in Russian: Reflections of Typological Constraints in a Single Language. *Journal of Linguistics.* 24: 31–64.

CROFT, WILLIAM (1990). *Typology and Universals.* Cambridge: Cambridge University Press.

CROWLEY, TERRY (1978). *The Middle Clarence Dialects of Bandjalang.* Canberra: Australian Institute of Aboriginal Studies.

CRUSE, D. A. (1986). *Lexical Semantics.* Cambridge: Cambridge University Press.

—— (1992–3). On Polylexy. *Dictionaries.* 14. 88–96.

DAVIS, PHILIP (1993/1994) (ed.) Alternative Modes in Linguistics: Reinterpreting Language. (= Language Sciences 15.4 and 16.1) Cambridge: Pergamon Press.

DAVIS, S. L. (1982). Colour Classification and the Aboriginal Classroom. In G. B. McKay and B. A. Sommers, (eds.). *Application of Linguistics to Australian Aboriginal Contexts.* ALAA Occasional Papers. No. 5. 68–77 Clayton, Vicoria: Applied Linguistics Association of Australia.

DESCARTES, RENÉ (1701/1931). The Search after Truth by the Light of Nature. In *The Philosophical Works of Descartes.* Trans. Elizabeth S. Haldane and G. R. T. Ross. 2 vols. Cambridge: Cambridge University Press. i. 305–27.

Dictionaries: Journal of the Dictionary Society of North America. (1992–3), ed. William S. Chisholm. No. 14. Cleveland: Cleveland State University.

Die Bibel: die gute Nachricht in heutigem Deutsch.

DILLER, ANTHONY (1994). Thai. In Goddard and Wierzbicka (1994), 149–70.

—— and P. JUNTANAMALAGA (forthcoming). An Introduction to Thai Grammar.

DIXON, ROBERT M. W. (1972). *The Dyirbal Language of North Queensland.* Cambridge: Cambridge University Press.

—— (1976a). Yidiny. In Dixon (1976c), 315–20.

—— (1976b). More on Yidiny. In Dixon (1976c), 327–9.

DIXON, ROBERT M. W. (1976c) (ed.). *Grammatical Categories in Australian Languages.* Canberra: AIAS.
—— (1977). *A Grammar of Yidin.* Cambridge: Cambridge University Press.
—— (1979). Ergativity. *Language.* 55: 59–138.
—— (1980). *The Languages of Australia.* Cambridge: Cambridge University Press.
—— (1982). *Where have all the Adjectives Gone? and Other Essays in Syntax and Semantics.* Janua Linguarum, Series maior. No. 107. The Hague: Mouton.
DOI, TAKEO (1974). Amae: A Key Concept for Understanding Japanese Personality Structure. In Takie S. Lebra and William P. Lebra (eds.). *Japanese Culture and Behavior.* Honolulu: University of Hawaii Press. 145–54.
—— (1981). *The Anatomy of Dependence.* Tokyo: Kodansha.
DOLEZAL, FREDRIC (1992). John Wilkins' and William Lloyd's *Alphabetical Dictionary* (1668): Towards a comprehensive, and systematically defined, lexicon. In Joseph L. Subbiondo (ed.). *John Wilkins and Seventeenth-Century British Linguistics: A Reader.* Amsterdam: John Benjamins. 309–28.
DONALDSON, MARGARET (1978). *Children's Minds.* New York: Norton.
DOUGHERTY, J. W. D. (1978). Salience and Relativity in Classification. *American Ethnologist.* 5/1: 66–80.
DOWTY, DAVID (1978). *Word Meaning and Montague Grammar.* Dordrecht: Reidel.
DUPRÉ, JOHN (1981). Natural Kinds and Biological Taxa. *Philosophical Review.* 90/1: 66–90.
DURIE, MARK, BUKHARI DAUD, and MAWARDI HASAN (1994). Acehnese. In Goddard and Wierzbicka (1994b), 171–201.
EDELMAN, GERALD M. (1992). *Bright Air, Brilliant Fire: On the Matter of the Mind.* New York: Basic Books.
EKMAN, PAUL (1973) (ed.). *Darwin and Facial Expression: A Century of Research in Review.* New York: Academic Press.
ELLEN, R. F. (1986). Ethnobiology, Cognition and the Structure of Prehension: Some General Theoretical Notes. *Journal of Ethnobiology.* 6: 83–98.
Encyclopaedia Britannica (1969). Chicago: Encyclopaedia Britannica.
ERNOUT, A., and A. MEILLET (1963). *Dictionnaire étymologique de la langue latine.* Paris: Klinksieck.
ERVIN-TRIPP, SUSAN (1970). Discourse Agreement: How Children Answer Questions. In J. R. Hayes (ed.). *Cognition and the Development of Language.* New York: Wiley.
EVANS, JULIAN (1993). *Transit of Venus.* London: Minerva.
EVANS, NICOLAS (1985). Kayardild: The Language of the Bentinck Islanders of North West Queensland. Ph.D. thesis. Australian National University.
—— (1986). On the Unimportance of 'Cause' in Kayardild. *Language in Aboriginal Australia.* 2: 9–17.
—— (1994). Kayardild. In Goddard and Wierzbicka (1994b), 203–28.
—— (forthcoming). A-Quantifiers and Scope in Mayali. In Bach *et al.* (forthcoming).
FALTZ, LEONARD M. (1985). *Reflexivisation.* New York: Garland.
FETZER, JAMES H. (1991). Primitive Concepts: Habits, Conventions, and Laws. In James H. Fetzer, David Shatz, and George N. Schlesinger (eds.). *Definitions and Definability: Philosophical Perspectives.* Dordrecht: Kluwer. 51–68.

FILLMORE, CHARLES J. (1971). Verbs of Judging: An Exercise in Semantic Description. In Charles J. Fillmore and D. Terence Langendoen (eds.). *Studies in Linguistic Semantics.* New York: Holt, Rinehart & Winston. 273–89.

—— (1975*a*). Santa Cruz Lectures on Deixis 1971. Bloomington: Indiana University Linguistics Club.

—— (1975*b*). An Alternative to Check List Theories of Meaning. *Proceedings of the First Annual Meeting of the Berkeley Linguistic Society.* 123–31.

—— (1977). Topics in Lexical Semantics. In R. W. Cole (1977). 76–138.

—— (1978). On the Organization of Semantic Information in the Lexicon. Parassession on the Lexicon. Chicago: Chicago Linguistic Society. 148–73.

—— (1982). Towards a Descriptive Framework for Spatial Deixis. In Robert J. Jarvella and Wolfgang Klein (eds.). *Speech, Place and Action.* London: Wiley. 31–59.

—— (1985). Semantic Fields and Semantic Frames. *Quaderni di semantica.* 6/2: 222–54.

FLETCHER, PAUL A. (1979). The development of the verb phrase. In Paul Fletcher and Michael Garman (eds.). *Language acquisition: studies in first language development.* Cambridge: Cambridge University Press. 261–284.

FODOR, JERRY A. (1981). *Representations.* Brighton: Harvester.

—— M. F. GARRETT, E. C. WALKER, and C. H. PARKES (1980). Against Definitions. *Cognition.* 8/3: 263–7.

FOLEY, WILLIAM A. (1991). *The Yimas Language of New Guinea.* Stanford: Stanford University Press.

FRAKE, CHARLES O. (1962). The Ethnographic Study of Cognitive Systems. In Thomas Gladwin and William Sturtevant (eds.). *Anthropology and Human Behavior.* Washington: Anthropological Society of Washington. 72–85.

FRAWLEY, WILLIAM (1981). Discussion: In Defense of the Dictionary: A Response to Haiman. *Lingua.* 55: 53–61.

FRENCH, LUCIA A., and KATHERINE NELSON (1985). *Young Children's Knowledge of Relational Terms: Some Ifs, Ors and Buts.* New York: Springer Verlag.

FRIEDMAN, VICTOR A. (1986). Evidentiality in the Balkans: Bulgarian, Macedonian, and Albanian. In Chafe and Nichols (1986), 168–87.

FRIES, CHARLES CARPENTER (1952). *The Structure of English: An Introduction to the Construction of English Sentences.* London: Longmans, Green.

FRUMKINA, RITA M. (1984). *Cvet, smysl, sxodstvo.* Moscow: Nauka.

—— and B. G. MIRKIN (1986). Semantika 'konkretnoj' leksiki: psixolingvističeskij podxod. *Izvestija Akademii Nauk SSSR, Seria Literatury i Jazyka.* 45/1: 12–22.

—— and A. D. MOSTOVAJA (1988). Ob opisanii otnošenij meždu imenami konkretnoj leksiki. *Izvestija Akademii Nauk SSSR, Seria Literatury i Jazyka.* 46/1: 52–62.

GAL, S. (1973). Inter-informant Variability in an Ethnozoological Taxonomy. *Anthropological Linguistics.* 15: 203–19.

GARDNER, P (1976). Birds, Words, and a Requiem for the Omniscient Informant. *American Ethnologist.* 3: 446–68.

GEERAERTS, D. (1993). Vagueness's Puzzles, Polysemy's Vagaries. *Cognitive Linguistics.* 4/3: 223–72.

GEERTZ, CLIFFORD (1966). *Person, Time and Conduct in Bali: An Essay in Cultural Analysis.* Monograph Series, Southeast Asia Studies. No. 14. New Haven: Yale University.

GELMAN, S. (1992). *Domain Specificity and the Representation of Knowledge.* Cambridge, Mass.: Bradford Books.

—— and J. COLEY (1991). Language and Categorization: The Acquisition of Natural Kind Terms. In S. A. Gelman, and J. P. Byrnes (eds.). *Perspectives on Language and Thought: Interrelations in Development.* Cambridge: Cambridge University Press. 146–96.

GENIUŠIENĖ, EMMA (1987). *The Typology of Reflexives.* Berlin: Mouton de Gruyter.

GIVÓN, TALMY (1989). *Mind, Code and Context.* Hillsdale, NJ: Lawrence Erlbaum.

—— (1990). *Syntax: A Functional-Typological Introduction,* ii. Amsterdam: John Benjamins.

GLASS, AMEE (1983). *Ngaanyatjarra Sentences.* Work Papers of SIL-AAB. Series A. 7. Darwin: Summer Institute of Linguistics, Australian Aborigines Branch.

—— and DOROTHY HACKETT (1970). *Pitjantjatjara Grammar.* Canberra: Australian Institute of Aboriginal Studies.

GLEASON, H. A. (1969). *An Introduction to Descriptive Linguistics.* Rev. edn. New York: Holt, Rinehart & Winston.

GODDARD, CLIFF (1986a). *Wild Ideas on Natural Semantic Metalanguage.* Paper presented at Australian Linguistics Society Annual Conference, Semantics Workshop, Adelaide.

—— (1986b). The Natural Semantics of *Too. Journal of Pragmatics.* 10/5: 635–43.

—— (1989a). Issues in Natural Semantic Metalanguage. *Quaderni di semantica.* 10/1: 51–64.

—— (1989b). Goals and Limits of Semantic Representation. *Quaderni di semantica.* 10/2: 297–308.

—— (1990). The Lexical Semantics of 'Good Feelings' in Yankunytjatjara. *Australian Journal of Linguistics* (Special Issue on the Semantics of Emotions). 10/2: 257–92.

—— (1991a). Testing the Translatability of Semantic Primitives into an Australian Aboriginal Language. *Anthropological Linguistics.* 33/1: 31–56.

—— (1991b). Anger in the Western Desert: A Case Study in the Cross-cultural Semantics of Emotion. *Man.* 26: 602–19.

—— (1992a). *Pitjantjatjara/Yankunytjatjara to English Dictionary.* 2nd edn. Alice Springs: Institute for Aboriginal Development.

—— (1992b). Traditional Yankunytjatjara Ways of Speaking: A Semantic Perspective. *Australian Journal of Linguistics.* 12/1: 93–122.

—— (1993). *Semantic Study Guide.* Department of Linguistics, University of New England. Armidale, NSW.

—— (1994a). Semantic Theory and Semantic Universals. In Goddard and Wierzbicka (1994), 7–29.

—— (1994b). Lexical Primitives in Yankunytjatjara. In Goddard and Wierzbicka (1994), 229–62.

—— (1994c). The Meaning of *Lah*: Understanding 'Emphasis' in Malay (Bahasa Melayu). *Oceanic Linguistics.* 33/1: 145–65.

—— (forthcoming *a*). Building a Semantic Metalanguage.

—— (forthcoming *b*). Cultural Values and Cultural Scripts in Malay (Bahasa Melayu).

—— (forthcoming *c*). The 'Social Emotions' of Malay (Bahasa Melayu). *Ethos*.

—— (1995). Who are We? The Natural Semantics of Pronouns. *Language Sciences*. 17/1: 99–121.

—— and ANNA WIERZBICKA (1994*a*). Introducing Lexical Primitives. In Goddard and Wierzbicka (1994*b*), 31–54.

—— —— (1994*b*) (eds.). *Semantic and Lexical Universals: Theory and Empirical Findings*. Amsterdam: John Benjamins.

—— —— (forthcoming). In Teun A. van Dijk (ed.). *Discourse: A Multidisciplinary Introduction*. London: Sage.

GOODENOUGH, WARD H. (1957). Cultural Anthropology and Linguistics. In Paul L. Garvin (ed.). *Report of the Seventh Annual Round Table Meeting on Linguistics and Language Study*. Monograph Series on Languages and Linguistics. No. 9. 167–73. Washington: Institute of Language and Linguistics, Georgetown University.

GOODMAN, NELSON (1951). *The Structure of Appearance*. Cambridge, Mass.: Harvard University Press.

GORDON, LYNN (1986). The Development of Evidentials in Maricopa. In Chafe and Nichols (1986), 75–88.

GRACE, GEORGE W. (1987). *The Linguistic Construction of Reality*. London: Croom Helm.

GREEN, DIANA (1993). Palikúr Numerals. Summer Institute of Linguistics.

GREEN, GEORGIA (1983). A Review of K. Bach and R. Harnish's 'Linguistic Communication and Speech Acts'. *Language*. 59: 627–35.

GREEN, IAN (1992). 'All' in Marrithiyel. Australian National University.

GREENBERG, JOSEPH H. (1966*a*). *Language Universals*. The Hague. Mouton.

—— (1966*b*). *Some Universals of Grammar with Particular Reference to the Order of Meaningful Elements*. In Greenberg (1966*c*), 73–113.

—— (1966*c*) (ed.). *Universals of Grammar*. Cambridge, Mass.: MIT Press.

—— (ed.) (1978). *Universals of Human Language*. 4 vols. Stanford: Stanford University Press.

GREGORY, R. L (1977). *Eye and Brain*. London: Weidenfeld.

GRICE, H. P. (1975). Logic and Conversation. In P. Cole and J. L. Morgan (eds.). *Syntax and Semantics: Speech Acts*. New York: Academic Press. 41–58.

GRUBER, JEFFREY S. (1965). Studies in Lexical Relations. Doctoral dissertation. MIT.

HAIMAN, JOHN (1980*a*). Dictionaries and Encyclopedias. *Lingua*. 50: 329–57.

—— (1980). *Hua: A Papuan Language of the Eastern Highlands of New Guinea*. Amsterdam: John Benjamins.

—— (1982). Discussion: Dictionaries and Encyclopedias Again. *Lingua*. 56: 353–5.

—— (1985). *Natural Syntax*. Cambridge: Cambridge University Press.

—— (1995). Grammatical Signs of the Divided Self: Evidence from Hua. In: Werner Abraham, Talmy Givón, and Sandra Thompson (1995), 213–34.

—— (1991). *Hua–English Dictionary*. Wiesbaden: Otto Harrassowitz.

HALE, KEN (1994). Preliminary Observations on Lexical and Semantic Primitives in the Misumalpan Languages of Nicaragua. In Goddard and Wierzbicka (1994*b*), 263–83.

HALE, KEN, MARY LAUGHREN, and DAVID NASH (forthcoming). *A Warlpiri Dictionary Project*. Cambridge, Mass.: MIT.

HALL, EDWARD (1983). *The Dance of Life*. New York: Doubleday.

HALLIDAY, MICHAEL A. K. (1975). *Learning how to Mean: Explorations in the Development of Language*. London: Arnold.

HALLIDAY, MICHAEL A. K. (1987). Spoken and Written Modes of Meaning. In Michael A. K. Halliday. *Comprehending Oral and Written Language*. New York: Academic Press. 55–82.

HALLPIKE, CHRISTOPHER ROBERT (1979). *The Foundations of Primitive Thought*. Oxford: Clarendon Press.

HANKS, PATRICK (1992/1993). Lexicography: Theory and Practice. *Dictionaries*. 14. 97–112.

HARGRAVE, SUSANNE (1982). *A Report on Colour Term Research in Five Aboriginal Languages*. Work Papers of SIL-AAB. Series B. 8. Darwin: Summer Institute of Linguistics, Australian Aborigines Branch.

HARKINS, JEAN (1986). Semantics and the Language Learner: Warlpiri Particles. *Journal of Pragmatics*. 10/5: 559–74.

—— (1991). A Bunch of Ambiguous Quantifiers: 'Many/All' Words in Several Australian Languages. Australian National University.

—— (1992). Throat and Desire in Arrernte: Metaphor or Polysemy? Australian National University.

—— (1994). *Desire in Language and Thought: A Study in Cross-linguistic Semantics*. Ph.D. thesis. Australian National University.

—— and DAVID P. WILKINS (1994). Mparntwe Arrernte and the Search for Lexical Universals. In Goddard and Wierzbicka (1994*b*), 285–310.

HARKNESS, SARA (1973). Universal Aspects of Learning Colour Codes: A Study in Two Cultures. *Ethos*. 1: 175–200.

HARRÉ, ROM (1993). Universals yet Again: A Test of the 'Wierzbicka Thesis'. *Language Sciences*. 15/3: 231–8.

—— and GRANT GILLETT (1994). *The Discursive Mind*. London: Sage.

HARRIS, RANDY ALLEN (1993). *The Linguistics Wars*. New York: Oxford University Press.

HARRIS, ZELLIG S. (1946). From Morpheme to Utterance. *Language*. 22: 161–83.

—— (1951). *Structural Linguistics*. Chicago: Phoenix.

HASADA, RIE (1994). *The Semantic Aspects of Onomatopoeia in Japanese*. MA thesis. Australian National University.

HAVILAND, JOHN (1979). Guugu Yimidhirr. In R. M. W. Dixon and Barry Blake (eds.). *Handbook of Australian Languages*, i. Canberra: ANU Press. 27–180.

—— (1991). *Projections, Transpositions, and Relativity*. Working Paper No. 3, Oct. Nijmegen: Cognitive Anthropology Research Group, Max Planck Institute for Psycholinguistics.

HAWKING, STEPHEN. W. (1989). *A Brief History of Time*. Toronto: Bantam Books.

HAYS, T (1976). An Empiricial Method for the Identification of Covert Categories in Ethnobiology. *American Ethnologist*. 3: 489–507.

HEATH, JEFFREY (1978*a*). Linguistic Approaches to Nunggubuyu Ethnology and Ethnobotany. In L. R. Hiatt (ed.). *Australian Aboriginal Concepts*. Canberra:

Australian Institute of Aboriginal Studies, and Atlantic Heights, NJ: Humanities Press. 40–55.

—— (1978*b*). *Ngandi Grammar, Texts, and Dictionary*. Canberra: Australian Institute of Aboriginal Studies, and Atlantic Heights, NJ: Humanities Press.

HEIDER, ELEANOR ROSCH (1972*a*). Probabilities, Sampling, and Ethnographic Method: The Case of Dani Colour Names. *Man*. 7/3: 448–66.

—— (1972*b*). Universals in Colour Naming and Memory. *Journal of Experimental Psychology*. 93/1: 10–20.

HEIDER, KARL G. (1970). *The Dugun Dani*. Chicago: Aldine.

HEINE, BERND, ULRIKE CLAUDI, and FRIEDERIKE HÜNNEMEYER (1991). *Grammaticalization: A Conceptual Framework*. Chicago: University of Chicago Press.

HEINEMANN, F. H. (1944). The Meaning of Negation. *Proceedings of the Aristotelian Society*. 44: 127–52.

HENDERSON, JOHN, and VERONICA DOBSON (1994). *Eastern and Central Arrernte to English Dictionary*. Alice Springs: Institute for Aboriginal Development.

HERING, E. (1920/1964). *Outlines of a Theory of the Light Sense*. Trans. L. M. Hurvich and D. Jameson. Cambridge, Mass.: Harvard University Press.

HERSCH, HENRY, and ALFONSO CARAMAZZA (1976). A Fuzzy Set Approach to Modifiers and Vagueness in Natural Language. *Journal of Experimental Psychology: General*. 105/3: 254–76.

HEWES, GORDON W. (1992). Comment on MacLaury's 'From Brightness to Hue: An Explanatory Model of Color-Category Evolution'. *Current Anthropology*. 33/2. Apr. 163.

HILL, DEBORAH (1987). A Cross-linguistic Study of Value Judgement Terms. MA thesis. Australian National University.

—— (1994). Longgu. In Goddard and Wierzbicka (1994*b*), 311–29.

HIRSCHFELD, LAWRENCE A., and SUSAN A. GELMAN (1994) (eds.). *Mapping the Mind: Domain Specificity in Cognition and Culture*. Cambridge: Cambridge University Press.

HJELMSLEV, LOUIS (1953). *Prolegomena to a Theory of Language*. Trans. Francis J. Whitfield. *International Journal of American Linguistics*, Memoir 7. Baltimore: Waverley.

HOCKETT, CHARLES (1970) (ed.). *A Leonard Bloomfield Anthology*. Bloomington: Indiana University Press.

Holy Bible, The (1966). King James version. Cleveland and New York: World Publishing Co.

HOPPER, PAUL J. (1982) (ed.). *Tense-Aspect: Between Semantics and Pragmatics*. Amsterdam: John Benjamins.

—— and SANDRA THOMPSON (1980). Transitivity in Grammar and Discourse. *Language*. 56/2: 251–99.

—— —— (1982) (eds.). *Studies in Transitivity*. Syntax and Semantics 15. New York: Academic Press.

—— and ELIZABETH CLOSS TRAUGOTT (1993). *Grammaticalization*. Cambridge: Cambridge University Press.

HORN, LAURENCE R. (1989). *A Natural History of Negation*. Chicago: University of Chicago Press.

HORROBIN, PETER, and GREG LEAVERS (1990). *Mission Praise*. London: Marshall Pickering.

HOWELL, SIGNE (1981). Rules not Words. In Paul Heelas and Andrew Lock (eds.). *Indigenous Psychologies: The Anthropology of the Self*. London: Academic Press. 133–43.

HOWES, D. (1991) (ed.). *The Varieties of Sensory Experience: A Sourcebook in the Anthropology of the Senses*. Toronto: University of Toronto Press.

HUDSON, RICHARD A. (1976). *Arguments for a Non-transformational Grammar*. Chicago: University of Chicago Press.

HUMBOLDT, WILHELM VON (1827/1973). Über den Dualis. In Wilhelm von Humboldt. *Schriften zur Sprache*. Stuttgart: Reclam. 21–9.

—— (1903–18). *Gesammelte Schriften*, i–vii. Ed. Albert Leitzmann. Berlin: B. Behr.

—— (1903–36). *Wilhelm von Humboldts Werke*. 17 vols. Ed. Albert Leitzmann. Berlin: B. Behr.

HUNN, EUGENE S. (1976). Toward a Perceptual Model of Folk Biological Classification. *American Ethnologist*. 3/3: 508–24.

—— (1977). *Tzeltal Folk Zoology: The Classification of Discontinuities in Nature*. New York: Academic Press.

—— (1982). The Utilitarian Factor in Folk Biological Classification. *American Anthropologist*. 84/4: 830–47.

—— (1987). Science and Common Sense: A Reply to Atran. *American Anthropologist*. 89/1: 146–9.

HURVICH, LEO (1981). *Color Vision*. Sunderland, Mass.: Sinauer.

HYMES, DELL, and JOHN FOUGHT (1975). American Structuralism. In T. Sebeok (ed.). *Historiography of Linguistics*. Current Trends in Linguistics. xiii. The Hague: Mouton. 25–54.

INGRAM, DAVID (1978). Typology and Universals of Personal Pronouns. In Greenberg (1978), iii. 213–47.

INOUE, KYOKO (1979). Japanese: A Story of Language and People. In T. Shopen (ed.). (1979). *Languages and Their Speakers*. Philadelphia: University of Pennsylvania Press. 24–300.

ISTOMINA, Z. M. (1963). Perception and Naming of Colour in Early Childhood. *Soviet Psychology and Psychiatry*. 1: 36–45.

JACKENDOFF, RAY (1983). *Semantics and Cognition*. Cambridge, Mass.: MIT Press.

—— (1985). Multiple Subcategorization: The Case of 'Climb'. *Natural Language and Linguistic Theory*. 3/3: 271–95.

—— (1990). *Semantic Structures*. Cambridge, Mass.: MIT Press.

—— (1992). *Languages of the Mind: Essays on Mental Representation*. Cambridge, Mass.: MIT Press.

JAKOBSON, ROMAN (1957). *Shifters, Verbal Categories and the Russian Verb*. Cambridge, Mass.: Harvard University Press.

—— (1962). *Selected Writings*. The Hague: Mouton.

JAUNCEY, DOROTHY (1990). *The Hidden Nature of Rabbits and the Essence of Bunnies*. Department of Linguistics, Australian National University.

JEFFCOTT, ANNA (1992). The Semantics of Lying. Australian National University.

JESPERSEN, OTTO (1917). *Negation in English and Other Languages*. Copenhagen: A. F. Høst.

—— (1924/1968). *The Philosophy of Grammar.* London: George Allen & Unwin.

JOHNSON, MARK (1987). *The Body in the Mind: The Bodily Basis of Meaning, Imagination and Reason.* Chicago: University of Chicago Press.

JOHNSTON, JUDITH R. (1985). Cognitive Prerequisites: The Evidence from Children Learning English. In Slobin (1985), i. 961–1004.

—— and DAN I. SLOBIN (1979). The Development of Locative Expressions in English, Italian, Serbo-Croatian and Turkish. *Journal of Child Language.* 6: 529–62.

JONES, RHYS and BETTY MEEHAN (1978). Anbarra Concept of Colour. In L. R. Hiatt (ed.). *Australian Aboriginal Concepts.* Canberra: Australian Institute of Aboriginal Studies. 20–9.

KATZ, DAVID (1935). *The World of Colour.* London: Kegan Paul.

KATZ, JERROLD (1972). *Semantic Theory.* New York: Harper & Row.

—— and JERRY FODOR (1963). The Structure of a Semantic Theory. *Language.* 39: 170–210.

KATZ, N., E. BAKER, and J. MACNAMARA (1974). What's in a Name? A Study of how Children Learn Common and Proper Names. *Child Development.* 45: 469–73.

KAY, PAUL, and CHAD MCDANIEL (1978). The Linguistic Significance of the Meaning of Basic Colour Terms. *Language.* 54: 610–46.

—— BRENT BERLIN, and WILLIAM MERRIFIELD (1991). Biocultural Implications of Systems of Colour Naming. *Journal of Linguistic Anthropology.* 1/1: 12–25.

KEENEN, E. L., and B. COMRIE (1977). NP Accessibility and Universal Grammar. *Linguistic Inquiry.* 8: 63–100.

KEESING, ROGER M. (1994). *Radical Cultural Difference: Anthropology's Myth?* In Martin Pütz (1994).

KEFER, MICHEL, and JOHANN VAN DER AUWERA (1991) (eds.). *Meaning and Grammar.* Berlin: Mouton de Gruyter.

KEIL, FRANK (1986). The Acquisition of Natural Kind and Artifact Terms. In A. Marras and W. Dernopoulos (eds.). *Language Learnability and Concept Acquisition.* Norwood, NJ: Ablex.

—— (1989). *Concepts, Kinds and Cognitive Development.* Cambridge, Mass.: MIT Press.

KELLER, HELEN (1956). *The Story of my Life.* London: Hodder & Stoughton.

Kenkyusha's New Japanese–English Dictionary (1954). Tokyo: Kenkyusha.

KIBRIK, ALEKSANDR (1977a). *Opyt strukturnogo opisanija arčinskogo jazyka,* ii. Moscow: Izdatel'stvo Moskovskogo Universiteta.

—— (1977b). *Opyt strukturnogo opisanija arčinskogo jazyka,* iii. Moscow: Izdatel'stvo Moskovskogo Universiteta.

—— (1991). *Semantically Ergative Languages in a Typological Perspective.* Working papers of the Summer Institute of Linguistics (University of South Dakota session) 35: 67–90.

—— (1992). *Očerki po obščim i prikladnym voprosam jazykoznanija.* Moscow: Izdatel'stvo Moskovskogo Universiteta.

KINNEAR, PAUL R., and J. B. DEREGOWSKI. (1992). Commentary on MacLaury's 'From Brightness to Hue: An Explanatory Model of Color-Category Evolution'. In *Current Anthropology.* 33/2. Apr. 163–4.

KLEIN, ERNEST (1966). *A Comprehensive Etymological Dictionary of the English Language.* 2 vols. Amsterdam: Elsevier.

KONDO, DORINNE K. (1990). *Crafting Selves: Power, Gender, and Discourses of Identity in a Japanese Workplace.* Chicago: University of Chicago Press.

KRIPKE, SAMUEL (1972). Naming and Necessity. In D. Davidson and G. Harman (eds.). *Semantics of Natural Language.* Dordrecht: Reidel. 253–355.

KRONHAUS, MAKSIM (1993). Semantika russkogo glagola. *Russian Linguistics.* 17: 15–36.

KUCZAJ, S. A., II, and M. J. DALEY (1979). The Development of Hypothetical Reference in the Speech of Young Children. *Journal of Child Language.* 6: 563–79.

KUSHNER, HAROLD S. (1982). *When Bad Things Happen to Good People.* London: Pan.

KWAPISZ, ZOFIA (1978). *Die Kontraste im Bereich der Reflexiven Konstruktionen im Polnischen und im Deutschen.* Wrocław: Ossolineum.

LABOV, WILLIAM (1973). The Boundaries of Words and their Meanings. In C. J. Bailey and R. Shuy (eds.). *New Ways of Analyzing Variation in English.* Washington: Georgetown University Press. 340–73.

—— (1981). Resolving the Neogrammarian controversy. *Language.* 57: 267–308.

LAKOFF, GEORGE (1973). Hedges: A Study in Meaning Criteria and the Logic of Fuzzy Concepts. *Journal of Philosophical Logic.* 2: 458–508.

—— (1986). Classifiers as a Reflection of Mind. In Colette Craig (ed.). *Noun Classes and Categorization.* Amsterdam: John Benjamins. 13–51.

—— (1987). *Women, Fire and Dangerous Things. What Categories Reveal about the Mind.* Chicago: Chicago University Press.

—— and MARK JOHNSON (1980). *Metaphors we Live By.* Chicago: Chicago University Press.

LANDAU, SIDNEY I. (1984). *Dictionaries: The Art and Craft of Lexicography.* New York: Scribner.

—— (1992–3). Wierzbicka's Theory and the Practice of Lexicography. *Dictionaries.* 14: 113–19.

LANDMAN, JANET (1993). *Regret.* New York: Oxford University Press.

LANGACKER, RONALD (1987). *Cognitive Grammar.* Stanford: Stanford University Press.

—— (1990). *Concept, Image and Symbol: The Cognitive Basis of Grammar.* Berlin: Mouton de Gruyter.

—— (1993). Grammatical Traces of Some 'Invisible' Semantic. In Davis (1993) (ed.), 323–56.

LAVE, JEAN (1981). How 'they' Think? Review of C. R. Hallpike, 'The Foundations of Primitive Thought'. *Contemporary Psychology.* 26: 788–9.

LDOCE (1978). *Longman Dictionary of Contemporary English.* Ed. Paul Procter. Harlow: Longman.

LDOTEL (1984). *Longman Dictionary of the English Language.* Ed. Heather Gay, Brian O'Kill, Katherine Seed, and Janet Whitcut. London: Longman.

LEACH, E. R. (1964). Anthropological Aspects of Language: Animal Categories and Verbal Abuse. In E. Lenneberg (ed.). *New Directions in the Study of Language.* Cambridge, Mass.: MIT Press. 23–63.

LEHRER, ADRIENNE (1974). *Semantic Fields and Lexical Structure*. Amsterdam: North-Holland.

—— (1983). *Wine and Conversation*. Bloomington: Indiana University Press.

—— (1988). Checklist for Verbs of Speaking. *Acta Linguistica Hungarica*. 38/1–4: 143–61.

—— (1990). Polysemy, Conventionality and the Structure of the Lexicon. *Cognitive Linguistics*, 1/1: 207–46.

LEIBNIZ, GOTTFRIED WILHELM (1704/1903). Table de définitions. In Leibniz (1903), 437–510.

—— (1765/1981). *New Essays on Human Understanding*. Trans. Peter Remnant and Jonathan Bennett. Cambridge: Cambridge University Press.

—— (1903). *Opuscules et fragments inédits de Leibniz*. Ed. Louis Couturat. Paris: Presses Universitaires de France. Repr. 1961. Hildesheim: Georg Olms.

—— (1966). *Logical Papers*, ed. and trans. G. H. R. Parkinson. Oxford: Clarendon Press.

—— (MSa/1903). Alphabetum Cogitationum Humanarum. In Leibniz (1903). 160–1.

LE PAN, DON (1989). *The Cognitive Revolution in Western Culture*, i. London: Macmillan.

LEVINSON, STEPHEN, and PENELOPE BROWN (1991). *Relativity and Spatial Conception and Description*. Working Paper No. 1. Oct. Nijmegen: Cognitive Anthropology Research Group, Max Planck Institute for Psycholinguistics.

—— —— (1992). *Immanuel Kant among the Tenejapans: Anthropology as Empirical Philosophy*. Working Paper No. 11. Aug. Nijmegen: Cognitive Anthropology Research Group, Max Planck Institute for Psycholinguistics.

LÉVY-BRUHL, LUCIEN (1926). *How Natives Think*. Trans. Lilian A. Clare from *Les Fonctions mentales dans les sociétés inférieures*. London: George Allen & Unwin. Repr. 1979, New York: Arno Press.

LEWIS, CLIVE STAPLES (1960). *Studies in Words*. Cambridge: Cambridge University Press.

LOCKE, J (1690/1959). *An Essay concerning Human Understanding*, ed. A. C. Fraser, ii. Oxford: Clarendon Press.

LONGACRE, ROBERT E. (1985). Sentences as Combinations of Clauses. In T. Shopen (ed.). *Language Typology and Syntactic Description, iii: Complex Constructions*. Cambridge: Cambridge University Press. 235–86.

LUCY, JOHN, and RICHARD SHWEDER (1979). Whorf and his Critics: Linguistic and Nonlinguistic Influences on Colour Memory. *American Anthropologist*. 81: 581–615.

LURIA, A. R. (1976). *Cognitive Development: Its Cultural and Social Foundations*. Cambridge, Mass.: Harvard University Press.

LUTZ, CATHERINE (1985). Ethnopsychology Compared to What? Explaining Behavior and Consciousness among the Ifaluk. In Geoffrey M. White and John Kirkpatrick (eds.). *Person, Self, and Experience: Exploring Pacific Ethnopsychologies*. Berkeley: University of California Press.

—— (1988). *Unnatural Emotions: Everyday Sentiments on a Micronesian Atoll and their Challenge to Western Theory*. Chicago: University of Chicago Press.

LYONS, JOHN (1977). *Semantics*. 2 vols. Cambridge: Cambridge University Press.

LYONS, W. (1981). *Language, Meaning and Context*. Bungay: Fontana.

McCAWLEY, JAMES D. (1973). *Grammar and Meaning*. Papers on Syntactic and Semantic Topics. New York: Academic Press.

—— (1981). *Everything that Linguists have always Wanted to Know about Logic* (*but were Ashamed to Ask)*. Chicago: Chicago University Press.

—— (1983). Review of Anna Wierzbicka's *Lingua Mentalis: The Semantics of Natural Language*. *Language*. 59/3: 654–9.

—— (1992–3). How to Achieve Lexicographic Virtue through Selective and Judicious Sinning. *Dictionaries*. 14. 120–9.

McCLOSKEY, M., and S. GLUCKSBERG (1978). Natural Categories: Welldefined or Fuzzy Set? *Memory and Cognition*. 6: 462–72.

McCONVELL, PATRICK (1991). Cultural Domain Separation: Two-Way Street or Blind Alley? Stephen Harris and the Neo-Whorfians on Aboriginal Education. *Australian Aboriginal Studies*. 1: 13–24.

MacLAURY, ROBERT E. (1987). Color-Category Evolution and Shurwap Yellow-with-Green. *American Anthropologist*. 89/1: 107–24.

—— (1991). Social and Cognitive Motivations of Change: Measuring Variability in Color Semantics. *Language*, 67/1: 34–62.

—— (1992). From Brightness to Hue: An Explanatory Model of Color-Category Evolution. *Current Anthropology*. 33/2: Apr. 137–86.

MACNAMARA, JOHN (1972). The Cognitive Basis of Language Learning in Infants. *Psychological Review*. 79: 1–13.

Macquarie Dictionary of Australian English, The (1981). Ed. Arthur Delbridge. Sydney: Macquarie Library.

McSHANE, JOHN (1991). *Cognitive Development: An Information Processing Approach*. Oxford: Blackwell.

MALKIEL, YAKOV (1980). The Lexicographer as a Mediator between Linguistics and Society. In Ladislav Zgusta (ed.). *Theory and Method in Lexicography: Western and Non-Western Perspectives*. Columbia, SC: Hornbeam. 43–58.

MALLINSON, G., and B. J. BLAKE (1981). *Language Typology: Cross-linguistic Studies in Syntax*. Amsterdam: North-Holland.

MALOTKI, EKKERART (1983). *Hopi Time: A Linguistic Analysis of the Temporal Concepts in the Hopi Language*. Berlin: Mouton.

MALT, BARBARA C. (1987). In Search of Word Meanings. (Review of Wierzbicka 1985.) *Contemporary Psychology*. 32/3: 266.

MANNING, CHRISTOPHER (1989). Semantic Primitives. Discussion paper, Australian National University.

MARANTZ, ALEC (1984). *On the Nature of Grammatical Relations*. Cambridge, Mass.: MIT Press.

MARTIN, GOTTFRIED (1964). *Leibniz: Logic and Metaphysics*. Trans. K. J. Northcott and P. G. Lucas. Manchester: Manchester University Press.

MATTHEWS, PETER HUGOE (1943). *Grammatical Theory in the United States from Bloomfield to Chomsky*. Cambridge: Cambridge University Press.

MEDIN, DOUGLAS (1989). Concepts and Conceptual Structure. *American Psychologist*. 44: 1469–81.

—— and ANDREW ORTONY (1989). Psychological Essentialism. In S. Vosniadou and A. Ortony (eds.). *Similarity and Analogical Reasoning*. New York: Cambridge University Press. 179–95.

MEL'ČUK, IGOR (1974a). O sintaksičeskom nule. In *Tipologia passivnyx konstrukcij*. Ed. A. A. Xolodovič. Leningrad: Nauka. 343–61.

—— (1974b). *Opyt teorii linguističeskix modelej: Smysl-tekst*. (An Outline of the Theory of the Linguistic Sense-Text model.) Moscow: Nauka.

—— (1981). Meaning-Text Models: A Recent Trend in Soviet Linguistics. *Annual Review of Anthropology*. 10: 27–62.

—— (1994). *Les Principes de Morphologie*. Montreal: Les Presses de l'Université de Montréal.

—— and ALEKSANDR ŽOLKOVSKIJ (1984). *Tolkovo-kombinatornyj slovar' sovremennogo russkogo jazyka*. xiv. Vienna: Wiener Slawistischer Almanach.

—— NADIA ARBATCHEWSKY-JUMARIE, LÉO ELNITSKY, LIDIJA IORDANSKAJA, and ADÈLE LESSARD (1984). *Dictionnaire explicatif et combinatoire du français contemporain*, i Recherches lexico-sémantiques, i. Montreal: Les Presses de l'Université de Montréal.

—— —— —— —— —— (1988). *Dictionnaire explicatif et combinatoire du français contemporain*, ii Recherches lexico-sémantiques, ii. Montreal: Les Presses de l'Université de Montréal.

—— —— —— —— —— (1992). *Dictionnaire explicatif et combinatoire du français contemporain*, iii Recherches lexico-sémantiques, iii. Montreal: Les Presses de l'Université de Montréal.

MILLER, GEORGE A. (1971a). Forward. In Michael Cole *et al.* (1971), vii–ix.

—— (1971b). *The Cultural Context of Learning and Thinking*. New York: Basic Books.

—— (1978). Semantic Relations among Words. In M. Halle, J. Bresnan, and G. Miller (eds.). *Linguistic Theory and Psychological Reality*. Cambridge, Mass.: MIT Press. 60–118.

MILLS, A. (1985). The Acquisition of German. In Slobin (1985), i. 141–254.

MIYOKAWA, YUKIKO (1989). Explicating Natural Kinds: The Case of the Japanese Nezumi. Australian National University.

MONDRY, H., and J. R. TAYLOR (1992). On Lying in Russian. *Language and Communication*. 12/2: 133–43.

MOORE, TERENCE, and CHRISTINE CARLING (1982). *Understanding Language: Towards a Post-Chomskyan Linguistics*. London: Macmillan.

MORAVCSIK, EDITH (1978). *On the Case Marking of Objects*. In Greenberg (1978), iv. 249–89.

—— (1991). Review of Anna Wierzbicka, *The Semantics of Grammar*. *Studies in Language*. 15/1: 129–48.

MOREHEAD, DONALD M., and ANN E. MOREHEAD (1976) (eds.). *Normal and Deficient Child Language*. Baltimore: University Park Press.

MORSBACH, H., and W. J. TYLER (1986). A Japanese Emotion: Amae. In Rom Harré (ed.). *The Social Construction of Emotions*. Oxford: Blackwell. 289–307.

MOSEL, ULRIKE (1984). *Tolai Syntax and its Historical Development*. Pacific Linguistics. Series B. No. 92. Canberra: Department of Linguistics Research School of Pacific Studies, Australian National University.

—— (1991). Transitivity and Reflexivity in Samoan. *Australian Journal of Linguistics*. 11: 175–94.

—— (1994). Samoan. In Goddard and Wierzbicka (1994b), 331–60.

Mosel, Ulrike (forthcoming). Where have all the Reflexives Gone in Samoan? —— and Even Hovdhaugen (1992). *Samoan Reference Grammar*. Oslo: Scandinavian University Press.

Moss, A. E (1989). *Basic Colour Terms: Problems and Hypotheses*. Amsterdam: Elsevier Science Publishers (North-Holland).

Needham, R. (1972). *Belief, Language, and Experience*. Oxford: Blackwell.

New English Bible, The (1961/1970). London: Oxford University Press.

Nida, Eugene A. (1947). *Bible Translating*. New York: American Bible Society.

—— (1975). *Exploring Semantic Structures*. Munich: Fink.

OAJD (1980). *The Oxford Australian Junior Dictionary*. Ed. Rosemary Sansome and Angela Ridsdale. Melbourne: Oxford University Press.

OED (1933). *The Oxford English Dictionary*. 12 vols. Oxford: Clarendon Press.

Ogden, C. K. and I. A. Richards (1923). *The Meaning of Meaning*. London: Routledge & Kegan Paul.

Ogloblin, A. K. (1988). Imperativ i zalog v javanskom jazyke. In Akademija Nauk (1988), 92–3.

Onishi, Masayuki (1994). Semantic Primitives in Japanese. In Goddard and Wierzbicka (1994*b*), 361–85.

OPD (1979). *The Oxford Paperback Dictionary*. Oxford: Oxford University Press.

Ortony, Andrew, Gerald L. Clore, and Mark A. Foss (1987). The Referential Structure of the Affective Lexicon. *Cognitive Science*. 11: 341–64.

Osherson, Daniel, and Edward Smith (1981). On the Adequacy of Prototype Theory as a Theory of Concepts. *Cognition*. 9: 35–58.

Oswalt, Robert L. (1986). The Evidential System of Kashaya. In Chafe and Nichols (1986), 29–45.

Palmer, F. (1990). The Semantics of Grammar. (Review of Wierzbicka 1988.) *Journal of Linguistics*. 26: 223–33.

Pascal, Blaise (1667/1954). De l'esprit géométrique et de l'art de persuader. In Œuvres complètes. Ed. J. Chevalier. Paris: Gallimard. 575–604.

Pawley, Andrew (1966). The Structure of Kalam: A Grammar of a New Guinea Highlands Language. Ph.D. dissertation. University of Auckland.

—— (1975). Kalam Verb Semantics. Seminar Handout. Australian National University.

—— (1986). Encoding Events in Kalam and English: Different Logics for Reporting Experience. In Ross Tomlin (ed.). *Grounding and Coherence in Discourse*. Amsterdam: John Benjamins. 329–60.

—— (1994). Kalam Exponents of Lexical and Semantic Primitives. In Goddard and Wierzbicka (1994*b*), 387–421.

Peeters, Bert (1994). Semantic and Lexical Universals in French. In Goddard and Wierzbicka (1994*b*), 423–42.

Pinker, Steven (1989). *Learnability and Cognition: The Acquisition of Argument Structure*. Cambridge, Mass.: MIT Press.

Plank, Frans (1984) (ed.). *Objects: Towards a Theory of Grammatical Relations*. London: Academic Press.

Plato (1970). *The Dialogues of Plato*. Trans. Benjamin Jowett. Ed. R. M. Hare and D. A. Russell. 2 vols. London: Sphere Books.

POMERANTZ, ANITA (1978). Compliment Responses: Notes on the Co-operation of Multiple Constraints. In Jim Schenkein (ed.). *Studies in the Organization of Conversational Interaction*. New York: Academic Press. 79–112.

POPJES, JACK, and JO POPJES (1986). Canela-Krahô. In D. C. Derbyshire and G. K. Pullum (eds.). *Handbook of Amazonian Languages*, i. Berlin: Mouton de Gruyter. 128–99.

POSNER, MICHAEL (1986). Empirical Studies of Prototypes. In Colette Craig (ed.). *Noun Classes and Categorization*. Amsterdam: John Benjamins. 53–61.

PUENTE B., BLAS (1972). *Quechua Tarmeño I: Textos*. Documento de trabajo. No. 2. Lima: Centro de Investigación de la Lingüística Aplicada.

PUTNAM, HILARY (1975). The Meaning of Meaning. In K. Gunderson (ed.). *Minnesota Studies in the Philosophy of Science*, vii. Minneapolis: University of Minnesota Press. 131–93.

—— (1977). Is Semantics Possible? In S. P. Schwartz (ed.). *Naming, Necessity and Natural Kinds*. Ithaca, NY: Cornell University Press. 102–18.

PÜTZ, MARTIN (1992) (ed.). *Thirty Years of Linguistic Evolution: A Festschrift for René Dirven*. Amsterdam: John Benjamins.

—— (1994) (ed.). *Language Contact and Language Conflict*. Amsterdam: John Benjamins.

RANDALL, R (1987). The Nature of Highly Inclusive Folk-Botanical Categories. *American Anthropologist*. 89: 143–6.

—— and E. S. HUNN (1984). Do Life Forms Evolve or do Uses for Life? Some Doubts about Brown's Universals Hypotheses. *American Ethnologist*. 11: 329–49.

RAPPAPORT, GILBERT (1988). On the Relationship between Prosodic and Syntactic Properties of Pronouns in Slavic Languages. In A. Schenker (ed.). *American Contributions to the Tenth International Congress of Slavists*, Sofia, Sep. 1988. Columbus, Ohio: Slavica. 301–28.

—— (forthcoming). *Slavic Reflexives: In Defense of Grammar*.

READ, K. E. (1955). Morality and the Concept of the Person among the Gahuku-Gama. *Oceania*. 25/4: 233–82.

REDDY, MICHAEL J. (1979). The Conduit Metaphor: A Case of Frame Conflict in our Language about Language. In Andrew Ortony (ed.). *Metaphor and Thought*. Cambridge: Cambridge University Press. 284–324.

REICHENBACH, HANS (1948). *Elements of Symbolic Logic*. New York: Macmillan.

REY, ALAIN (1983). La Lexicographie française: Rétrospective et perspectives. In Bernard Al and Jaap Spa (eds.). *Lexique 2: Le dictionnaire*. Lille: Presses universitaires de Lille. 11–24.

RIPS, L. J. (1989). Similarity, Typicality, and Categorization. In S. Vosniadou and A. Ortony (eds.). *Similarity and Analogical Reasoning*. Cambridge: Cambridge University Press. 21–59.

ROBINSON, RICHARD (1950). *Definition*. Oxford: Clarendon Press.

ROSALDO, MICHELLE Z. (1980). *Knowledge and Passion: Ilongot Notions of Self and Social Life*. Cambridge: Cambridge University Press.

ROSCH HEIDER, ELEANOR (1973). Natural Categories. *Cognitive Psychology*. 4: 328–50.

ROSCH, ELEANOR (1975a). Cognitive Representations of Semantic Categories. *Toward an Experimental Psychology: General*. 104: 192–233.

ROSCH, ELEANOR (1975*b*). Universals and Cultural Specifics in Human Categorization. In Richard Brislin, Stephen Bochner, and Walter Lonner (eds.). *Cross-cultural Perspectives on Learning*. New York: Wiley. 177–206.

—— (1978). Principles of Categorization. In E. Rosch and L. L. Lloyd (eds.). *Cognition and Categorization*. Hillsdale, NJ: Lawrence Erlbaum Associates.

—— and C. MERVIS (1975). Family Resemblances: Studies in the Internal Structure of Categories. *Cognitive Psychology*. 7: 573–605.

ROSS, J. R. (1970). On Declarative Sentences. In R. A. Jacobs and P. S. Rosenbaum (eds.). *Readings in English Transformational Grammar*. Waltham, Mass.: Ginn-Blaisdell.

ROTHSTEIN, ROBERT A. (1973). Sex, Gender and the October Revolution. In S. R. Anderson and P. Kiparsky (eds.). *A Festschrift for Morris Halle*. New York: Holt, Rinehart & Winston. 460–6.

ROYCE, J. (1917). Negation. *Encyclopaedia of Religion and Ethics*. Ed. J. Hastings. New York: Charles Scribner. ix. 264–71.

RUDZKA, BRYGIDA, JOANNA CHANNELL, Y. F. L. PUTSEYS, and P. OSTYN (1981). *Words you Need*. London: Macmillan.

RUSSELL, BERTRAND (1948). *Human Knowledge: Its Scope and Limits*. New York: Simon & Schuster.

—— (1964). The Philosophy of Logical Atomism. In *Logic and Knowledge*. London: George Allen & Unwin.

—— (1965). *An Inquiry into Meaning and Truth*. Baltimore: Penguin Books.

SACKS, OLIVER (1993). Making up the Mind. Review of Edelman 1992. *New York Review of Books*. 40/7. 8 Apr. 42–9.

SALONI, ZYGMUNT (1976). Cechy składniowe polskiego czasownika. Wrocław: Prace językoznawcze. Polska Akademia Nauk. Komitet Językoznawstwa.

SAPIR, EDWARD (1927). The Unconscious Patterning of Behaviour in Society. In Ethel S. Dummer (ed.). *The Unconscious: A Symposium*. New York: Knopf. 114–42.

—— (1949). *Selected Writings of Edward Sapir in Language, Culture and Personality*, ed. David Mandelbaum. Berkeley: University of California Press.

SAUNDERS, B. A. C. (1992). Comment on MacLaury's 'From Brightness to Hue: An Explanatory Model of Color-Category Evolution.' *Current Anthropology*. 33/2. Apr. 165–7.

SAVIĆ, S. (1975). Aspects of Adult–Child Communication: The Problem of Question Acquisition. *Journal of Child Language*. 2: 251–60.

SAYERS, BARBARA, and MARGARET BAIN (1989). A Communication Dilemma: Contrasting Orders of Abstraction and the Associated Logic. Paper presented to the Interdisciplinary Research Workshop on Logical Connections, Summer Institute of Linguistics, Dallas, May.

SCHANK, ROGER C., and ROBERT P. ABELSON (1977). *Scripts, Plans, Goals and Understanding: An Enquiry into Human Knowledge Structures*. Hillsdale, NJ: Lawrence Erlbaum Associates.

SCHLICHTER, ALICE (1986). The Origins and Deictic Nature of Wintu Evidentials. In Chafe and Nichols (1986), 46–59.

SCHLICK, MORITZ (1962). *Problems of Ethics*. Trans. David Rynin. New York: Dover.

SCHUCHARDT, HUGO (1895/1972). On Sound Laws: Against the Neogrammarians. In Vennemann and Wilbur (1972), 39–72.

SCHWARTZ, STEPHEN P. (1978). Putnam on Artifacts. *Philosophical Review.* 87/4: 566–74.

SEARLE, JOHN (1976). A Classification of Illocutionary Acts. *Language in Society.* 5: 1–23.

—— (1983). *Intentionality: An Essay in the Philosophy of Mind.* Cambridge: Cambridge University Press.

SEILER, HANSJAKOB (1986). *Apprehension: Language, Object, and Order.* Tübingen: Günther Narr.

SHOPEN, TIMOTHY (forthcoming). Semantic Invariants and the Russian Words Translated 'Truth' and 'Lie'.

SHWEDER, RICHARD A. (1982). On Savages and Other Children: Review of C. R. Hallpike's *The Foundations of Primitive Thought. American Anthropologist.* 84: 354–66.

—— and EDMUND J. BOURNE (1984). Does the Concept of the Person Vary Cross-culturally? In Richard A. Shweder and Robert A. LeVine (eds.). *Culture Theory: Essays on Mind, Self, and Emotion.* Cambridge: Cambridge University Press. 158–99.

—— and MARIA A. SULLIVAN (1990). The Semiotic Subject of Cultural Psychology. In L. Pervin (ed.). *Handbook of Personality.* New York: Guilford. 399–416.

SILVERSTEIN, MICHAEL (1976). Hierarchy of Features and Ergativity. In Dixon (1976c), 112–71.

—— (1981). Case Marking and the Nature of Language. *Australian Journal of Linguistics.* 1: 227–44.

SIMPSON, JANE (1989). Warlpiri Colour Terms. Sydney University.

SLEDD, JAMES (1972). Dollars and Dictionaries: The Limits of Commercial Lexicography. In Howard D. Weinbrot (ed.). *New Aspects of Lexicography.* Carbondale, Ill.: Southern Illinois University Press. 119–37.

SLOBIN, DAN ISAAC (1971) (ed.). *The Ontogenesis of Grammar.* New York: Academic Press.

—— (1982). The Origin of Grammatical Encoding of Events. In Paul Hopper and Sandra Thompson (eds.). *Studies in Transitivity, Syntax and Semantics,* xv. New York: Academic Press. 409–22.

—— (1985a). Cross-linguistic Evidence for the Language-making Capacity. In Slobin (1985), ii. 1157–256.

—— (1985b) (ed.) *The Cross-linguistic Study of Language Acquisition, i: The Data, ii: Theoretical Issues.* Hillsdale, NJ: Lawrence Erlbaum Associates.

SOED (1964). *The Shorter Oxford English Dictionary.* Oxford: Clarendon Press.

SØRENSEN, HOLGER STEEN (1963). *The Meaning of Proper Names.* Copenhagen: Gad.

SOVRAN, TAMAR (1992). Between Similarity and Sameness. *Journal of Pragmatics.* 18/4: 329–44.

SPIRO, MELFORD E. (1993). Is the Western Conception of the Self 'Peculiar' within the Context of World Cultures? *Ethos.* 21/2: 107–53.

STANLAW, JAMES (1992). Comment on MacLaury's 'From Brightness to Hue: An Explanatory Model of Color-Category Evolution'. *Current Anthropology.* 33/2: Apr. 167–8.

STEVENSON, BURTON (1946). *Stevenson's Book of Quotations.* London: Cassell.

SUZUKI, T. (1978). *Japanese and the Japanese: Words in Culture.* Trans. Akira Kiura. Tokyo: Kodansha International.

SWADESH, M. (1941). Observations of Pattern Impact on the Phonetics of Bi-linguals. In *Language, Culture and Personality: Essays in Memory of Edward Sapir.* Ed. L. Spier. Menasha, Wis.: Sapir Memorial Publication Fund. 59–65.

—— (1972). *The Origin and Diversification of Language.* London: Routledge & Kegan Paul.

SWEETSER, EVE (1987). The Definition of *Lie*: An Examination of the Folk Models Underlying a Prototype. In D. N. Holland and N. Quinn (eds.). *Cultural Models in Language and Thought.* Cambridge: Cambridge University Press. 43–66.

SWIFT, JONATHAN (1728/1931). *Gulliver's Travels,* ed. A. B. Gough. Oxford: Clarendon Press.

SZOBER, STANISŁAW (1966). *Gramatyka języka polskiego.* Warsaw: Państwowe Wydawnictwo Naukowe.

Takenobu Japanese–English Dictionary (1918). Tokyo: Kenkyusha.

TALMY, LEONARD (1985). Lexicalization Patterns: Semantic Structure in Lexical Forms. In *Language Typology and Syntactic Description: Grammatical Categories and the Lexicon.* iii. Ed. T. Shopen. Cambridge University Press. 57–149.

TAYLOR, JOHN R. (1989). *Linguistic Categorization: Prototypes in Linguistic Theory.* Oxford: Clarendon Press.

TIEN, ADRIAN (1994). Semantic Primitives in Taiwanese Chinese. BA Hons. thesis. Australian National University.

TOREN, CHRISTINA (1992). Comment on MacLaury's 'From Brightness to Hue: An Explanatory Model of Color-Category Evolution.' *Current Anthropology.* 33/2: Apr. 168–9.

TRAUGOTT, ELIZABETH CLOSS, ALICE TER MEULEN, JUDY SNITZER REILLY, and CHARLES A. FERGUSON (1986) (eds.). *On Conditionals.* Cambridge: Cambridge University Press.

TRAVIS, CATHERINE (1992). How to be Kind, Compassionate and Considerate in Japanese. BA Hons. thesis. Australian National University.

TREERAT, WIPA (1986). The Semantics of 'I' and 'You' in Thai. Australian National University.

TRIER, J. (1931). *Der deutsche Wortschatz im Sinnbezirk des Verstandes.* Die Geschichte eines sprachlichen Feldes. Heidelberg: Winter.

TSOHATZIDIS, S. L. (1990). A Few Truths about 'Lie'. In S. L. Tsohatzidis (ed.). *Meanings and Prototypes. Studies in Linguistic Categorization.* London: Routledge. 438–46.

TSUNODA, TASAKU (1981). Split Case-Marking Patterns in Verb Types and Tense/Aspect/Mood. *Linguistics.* 19/5–6: 389–438.

TURNER, VICTOR W. (1966). Color Classification in Ndembu Ritual. In Michael Banton (ed.). *Anthropological Approaches to the Study of Religion.* London: Tavistock. 47–87.

TYACK, D. and D. INGRAM, (1977). Children's Production and Comprehension of Questions. *Journal of Child Language.* 4: 211–24.

TYLER, STEPHEN (1978). *The Said and the Unsaid.* New York: Academic Press.

VAN BRAKEL, J. (1991). Meaning, Prototype and the Future of Cognitive Science. *Minds and Machines.* 1: 233–57.

—— (1992). Comment on MacLaury's 'From Brightness to Hue: An Explanatory Model of Color-Category Evolution.' In *Current Anthropology.* 33/2. Apr. 169–72.

—— (1993). The Plasticity of Categories: The Case of Colour. *British Journal for the Philosophy of Science.* 44: 103–35.

VENNEMAN, THEO, and TERENCE H. WILBUR (1972) (eds.). *Schuchardt, the Neogrammarians, and the Transformational Theory of Phonological Change.* Frankfurt: Athenäum.

VERCORS [JEAN BRULLER] (1956). *Les Animaux dénaturés suivi de la marche à l'étoile.* Paris: Michel.

VERHAAR, JOHN W. M. (1966–73) (ed.). *The Verb 'Be' and its Synonyms: Philosophical and Grammatical Studies.* Dordrecht: Reidel. i–iv.

—— (1990). How Transitive is Intransitive. *Studies in Language.* 14/1: 93–168.

VERSCHUEREN, JEFF (1985). *What People Say they do with Words.* Norwood, NJ: Ablex.

WAKE, C. S. (1872). The Mental Characteristics of Primitive Man as Exemplified by the Australian Aborigines. *Journal of the Anthropological Institute.* 1: 74–84, 102–4.

WEBER, DAVID J. (1986). Information Perspective, Profile, and Patterns in Quechua. In Chafe and Nichols (1986), 137–58.

WEBER, MAX (1930/1968). *The Protestant Ethic and the Spirit of Capitalism.* Trans. Talcott Parsons. London: George Allen & Unwin.

Webster's New School and Office Dictionary (1959). Greenwich, Conn.: Fawcett.

Webster's New School and Office Dictionary (1965). New York: World and Crest.

Webster's New World Dictionary (1977). Pocket-size edn. Sydney: Fontana–Collins.

Webster's New World Dictionary (1988). 3rd college edn. New York: Simon & Schuster.

Webster's Third New International Dictionary of the English Language (1976). Springfield, Mass.: Merriam.

WEIL, SIMONE (1972). *Gravity and Grace.* London: Routledge & Kegan Paul.

WEINREICH, URIEL (1963). On the Semantic Structure of Language. In J. Greenberg J. (ed.) *Universals of Language.* Cambridge, Mass.: MIT Press.

—— (1980). *On Semantics.* William Labov and Beatrice S. Weinreich (eds.). Philadelphia: University of Pennsylvania Press.

WELLMAN, HENRY M. (1990). *The Child's Theory of Mind.* Cambridge, Mass.: MIT Press.

—— (1994). In J. Russell (ed.). *Everyday Conceptions of Emotion.* NATO AS1 series. Dordrecht: Kluwer. 289–314.

WESTPHAL, JONATHAN (1987). *Colour: Some Philosophical Problems from Wittgenstein.* Aristotelian Society series, vii. Oxford: Blackwell.

WHORF, BENJAMIN LEE (1956). *Language, Thought and Reality: Selected Writings of Benjamin Lee Whorf.* Ed. John B. Carroll. New York: Wiley.

WIERZBICKA, ANNA (1967a). Negation: A Study in Deep Grammar. Mimeographed paper. Cambridge Mass.: MIT.

—— (1967b). Against "Conjunction Reduction". Mimeographed paper. Cambridge, Mass.: MIT.

WIERZBICKA, ANNA (1971). The Deep or Semantic Structure of the Comparative. In Arnim von Stechow (ed.). *Linguistische Berichte 16*. Braunschweig: Viewig. 39–45.

—— (1972). *Semantic Primitives*. Linguistische Forschungen. No. 22. Frankfurt: Athenäum.

—— (1975). W poszukiwaniu tradycji: Idee semantyczne Leibniza. (The Aristotelian and Leibnizian tradition in semantics.) *Pamiętnik Literacki*. 66/1: 109–26.

—— (1976a). In Defense of YOU and ME. In Wolfgang Girke and Helmut Jachnow (eds.). *Theoretische Linguistik in Osteuropa*. Tübingen: Max Niemeyer. 1–21.

—— (1976b). Mind and Body. In James D. McCawley (ed.). *Syntax and Semantics: Notes from the Linguistic Underground*, vii. New York: Academic Press. 129–57.

—— (1976c). Particles and Linguistic Relativity. *International Review of Slavic Linguistics*. 1/2–3: 327–67.

—— (1976d). Review of J. D. Apresjan's *Leksičeskaja semantika: Sinonimičeskie sredstva jazyka*. *International Review of Slavic Linguistics*. 1/10: 141–63.

—— (1980). *Lingua Mentalis: The Semantics of Natural Language*. Sydney: Academic Press.

—— (1981). Case Marking and Human Nature. *Australian Journal of Linguistics*. 1: 43–80.

—— (1983a). Semantics and Lexicography: Some Comments on the Warlpiri Dictionary Project. In Peter Austin (ed.). *Papers in Australian Linguistics, xv: Australian Aboriginal Lexicography*. Pacific Linguistics. Series A. No. 66. Canberra: Linguistics Department Research School of Pacific Studies, Australian National University. 135–44.

—— (1983b). The Semantics of Case Marking. *Studies in Language*. 7/2: 247–75.

—— (1984). Apples are not a Kind of Fruit: The Semantics of Human Categorization. *American Ethnologist*. 11/2: 313–28.

—— (1985). *Lexicography and Conceptual Analysis*. Ann Arbor: Karoma.

—— (1986a). Human Emotions: Universal or Culture-Specific? *American Anthropologist*. 88/3: 584–94.

—— (1986b). Metaphors Linguists Live By: Lakoff and Johnson contra Aristotle. (Review of Lakoff and Johnson 1980.) *Papers in Linguistics* 19/2: 287–313.

—— (1986c). Precision in Vagueness: The Semantics of English Approximatives. *Journal of Pragmatics*. 10/2: 597–613.

—— (1986d). The Semantics of Quantitative Particles in Polish and in English. In Andrzej Bogusławski and Bożenna Bojar (eds.). *Od kodu do kodu*. (Festschrift for Olgierd Wojtasiewicz.) Warsaw: Państwowe Wydawnictwo Naukowe. 175–89.

—— (1986e). Review of Igor Mel'čuk et al. *Dictionnaire explicatif et combinatoire du français contemporain* and Igor Mel'čuk and Aleksandr Žolkovskij. *Tolkovo-kombinatornyj slovar' sovremennogo russkogo jazyka*. *Australian Journal of Linguistics*. 6/1: 139–47.

—— (1986f). Review of Igor Mel'čuk and Aleksandr Žolkovskij. *Tolkovo-kombinatornyj slovar' sovremennogo russkogo jazyka*. *Language*. 62/3: 684–7.

—— (1987a). *English Speech Act Verbs: A Semantic Dictionary*. Sydney: Academic Press.

—— (1987b). The Semantics of Modality. *Folia Linguistica*. 21/1: 25–43.

—— (1988). *The Semantics of Grammar*. Amsterdam: John Benjamins.

—— (1989*a*). Soul and Mind: Linguistic Evidence for Ethnopsychology and Cultural History. *American Anthropologist*. 90/4: 982–3.

—— (1989*b*). Semantic Primitives and Lexical Universals. *Quaderni di semantica*. 10/1: 103–21.

—— (1989*c*). Semantic Primitives: The Expanding Set. *Quaderni di semantica* (Round Table on Semantic Primitives 2). 10/2: 309–32.

—— (1990*a*). The Meaning of Colour Terms: Semantics, Culture and Cognition. *Cognitive Linguistics*. 1/1: 99–150.

—— (1990*b*). 'Prototypes Save': On the Uses and Abuses of the Notion of 'Prototype' in Linguistics and Related Fields. In Savas L. Tsohatzidis (ed.). *Meanings and Prototypes: Studies in Linguistic Categorization*. London: Routledge & Kegan Paul. 347–67.

—— (1990*c*). The Semantics of Emotion: *Fear* and its Relatives in English. *Australian Journal of Linguistics* (Special Issue on the Semantics of Emotions). 10/2: 359–75.

—— (1991*a*). *Cross-cultural Pragmatics: The Semantics of Human Interaction*. Berlin: Mouton de Gruyter.

—— (1991*b*). Japanese Key Words and Core Cultural Values. *Language in Society*. 20: 333–85.

—— (1991*c*). Lexical Universals and Universals of Grammar. In Kefer and van der Auwera (1991), 383–415.

—— (1992*a*). *Semantics, Culture and Cognition: Universal Human Concepts in Culture-Specific Configurations*. New York: Oxford University Press.

—— (1992*b*). Furniture and Birds: A Reply to Dwight Bolinger. *Cognitive Linguistics*. 3/1: 119–23.

—— (1992*c*). Talking about Emotions: Semantics, Culture and Cognition. *Cognition and Emotion*. (Special Issue on Basic Emotions) 6/3–4: 289–319.

—— (1992*d*). The Search for Universal Semantic Primitives. In Pütz (1992), 215–42.

—— (1992*e*). Defining Emotion Concepts. *Cognitive Science*. 16: 539–81.

—— (1993*a*). Reading Human Faces: Emotion Components and Universal Semantics. *Pragmatics and Cognition*. 1/1: 1–23.

—— (1993*b*). A Conceptual Basis for Cultural Psychology. *Ethos*. 21/2: 205–31.

—— (1993*c*). Why do we Say *IN* April, *ON* Thursday, *AT* 10 o'clock? In Search of an Explanation. *Studies in Language*. 17/2: 437–54.

—— (1993*d*). What is Prayer? In Search of a Definition. In L. N. Brown (ed.) *The Human Side of Prayer: The Psychology of Praying*. Birmingham, Ala.: Religious Education Press. 25–46.

—— (1993*e*). Intercultural Communication in Australia. In G. Schultz (ed.). *The Languages of Australia. Papers from the Australian Academy of Humanities Symposium 1992*. 83–103. Canberra: Australian Academy of the Humanities.

—— (1994*a*). 'Cultural Scripts': A Semantic Approach to Cultural Analysis and Cross-cultural Communication. *Pragmatics and Language Learning*. Monograph Series, v. Urbana-Champaign: DEIL University of Illinois.

—— (1994*b*). Semantic Primitives across Languages: A Critical Review. In Goddard and Wierzbicka (1994*b*), 445–500.

WIERZBICKA, ANNA (1994*c*). Cognitive Domains and the Structure of the Lexicon: The Case of Emotions. In Hirschfeld and Gelman (1994), 771–97.

—— (1994*d*). 'Cultural Scripts': A New Approach to the Study of Cross-cultural Communication. In Pütz (1994), 69–87.

—— (1994*e*). Emotion, Language and 'Cultural Scripts'. In S. Kitayama and H. Markus (eds.). *Emotion and Culture: Empirical Studies of Mutual Influence.* Washington: American Psychological Association. 130–98.

—— (1994*f*). In Search of Tradition: The Semantic Ideas of Leibniz. *Lexicographica.* 8: 10–25.

—— (1994*g*). Semantic Universals and 'Primitive Thought': The Question of the Psychic Unity of Humankind. In *Journal of Linguistic Anthropology.* 4/1: 1–27.

—— (1994*h*). Everday Conceptions of Emotion (a Semantic Perspective). In J. Russell (ed.). *Everyday Conceptions of Emotion.* Dordrecht: Kluwer. 17–48.

—— (1995*a*). Kisses, Handshakes, Bows: The Semantics of Nonverbal Communication. *Semiotica.* 103/3–4: 207–52.

—— (1995*b*). Emotion and Facial Expression: A Semantic Perspective. *Culture and Psychology.* 1/2. 227–258.

—— (forthcoming *a*). Contrastive Sociolinguistics and the Theory of 'Cultural Scripts': Chinese versus English. In Marlis Hellinger and Ulrich Ammon (eds.). *Contrastive Sociolinguistics,* Contributions to the Sociology of Language. Gen. ed. Joshua A. Fishman. The Hague: Mouton.

—— (forthcoming *b*). What did Jesus Mean? The Lord's Prayer Translated into Universal Human Concepts.

—— (forthcoming *c*). Japanese Cultural Scripts: Cultural Psychology and Cultural Grammar. *Ethos.*

—— (forthcoming *d*). The Universality of Taxonomic Categorization and the Indispensability of the Concept 'Kind'. *Rivista di Linguistica.* 6/2.

—— (forthcoming *e*). *Understanding Cultures through their Key Words.* New York: Oxford University Press.

—— (forthcoming *f*). THINK: A Universal Human Concept and a Conceptual Primitive. In Jacek Jadacki (ed.). *Festschrift for Jerzy Pelc.* Warsaw: Państwowe Wydawnictwo Naukowe.

—— (forthcoming *g*). Conditionals and Counterfactuals: Conceptual Primitives and Linguistic Universals. In Angeliki Athanesiadou and René Dirven (eds.). *On Conditionals Again.* Amsterdam: John Benjamins.

WILKINS, D. (1981). Towards a Theory of Semantic Change. BA Hons. thesis. Australian National University.

—— (1986). Particle/Clitics for Criticism and Complaint in Mparntwe Arrernte (Aranda). *Journal of Pragmatics.* 19/5: 575–96.

—— (1989). Mparntwe Arrernte (Aranda): Studies in the Structure and Semantics of Grammar. Ph.D. thesis. Australian National University.

—— (1992). Interjections as Deictics. *Journal of Pragmatics* (special Issue on Interjections, ed. Felix Ameka). 16: 119–58.

—— (1993). Predicting Syntactic Structure from Semantic Representations: *Remember* in English and its Equivalents in Mparntwe Arrernte. In R. D. Van Valin, Jr. and David F. Wilkins (eds.). *Advances in Role and Reference Grammar.* Amsterdam: John Benjamins. 499–534.

WILKINS, JOHN (1668). *An Essay towards a Real Character and a Philosophical Language*. London: Gellibrand.

WITKOWSKI, STANLEY R., and CECIL H. BROWN (1978). Lexical Universals. *Annual Review of Anthropology*. 7: 427–51.

WITTGENSTEIN, LUDWIG (1953). *Philosophical Investigations*. Trans. G. E. M. Anscombe. Oxford: Blackwell.

—— (1977). *Remarks on Color*, Ed. G. E. M. Anscombe. Trans. from the German by Linda L. McAlister and Margaret Schättle. Oxford: Blackwell.

World of Science (n.d.) Sydney: Bay Books.

WRIGHT, DAVID (1993). *Deafness: an Autobiography*. London: Mandarin.

XU, W. (1994). Chinese Colour Semantics. Ph.D. dissertation. Australian National University.

ZGUSTA, LADISLAV (1922/1993). Lexicography: Its Theory and Linguistics. *Dictionaries*. No. 14. 130–8.

—— (1971). *Manual of Lexicography*. The Hague: Mouton.

ZIPF, G. K. (1949). *Human Behaviour and the Principle of Least Effort*. Cambridge, Mass.: Addison-Wesley.

ŽOLKOVSKIJ, ALEKSANDR (1964a). Predislovie. *Mašinnyj Perevod i Prikladnaja Lingvistika*. 8: 3–16.

—— (1964b). Leksika celesoobraznoj dejatel'nosti. *Mašinnyj Perevod i Prikladnaja Lingvistika*. 8: 67–103.

ZUBIN, DAVID, and KLAUS-MICHAEL KÖPCKE (1986). Gender and Folk Taxonomy: The Indexical Relation between Grammatical and Lexical Categorization. In Colette Craig (ed.). *Noun Classes and Categorization*. Amsterdam: John Benjamins.

Index